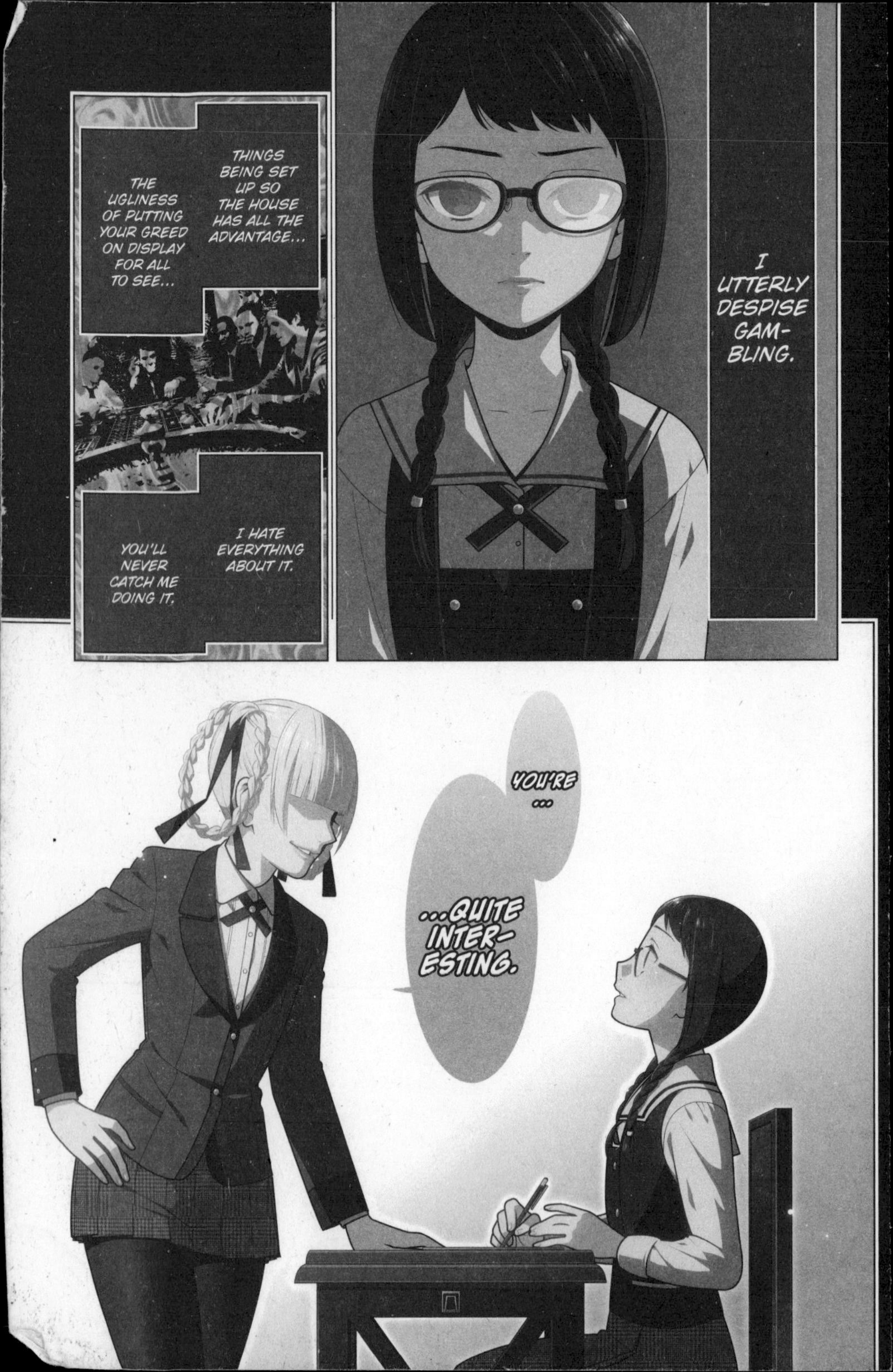
I UTTERLY DESPISE GAMBLING.
THINGS BEING SET UP SO THE HOUSE HAS ALL THE ADVANTAGE...
THE UGLINESS OF PUTTING YOUR GREED ON DISPLAY FOR ALL TO SEE...
I HATE EVERYTHING ABOUT IT.
YOU'LL NEVER CATCH ME DOING IT.
YOU'RE...
...QUITE INTERESTING.

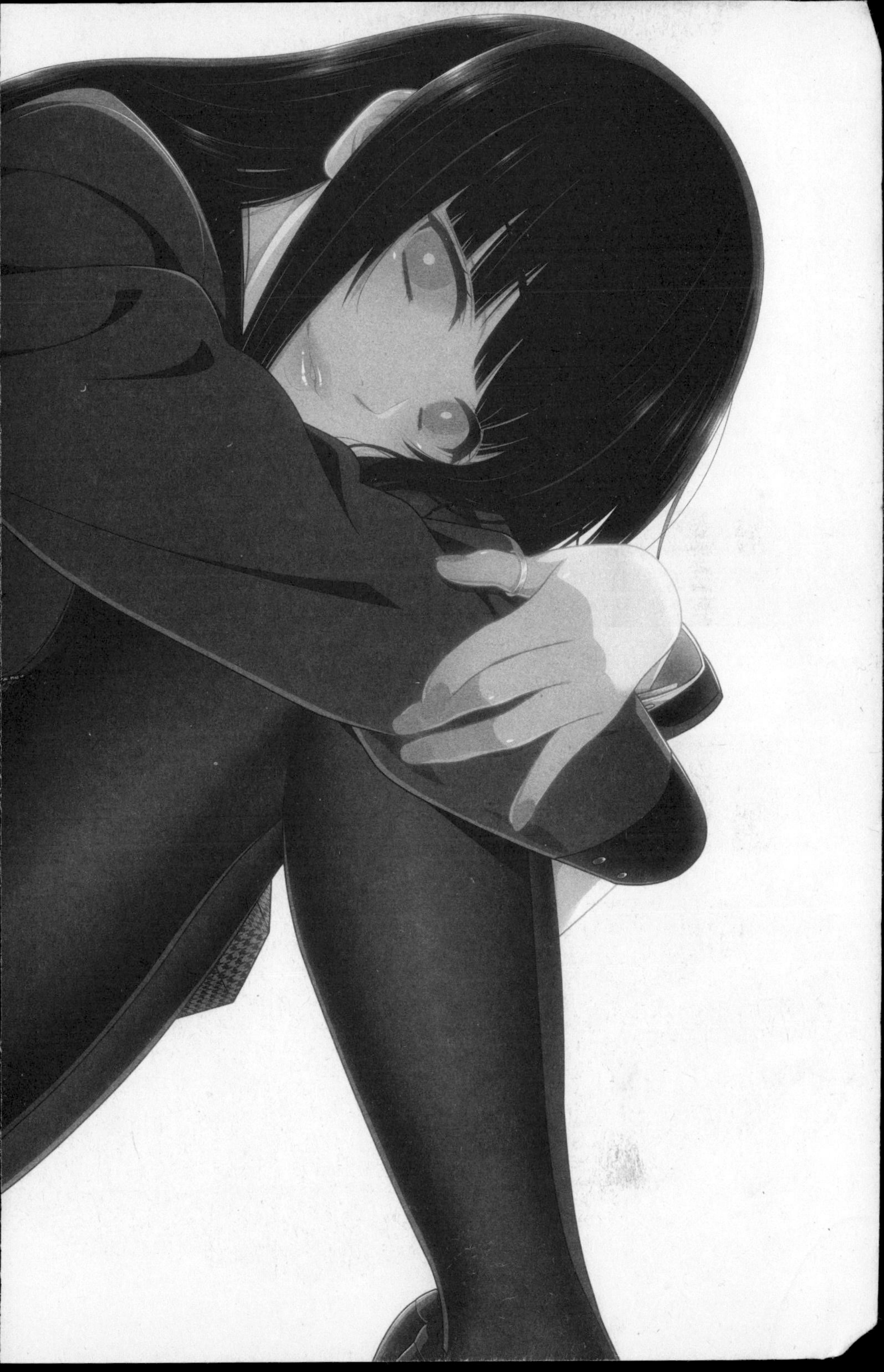

CHAPTER TWENTY-EIGHT
THE PASSING GIRL

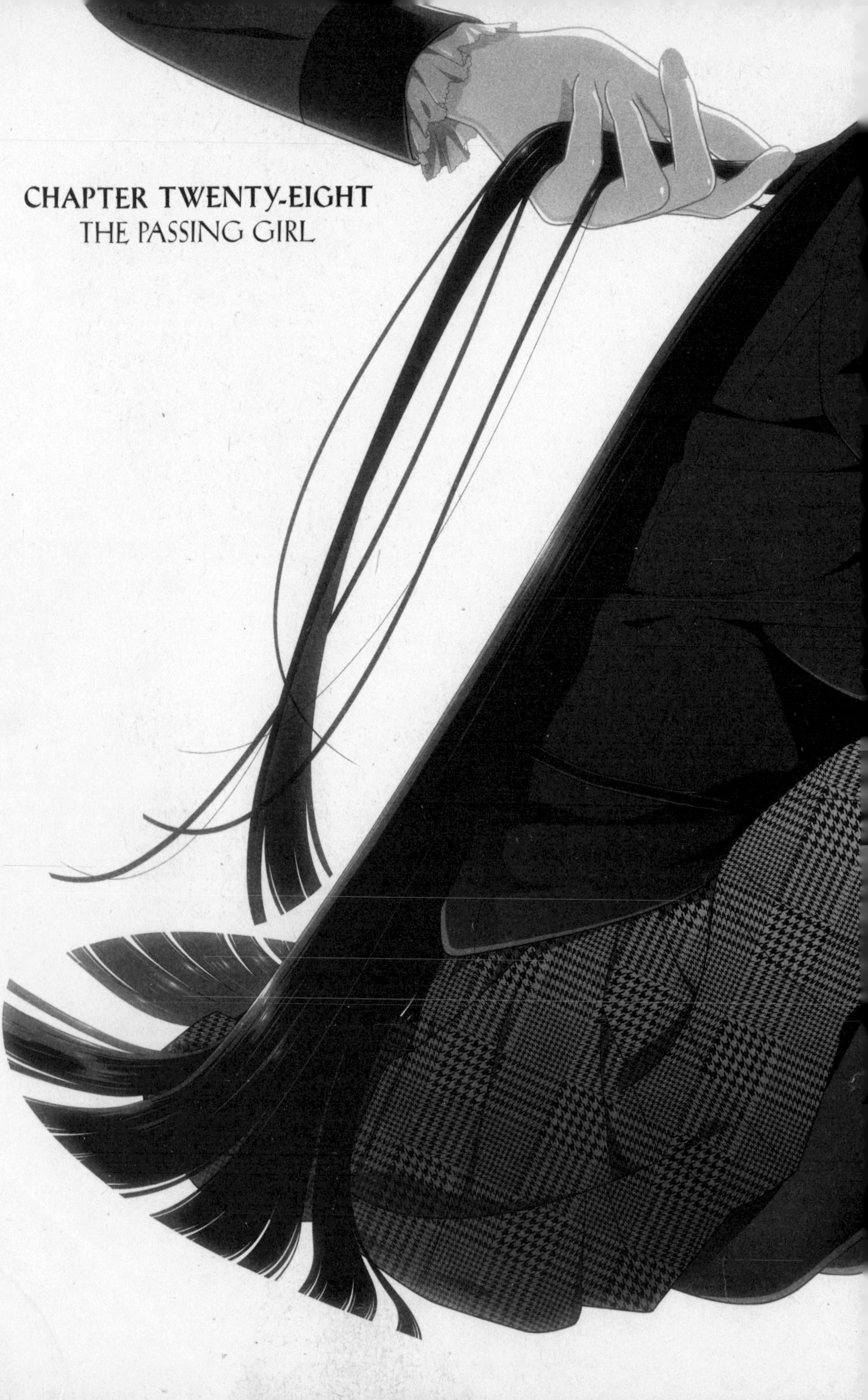

KAKEGURUI

— Compulsive Gambler —

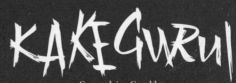

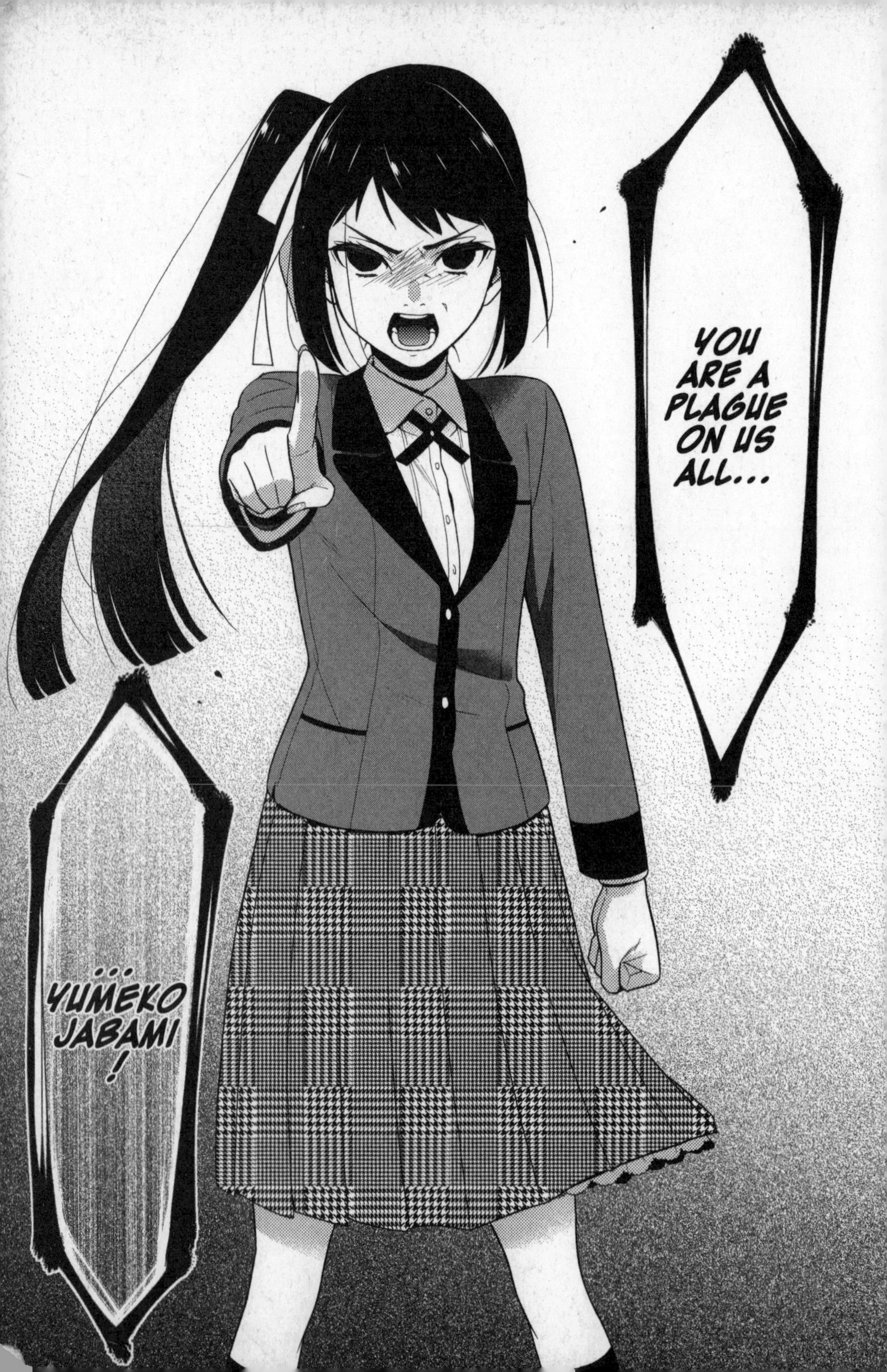
YOU ARE A PLAGUE ON US ALL...
...YUMEKO JABAMI!

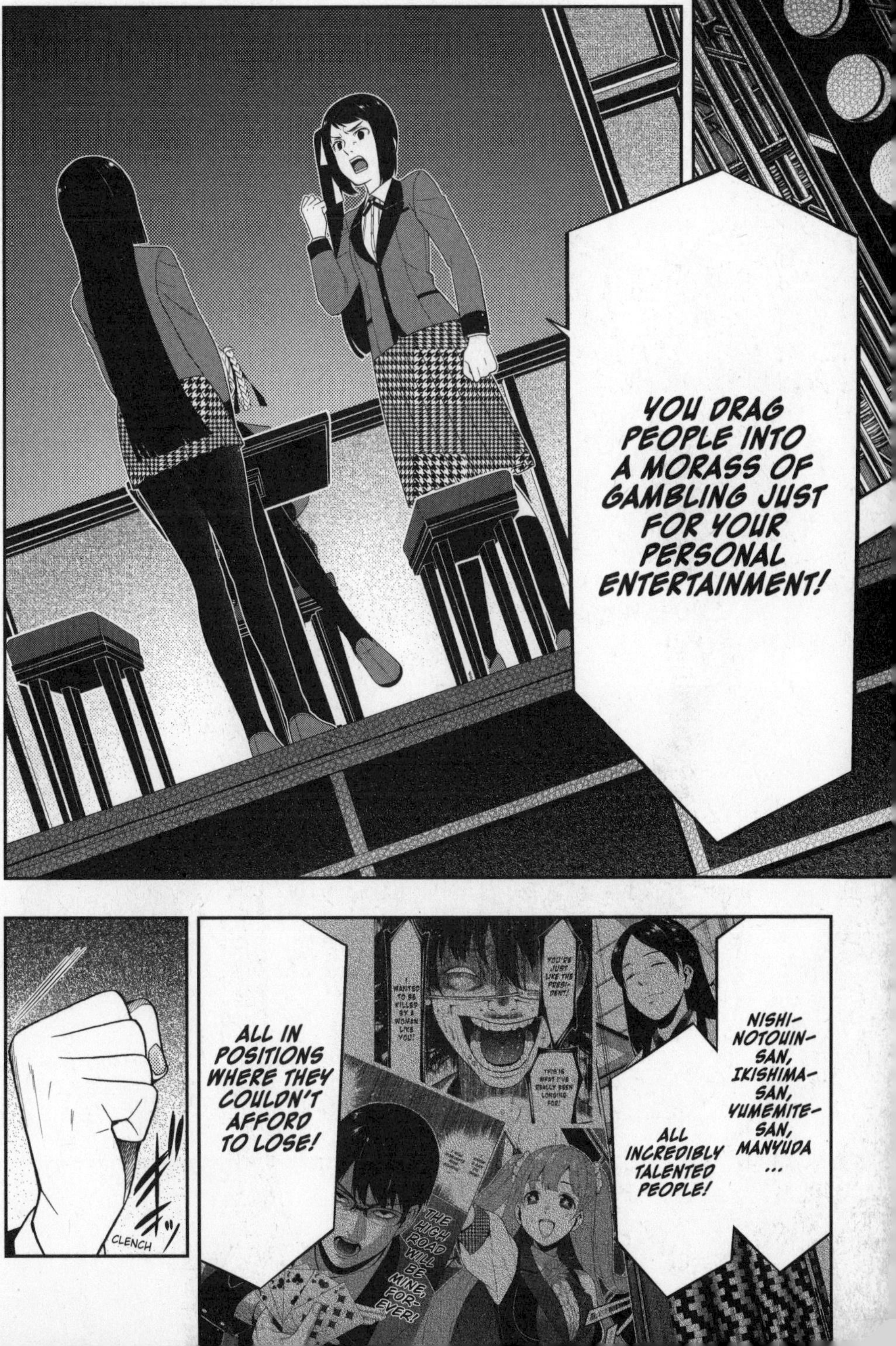
YOU DRAG PEOPLE INTO A MORASS OF GAMBLING JUST FOR YOUR PERSONAL ENTERTAINMENT!
NISHI-NOTOUIN-SAN, IKISHIMA-SAN, YUMEMITE-SAN, MANYUDA...
ALL INCREDIBLY TALENTED PEOPLE!
YOU'RE JUST LIKE THE PRESI-DENT!
THIS IS WHAT I'VE REALLY BEEN LONGING FOR!
I WANTED TO BE KILLED BY A WOMAN LIKE YOU!
THE HIGH ROAD WILL BE MINE, FOR-EVER!
ALL IN POSITIONS WHERE THEY COULDN'T AFFORD TO LOSE!
CLENCH

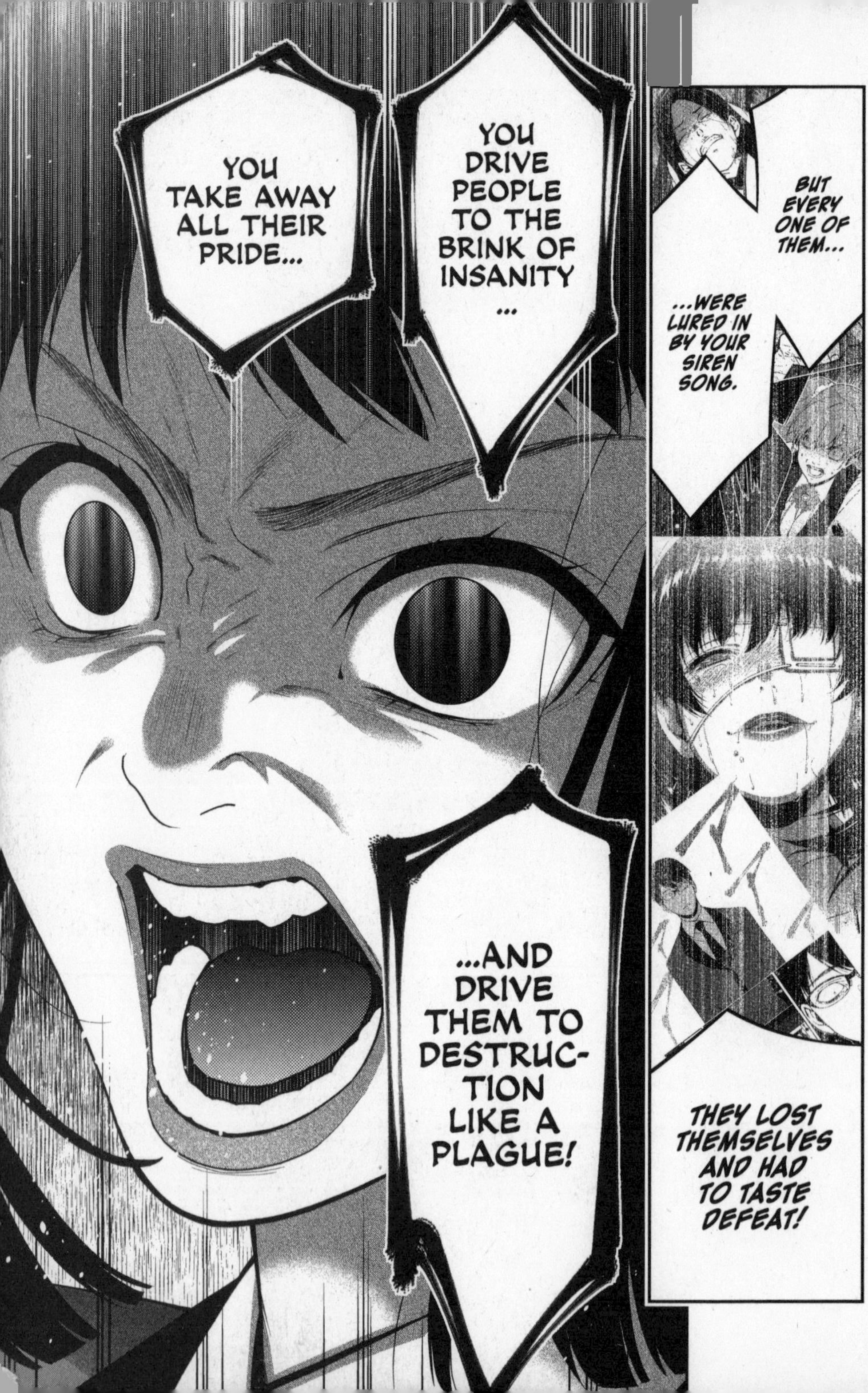
BUT EVERY ONE OF THEM...
...WERE LURED IN BY YOUR SIREN SONG.
THEY LOST THEMSELVES AND HAD TO TASTE DEFEAT!
YOU DRIVE PEOPLE TO THE BRINK OF INSANITY...
YOU TAKE AWAY ALL THEIR PRIDE...
...AND DRIVE THEM TO DESTRUC-TION LIKE A PLAGUE!

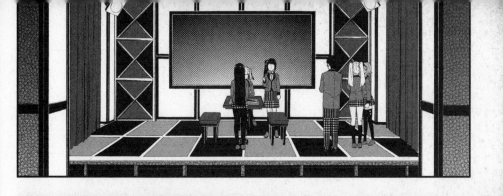

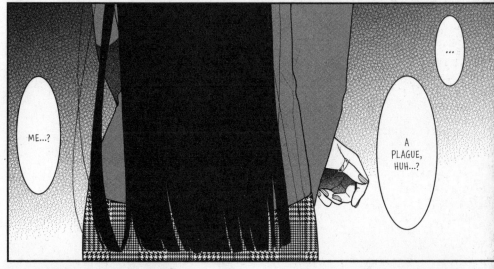

...

ME...?

A PLAGUE, HUH...?

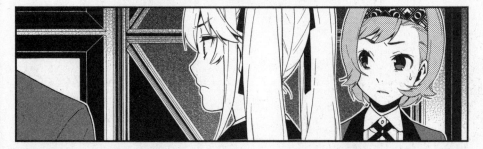

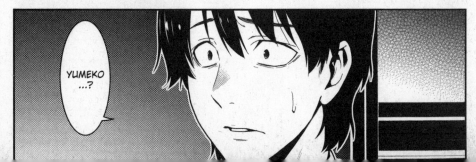

YUMEKO ....?

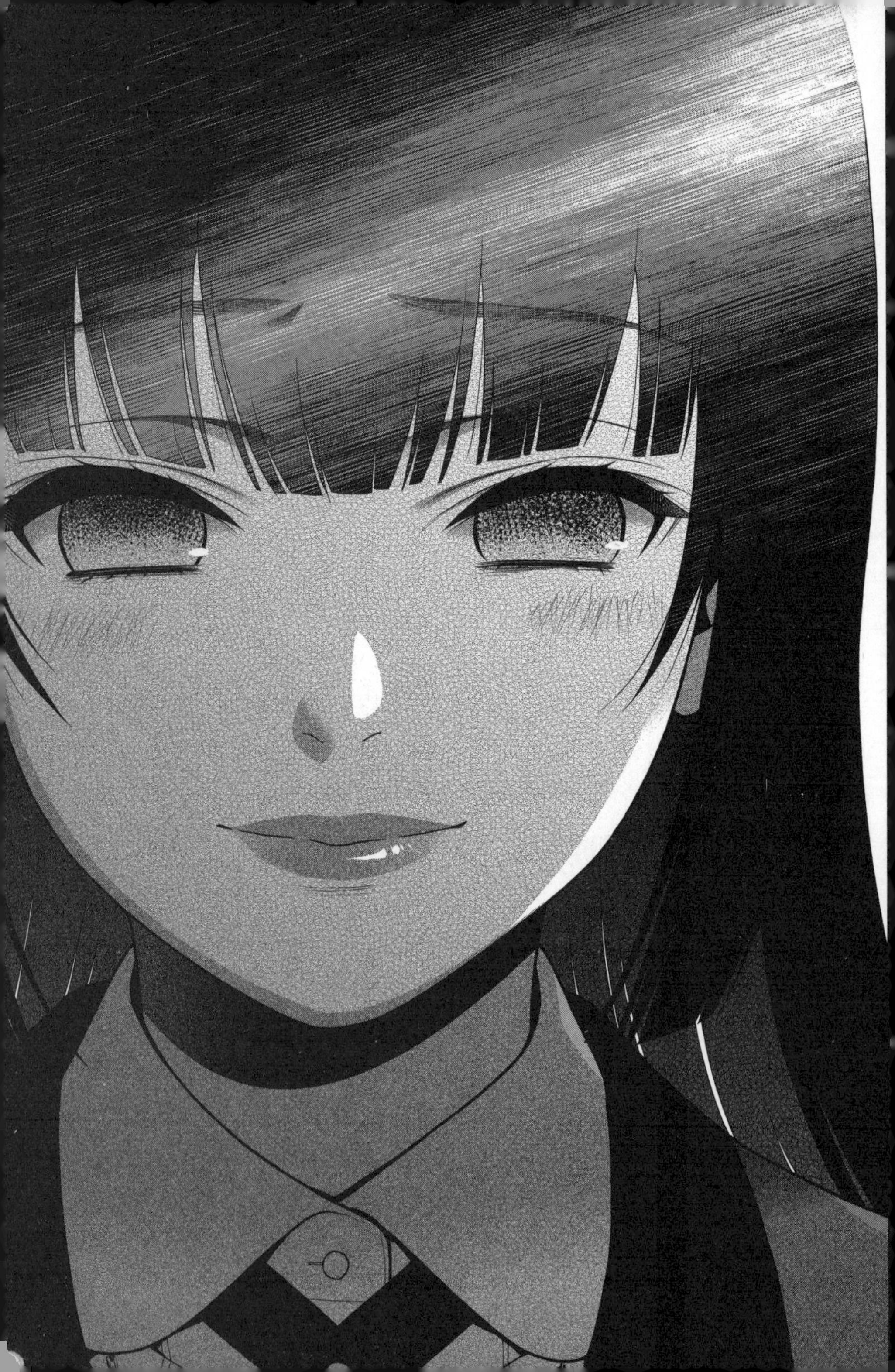

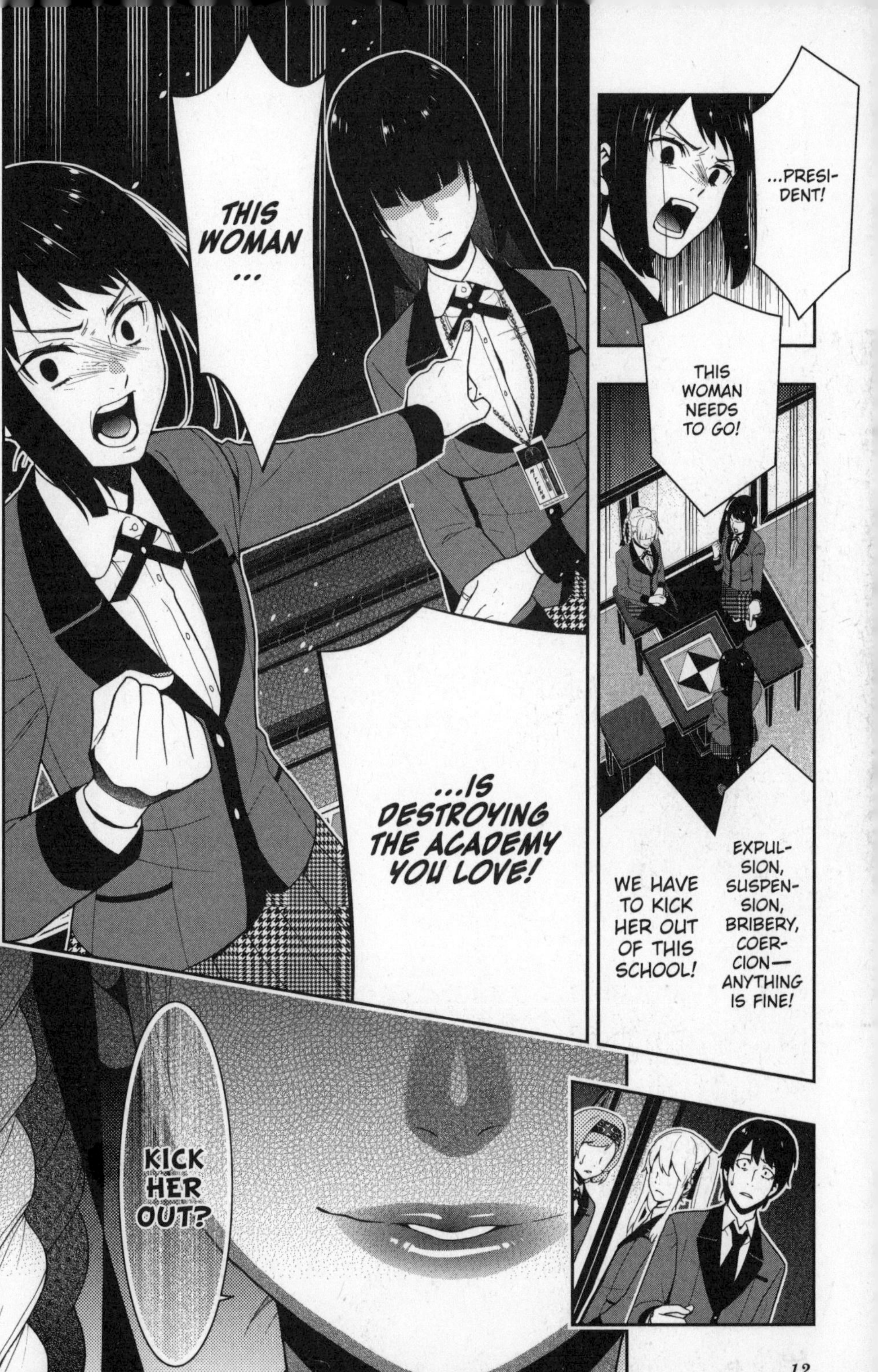
...PRESI-DENT!
THIS WOMAN NEEDS TO GO!
EXPUL-SION, SUSPEN-SION, BRIBERY, COER-CION—ANYTHING IS FINE!
WE HAVE TO KICK HER OUT OF THIS SCHOOL!
THIS WOMAN ...
...IS DESTROYING THE ACADEMY YOU LOVE!
KICK HER OUT?

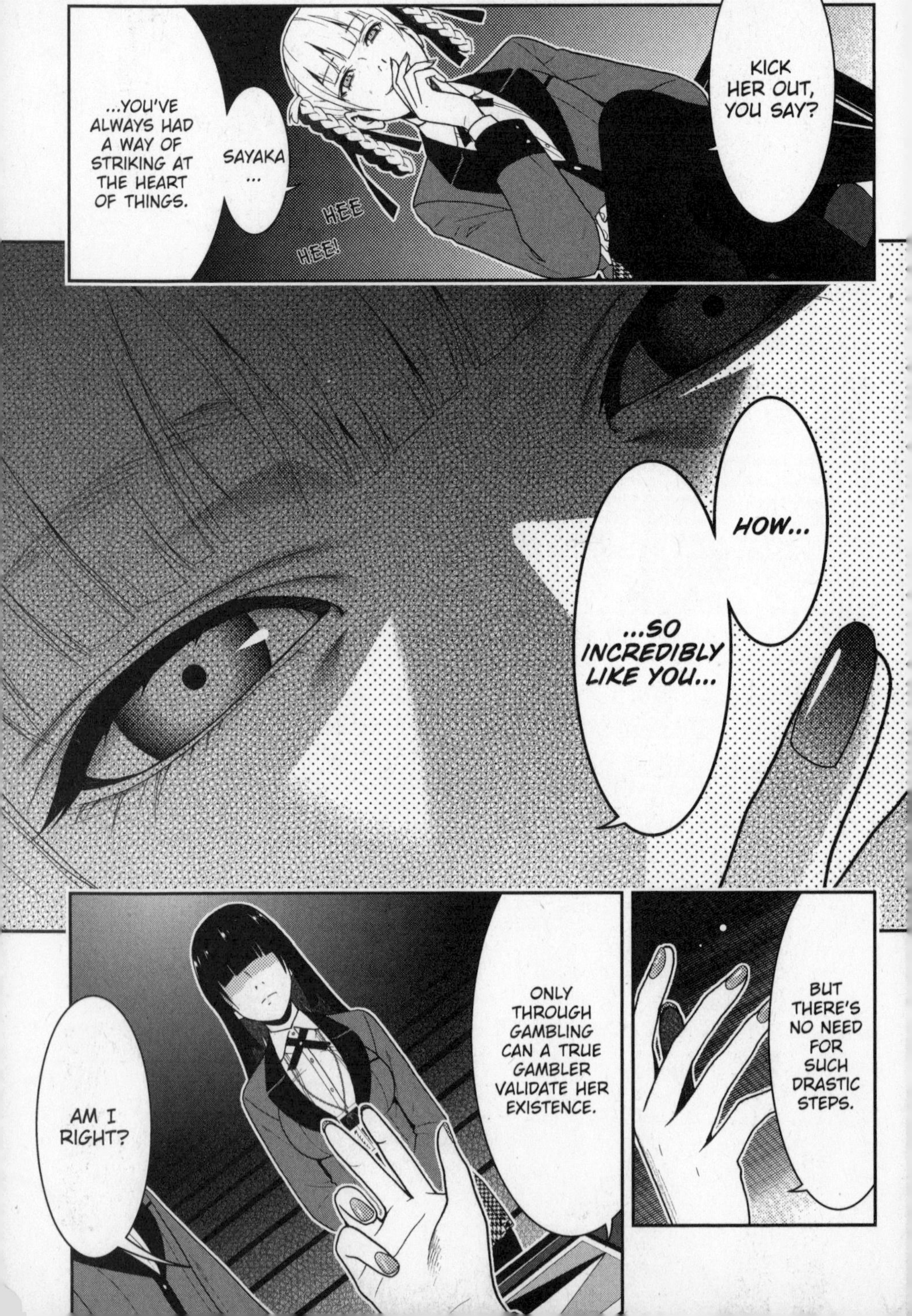
KICK HER OUT, YOU SAY?
SAYAKA...
...YOU'VE ALWAYS HAD A WAY OF STRIKING AT THE HEART OF THINGS.
HEE HEE!
HOW...
...SO INCREDIBLY LIKE YOU...
BUT THERE'S NO NEED FOR SUCH DRASTIC STEPS.
ONLY THROUGH GAMBLING CAN A TRUE GAMBLER VALIDATE HER EXISTENCE.
AM I RIGHT?

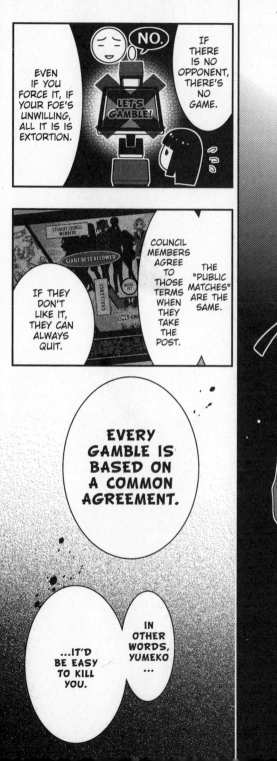

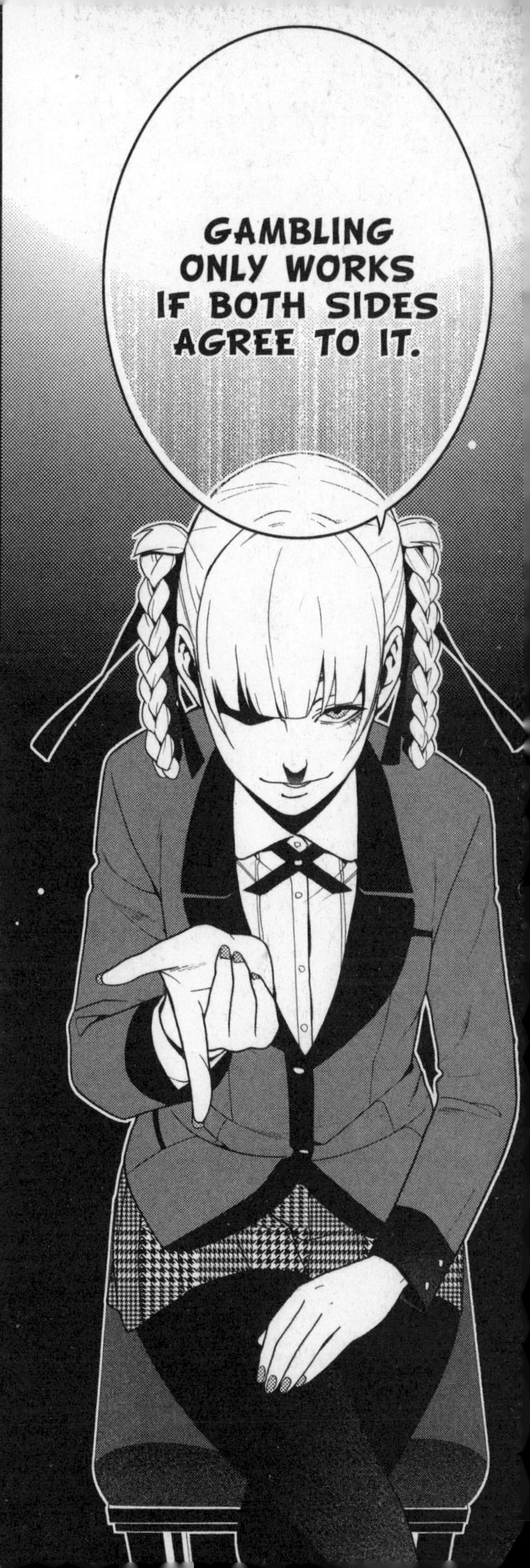
GAMBLING ONLY WORKS IF BOTH SIDES AGREE TO IT.
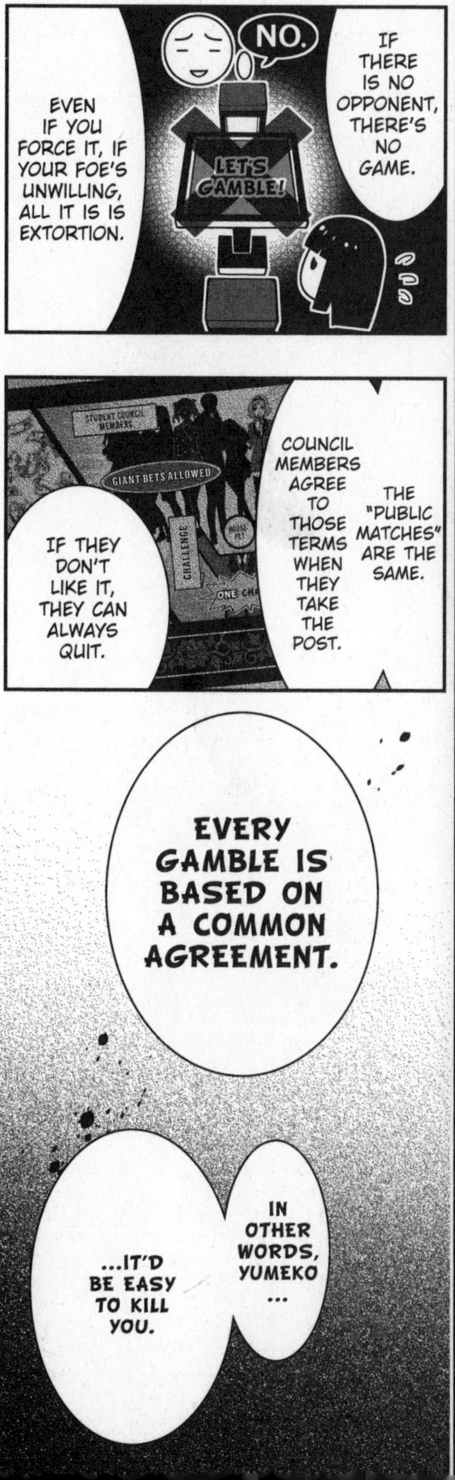
IF THERE IS NO OPPONENT, THERE'S NO GAME.
NO.
LET'S GAMBLE!
EVEN IF YOU FORCE IT, IF YOUR FOE'S UNWILLING, ALL IT IS IS EXTORTION.
THE "PUBLIC MATCHES" ARE THE SAME.
COUNCIL MEMBERS AGREE TO THOSE TERMS WHEN THEY TAKE THE POST.
STUDENT COUNCIL MEMBERS
GIANT BETS ALLOWED
CHALLENGE
HOUSE PET
IF THEY DON'T LIKE IT, THEY CAN ALWAYS QUIT.
EVERY GAMBLE IS BASED ON A COMMON AGREEMENT.
IN OTHER WORDS, YUMEKO...
...IT'D BE EASY TO KILL YOU.

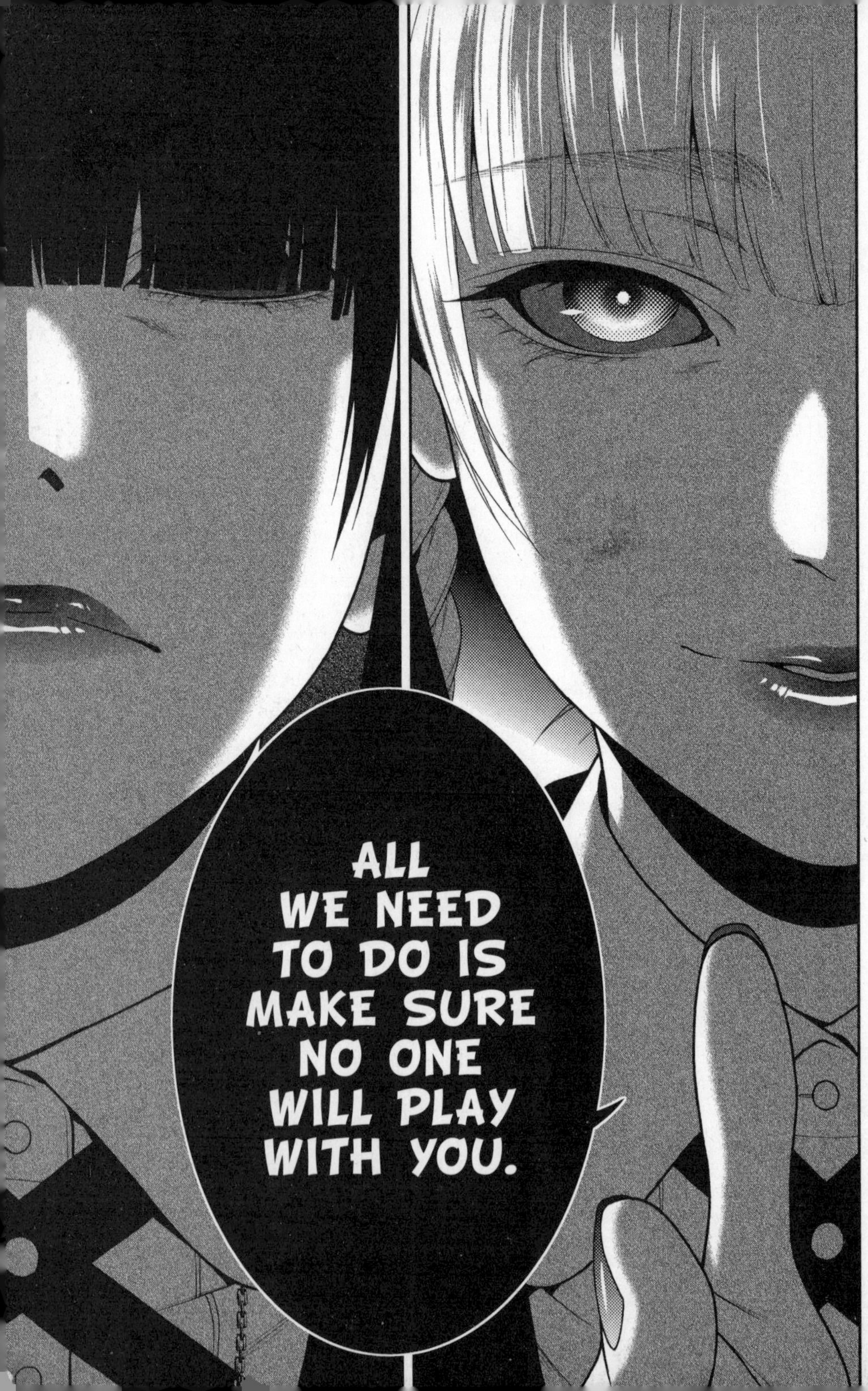
ALL WE NEED TO DO IS MAKE SURE NO ONE WILL PLAY WITH YOU.

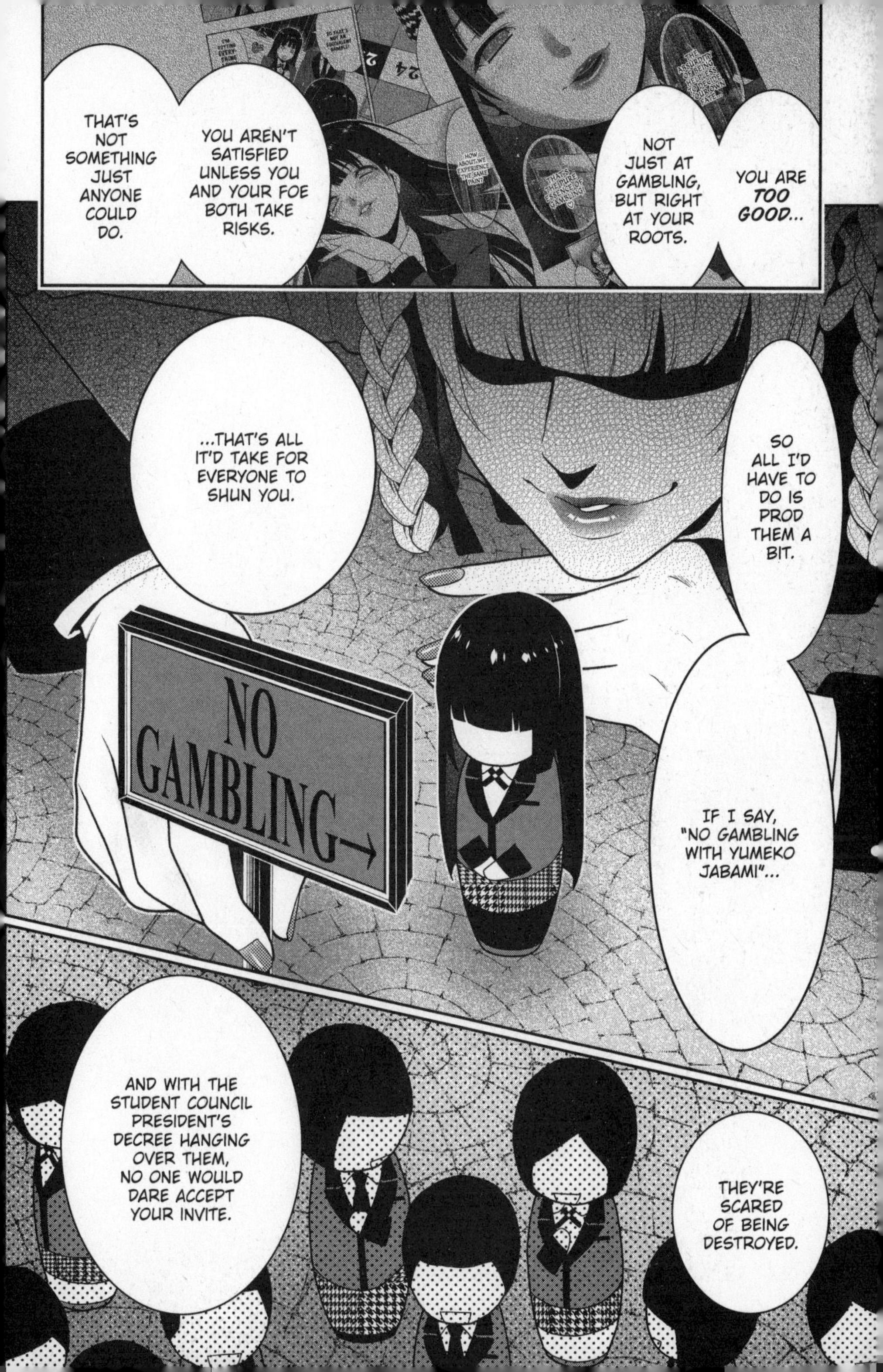
YOU ARE TOO GOOD...
THE ABSURDITY OF BEING HELPLESS TO DECIDE YOUR OWN FATE...
NOT JUST AT GAMBLING, BUT RIGHT AT YOUR ROOTS.
THAT'S THE PURE ESSENCE OF GAMBLING! ♡
HOW ABOUT WE EXPERIENCE THE SAME PAIN?
YOU AREN'T SATISFIED UNLESS YOU AND YOUR FOE BOTH TAKE RISKS.
THAT'S NOT SOMETHING JUST ANYONE COULD DO.
SO ALL I'D HAVE TO DO IS PROD THEM A BIT.
IF I SAY, "NO GAMBLING WITH YUMEKO JABAMI"...
...THAT'S ALL IT'D TAKE FOR EVERYONE TO SHUN YOU.
NO GAMBLING→
AND WITH THE STUDENT COUNCIL PRESIDENT'S DECREE HANGING OVER THEM, NO ONE WOULD DARE ACCEPT YOUR INVITE.
THEY'RE SCARED OF BEING DESTROYED.

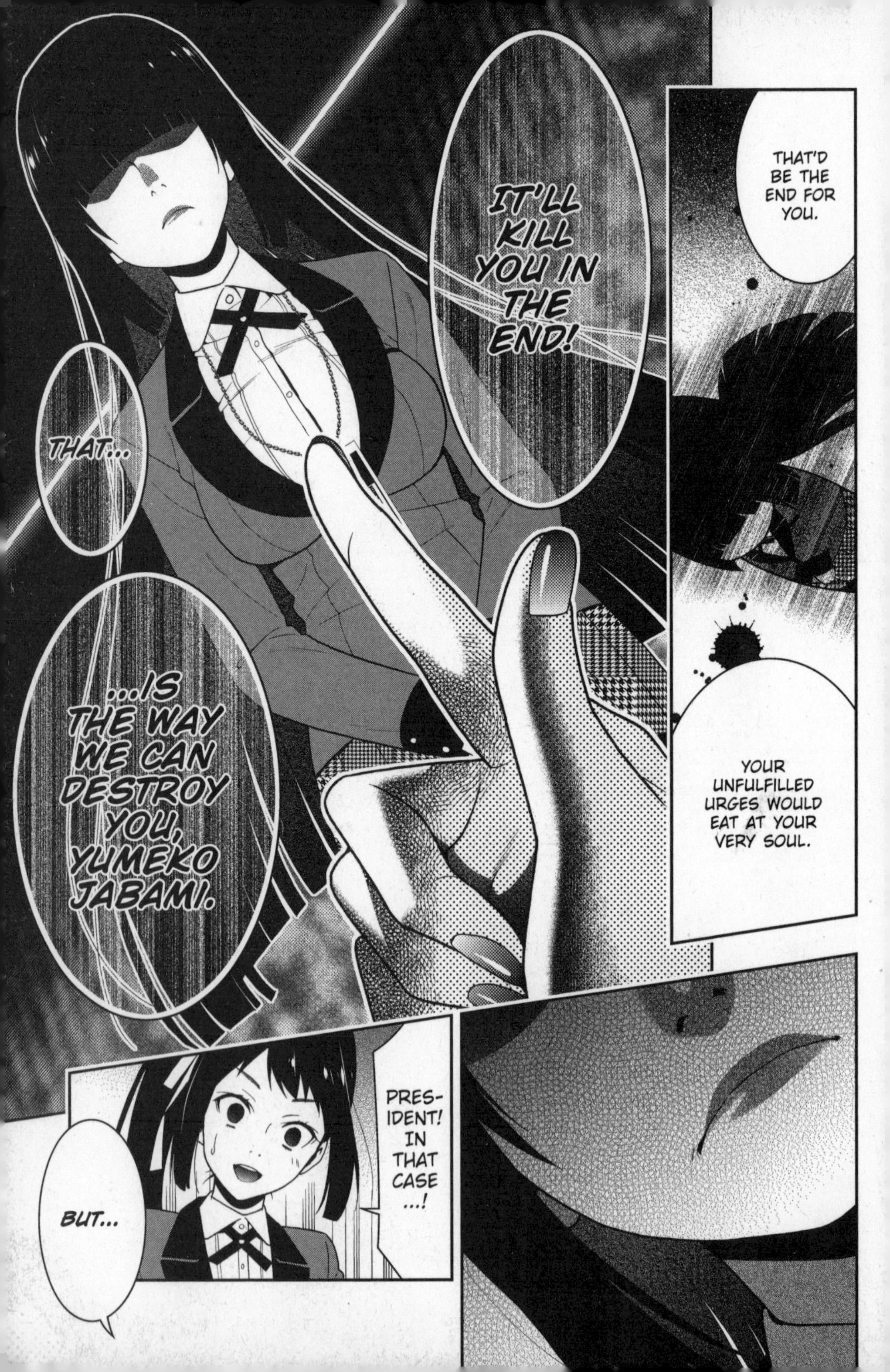
THAT'D BE THE END FOR YOU.
YOUR UNFULFILLED URGES WOULD EAT AT YOUR VERY SOUL.
IT'LL KILL YOU IN THE END!
THAT...
...IS THE WAY WE CAN DESTROY YOU, YUMEKO JABAMI.
PRES-IDENT! IN THAT CASE...!
BUT...

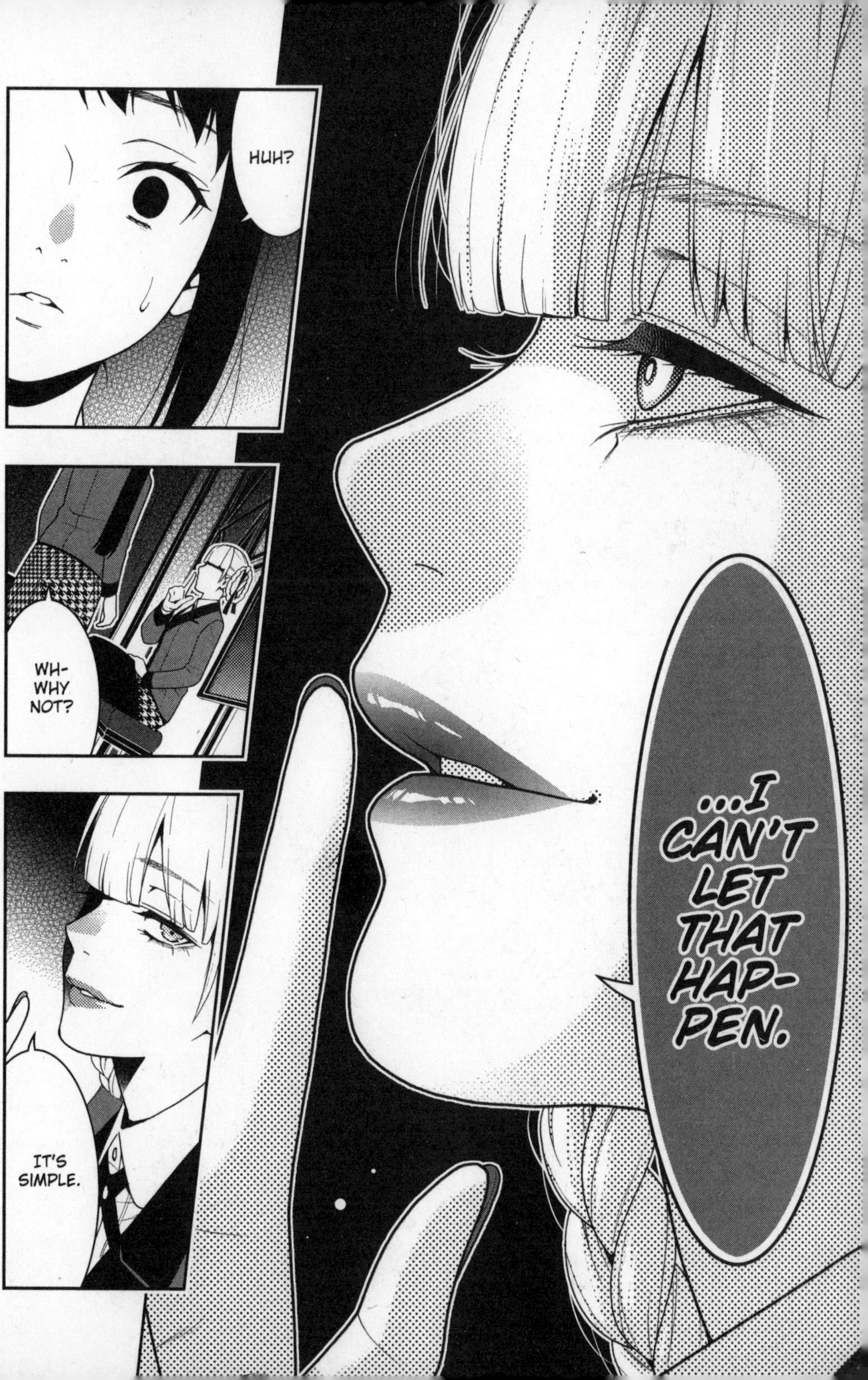
...I CAN'T LET THAT HAP-PEN.
HUH?
WH-WHY NOT?
IT'S SIMPLE.

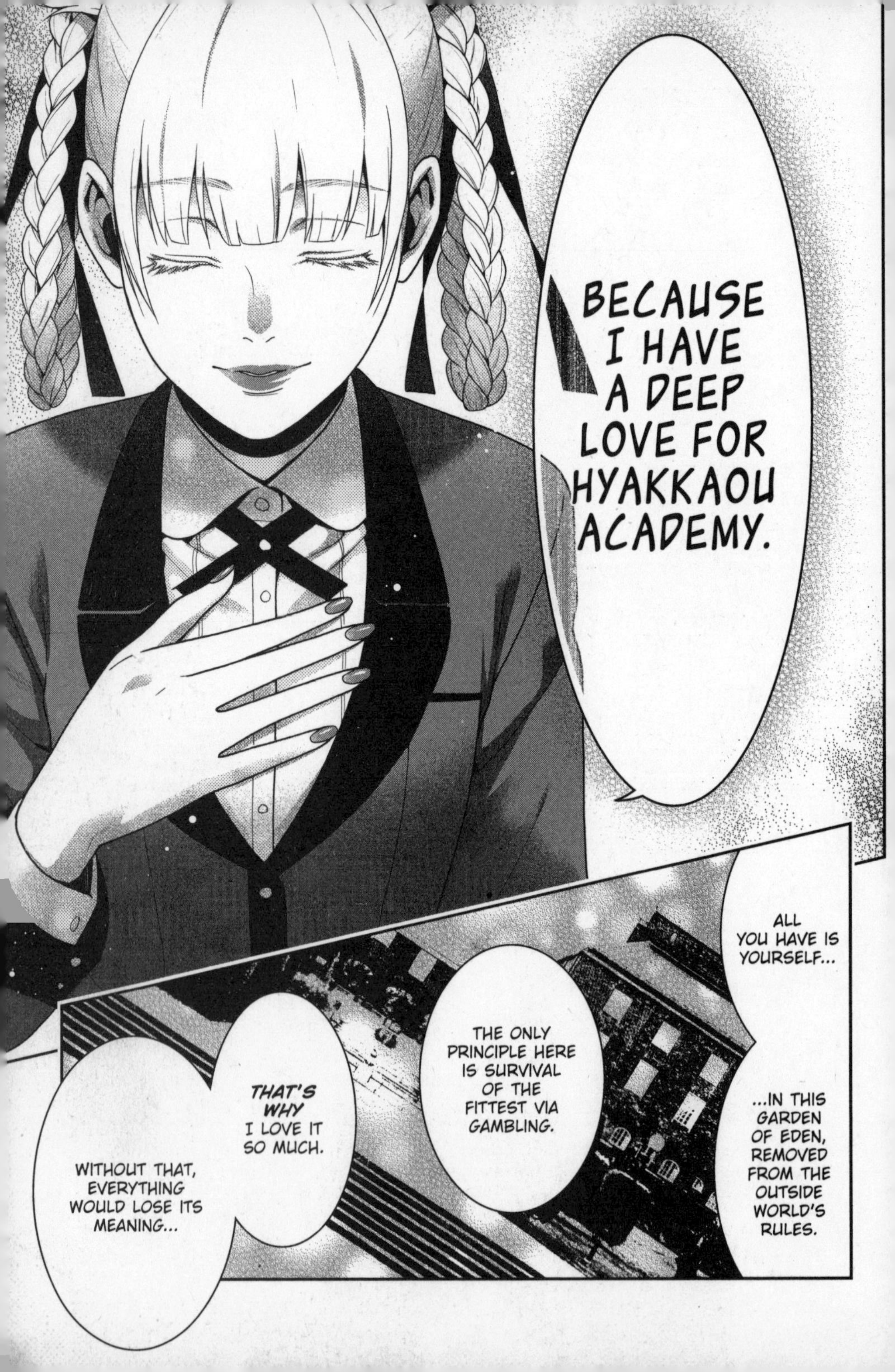
BECAUSE I HAVE A DEEP LOVE FOR HYAKKAOU ACADEMY.
ALL YOU HAVE IS YOURSELF...
...IN THIS GARDEN OF EDEN, REMOVED FROM THE OUTSIDE WORLD'S RULES.
THE ONLY PRINCIPLE HERE IS SURVIVAL OF THE FITTEST VIA GAMBLING.
THAT'S WHY I LOVE IT SO MUCH.
WITHOUT THAT, EVERYTHING WOULD LOSE ITS MEANING...

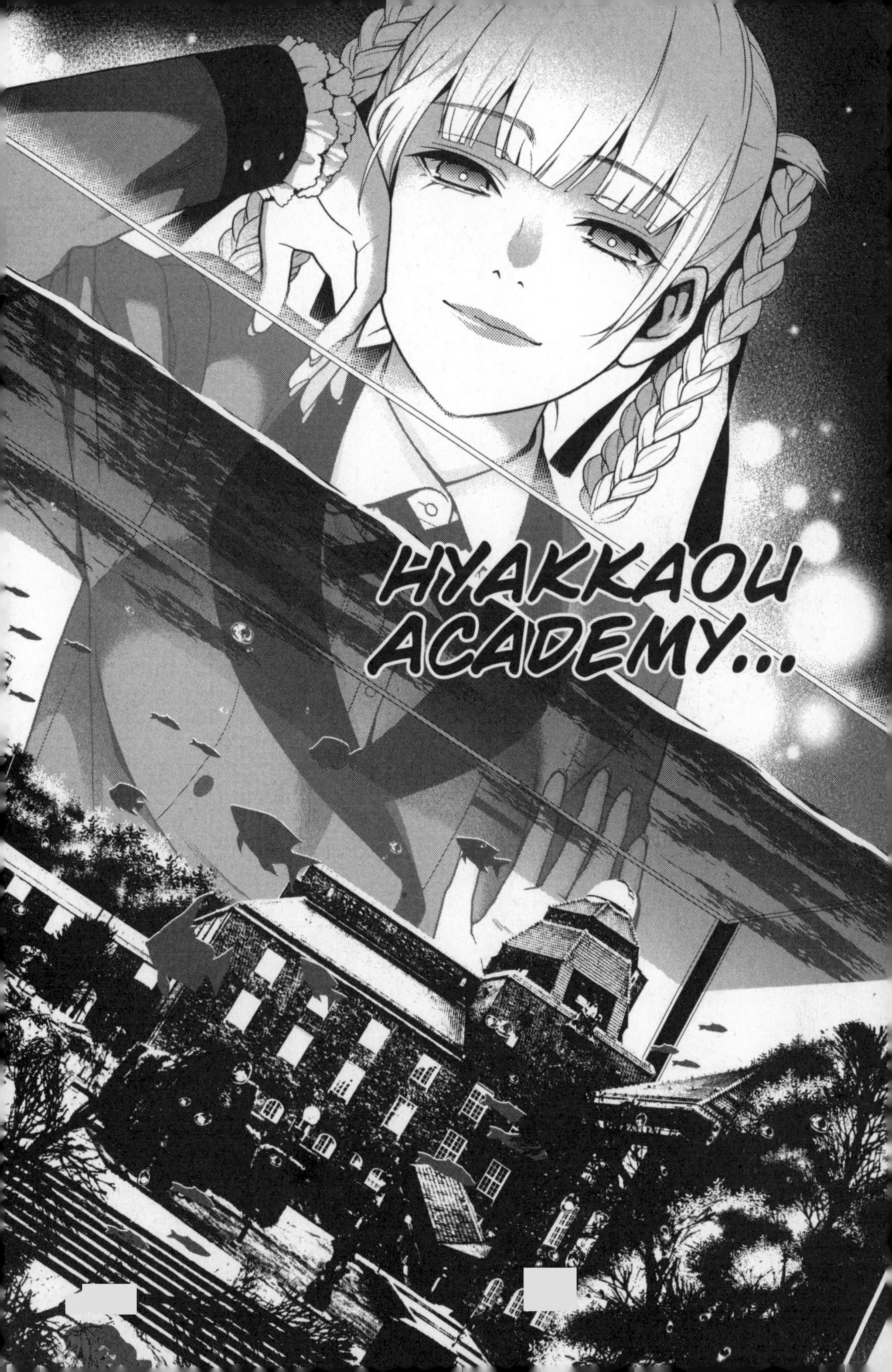
HYAKKAOU ACADEMY...

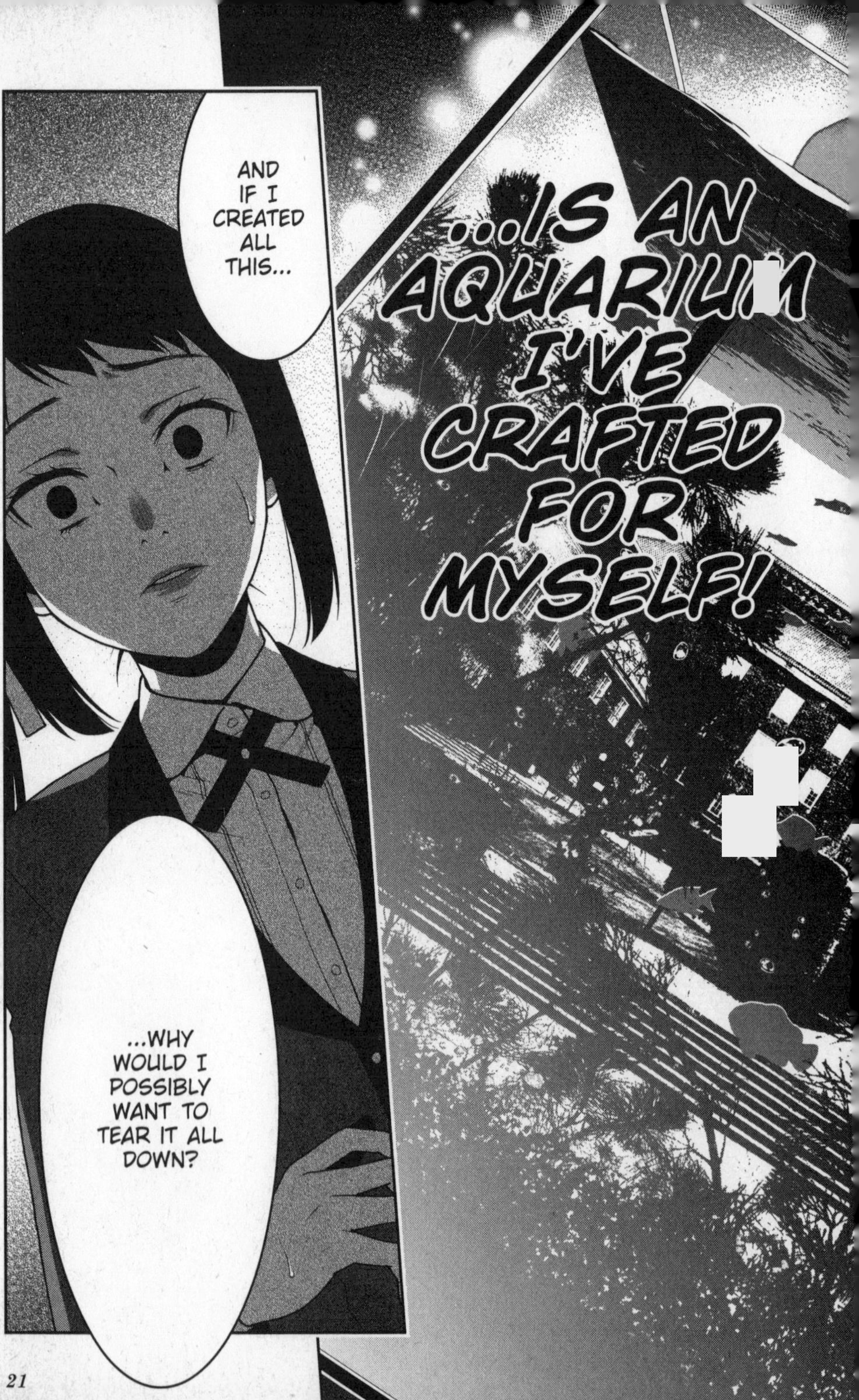
...IS AN AQUARIUM I'VE CRAFTED FOR MYSELF!
AND IF I CREATED ALL THIS...
...WHY WOULD I POSSIBLY WANT TO TEAR IT ALL DOWN?

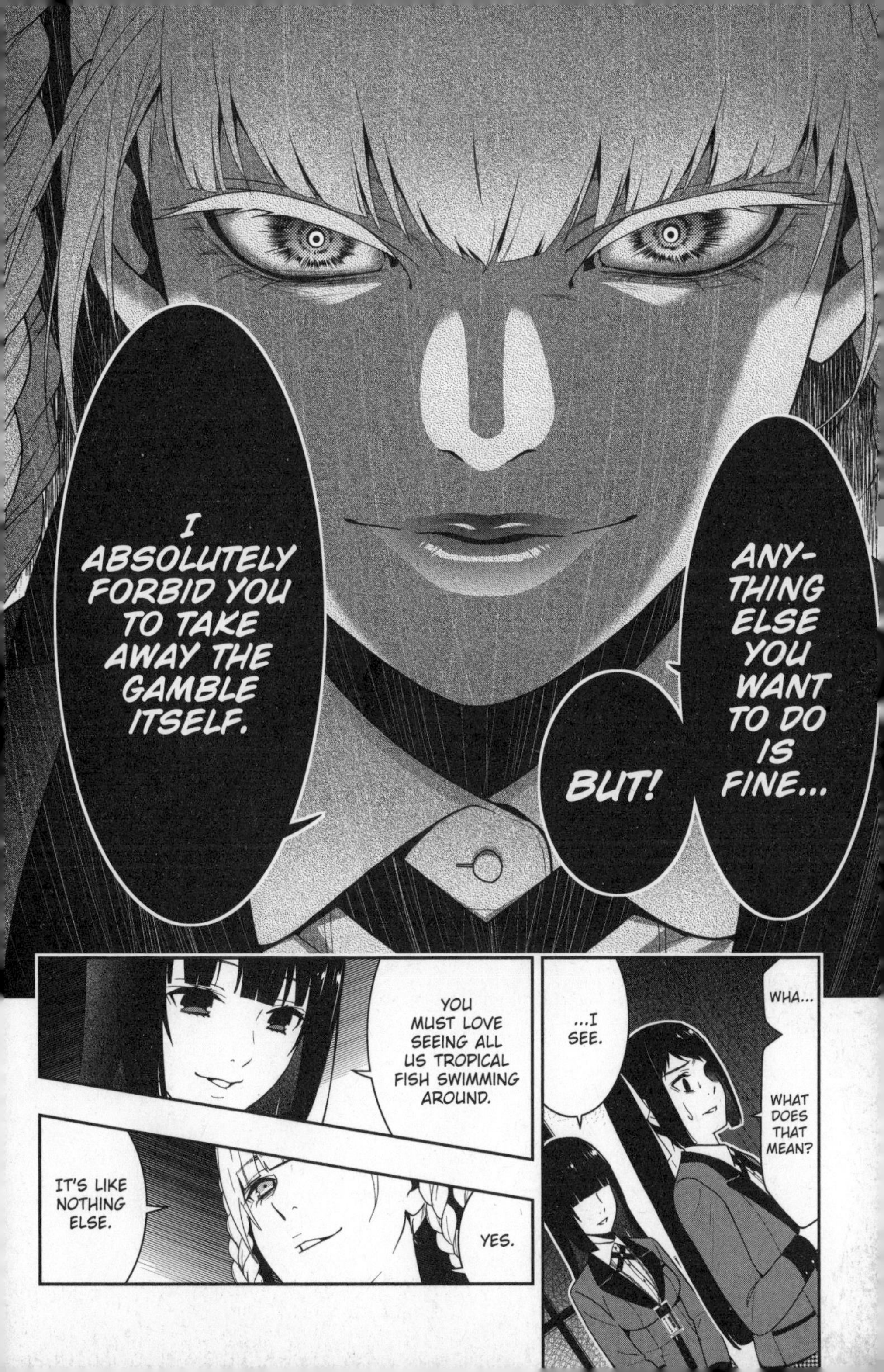
ANY-THING ELSE YOU WANT TO DO IS FINE...
BUT!
I ABSOLUTELY FORBID YOU TO TAKE AWAY THE GAMBLE ITSELF.
WHA...
...I SEE.
WHAT DOES THAT MEAN?
YOU MUST LOVE SEEING ALL US TROPICAL FISH SWIMMING AROUND.
YES.
IT'S LIKE NOTHING ELSE.

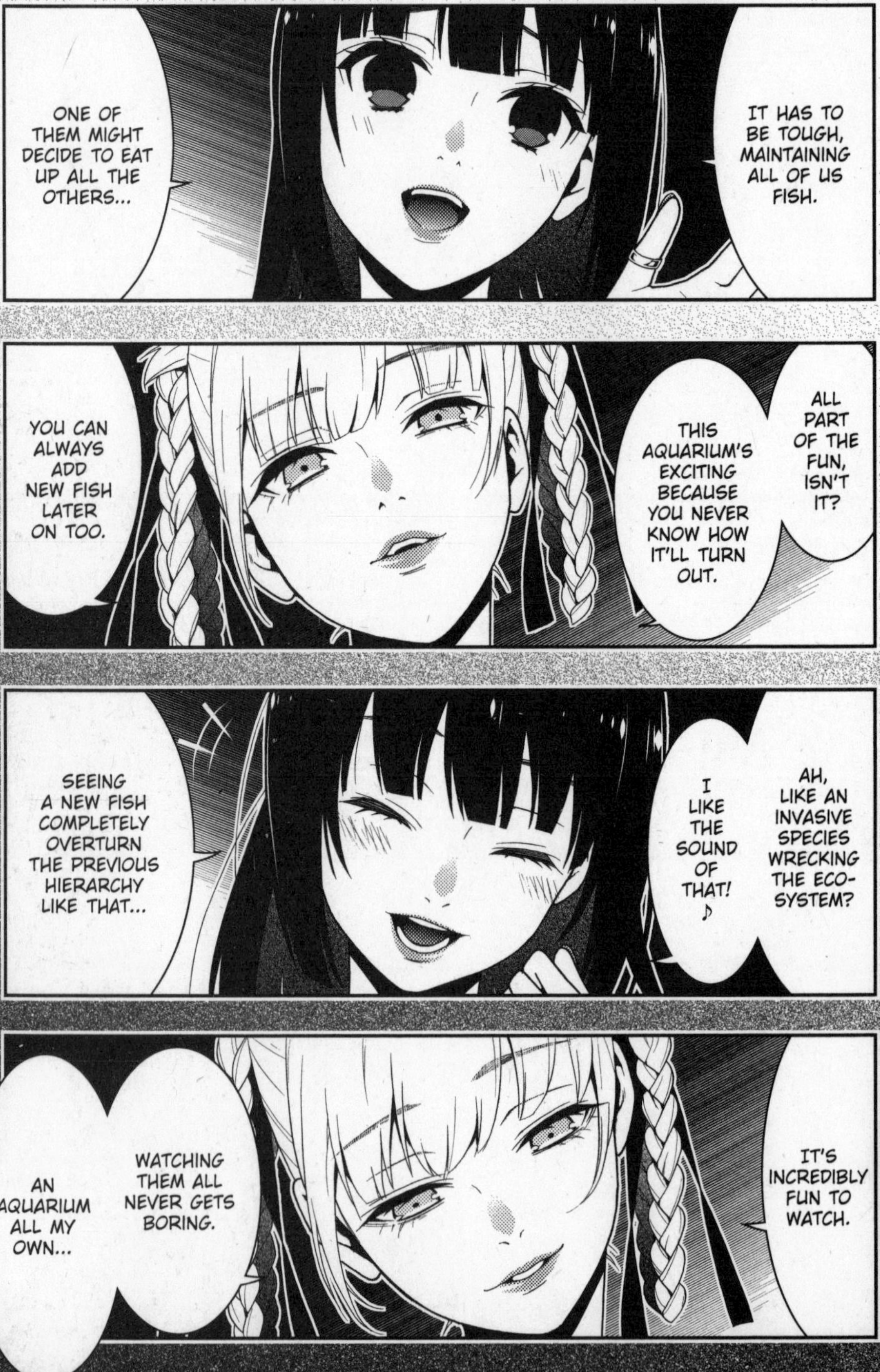
IT HAS TO BE TOUGH, MAINTAINING ALL OF US FISH.
ONE OF THEM MIGHT DECIDE TO EAT UP ALL THE OTHERS...
ALL PART OF THE FUN, ISN'T IT?
THIS AQUARIUM'S EXCITING BECAUSE YOU NEVER KNOW HOW IT'LL TURN OUT.
YOU CAN ALWAYS ADD NEW FISH LATER ON TOO.
AH, LIKE AN INVASIVE SPECIES WRECKING THE ECO-SYSTEM?
I LIKE THE SOUND OF THAT! ♪
SEEING A NEW FISH COMPLETELY OVERTURN THE PREVIOUS HIERARCHY LIKE THAT...
IT'S INCREDIBLY FUN TO WATCH.
WATCHING THEM ALL NEVER GETS BORING.
AN AQUARIUM ALL MY OWN...

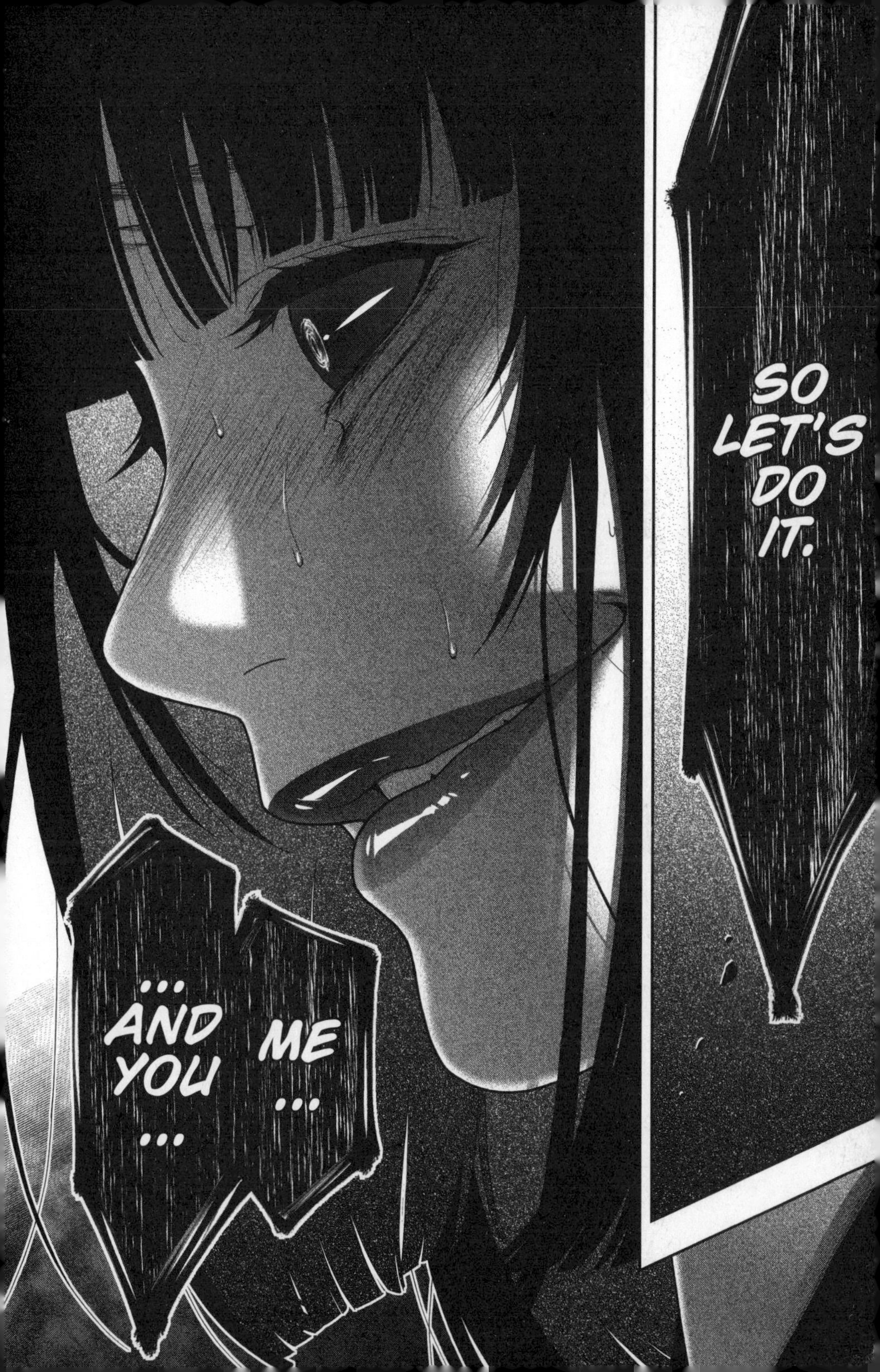
SO LET'S DO IT.
...AND YOU... ME...

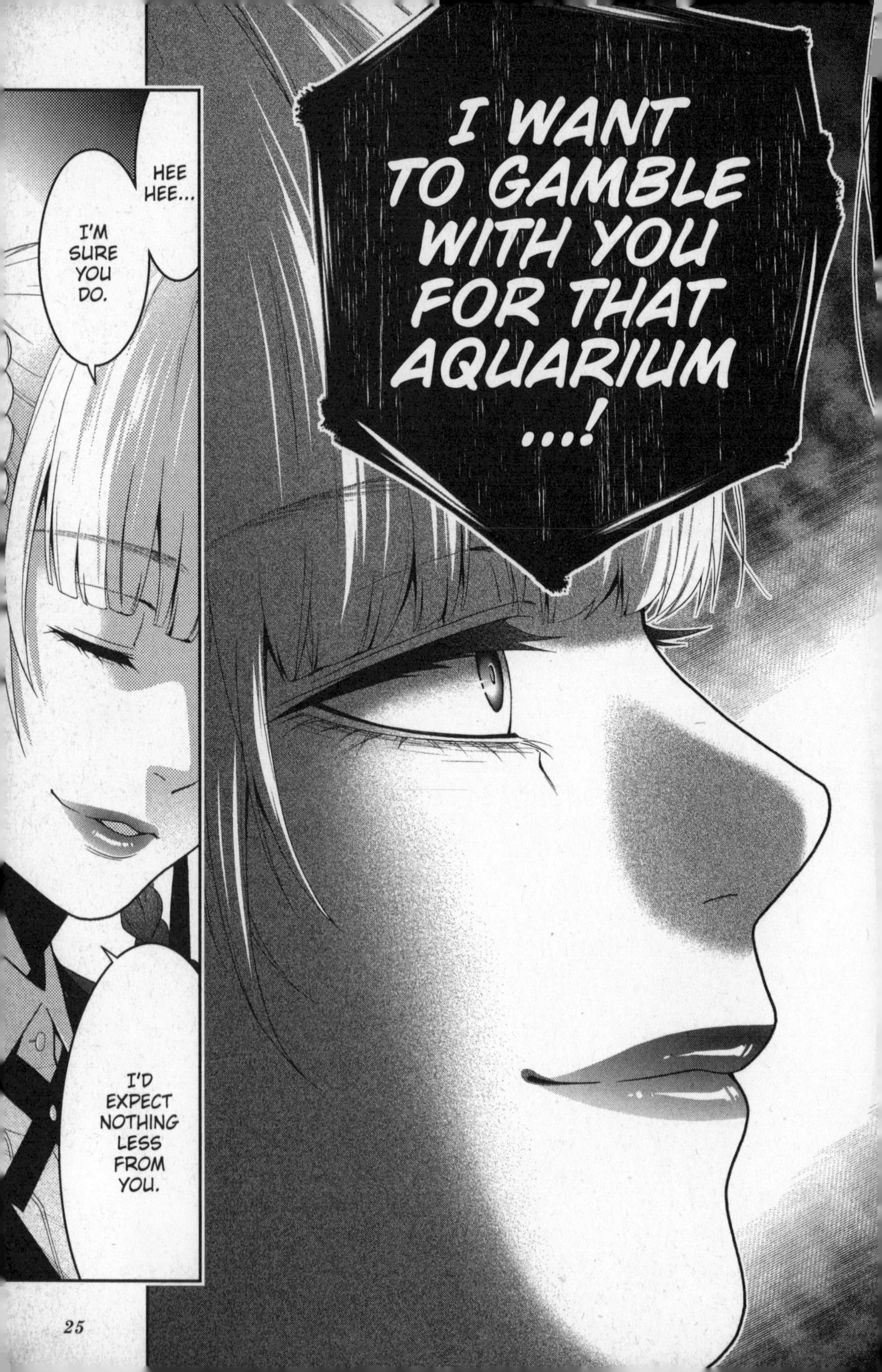
I WANT TO GAMBLE WITH YOU FOR THAT AQUARIUM ...!
HEE HEE...
I'M SURE YOU DO.
I'D EXPECT NOTHING LESS FROM YOU.

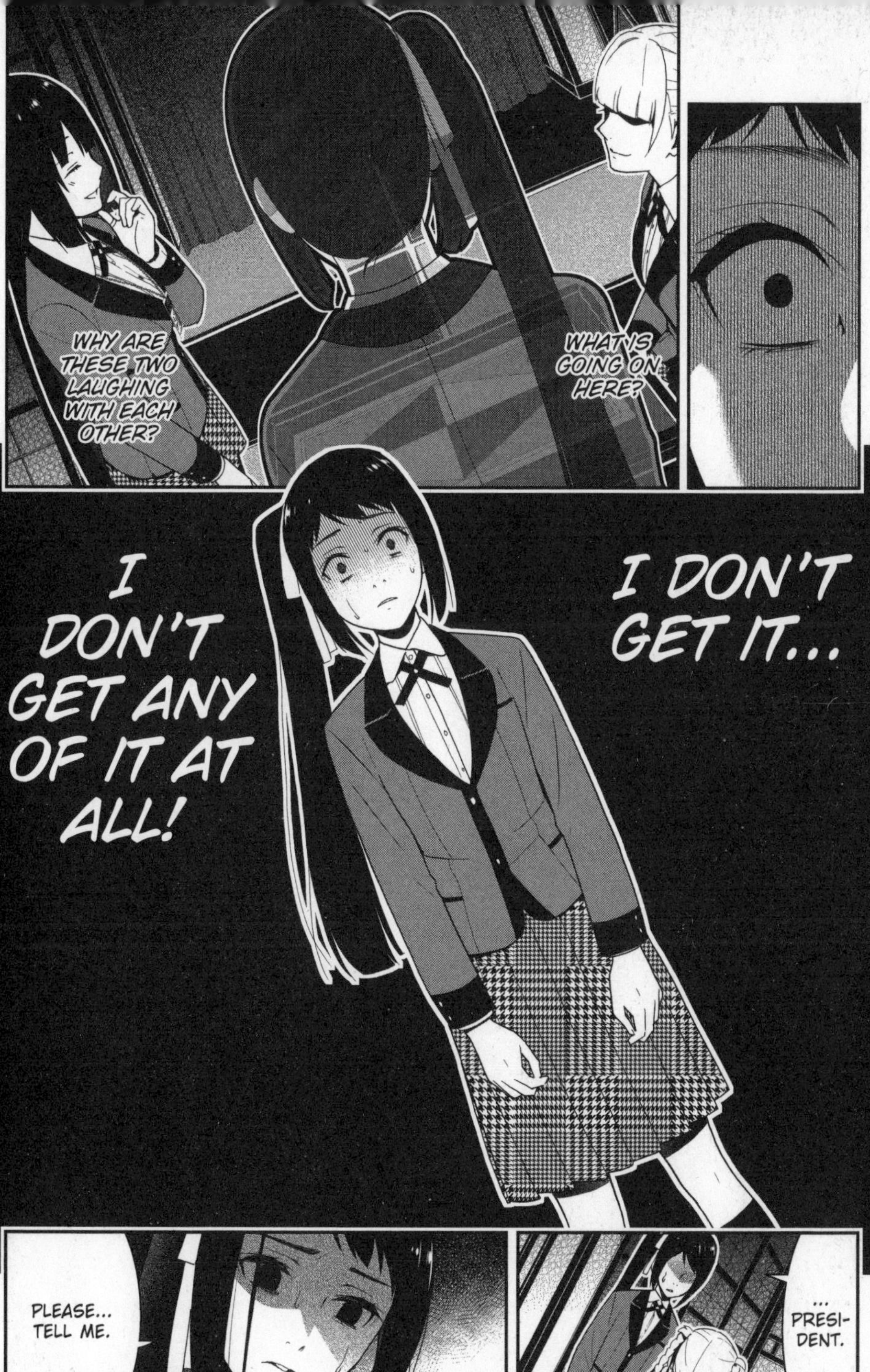
WHAT IS GOING ON HERE?
WHY ARE THESE TWO LAUGHING WITH EACH OTHER?
I DON'T GET IT...
I DON'T GET ANY OF IT AT ALL!
...PRESIDENT.
PLEASE... TELL ME.

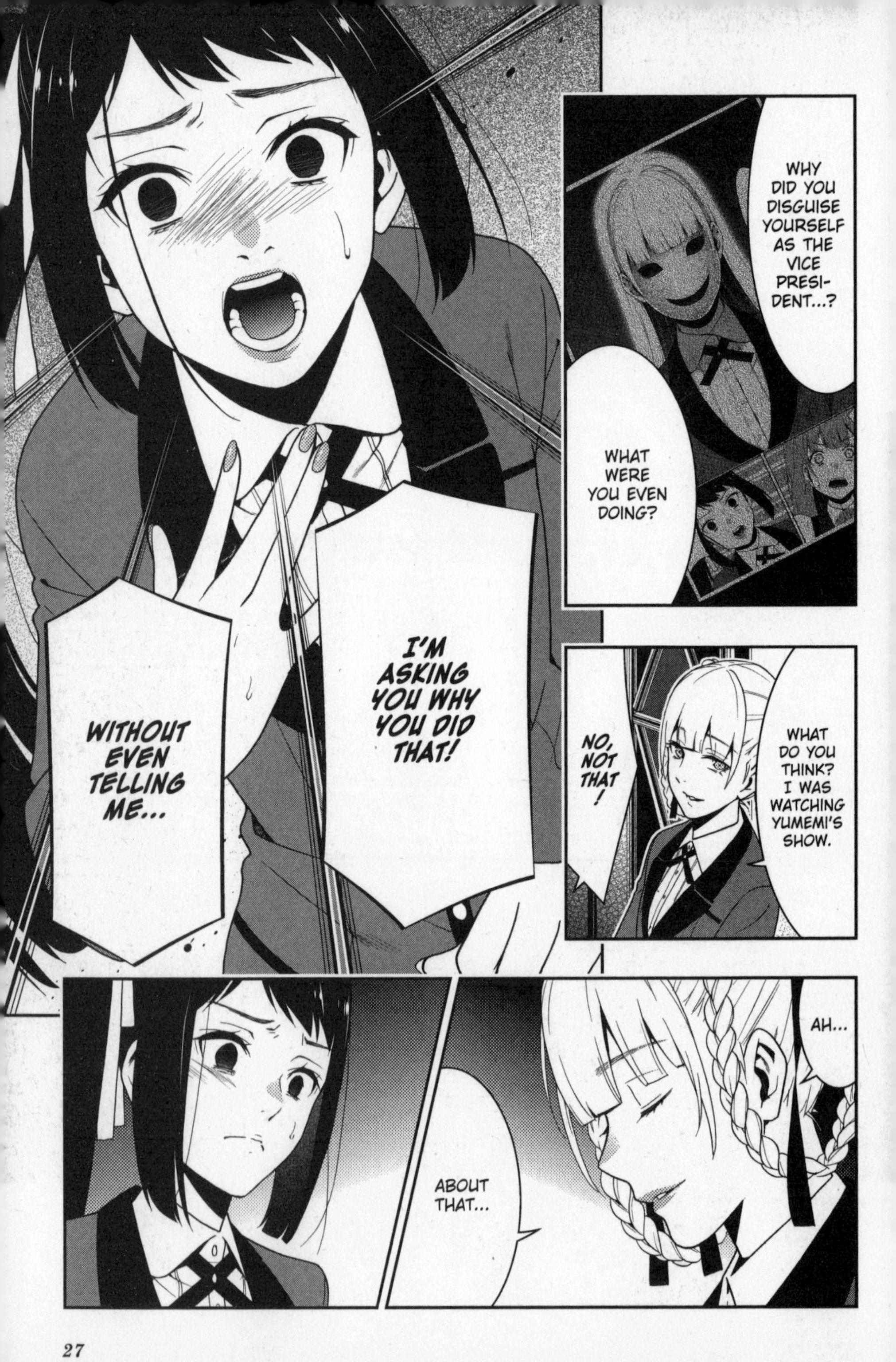
WHY DID YOU DISGUISE YOURSELF AS THE VICE PRESIDENT...?
WHAT WERE YOU EVEN DOING?
WHAT DO YOU THINK? I WAS WATCHING YUMEMI'S SHOW.
NO, NOT THAT!
I'M ASKING YOU WHY YOU DID THAT!
WITHOUT EVEN TELLING ME...
AH...
ABOUT THAT...

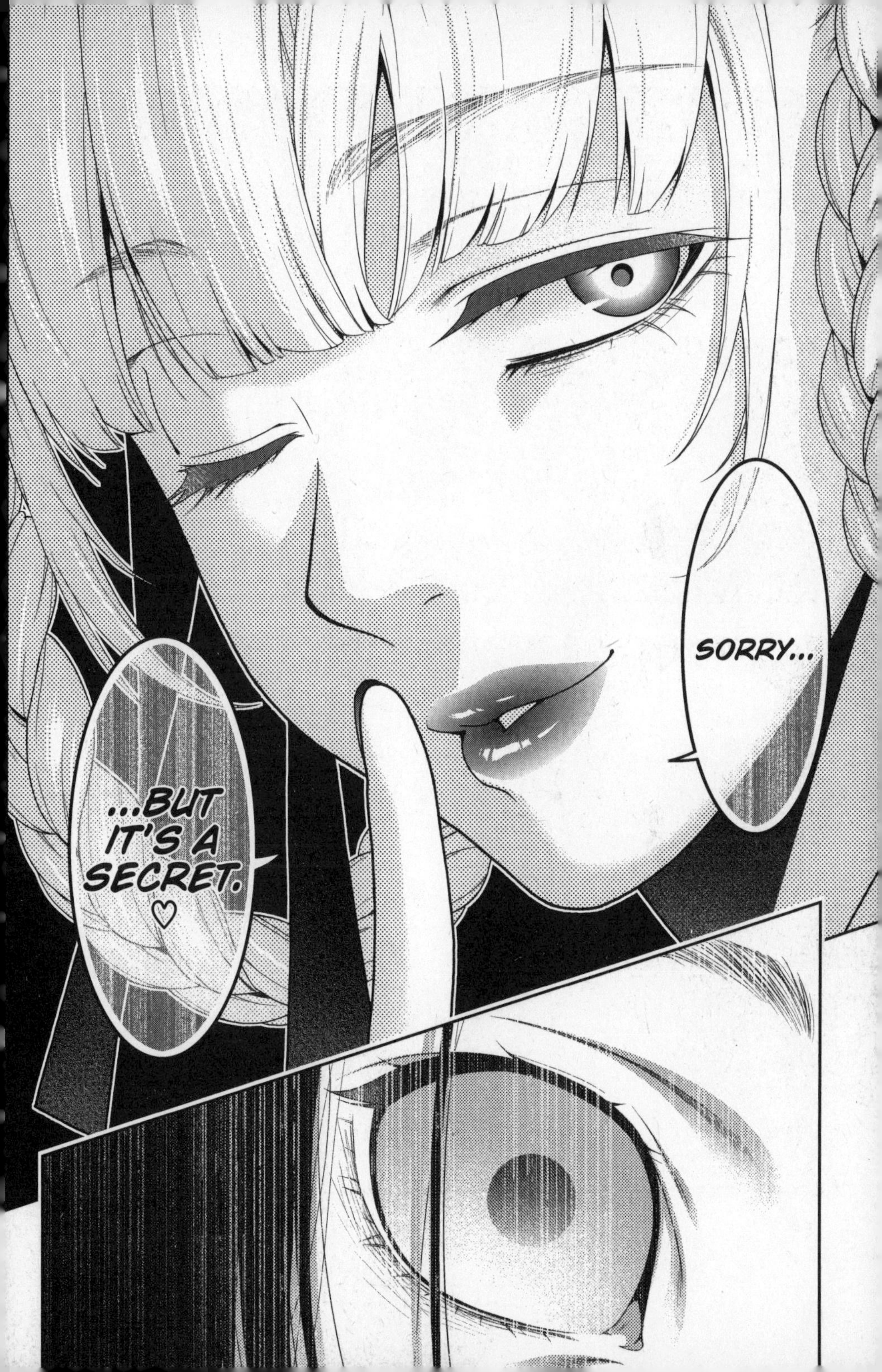
SORRY...
...BUT IT'S A SECRET. ♡

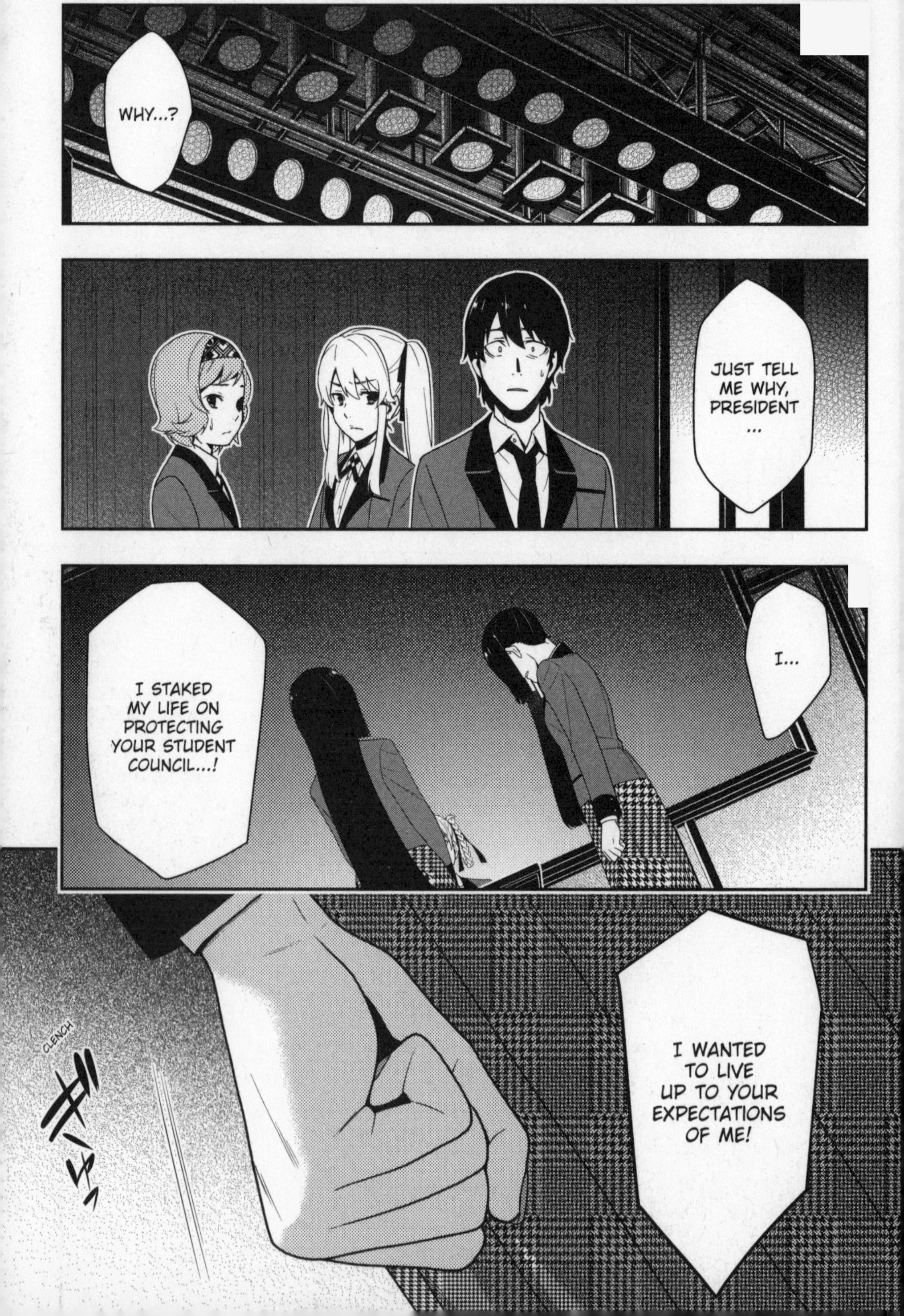
WHY...?
JUST TELL ME WHY, PRESIDENT ...
I...
I STAKED MY LIFE ON PROTECTING YOUR STUDENT COUNCIL...!
I WANTED TO LIVE UP TO YOUR EXPECTATIONS OF ME!
CLENCH

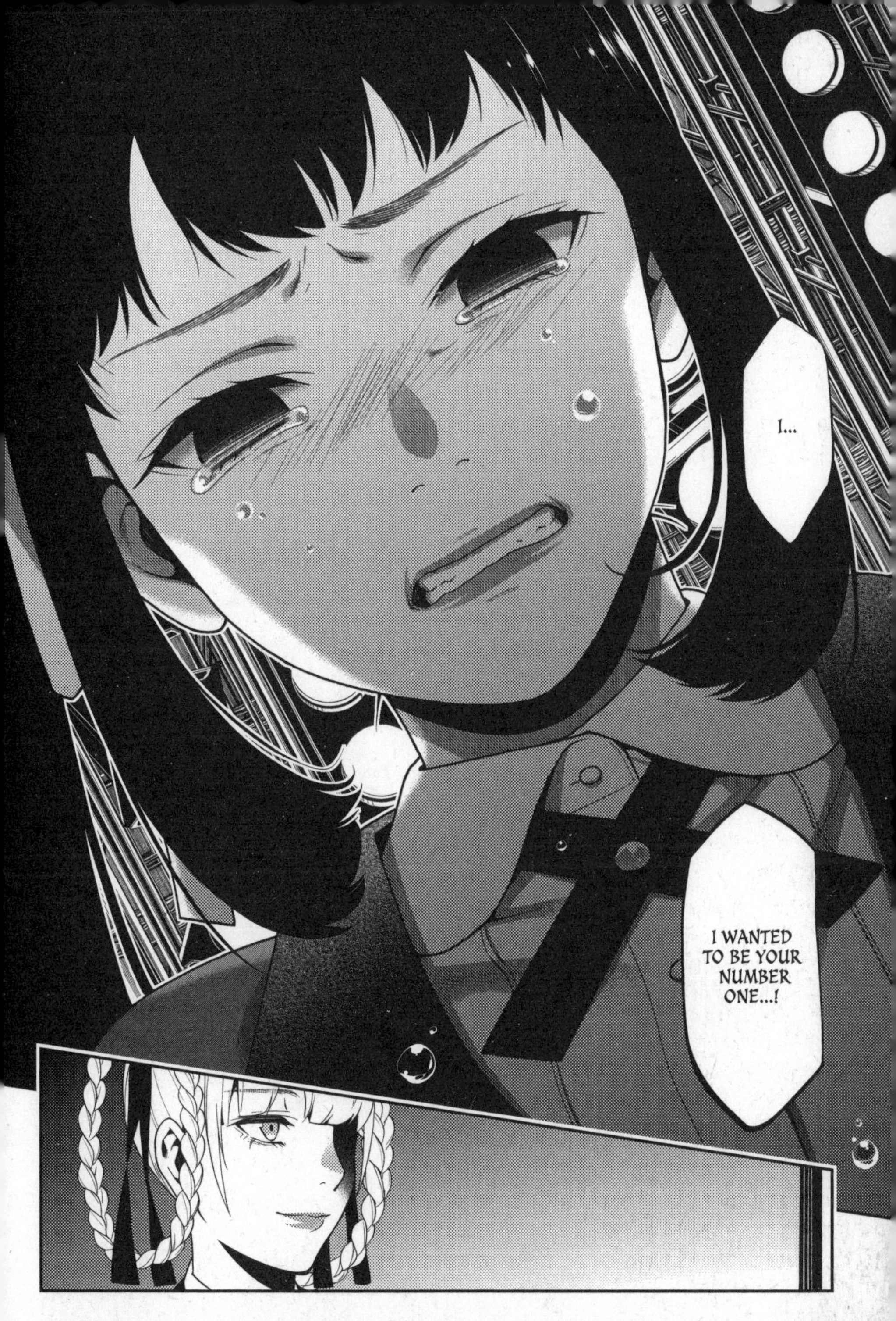
I...
I WANTED TO BE YOUR NUMBER ONE...!

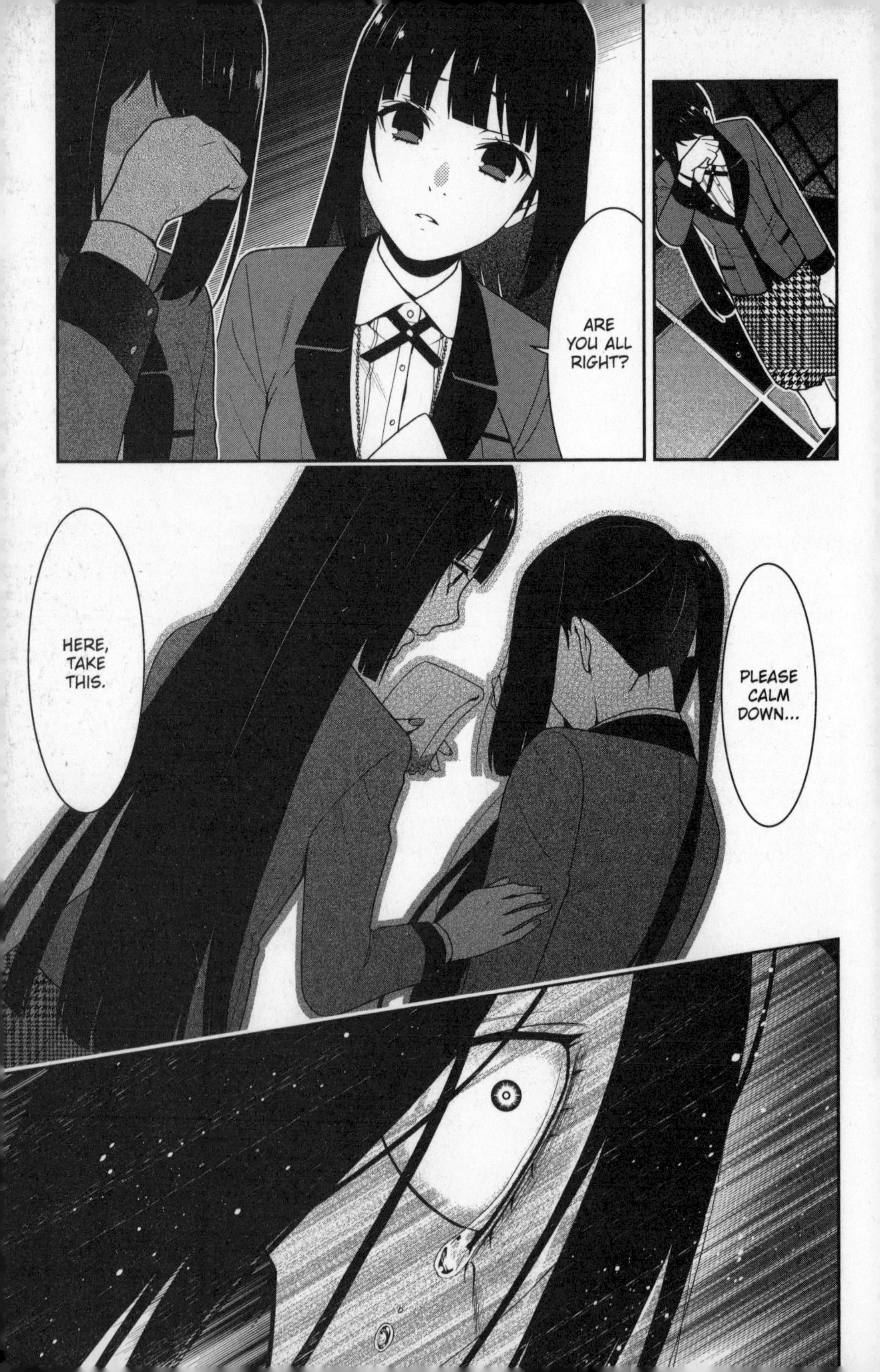
ARE YOU ALL RIGHT?
PLEASE CALM DOWN...
HERE, TAKE THIS.

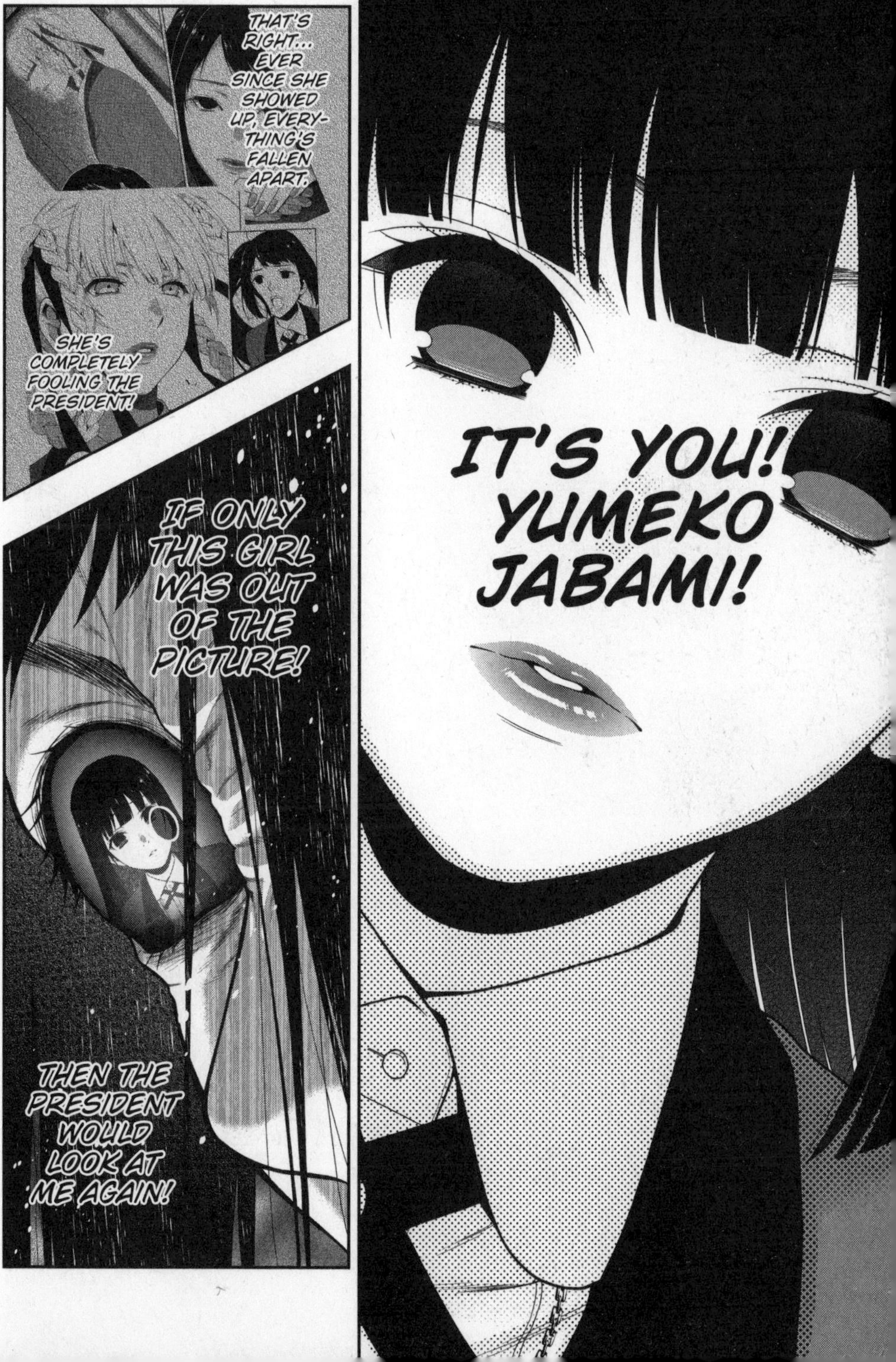
IT'S YOU! YUMEKO JABAMI!
THAT'S RIGHT... EVER SINCE SHE SHOWED UP, EVERY-THING'S FALLEN APART.
SHE'S COMPLETELY FOOLING THE PRESIDENT!
IF ONLY THIS GIRL WAS OUT OF THE PICTURE!
THEN THE PRESIDENT WOULD LOOK AT ME AGAIN!

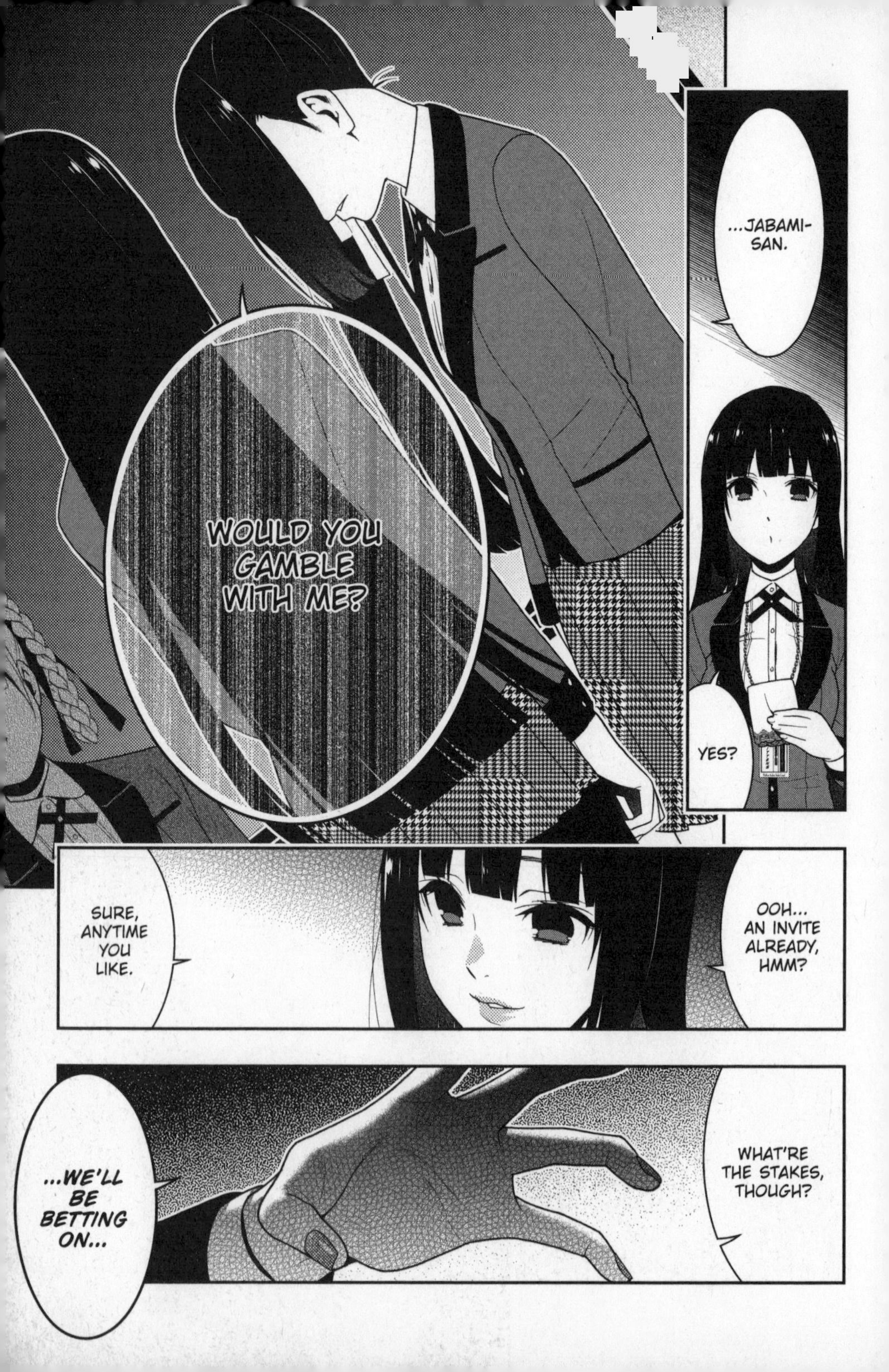
...JABAMI-SAN.
YES?
WOULD YOU GAMBLE WITH ME?
OOH... AN INVITE ALREADY, HMM?
SURE, ANYTIME YOU LIKE.
WHAT'RE THE STAKES, THOUGH?
...WE'LL BE BETTING ON...

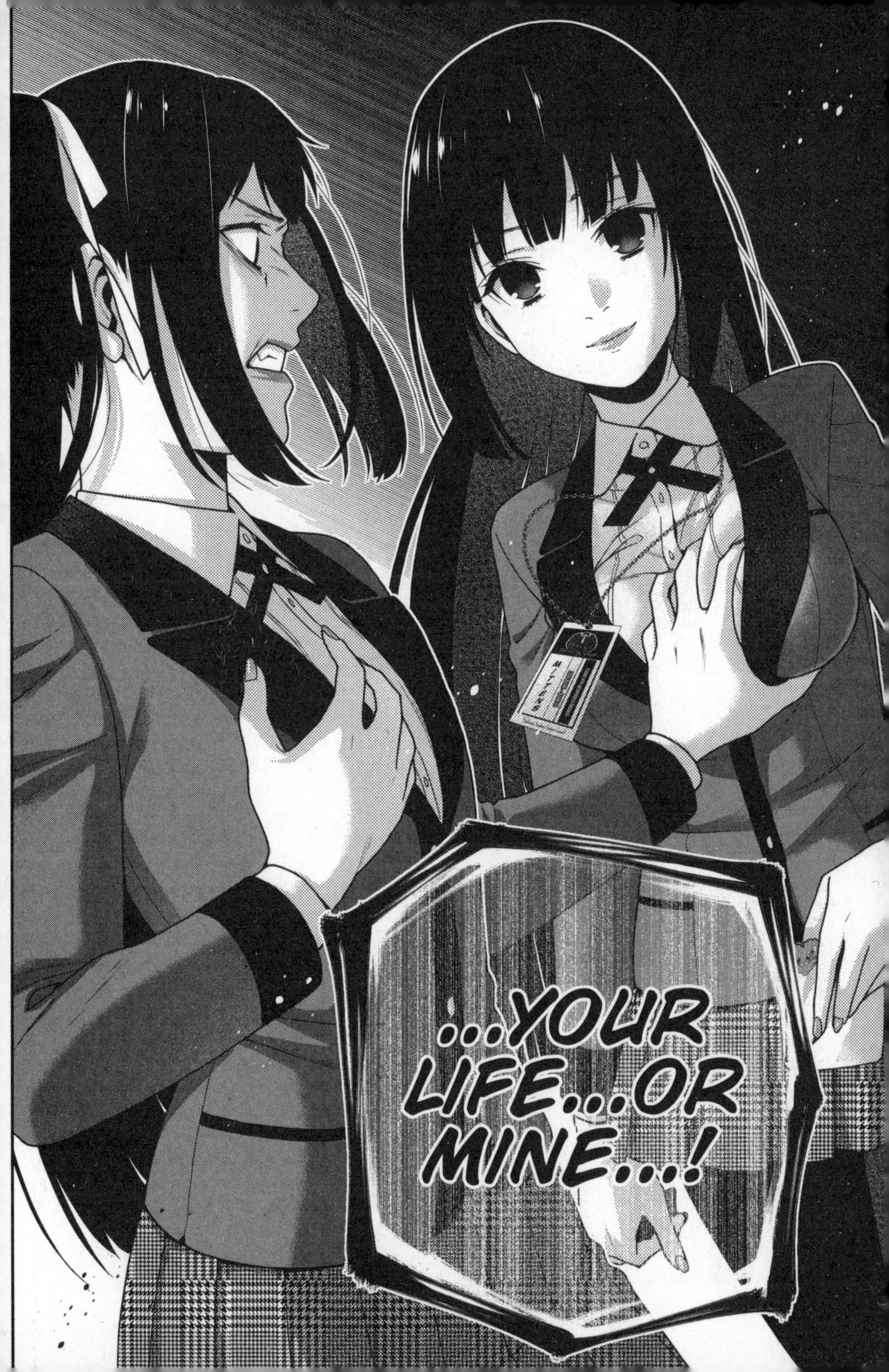
...YOUR LIFE...OR MINE...!

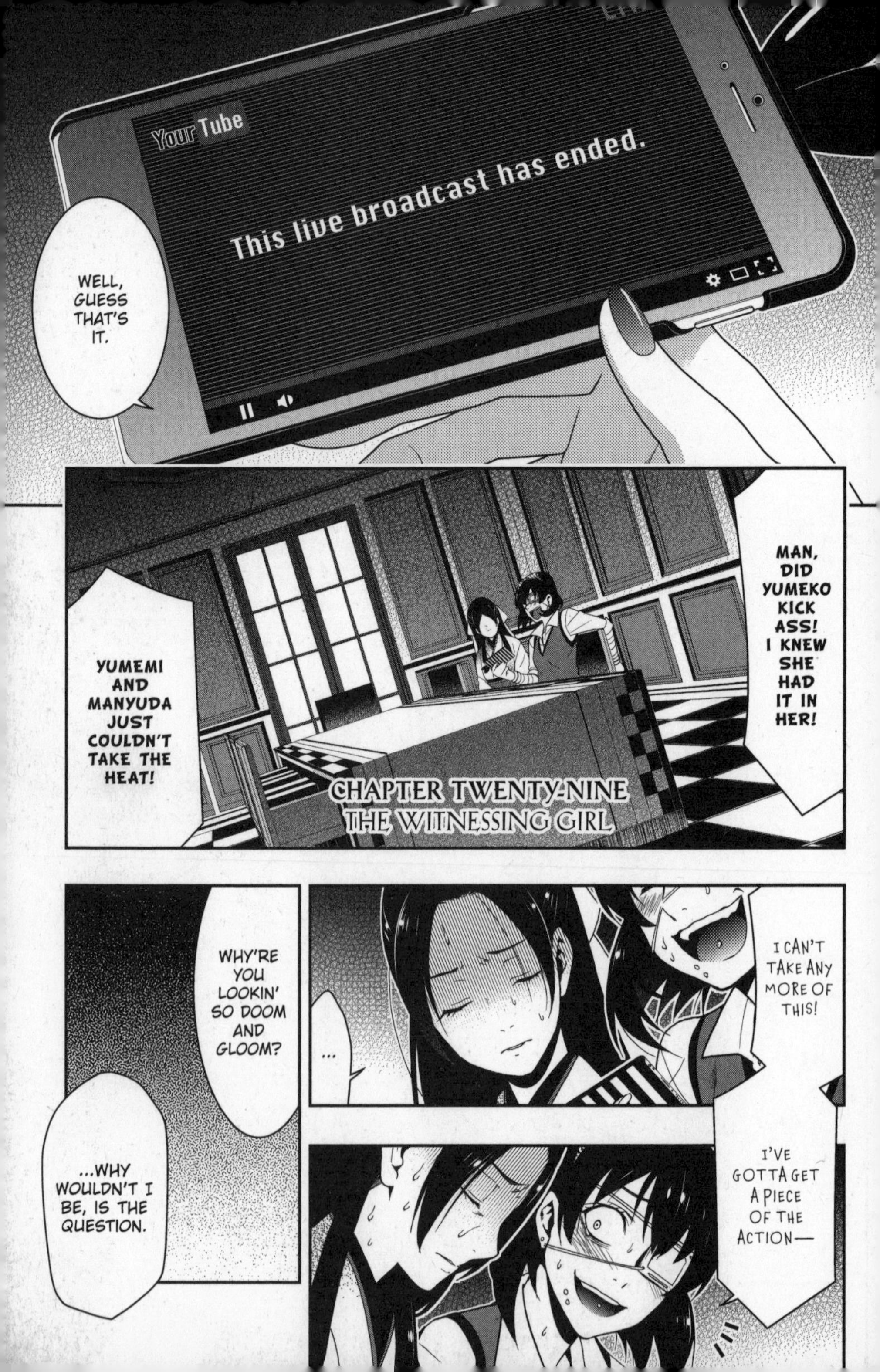
YourTube
This live broadcast has ended.
WELL, GUESS THAT'S IT.
MAN, DID YUMEKO KICK ASS! I KNEW SHE HAD IT IN HER!
YUMEMI AND MANYUDA JUST COULDN'T TAKE THE HEAT!
CHAPTER TWENTY-NINE
THE WITNESSING GIRL
I CAN'T TAKE ANY MORE OF THIS!
...
WHY'RE YOU LOOKIN' SO DOOM AND GLOOM?
I'VE GOTTA GET A PIECE OF THE ACTION—
...WHY WOULDN'T I BE, IS THE QUESTION.

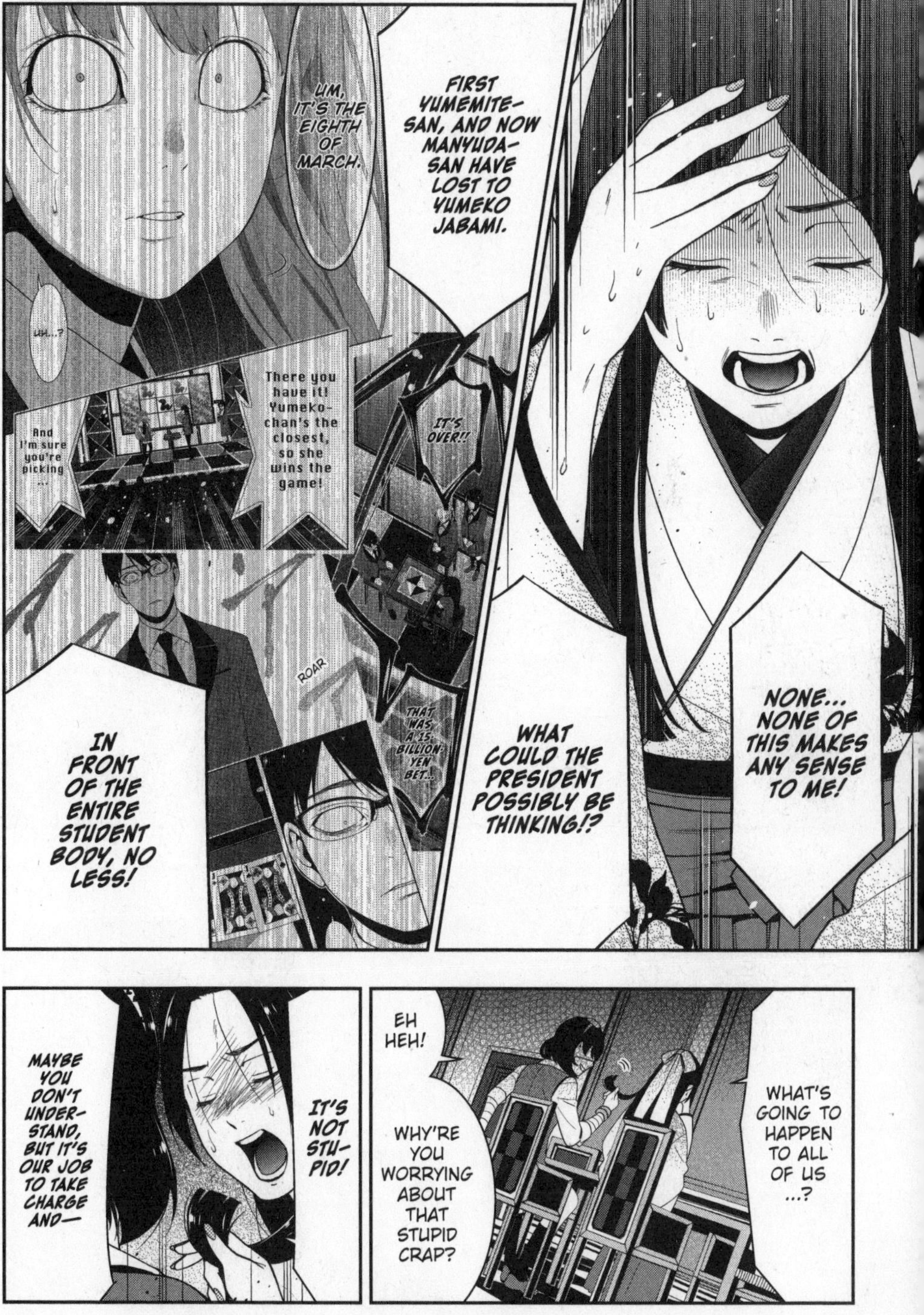
FIRST YUMEMITE-SAN, AND NOW MANYUDA-SAN HAVE LOST TO YUMEKO JABAMI.
NONE... NONE OF THIS MAKES ANY SENSE TO ME!
WHAT COULD THE PRESIDENT POSSIBLY BE THINKING!?
UM, IT'S THE EIGHTH OF MARCH.
UH...?
There you have it! Yumeko-chan's the closest, so she wins the game!
And I'm sure you're picking ...
IT'S OVER!!
ROAR
THAT WAS A 15-BILLION-YEN BET...
IN FRONT OF THE ENTIRE STUDENT BODY, NO LESS!
WHAT'S GOING TO HAPPEN TO ALL OF US ...?
EH HEH!
WHY'RE YOU WORRYING ABOUT THAT STUPID CRAP?
IT'S NOT STU-PID!
MAYBE YOU DON'T UNDER-STAND, BUT IT'S OUR JOB TO TAKE CHARGE AND—

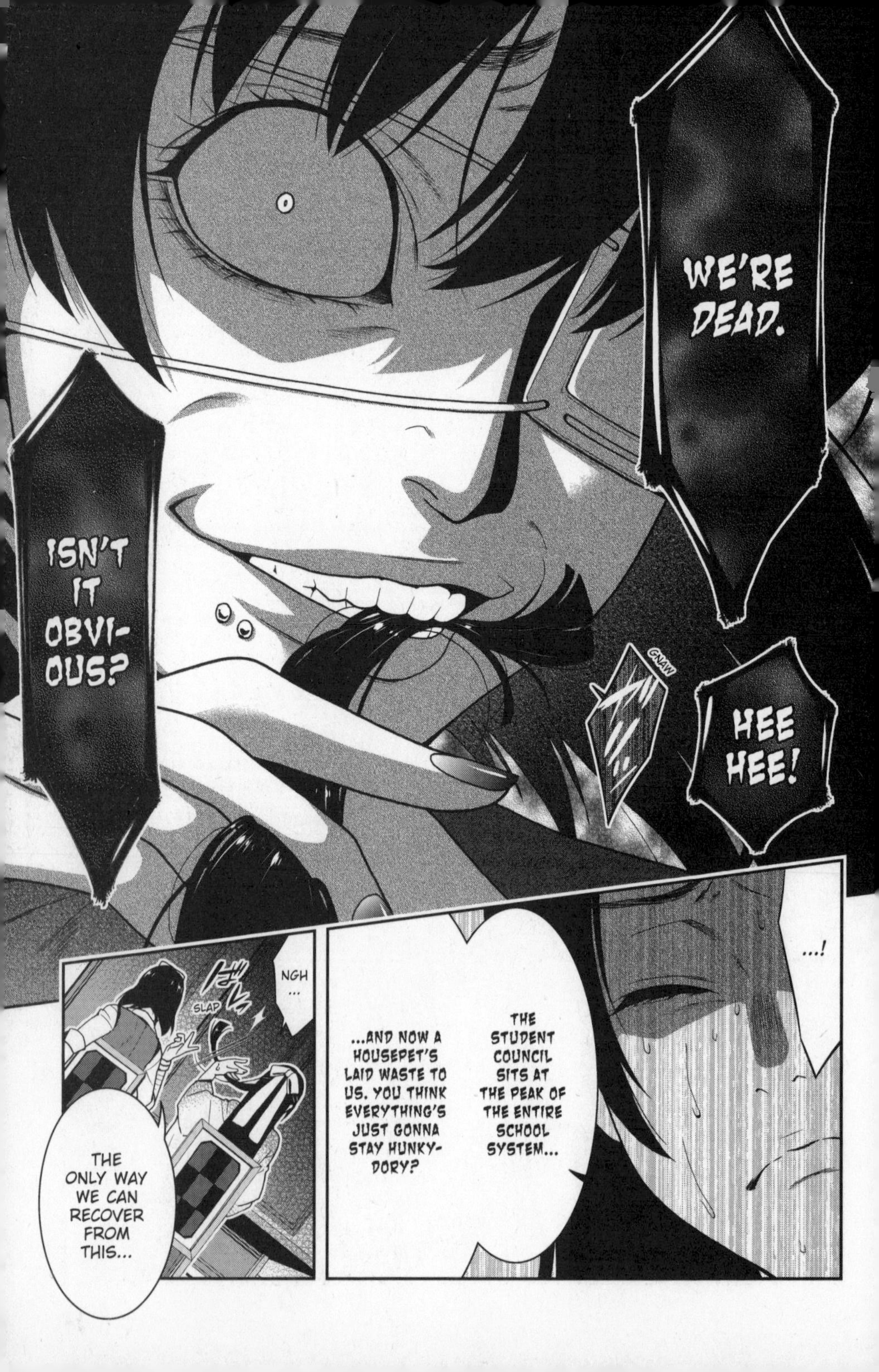
WE'RE DEAD.
ISN'T IT OBVI-OUS?
GNAW
HEE HEE!
...!
THE STUDENT COUNCIL SITS AT THE PEAK OF THE ENTIRE SCHOOL SYSTEM...
...AND NOW A HOUSEPET'S LAID WASTE TO US. YOU THINK EVERYTHING'S JUST GONNA STAY HUNKY-DORY?
NGH...
SLAP
THE ONLY WAY WE CAN RECOVER FROM THIS...

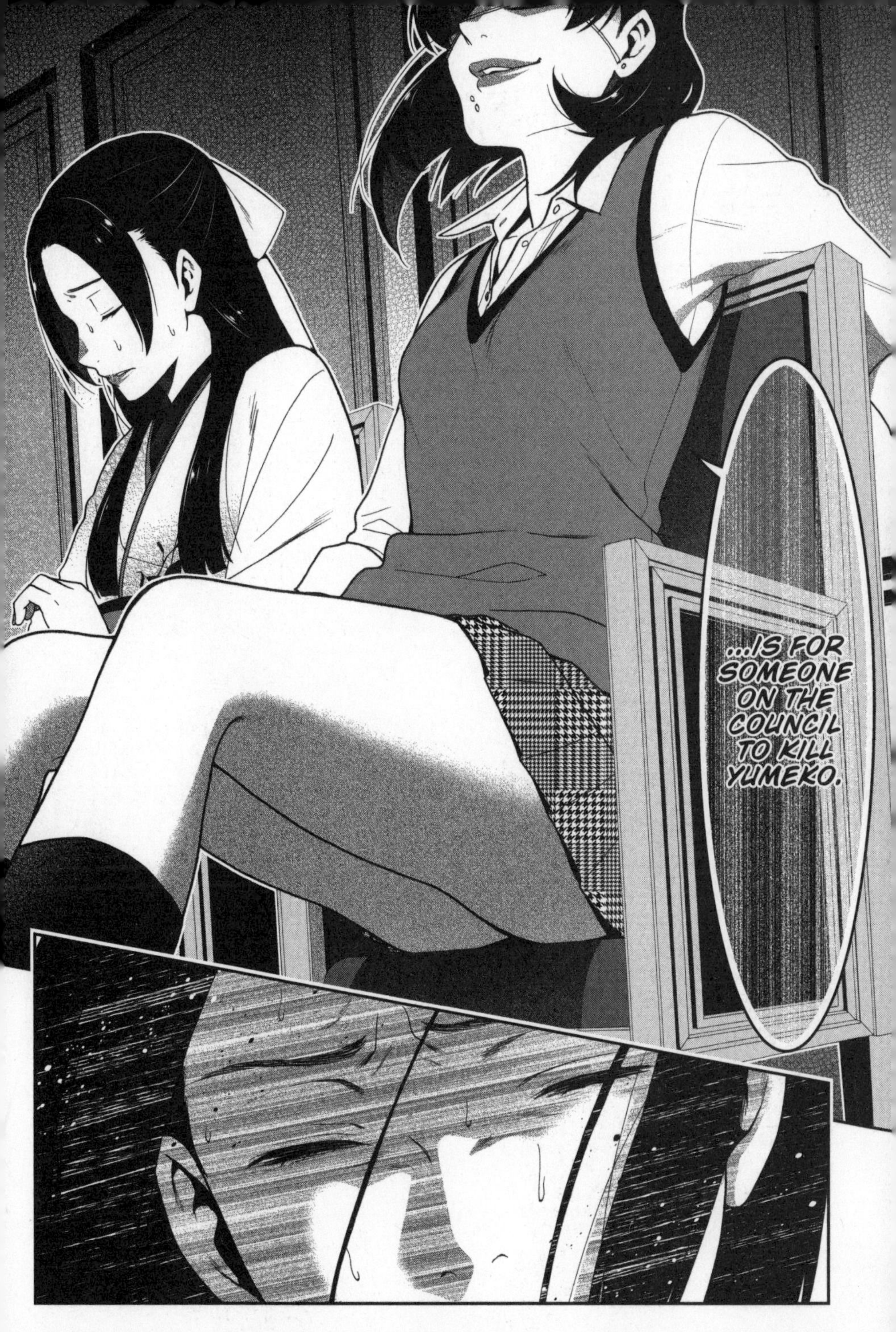
...IS FOR SOMEONE ON THE COUNCIL TO KILL YUMEKO.

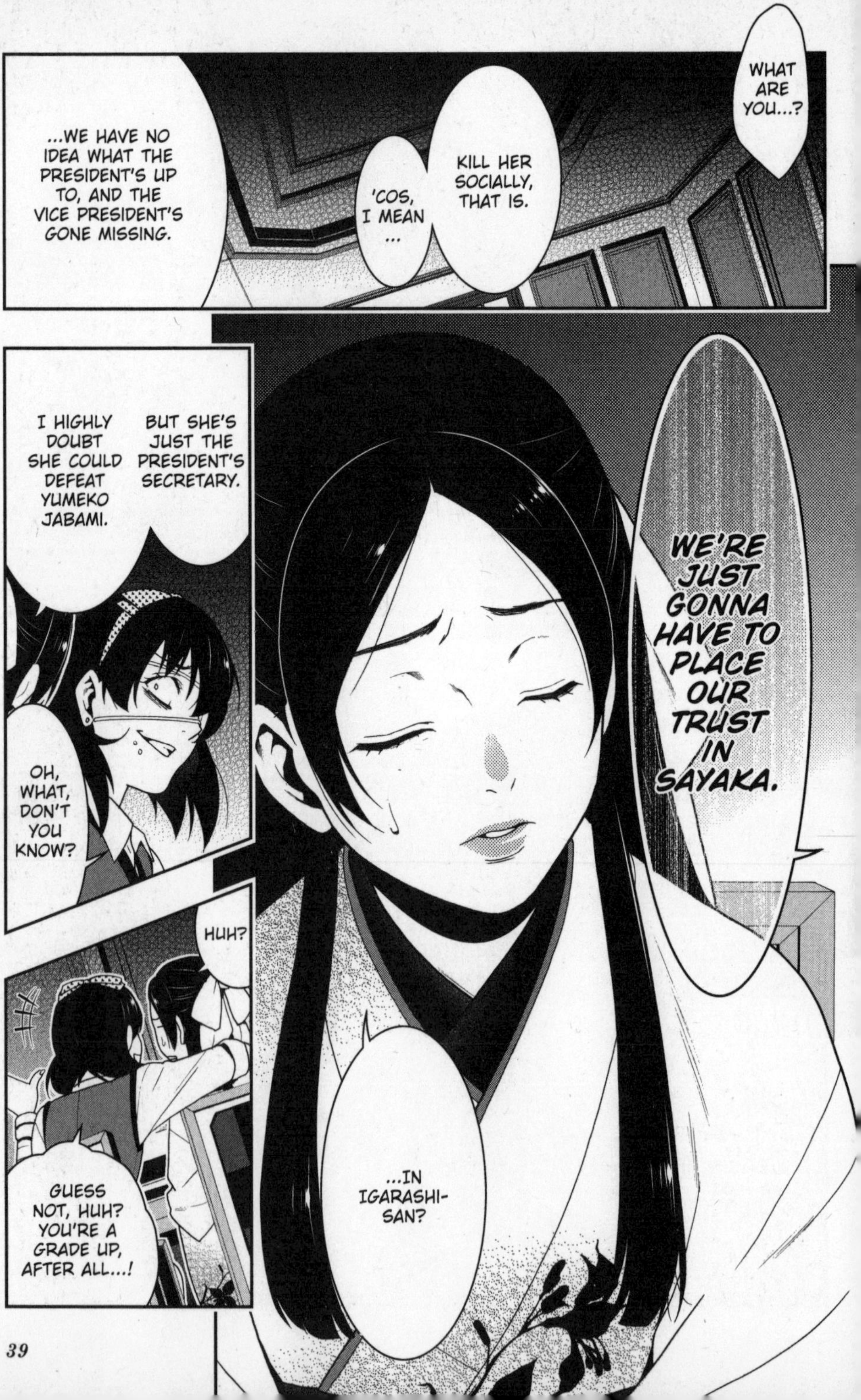
WHAT ARE YOU...?
KILL HER SOCIALLY, THAT IS.
'COS, I MEAN ...
...WE HAVE NO IDEA WHAT THE PRESIDENT'S UP TO, AND THE VICE PRESIDENT'S GONE MISSING.
WE'RE JUST GONNA HAVE TO PLACE OUR TRUST IN SAYAKA.
...IN IGARASHI-SAN?
BUT SHE'S JUST THE PRESIDENT'S SECRETARY.
I HIGHLY DOUBT SHE COULD DEFEAT YUMEKO JABAMI.
OH, WHAT, DON'T YOU KNOW?
HUH?
GUESS NOT, HUH? YOU'RE A GRADE UP, AFTER ALL...!

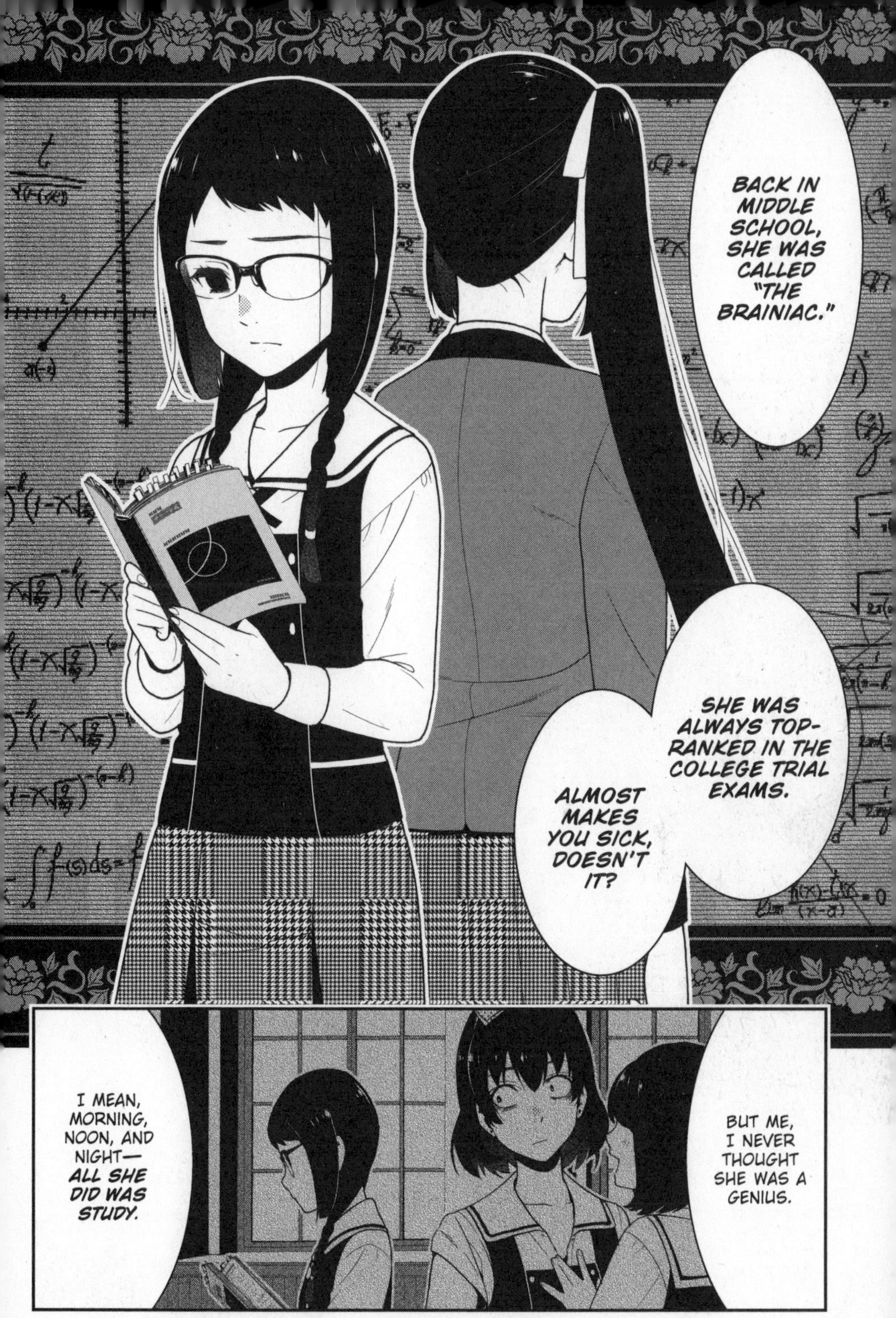
BACK IN MIDDLE SCHOOL, SHE WAS CALLED "THE BRAINIAC."
SHE WAS ALWAYS TOP-RANKED IN THE COLLEGE TRIAL EXAMS.
ALMOST MAKES YOU SICK, DOESN'T IT?
BUT ME, I NEVER THOUGHT SHE WAS A GENIUS.
I MEAN, MORNING, NOON, AND NIGHT—ALL SHE DID WAS STUDY.

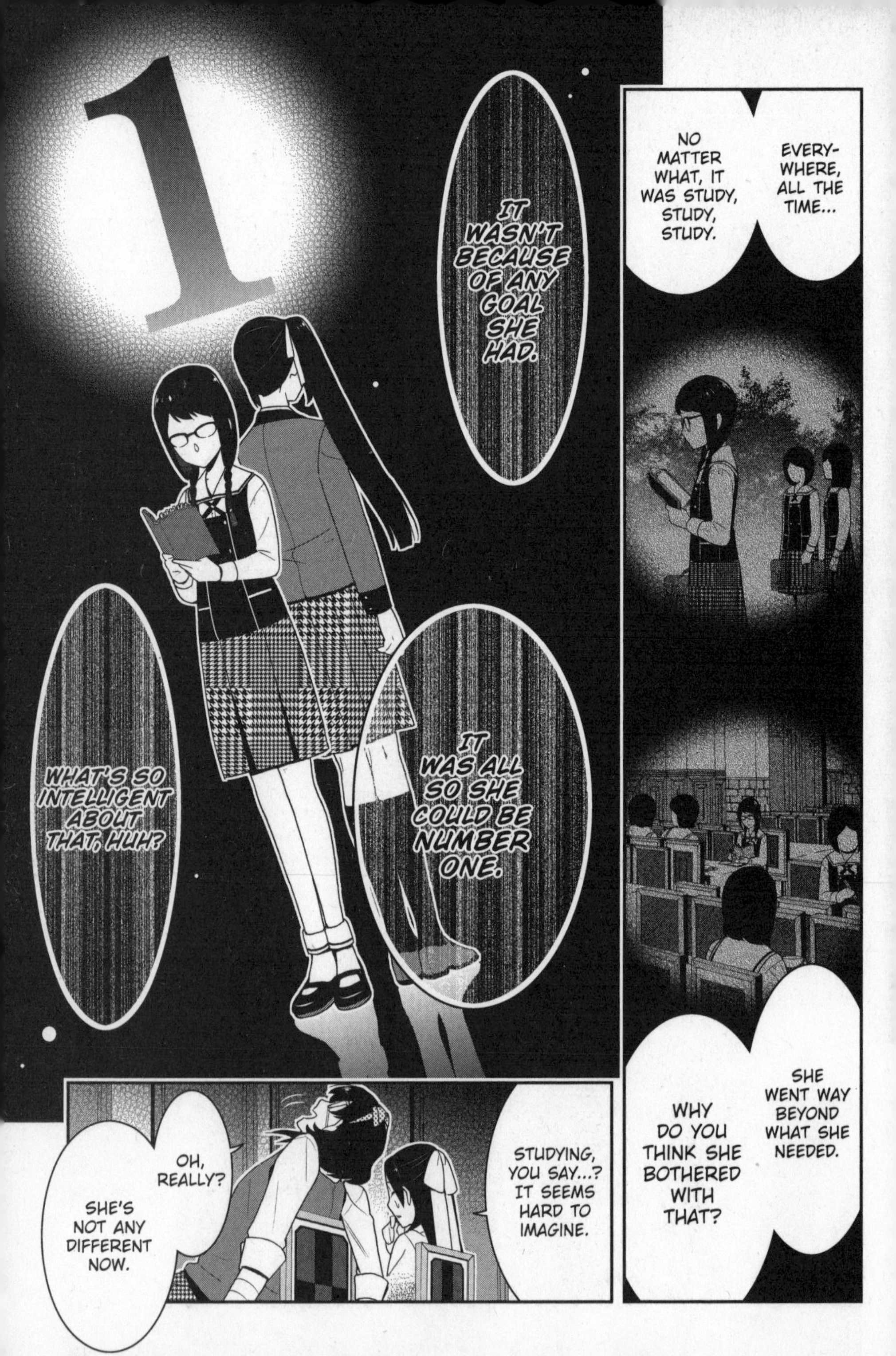
EVERY-WHERE, ALL THE TIME...
NO MATTER WHAT, IT WAS STUDY, STUDY, STUDY.
SHE WENT WAY BEYOND WHAT SHE NEEDED.
WHY DO YOU THINK SHE BOTHERED WITH THAT?
1
IT WASN'T BECAUSE OF ANY GOAL SHE HAD.
IT WAS ALL SO SHE COULD BE NUMBER ONE.
WHAT'S SO INTELLIGENT ABOUT THAT, HUH?
STUDYING, YOU SAY...? IT SEEMS HARD TO IMAGINE.
OH, REALLY?
SHE'S NOT ANY DIFFERENT NOW.

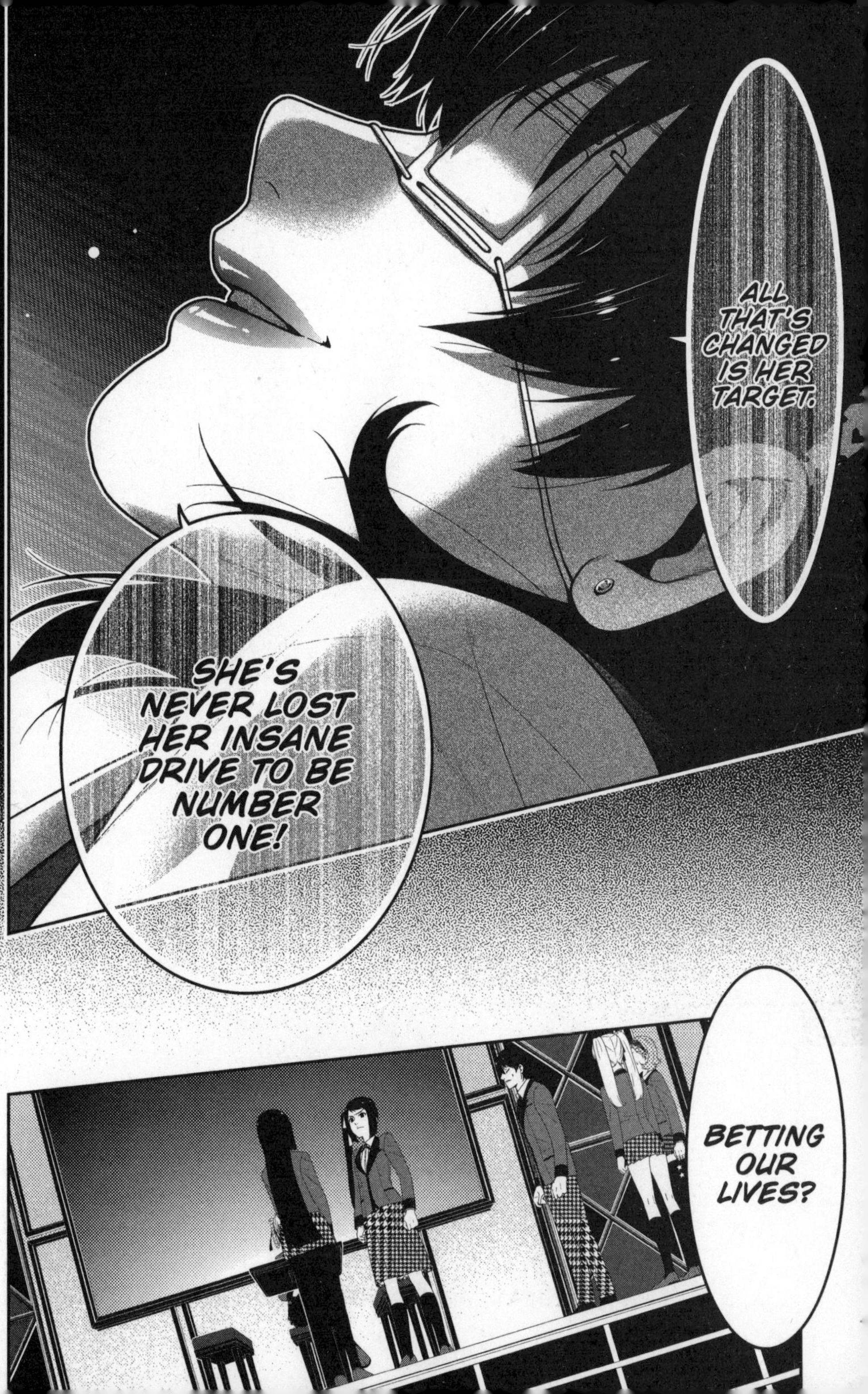
ALL THAT'S CHANGED IS HER TARGET.
SHE'S NEVER LOST HER INSANE DRIVE TO BE NUMBER ONE!
BETTING OUR LIVES?

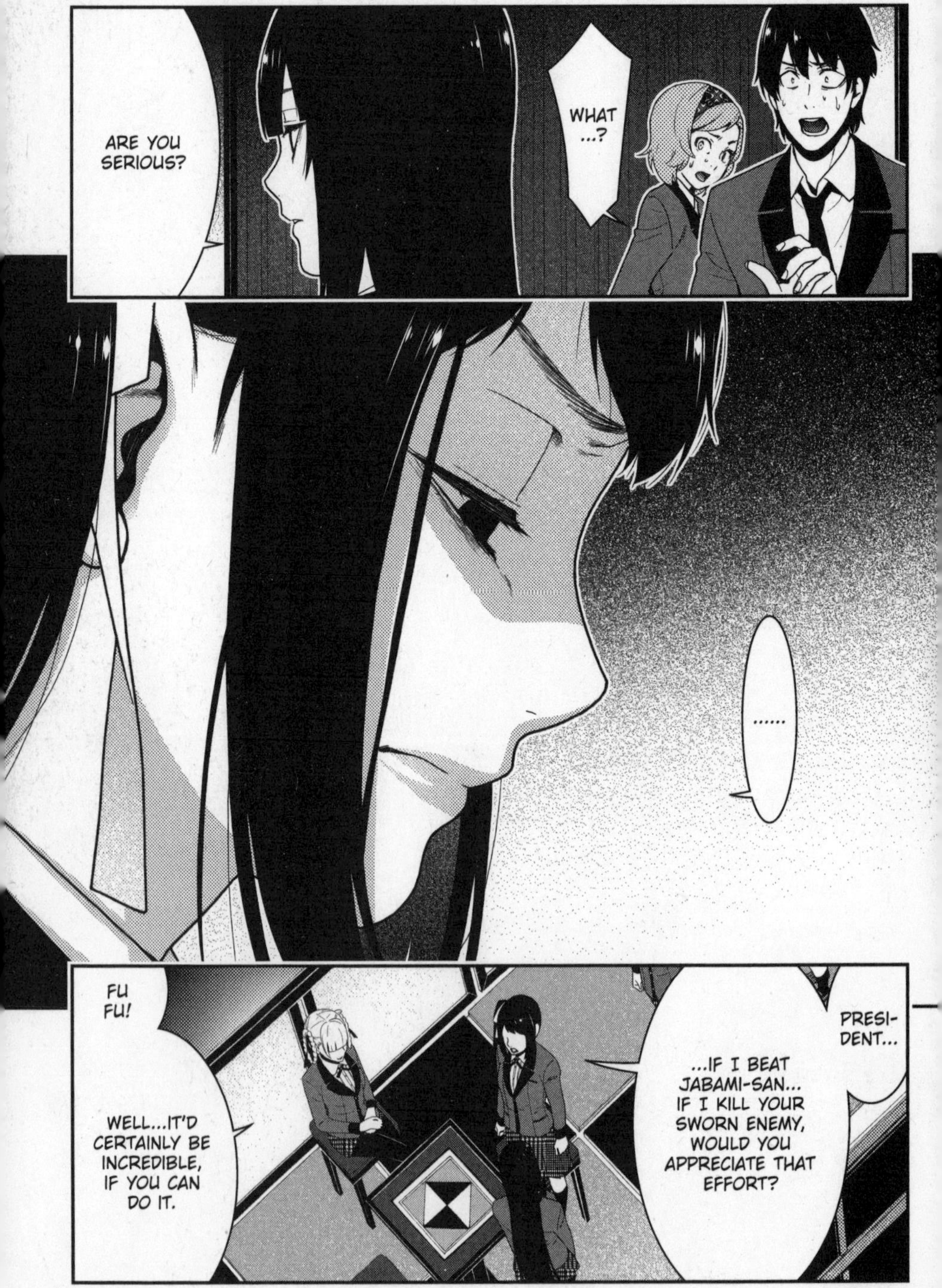
WHAT ...?
ARE YOU SERIOUS?
......
PRESI-DENT...
...IF I BEAT JABAMI-SAN... IF I KILL YOUR SWORN ENEMY, WOULD YOU APPRECIATE THAT EFFORT?
FU FU!
WELL...IT'D CERTAINLY BE INCREDIBLE, IF YOU CAN DO IT.

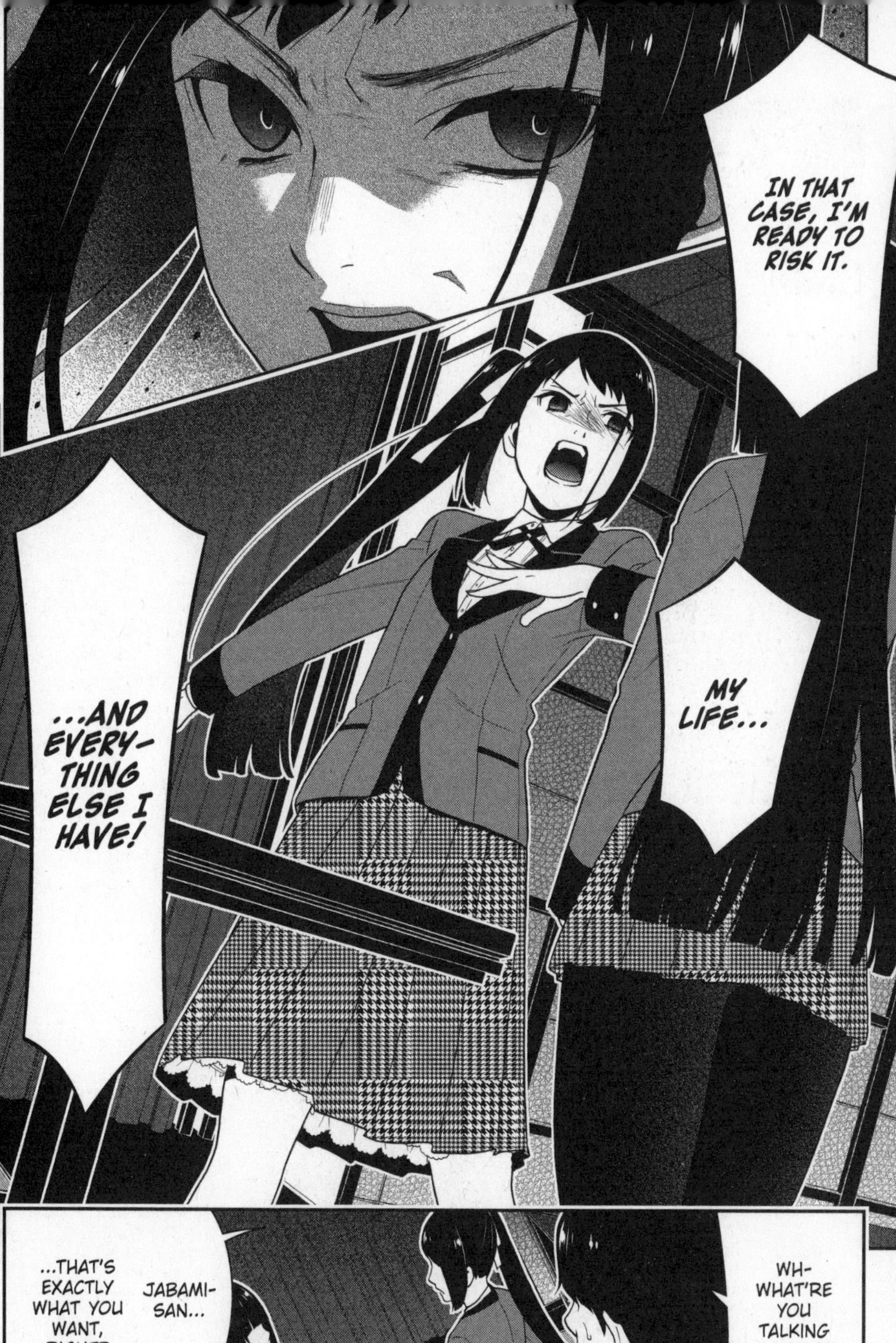
IN THAT CASE, I'M READY TO RISK IT.
MY LIFE...
...AND EVERY-THING ELSE I HAVE!
WH-WHAT'RE YOU TALKING ABOUT!?
JABAMI-SAN...
...THAT'S EXACTLY WHAT YOU WANT, RIGHT?

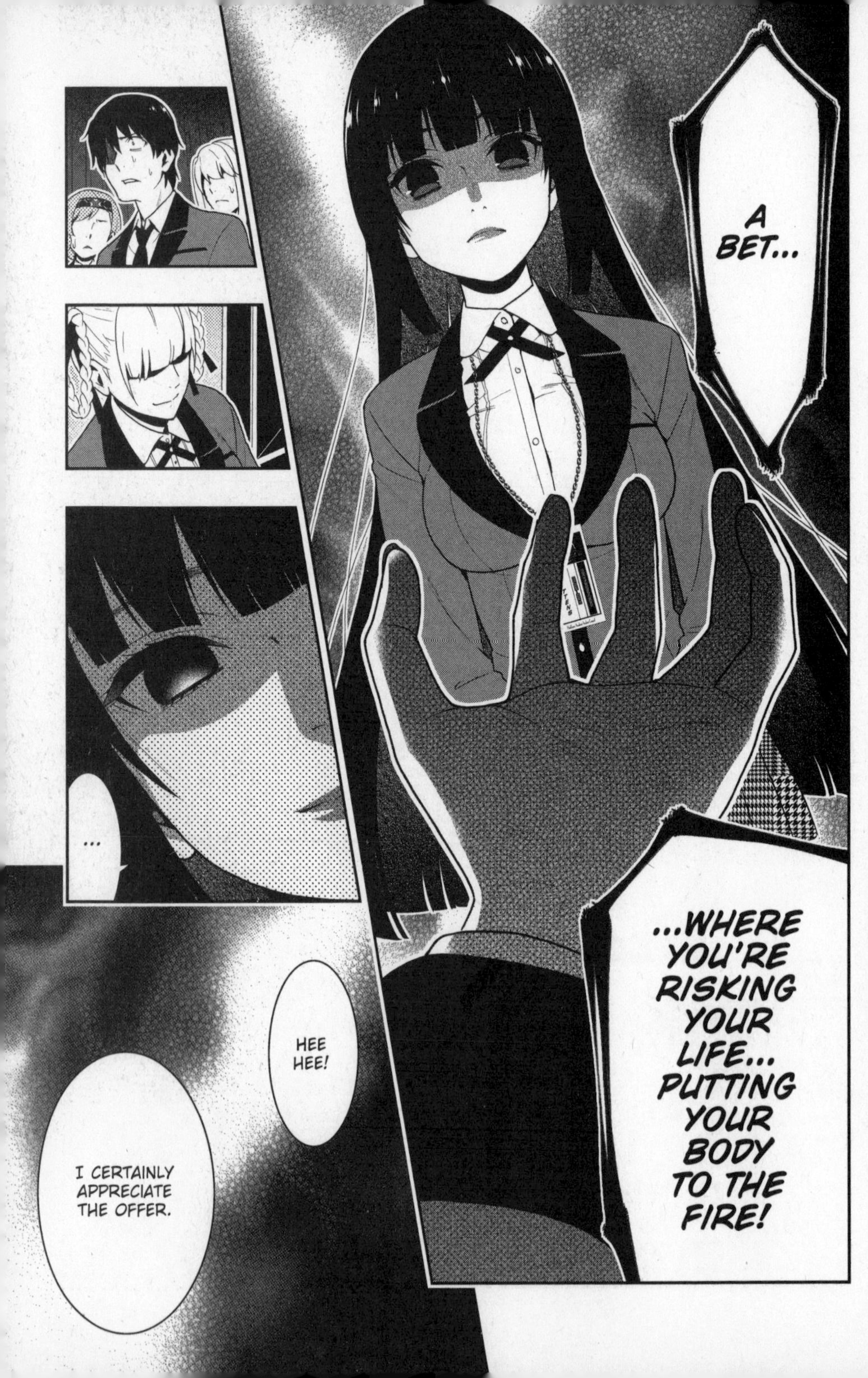
A BET...
...WHERE YOU'RE RISKING YOUR LIFE... PUTTING YOUR BODY TO THE FIRE!
...
HEE HEE!
I CERTAINLY APPRECIATE THE OFFER.

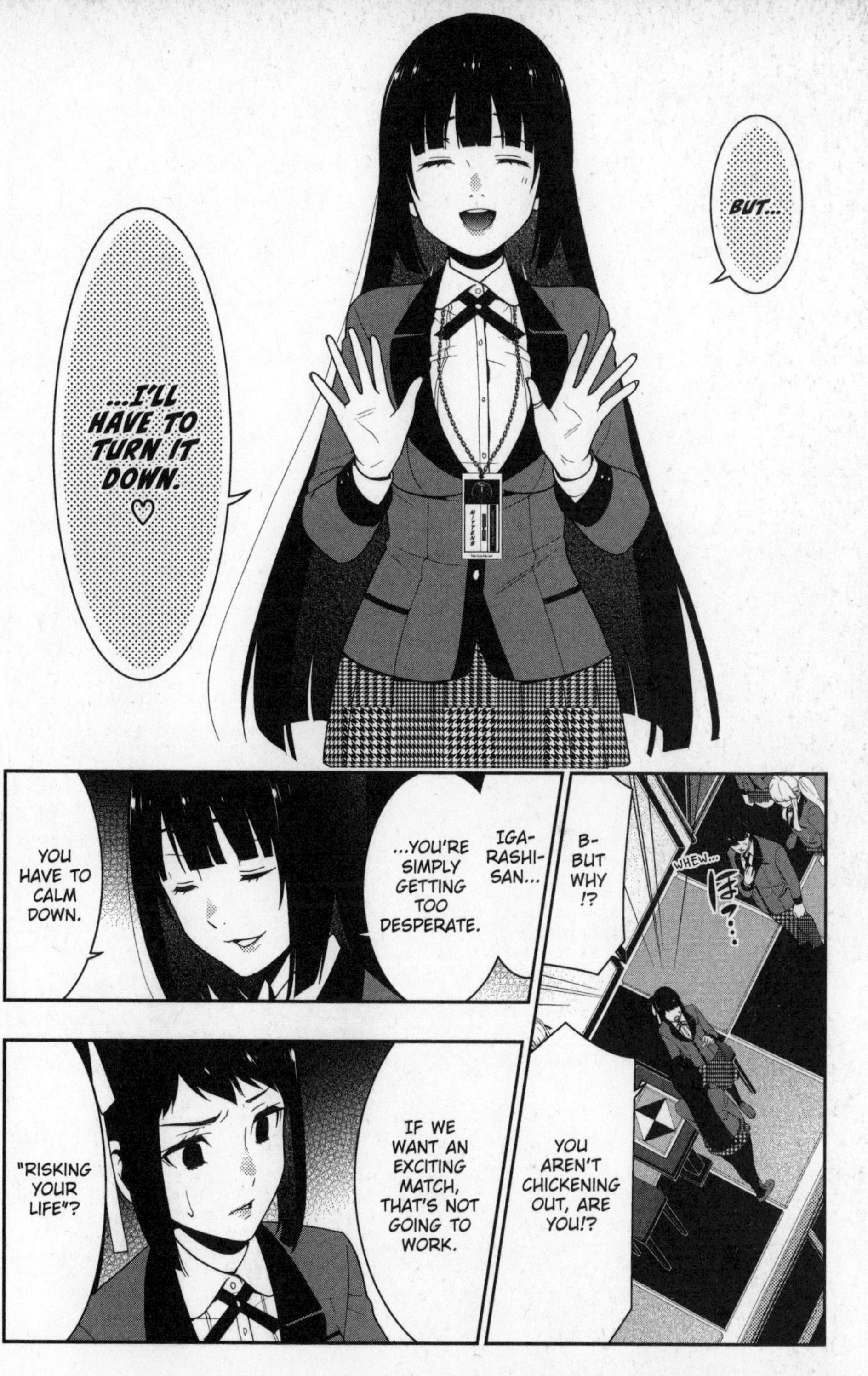
BUT...
...I'LL HAVE TO TURN IT DOWN. ♡
B-BUT WHY!?
WHEW...
YOU AREN'T CHICKENING OUT, ARE YOU!?
IGA-RASHI-SAN...
...YOU'RE SIMPLY GETTING TOO DESPERATE.
YOU HAVE TO CALM DOWN.
IF WE WANT AN EXCITING MATCH, THAT'S NOT GOING TO WORK.
"RISKING YOUR LIFE"?

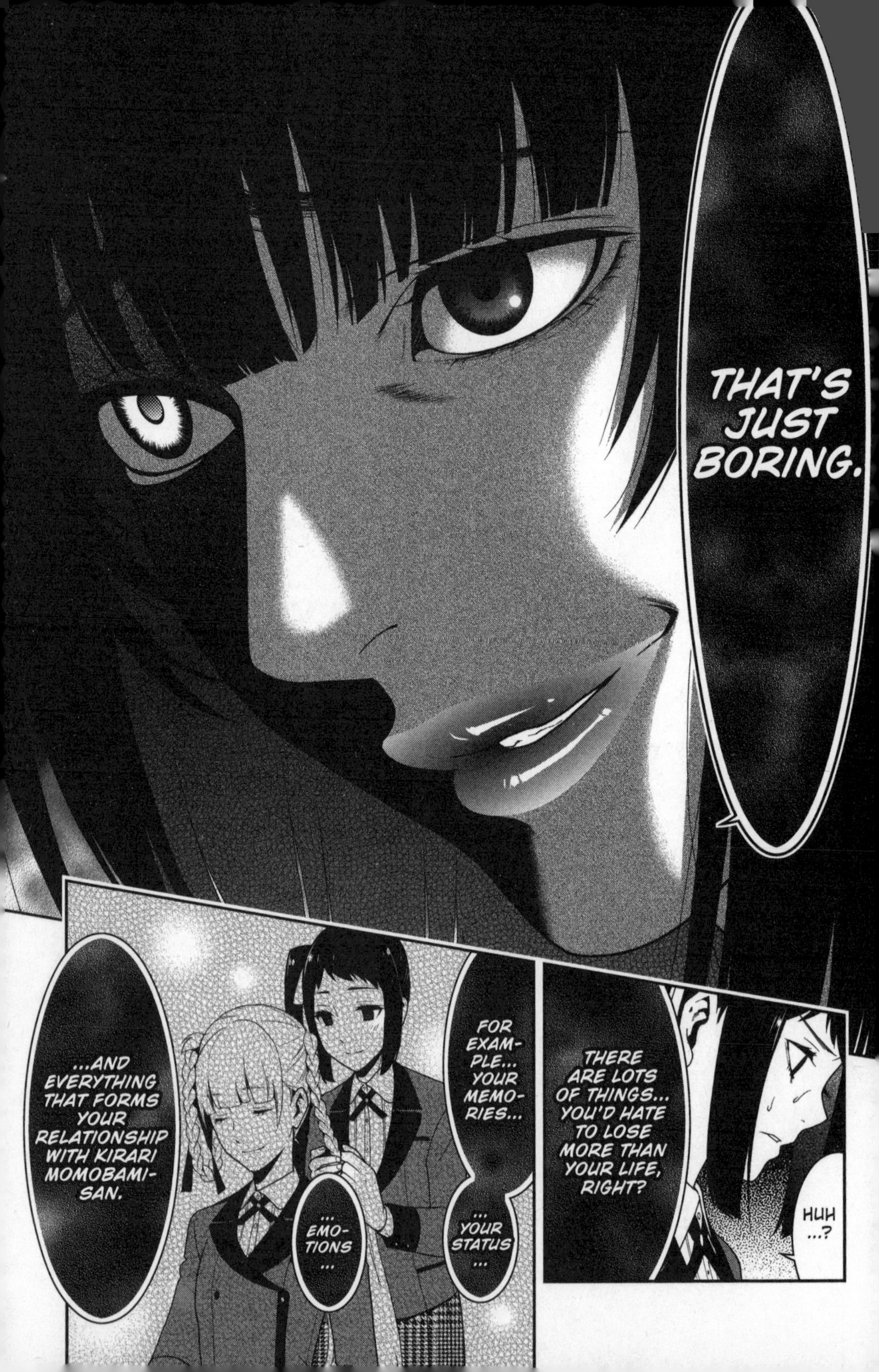
THAT'S JUST BORING.
THERE ARE LOTS OF THINGS... YOU'D HATE TO LOSE MORE THAN YOUR LIFE, RIGHT?
HUH ...?
FOR EXAM-PLE... YOUR MEMO-RIES...
... YOUR STATUS ...
... EMO-TIONS ...
...AND EVERYTHING THAT FORMS YOUR RELATIONSHIP WITH KIRARI MOMOBAMI-SAN.

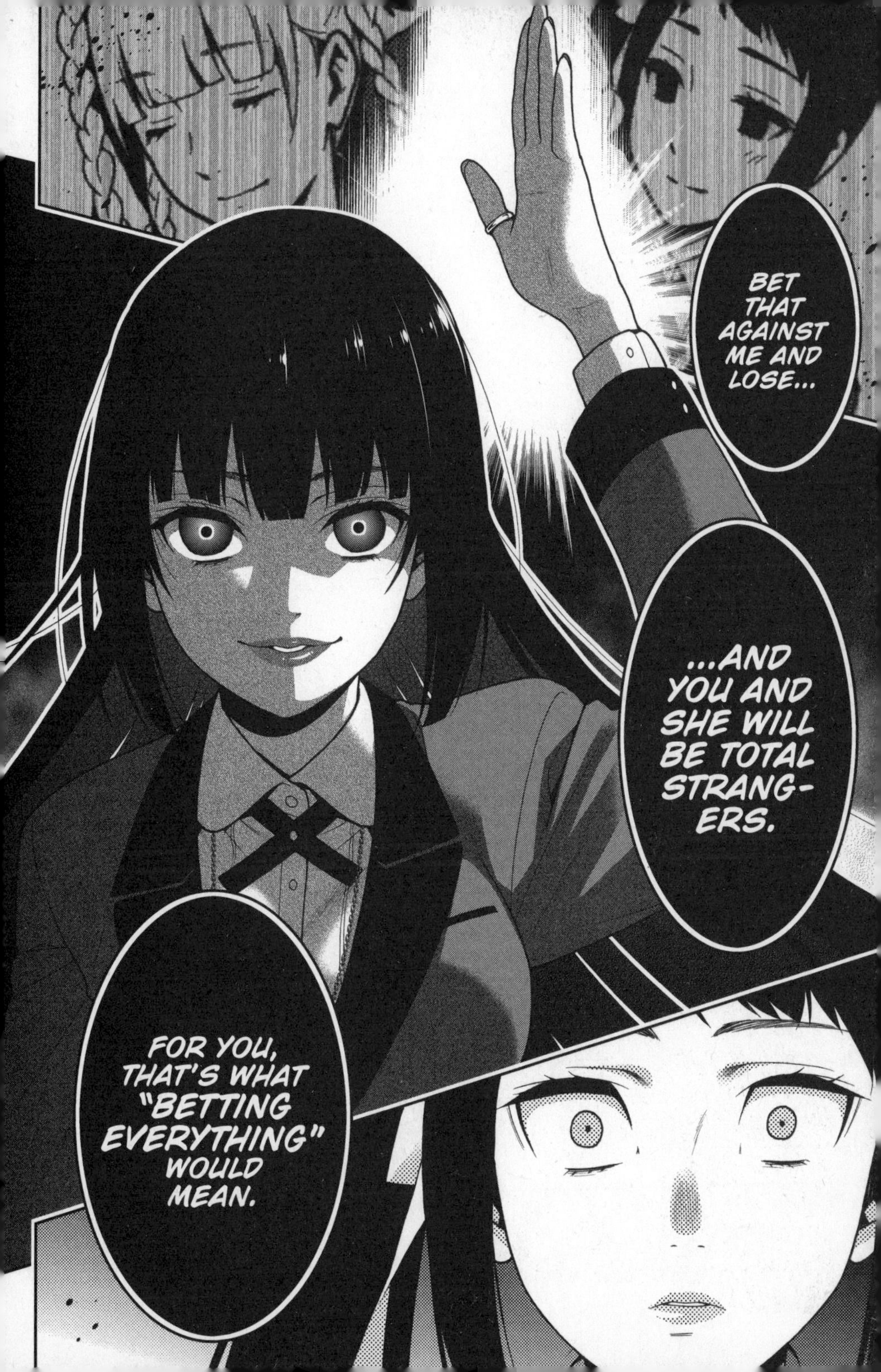
BET THAT AGAINST ME AND LOSE...
...AND YOU AND SHE WILL BE TOTAL STRANG-ERS.
FOR YOU, THAT'S WHAT "BETTING EVERYTHING" WOULD MEAN.

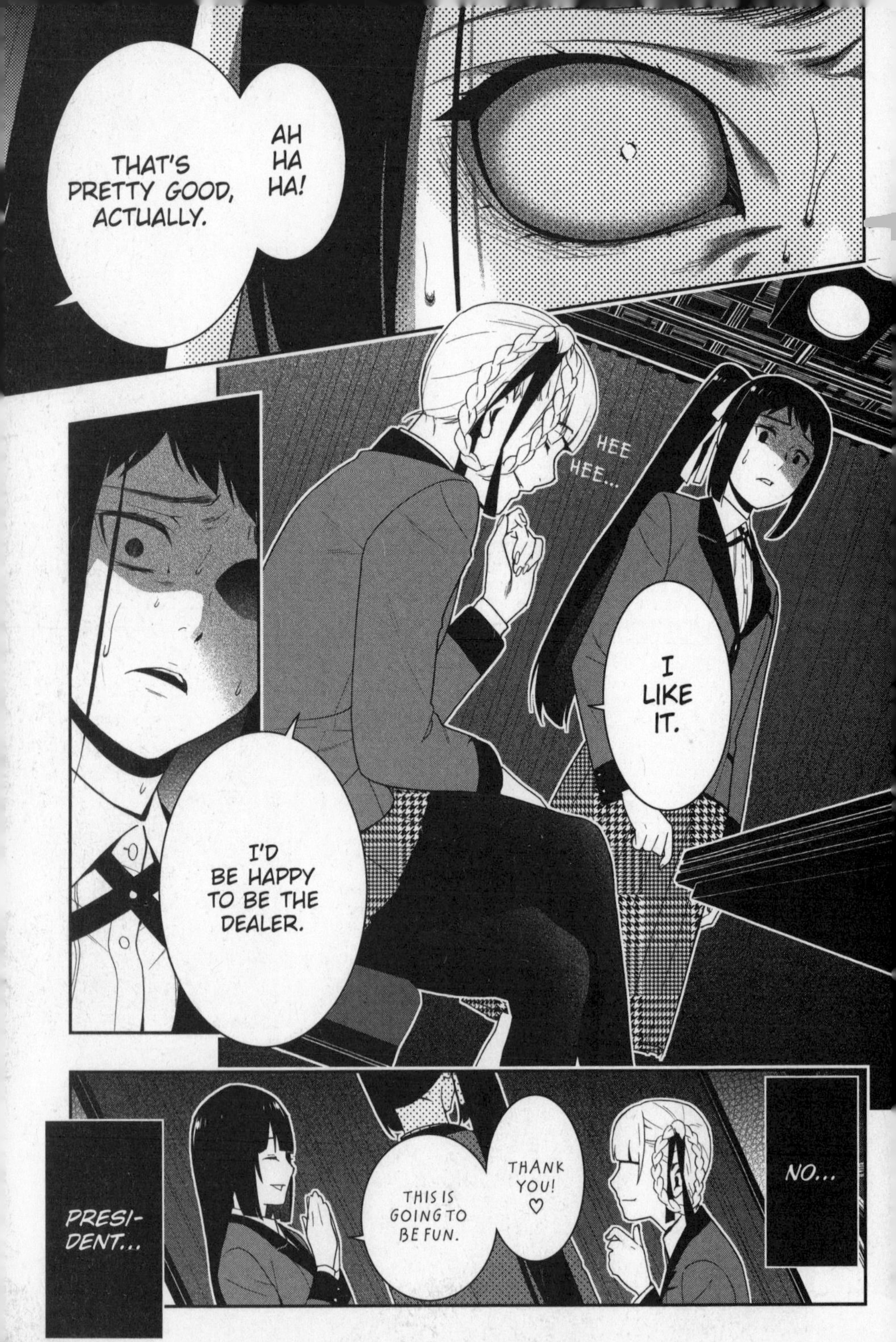
AH HA HA!
THAT'S PRETTY GOOD, ACTUALLY.
HEE HEE...
I LIKE IT.
I'D BE HAPPY TO BE THE DEALER.
NO...
THANK YOU! ♡
THIS IS GOING TO BE FUN.
PRESIDENT...

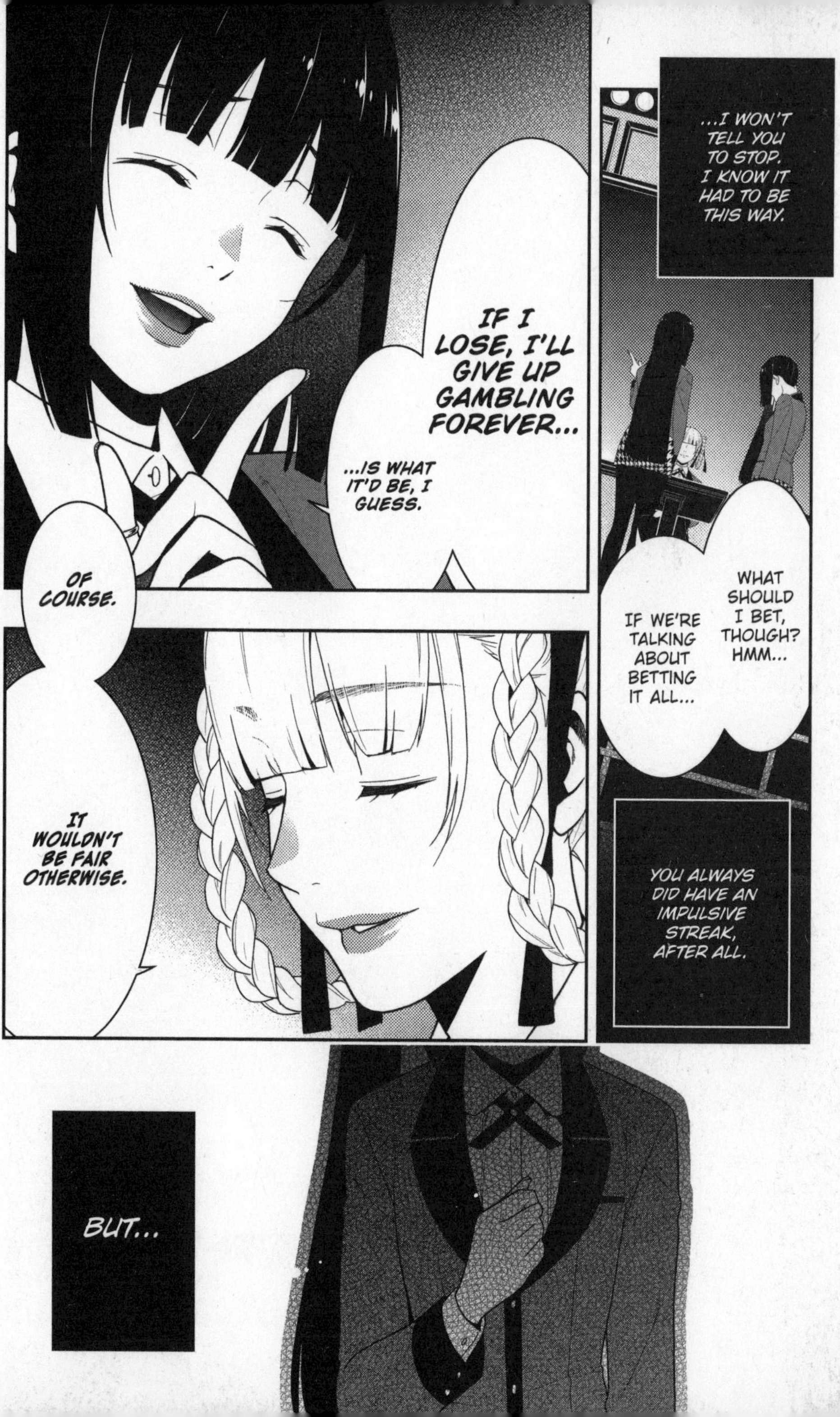
...I WON'T TELL YOU TO STOP. I KNOW IT HAD TO BE THIS WAY.
WHAT SHOULD I BET, THOUGH? HMM...
IF WE'RE TALKING ABOUT BETTING IT ALL...
YOU ALWAYS DID HAVE AN IMPULSIVE STREAK, AFTER ALL.
IF I LOSE, I'LL GIVE UP GAMBLING FOREVER...
...IS WHAT IT'D BE, I GUESS.
OF COURSE.
IT WOULDN'T BE FAIR OTHERWISE.
BUT...

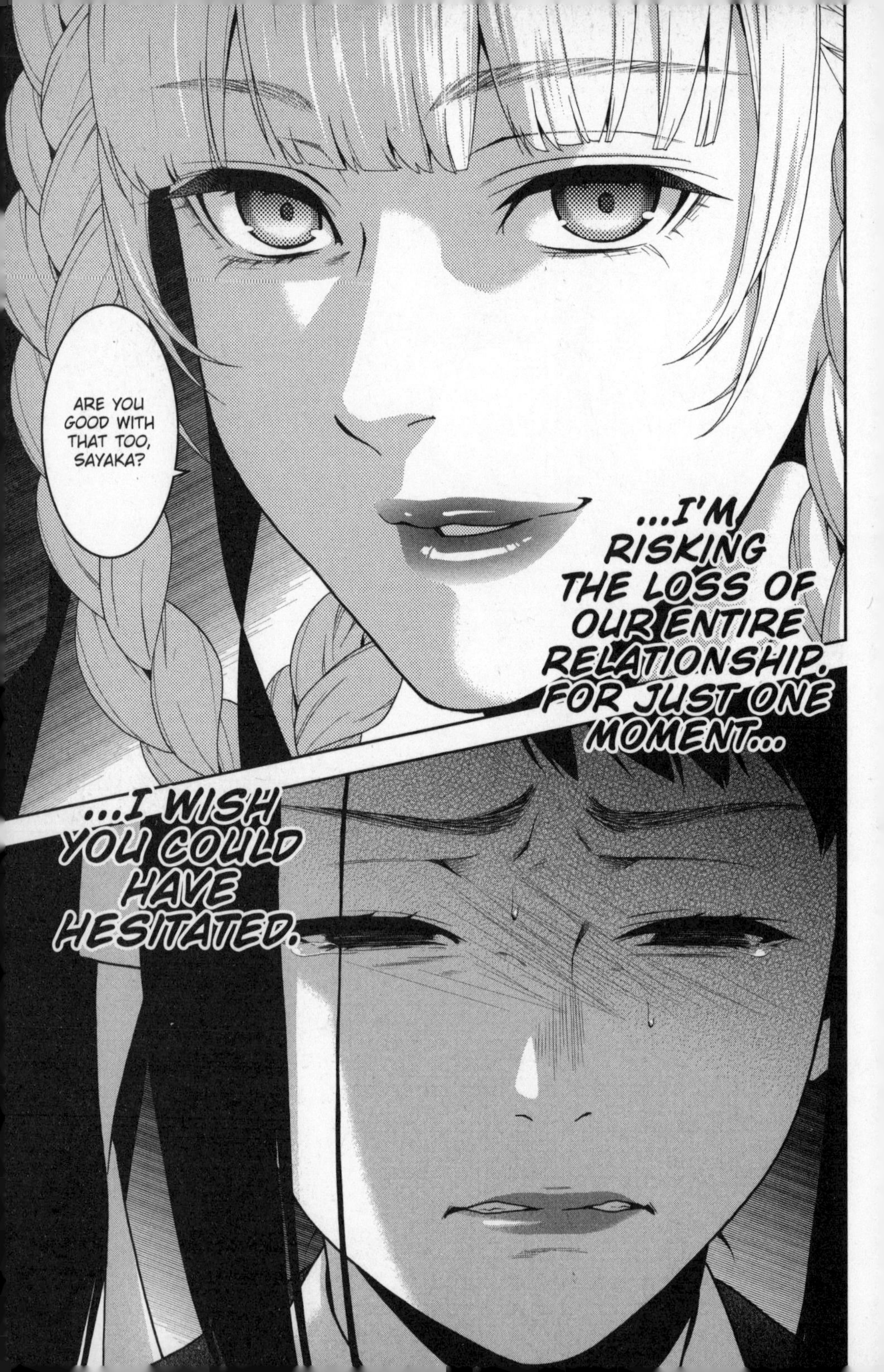
ARE YOU GOOD WITH THAT TOO, SAYAKA?
...I'M RISKING THE LOSS OF OUR ENTIRE RELATIONSHIP. FOR JUST ONE MOMENT...
...I WISH YOU COULD HAVE HESITATED.

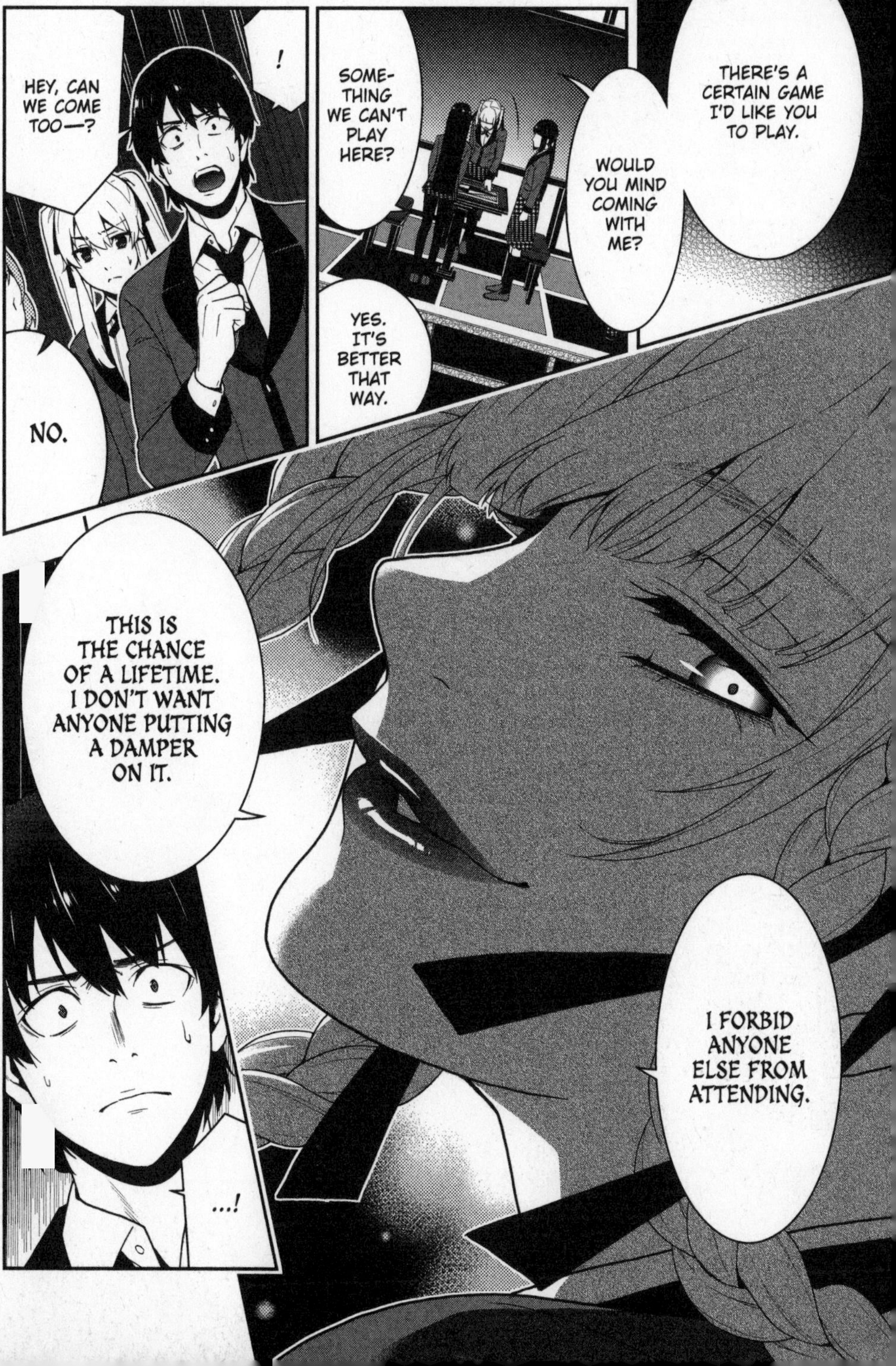
THERE'S A CERTAIN GAME I'D LIKE YOU TO PLAY.
WOULD YOU MIND COMING WITH ME?
SOME-THING WE CAN'T PLAY HERE?
YES. IT'S BETTER THAT WAY.
!
HEY, CAN WE COME TOO—?
NO.
THIS IS THE CHANCE OF A LIFETIME. I DON'T WANT ANYONE PUTTING A DAMPER ON IT.
I FORBID ANYONE ELSE FROM ATTENDING.
...!

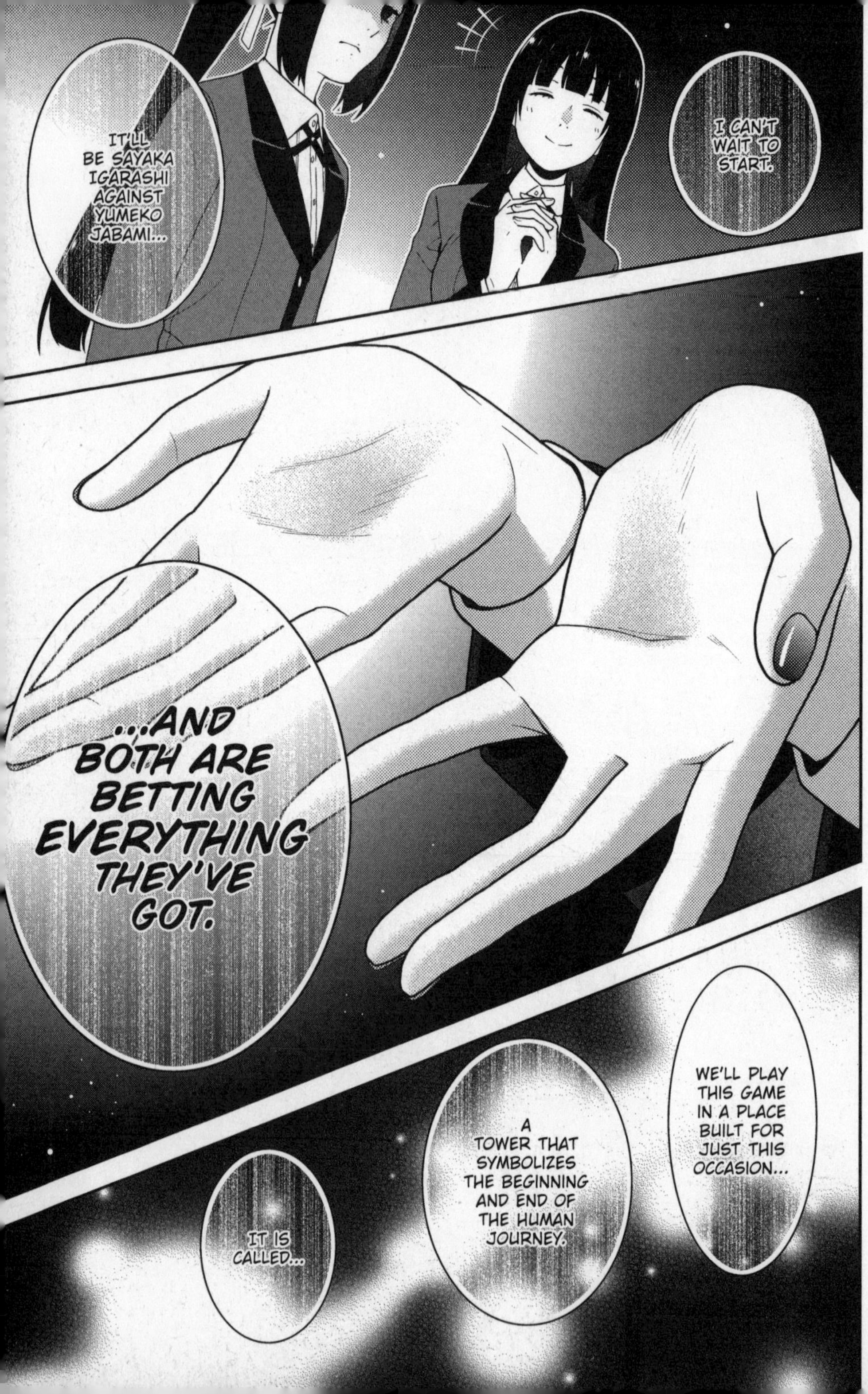
I CAN'T WAIT TO START.
IT'LL BE SAYAKA IGARASHI AGAINST YUMEKO JABAMI...
...AND BOTH ARE BETTING EVERYTHING THEY'VE GOT.
WE'LL PLAY THIS GAME IN A PLACE BUILT FOR JUST THIS OCCASION...
A TOWER THAT SYMBOLIZES THE BEGINNING AND END OF THE HUMAN JOURNEY.
IT IS CALLED...

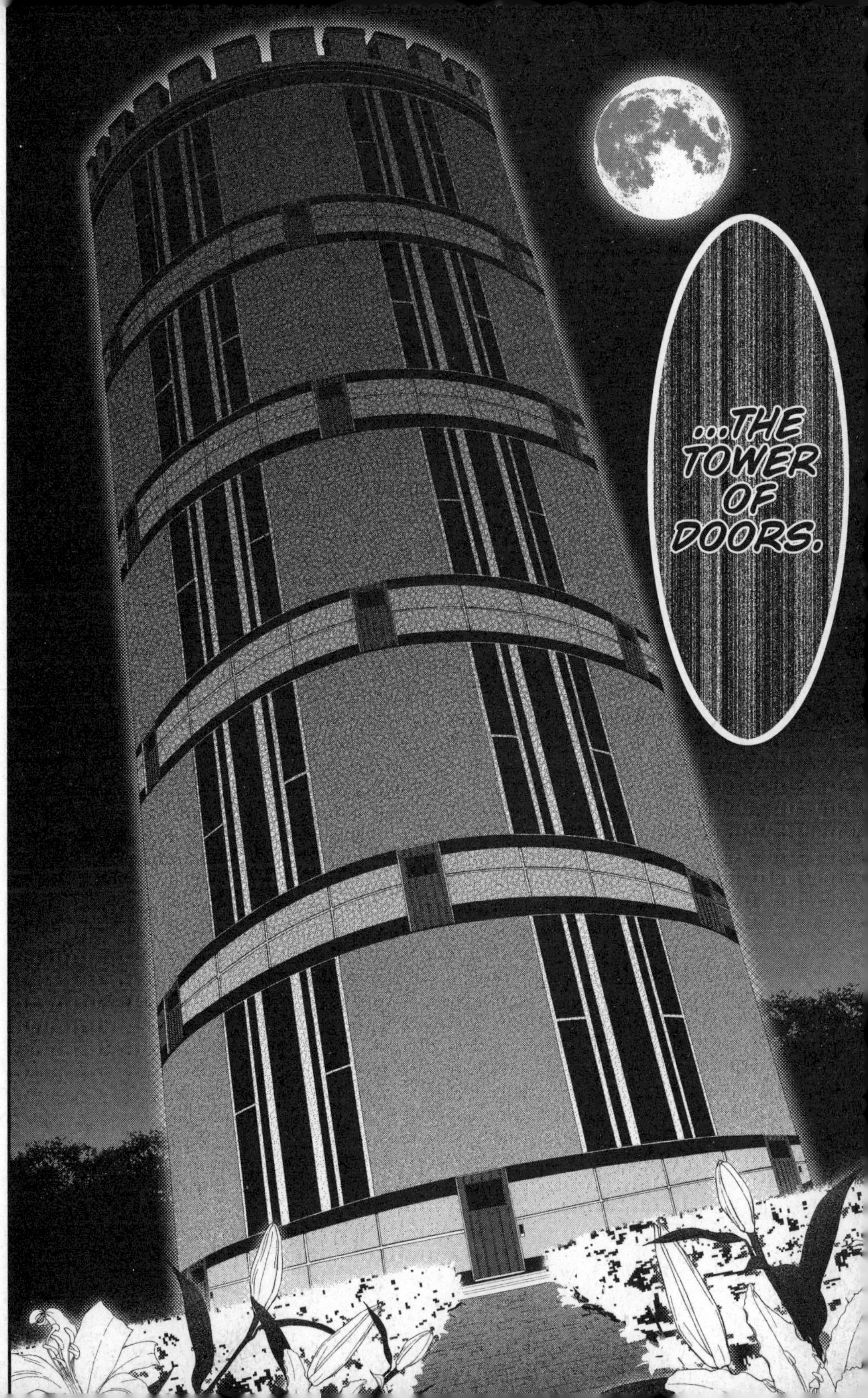
...THE TOWER OF DOORS.

KAKEGURUI

— Compulsive Gambler —

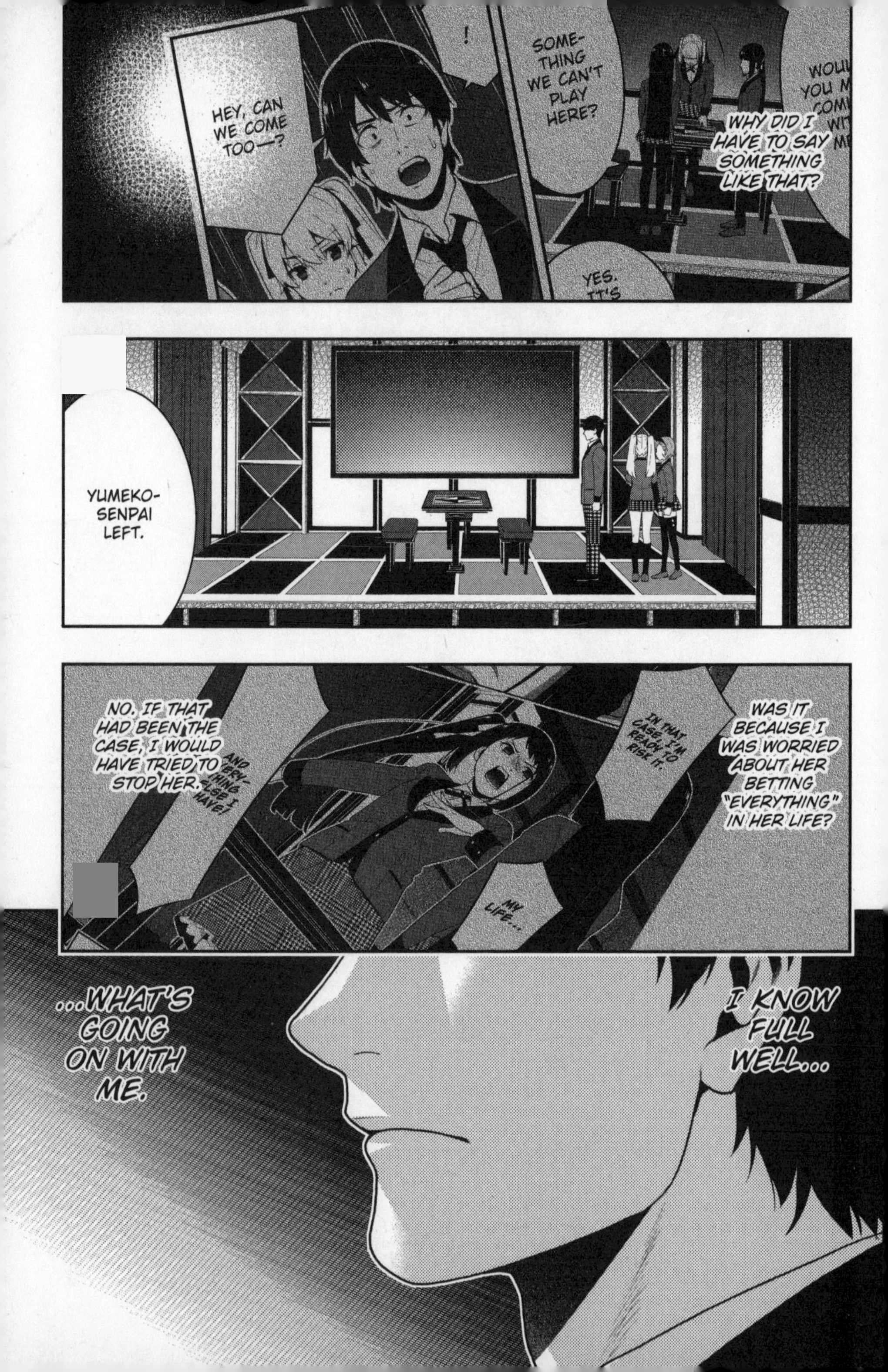
SOMETHING WE CAN'T PLAY HERE?
WHY DID I HAVE TO SAY SOMETHING LIKE THAT?
YES. IT'S
!
HEY, CAN WE COME TOO—?
YUMEKO-SENPAI LEFT.
WAS IT BECAUSE I WAS WORRIED ABOUT HER BETTING "EVERYTHING" IN HER LIFE?
IN THAT CASE, I'M READY TO RISK IT.
AND EVERYTHING ELSE I HAVE!
NO. IF THAT HAD BEEN THE CASE, I WOULD HAVE TRIED TO STOP HER.
MY LIFE...
I KNOW FULL WELL...
...WHAT'S GOING ON WITH ME.

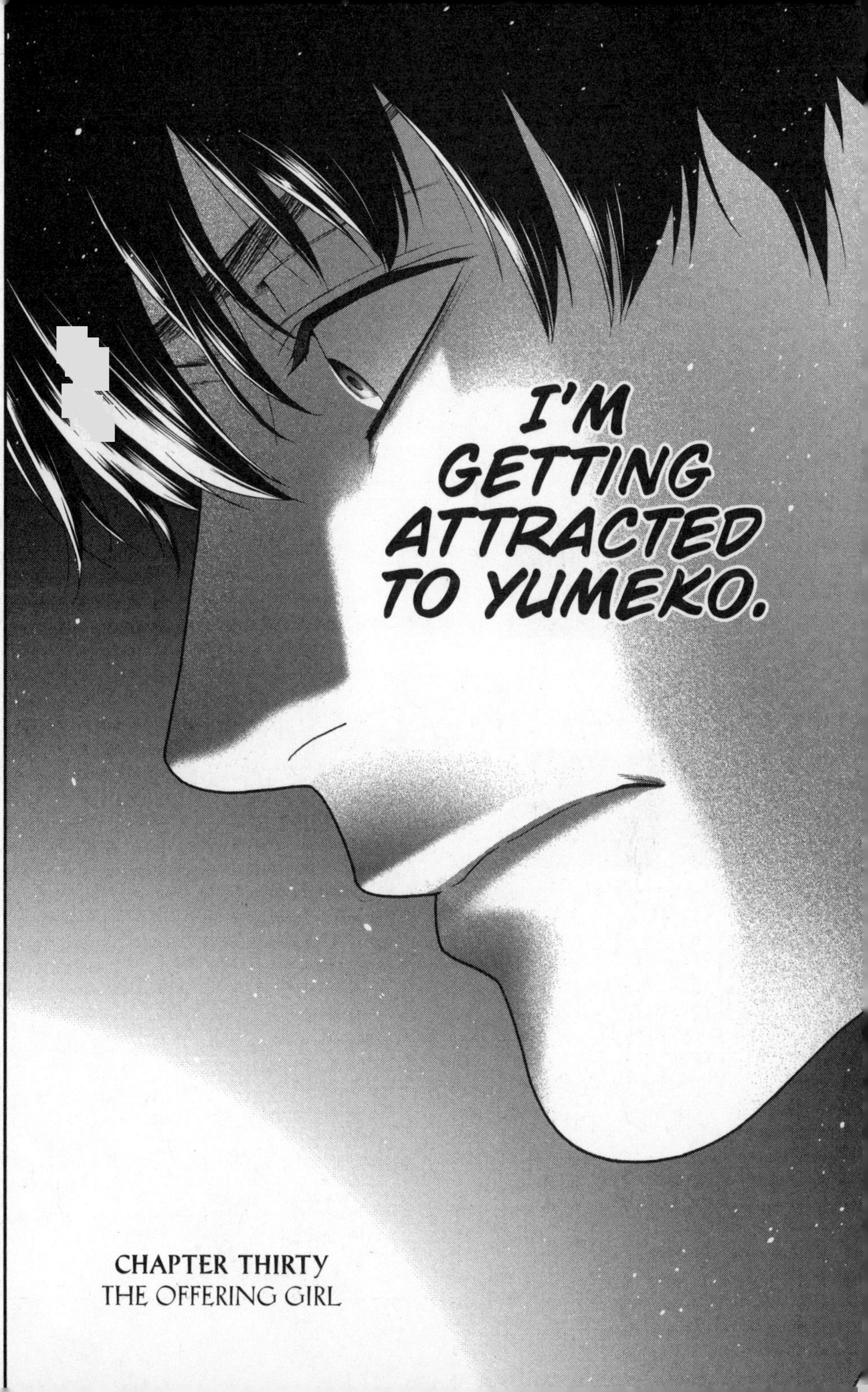
I'M GETTING ATTRACTED TO YUMEKO.
CHAPTER THIRTY
THE OFFERING GIRL

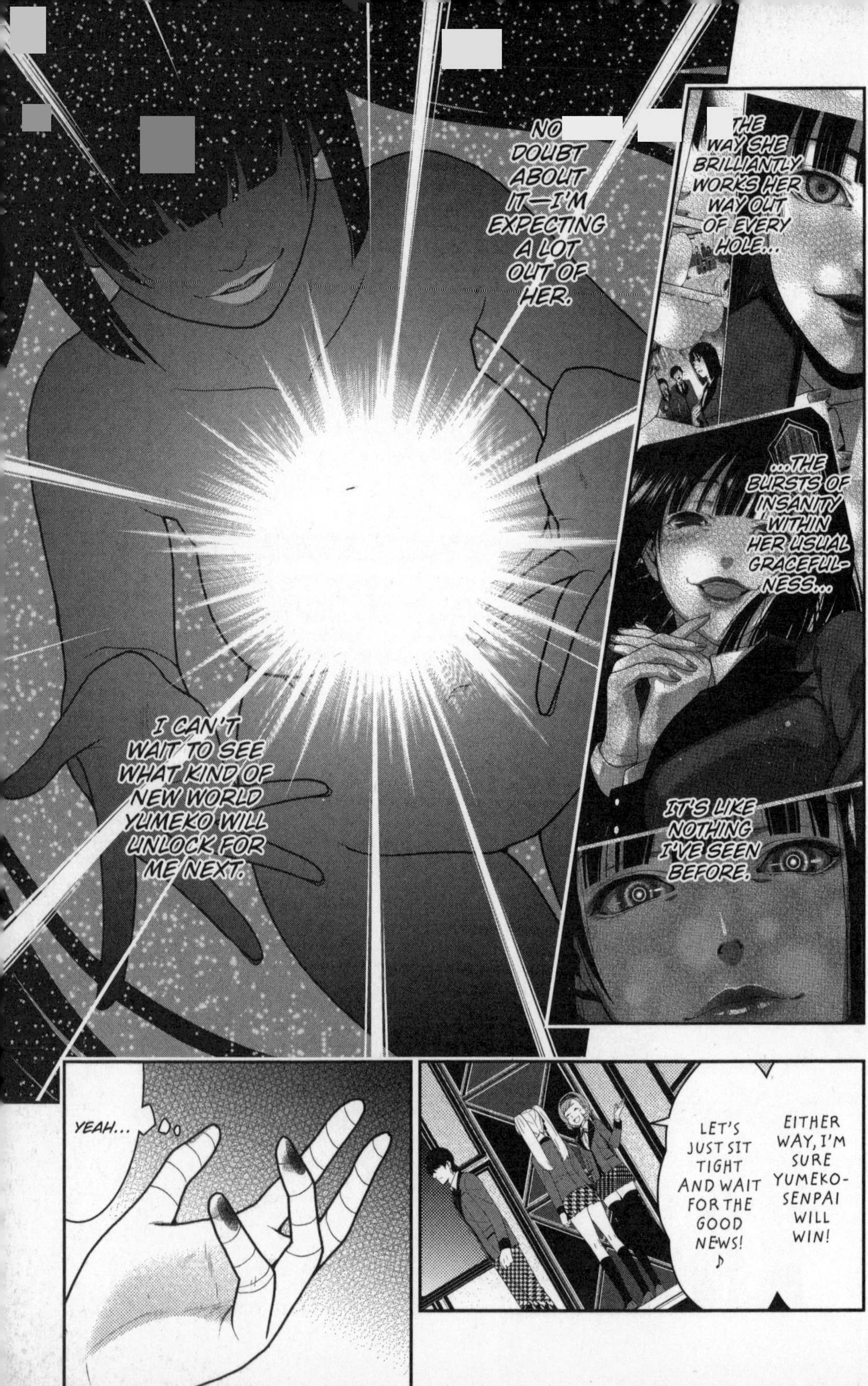
THE WAY SHE BRILLIANTLY WORKS HER WAY OUT OF EVERY HOLE...
...THE BURSTS OF INSANITY WITHIN HER USUAL GRACEFULNESS...
IT'S LIKE NOTHING I'VE SEEN BEFORE.
NO DOUBT ABOUT IT—I'M EXPECTING A LOT OUT OF HER.
I CAN'T WAIT TO SEE WHAT KIND OF NEW WORLD YUMEKO WILL UNLOCK FOR ME NEXT.
EITHER WAY, I'M SURE YUMEKO-SENPAI WILL WIN!
LET'S JUST SIT TIGHT AND WAIT FOR THE GOOD NEWS! ♪
YEAH...

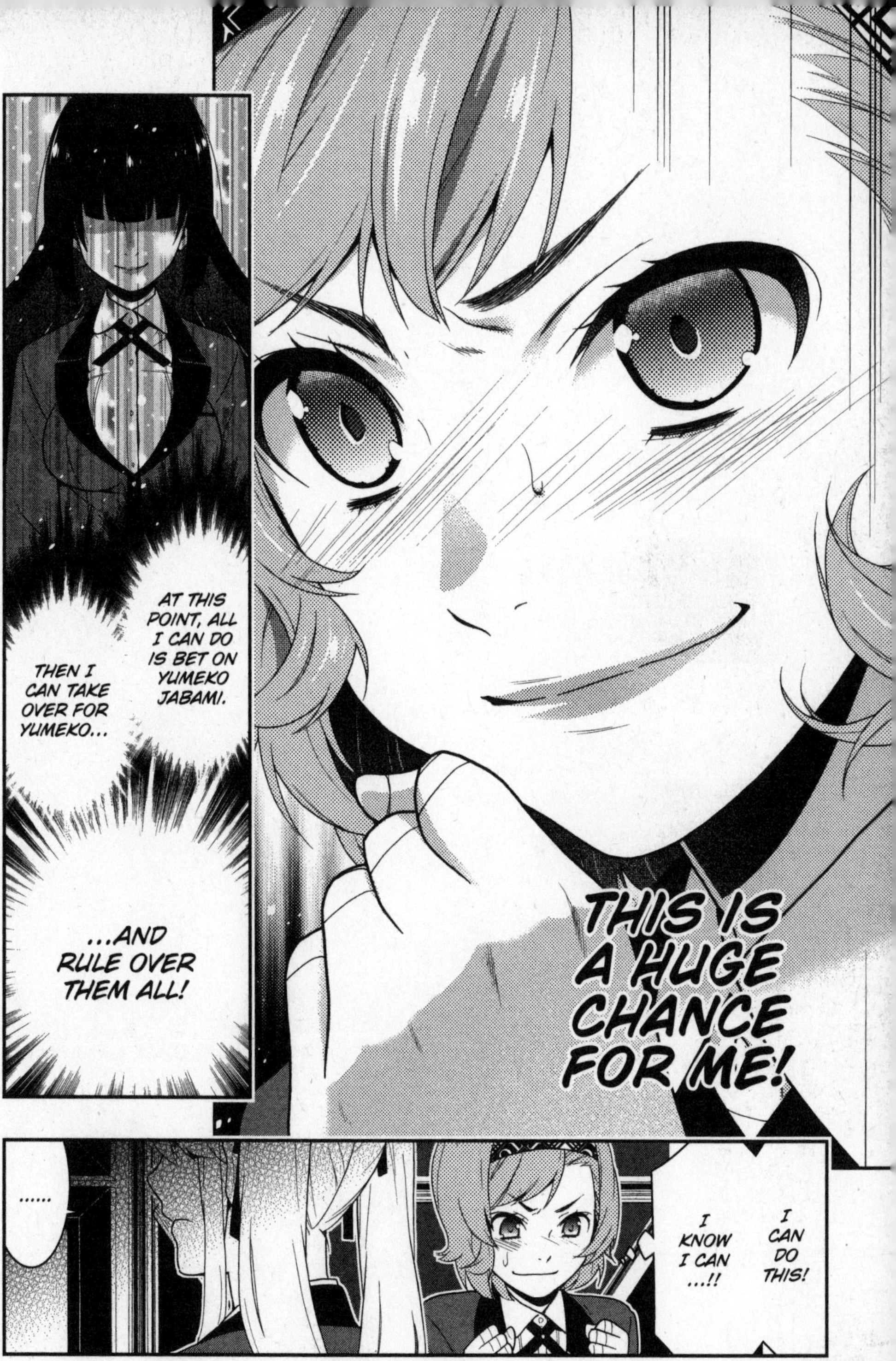
THIS IS A HUGE CHANCE FOR ME!
AT THIS POINT, ALL I CAN DO IS BET ON YUMEKO JABAMI.
THEN I CAN TAKE OVER FOR YUMEKO...
...AND RULE OVER THEM ALL!
I CAN DO THIS!
I KNOW I CAN ...!!
......

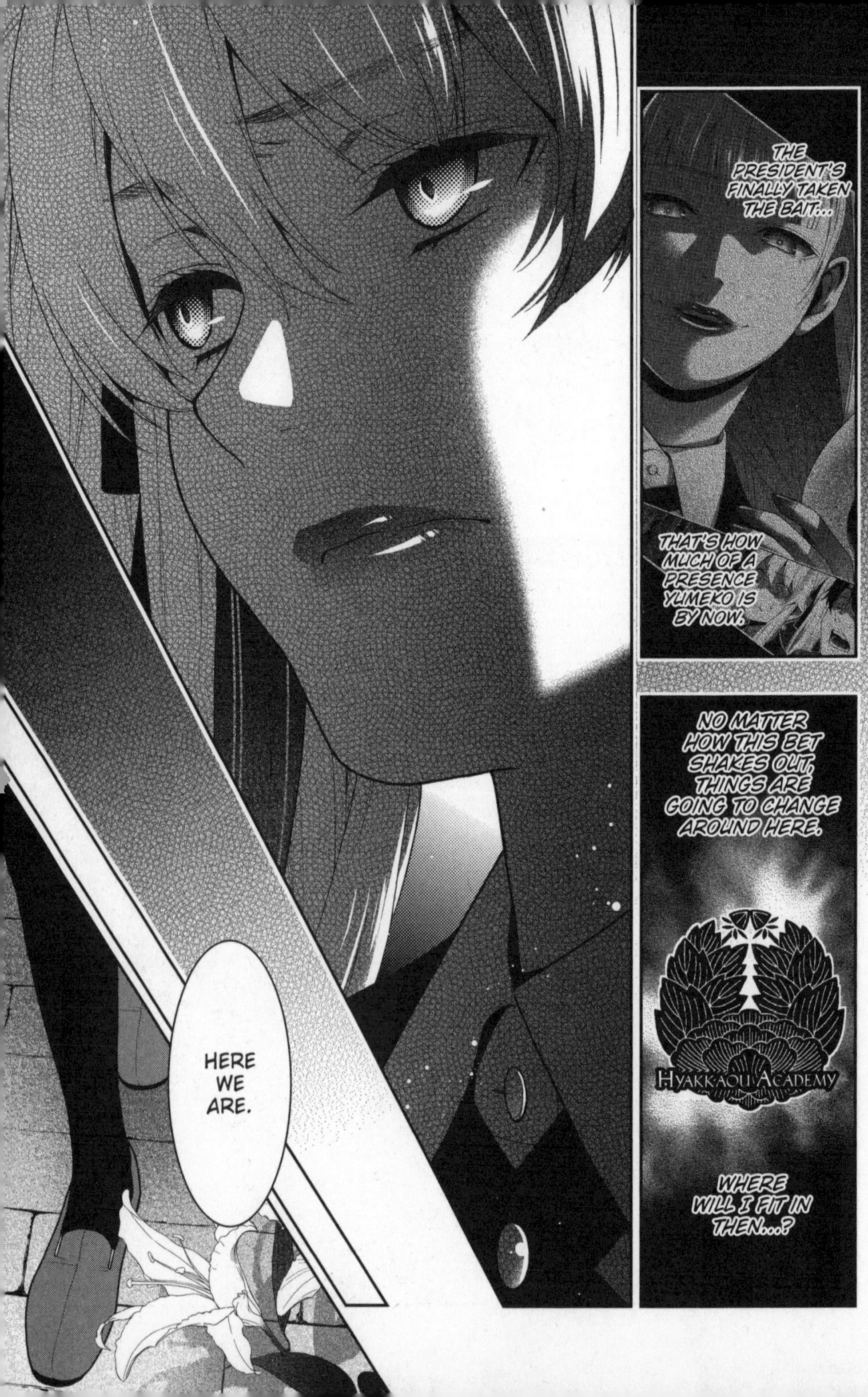
THE PRESIDENT'S FINALLY TAKEN THE BAIT...
THAT'S HOW MUCH OF A PRESENCE YUMEKO IS BY NOW.
NO MATTER HOW THIS BET SHAKES OUT, THINGS ARE GOING TO CHANGE AROUND HERE.
HYAKKAOU ACADEMY
WHERE WILL I FIT IN THEN...?
HERE WE ARE.

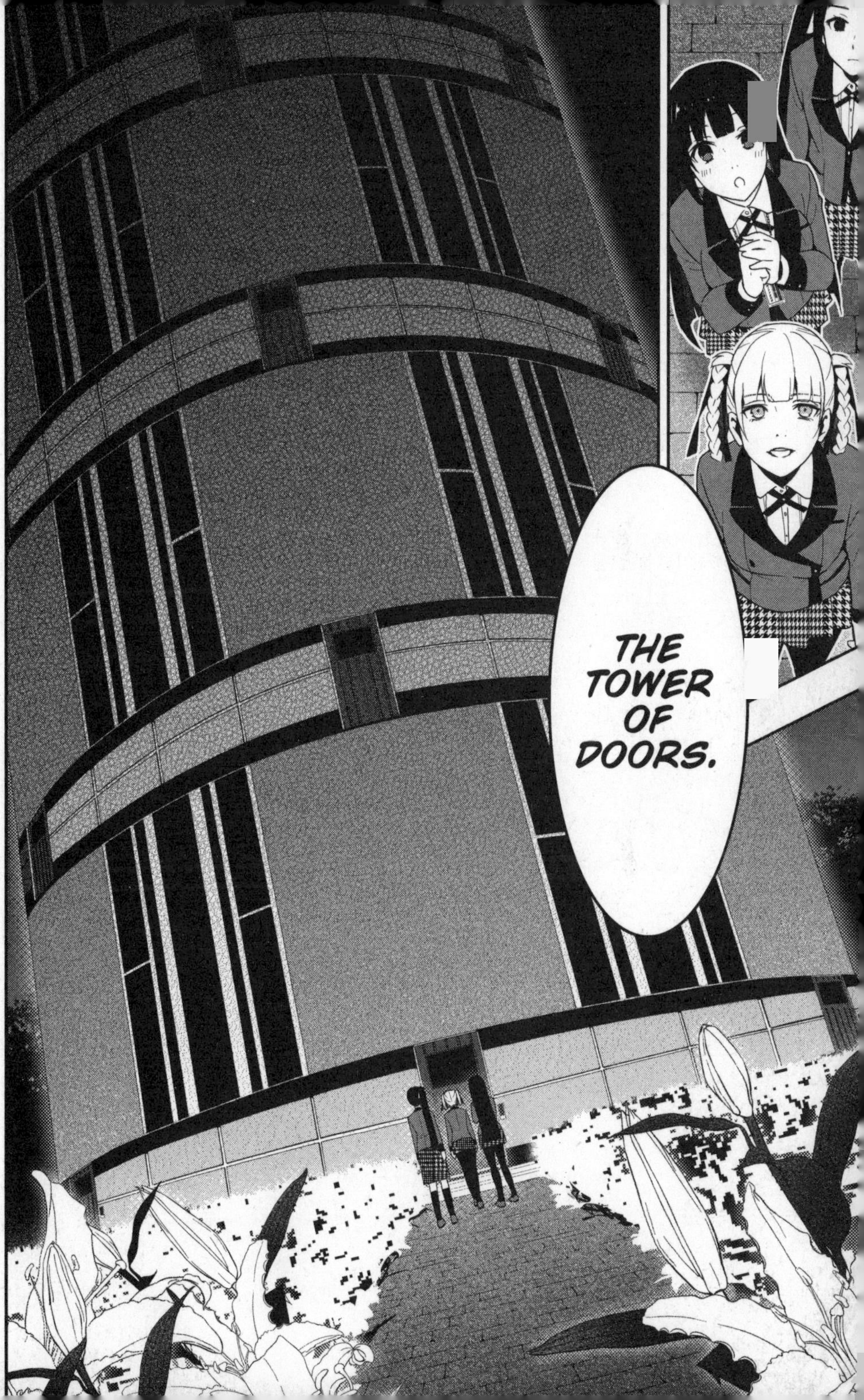
THE TOWER OF DOORS.

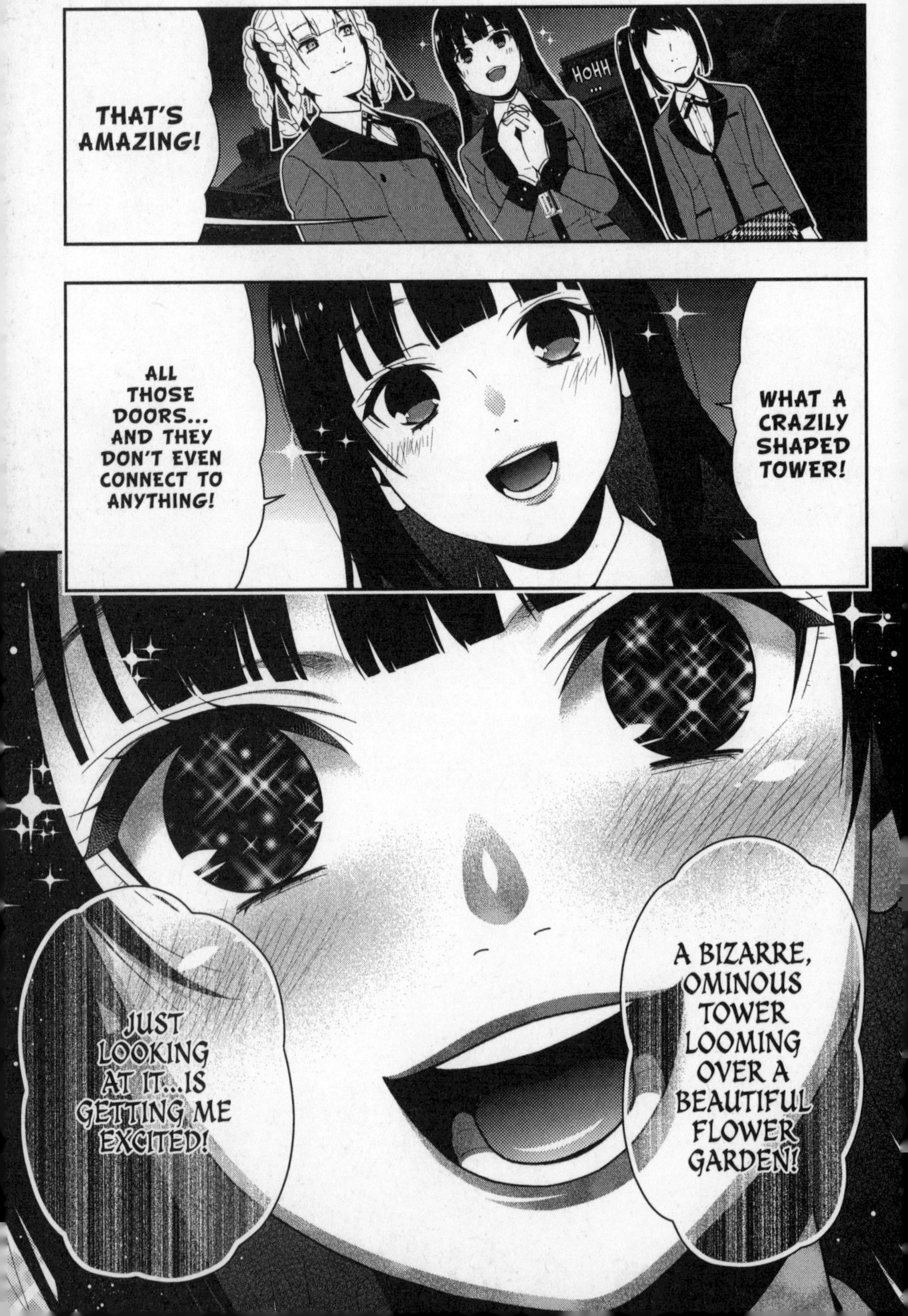
HOHH ...
THAT'S AMAZING!
WHAT A CRAZILY SHAPED TOWER!
ALL THOSE DOORS... AND THEY DON'T EVEN CONNECT TO ANYTHING!
A BIZARRE, OMINOUS TOWER LOOMING OVER A BEAUTIFUL FLOWER GARDEN!
JUST LOOKING AT IT...IS GETTING ME EXCITED!

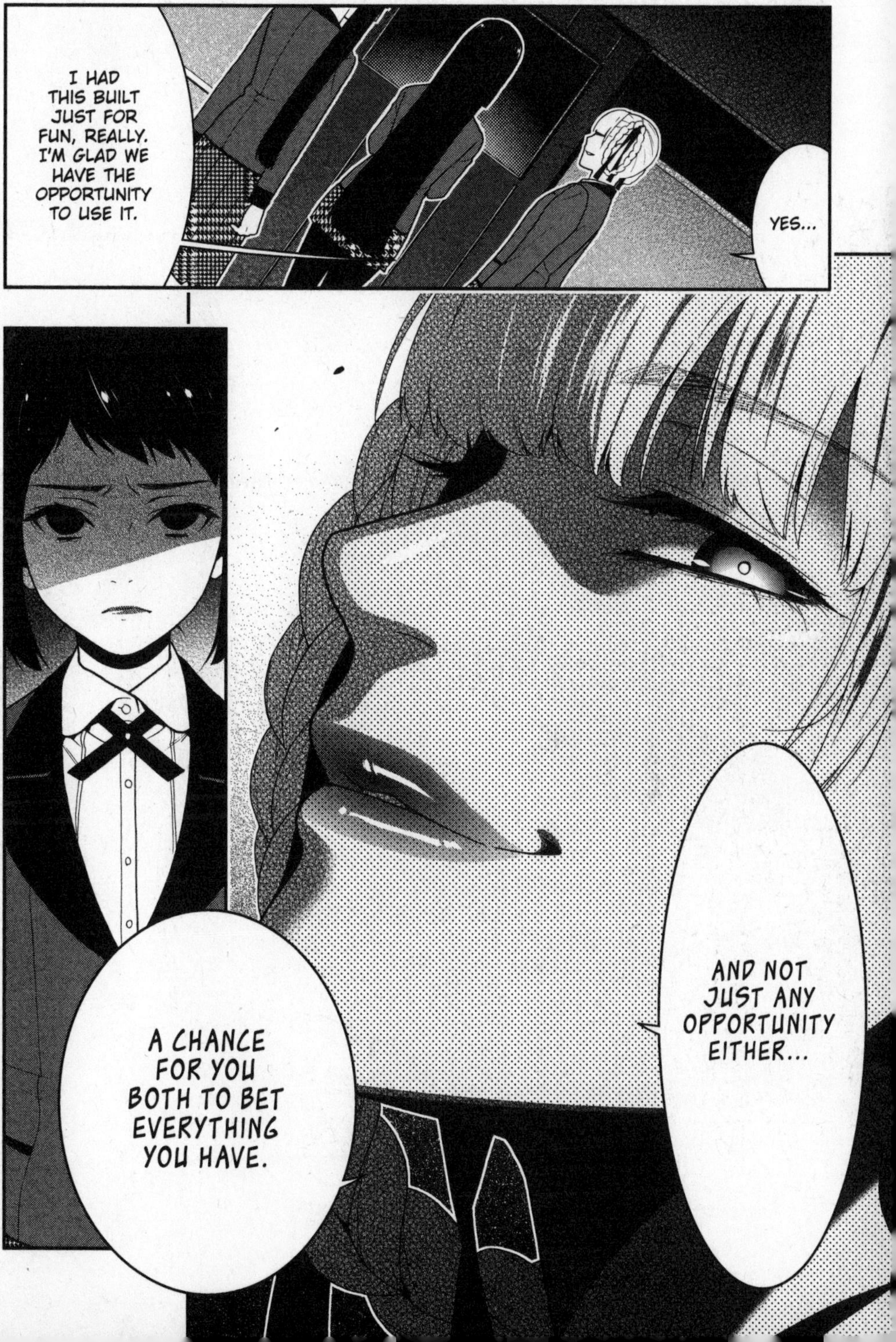
I HAD THIS BUILT JUST FOR FUN, REALLY. I'M GLAD WE HAVE THE OPPORTUNITY TO USE IT.
YES...
AND NOT JUST ANY OPPORTUNITY EITHER...
A CHANCE FOR YOU BOTH TO BET EVERYTHING YOU HAVE.

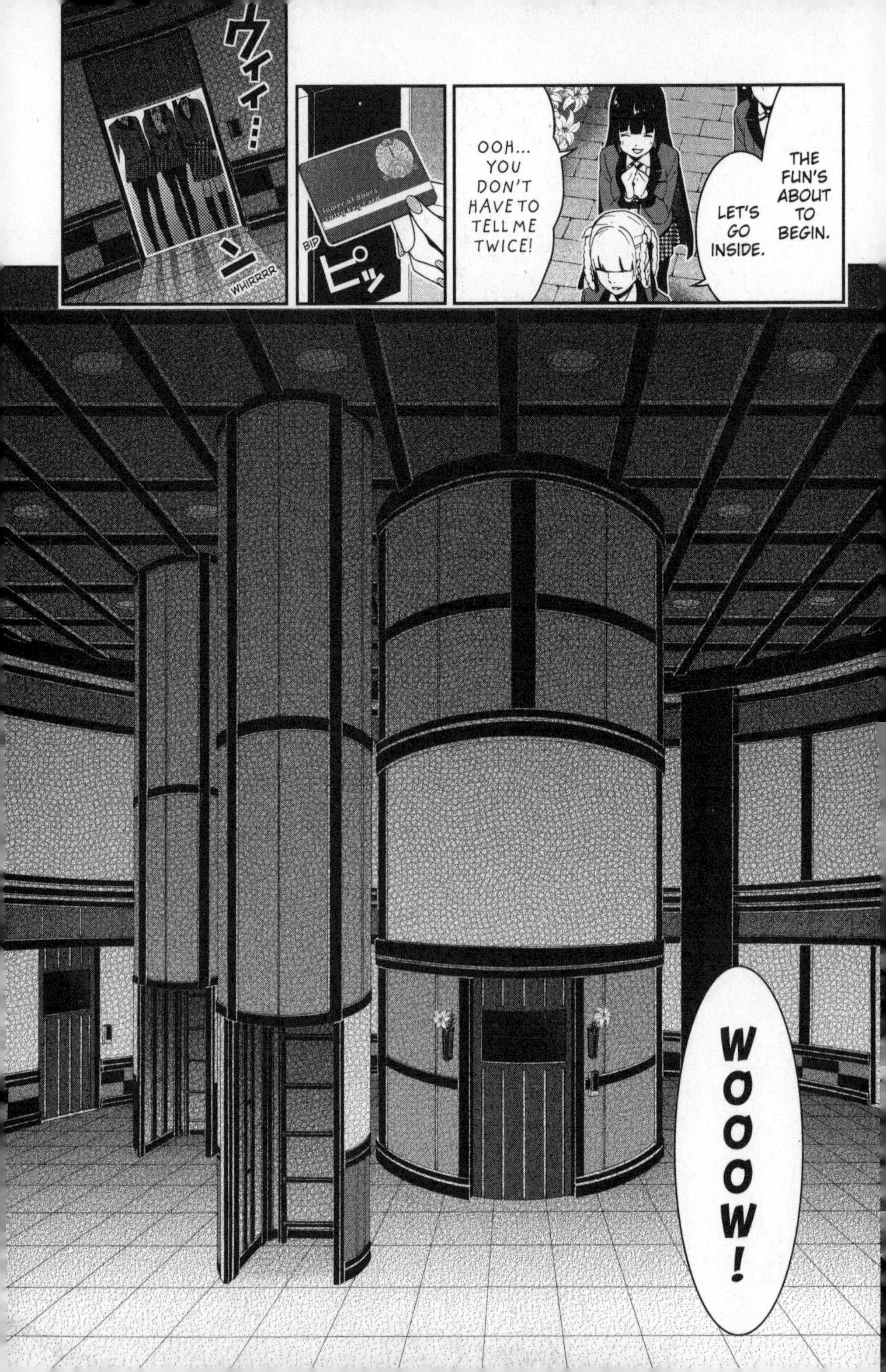
THE FUN'S ABOUT TO BEGIN.
LET'S GO INSIDE.
OOH... YOU DON'T HAVE TO TELL ME TWICE!
ピッ
BIP
ウィィ…ン
WHIRRRR
WOOOW!

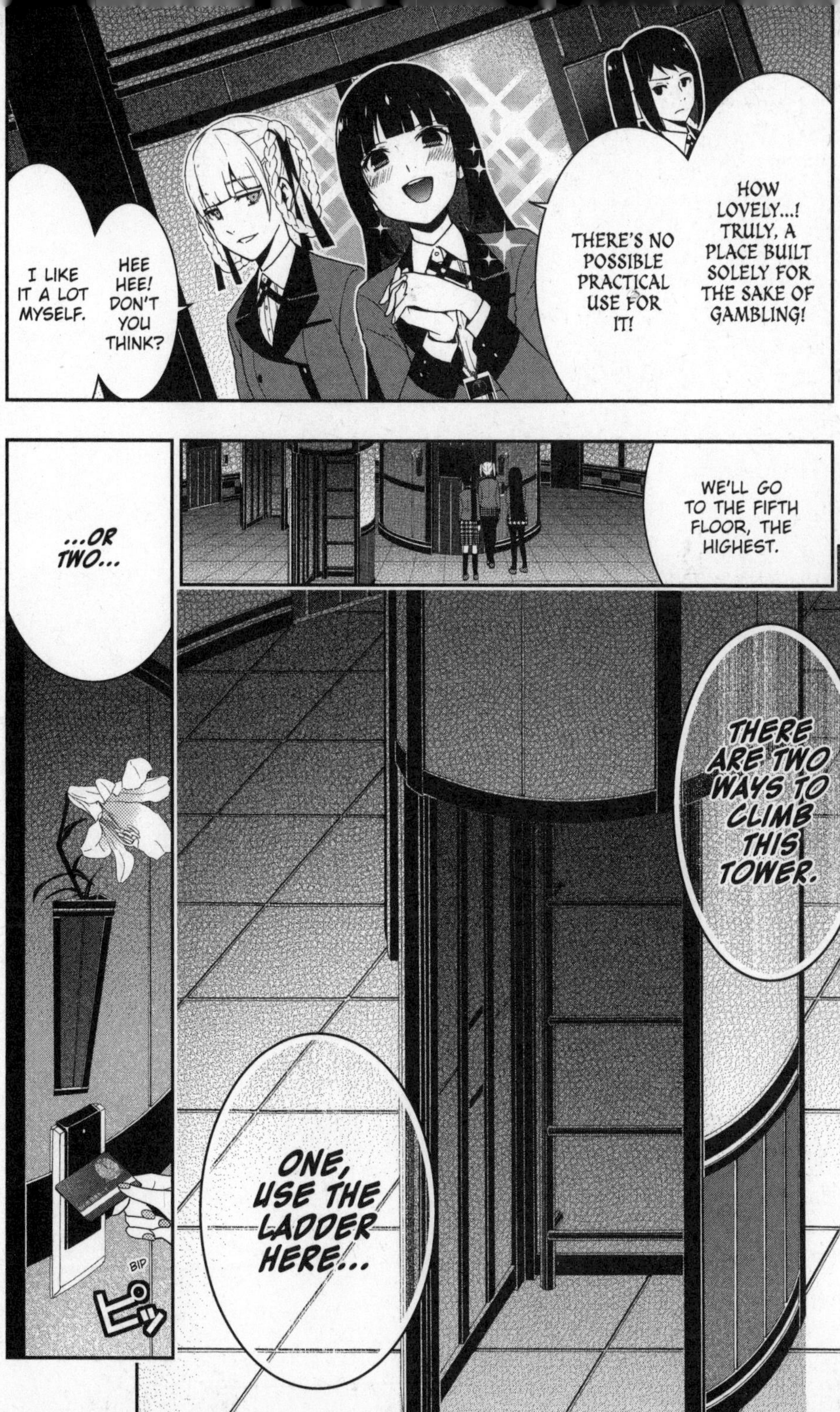
HOW LOVELY...! TRULY, A PLACE BUILT SOLELY FOR THE SAKE OF GAMBLING!
THERE'S NO POSSIBLE PRACTICAL USE FOR IT!
HEE HEE! DON'T YOU THINK?
I LIKE IT A LOT MYSELF.
WE'LL GO TO THE FIFTH FLOOR, THE HIGHEST.
THERE ARE TWO WAYS TO CLIMB THIS TOWER.
ONE, USE THE LADDER HERE...
...OR TWO...
BIP
ピッ

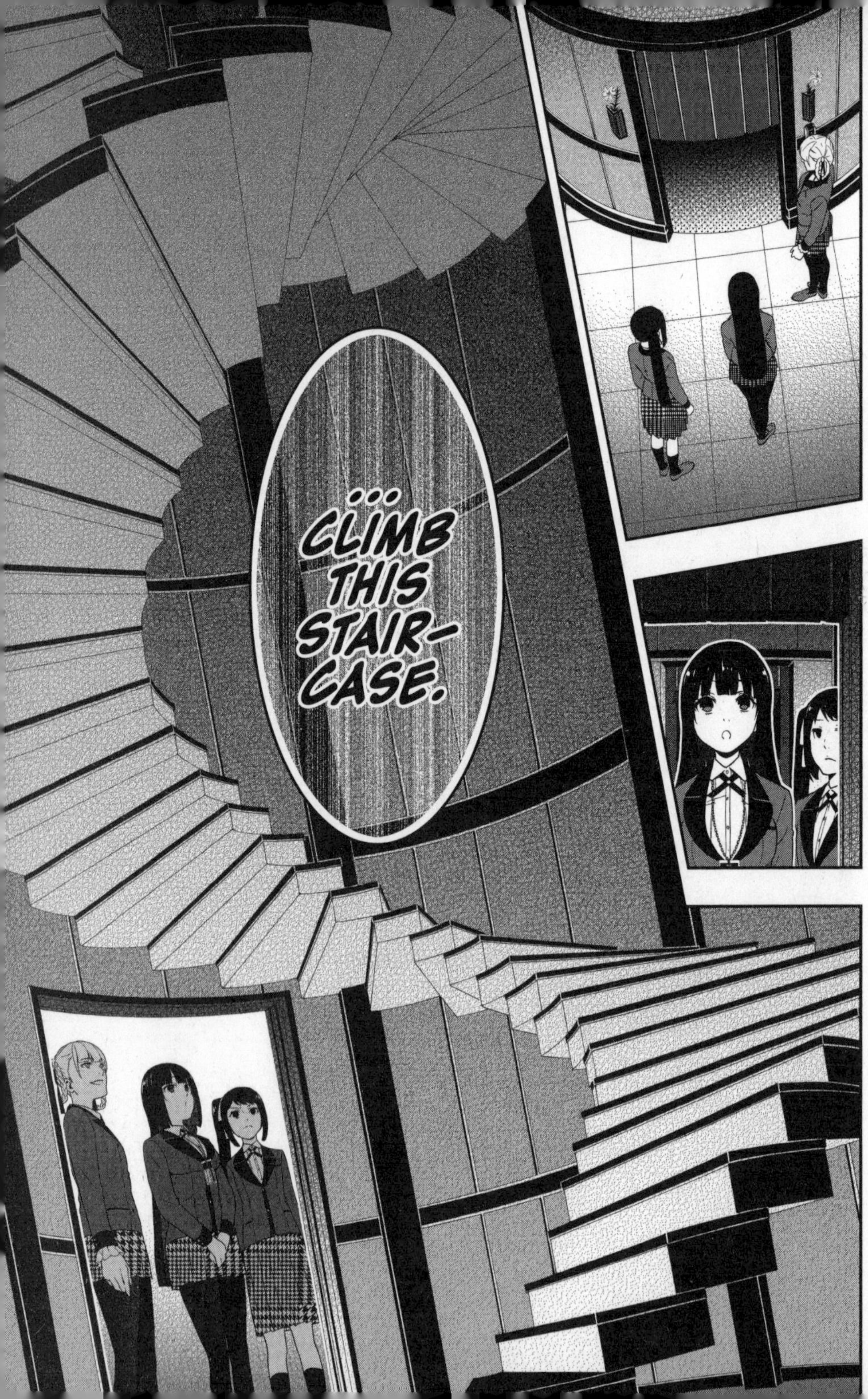
...CLIMB THIS STAIR-CASE.

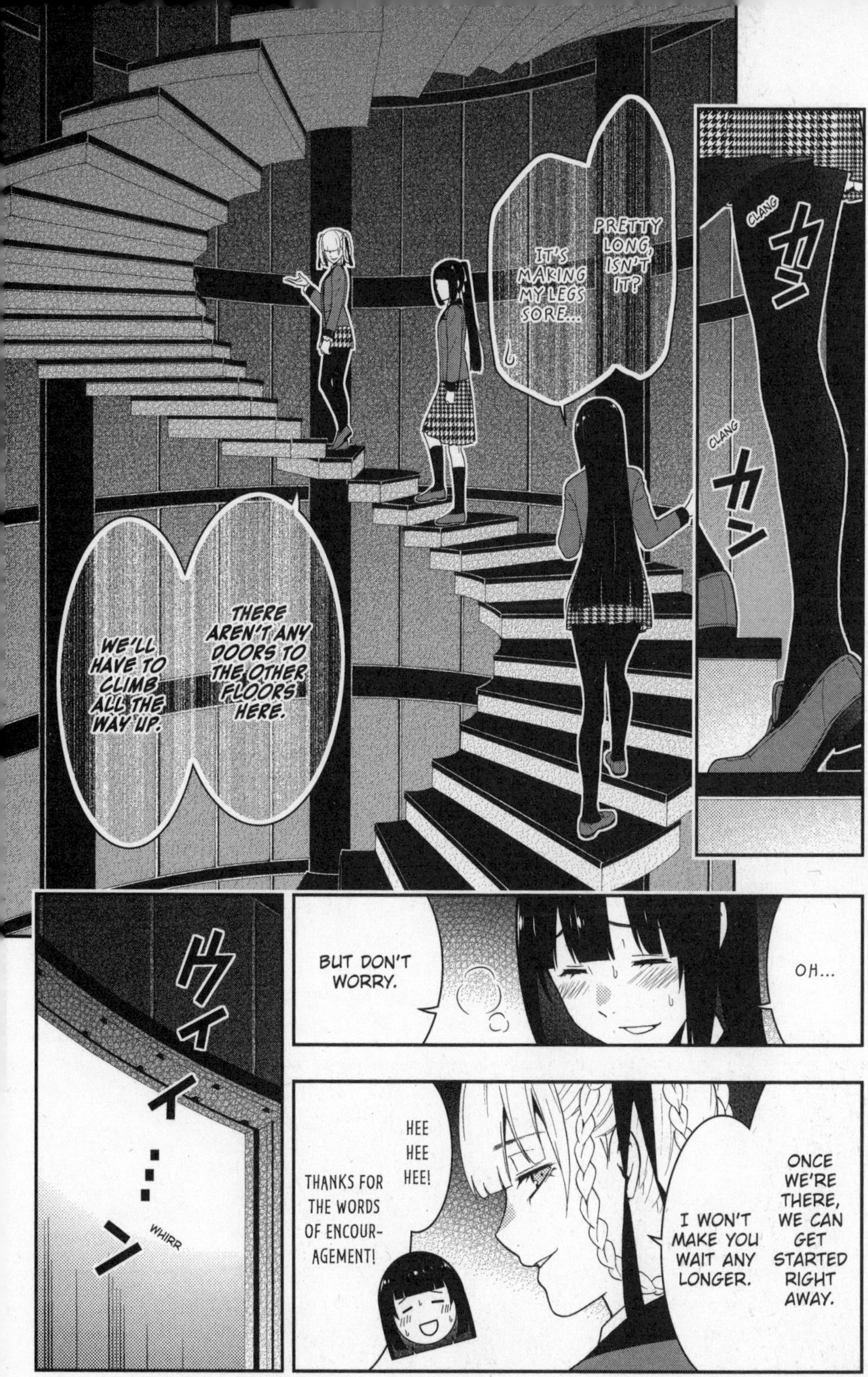
CLANG
カン
CLANG
カン
PRETTY LONG, ISN'T IT?
IT'S MAKING MY LEGS SORE...
THERE AREN'T ANY DOORS TO THE OTHER FLOORS HERE.
WE'LL HAVE TO CLIMB ALL THE WAY UP.
OH...
BUT DON'T WORRY.
ONCE WE'RE THERE, WE CAN GET STARTED RIGHT AWAY.
I WON'T MAKE YOU WAIT ANY LONGER.
HEE HEE HEE!
THANKS FOR THE WORDS OF ENCOUR-AGEMENT!
ウィィ…ン
WHIRR

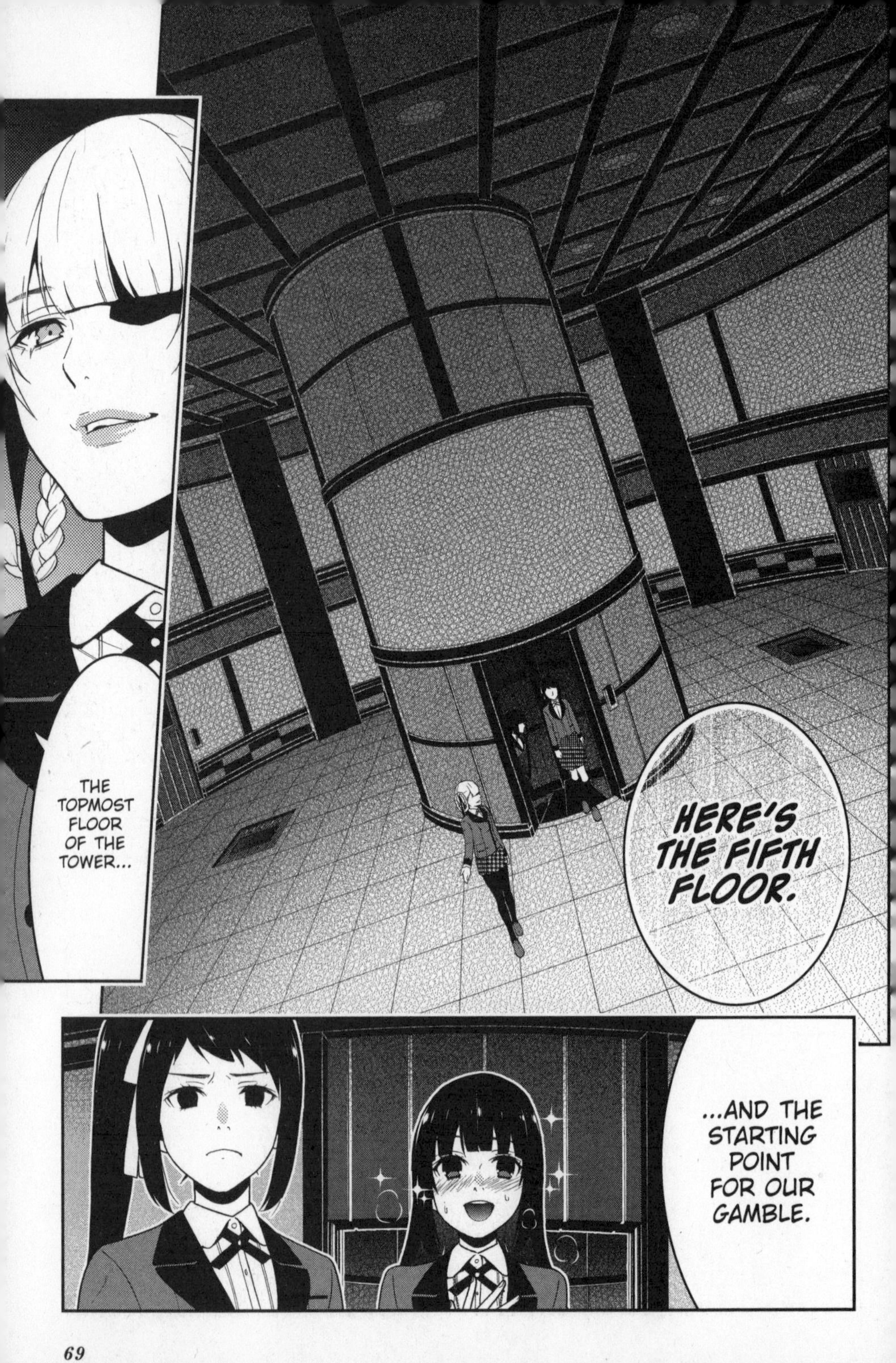
HERE'S THE FIFTH FLOOR.
THE TOPMOST FLOOR OF THE TOWER...
...AND THE STARTING POINT FOR OUR GAMBLE.

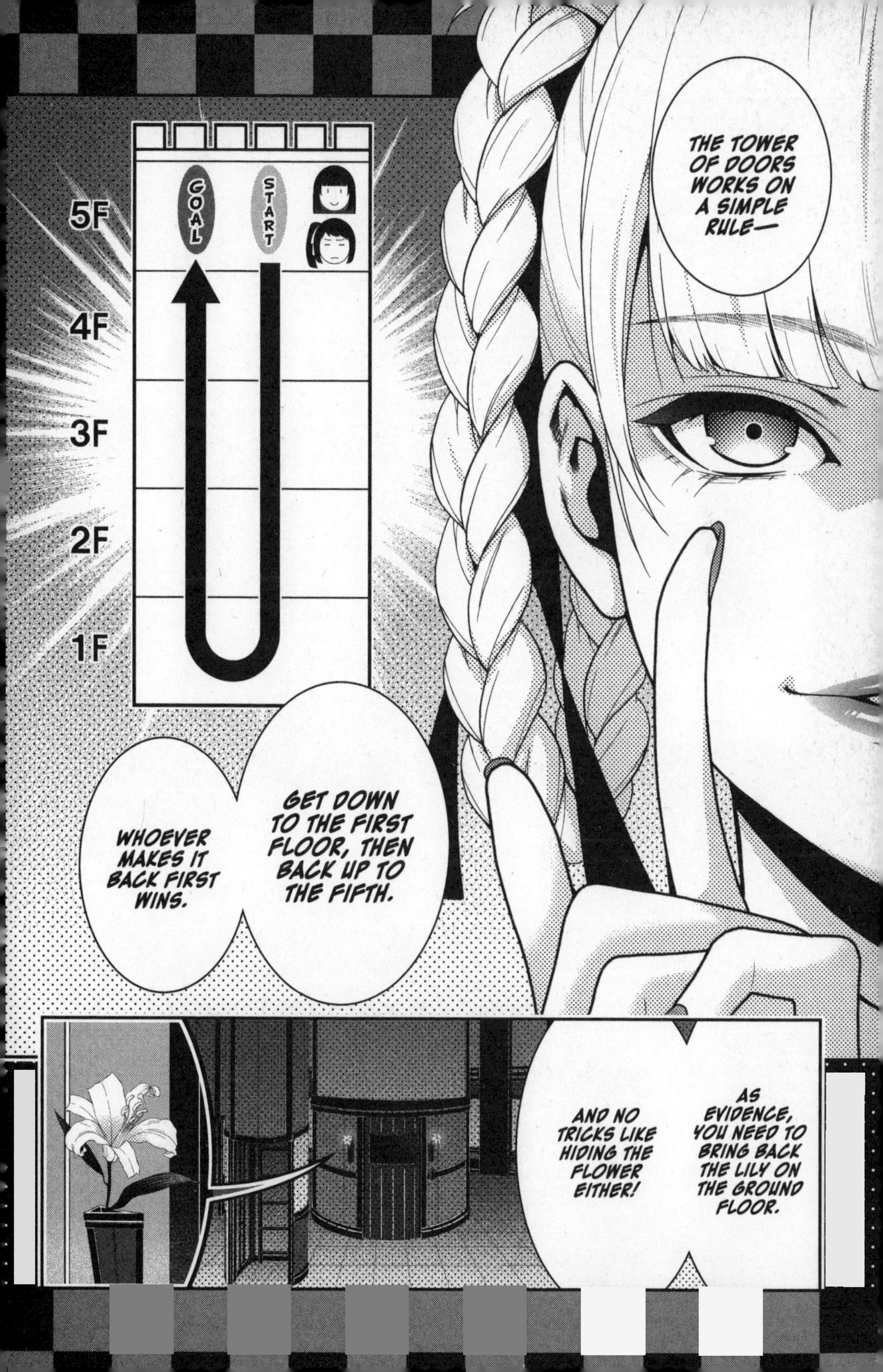
THE TOWER OF DOORS WORKS ON A SIMPLE RULE—
5F
4F
3F
2F
1F
START
GOAL
GET DOWN TO THE FIRST FLOOR, THEN BACK UP TO THE FIFTH.
WHOEVER MAKES IT BACK FIRST WINS.
AS EVIDENCE, YOU NEED TO BRING BACK THE LILY ON THE GROUND FLOOR.
AND NO TRICKS LIKE HIDING THE FLOWER EITHER!

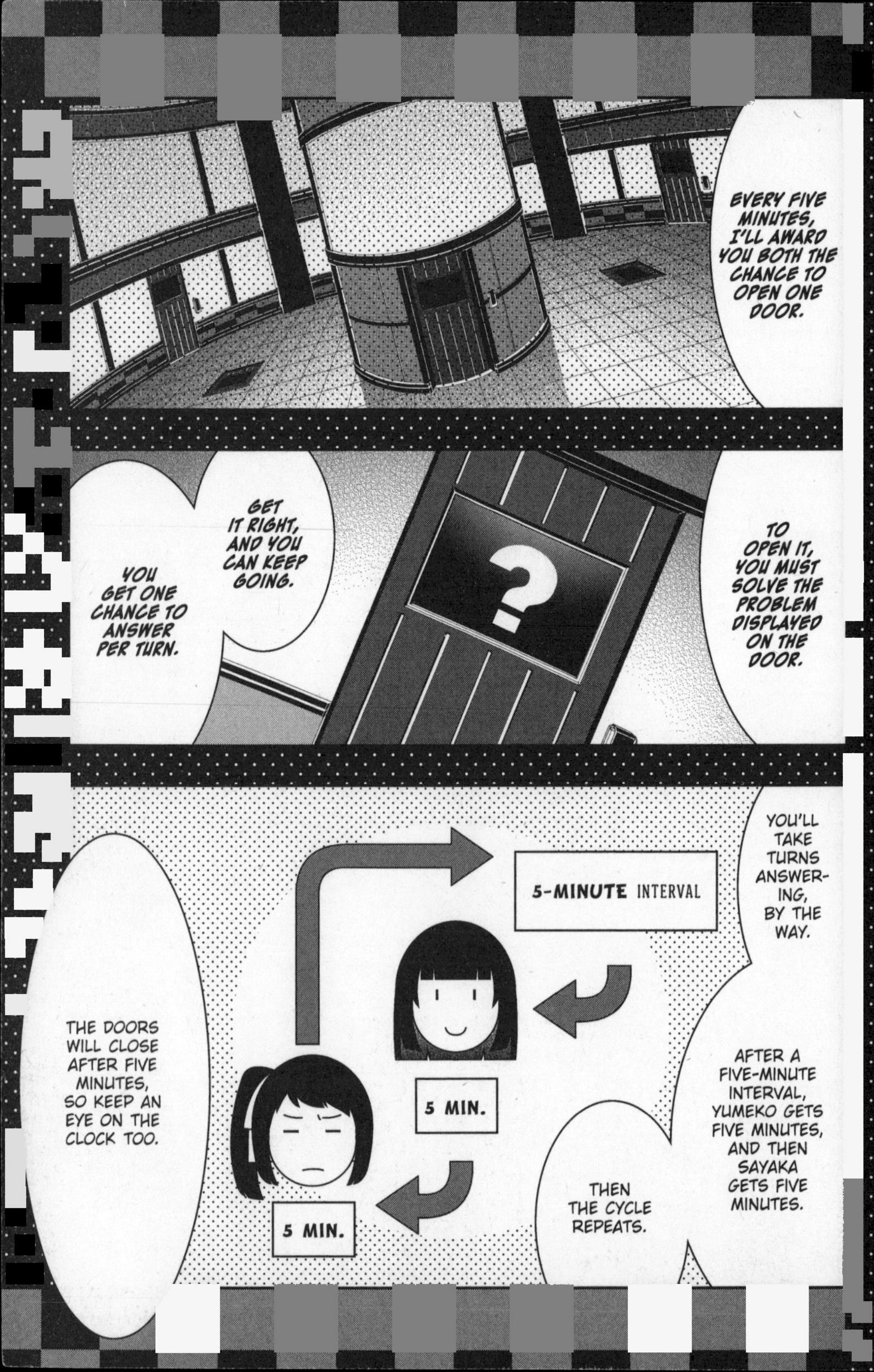
EVERY FIVE MINUTES, I'LL AWARD YOU BOTH THE CHANCE TO OPEN ONE DOOR.
TO OPEN IT, YOU MUST SOLVE THE PROBLEM DISPLAYED ON THE DOOR.
?
GET IT RIGHT, AND YOU CAN KEEP GOING.
YOU GET ONE CHANCE TO ANSWER PER TURN.
YOU'LL TAKE TURNS ANSWERING, BY THE WAY.
5-MINUTE INTERVAL
AFTER A FIVE-MINUTE INTERVAL, YUMEKO GETS FIVE MINUTES, AND THEN SAYAKA GETS FIVE MINUTES.
THEN THE CYCLE REPEATS.
5 MIN.
5 MIN.
THE DOORS WILL CLOSE AFTER FIVE MINUTES, SO KEEP AN EYE ON THE CLOCK TOO.

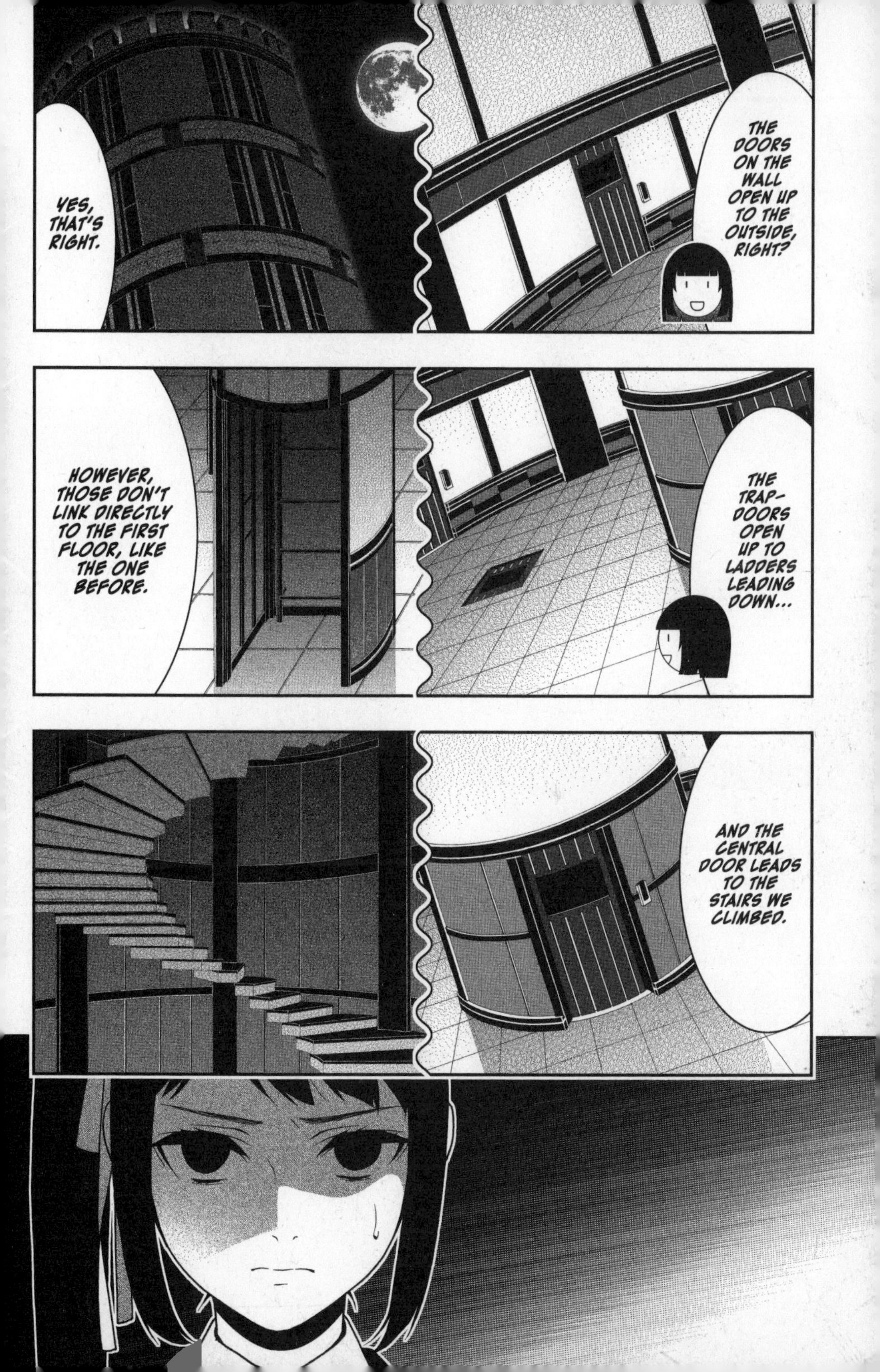
THE DOORS ON THE WALL OPEN UP TO THE OUTSIDE, RIGHT?
YES, THAT'S RIGHT.
THE TRAP-DOORS OPEN UP TO LADDERS LEADING DOWN...
HOWEVER, THOSE DON'T LINK DIRECTLY TO THE FIRST FLOOR, LIKE THE ONE BEFORE.
AND THE CENTRAL DOOR LEADS TO THE STAIRS WE CLIMBED.

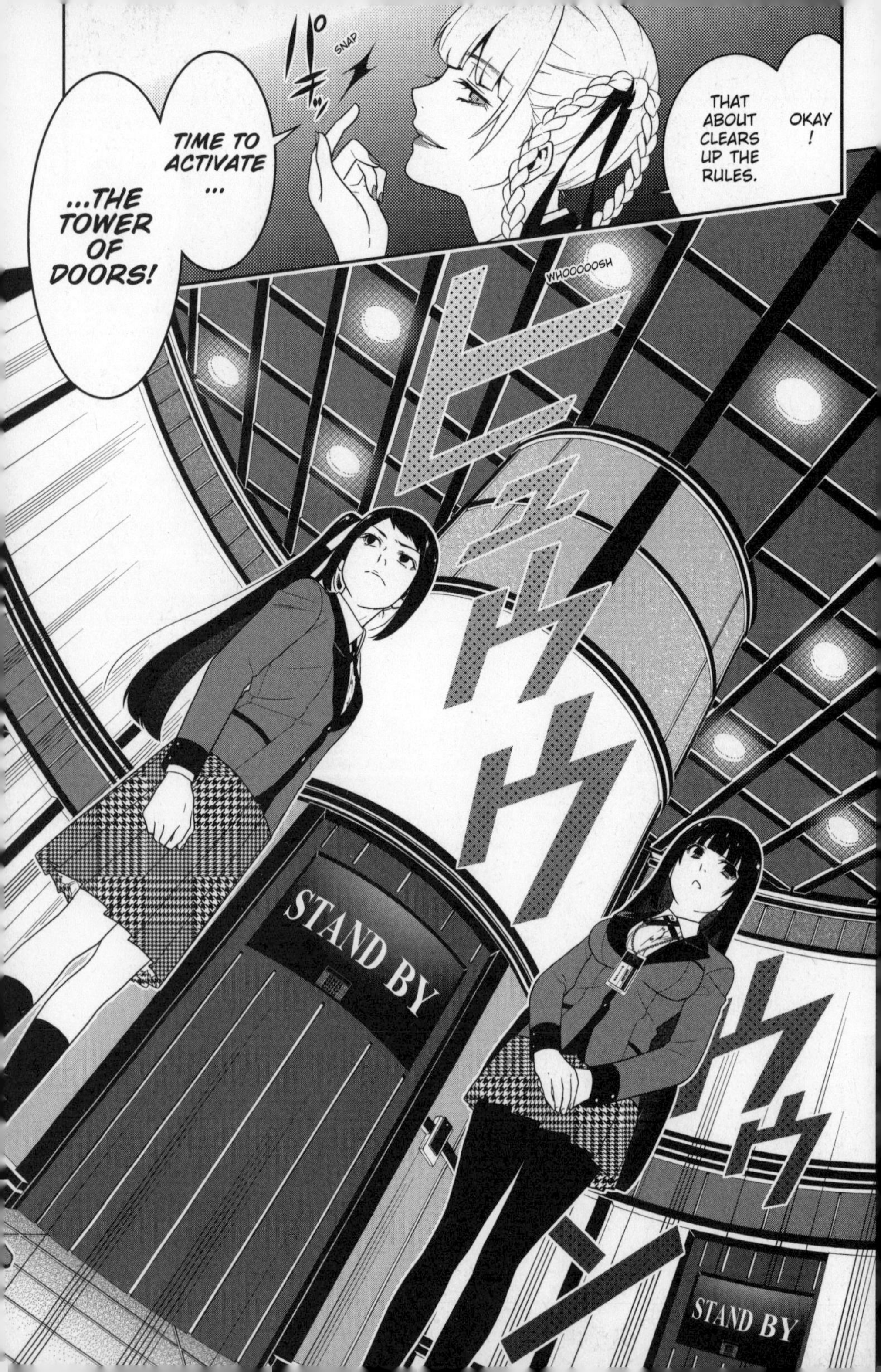
OKAY!
THAT ABOUT CLEARS UP THE RULES.
SNAP
TIME TO ACTIVATE ...
...THE TOWER OF DOORS!
WHOOOOOSH
STAND BY
STAND BY

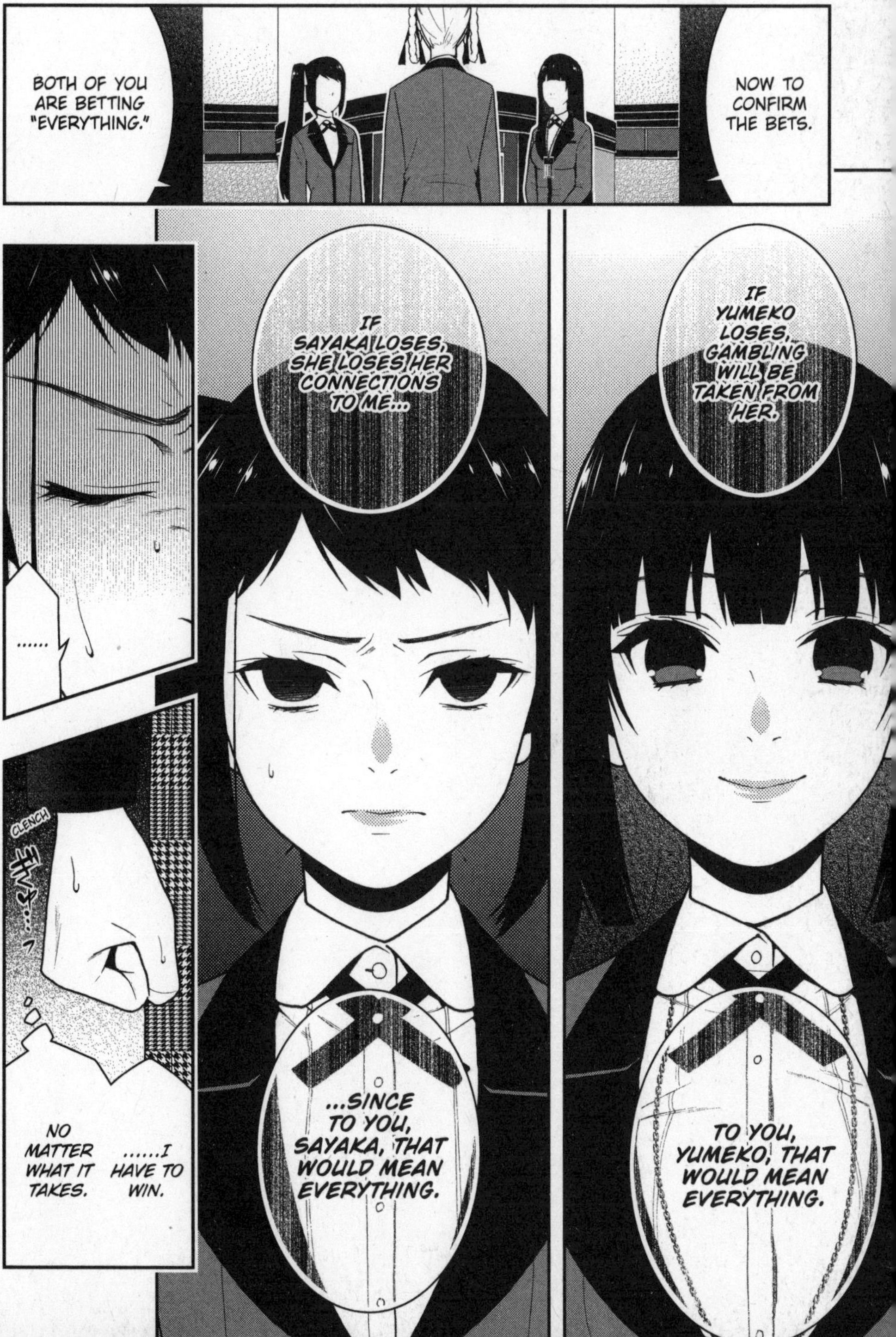
NOW TO CONFIRM THE BETS.
BOTH OF YOU ARE BETTING "EVERYTHING."
IF YUMEKO LOSES, GAMBLING WILL BE TAKEN FROM HER.
TO YOU, YUMEKO, THAT WOULD MEAN EVERYTHING.
IF SAYAKA LOSES, SHE LOSES HER CONNECTIONS TO ME...
...SINCE TO YOU, SAYAKA, THAT WOULD MEAN EVERYTHING.
......
CLENCH
......I HAVE TO WIN.
NO MATTER WHAT IT TAKES.

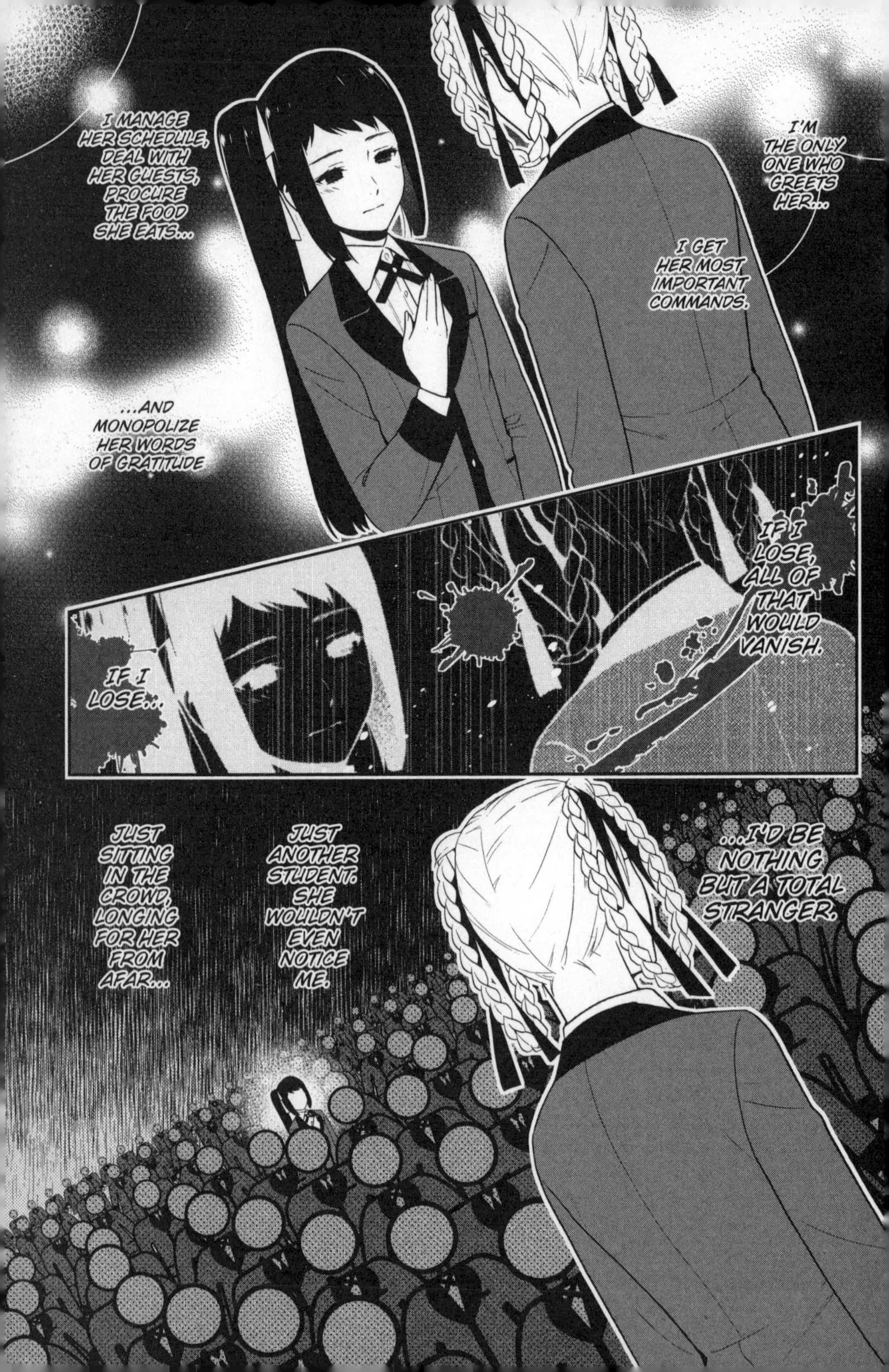
I'M THE ONLY ONE WHO GREETS HER...
I GET HER MOST IMPORTANT COMMANDS.
I MANAGE HER SCHEDULE, DEAL WITH HER GUESTS, PROCURE THE FOOD SHE EATS...
...AND MONOPOLIZE HER WORDS OF GRATITUDE
IF I LOSE, ALL OF THAT WOULD VANISH.
IF I LOSE...
...I'D BE NOTHING BUT A TOTAL STRANGER.
JUST ANOTHER STUDENT. SHE WOULDN'T EVEN NOTICE ME.
JUST SITTING IN THE CROWD, LONGING FOR HER FROM AFAR...

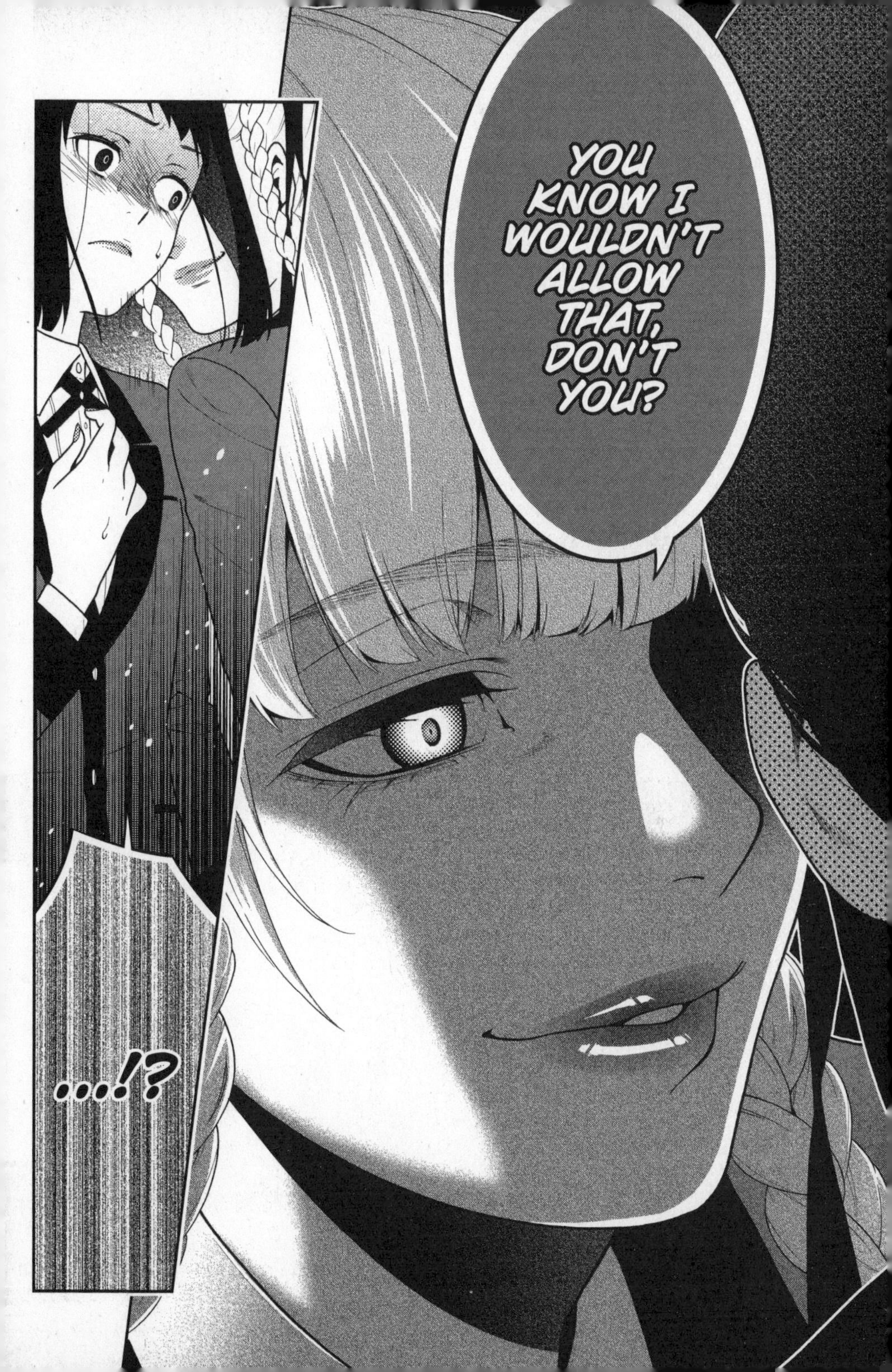
YOU KNOW I WOULDN'T ALLOW THAT, DON'T YOU?
...!?

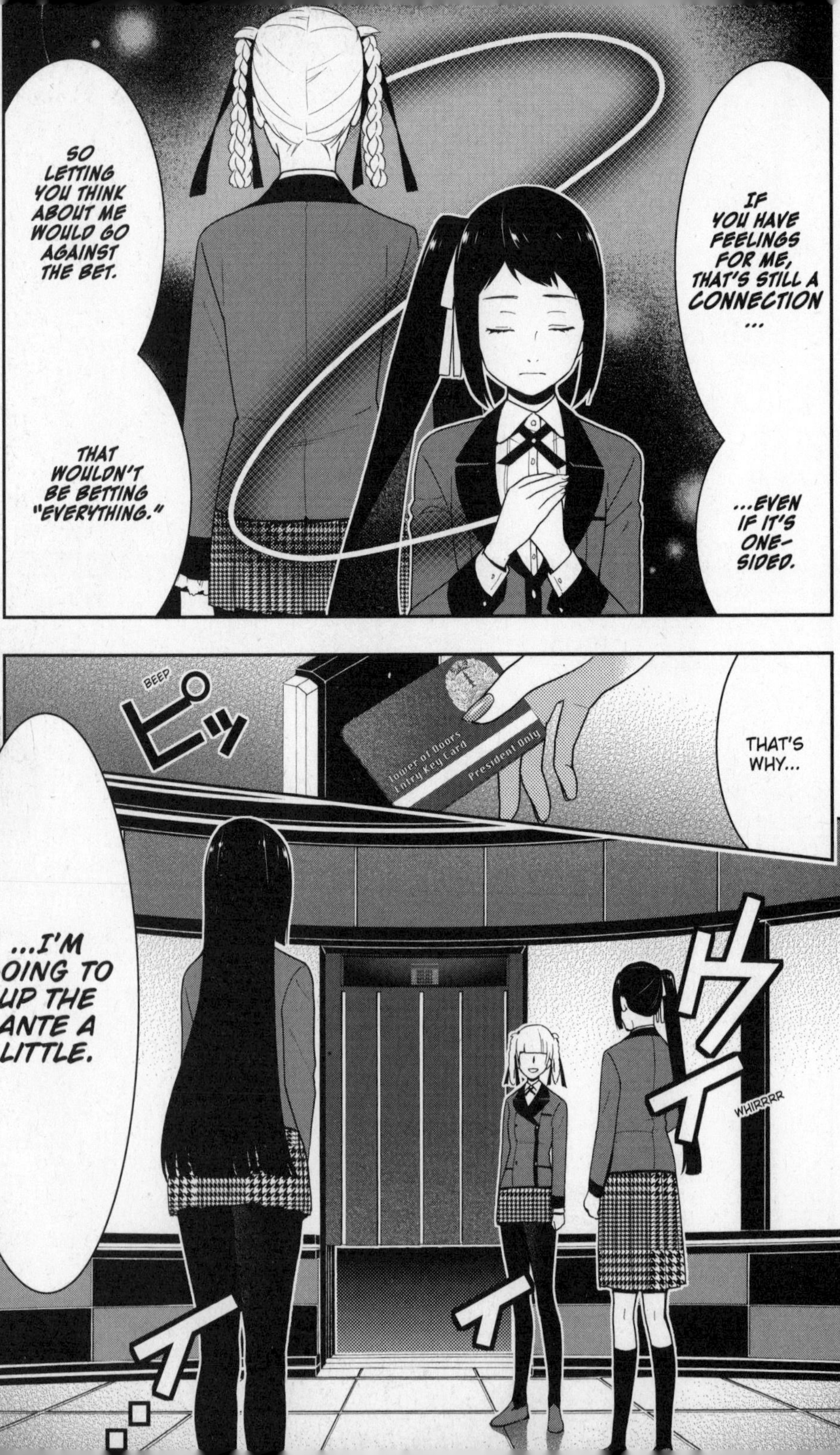
IF YOU HAVE FEELINGS FOR ME, THAT'S STILL A CONNECTION...
...EVEN IF IT'S ONE-SIDED.
SO LETTING YOU THINK ABOUT ME WOULD GO AGAINST THE BET.
THAT WOULDN'T BE BETTING "EVERYTHING."
THAT'S WHY...
Tower of Doors Entry Key Card
President Only
ピッ
BEEP
...I'M GOING TO UP THE ANTE A LITTLE.
WHIRRRR

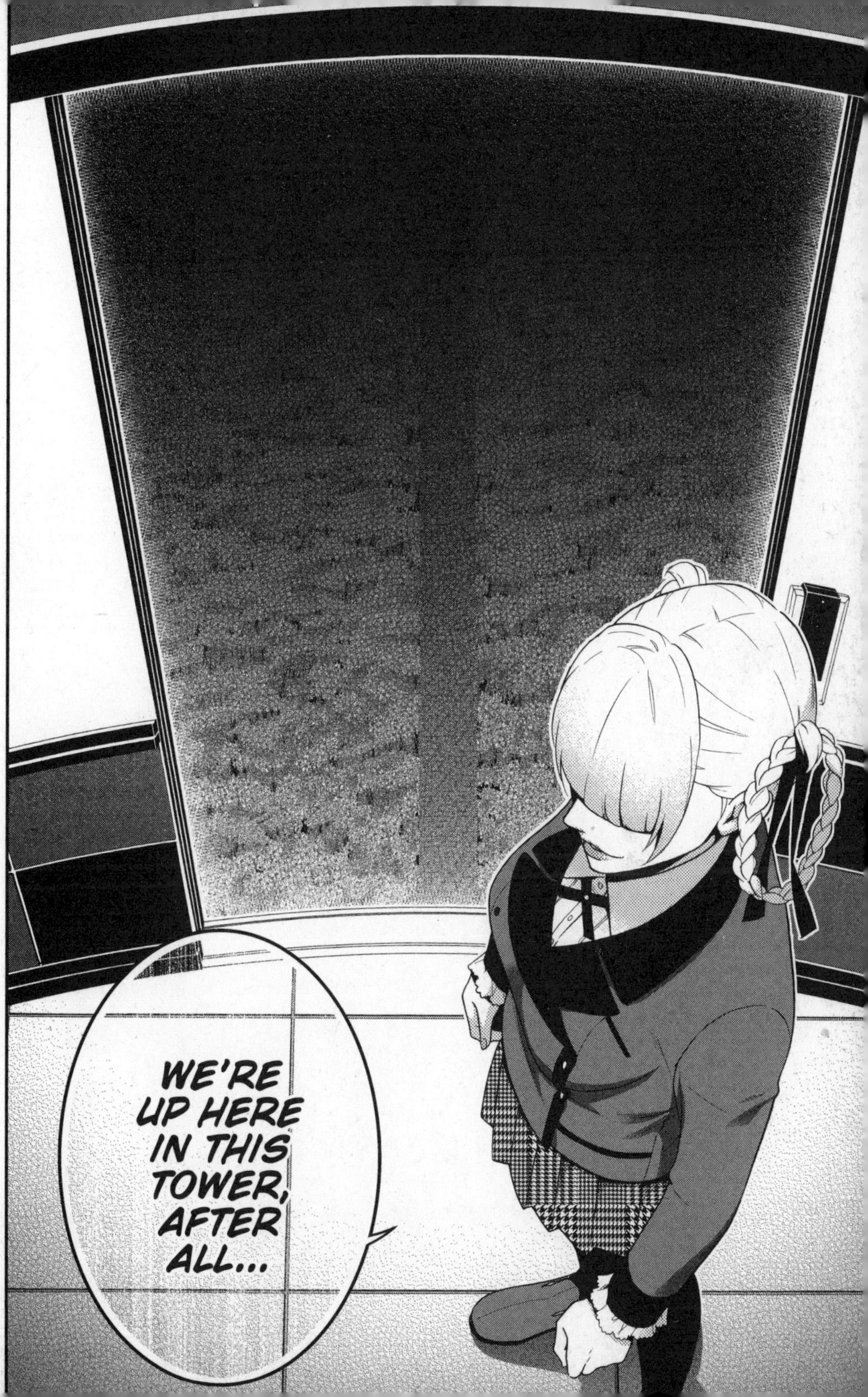
WE'RE UP HERE IN THIS TOWER, AFTER ALL...

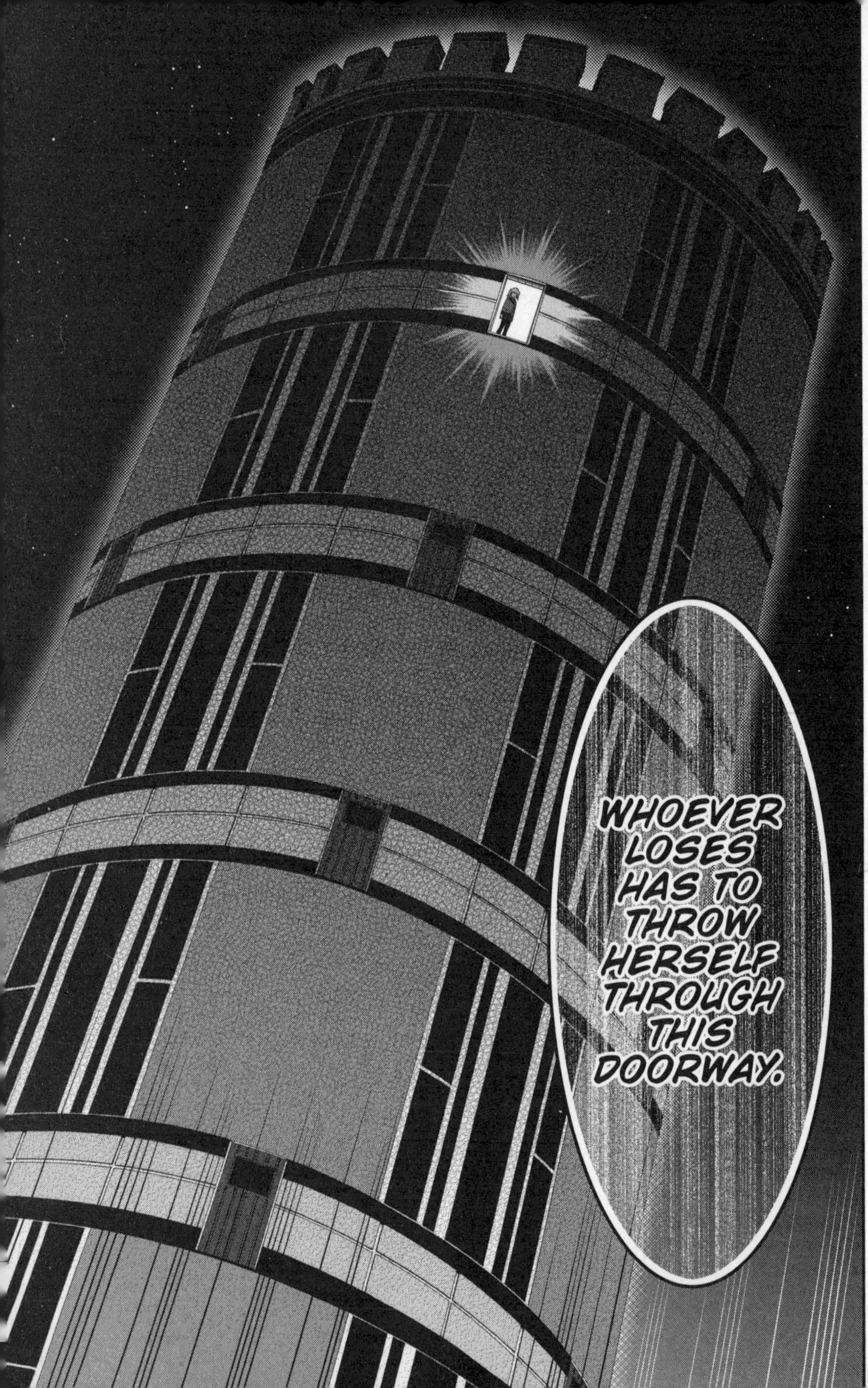
WHOEVER LOSES HAS TO THROW HERSELF THROUGH THIS DOORWAY.

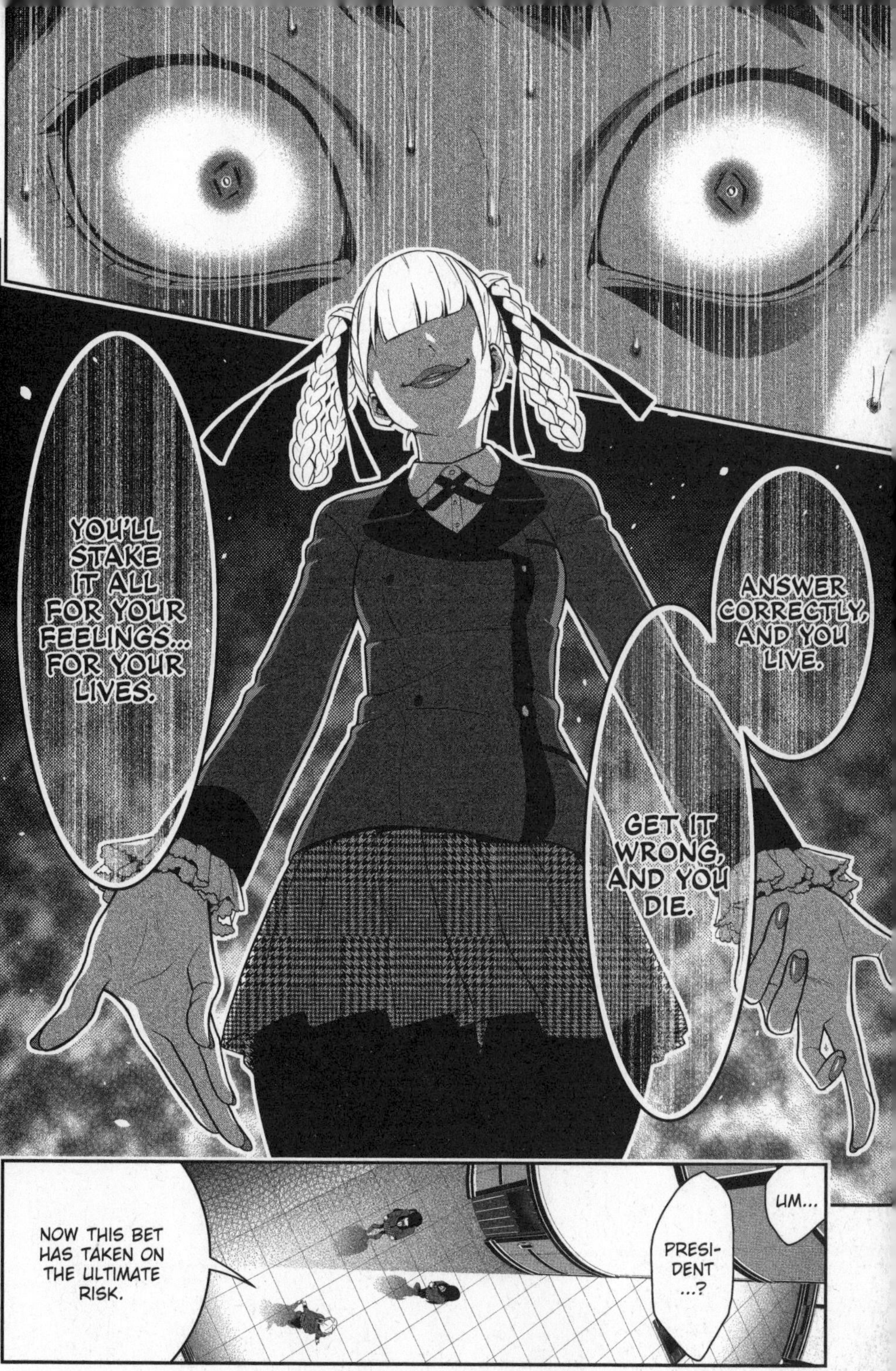
ANSWER CORRECTLY, AND YOU LIVE.
GET IT WRONG, AND YOU DIE.
YOU'LL STAKE IT ALL FOR YOUR FEELINGS... FOR YOUR LIVES.
UM...
PRESI-DENT ...?
NOW THIS BET HAS TAKEN ON THE ULTIMATE RISK.

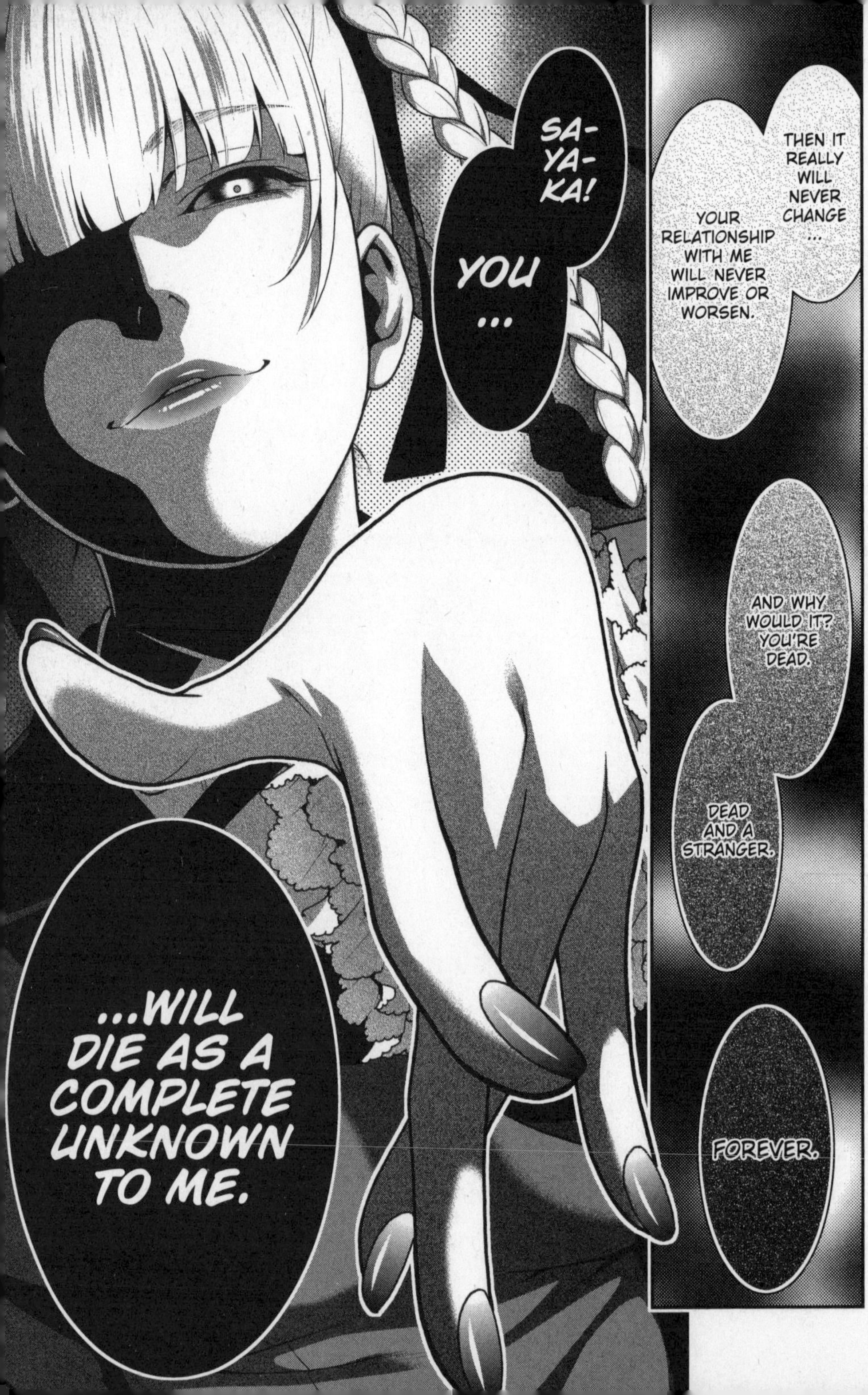
THEN IT REALLY WILL NEVER CHANGE ...
YOUR RELATIONSHIP WITH ME WILL NEVER IMPROVE OR WORSEN.
AND WHY WOULD IT? YOU'RE DEAD.
DEAD AND A STRANGER.
FOREVER.
SA-YA-KA!
YOU ...
...WILL DIE AS A COMPLETE UNKNOWN TO ME.

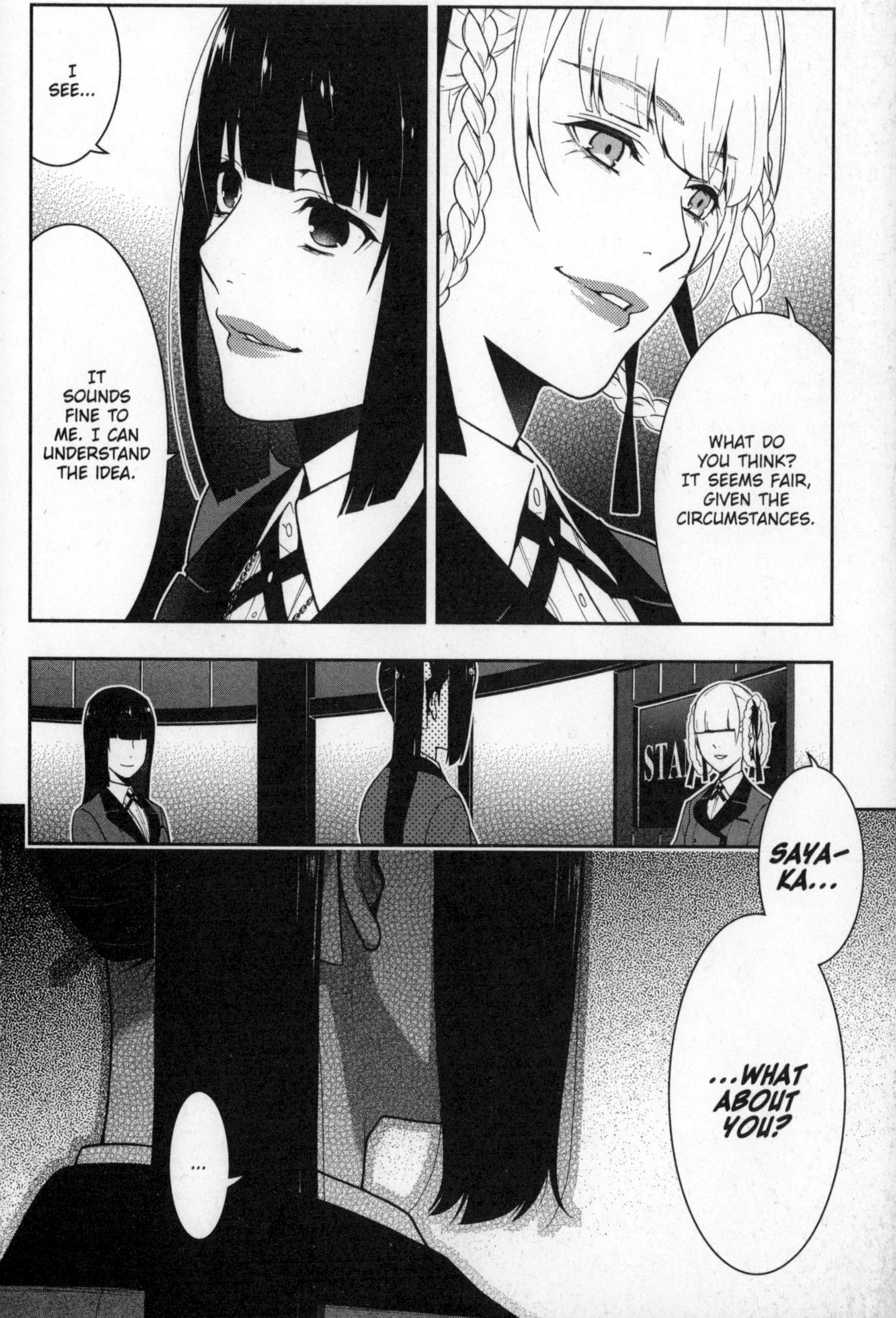
WHAT DO YOU THINK? IT SEEMS FAIR, GIVEN THE CIRCUMSTANCES.
I SEE...
IT SOUNDS FINE TO ME. I CAN UNDERSTAND THE IDEA.
SAYA-KA...
...WHAT ABOUT YOU?
...

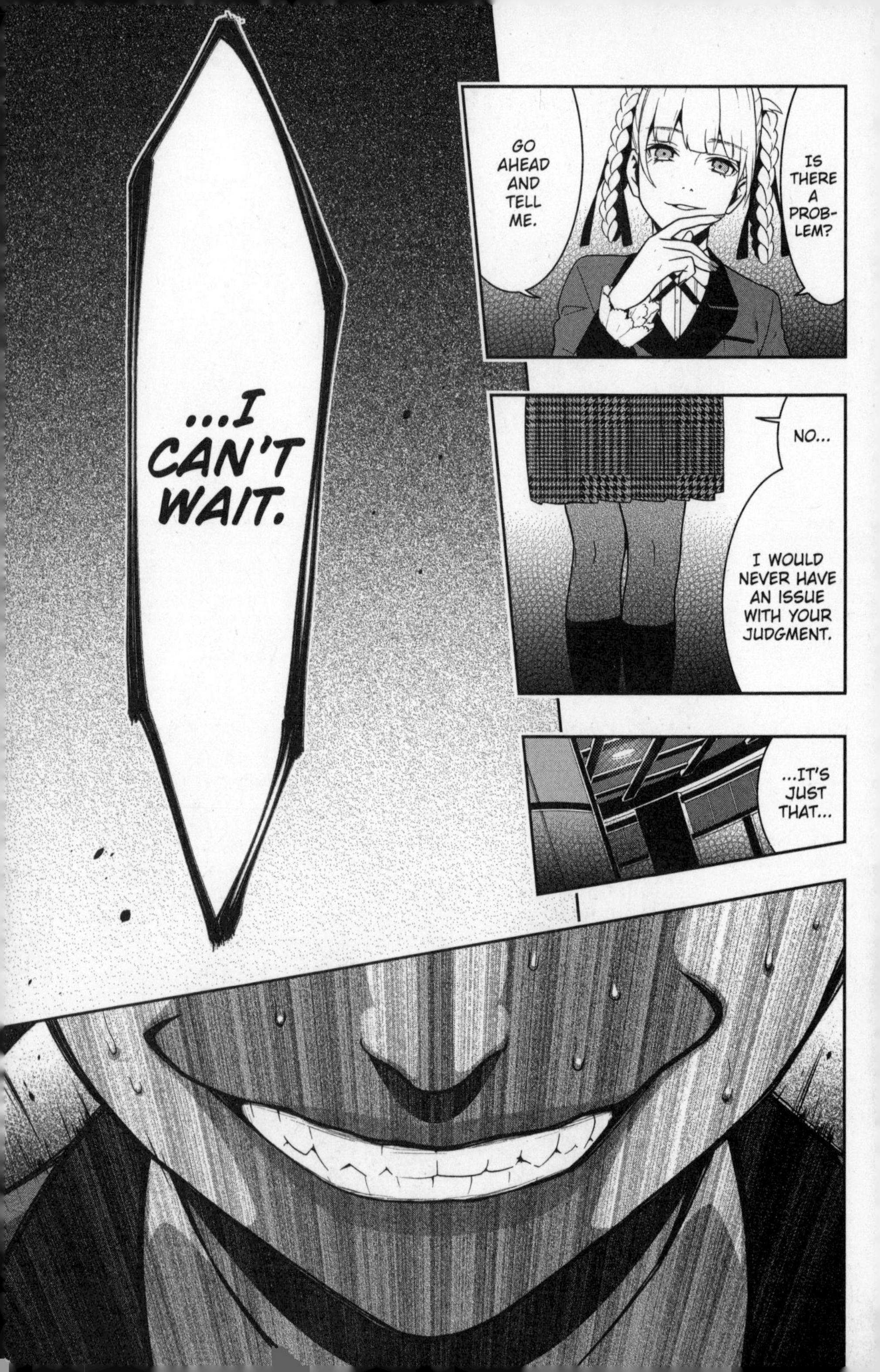
IS THERE A PROBLEM?
GO AHEAD AND TELL ME.
NO...
I WOULD NEVER HAVE AN ISSUE WITH YOUR JUDGMENT.
...IT'S JUST THAT...
...I CAN'T WAIT.

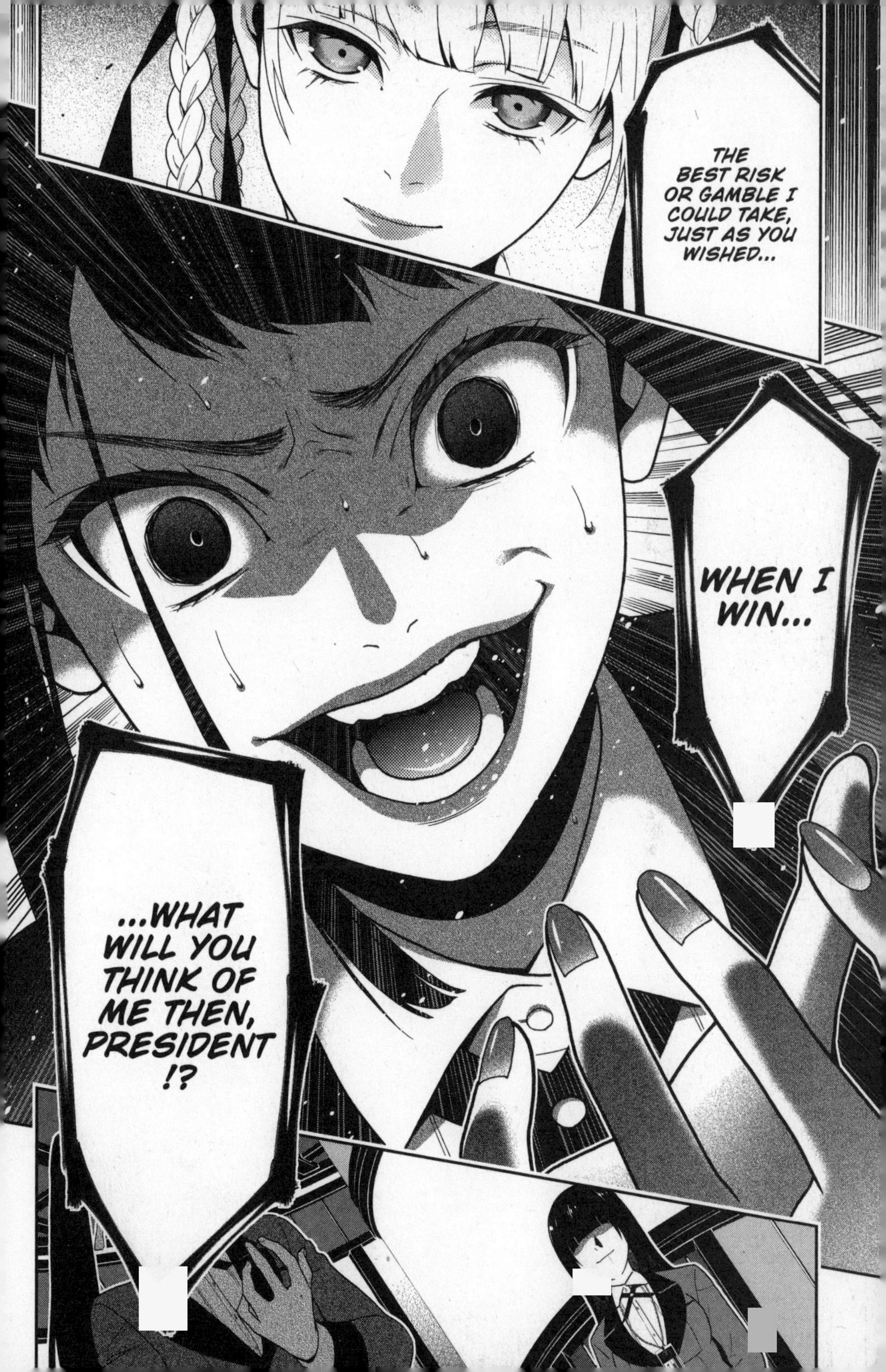
THE BEST RISK OR GAMBLE I COULD TAKE, JUST AS YOU WISHED...
WHEN I WIN...
...WHAT WILL YOU THINK OF ME THEN, PRESIDENT!?

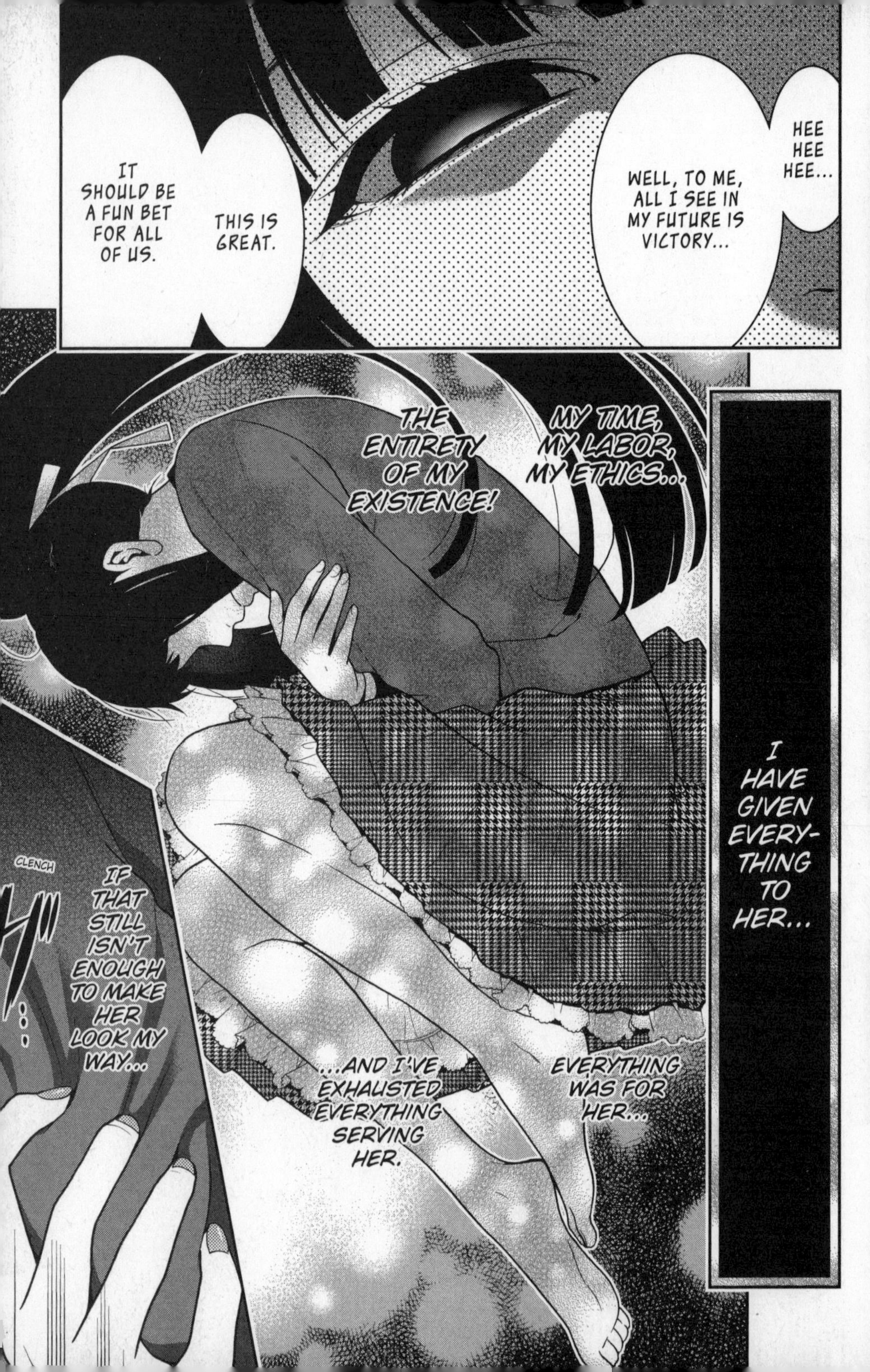
HEE HEE HEE...
WELL, TO ME, ALL I SEE IN MY FUTURE IS VICTORY...
THIS IS GREAT.
IT SHOULD BE A FUN BET FOR ALL OF US.
I HAVE GIVEN EVERY-THING TO HER...
MY TIME, MY LABOR, MY ETHICS...
THE ENTIRETY OF MY EXISTENCE!
EVERYTHING WAS FOR HER...
...AND I'VE EXHAUSTED EVERYTHING SERVING HER.
IF THAT STILL ISN'T ENOUGH TO MAKE HER LOOK MY WAY...
CLENCH

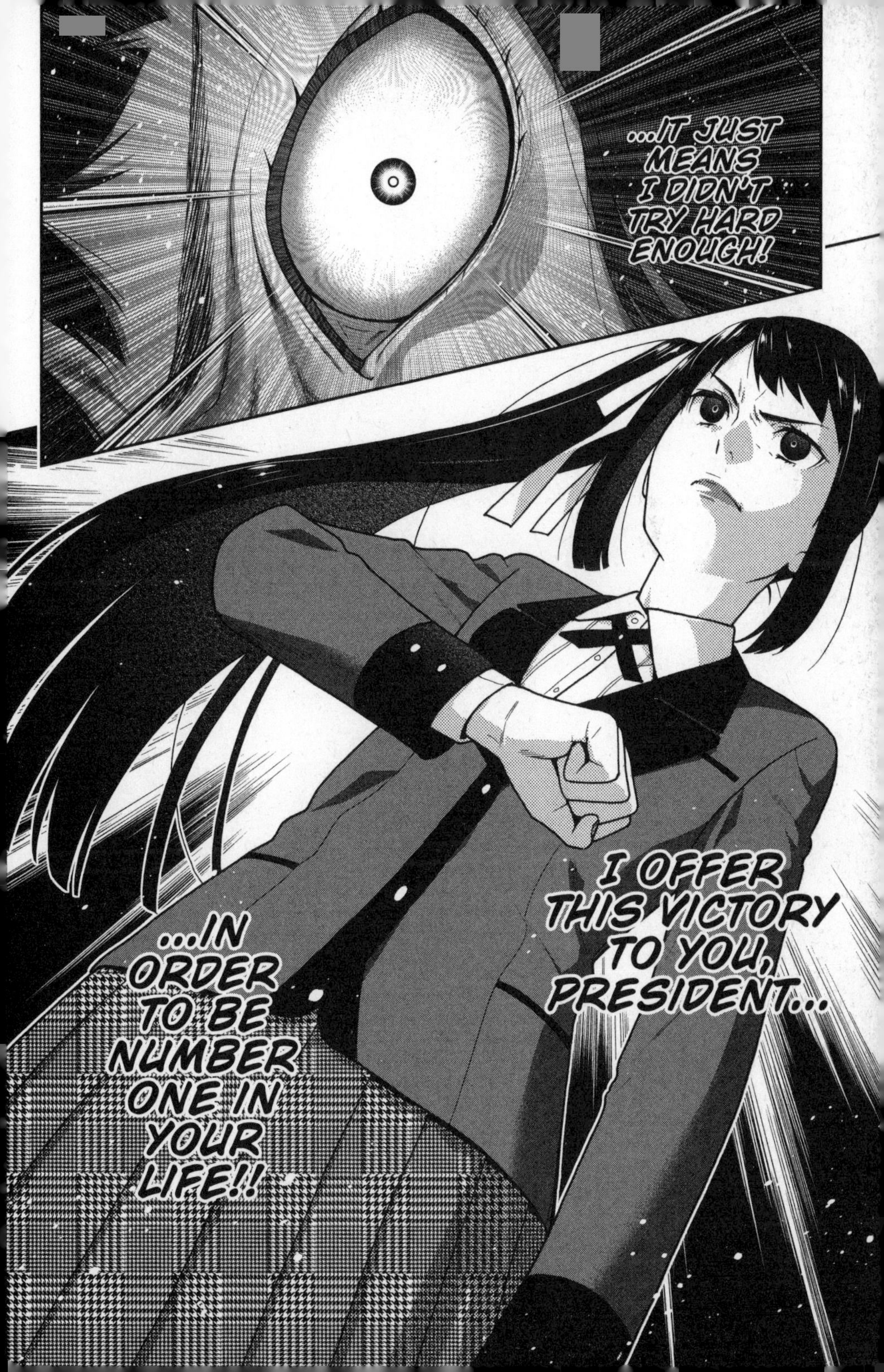
...IT JUST MEANS I DIDN'T TRY HARD ENOUGH!
I OFFER THIS VICTORY TO YOU, PRESIDENT...
...IN ORDER TO BE NUMBER ONE IN YOUR LIFE!!

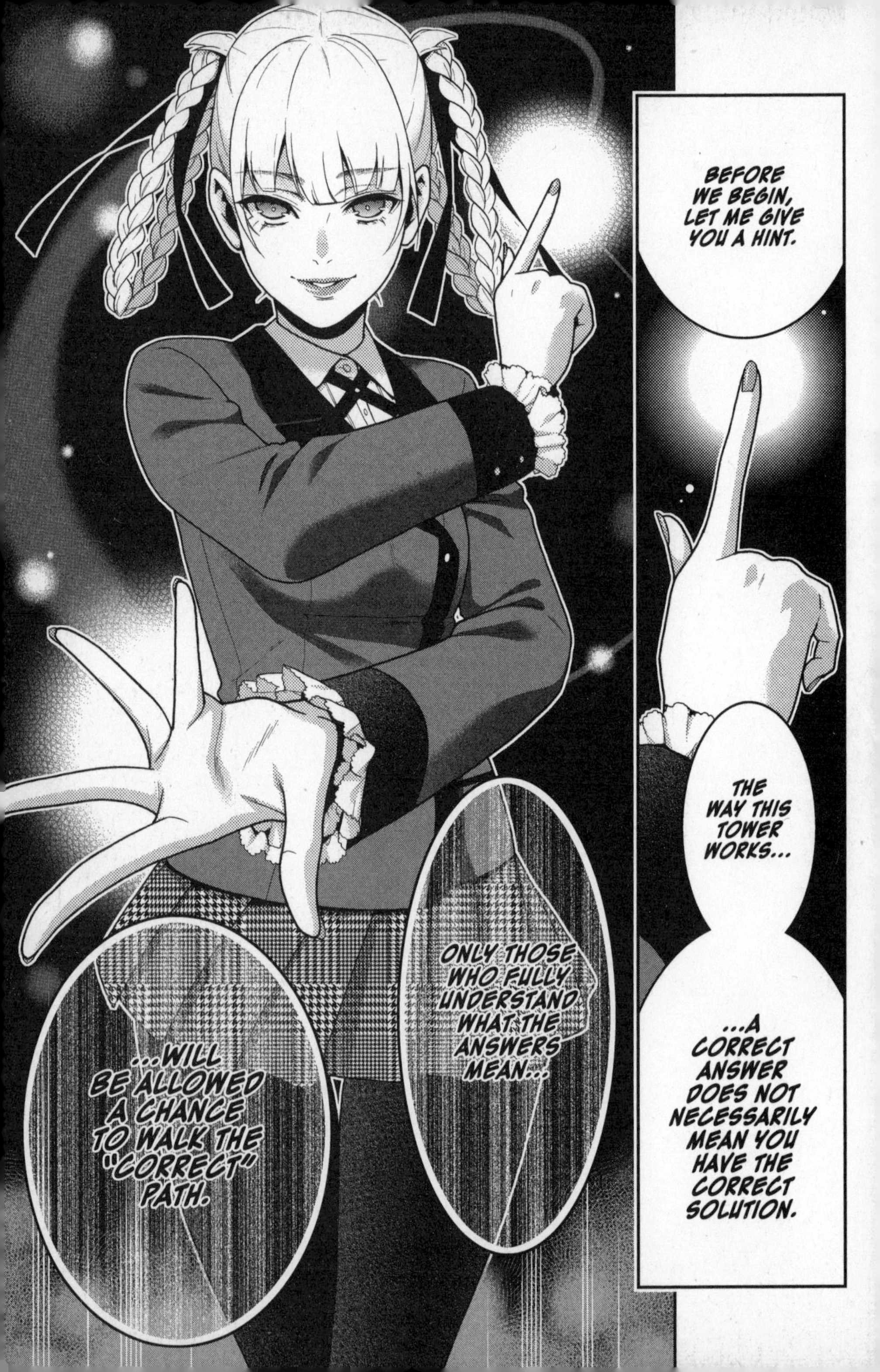
BEFORE WE BEGIN, LET ME GIVE YOU A HINT.
THE WAY THIS TOWER WORKS...
...A CORRECT ANSWER DOES NOT NECESSARILY MEAN YOU HAVE THE CORRECT SOLUTION.
ONLY THOSE WHO FULLY UNDERSTAND WHAT THE ANSWERS MEAN...
...WILL BE ALLOWED A CHANCE TO WALK THE "CORRECT" PATH.

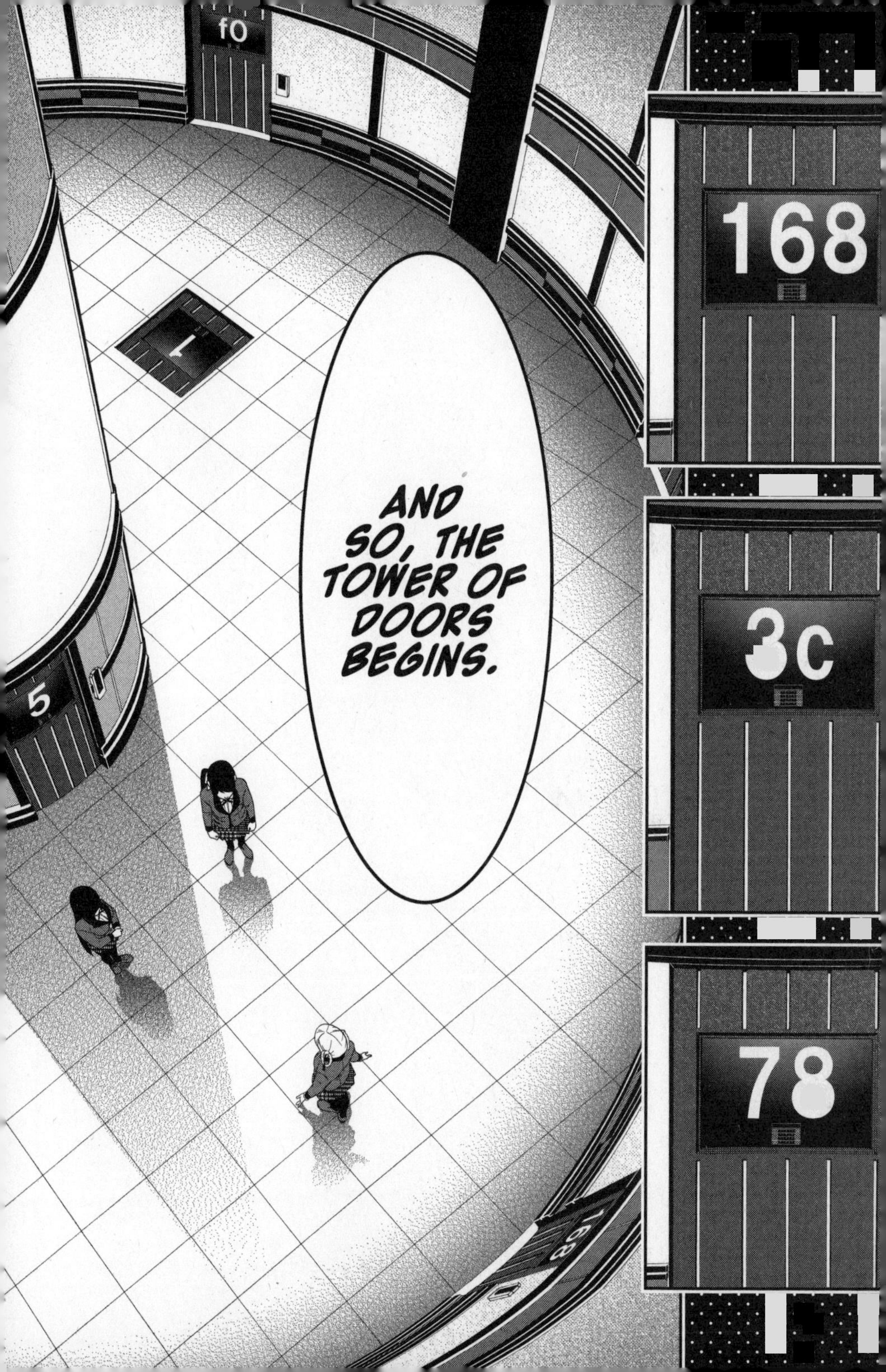
168
3c
78
AND SO, THE TOWER OF DOORS BEGINS.
fO
5

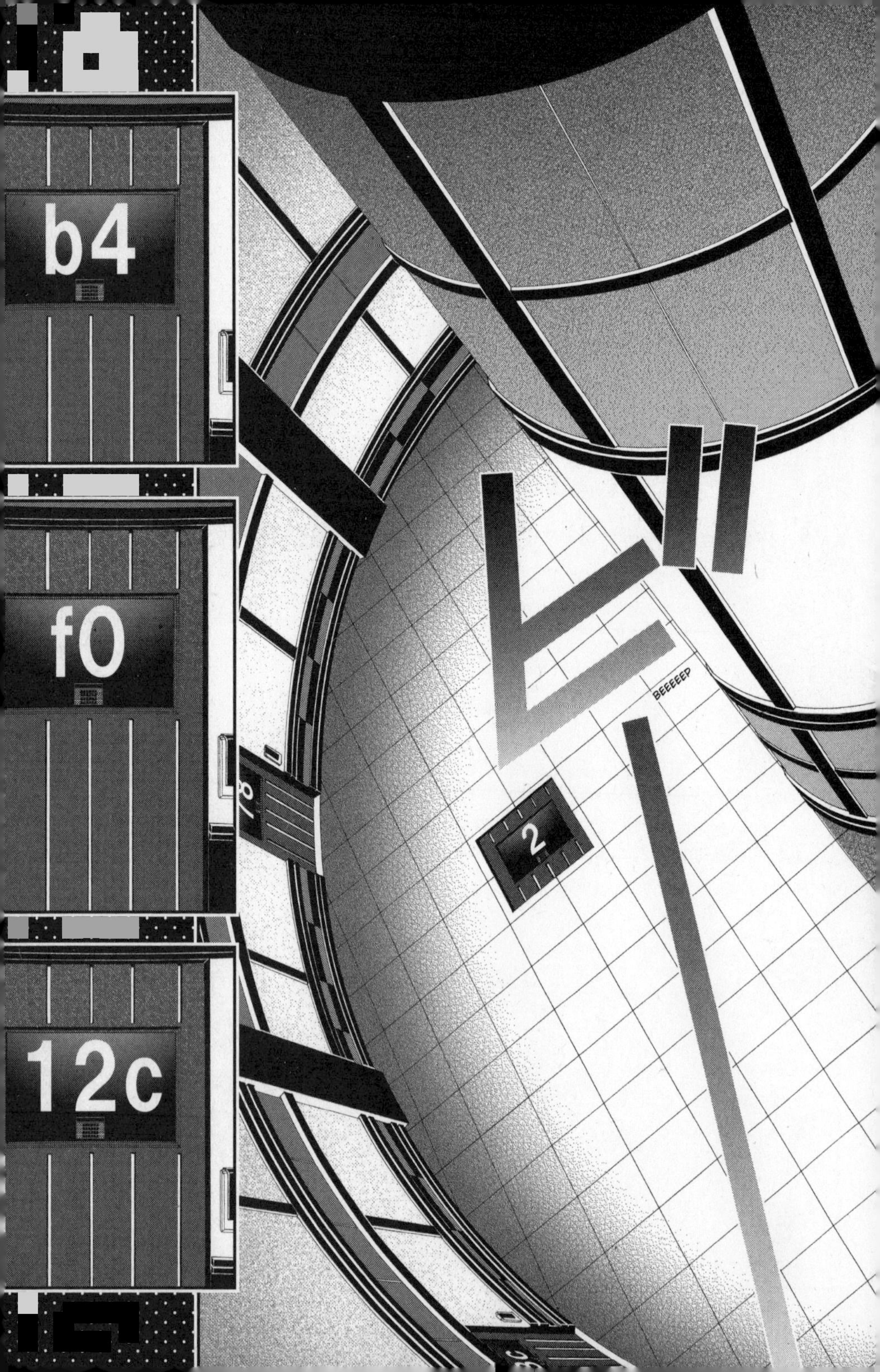
BEEEEEP
2
b4
f0
12c

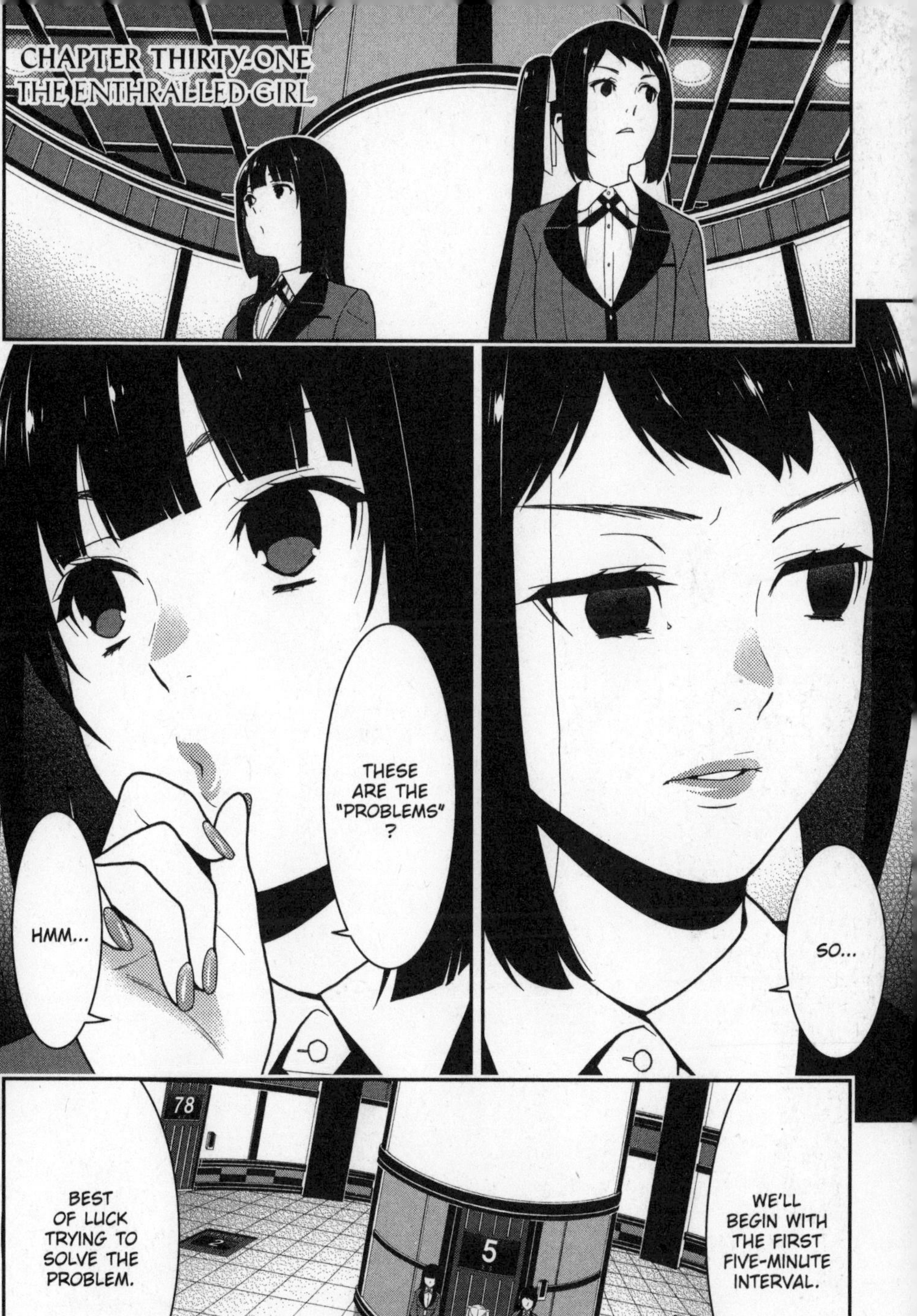
CHAPTER THIRTY-ONE
THE ENTHRALLED GIRL
SO...
THESE ARE THE "PROBLEMS"?
HMM...
WE'LL BEGIN WITH THE FIRST FIVE-MINUTE INTERVAL.
BEST OF LUCK TRYING TO SOLVE THE PROBLEM.

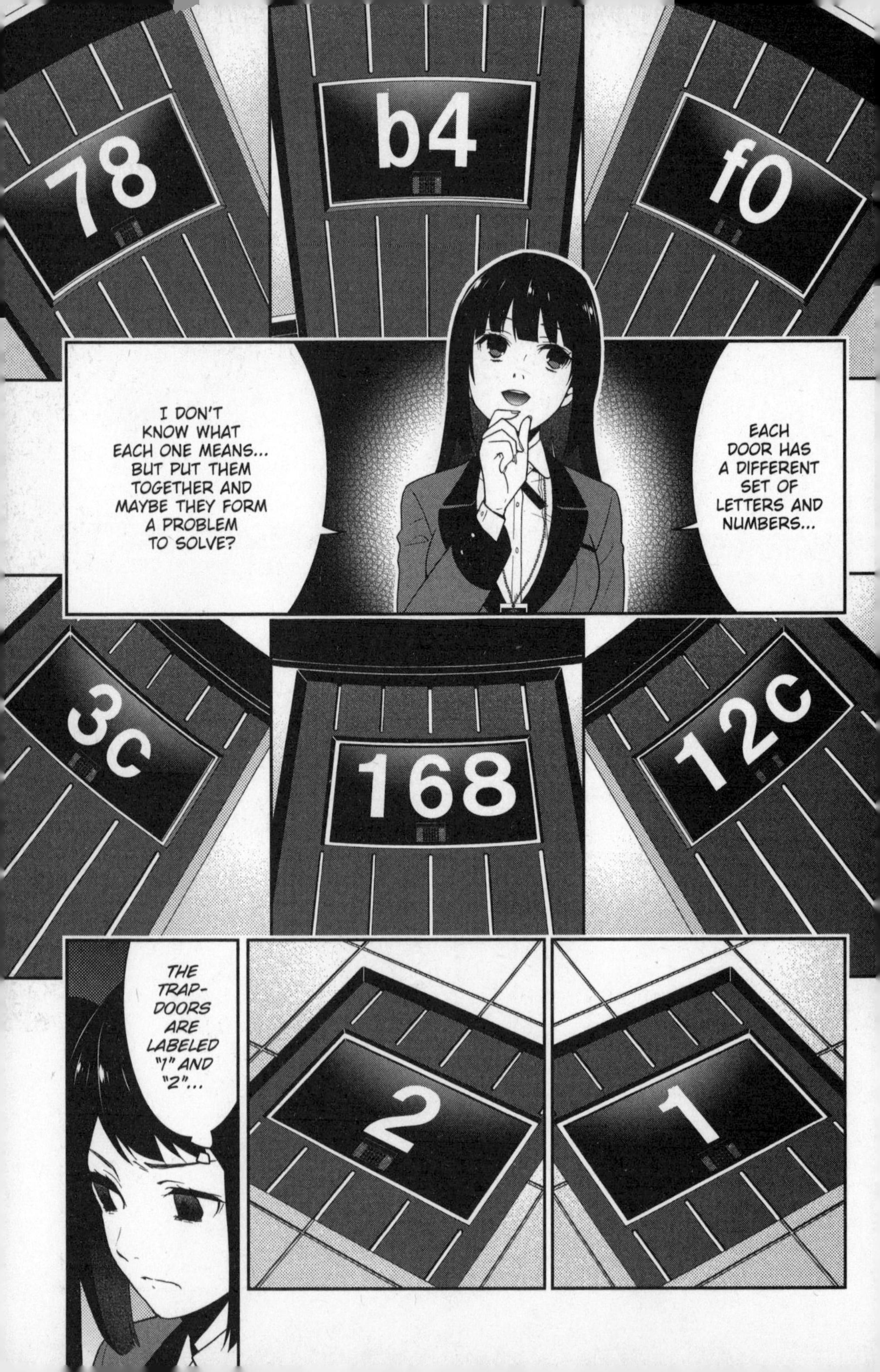
f0
b4
78
EACH DOOR HAS A DIFFERENT SET OF LETTERS AND NUMBERS...
I DON'T KNOW WHAT EACH ONE MEANS... BUT PUT THEM TOGETHER AND MAYBE THEY FORM A PROBLEM TO SOLVE?
12c
168
3c
1
2
THE TRAP-DOORS ARE LABELED "1" AND "2"...

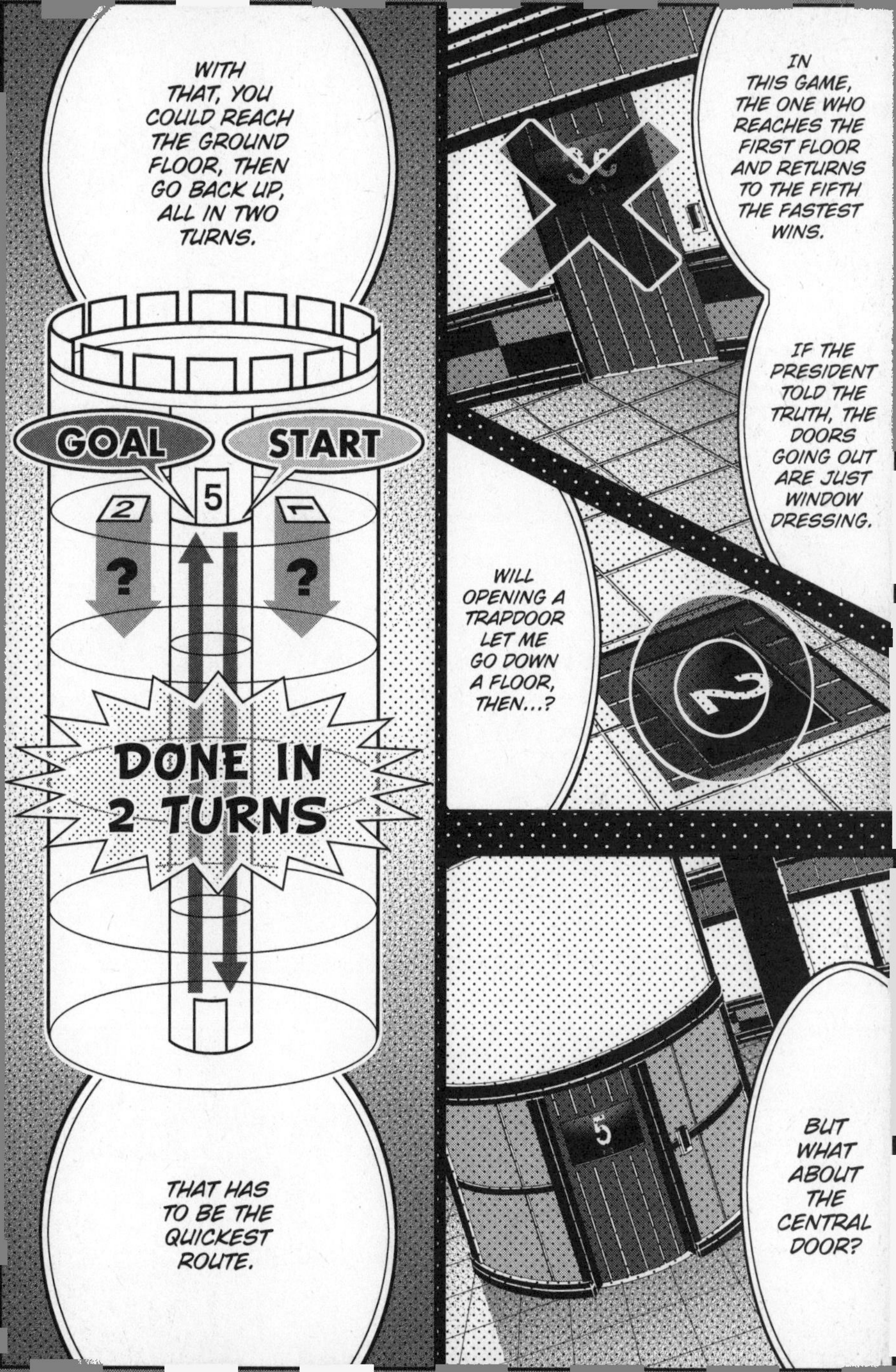
IN THIS GAME, THE ONE WHO REACHES THE FIRST FLOOR AND RETURNS TO THE FIFTH THE FASTEST WINS.
IF THE PRESIDENT TOLD THE TRUTH, THE DOORS GOING OUT ARE JUST WINDOW DRESSING.
WILL OPENING A TRAPDOOR LET ME GO DOWN A FLOOR, THEN...?
BUT WHAT ABOUT THE CENTRAL DOOR?
WITH THAT, YOU COULD REACH THE GROUND FLOOR, THEN GO BACK UP, ALL IN TWO TURNS.
START
GOAL
5
1
2
?
?
DONE IN 2 TURNS
THAT HAS TO BE THE QUICKEST ROUTE.

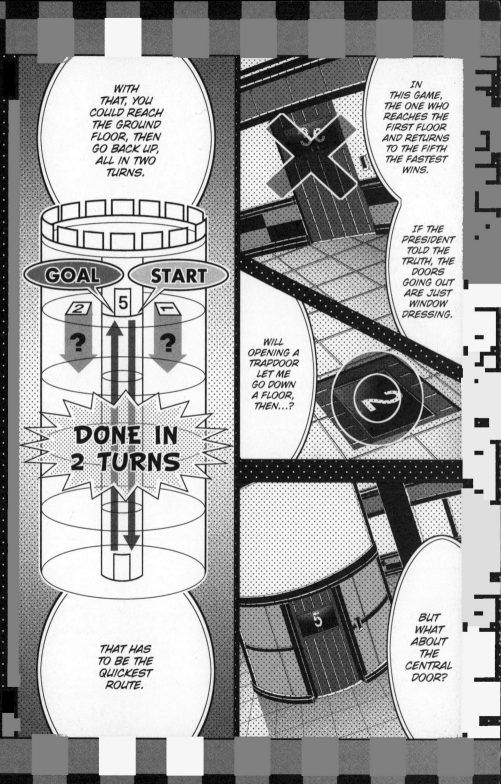

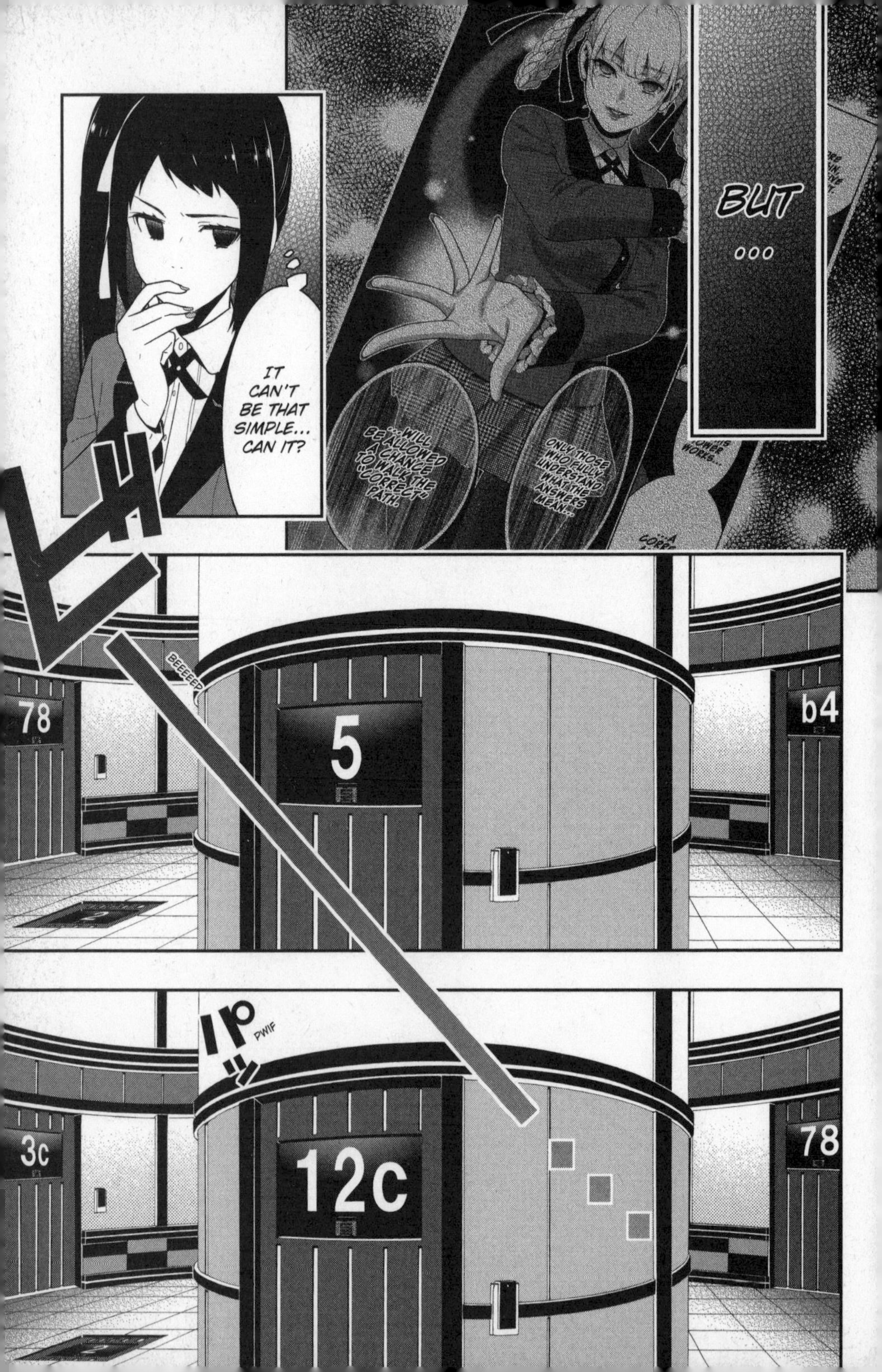
BUT
...
ONLY THOSE WHO FULLY UNDERSTAND WHAT THE ANSWERS MEAN...
...WILL BE ALLOWED A CHANCE TO WALK THE "CORRECT" PATH.
IT CAN'T BE THAT SIMPLE... CAN IT?
BEEEEEP
b4
5
78
DWIF
78
12c
3c

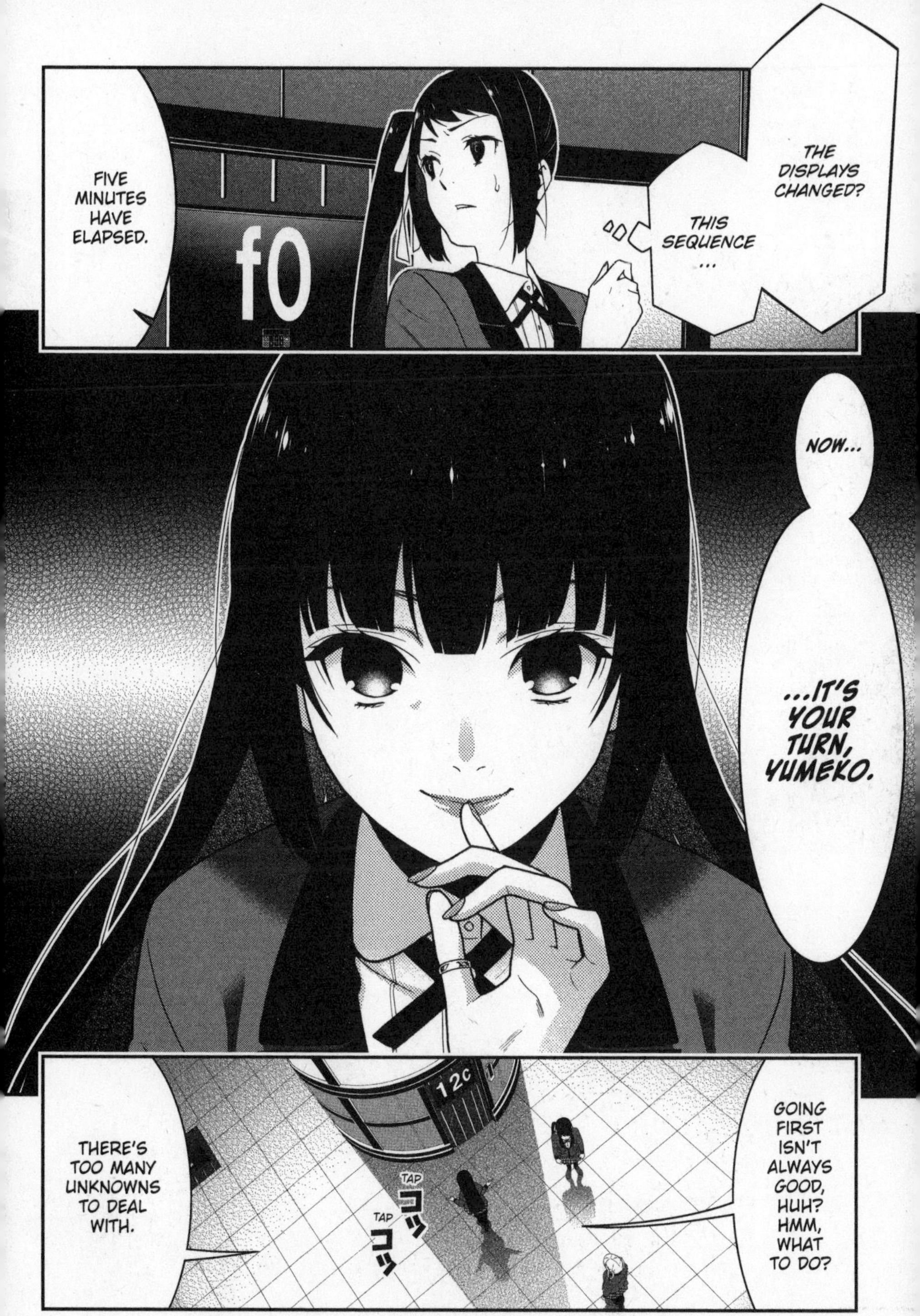

THE DISPLAYS CHANGED?
THIS SEQUENCE ...
FIVE MINUTES HAVE ELAPSED.
fO
NOW...
...IT'S YOUR TURN, YUMEKO.
12c
GOING FIRST ISN'T ALWAYS GOOD, HUH? HMM, WHAT TO DO?
TAP コツ
TAP コツ
THERE'S TOO MANY UNKNOWNS TO DEAL WITH.

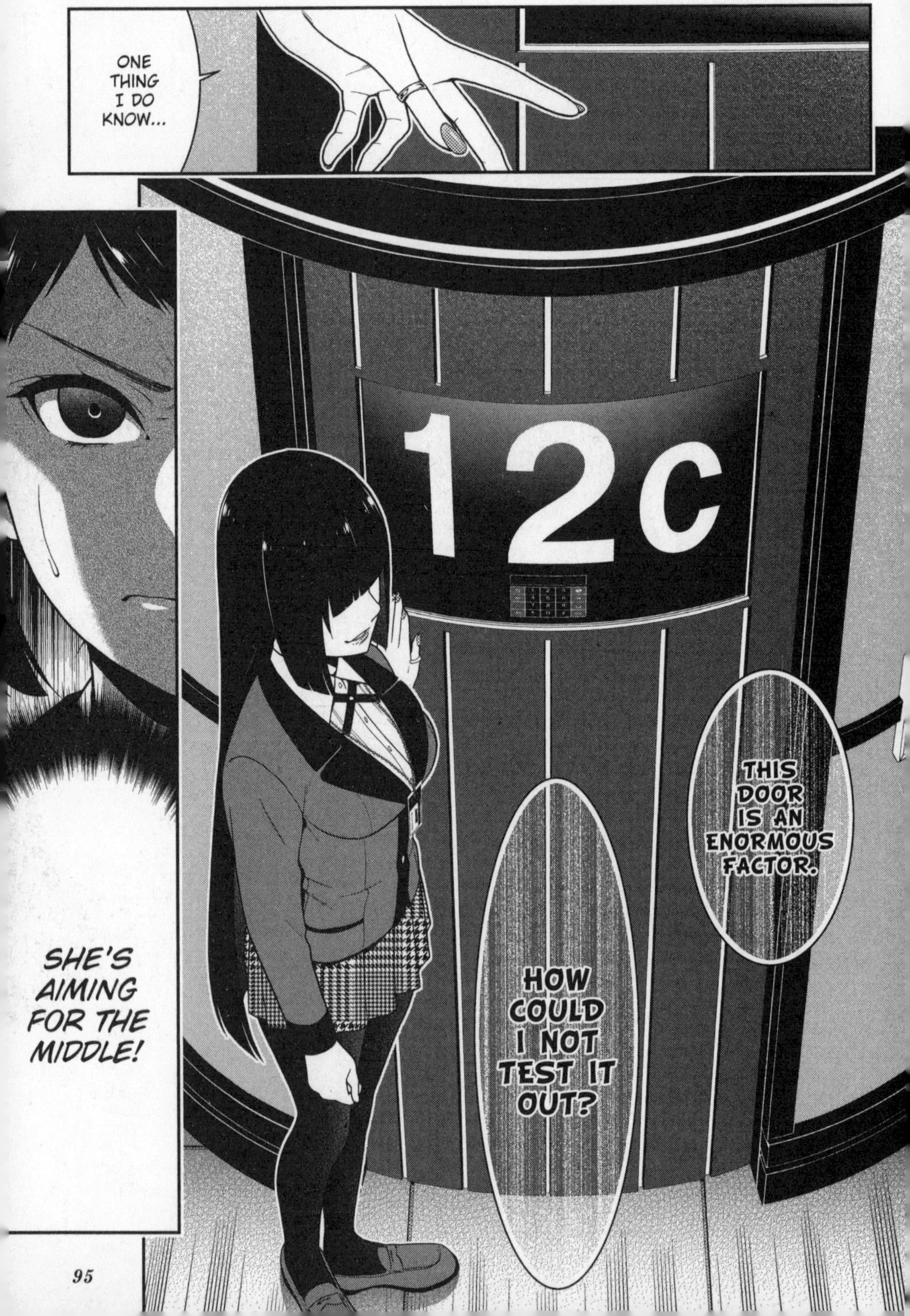
ONE THING I DO KNOW...
THIS DOOR IS AN ENORMOUS FACTOR.
HOW COULD I NOT TEST IT OUT?
SHE'S AIMING FOR THE MIDDLE!

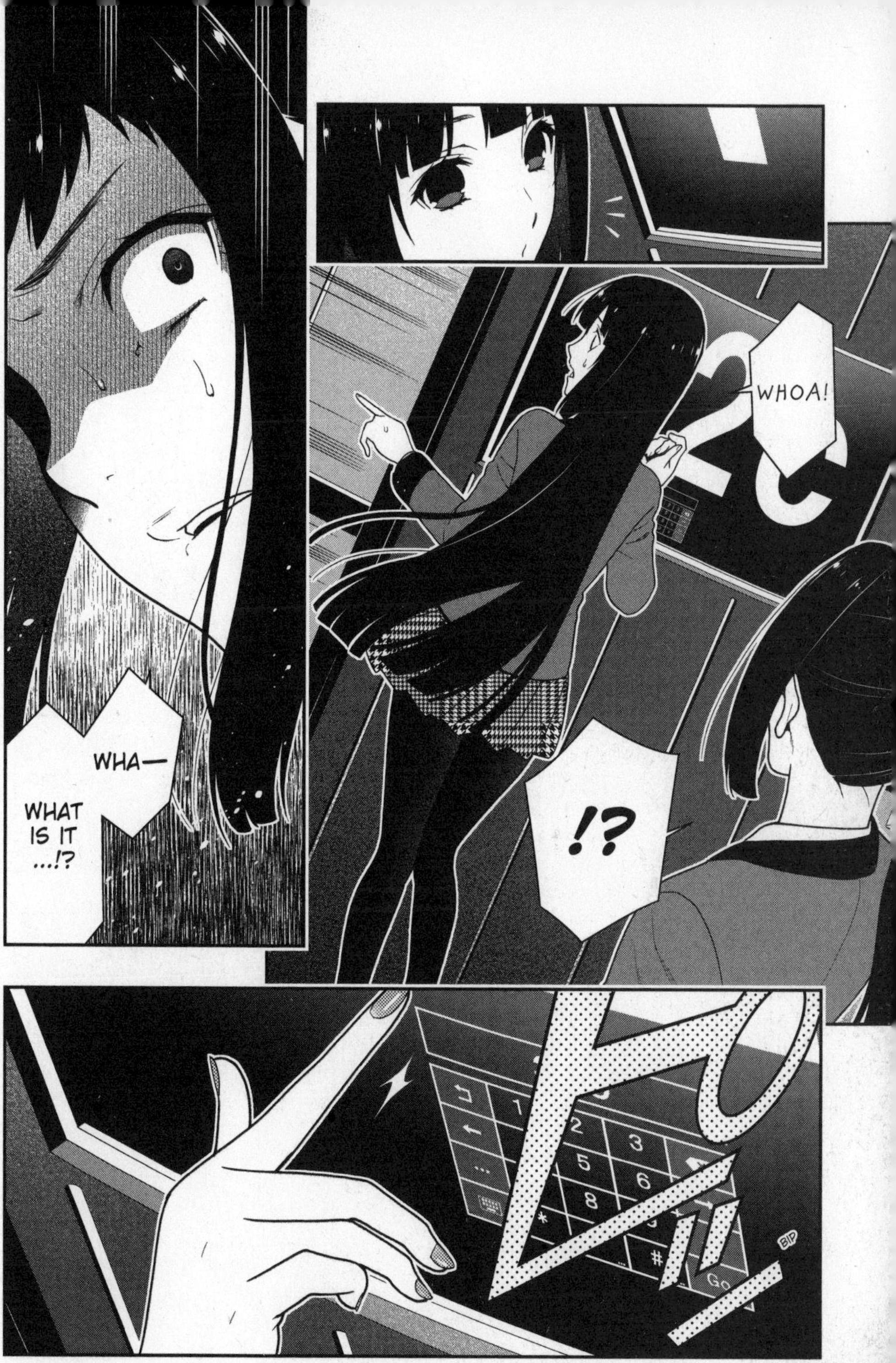
WHOA!
!?
WHA—
WHAT IS IT ...!?
BIP

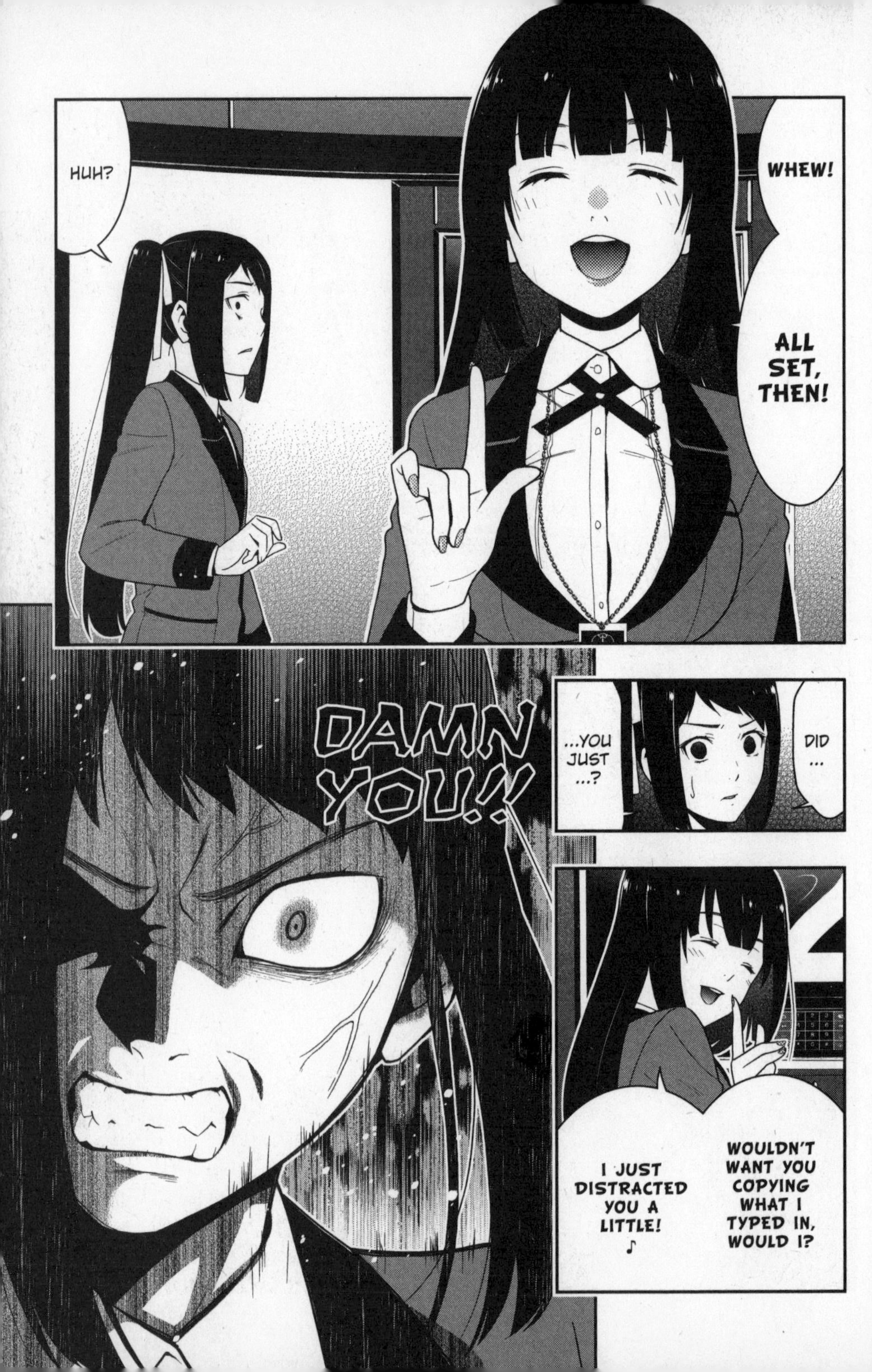
WHEW!
ALL SET, THEN!
HUH?
DID ...
...YOU JUST ...?
WOULDN'T WANT YOU COPYING WHAT I TYPED IN, WOULD I?
I JUST DISTRACTED YOU A LITTLE! ♪
DAMN YOU!!

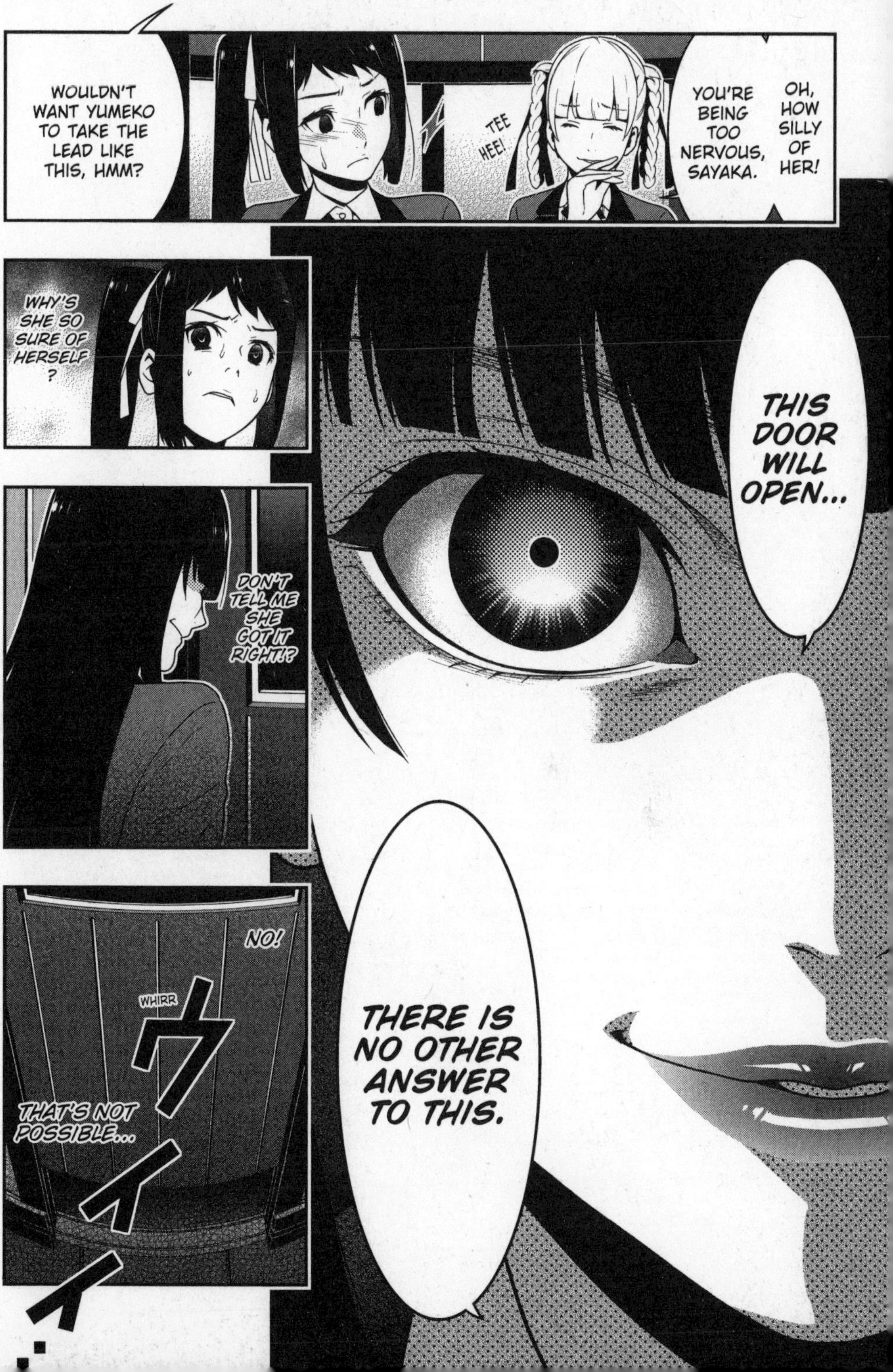

OH, HOW SILLY OF HER!
YOU'RE BEING TOO NERVOUS, SAYAKA.
TEE HEE!
WOULDN'T WANT YUMEKO TO TAKE THE LEAD LIKE THIS, HMM?
THIS DOOR WILL OPEN...
THERE IS NO OTHER ANSWER TO THIS.
WHY'S SHE SO SURE OF HERSELF?
DON'T TELL ME SHE GOT IT RIGHT!?
NO!
WHIRR
THAT'S NOT POSSIBLE...

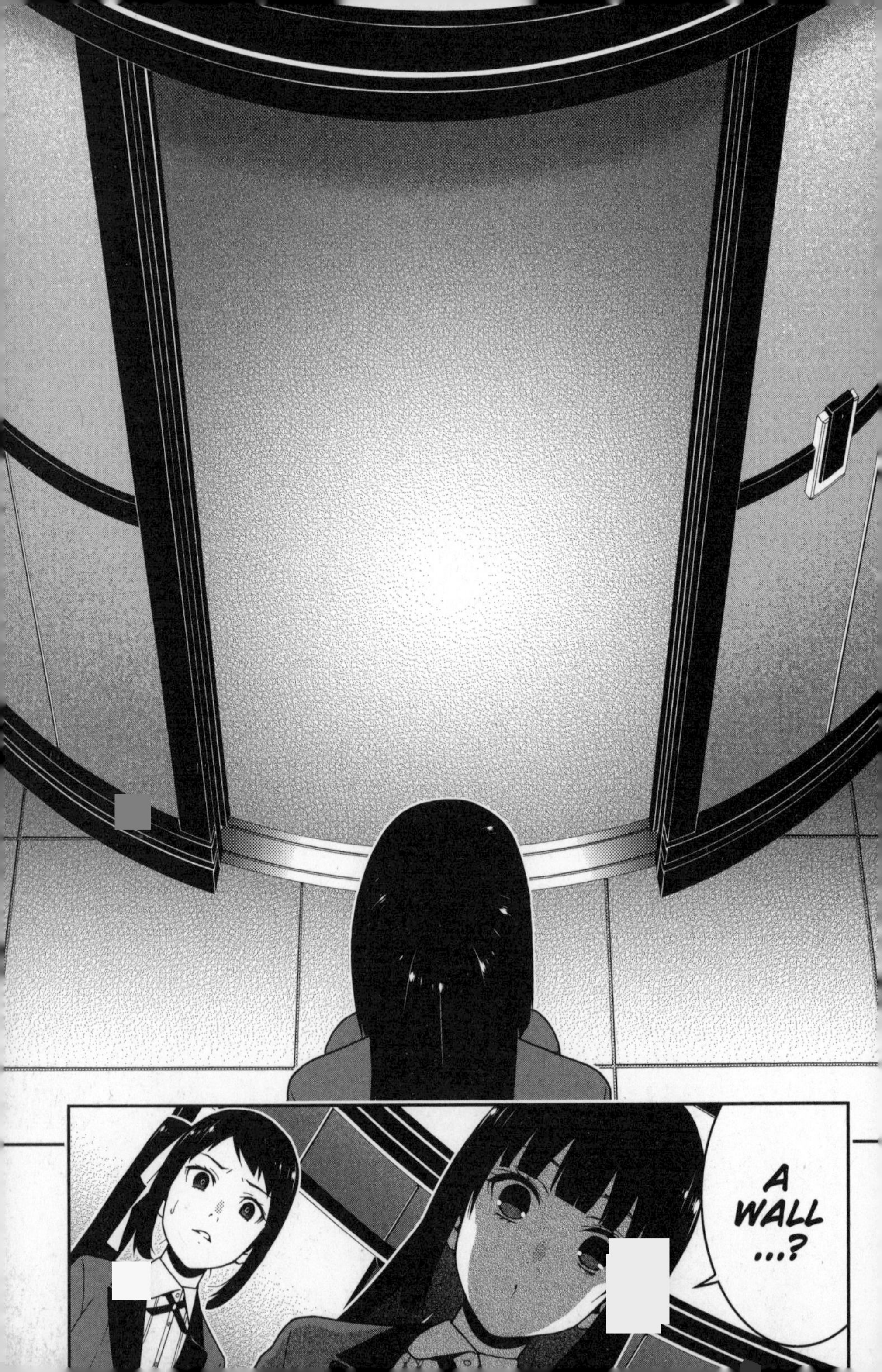
A WALL ...?

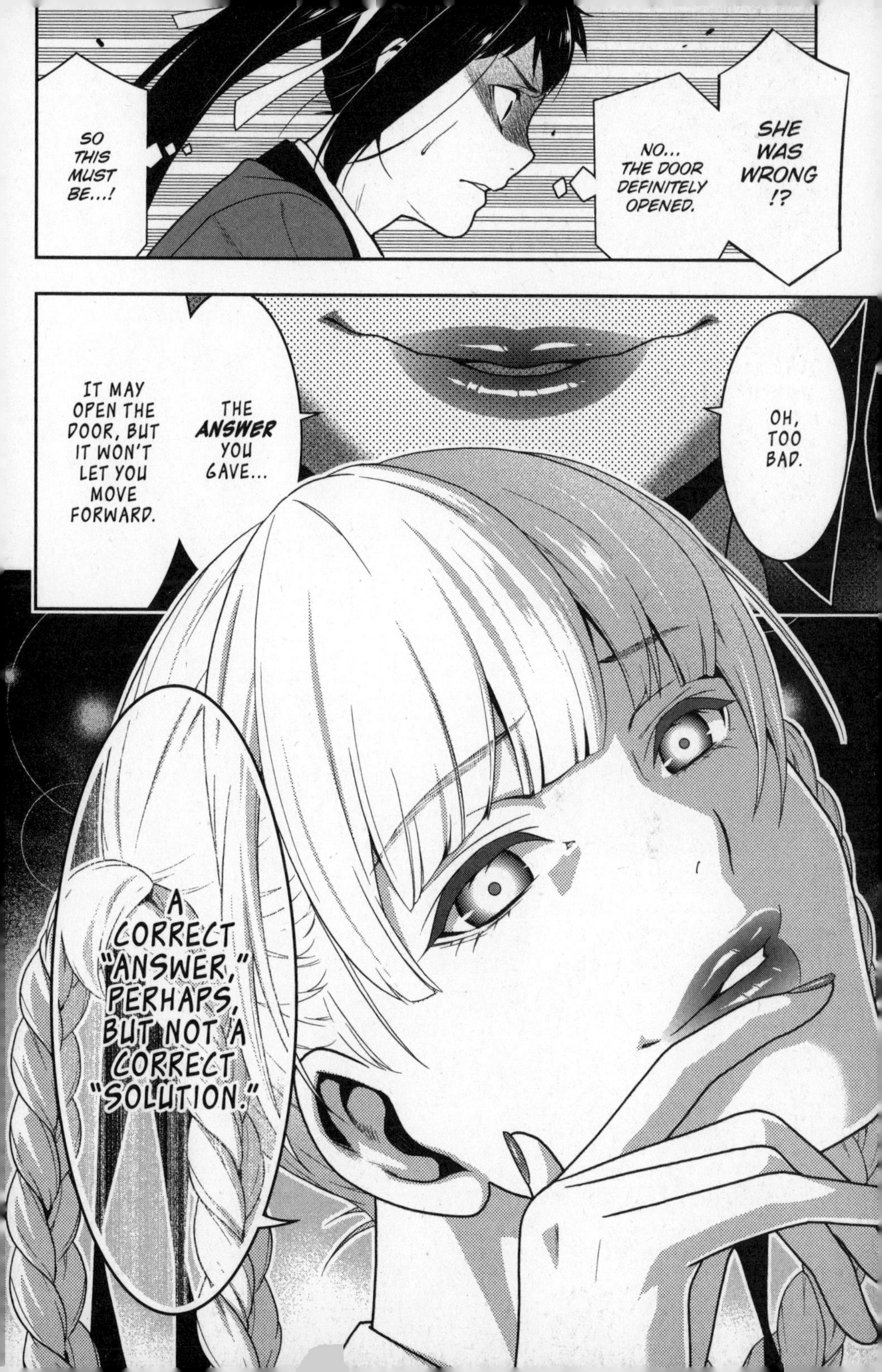
SHE WAS WRONG!?
NO... THE DOOR DEFINITELY OPENED.
SO THIS MUST BE...!
OH, TOO BAD.
THE ANSWER YOU GAVE...
IT MAY OPEN THE DOOR, BUT IT WON'T LET YOU MOVE FORWARD.
A CORRECT "ANSWER," PERHAPS, BUT NOT A CORRECT "SOLUTION."

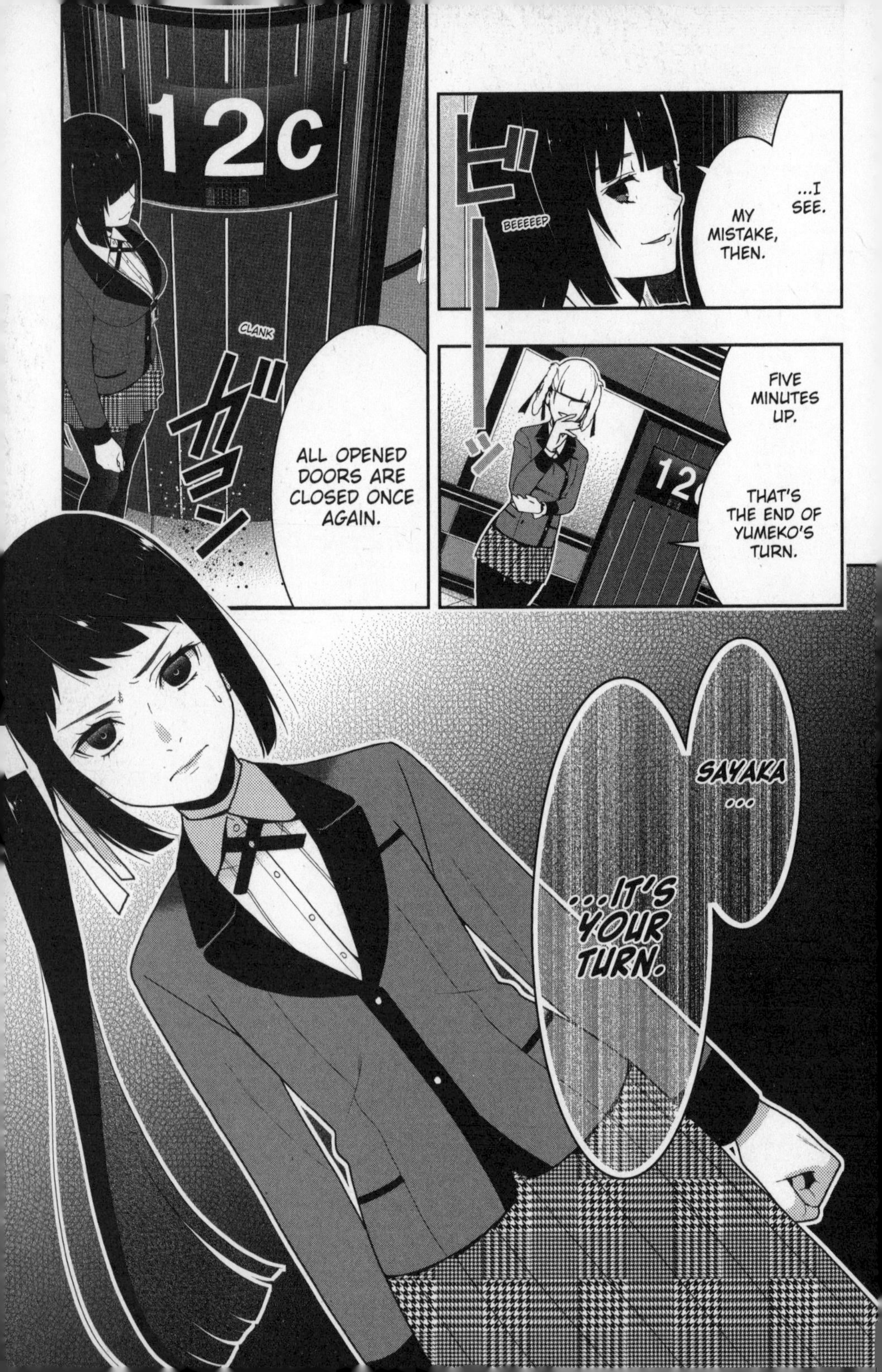
BEEEEEP
...I SEE.
MY MISTAKE, THEN.
FIVE MINUTES UP.
THAT'S THE END OF YUMEKO'S TURN.
CLANK
ALL OPENED DOORS ARE CLOSED ONCE AGAIN.
SAYAKA...
...IT'S YOUR TURN.

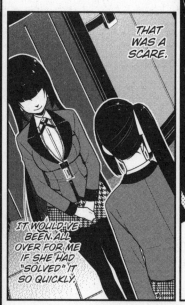

...
THAT WAS A SCARE.
IT WOULD'VE BEEN ALL OVER FOR ME IF SHE HAD "SOLVED" IT SO QUICKLY.
BUT THAT NEVER COULD'VE HAPPENED.
THERE'S NOWHERE NEAR ENOUGH INFORMATION TO SOLVE IT YET.
YUMEKO AND I ARE STILL AT THE SAME POINT.
AND I KNEW WHAT THE NUMBERS ON THE DOORS WERE FROM THE VERY START.

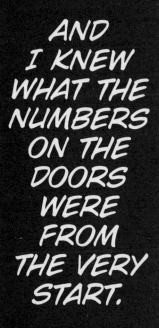

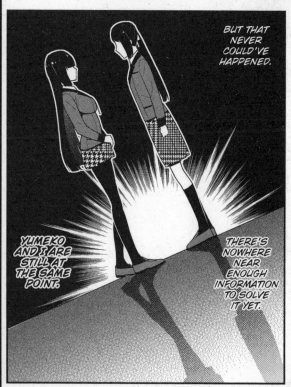

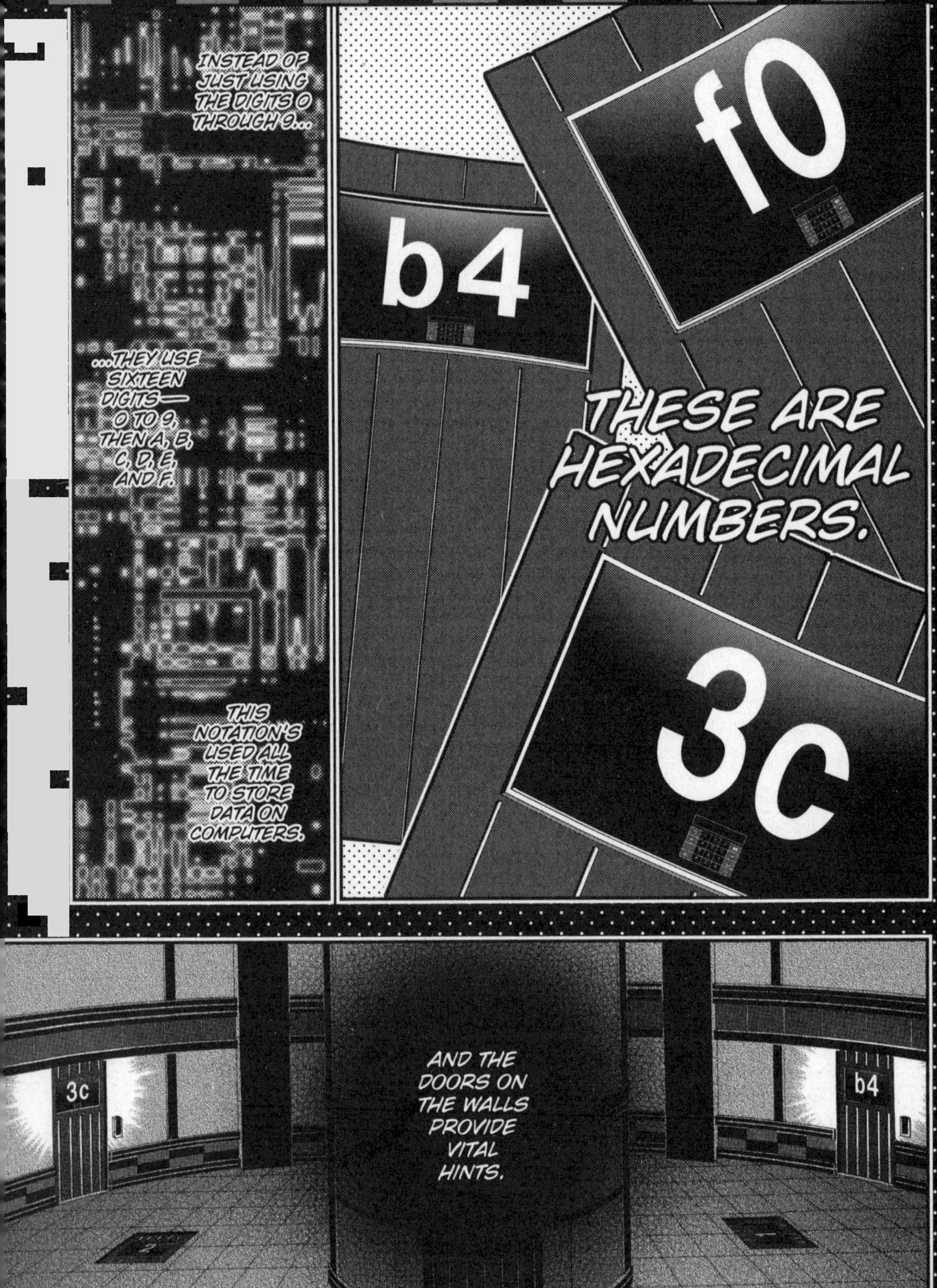
f0
b4
THESE ARE HEXADECIMAL NUMBERS.
3c
INSTEAD OF JUST USING THE DIGITS 0 THROUGH 9...
...THEY USE SIXTEEN DIGITS—0 TO 9, THEN A, B, C, D, E, AND F.
THIS NOTATION'S USED ALL THE TIME TO STORE DATA ON COMPUTERS.
b4
AND THE DOORS ON THE WALLS PROVIDE VITAL HINTS.
3c

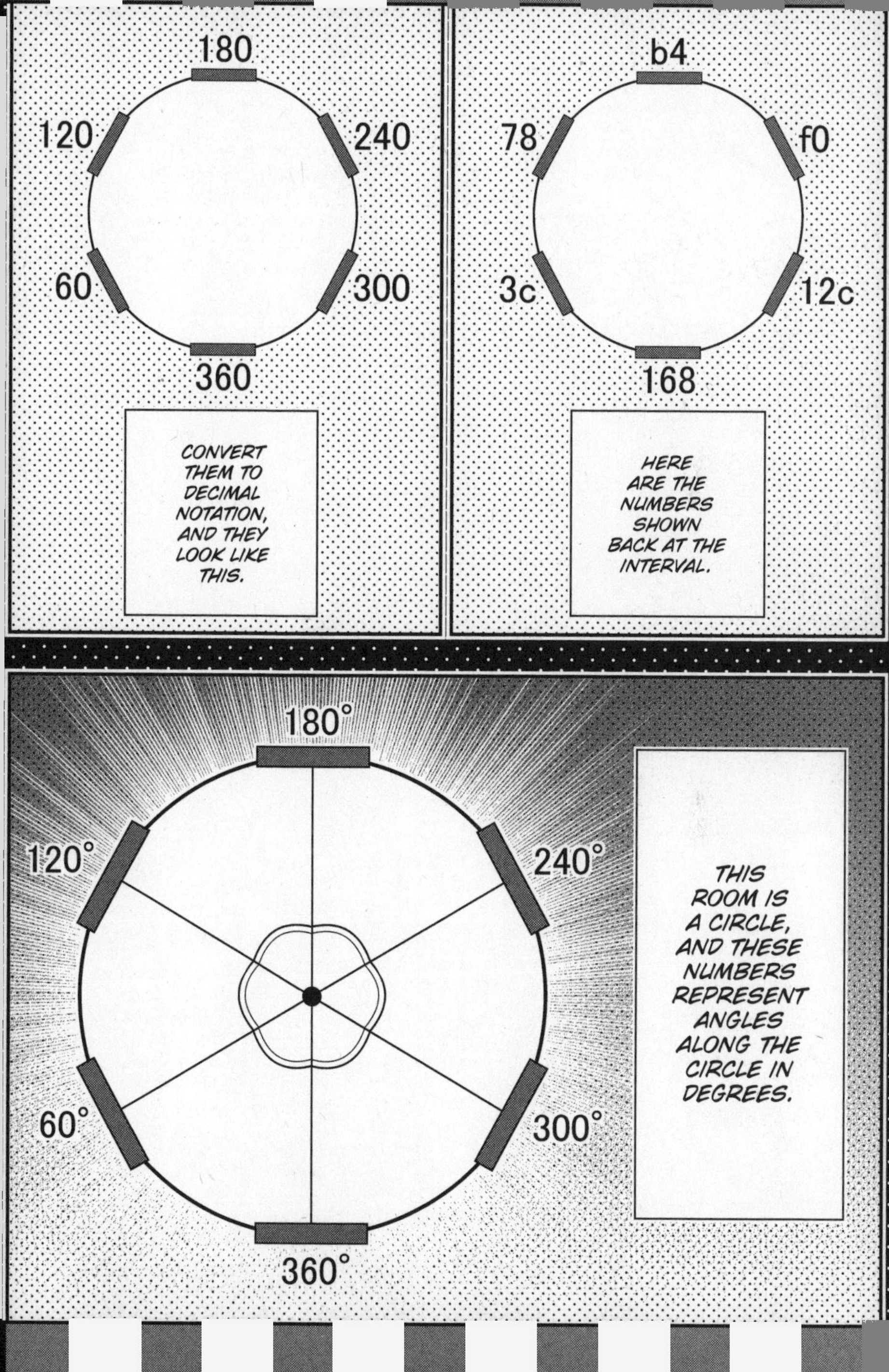
b4
78
f0
3c
12c
168
HERE ARE THE NUMBERS SHOWN BACK AT THE INTERVAL.
180
120
240
60
300
360
CONVERT THEM TO DECIMAL NOTATION, AND THEY LOOK LIKE THIS.
180°
120°
240°
60°
300°
360°
THIS ROOM IS A CIRCLE, AND THESE NUMBERS REPRESENT ANGLES ALONG THE CIRCLE IN DEGREES.

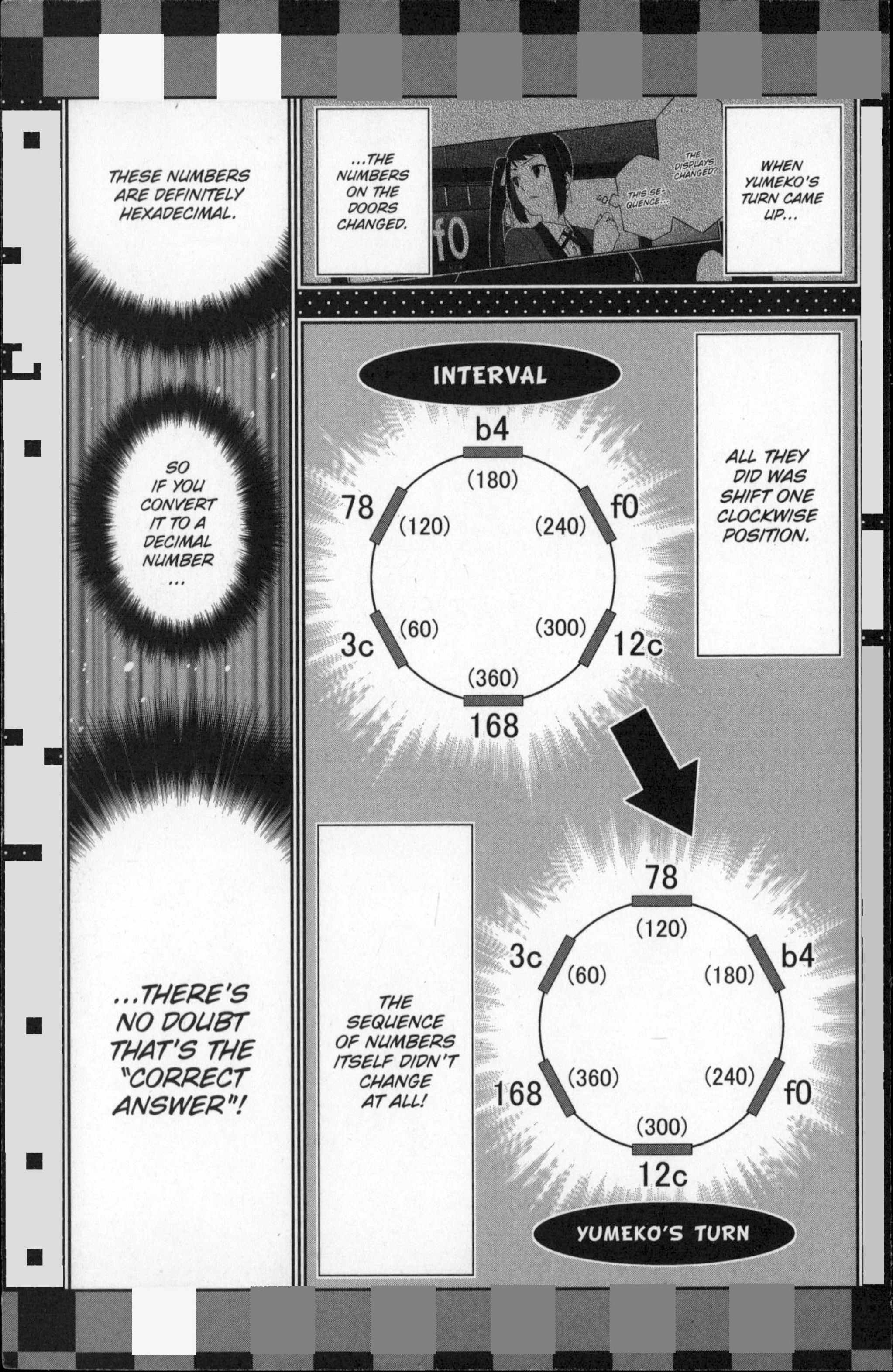
WHEN YUMEKO'S TURN CAME UP...
THE DISPLAYS CHANGED?
THIS SE-QUENCE...
f0
...THE NUMBERS ON THE DOORS CHANGED.
ALL THEY DID WAS SHIFT ONE CLOCKWISE POSITION.
INTERVAL
b4 (180)
f0 (240)
12c (300)
168 (360)
3c (60)
78 (120)
78 (120)
b4 (180)
f0 (240)
12c (300)
168 (360)
3c (60)
YUMEKO'S TURN
THE SEQUENCE OF NUMBERS ITSELF DIDN'T CHANGE AT ALL!
THESE NUMBERS ARE DEFINITELY HEXADECIMAL.
SO IF YOU CONVERT IT TO A DECIMAL NUMBER...
...THERE'S NO DOUBT THAT'S THE "CORRECT ANSWER"!

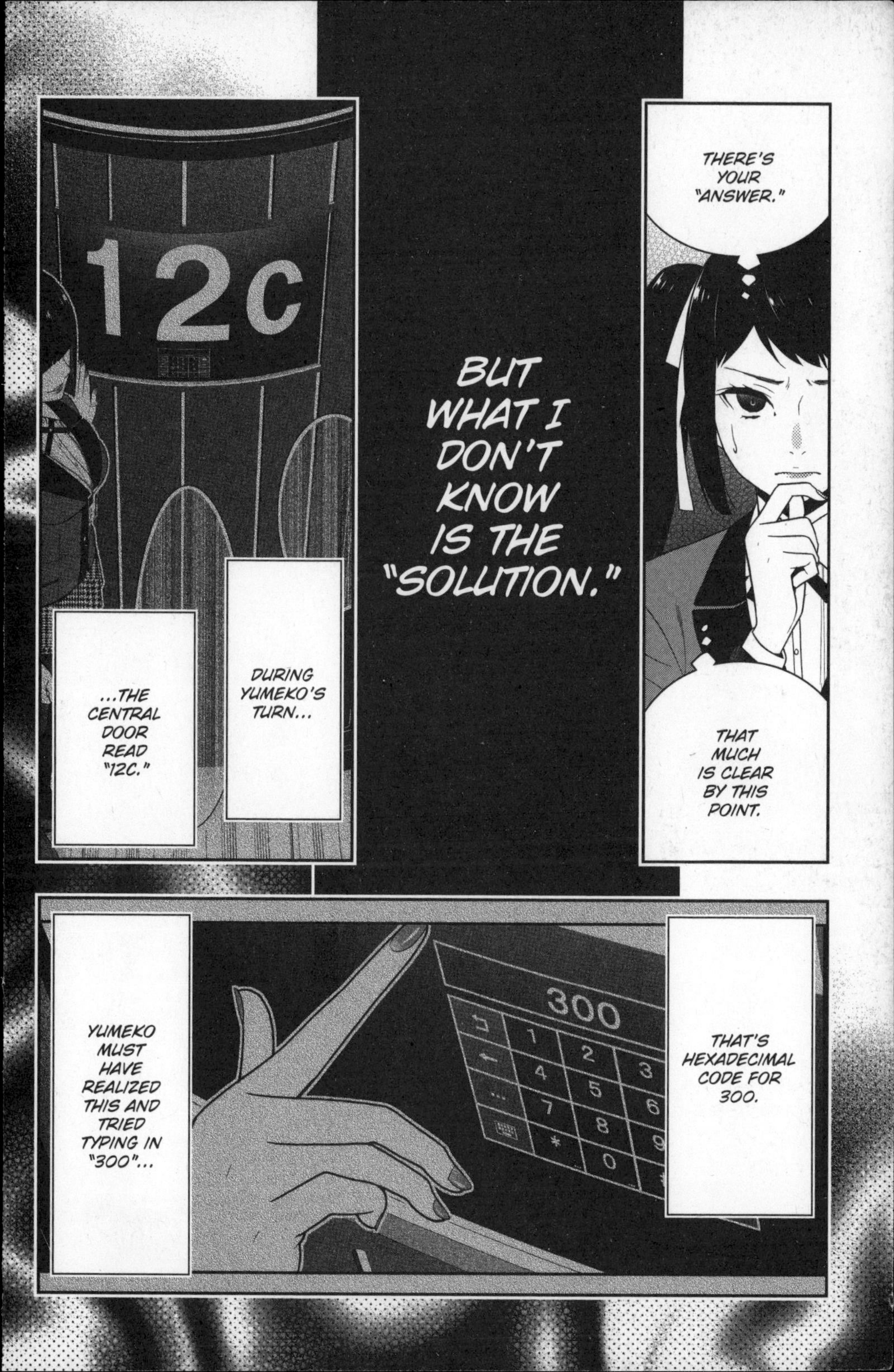
THERE'S YOUR "ANSWER."
THAT MUCH IS CLEAR BY THIS POINT.
BUT WHAT I DON'T KNOW IS THE "SOLUTION."
12c
DURING YUMEKO'S TURN...
...THE CENTRAL DOOR READ "12C."
THAT'S HEXADECIMAL CODE FOR 300.
300
YUMEKO MUST HAVE REALIZED THIS AND TRIED TYPING IN "300"...

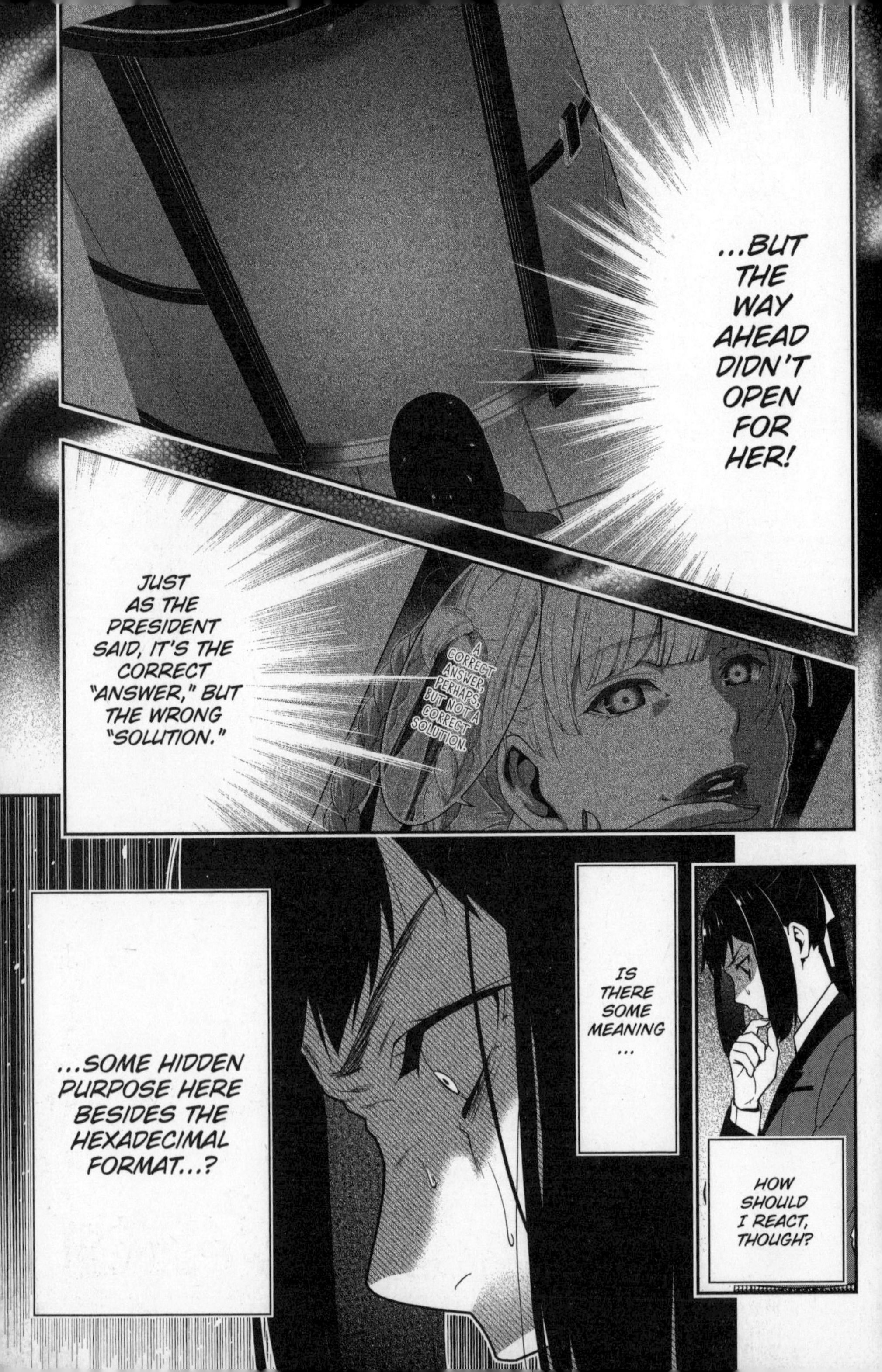
...BUT THE WAY AHEAD DIDN'T OPEN FOR HER!
A CORRECT ANSWER, PERHAPS, BUT NOT A CORRECT SOLUTION.
JUST AS THE PRESIDENT SAID, IT'S THE CORRECT "ANSWER," BUT THE WRONG "SOLUTION."
HOW SHOULD I REACT, THOUGH?
IS THERE SOME MEANING...
...SOME HIDDEN PURPOSE HERE BESIDES THE HEXADECIMAL FORMAT...?

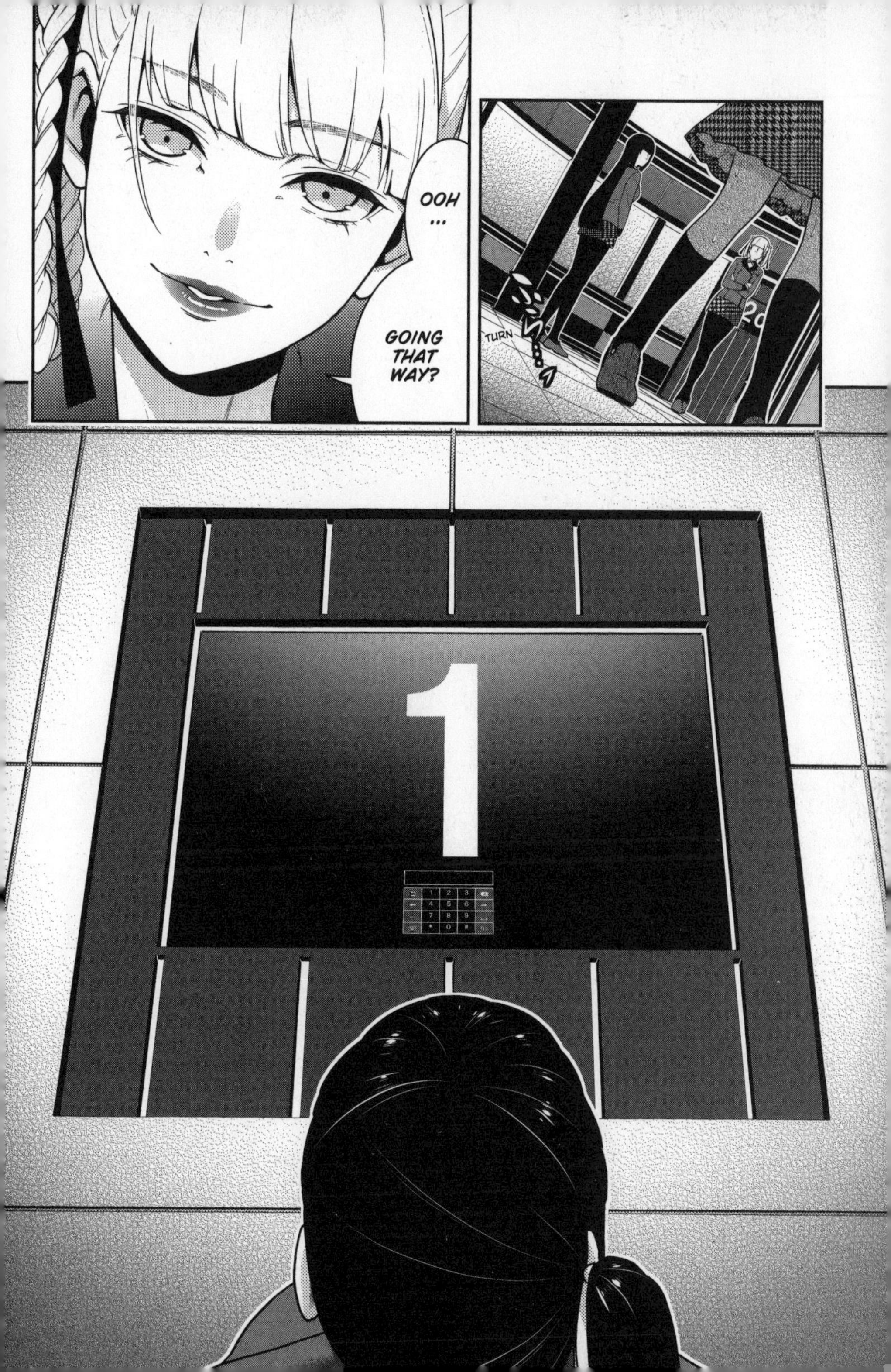
TURN
OOH ...
GOING THAT WAY?
1

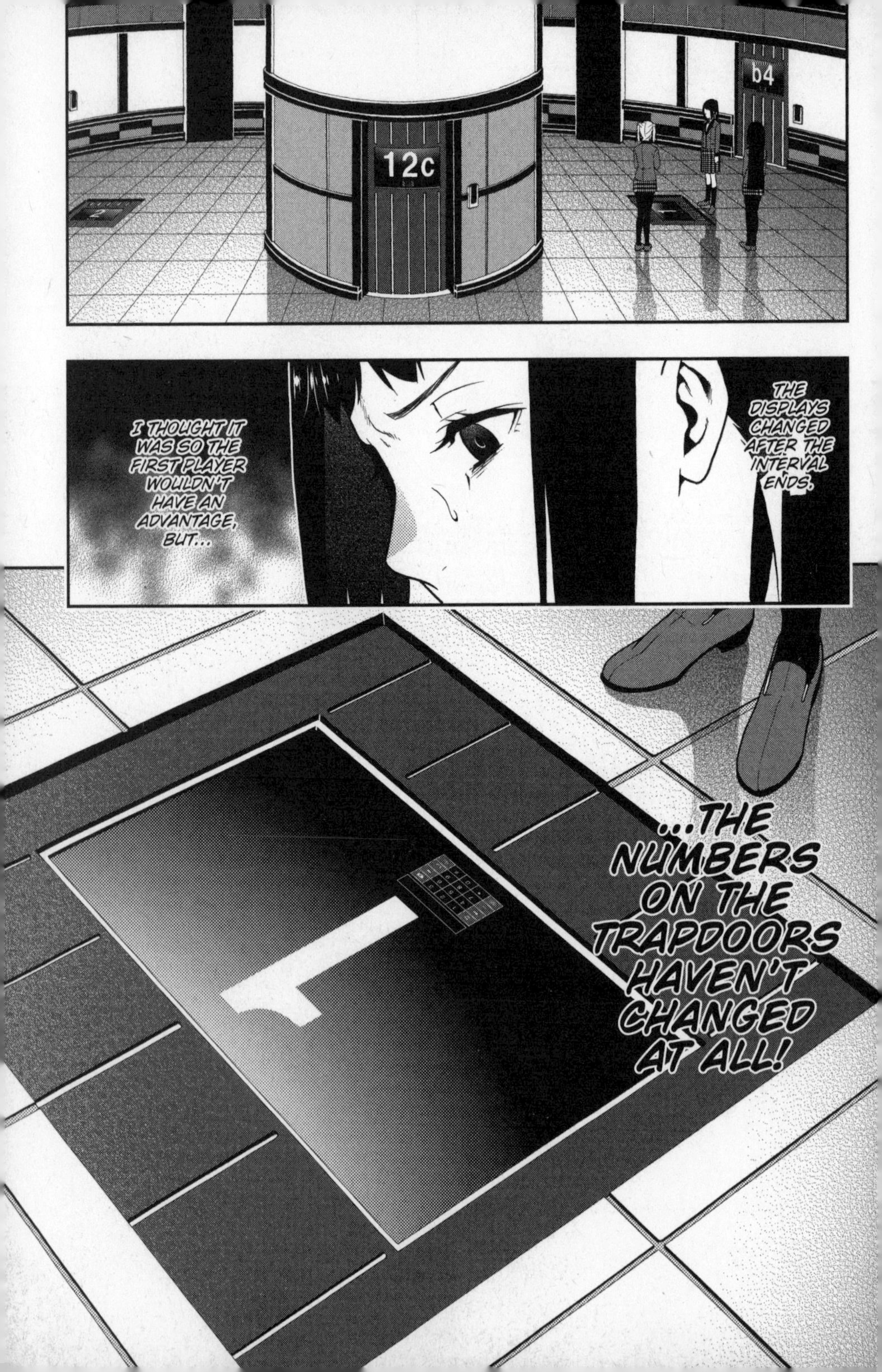
b4
12c
THE DISPLAYS CHANGED AFTER THE INTERVAL ENDS.
I THOUGHT IT WAS SO THE FIRST PLAYER WOULDN'T HAVE AN ADVANTAGE, BUT...
...THE NUMBERS ON THE TRAPDOORS HAVEN'T CHANGED AT ALL!

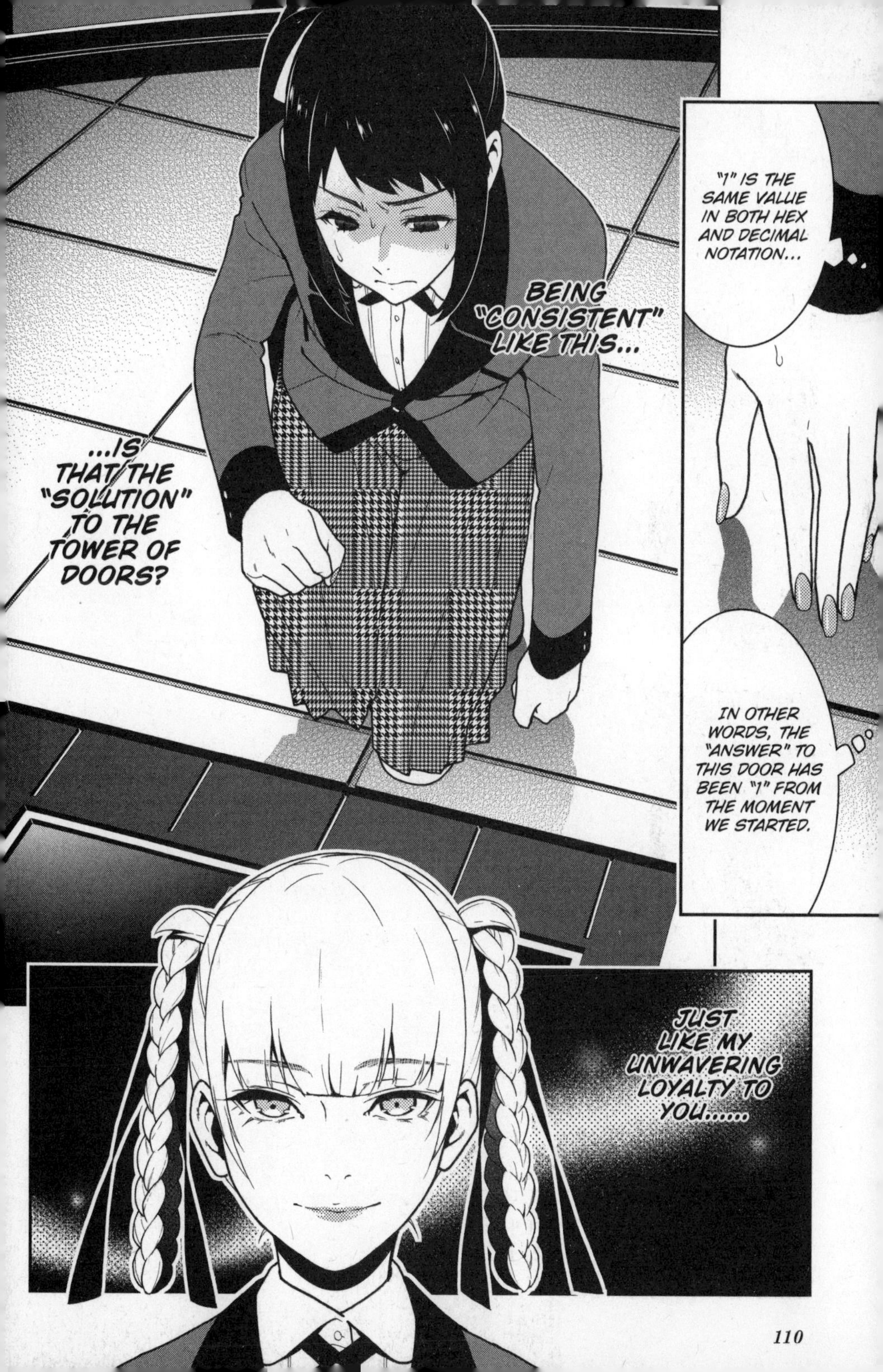
"1" IS THE SAME VALUE IN BOTH HEX AND DECIMAL NOTATION...
IN OTHER WORDS, THE "ANSWER" TO THIS DOOR HAS BEEN "1" FROM THE MOMENT WE STARTED.
BEING "CONSISTENT" LIKE THIS...
...IS THAT THE "SOLUTION" TO THE TOWER OF DOORS?
JUST LIKE MY UNWAVERING LOYALTY TO YOU......

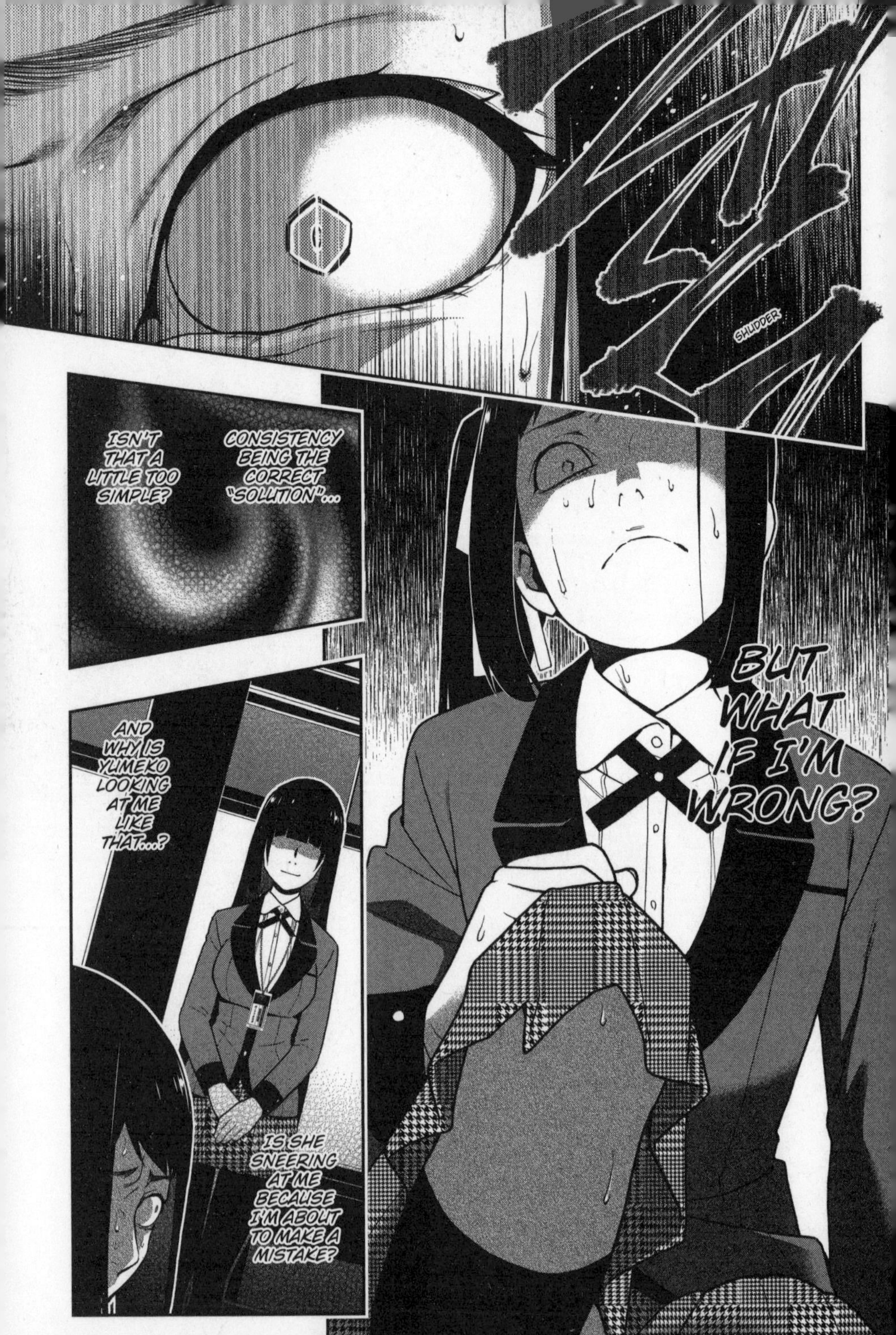
SHUDDER
BUT WHAT IF I'M WRONG?
CONSISTENCY BEING THE CORRECT "SOLUTION"...
ISN'T THAT A LITTLE TOO SIMPLE?
AND WHY IS YUMEKO LOOKING AT ME LIKE THAT...?
IS SHE SNEERING AT ME BECAUSE I'M ABOUT TO MAKE A MISTAKE?

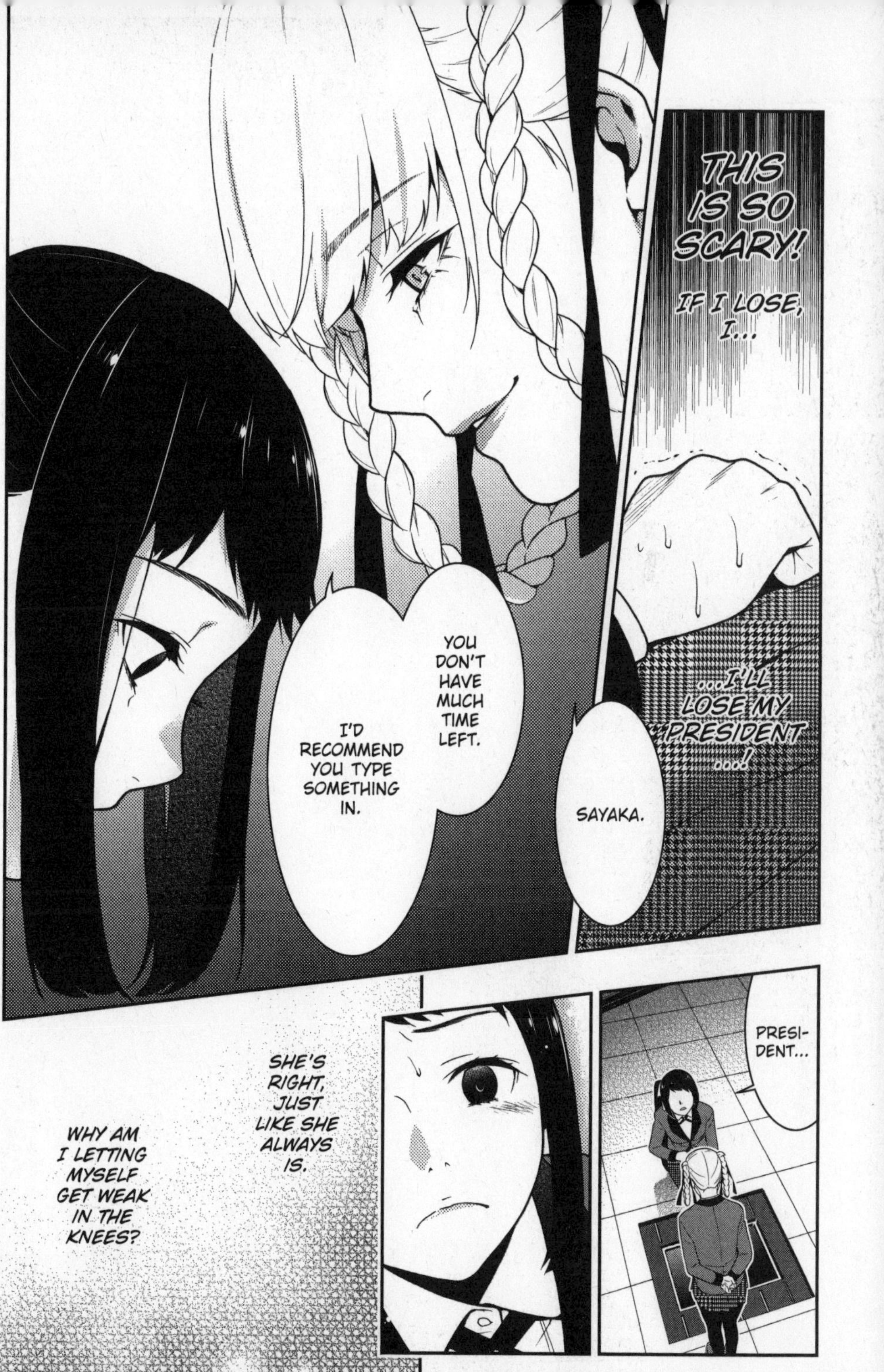
THIS IS SO SCARY!
IF I LOSE, I...
...I'LL LOSE MY PRESIDENT...!
SAYAKA.
YOU DON'T HAVE MUCH TIME LEFT.
I'D RECOMMEND YOU TYPE SOMETHING IN.
PRESI-DENT...
SHE'S RIGHT, JUST LIKE SHE ALWAYS IS.
WHY AM I LETTING MYSELF GET WEAK IN THE KNEES?

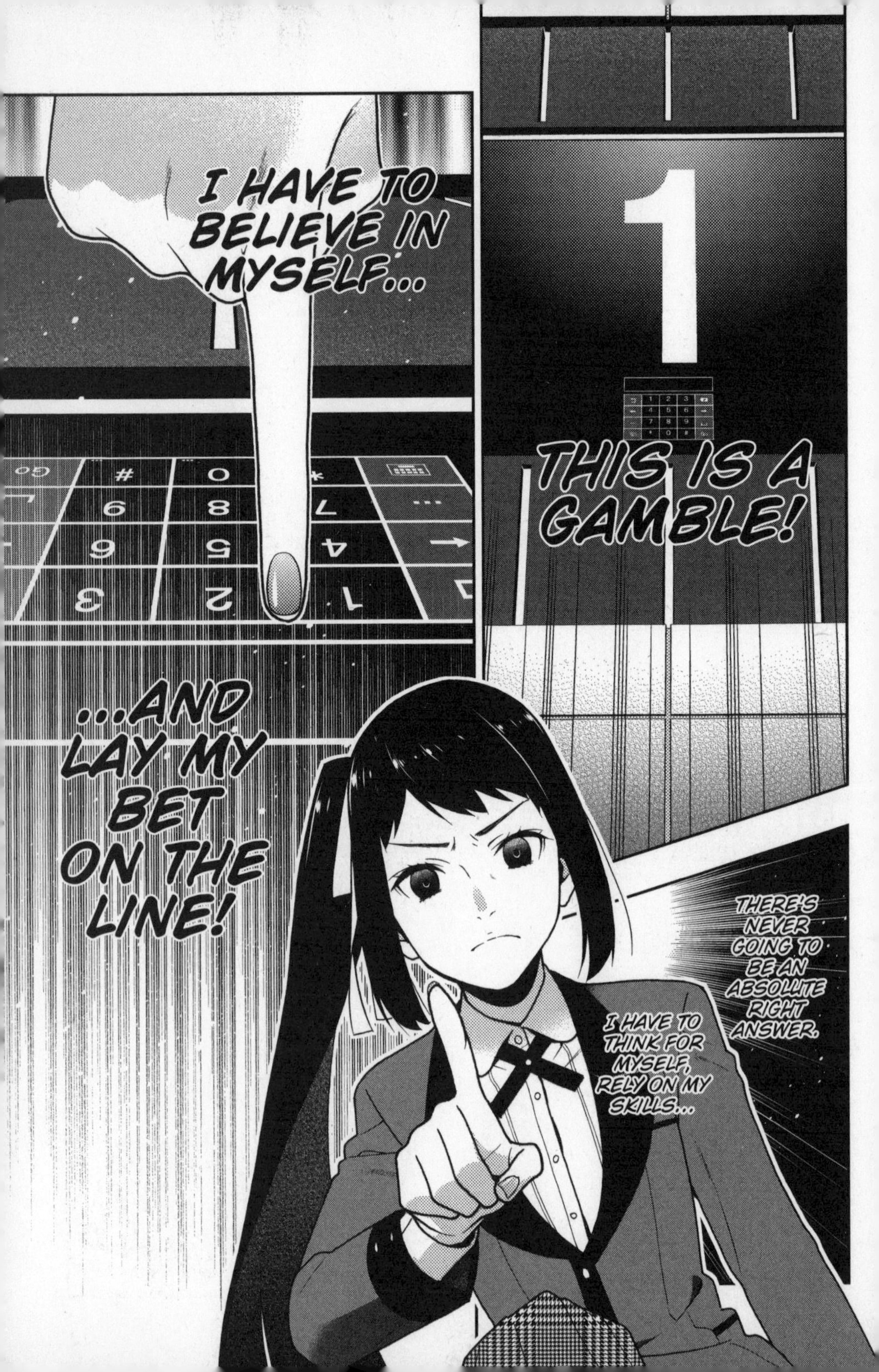
1
THIS IS A GAMBLE!
I HAVE TO BELIEVE IN MYSELF...
THERE'S NEVER GOING TO BE AN ABSOLUTE RIGHT ANSWER.
I HAVE TO THINK FOR MYSELF, RELY ON MY SKILLS...
...AND LAY MY BET ON THE LINE!

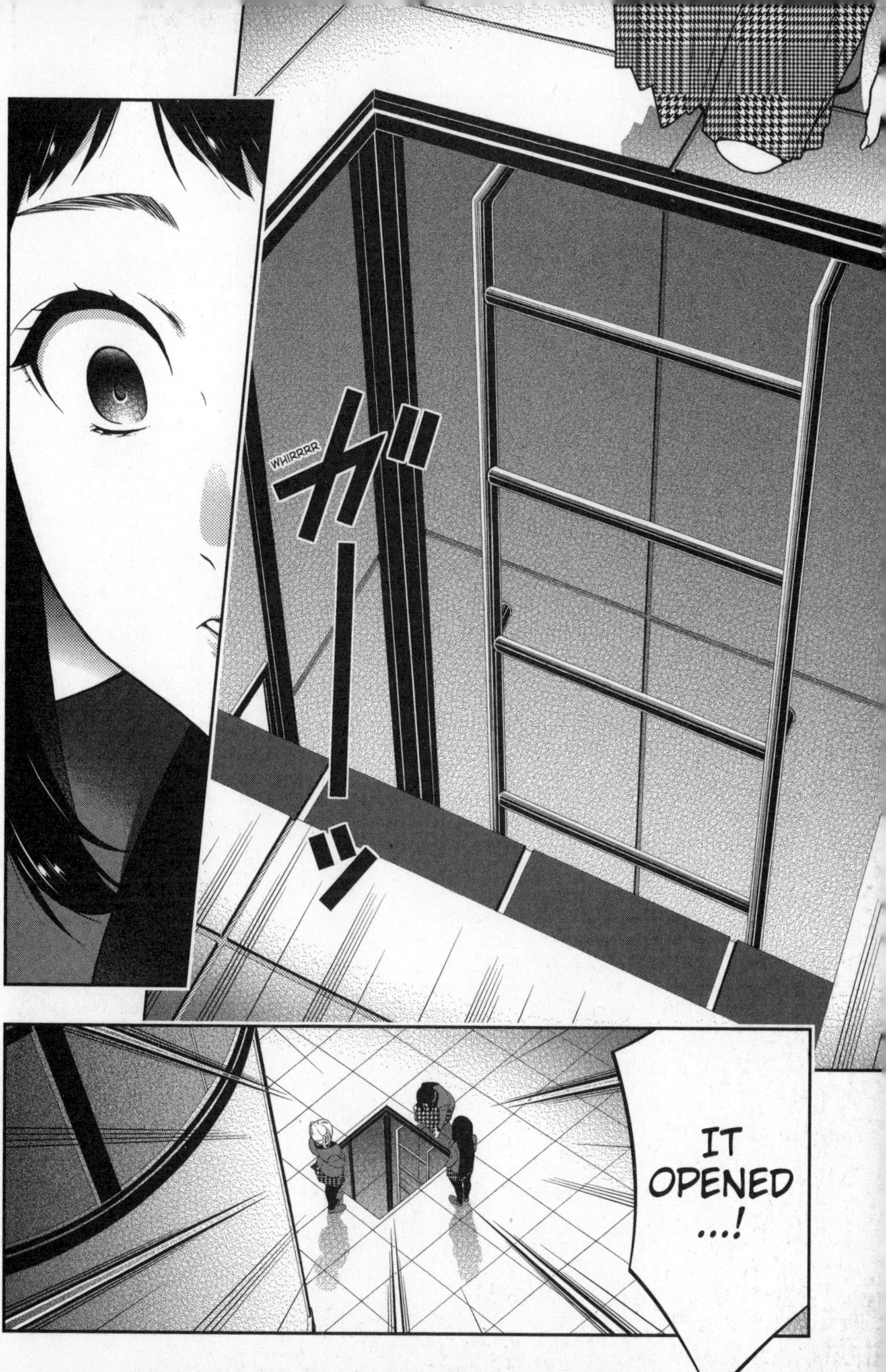
WHIRRRR
ガゴーッ
IT OPENED ...!

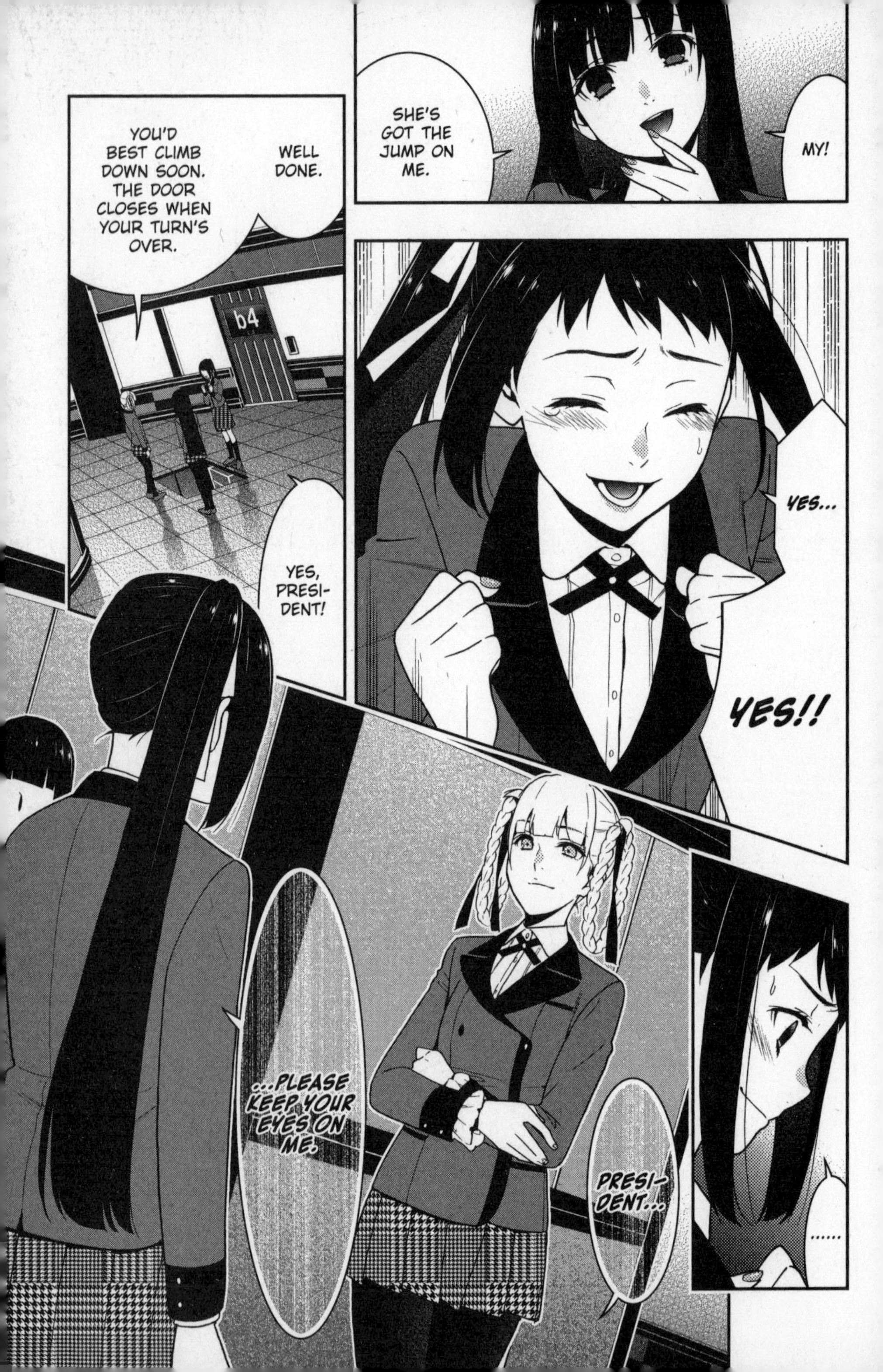
MY!
SHE'S GOT THE JUMP ON ME.
WELL DONE.
YOU'D BEST CLIMB DOWN SOON. THE DOOR CLOSES WHEN YOUR TURN'S OVER.
b4
YES...
YES!!
YES, PRESIDENT!
......
PRESI-DENT...
...PLEASE KEEP YOUR EYES ON ME.

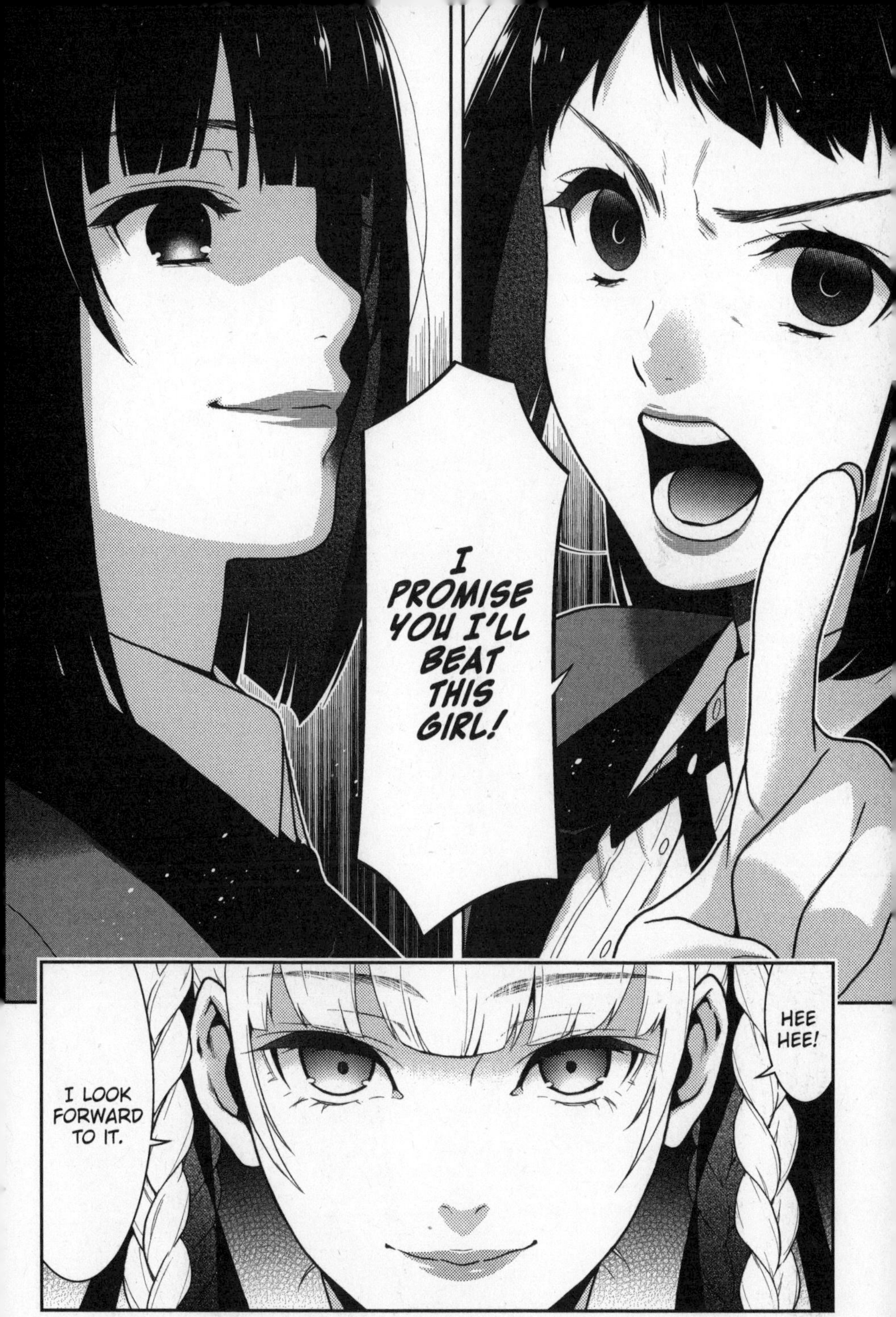
I PROMISE YOU I'LL BEAT THIS GIRL!
HEE HEE!
I LOOK FORWARD TO IT.

CHAPTER THIRTY-TWO THE CLINGING GIRL

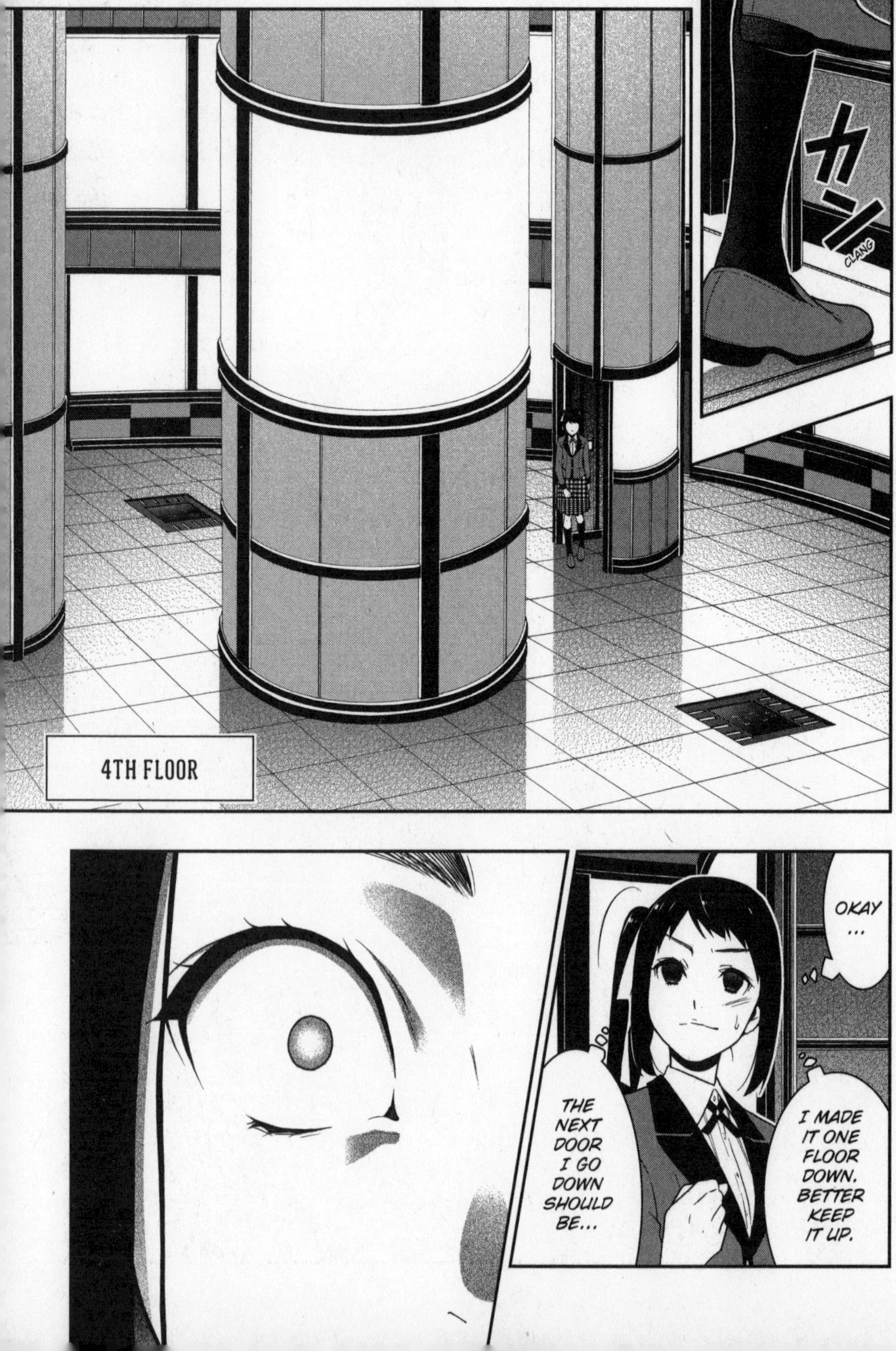
CLANG
4TH FLOOR
OKAY...
I MADE IT ONE FLOOR DOWN. BETTER KEEP IT UP.
THE NEXT DOOR I GO DOWN SHOULD BE...

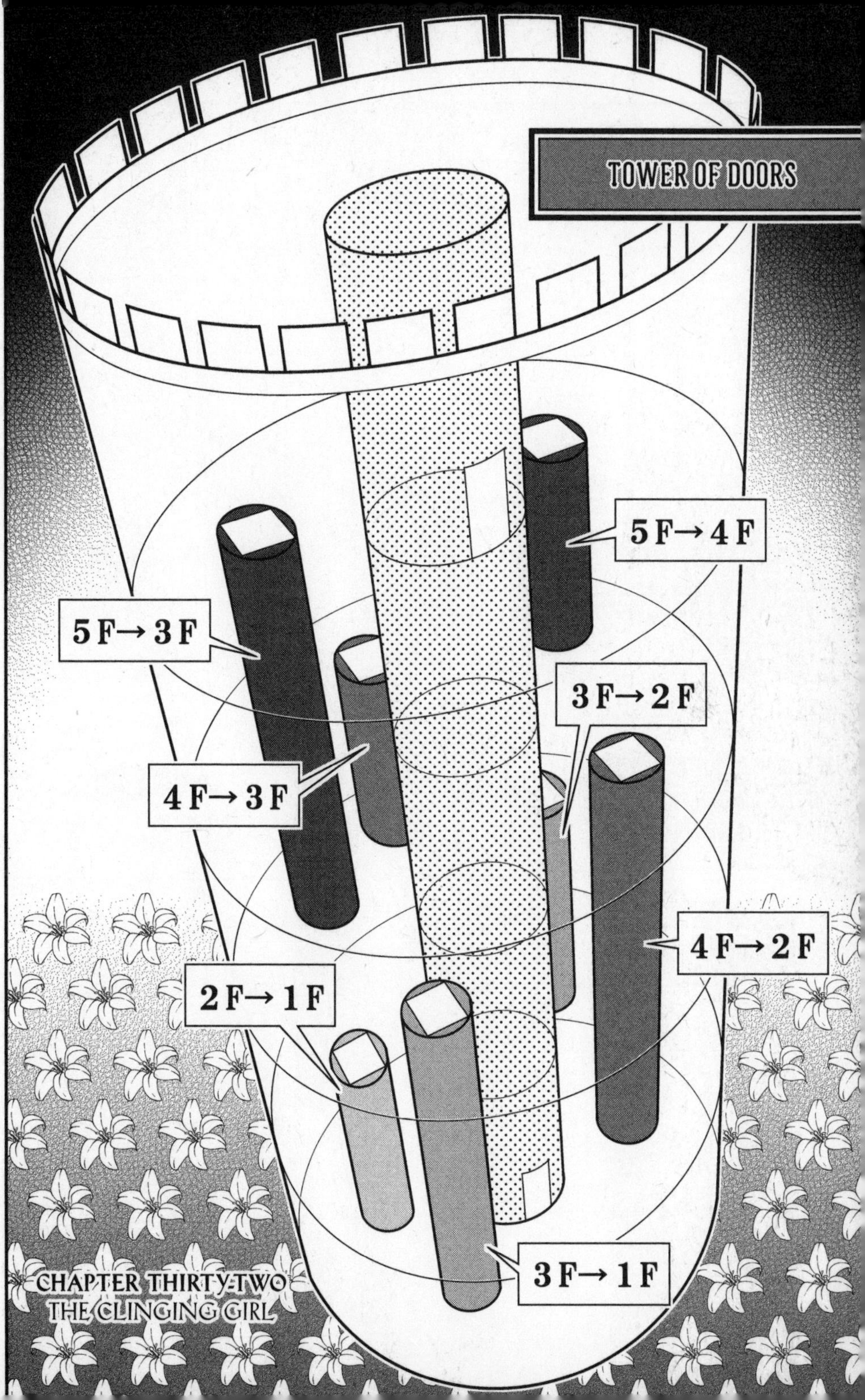
TOWER OF DOORS
5F→4F
5F→3F
3F→2F
4F→3F
4F→2F
2F→1F
3F→1F
CHAPTER THIRTY-TWO
THE CLINGING GIRL

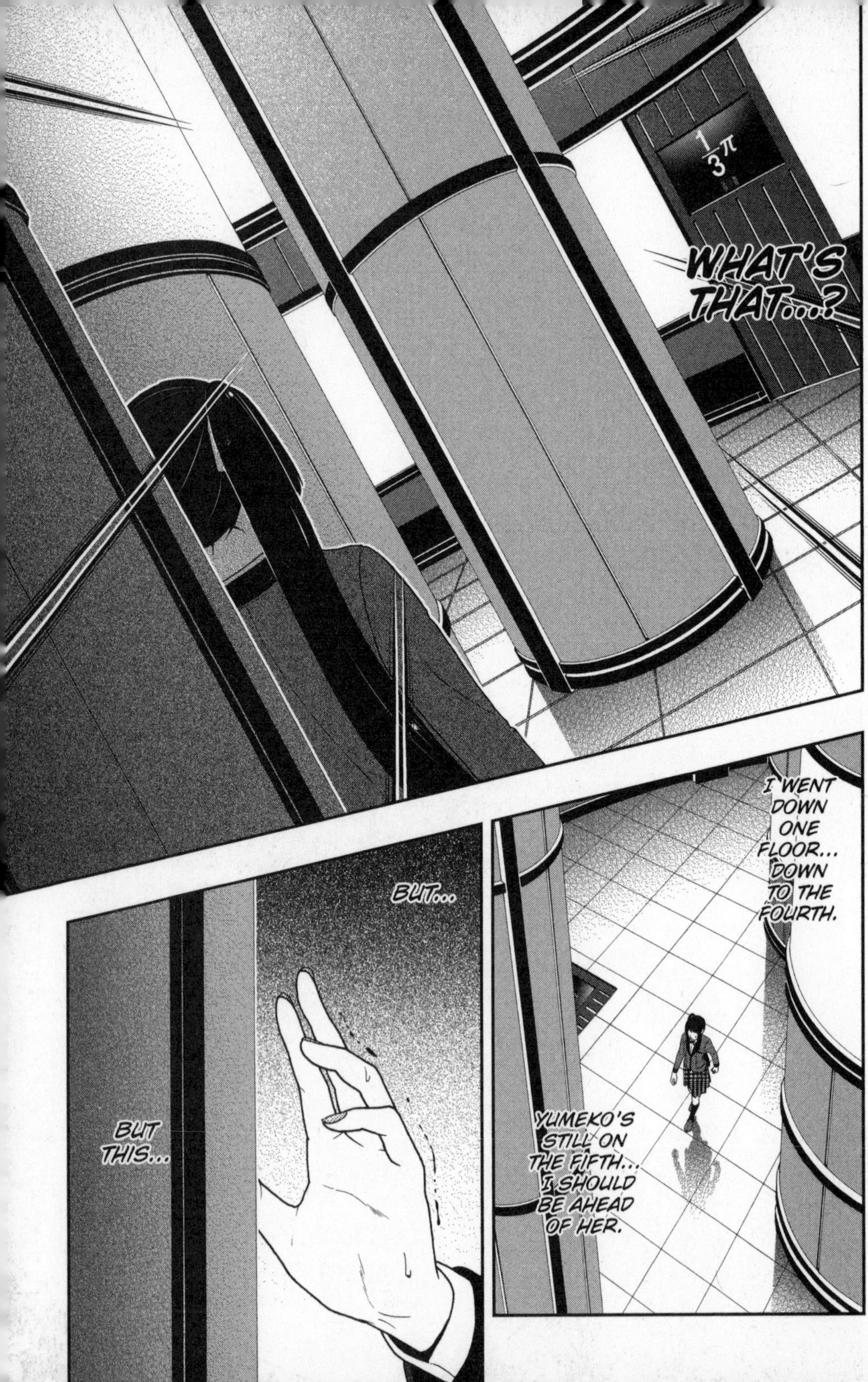
1/3π
WHAT'S THAT...?
I WENT DOWN ONE FLOOR... DOWN TO THE FOURTH.
YUMEKO'S STILL ON THE FIFTH... I SHOULD BE AHEAD OF HER.
BUT...
BUT THIS...

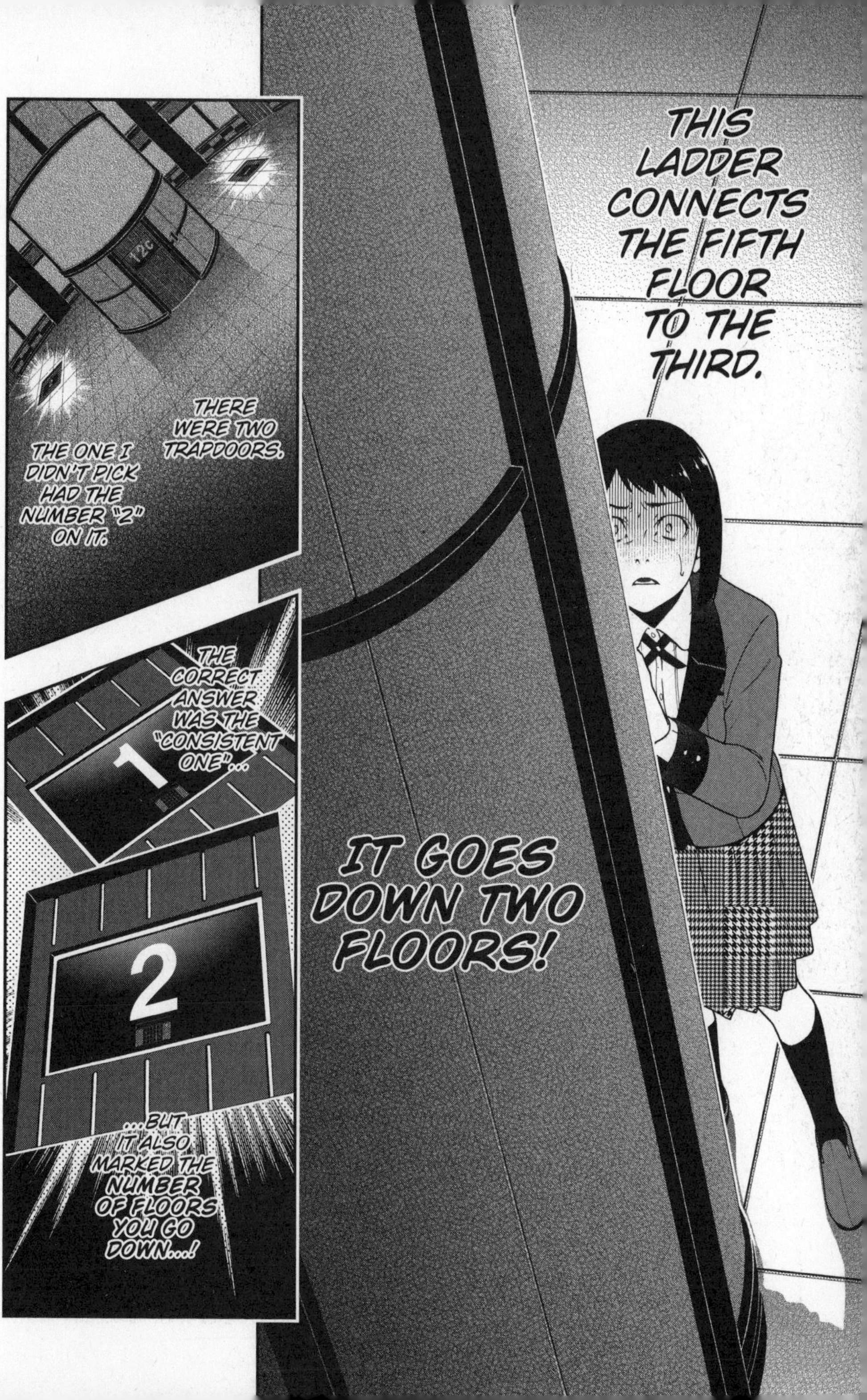
THIS LADDER CONNECTS THE FIFTH FLOOR TO THE THIRD.
IT GOES DOWN TWO FLOORS!
THERE WERE TWO TRAPDOORS.
THE ONE I DIDN'T PICK HAD THE NUMBER "2" ON IT.
THE CORRECT ANSWER WAS THE "CONSISTENT ONE"...
...BUT IT ALSO MARKED THE NUMBER OF FLOORS YOU GO DOWN...!

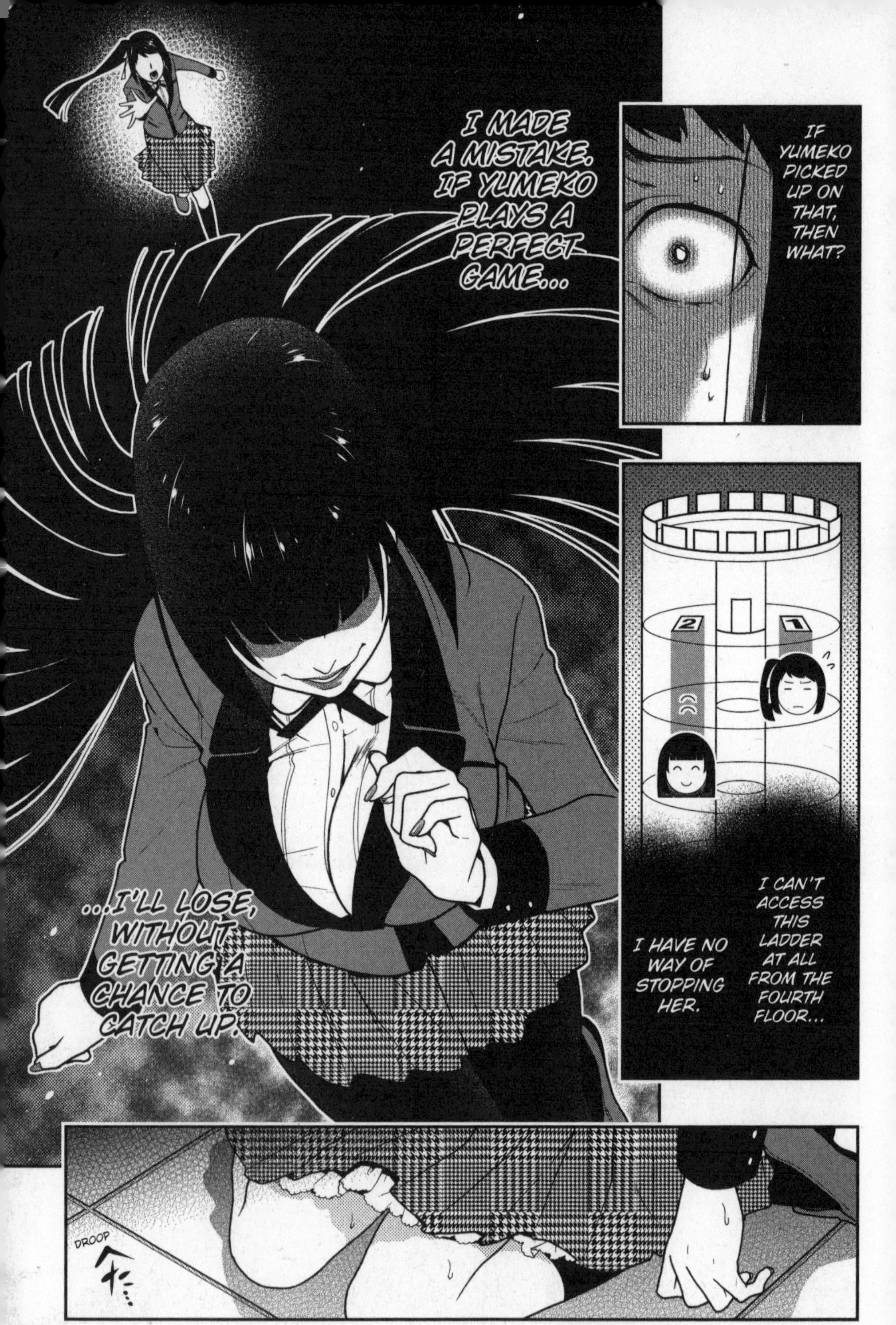
IF YUMEKO PICKED UP ON THAT, THEN WHAT?
I CAN'T ACCESS THIS LADDER AT ALL FROM THE FOURTH FLOOR...
I HAVE NO WAY OF STOPPING HER.
I MADE A MISTAKE. IF YUMEKO PLAYS A PERFECT GAME...
...I'LL LOSE, WITHOUT GETTING A CHANCE TO CATCH UP.
DROOP

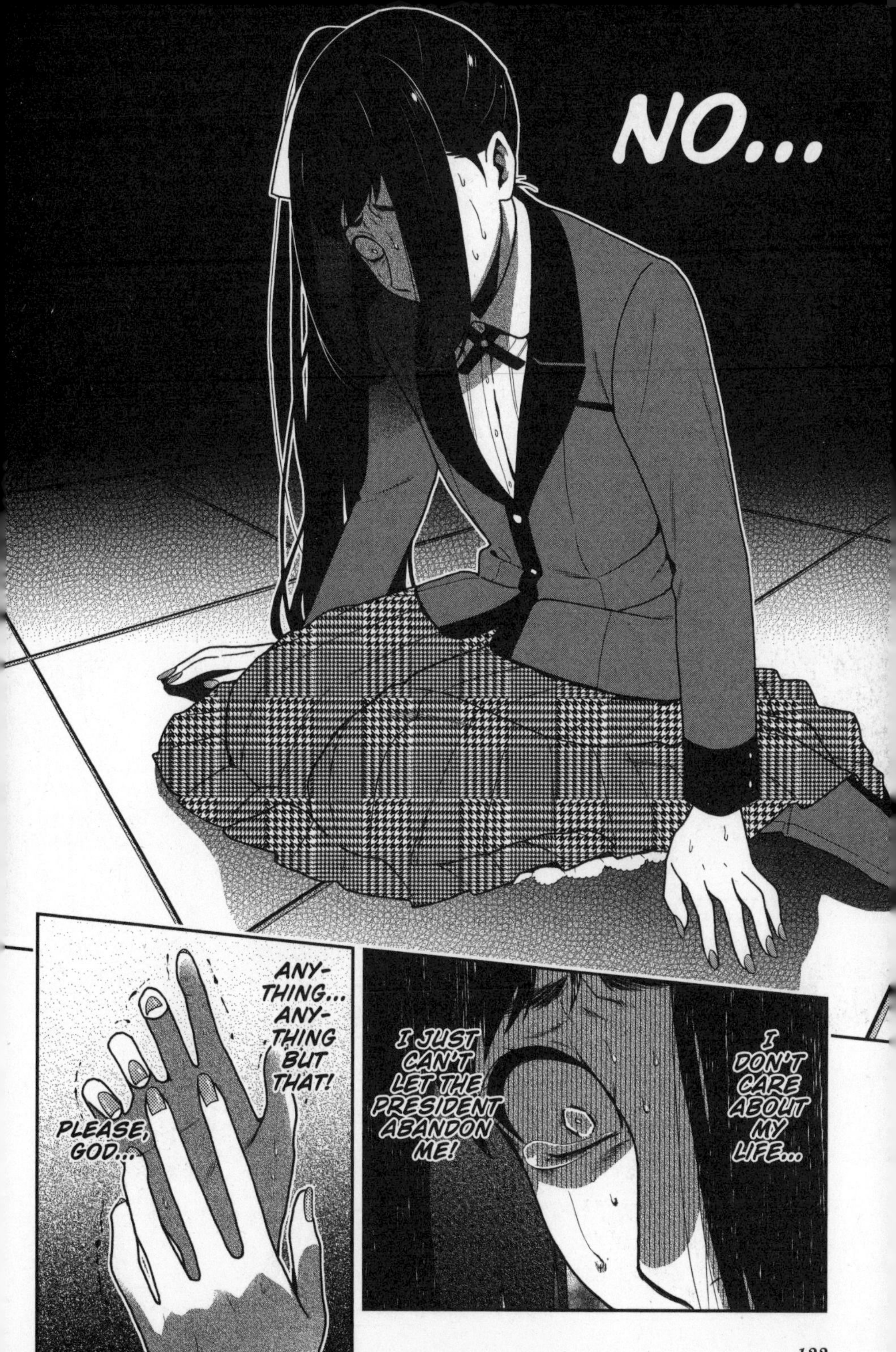
NO...
I DON'T CARE ABOUT MY LIFE...
I JUST CAN'T LET THE PRESIDENT ABANDON ME!
ANY-THING... ANY-THING BUT THAT!
PLEASE, GOD...

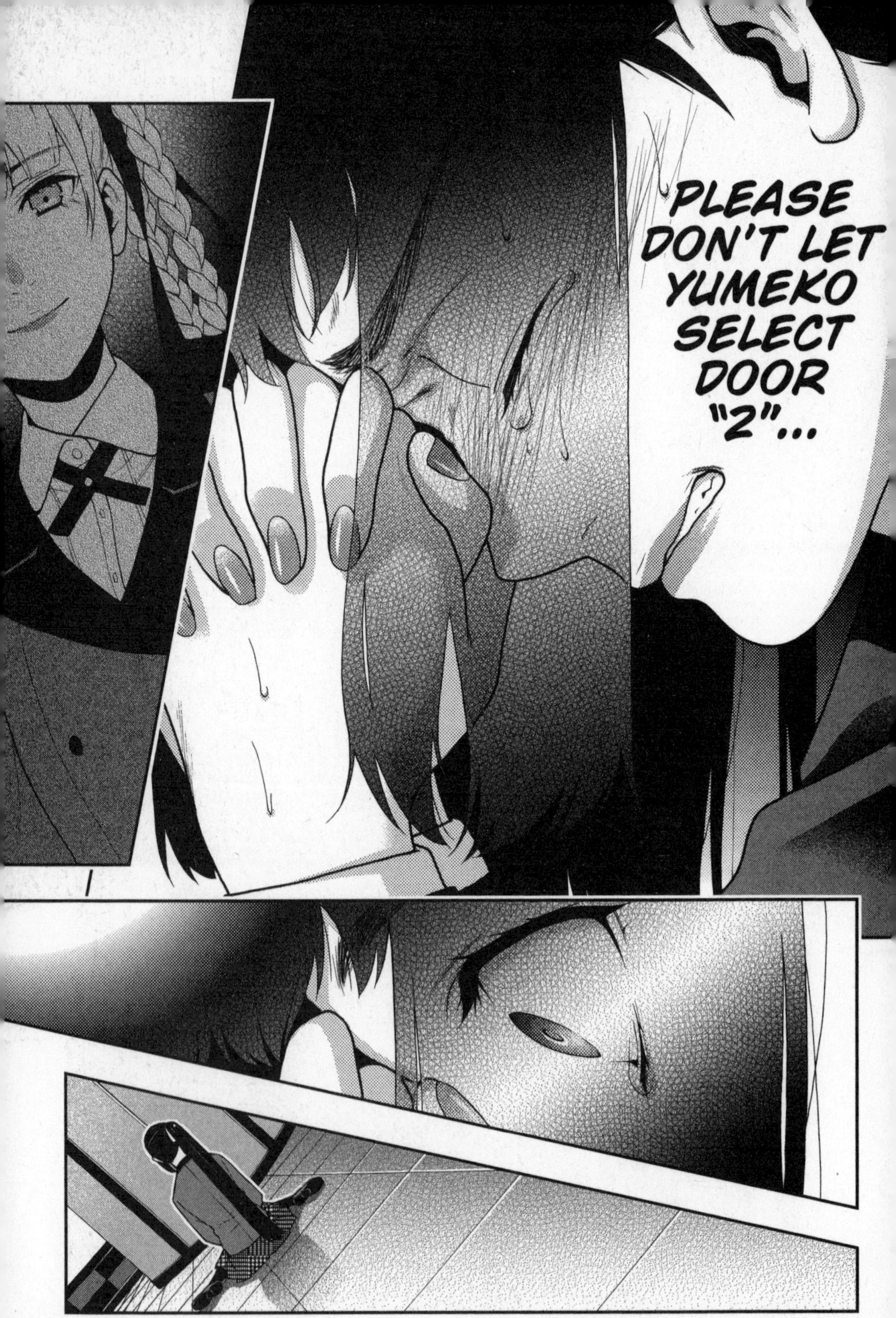
PLEASE DON'T LET YUMEKO SELECT DOOR "2"...

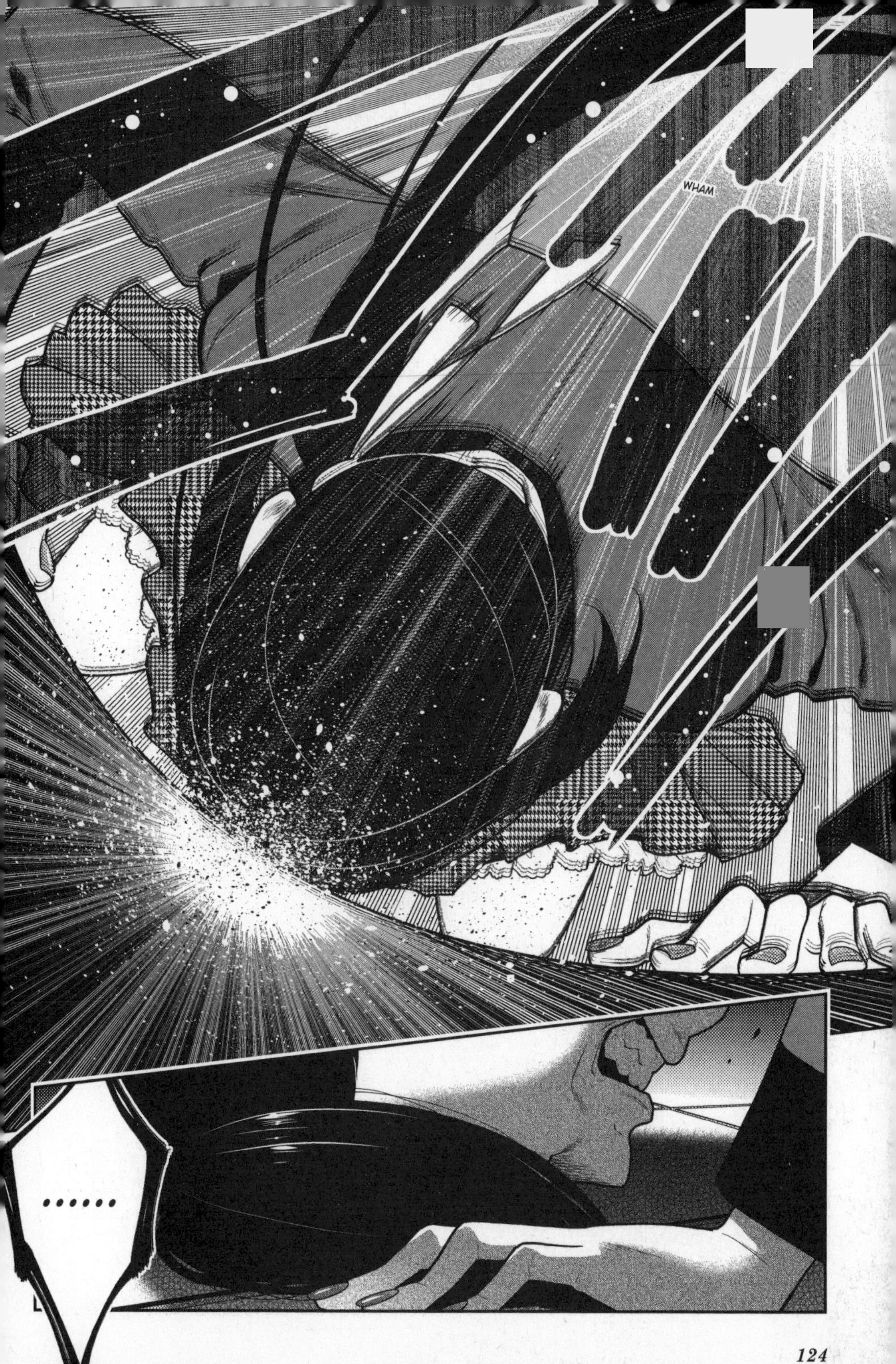
WHAM
......

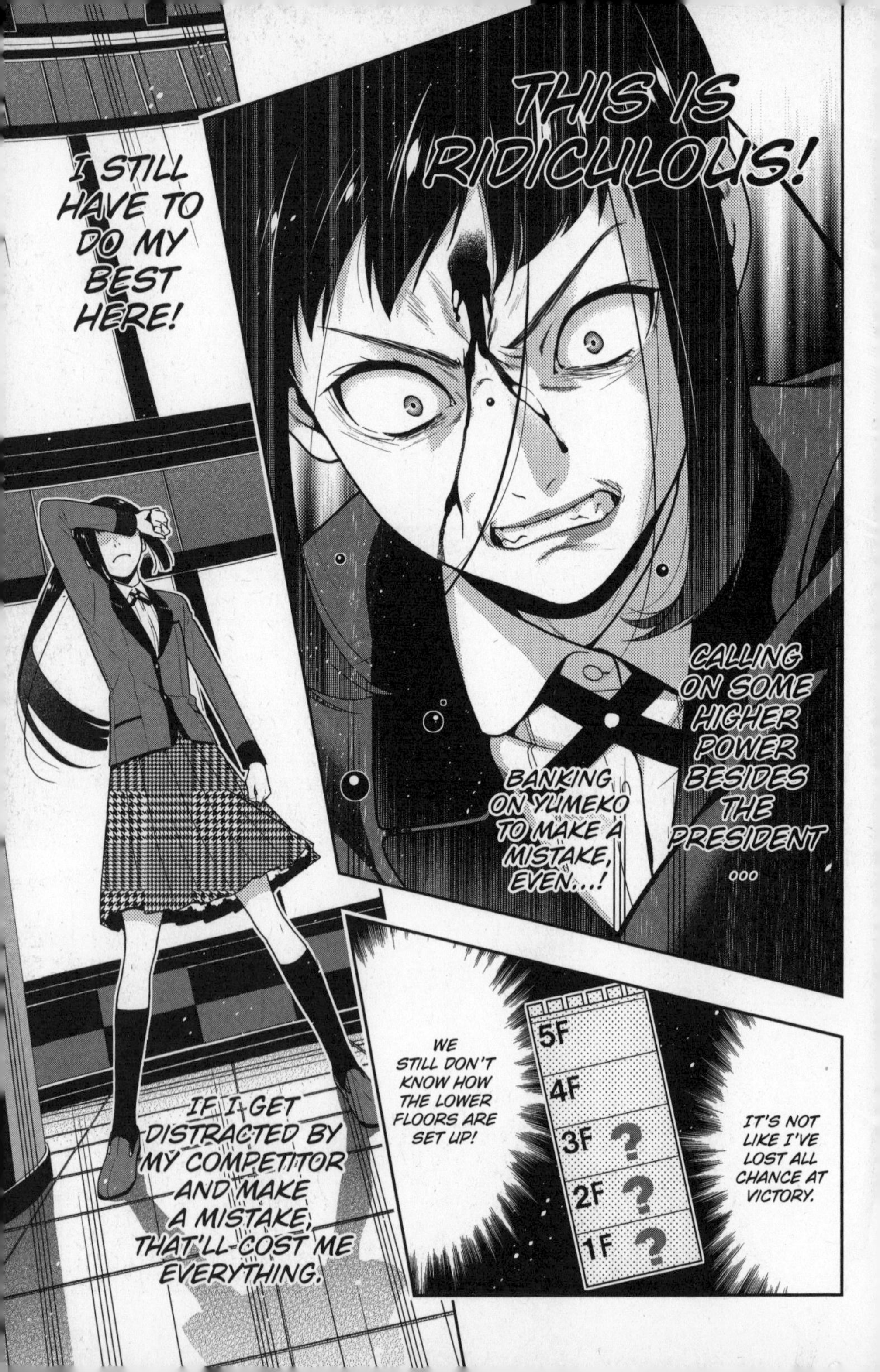
THIS IS RIDICULOUS!
CALLING ON SOME HIGHER POWER BESIDES THE PRESIDENT...
BANKING ON YUMEKO TO MAKE A MISTAKE, EVEN...!
IT'S NOT LIKE I'VE LOST ALL CHANCE AT VICTORY.
WE STILL DON'T KNOW HOW THE LOWER FLOORS ARE SET UP!
5F
4F
3F ?
2F ?
1F ?
I STILL HAVE TO DO MY BEST HERE!
IF I GET DISTRACTED BY MY COMPETITOR AND MAKE A MISTAKE, THAT'LL COST ME EVERYTHING.

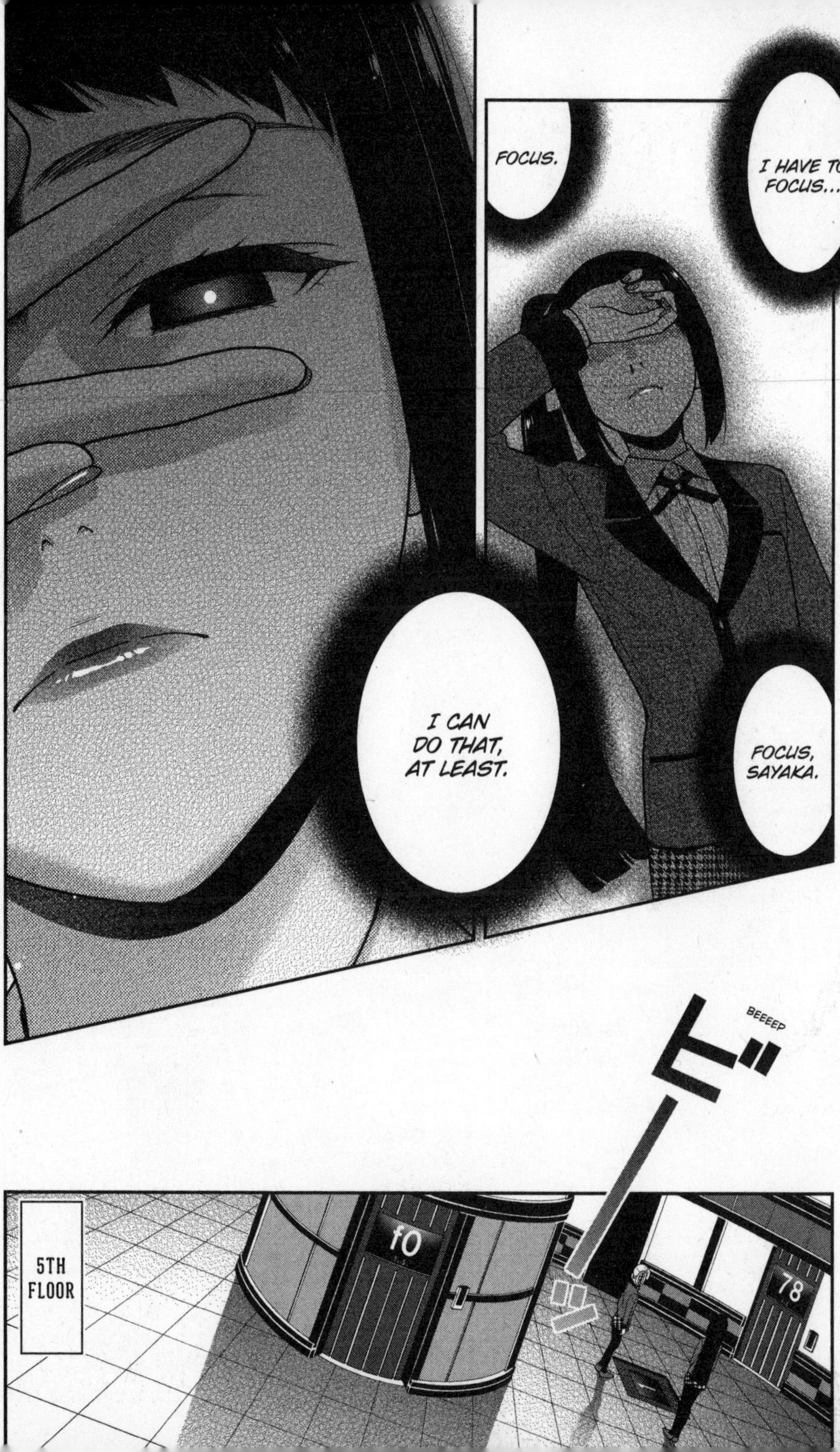
I HAVE TO FOCUS...
FOCUS.
FOCUS, SAYAKA.
I CAN DO THAT, AT LEAST.
BEEEEP
5TH FLOOR

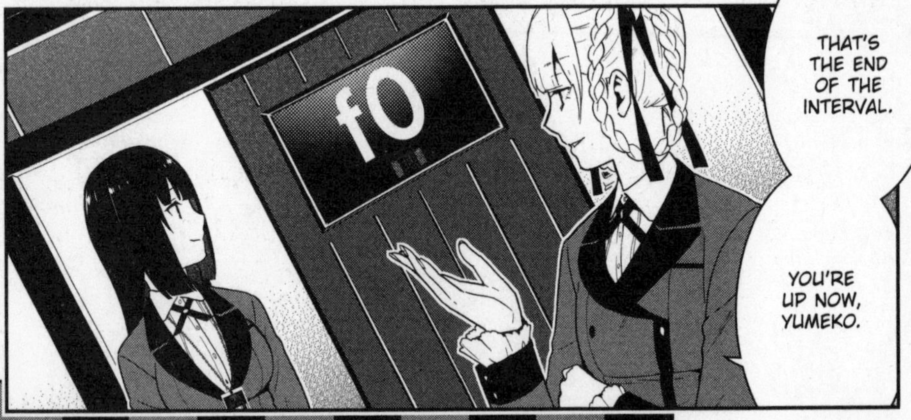
THAT'S THE END OF THE INTERVAL.
YOU'RE UP NOW, YUMEKO.
f0
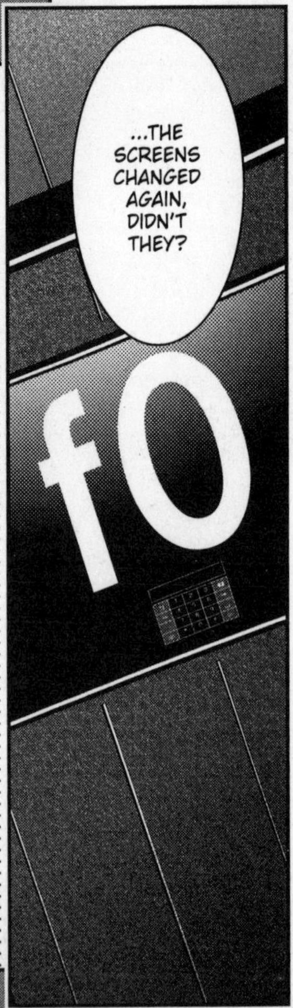
...THE SCREENS CHANGED AGAIN, DIDN'T THEY?
f0
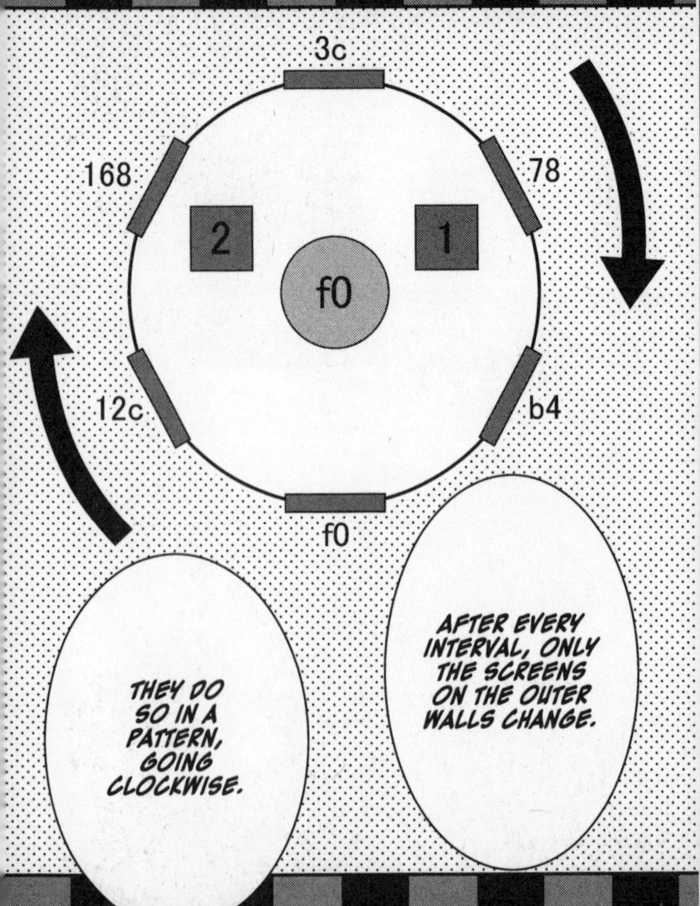
3c
78
b4
f0
12c
168
1
2
f0
AFTER EVERY INTERVAL, ONLY THE SCREENS ON THE OUTER WALLS CHANGE.
THEY DO SO IN A PATTERN, GOING CLOCKWISE.

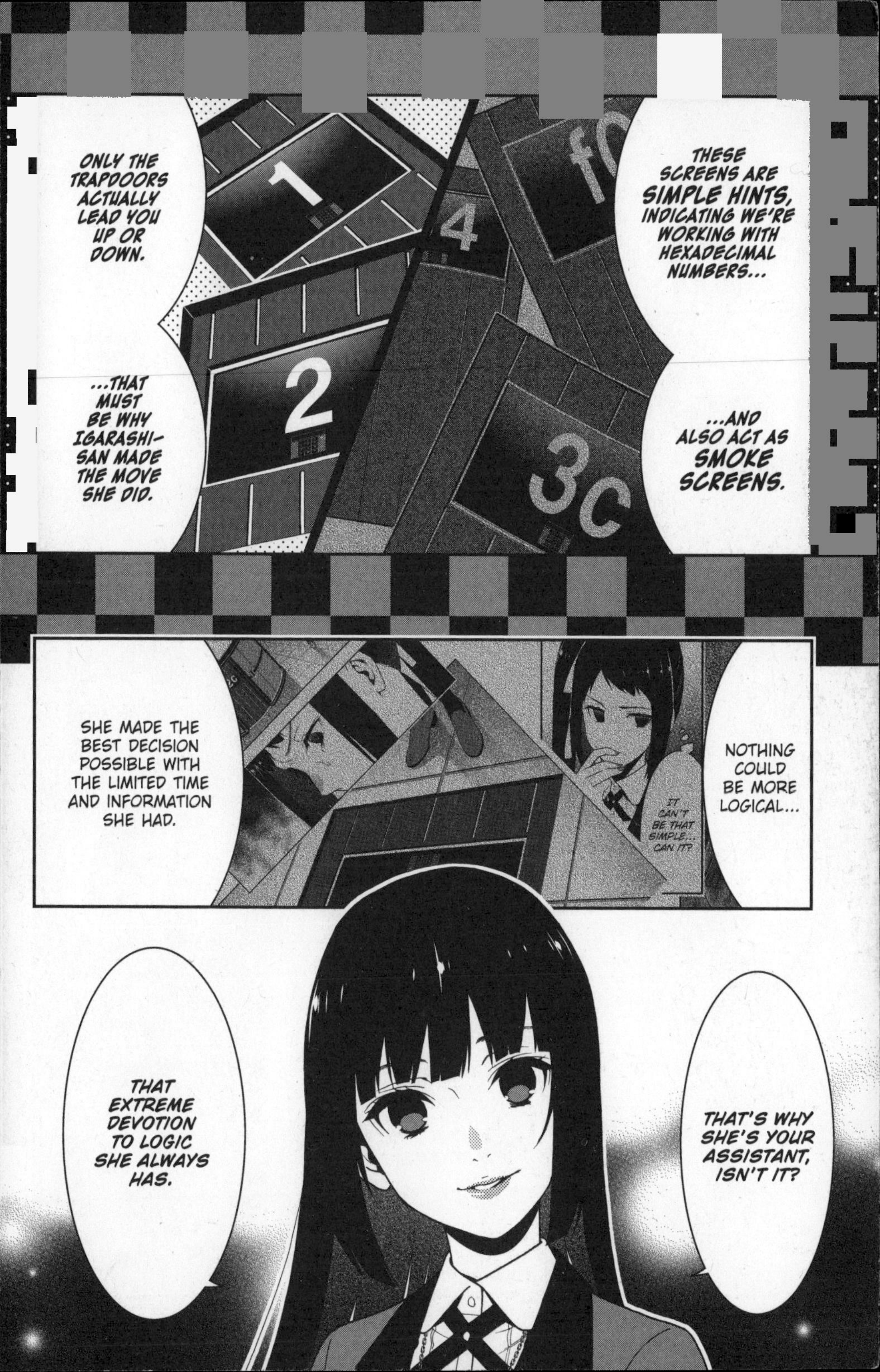
THESE SCREENS ARE SIMPLE HINTS, INDICATING WE'RE WORKING WITH HEXADECIMAL NUMBERS...
...AND ALSO ACT AS SMOKE SCREENS.
ONLY THE TRAPDOORS ACTUALLY LEAD YOU UP OR DOWN.
...THAT MUST BE WHY IGARASHI-SAN MADE THE MOVE SHE DID.
NOTHING COULD BE MORE LOGICAL...
IT CAN'T BE THAT SIMPLE... CAN IT?
SHE MADE THE BEST DECISION POSSIBLE WITH THE LIMITED TIME AND INFORMATION SHE HAD.
THAT EXTREME DEVOTION TO LOGIC SHE ALWAYS HAS.
THAT'S WHY SHE'S YOUR ASSISTANT, ISN'T IT?

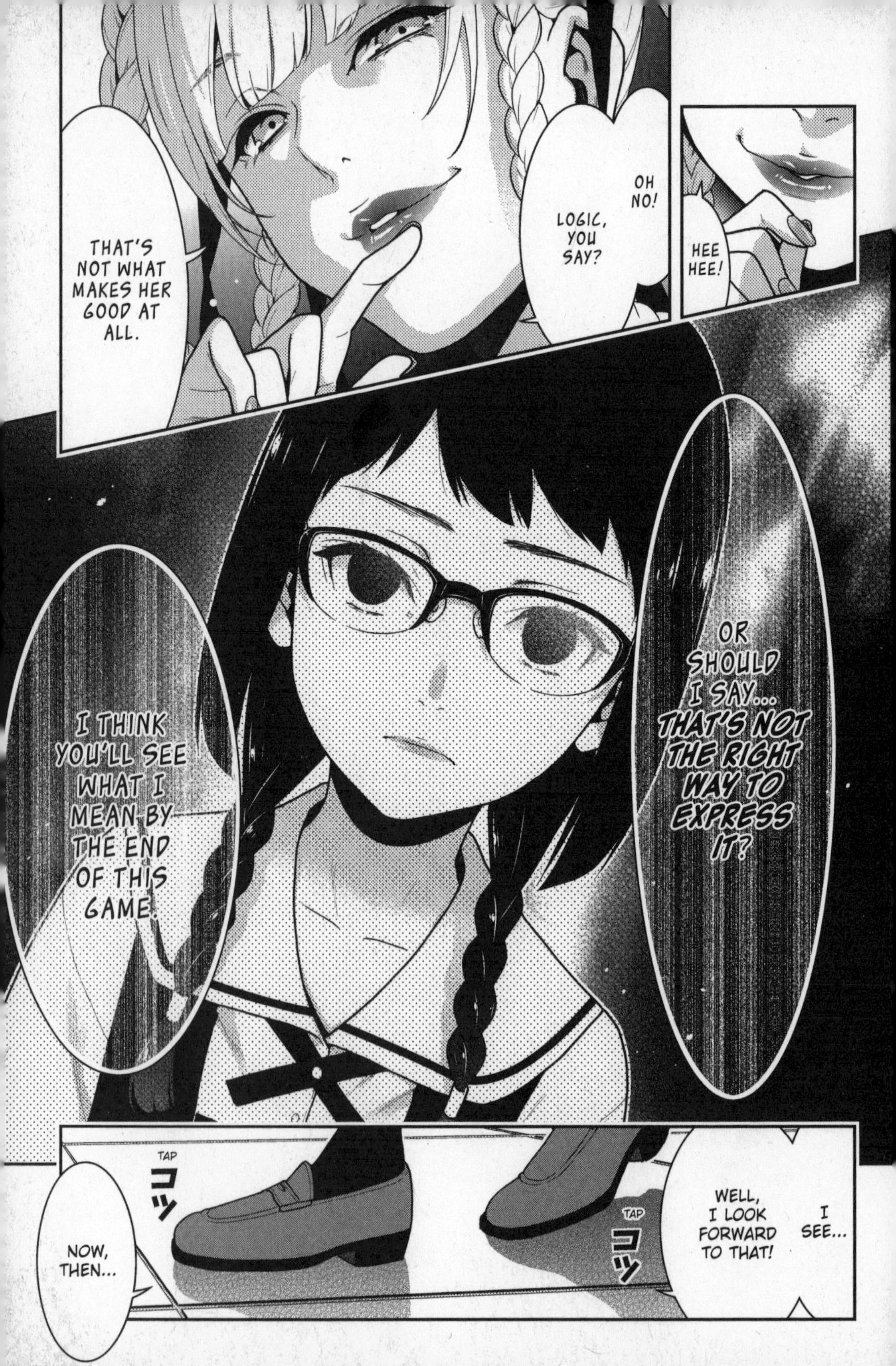
HEE HEE!
OH NO! LOGIC, YOU SAY?
THAT'S NOT WHAT MAKES HER GOOD AT ALL.
OR SHOULD I SAY... THAT'S NOT THE RIGHT WAY TO EXPRESS IT?
I THINK YOU'LL SEE WHAT I MEAN BY THE END OF THIS GAME.
I SEE... WELL, I LOOK FORWARD TO THAT!
TAP コッ
TAP コッ
NOW, THEN...

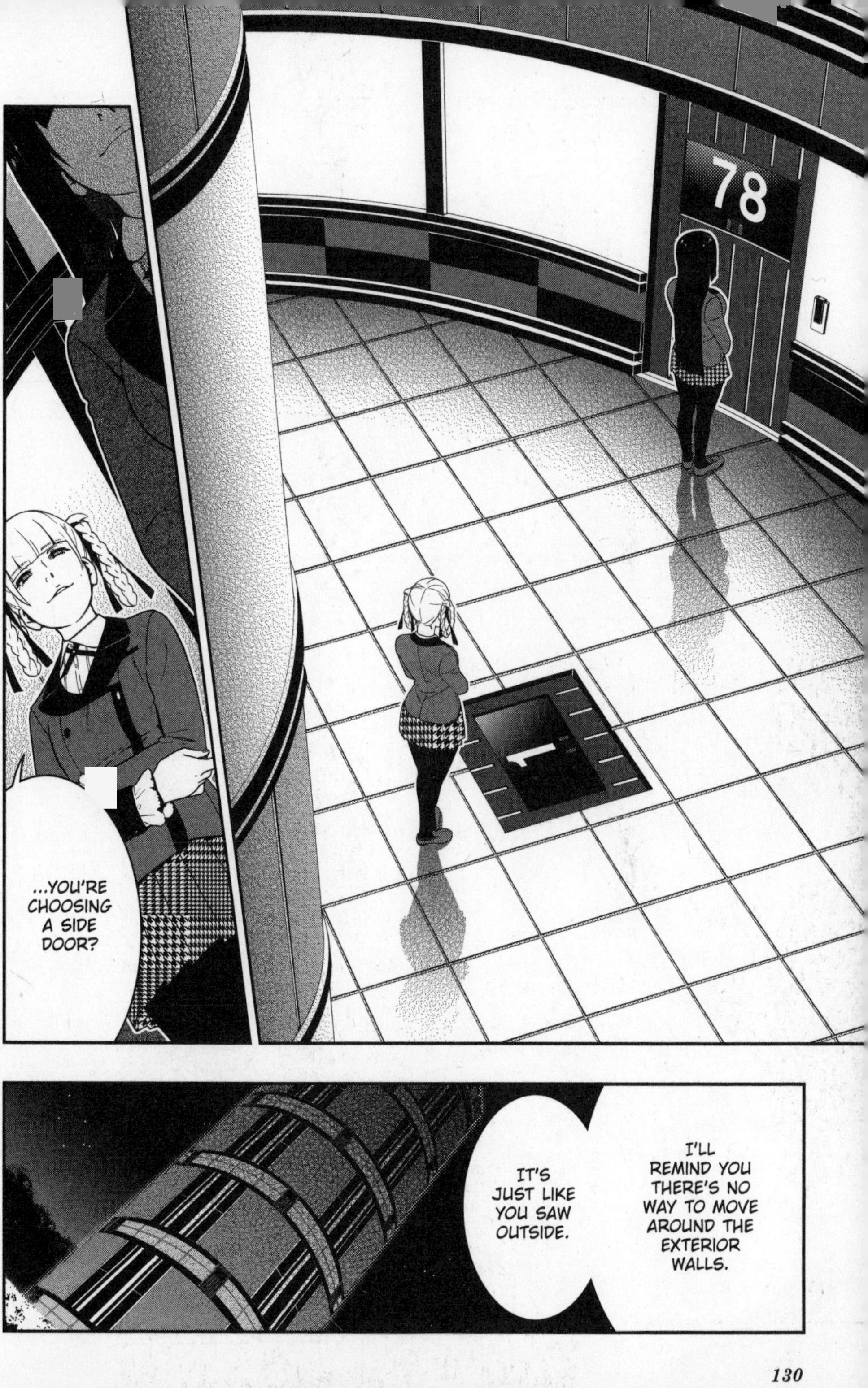
...YOU'RE CHOOSING A SIDE DOOR?
I'LL REMIND YOU THERE'S NO WAY TO MOVE AROUND THE EXTERIOR WALLS.
IT'S JUST LIKE YOU SAW OUTSIDE.

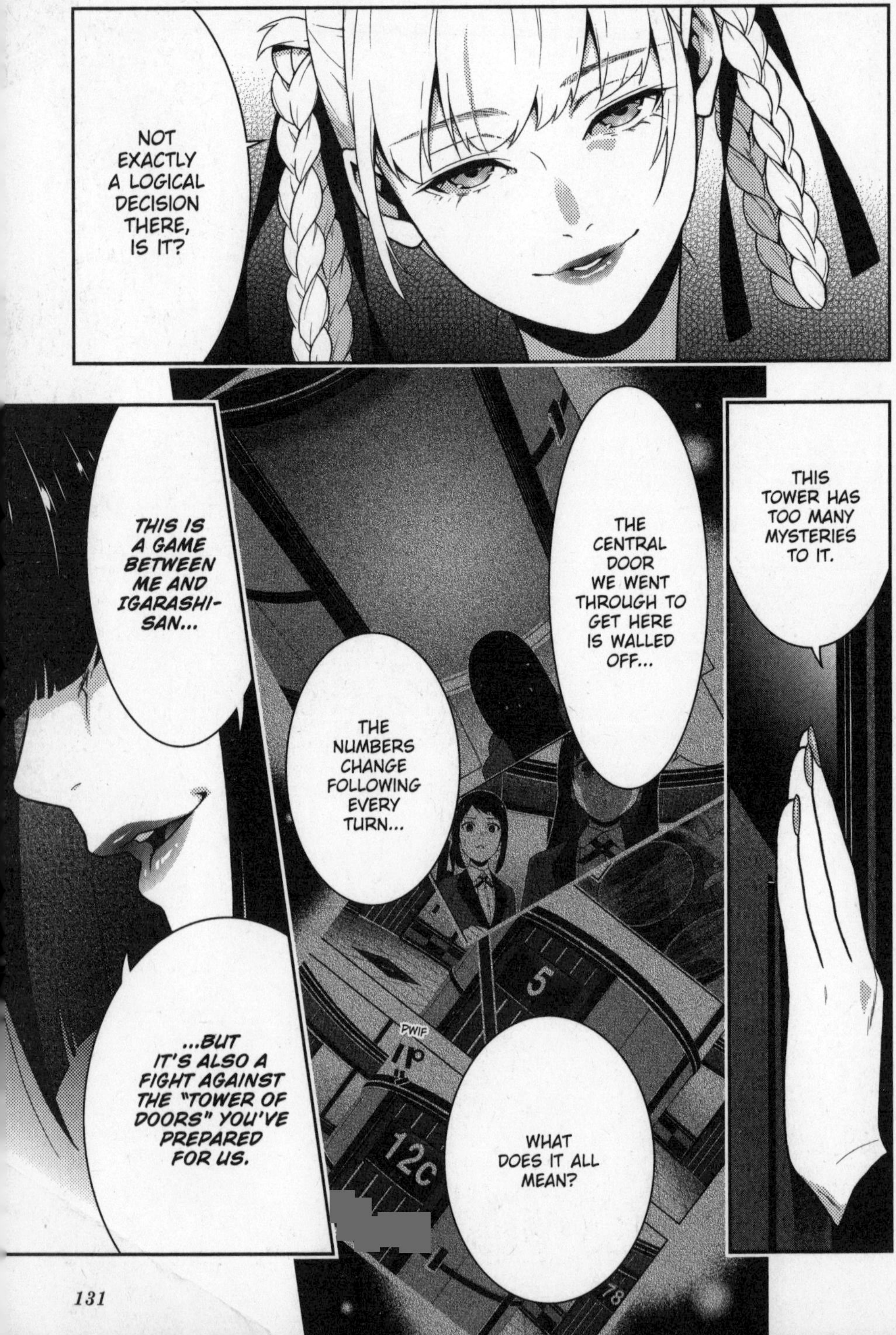
NOT EXACTLY A LOGICAL DECISION THERE, IS IT?
THIS TOWER HAS TOO MANY MYSTERIES TO IT.
THE CENTRAL DOOR WE WENT THROUGH TO GET HERE IS WALLED OFF...
THE NUMBERS CHANGE FOLLOWING EVERY TURN...
PWIF
WHAT DOES IT ALL MEAN?
THIS IS A GAME BETWEEN ME AND IGARASHI-SAN...
...BUT IT'S ALSO A FIGHT AGAINST THE "TOWER OF DOORS" YOU'VE PREPARED FOR US.

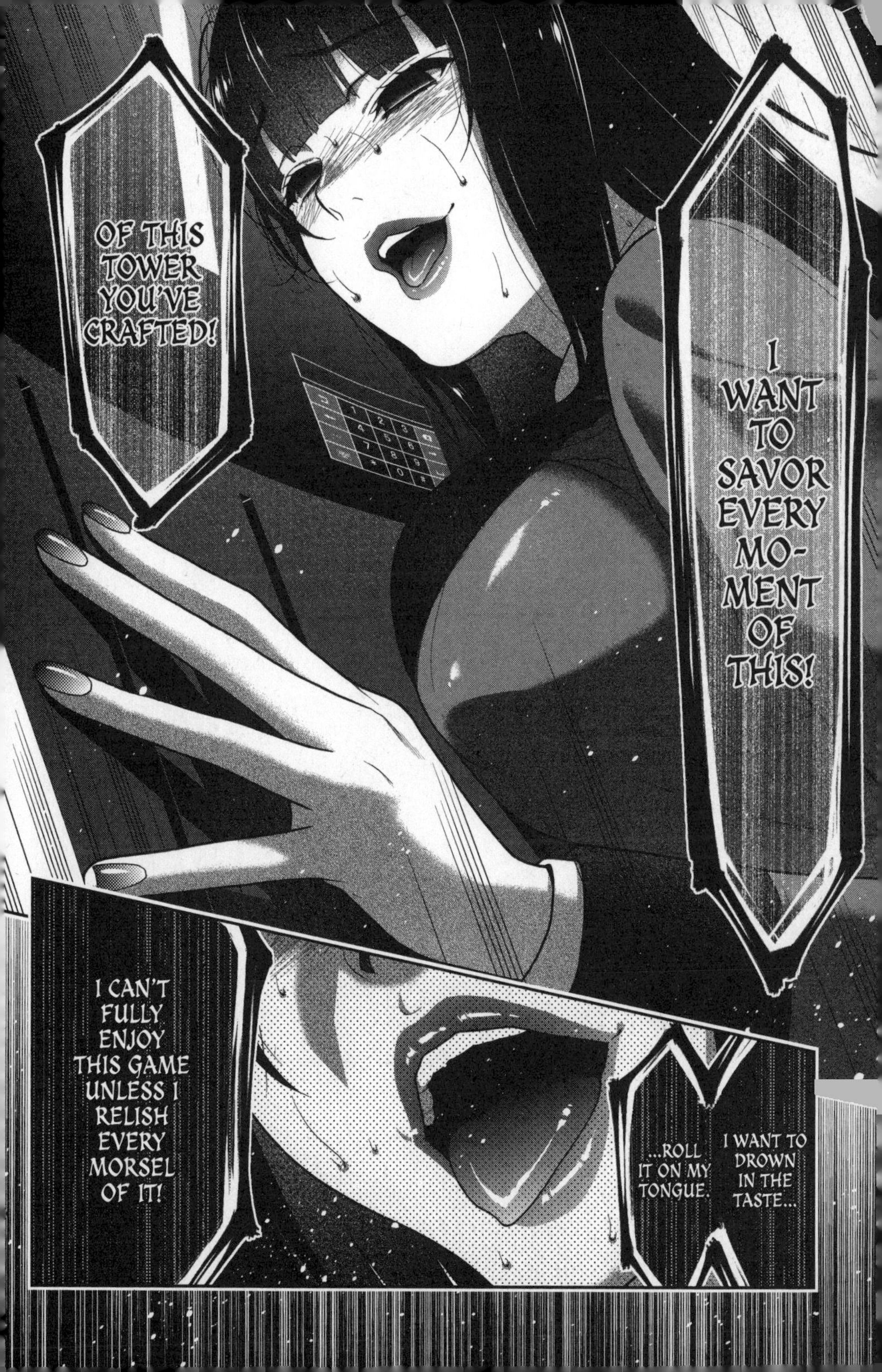
I WANT TO SAVOR EVERY MO-MENT OF THIS!
OF THIS TOWER YOU'VE CRAFTED!
I WANT TO DROWN IN THE TASTE...
...ROLL IT ON MY TONGUE.
I CAN'T FULLY ENJOY THIS GAME UNLESS I RELISH EVERY MORSEL OF IT!

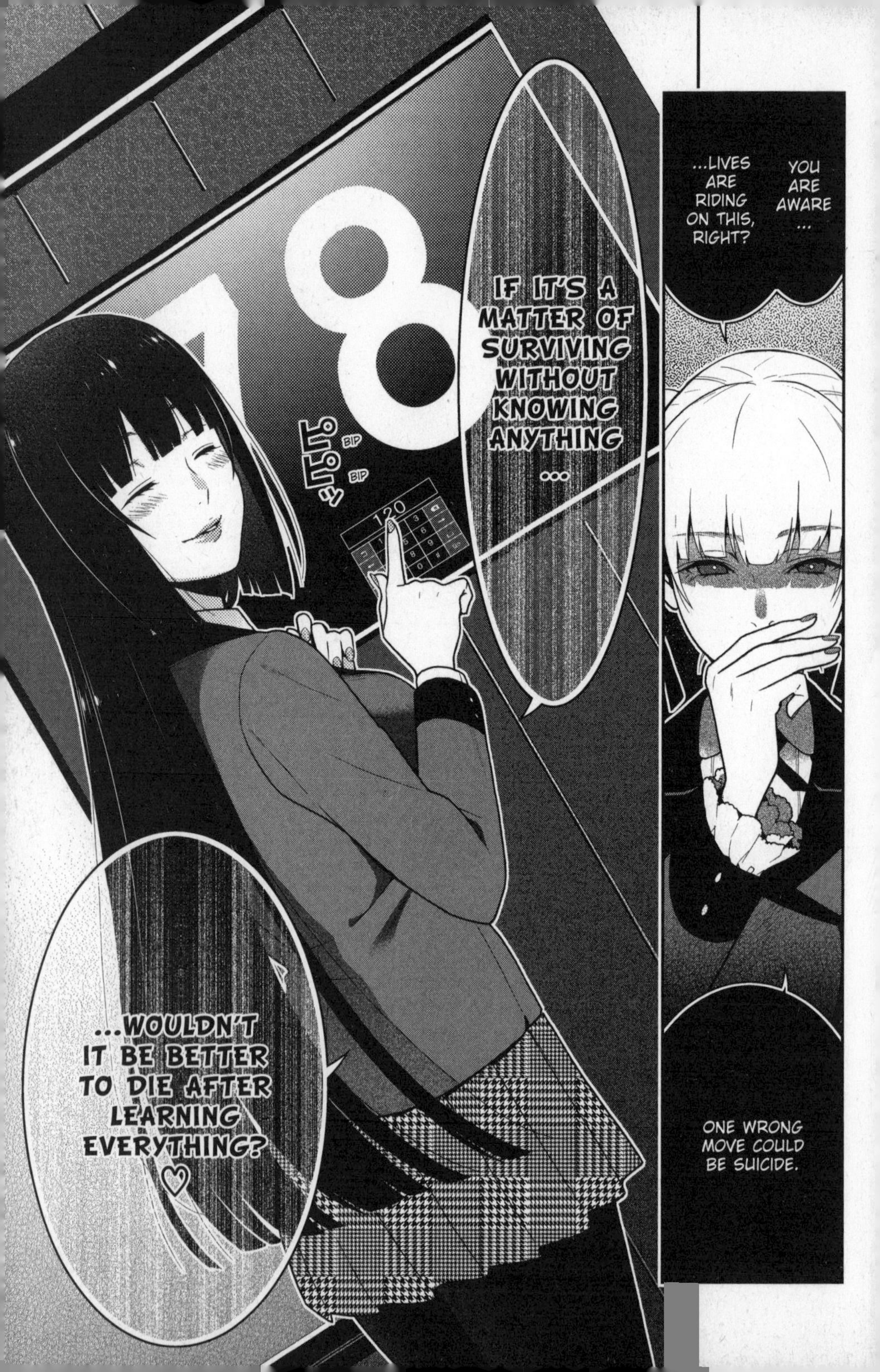
YOU ARE AWARE...
...LIVES ARE RIDING ON THIS, RIGHT?
ONE WRONG MOVE COULD BE SUICIDE.
IF IT'S A MATTER OF SURVIVING WITHOUT KNOWING ANYTHING...
BIP BIP
...WOULDN'T IT BE BETTER TO DIE AFTER LEARNING EVERYTHING? ♡

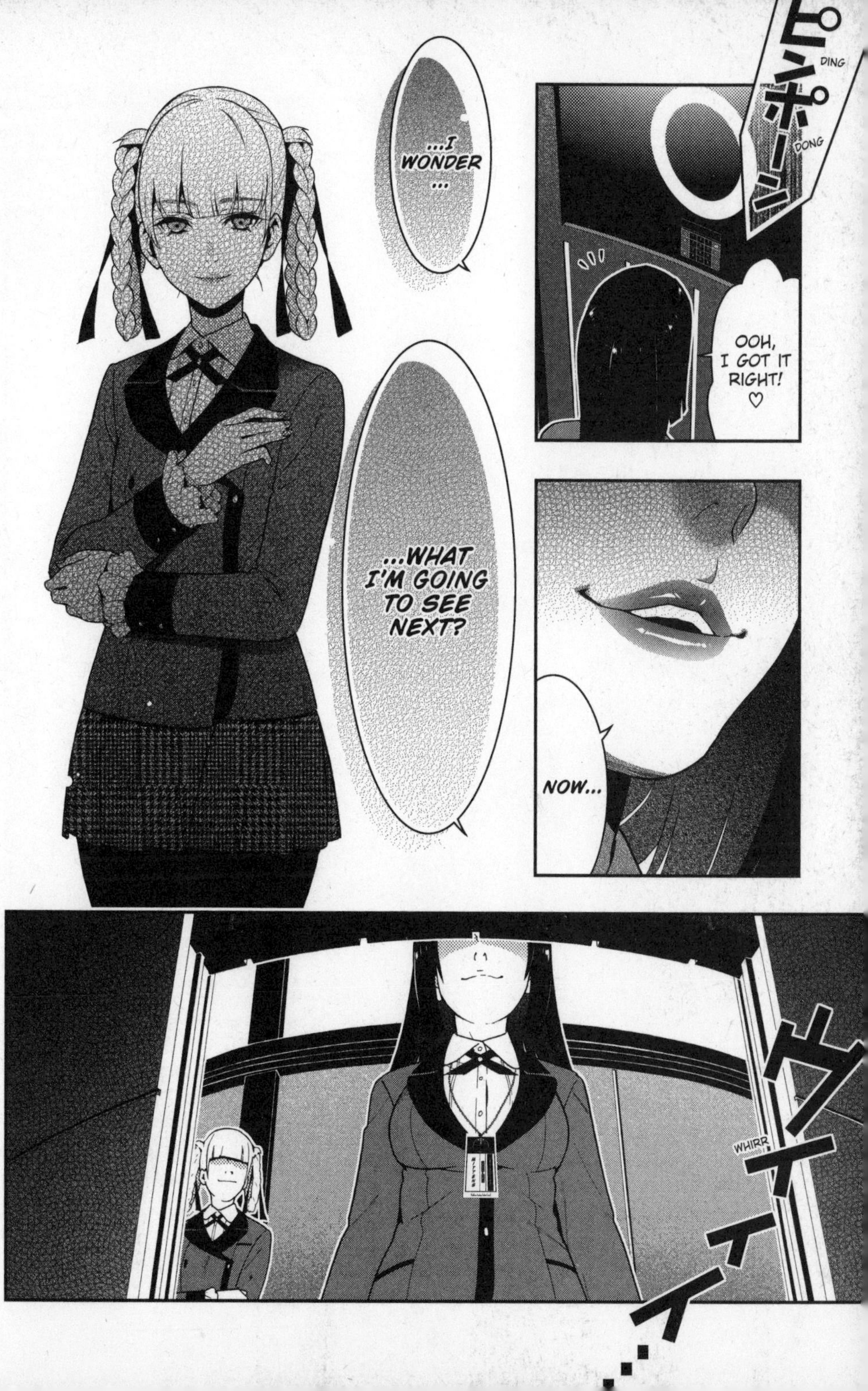
DING
DONG
OOH, I GOT IT RIGHT! ♡
NOW...
...I WONDER...
...WHAT I'M GOING TO SEE NEXT?
WHIRR

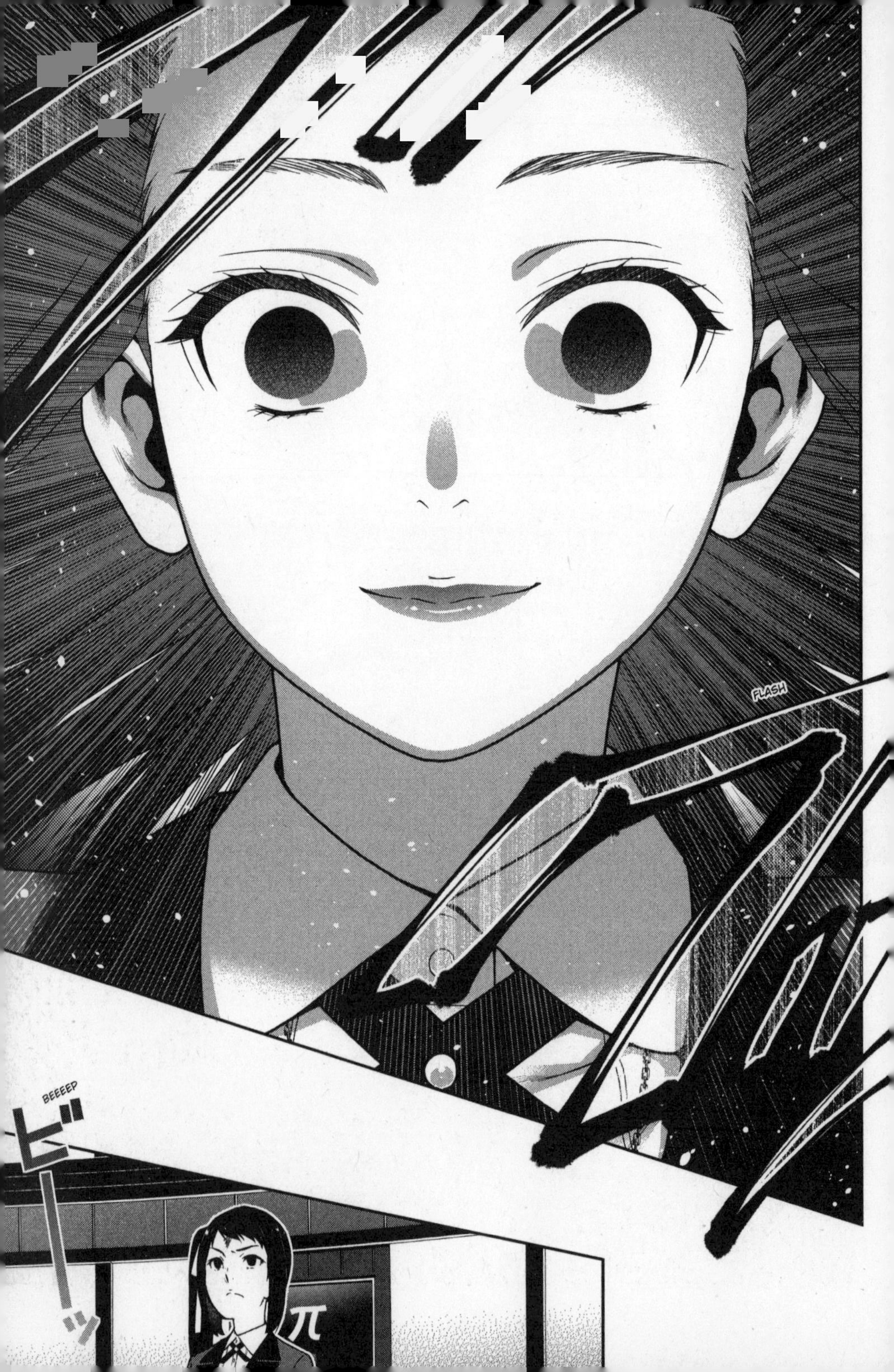
FLASH
BEEEEP
ビーーッ

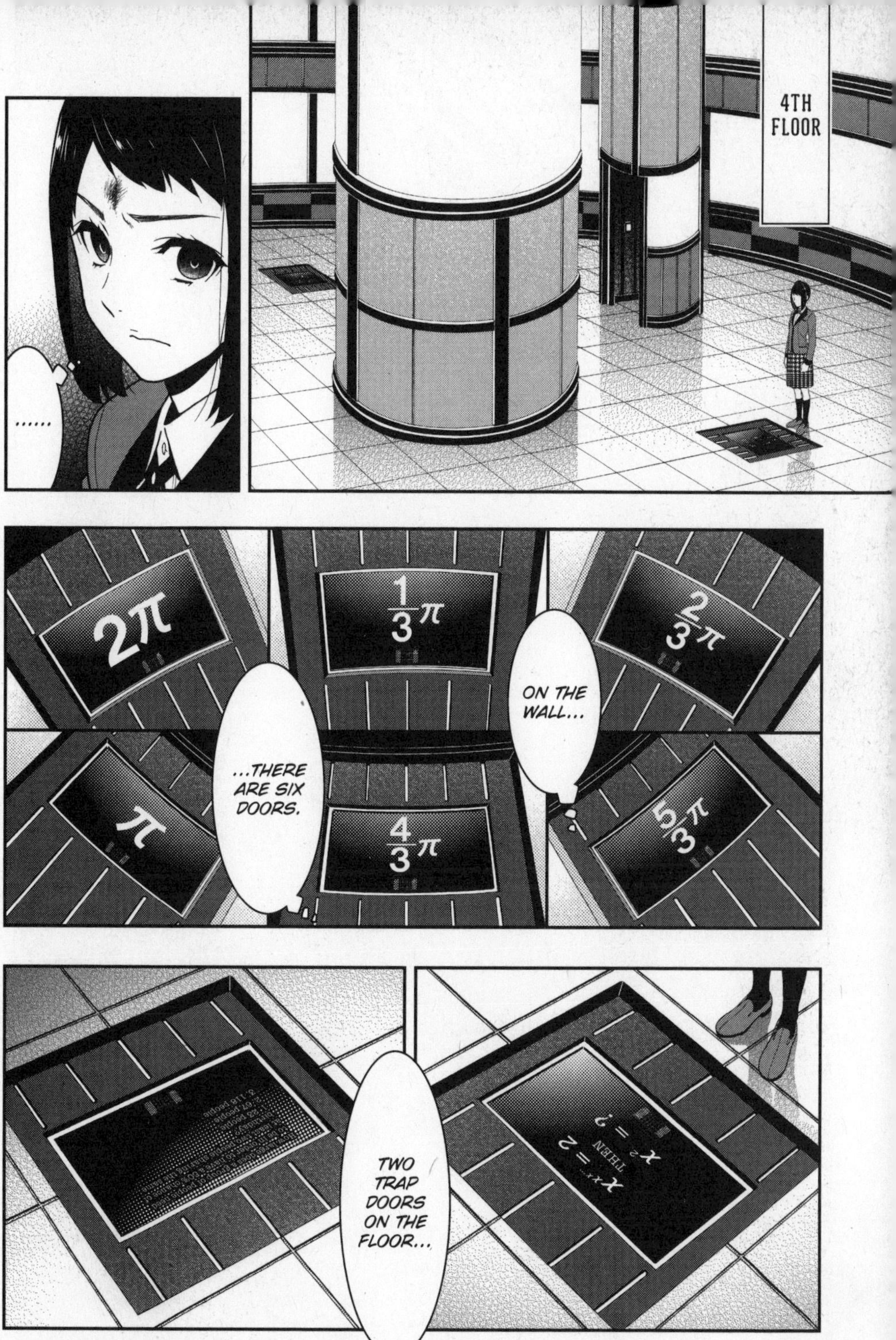
4TH FLOOR
......
ON THE WALL...
...THERE ARE SIX DOORS.
2/3 π
1/3 π
2π
5/3 π
4/3 π
π
TWO TRAP DOORS ON THE FLOOR...

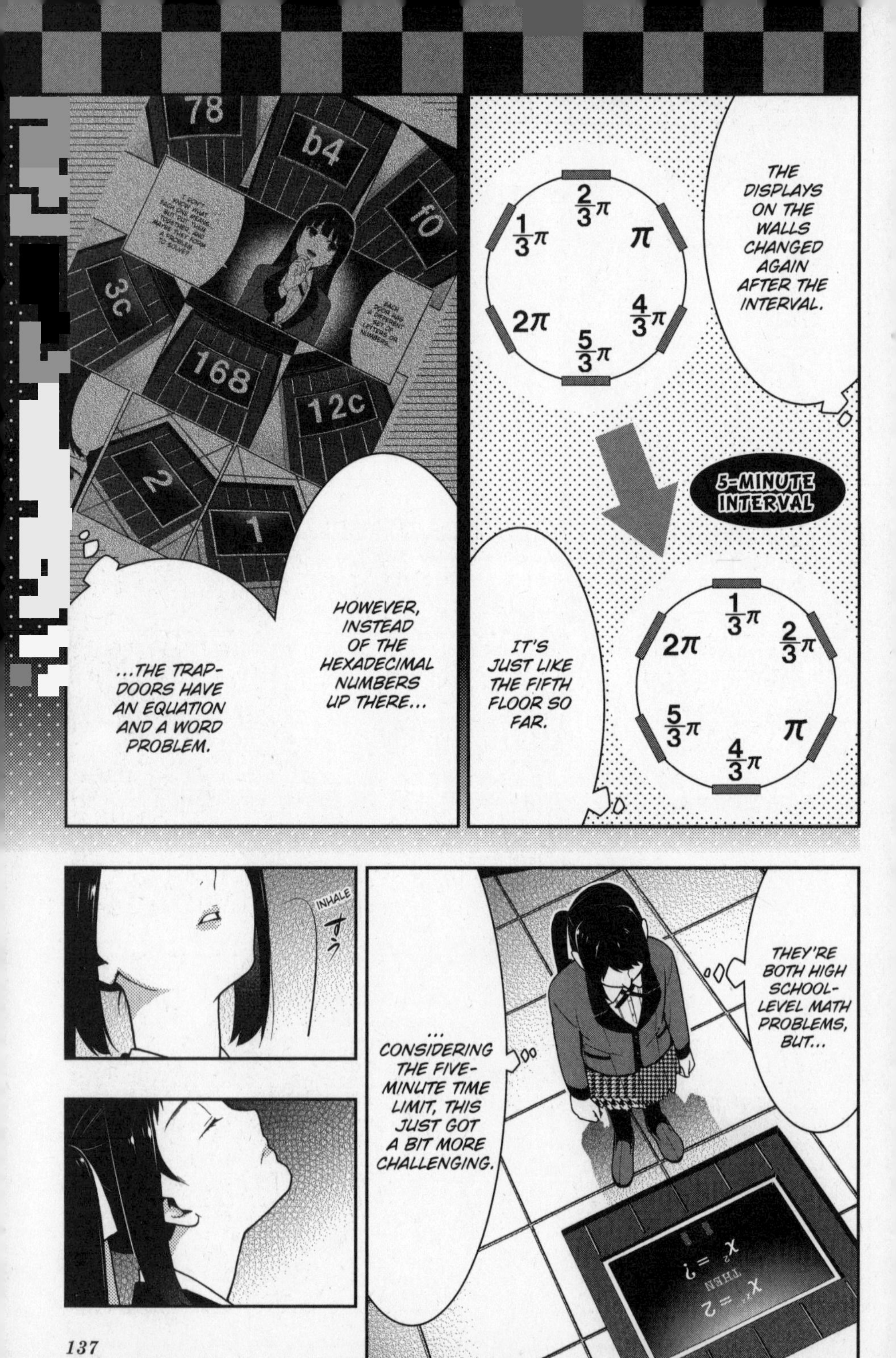
THE DISPLAYS ON THE WALLS CHANGED AGAIN AFTER THE INTERVAL.
2/3π
π
4/3π
5/3π
2π
1/3π
5-MINUTE INTERVAL
1/3π
2/3π
π
4/3π
5/3π
2π
IT'S JUST LIKE THE FIFTH FLOOR SO FAR.
78
b4
f0
EACH DOOR HAS A DIFFERENT SET OF LETTERS OR NUMBERS...
I DON'T KNOW WHAT EACH ONE MEANS, BUT PUT THEM TOGETHER, AND MAYBE THEY FORM A PROBLEM TO SOLVE?
3c
168
12c
2
1
HOWEVER, INSTEAD OF THE HEXADECIMAL NUMBERS UP THERE...
...THE TRAPDOORS HAVE AN EQUATION AND A WORD PROBLEM.
THEY'RE BOTH HIGH SCHOOL-LEVEL MATH PROBLEMS, BUT...
...CONSIDERING THE FIVE-MINUTE TIME LIMIT, THIS JUST GOT A BIT MORE CHALLENGING.
INHALE
すう

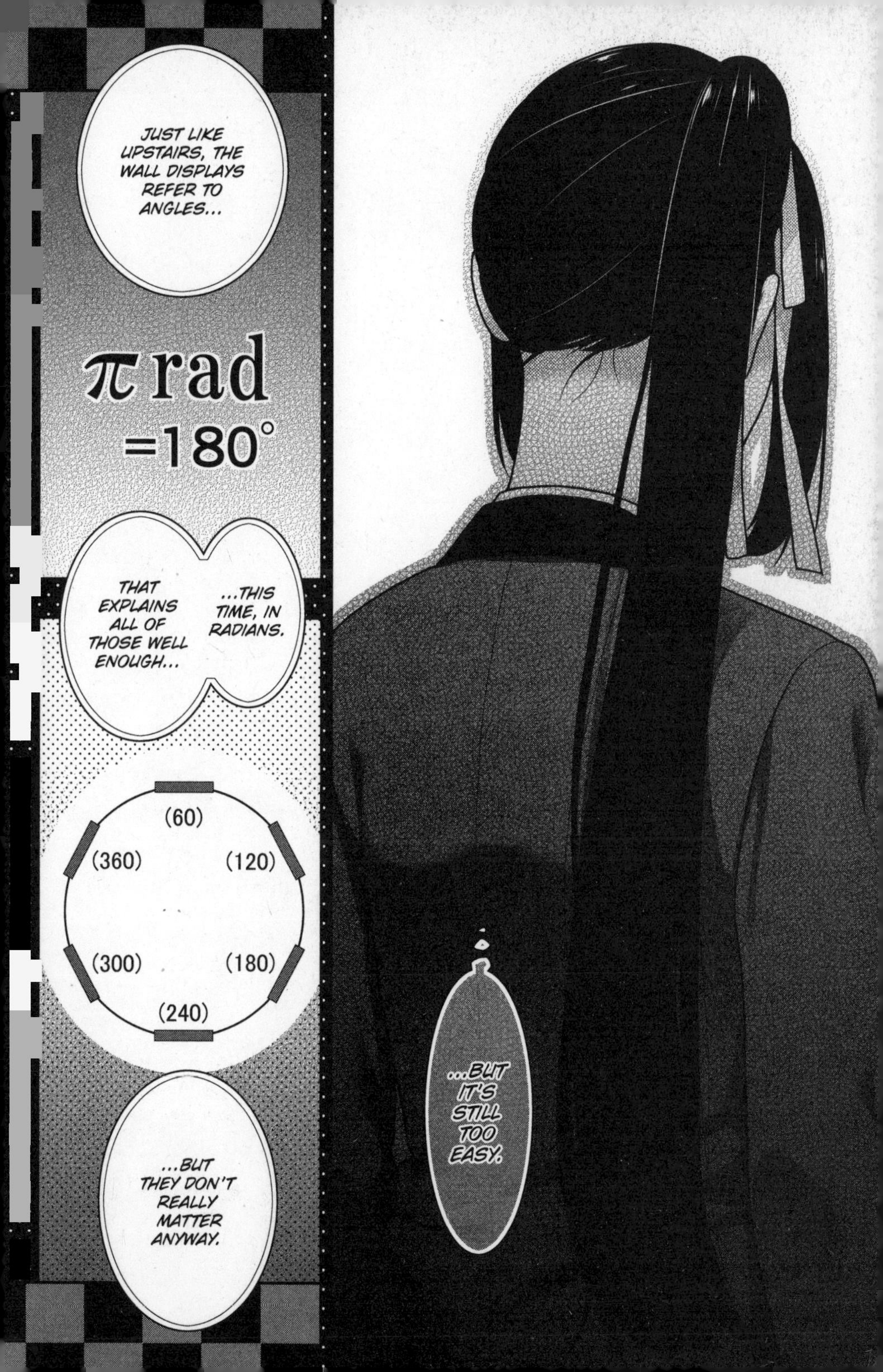
...BUT IT'S STILL TOO EASY.
JUST LIKE UPSTAIRS, THE WALL DISPLAYS REFER TO ANGLES...
π rad =180°
THAT EXPLAINS ALL OF THOSE WELL ENOUGH...
...THIS TIME, IN RADIANS.
(60)
(120)
(180)
(240)
(300)
(360)
...BUT THEY DON'T REALLY MATTER ANYWAY.

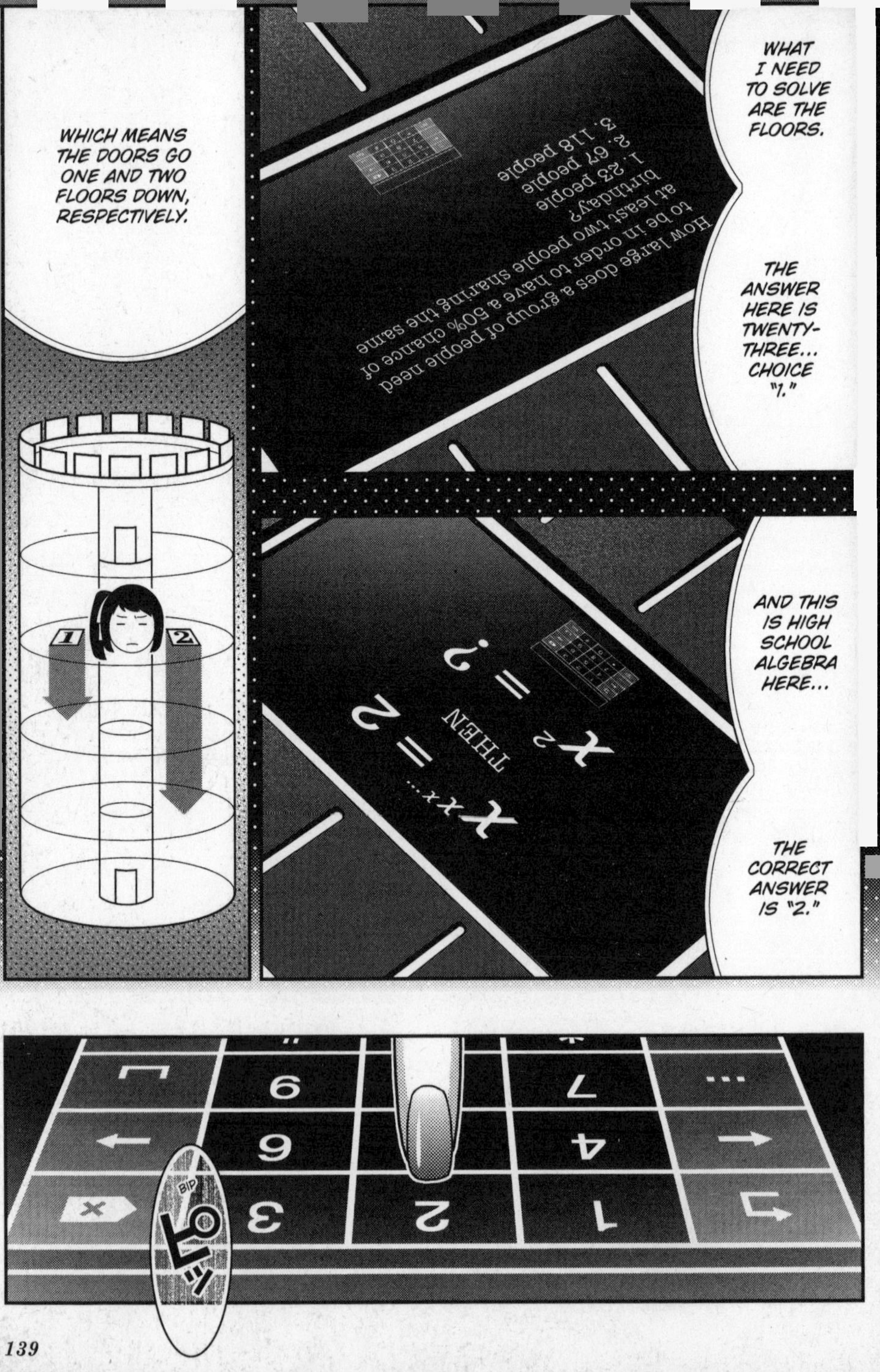
WHAT I NEED TO SOLVE ARE THE FLOORS.
How large does a group of people need to be in order to have a 50% chance of at least two people sharing the same birthday?
1. 23 people
2. 67 people
3. 118 people
THE ANSWER HERE IS TWENTY-THREE... CHOICE "1."
AND THIS IS HIGH SCHOOL ALGEBRA HERE...
$x^{x^{x\cdots}} = 2$ THEN $x^2 = ?$
THE CORRECT ANSWER IS "2."
WHICH MEANS THE DOORS GO ONE AND TWO FLOORS DOWN, RESPECTIVELY.
BIP
ピッ

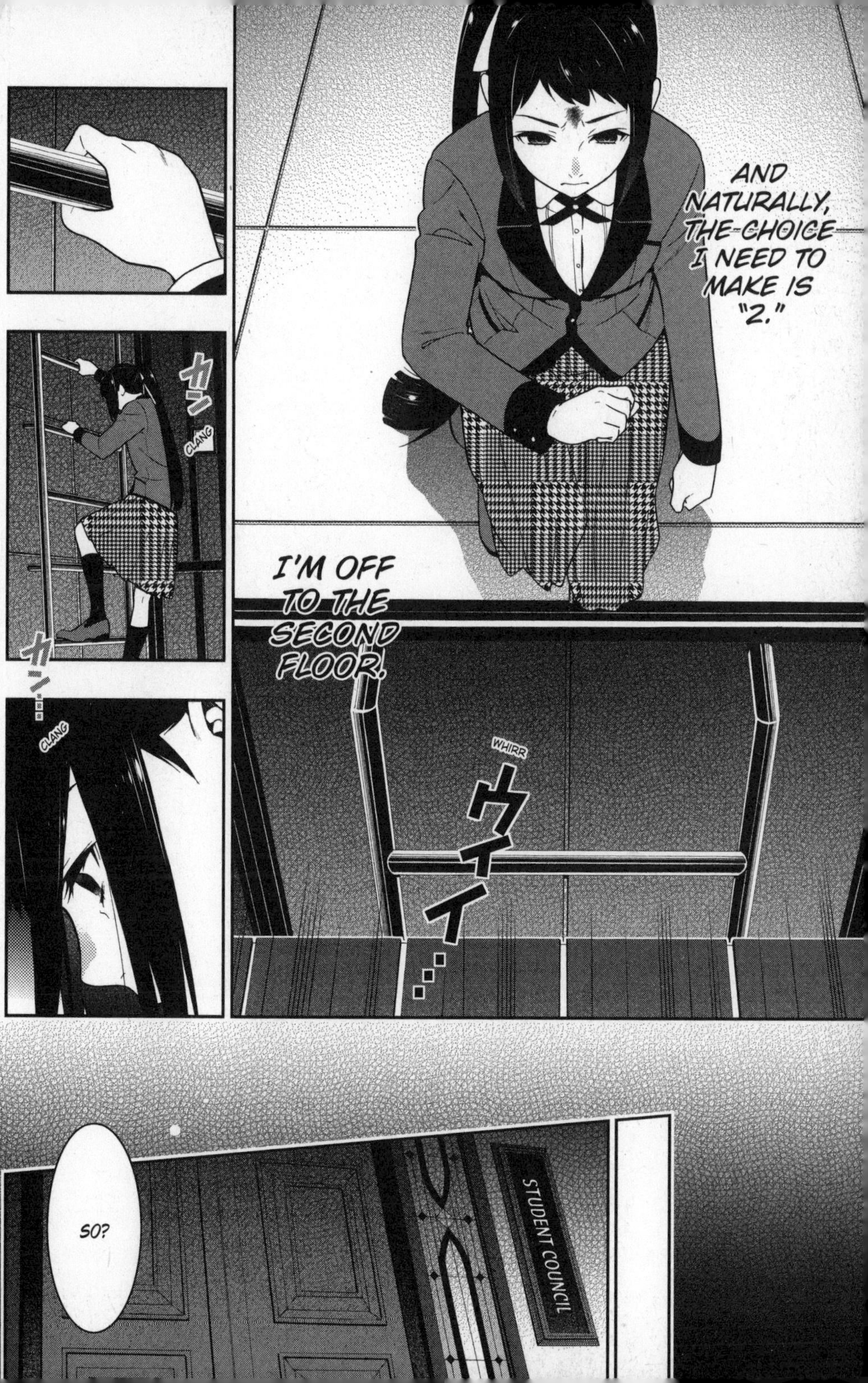
AND NATURALLY, THE CHOICE I NEED TO MAKE IS "2."
I'M OFF TO THE SECOND FLOOR.
WHIRR
CLANG
CLANG
SO?
STUDENT COUNCIL

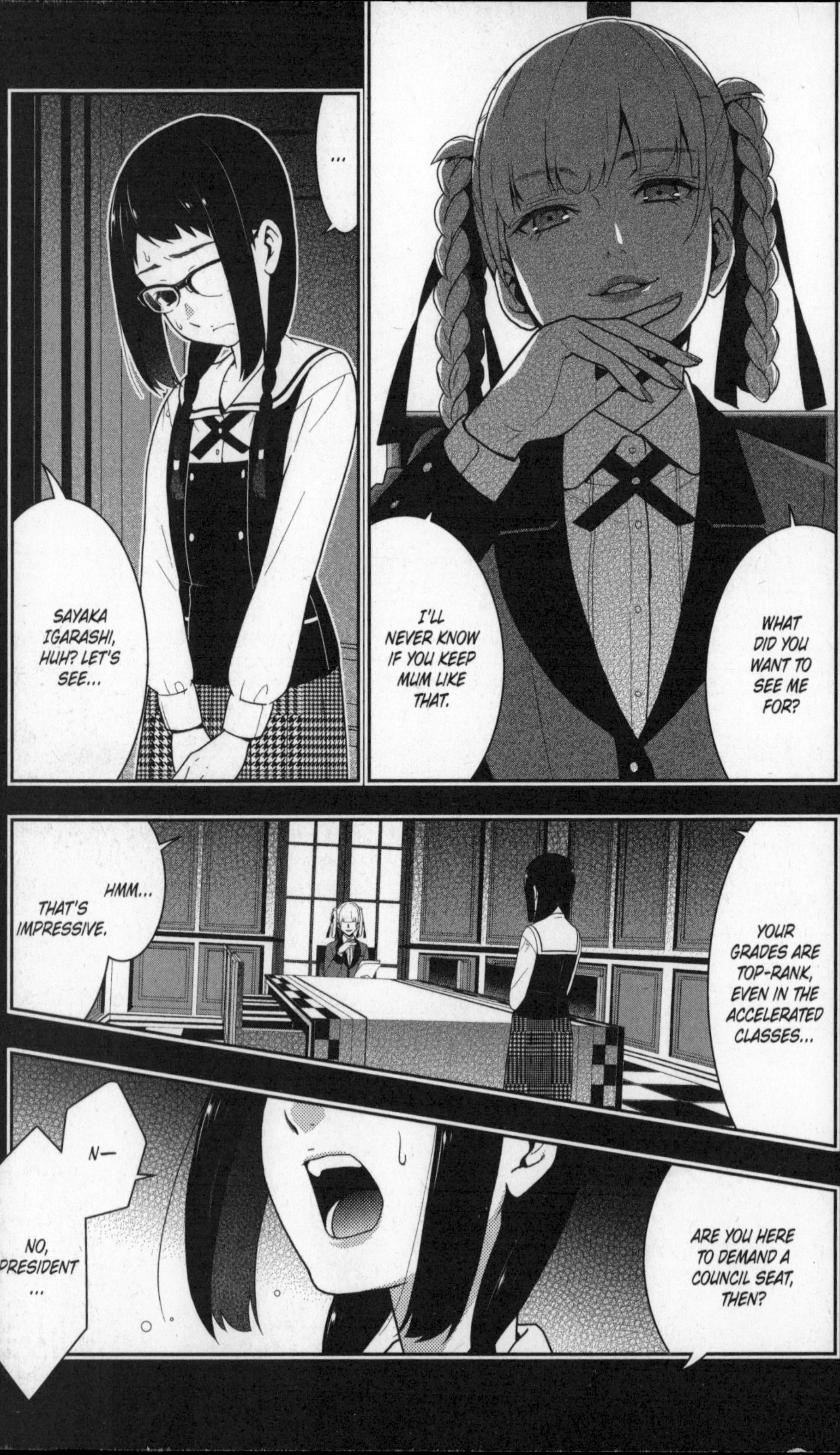
WHAT DID YOU WANT TO SEE ME FOR?
I'LL NEVER KNOW IF YOU KEEP MUM LIKE THAT.
...
SAYAKA IGARASHI, HUH? LET'S SEE...
YOUR GRADES ARE TOP-RANK, EVEN IN THE ACCELERATED CLASSES...
HMM... THAT'S IMPRESSIVE.
ARE YOU HERE TO DEMAND A COUNCIL SEAT, THEN?
N—
NO, PRESIDENT ...

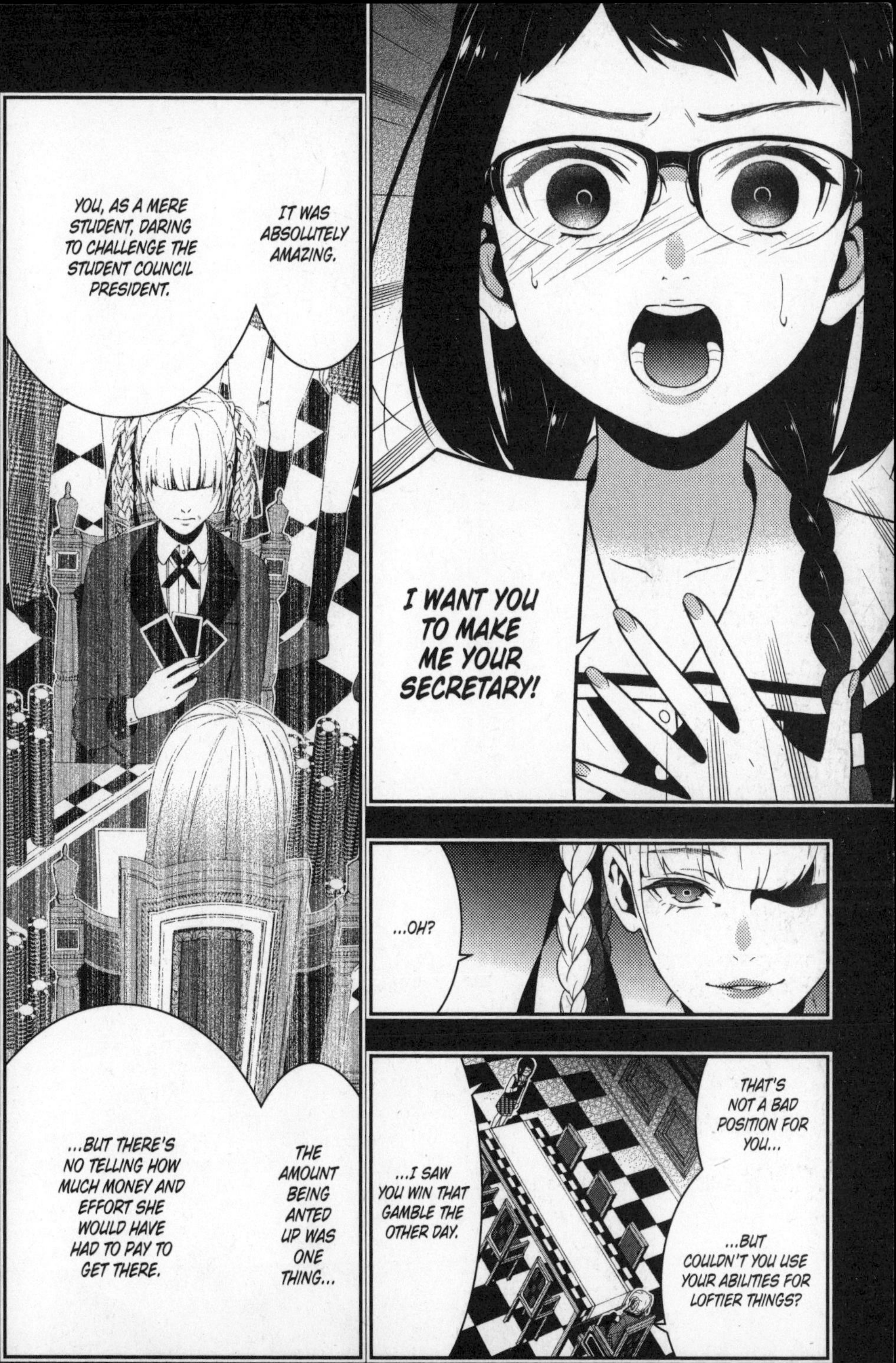
I WANT YOU TO MAKE ME YOUR SECRETARY!
...OH?
THAT'S NOT A BAD POSITION FOR YOU...
...I SAW YOU WIN THAT GAMBLE THE OTHER DAY.
...BUT COULDN'T YOU USE YOUR ABILITIES FOR LOFTIER THINGS?
IT WAS ABSOLUTELY AMAZING.
YOU, AS A MERE STUDENT, DARING TO CHALLENGE THE STUDENT COUNCIL PRESIDENT.
THE AMOUNT BEING ANTED UP WAS ONE THING...
...BUT THERE'S NO TELLING HOW MUCH MONEY AND EFFORT SHE WOULD HAVE HAD TO PAY TO GET THERE.

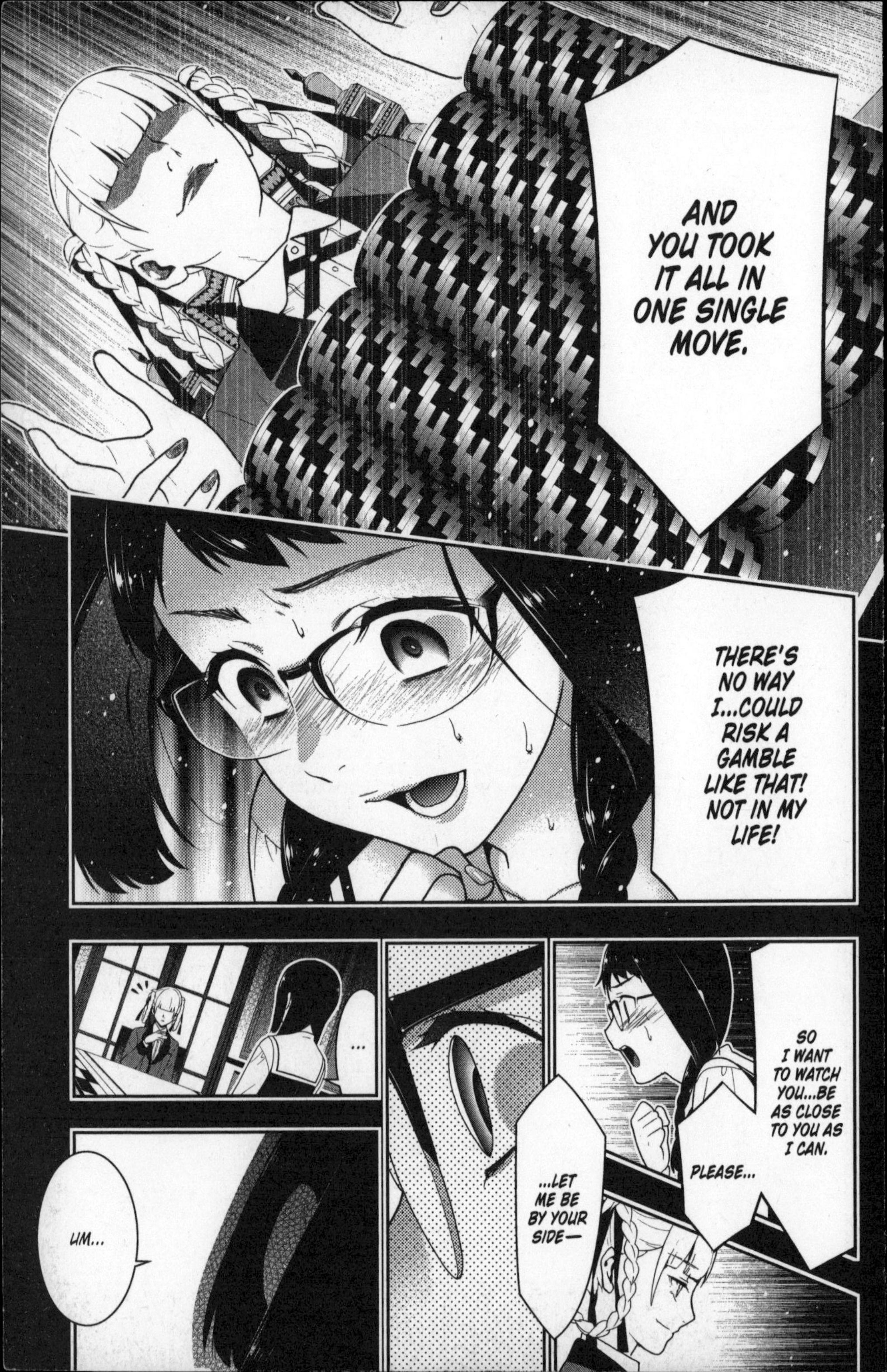
AND YOU TOOK IT ALL IN ONE SINGLE MOVE.
THERE'S NO WAY I...COULD RISK A GAMBLE LIKE THAT! NOT IN MY LIFE!
SO I WANT TO WATCH YOU...BE AS CLOSE TO YOU AS I CAN.
PLEASE...
...LET ME BE BY YOUR SIDE—
...
UM...

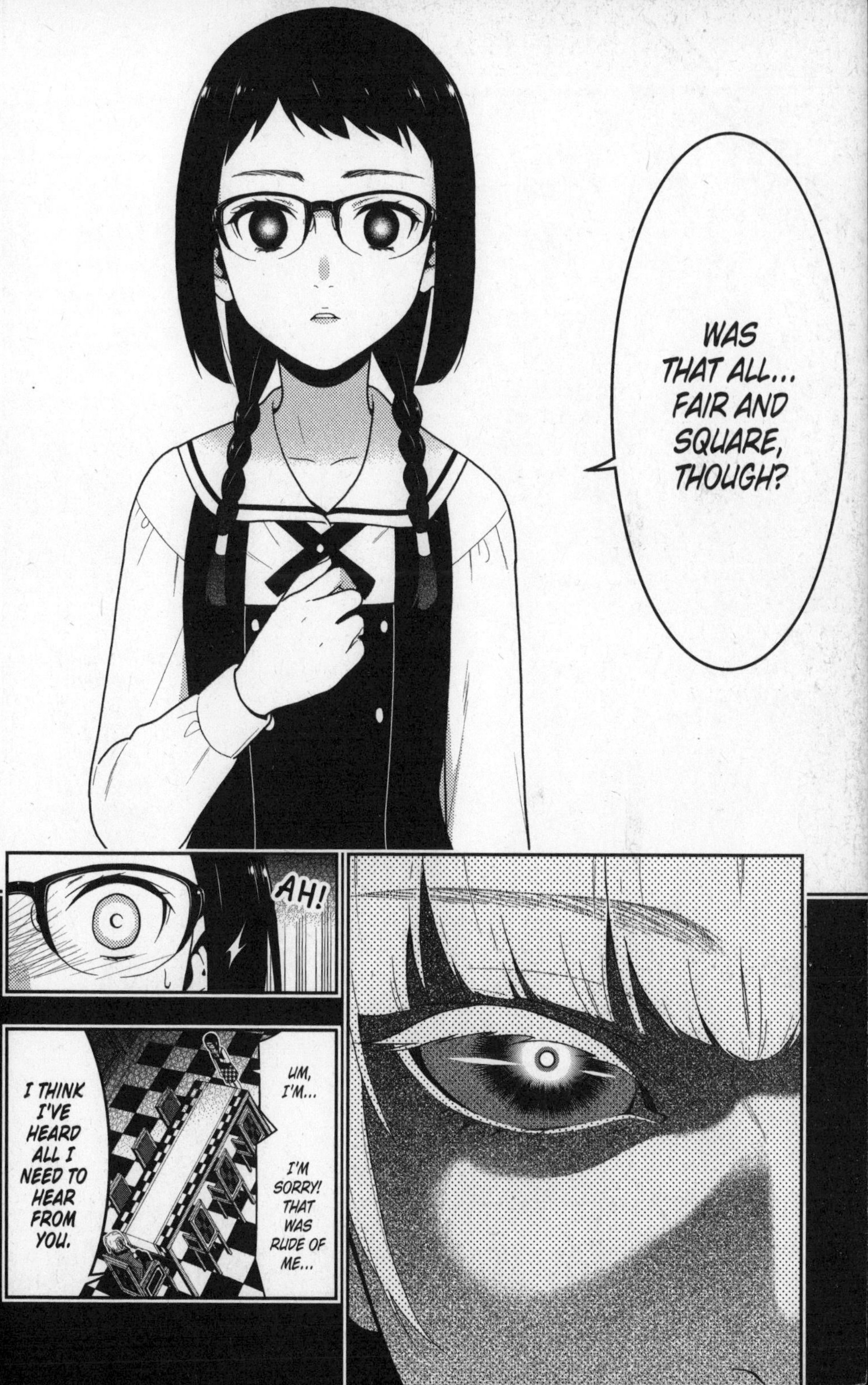
WAS THAT ALL... FAIR AND SQUARE, THOUGH?
AH!
UM, I'M...
I'M SORRY! THAT WAS RUDE OF ME...
I THINK I'VE HEARD ALL I NEED TO HEAR FROM YOU.

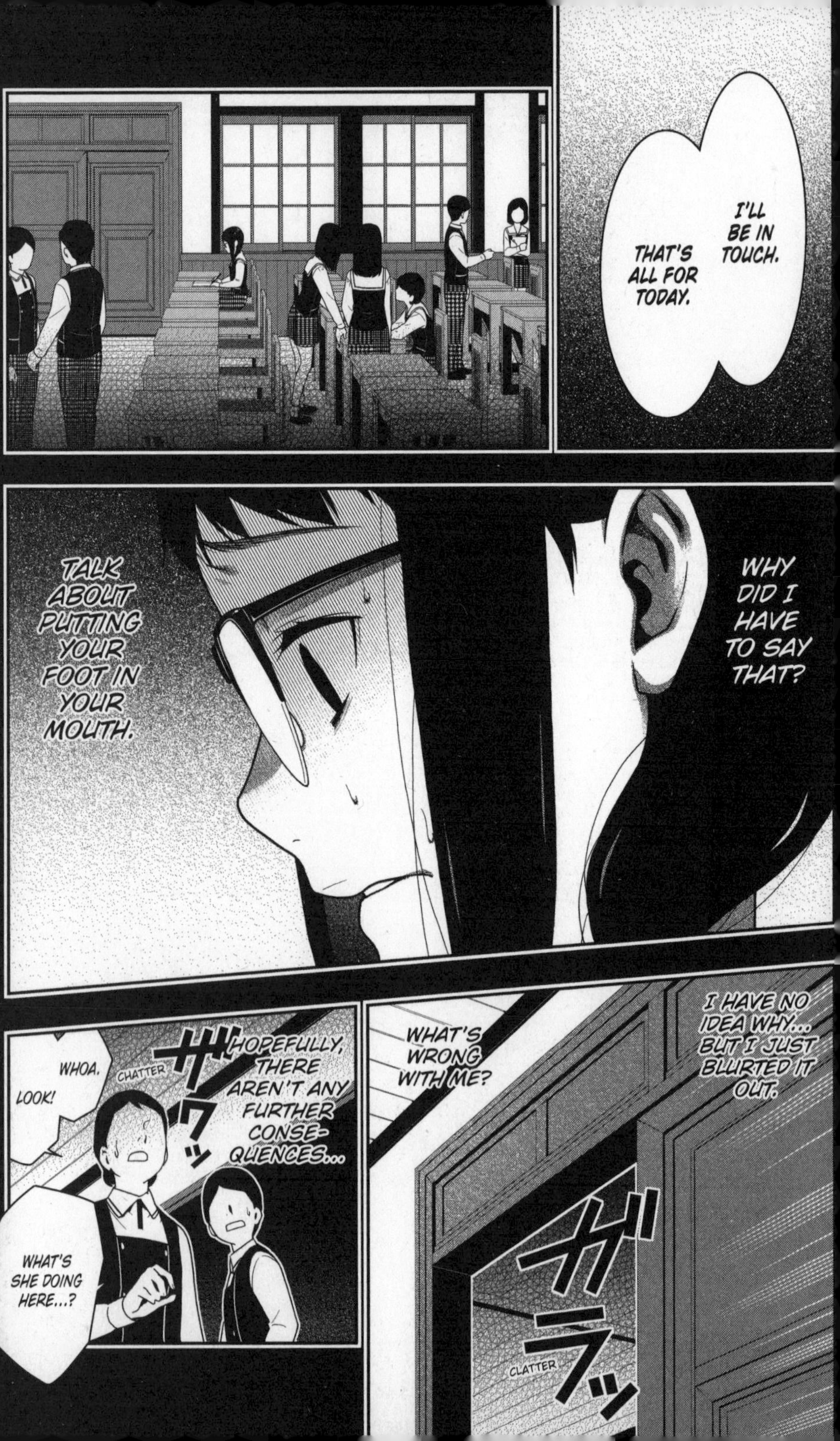
I'LL BE IN TOUCH.
THAT'S ALL FOR TODAY.
WHY DID I HAVE TO SAY THAT?
TALK ABOUT PUTTING YOUR FOOT IN YOUR MOUTH.
I HAVE NO IDEA WHY... BUT I JUST BLURTED IT OUT.
WHAT'S WRONG WITH ME?
CLATTER
HOPEFULLY, THERE AREN'T ANY FURTHER CONSE-QUENCES...
CHATTER
WHOA.
LOOK!
WHAT'S SHE DOING HERE...?

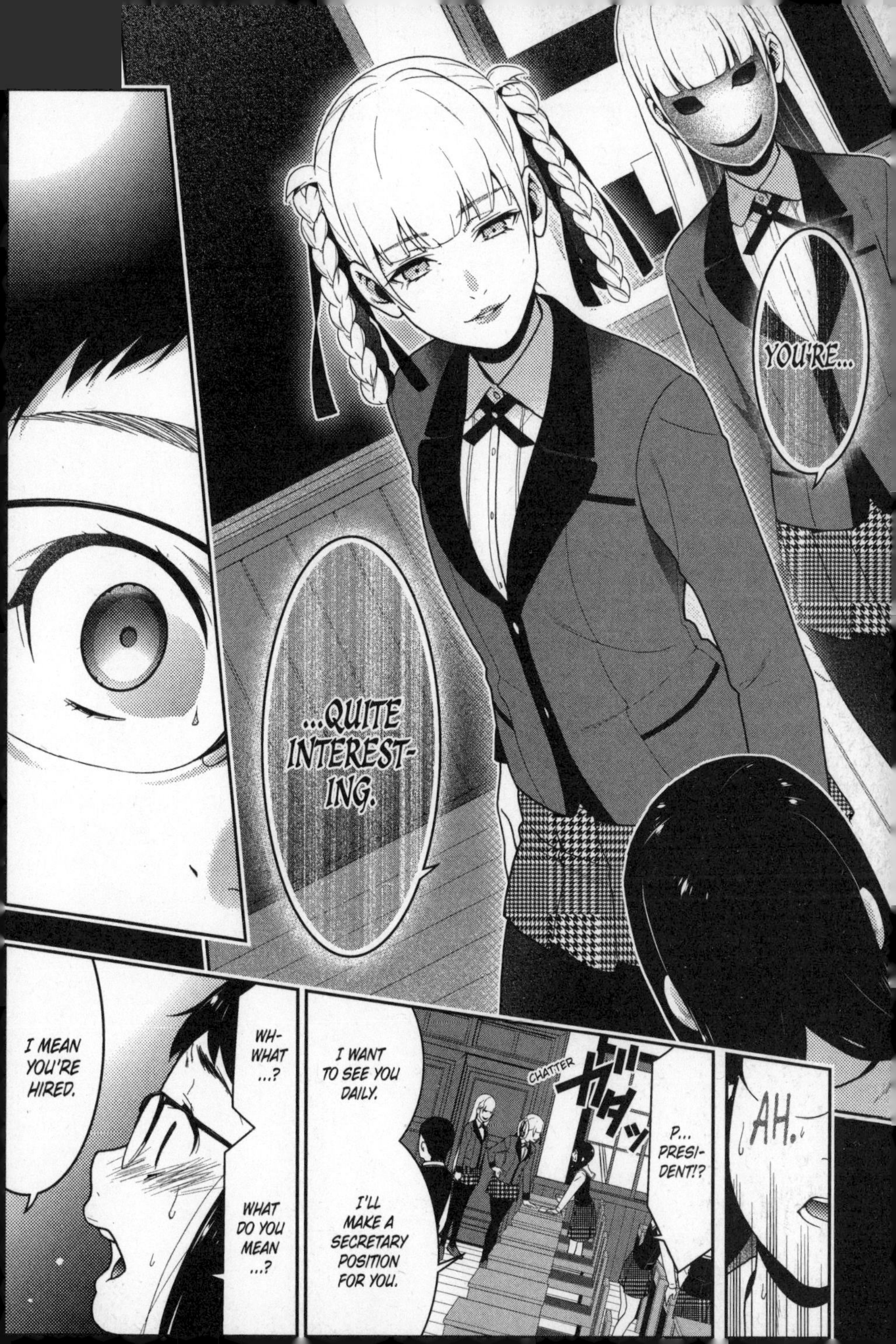
YOU'RE...
...QUITE INTEREST-ING.
AH.
P... PRESI-DENT!?
ガタッ
CHATTER
I WANT TO SEE YOU DAILY.
I'LL MAKE A SECRETARY POSITION FOR YOU.
WH-WHAT ...?
WHAT DO YOU MEAN ...?
I MEAN YOU'RE HIRED.

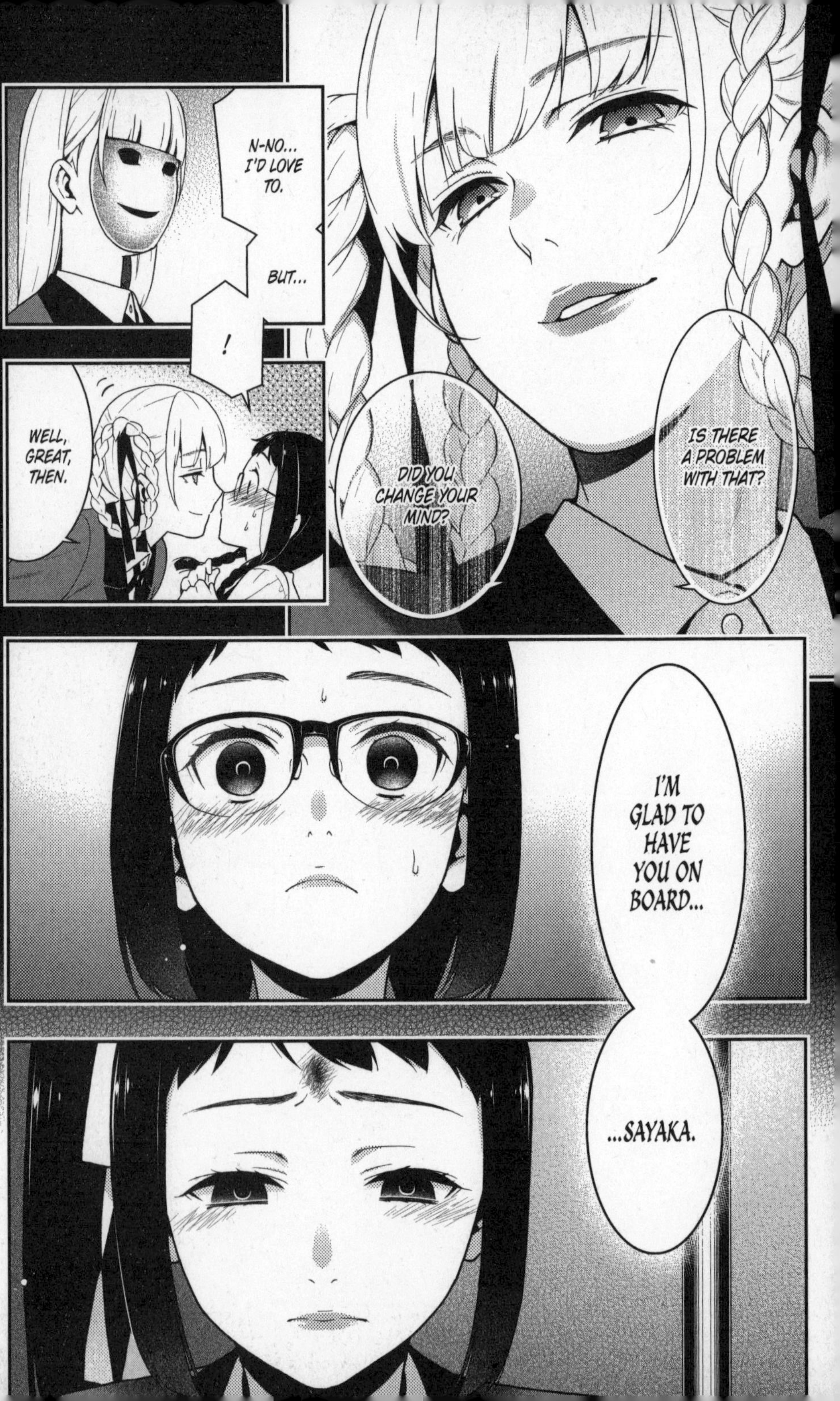
IS THERE A PROBLEM WITH THAT?
DID YOU CHANGE YOUR MIND?
N-NO... I'D LOVE TO.
BUT...
!
WELL, GREAT, THEN.
I'M GLAD TO HAVE YOU ON BOARD...
...SAYAKA.

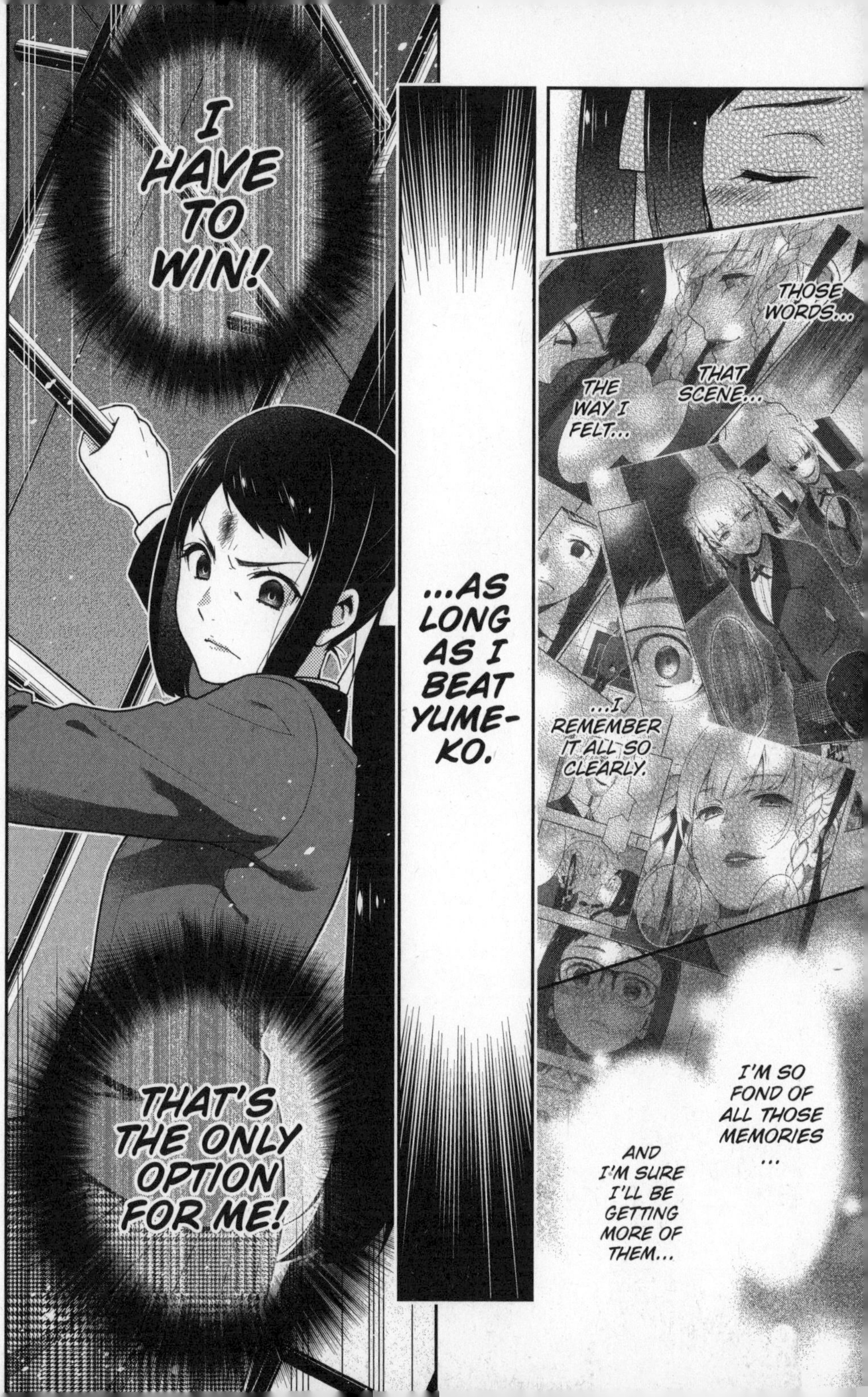
THOSE WORDS...
THAT SCENE...
THE WAY I FELT...
...I REMEMBER IT ALL SO CLEARLY.
I'M SO FOND OF ALL THOSE MEMORIES...
AND I'M SURE I'LL BE GETTING MORE OF THEM...
...AS LONG AS I BEAT YUME-KO.
I HAVE TO WIN!
THAT'S THE ONLY OPTION FOR ME!

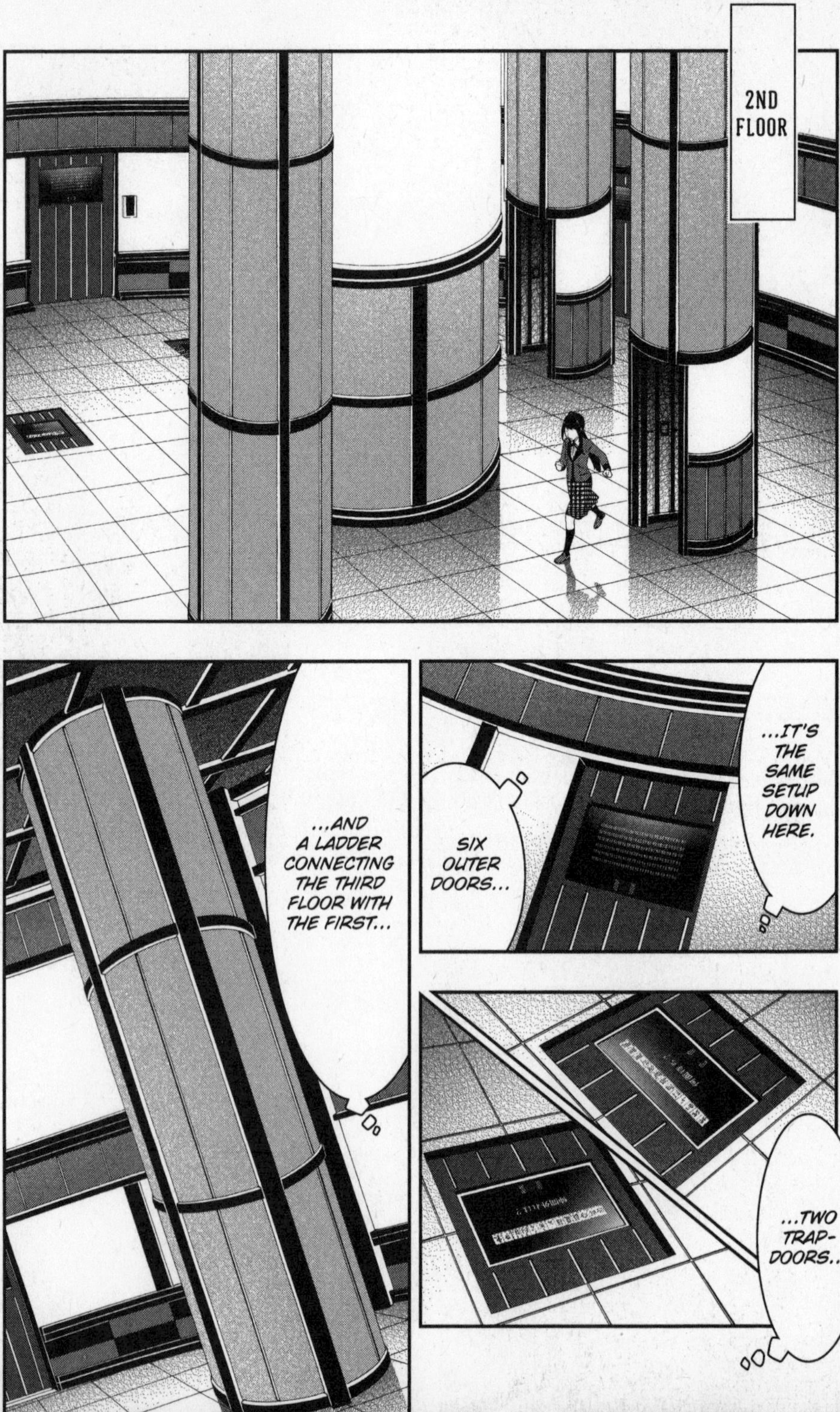
2ND FLOOR
...IT'S THE SAME SETUP DOWN HERE.
SIX OUTER DOORS...
...TWO TRAP-DOORS...
...AND A LADDER CONNECTING THE THIRD FLOOR WITH THE FIRST...

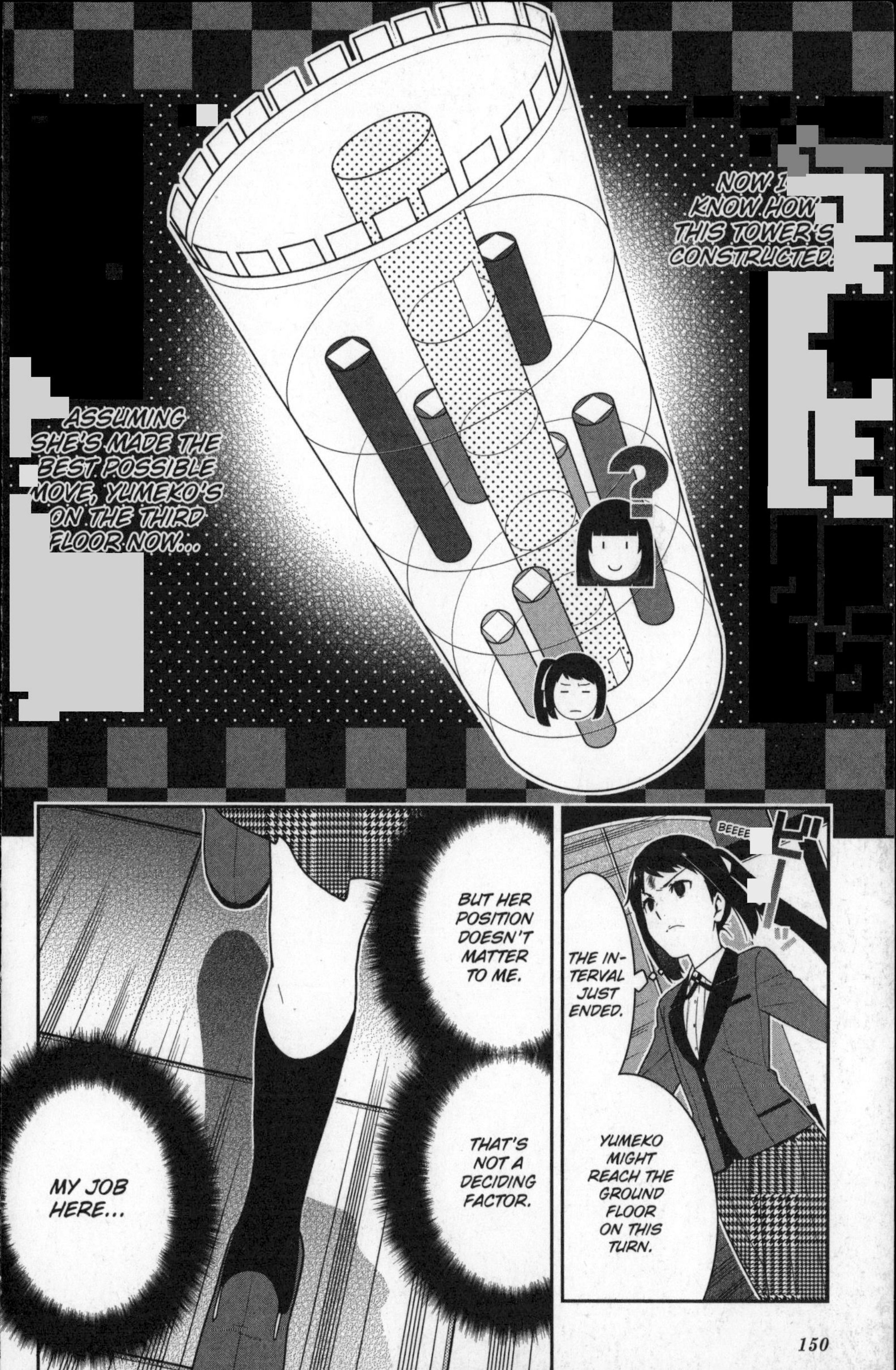
NOW I KNOW HOW THIS TOWER'S CONSTRUCTED.
ASSUMING SHE'S MADE THE BEST POSSIBLE MOVE, YUMEKO'S ON THE THIRD FLOOR NOW...
THE IN-TERVAL JUST ENDED.
YUMEKO MIGHT REACH THE GROUND FLOOR ON THIS TURN.
BUT HER POSITION DOESN'T MATTER TO ME.
THAT'S NOT A DECIDING FACTOR.
MY JOB HERE...

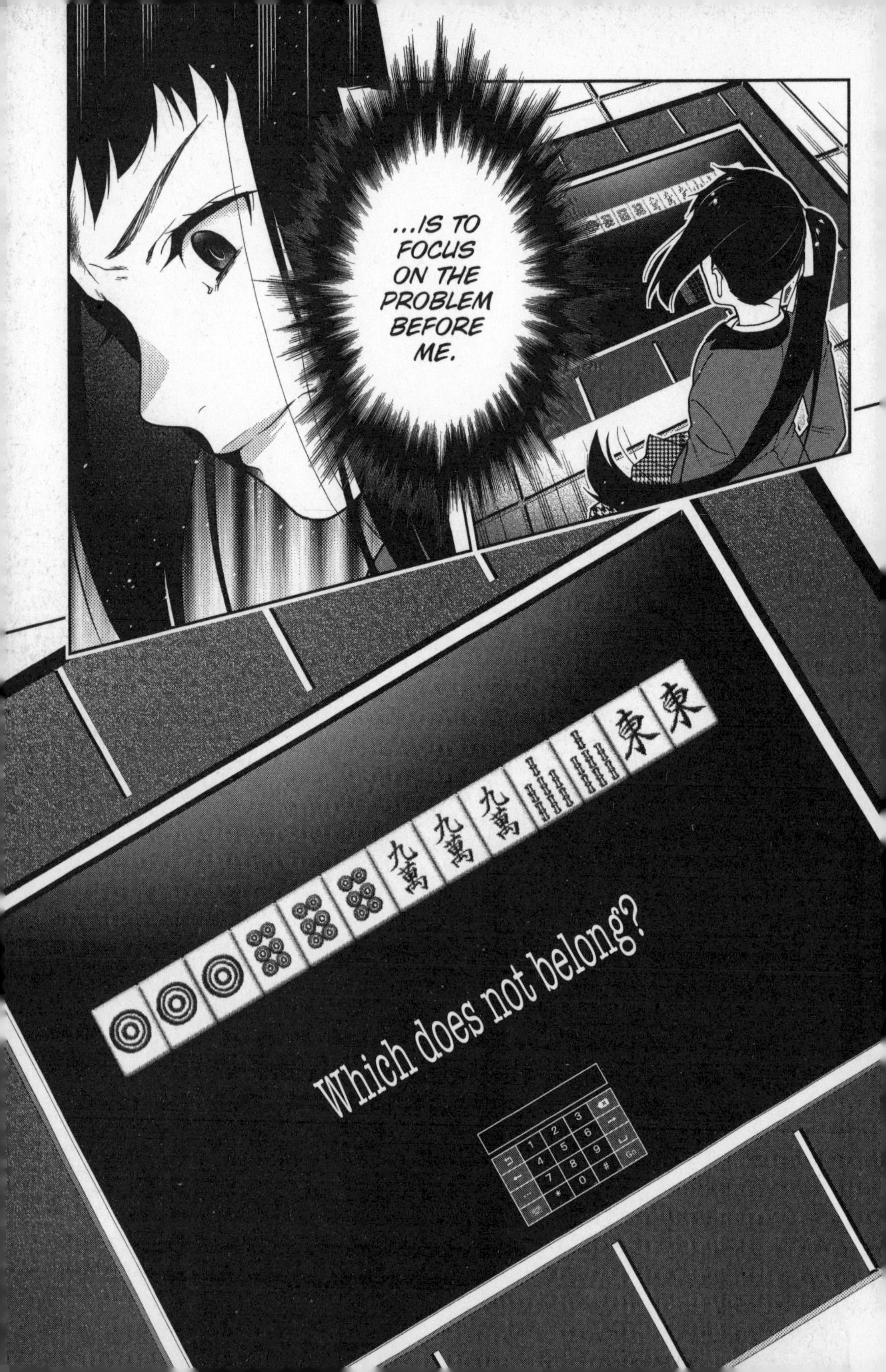
...IS TO FOCUS ON THE PROBLEM BEFORE ME.
九萬
九萬
九萬
東
東
Which does not belong?
1
2
3
4
5
6
7
8
9
*
0
#
Go

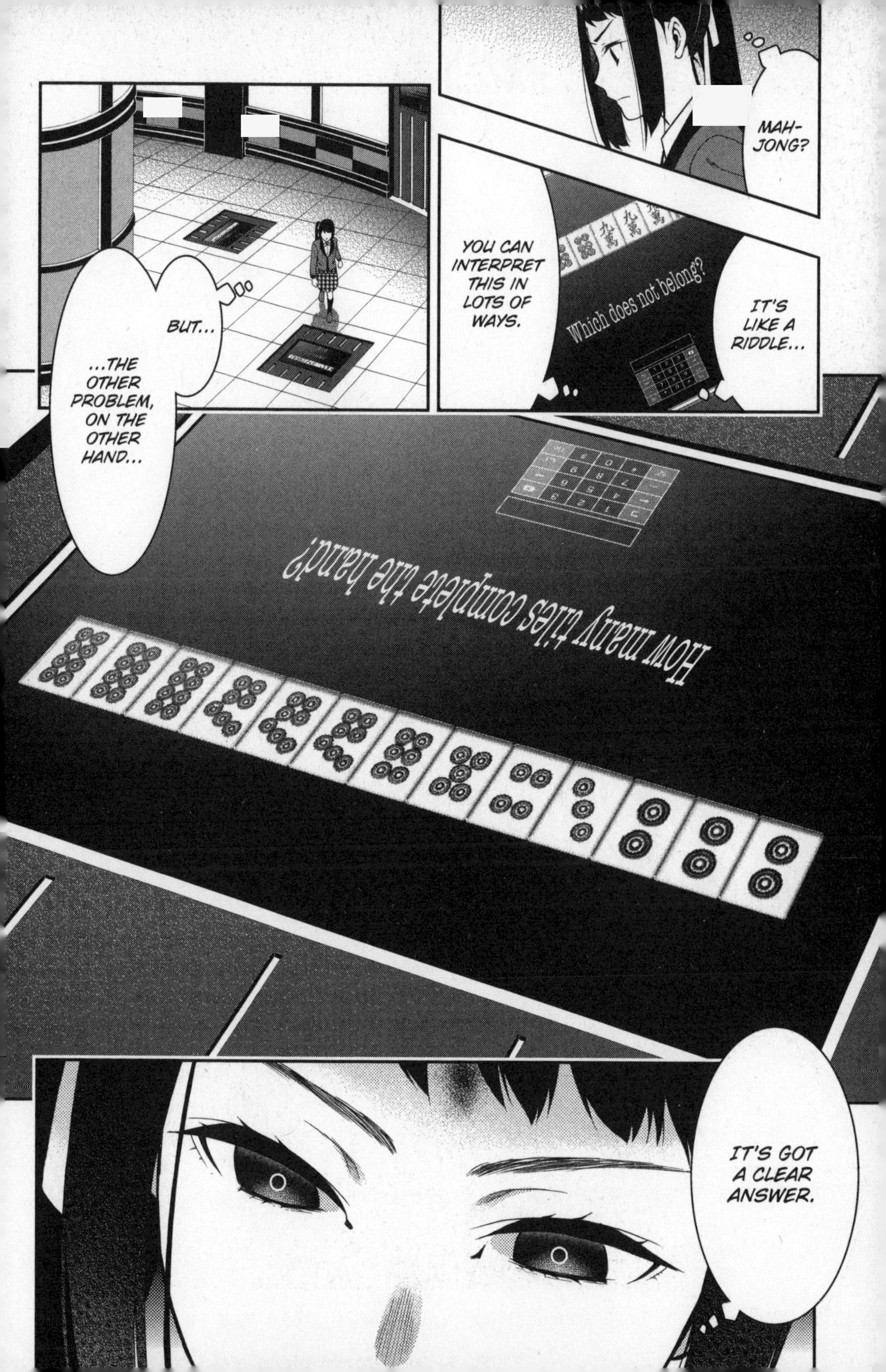
MAH-JONG?
Which does not belong?
IT'S LIKE A RIDDLE...
YOU CAN INTERPRET THIS IN LOTS OF WAYS.
BUT...
...THE OTHER PROBLEM, ON THE OTHER HAND...
How many tiles complete the hand?
IT'S GOT A CLEAR ANSWER.

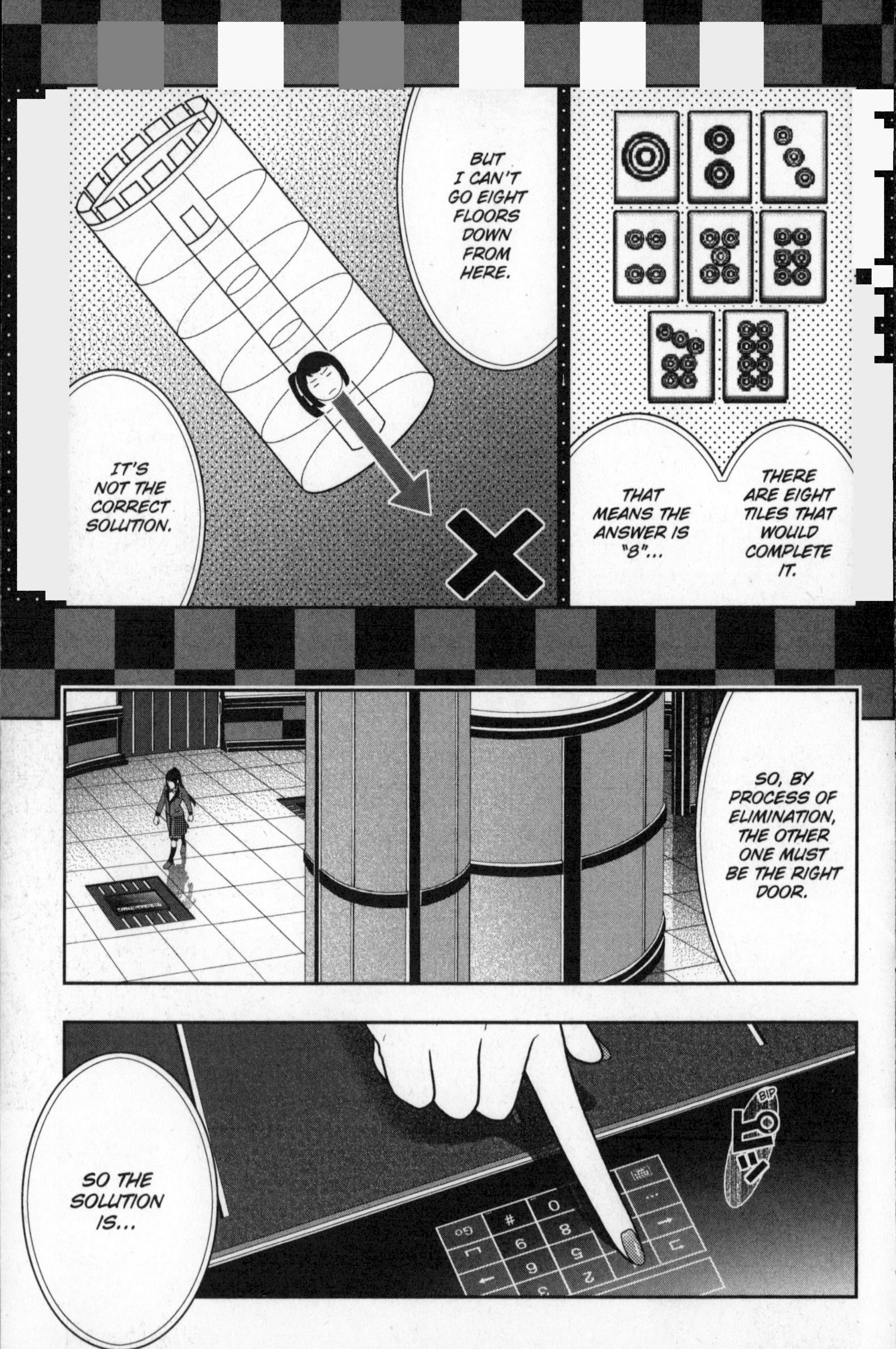
THERE ARE EIGHT TILES THAT WOULD COMPLETE IT.
THAT MEANS THE ANSWER IS "8"...
BUT I CAN'T GO EIGHT FLOORS DOWN FROM HERE.
IT'S NOT THE CORRECT SOLUTION.
SO, BY PROCESS OF ELIMINATION, THE OTHER ONE MUST BE THE RIGHT DOOR.
BIP
SO THE SOLUTION IS...

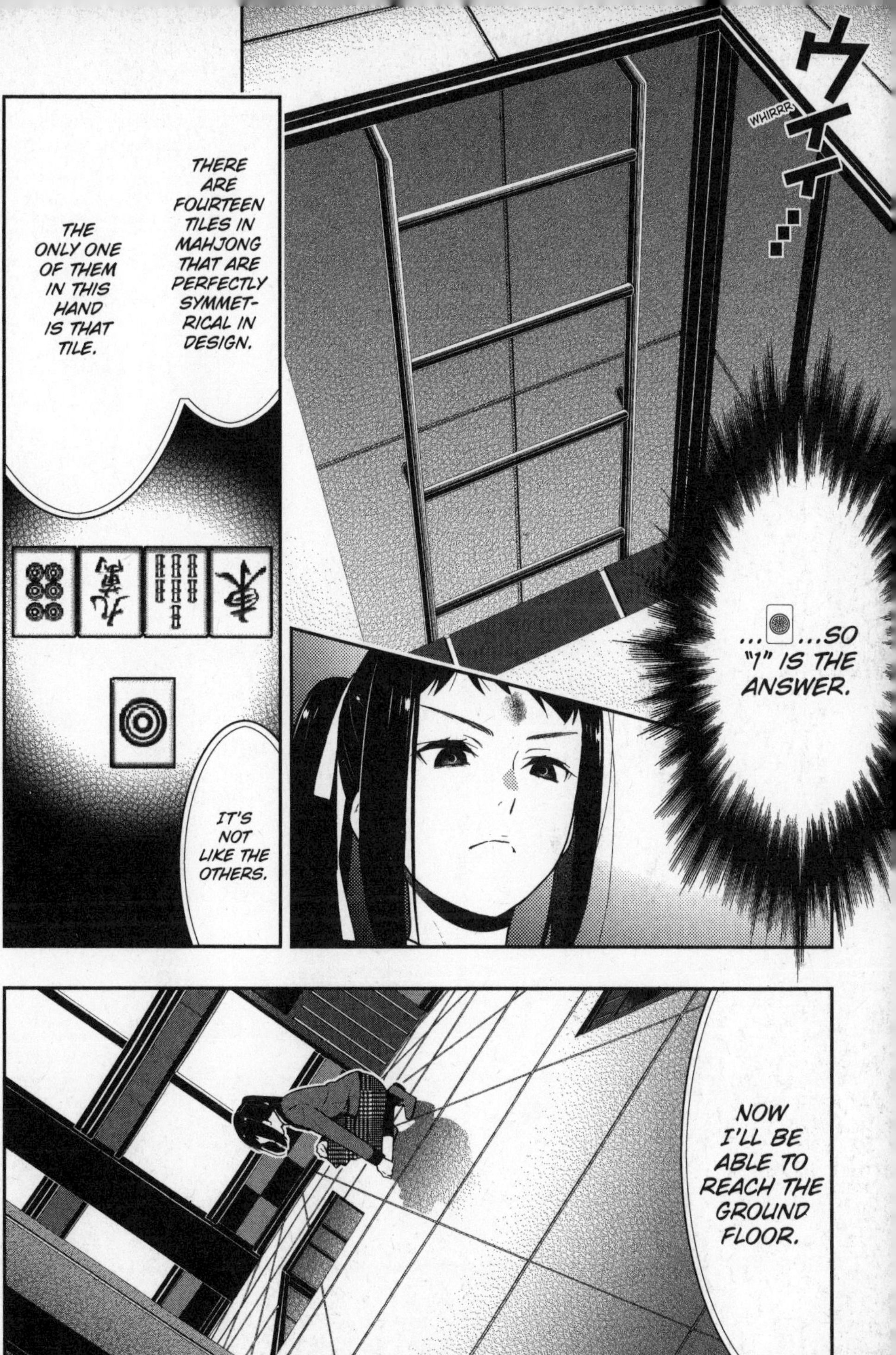
WHIRRR
... ...SO "1" IS THE ANSWER.
THERE ARE FOURTEEN TILES IN MAHJONG THAT ARE PERFECTLY SYMMET-RICAL IN DESIGN.
THE ONLY ONE OF THEM IN THIS HAND IS THAT TILE.
IT'S NOT LIKE THE OTHERS.
NOW I'LL BE ABLE TO REACH THE GROUND FLOOR.

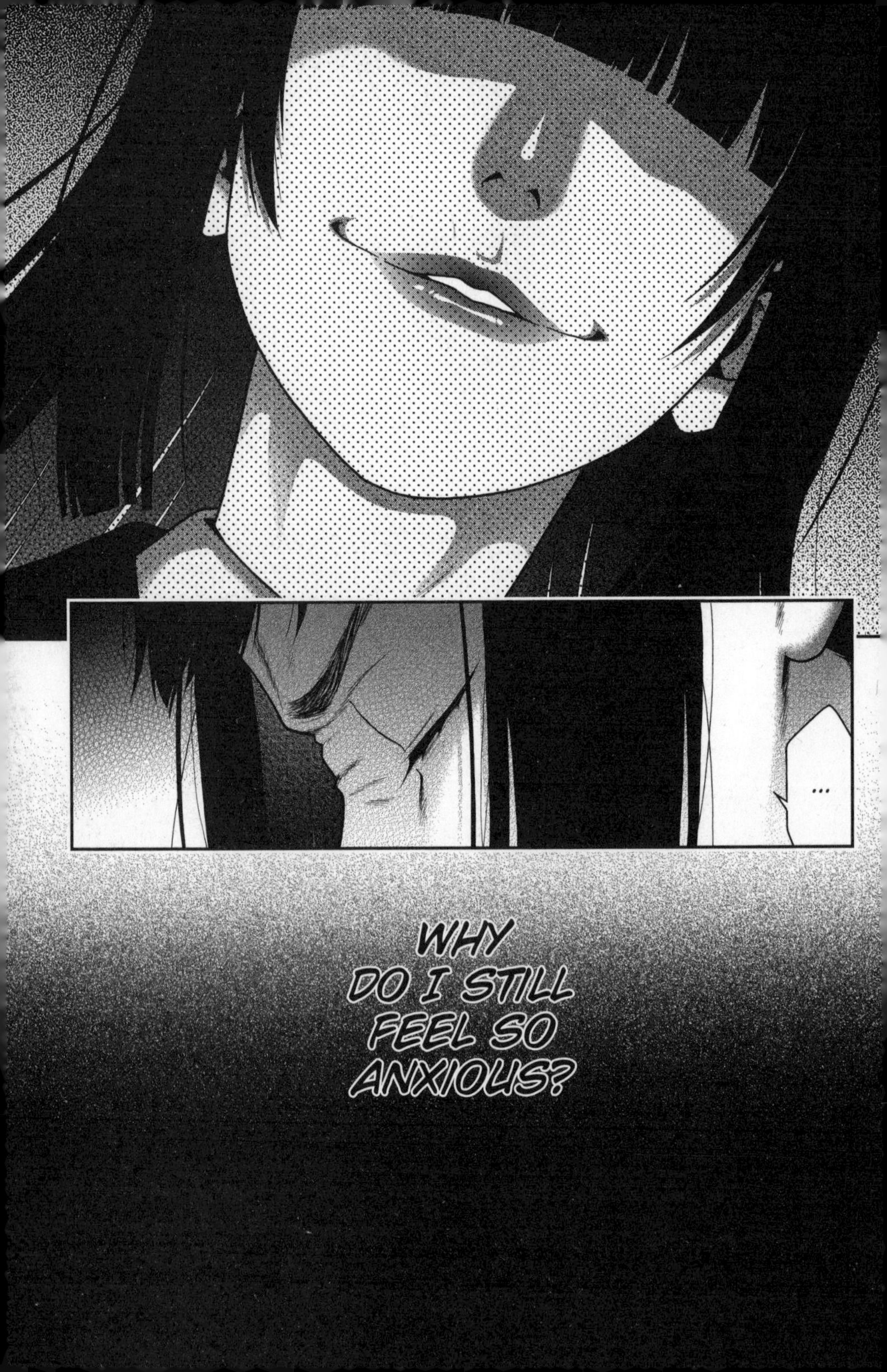
...
WHY DO I STILL FEEL SO ANXIOUS?

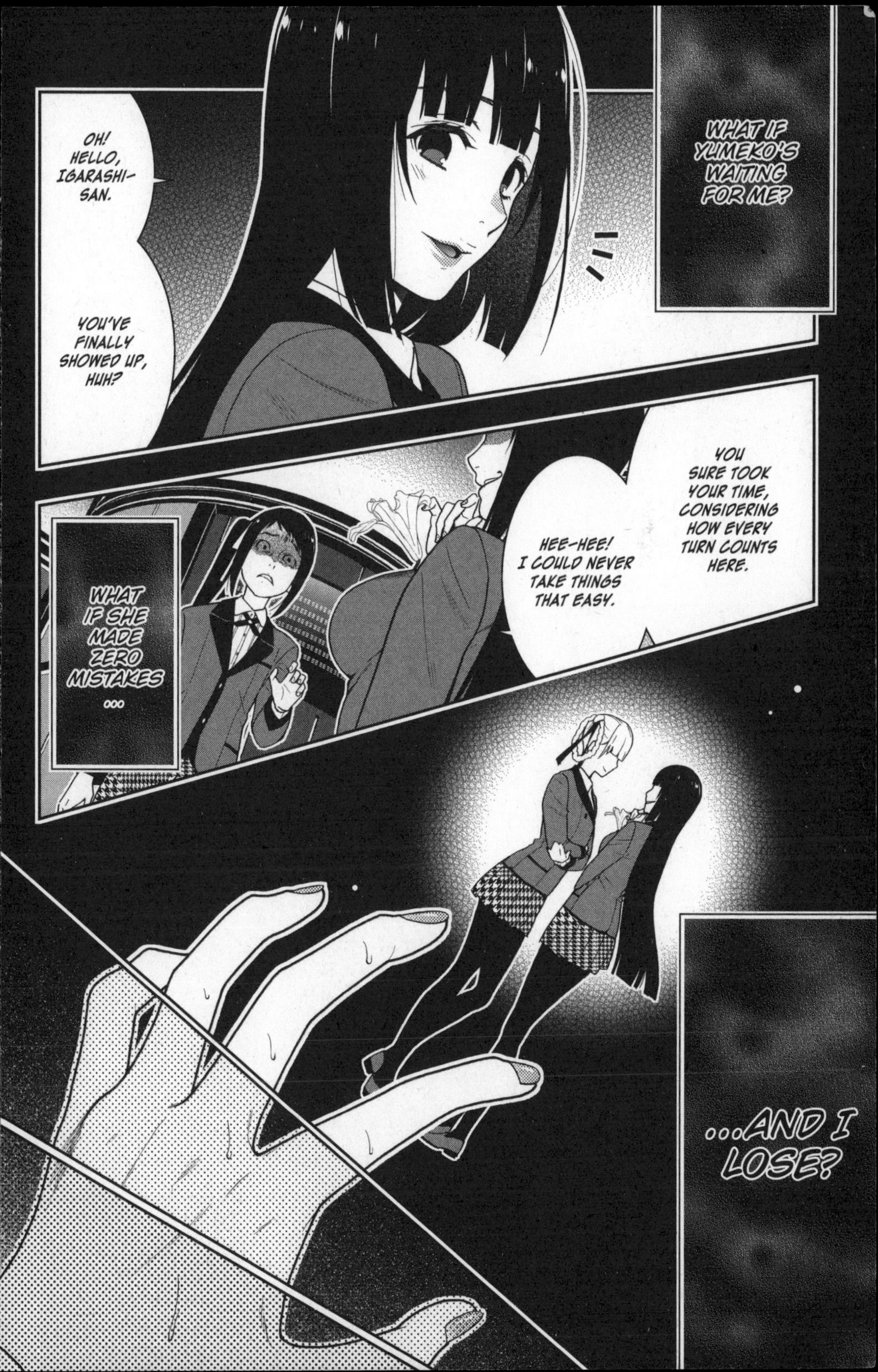
WHAT IF YUMEKO'S WAITING FOR ME?
OH! HELLO, IGARASHI-SAN.
YOU'VE FINALLY SHOWED UP, HUH?
YOU SURE TOOK YOUR TIME, CONSIDERING HOW EVERY TURN COUNTS HERE.
HEE-HEE! I COULD NEVER TAKE THINGS THAT EASY.
WHAT IF SHE MADE ZERO MISTAKES...
...AND I LOSE?

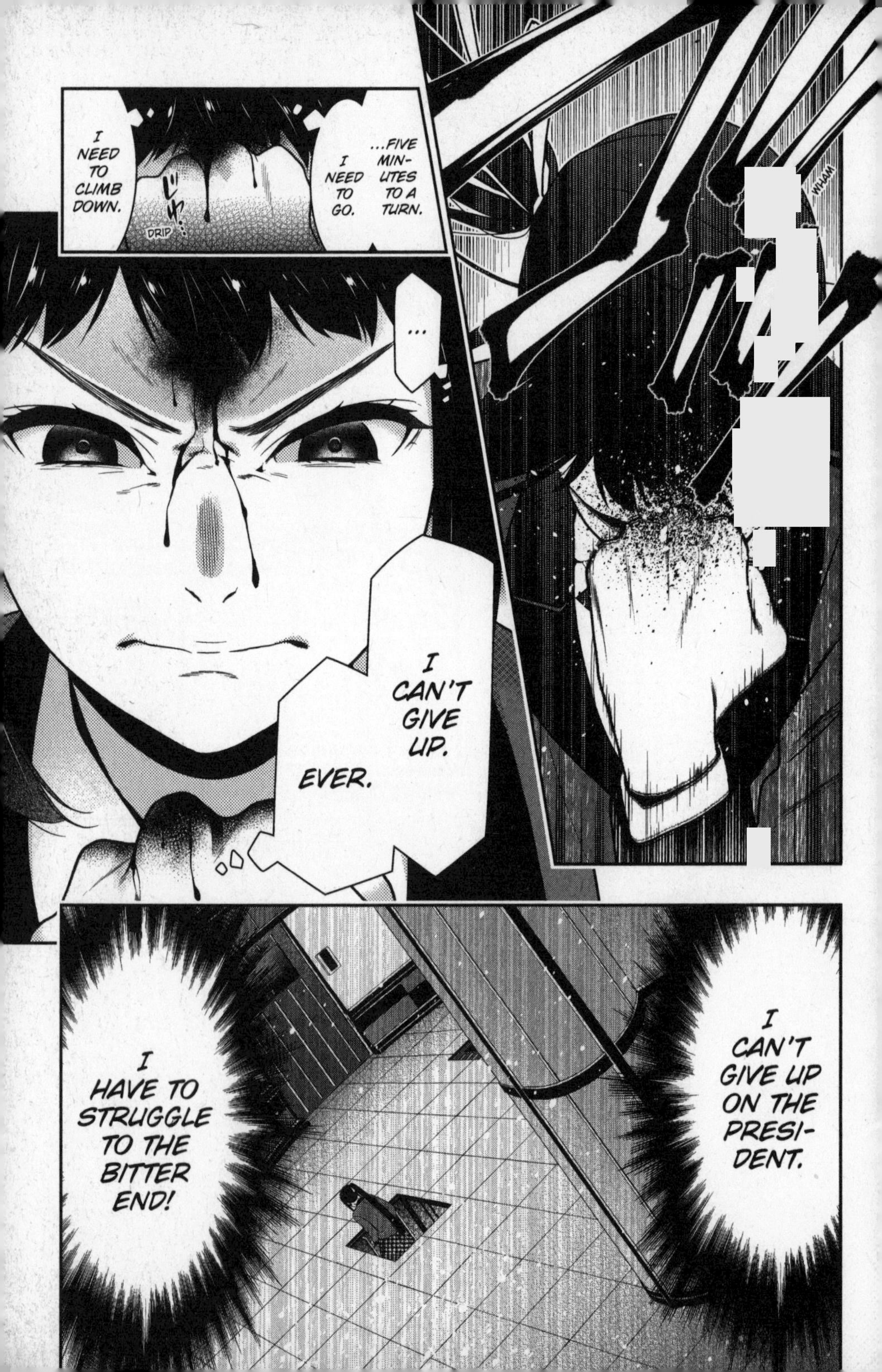
WHAM
...FIVE MIN-UTES TO A TURN.
I NEED TO GO.
DRIP
I NEED TO CLIMB DOWN.
...
I CAN'T GIVE UP.
EVER.
I CAN'T GIVE UP ON THE PRESI-DENT.
I HAVE TO STRUGGLE TO THE BITTER END!

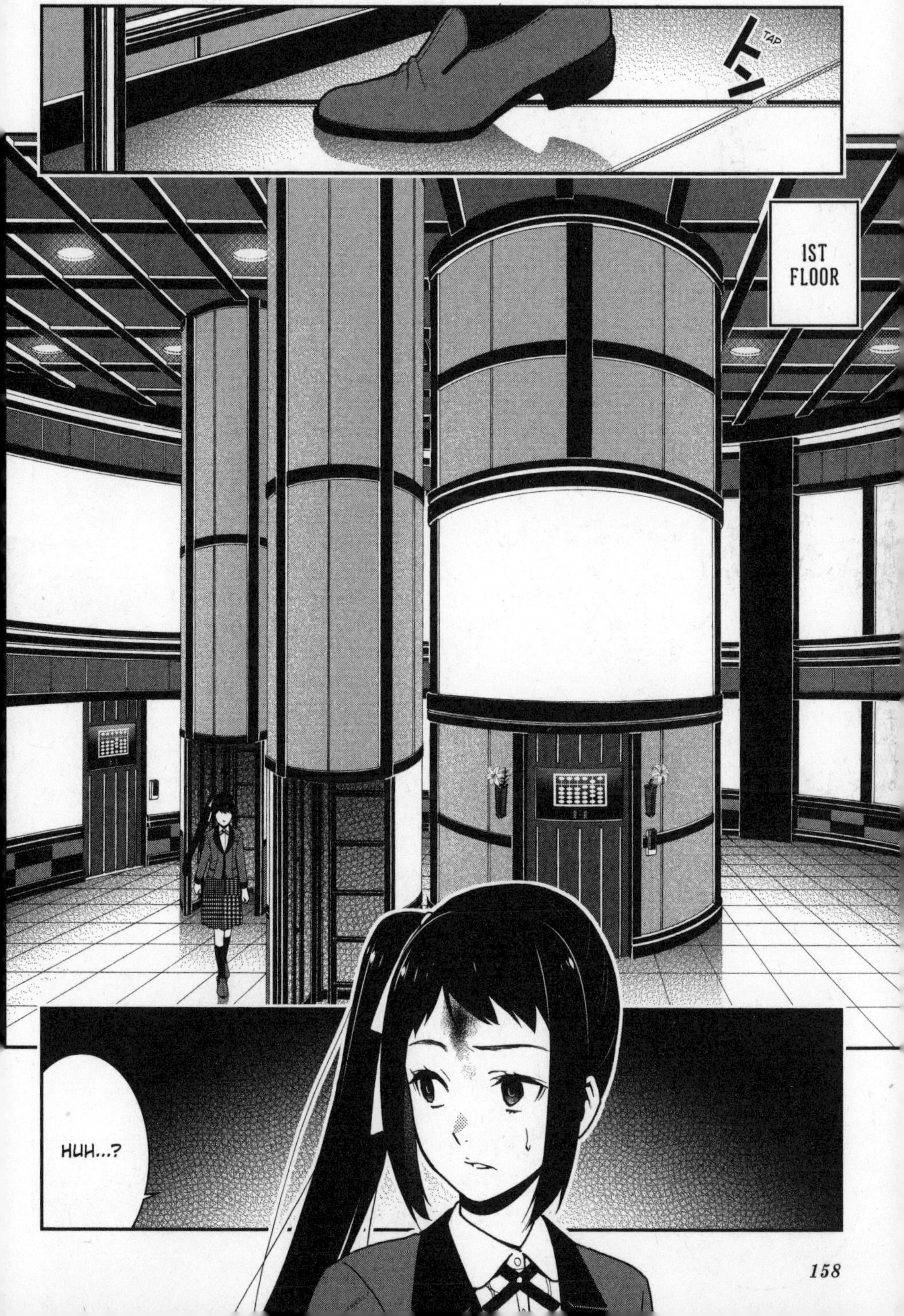
トン
TAP
1ST
FLOOR
HUH...?

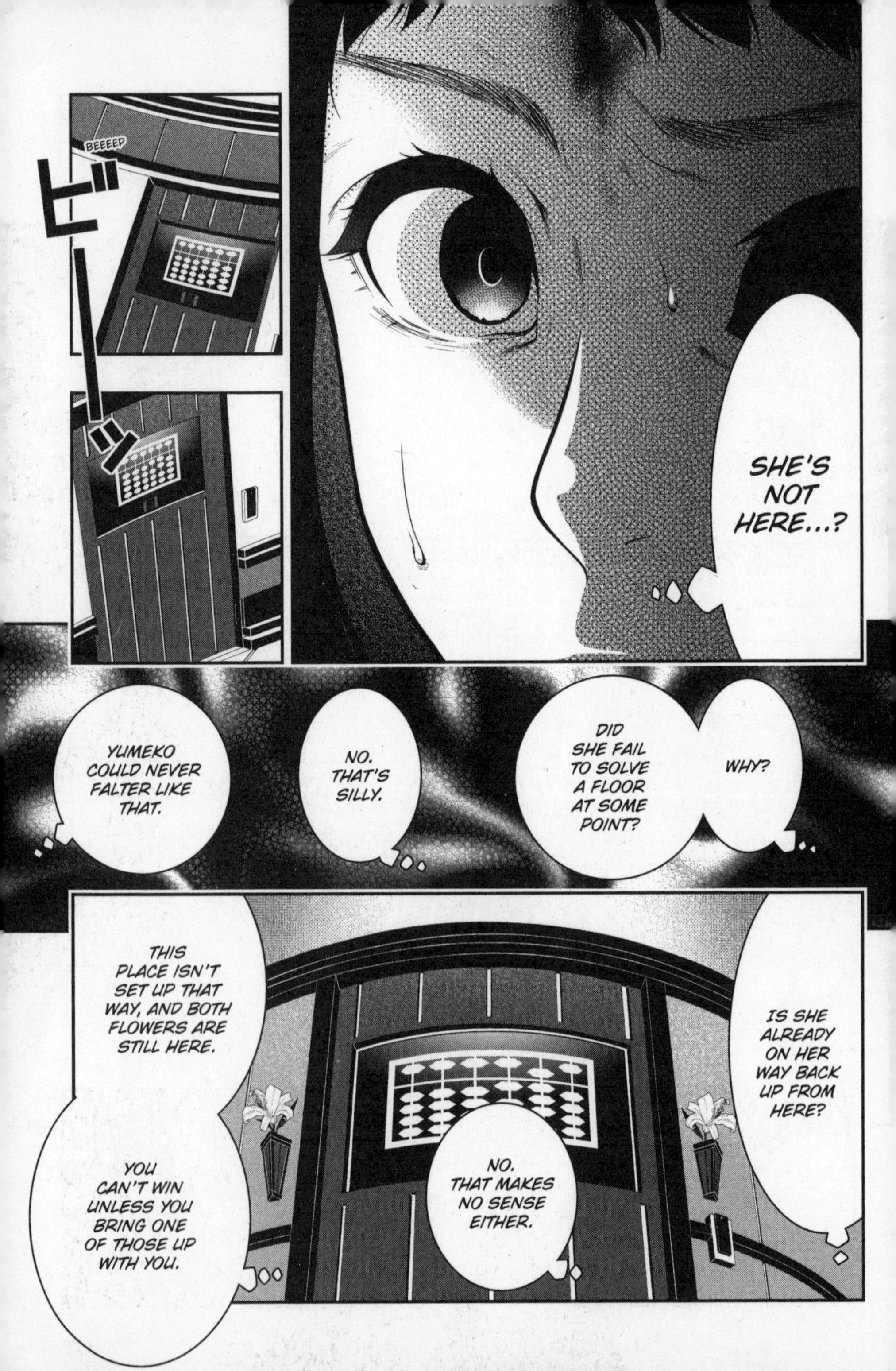
SHE'S NOT HERE...?
BEEEEP
WHY?
DID SHE FAIL TO SOLVE A FLOOR AT SOME POINT?
NO. THAT'S SILLY.
YUMEKO COULD NEVER FALTER LIKE THAT.
IS SHE ALREADY ON HER WAY BACK UP FROM HERE?
NO. THAT MAKES NO SENSE EITHER.
THIS PLACE ISN'T SET UP THAT WAY, AND BOTH FLOWERS ARE STILL HERE.
YOU CAN'T WIN UNLESS YOU BRING ONE OF THOSE UP WITH YOU.

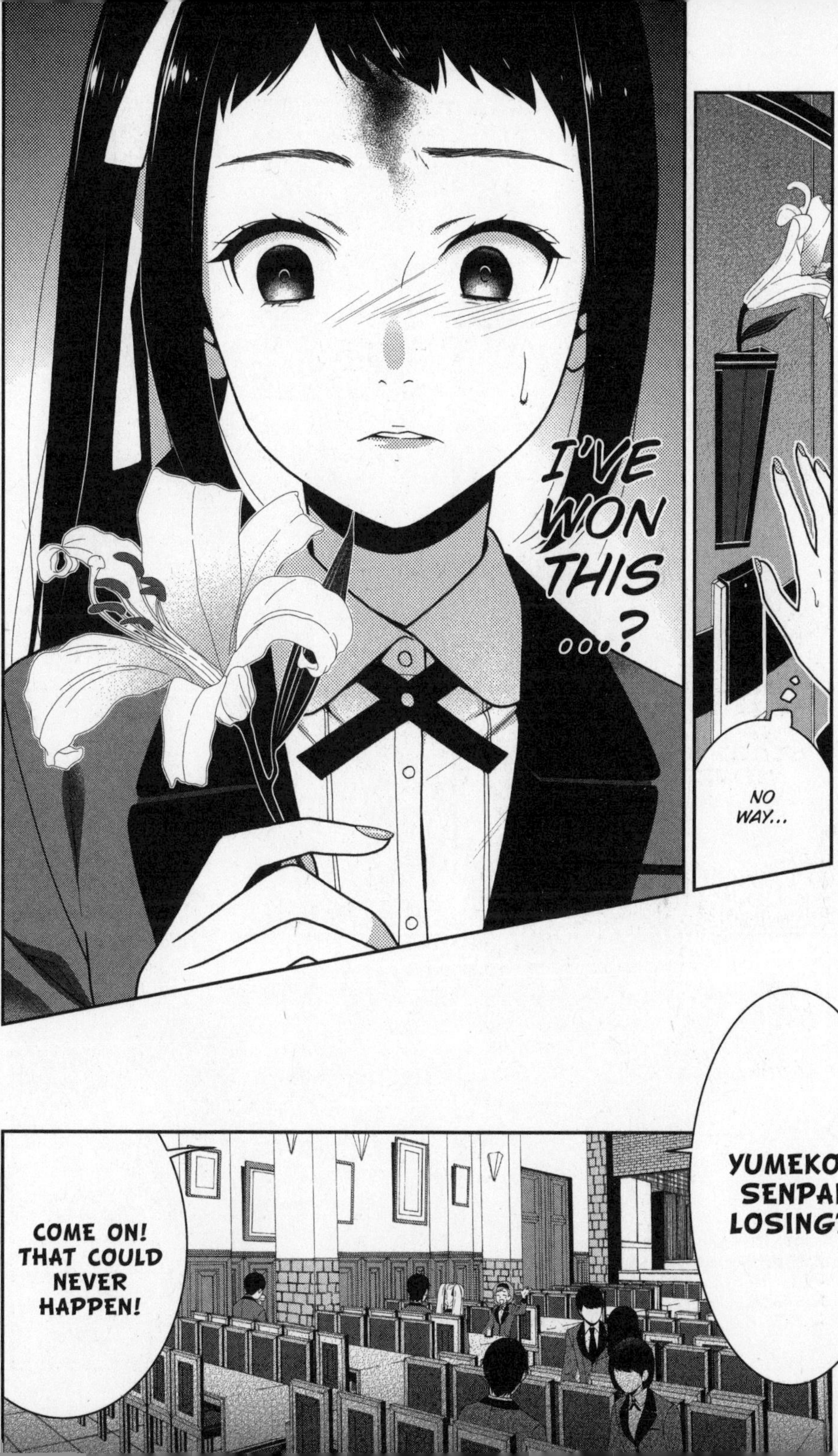
NO WAY...
I'VE WON THIS ...?
YUMEKO-SENPAI LOSING?
COME ON! THAT COULD NEVER HAPPEN!

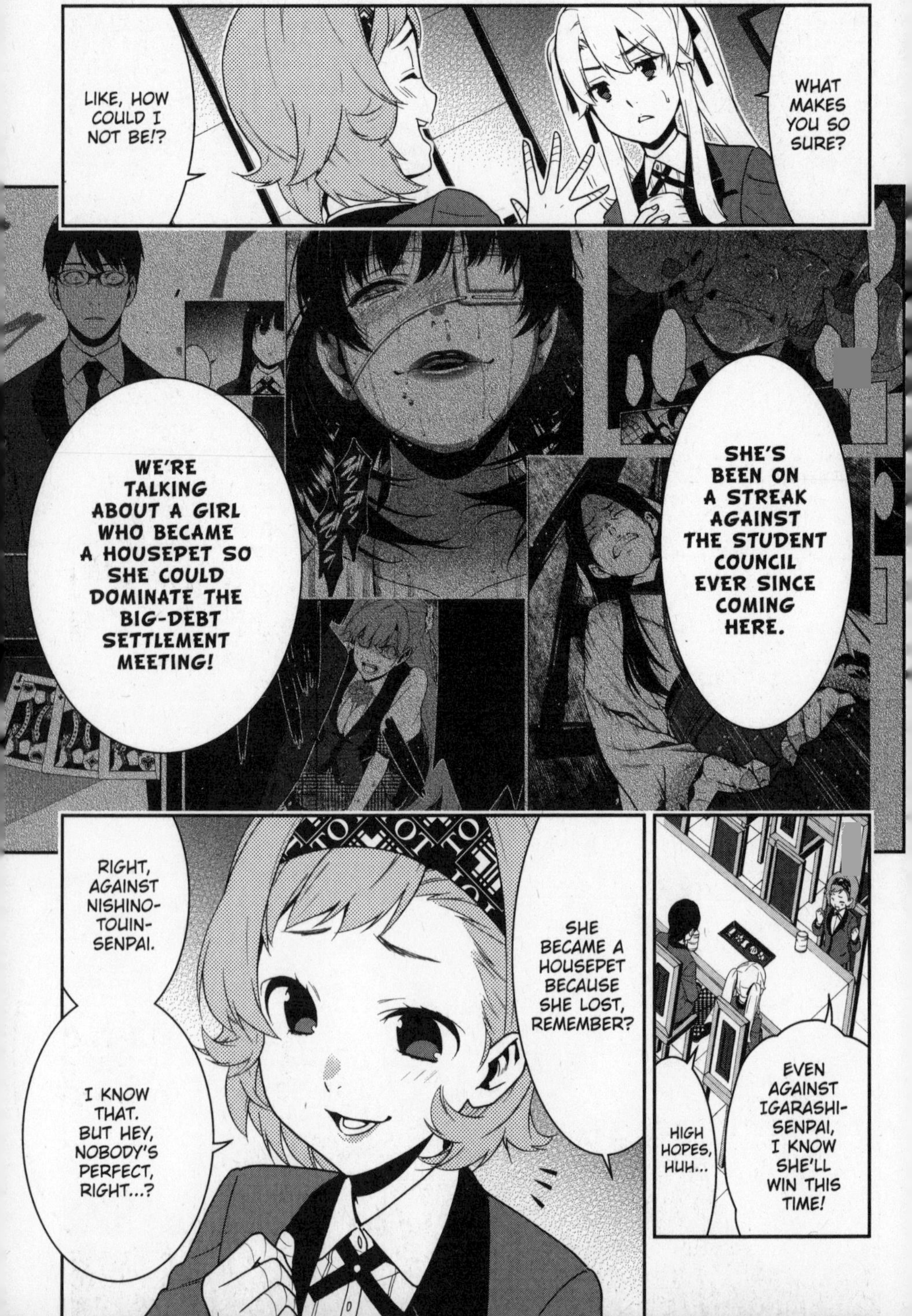
WHAT MAKES YOU SO SURE?
LIKE, HOW COULD I NOT BE!?
SHE'S BEEN ON A STREAK AGAINST THE STUDENT COUNCIL EVER SINCE COMING HERE.
WE'RE TALKING ABOUT A GIRL WHO BECAME A HOUSEPET SO SHE COULD DOMINATE THE BIG-DEBT SETTLEMENT MEETING!
EVEN AGAINST IGARASHI-SENPAI, I KNOW SHE'LL WIN THIS TIME!
HIGH HOPES, HUH...
SHE BECAME A HOUSEPET BECAUSE SHE LOST, REMEMBER?
RIGHT, AGAINST NISHINO-TOUIN-SENPAI.
I KNOW THAT. BUT HEY, NOBODY'S PERFECT, RIGHT...?

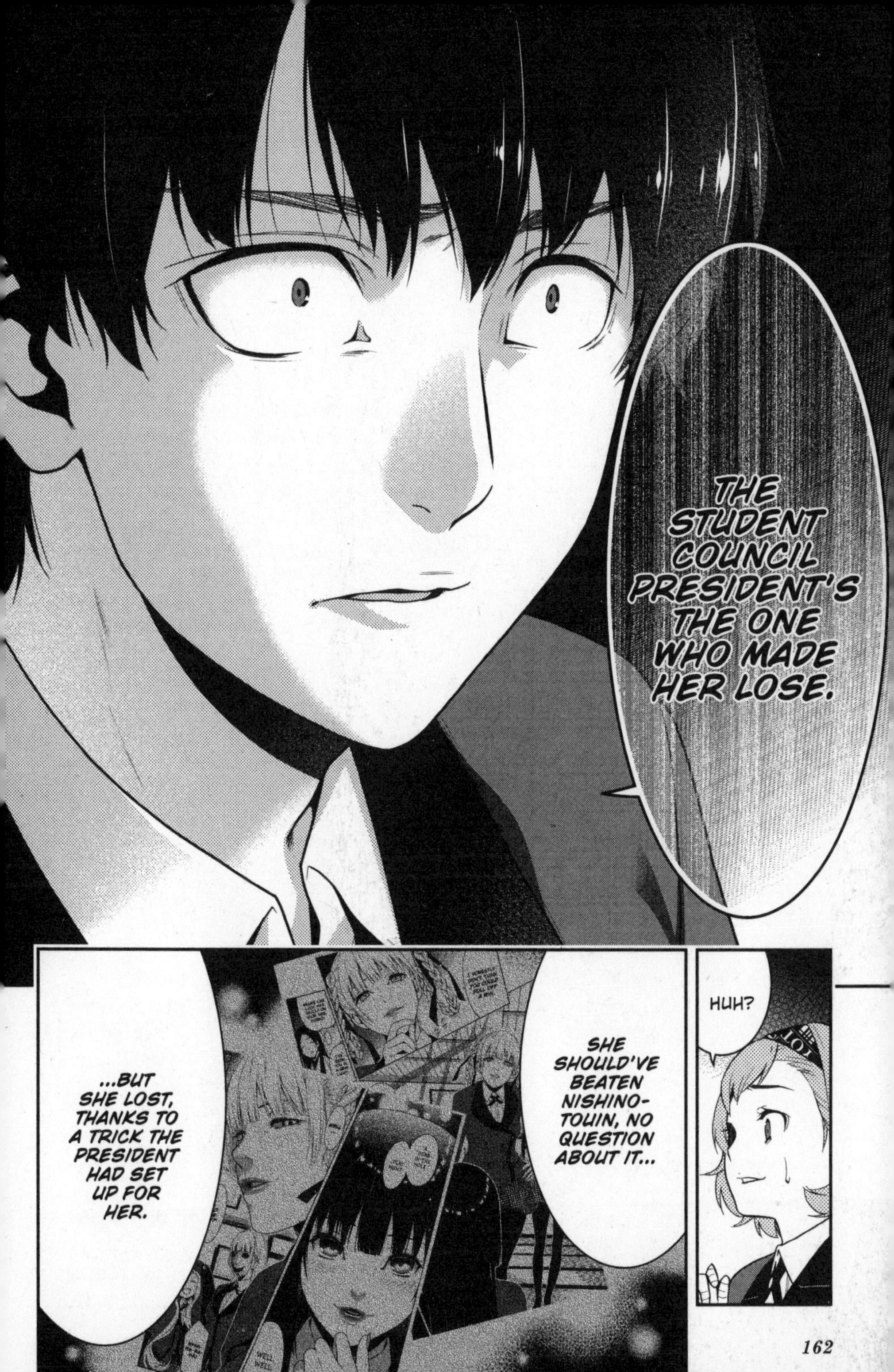
THE STUDENT COUNCIL PRESIDENT'S THE ONE WHO MADE HER LOSE.
HUH?
SHE SHOULD'VE BEATEN NISHINO-TOUIN, NO QUESTION ABOUT IT...
...BUT SHE LOST, THANKS TO A TRICK THE PRESIDENT HAD SET UP FOR HER.

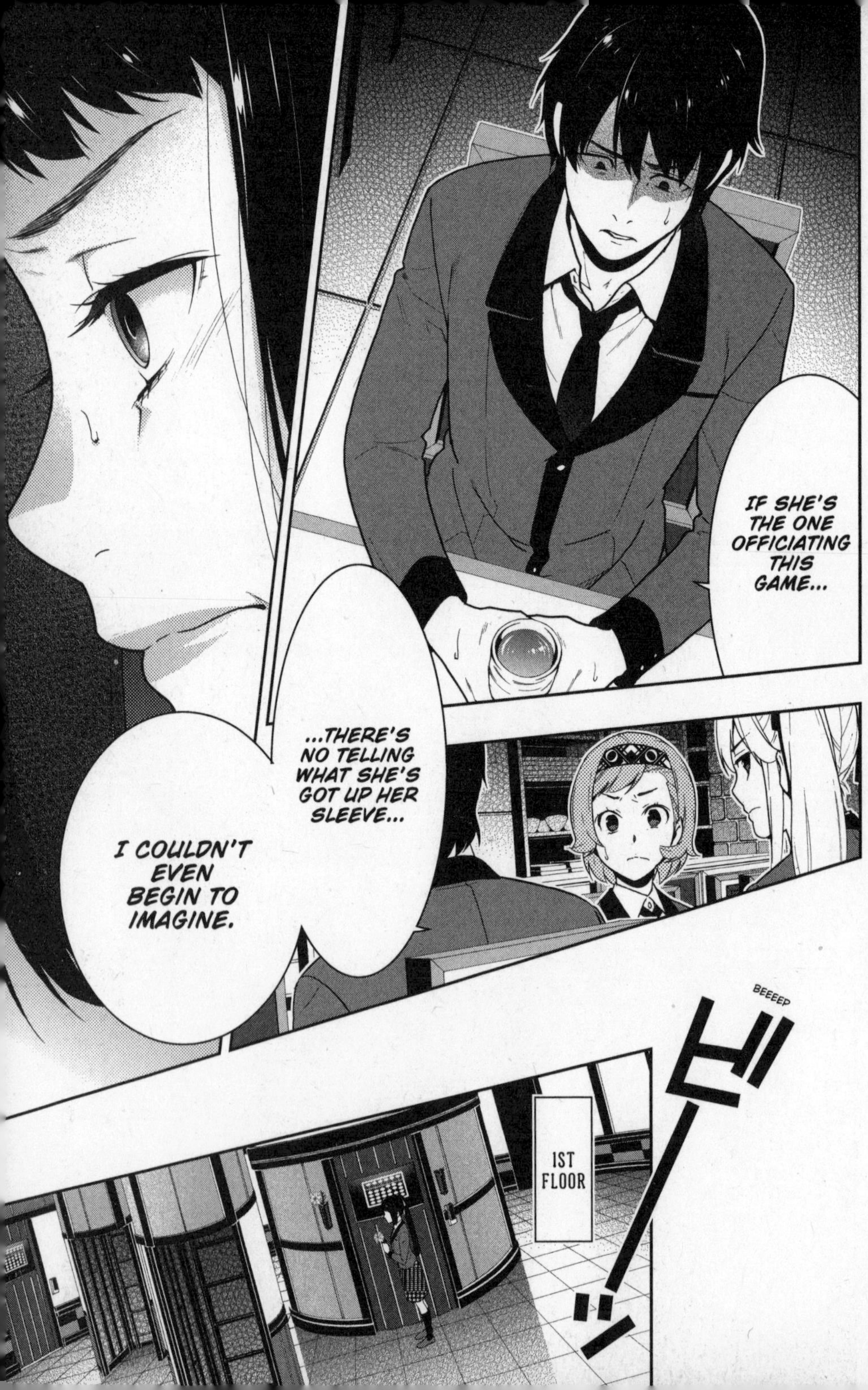
IF SHE'S THE ONE OFFICIATING THIS GAME...
...THERE'S NO TELLING WHAT SHE'S GOT UP HER SLEEVE...
I COULDN'T EVEN BEGIN TO IMAGINE.
BEEEEP
1ST FLOOR

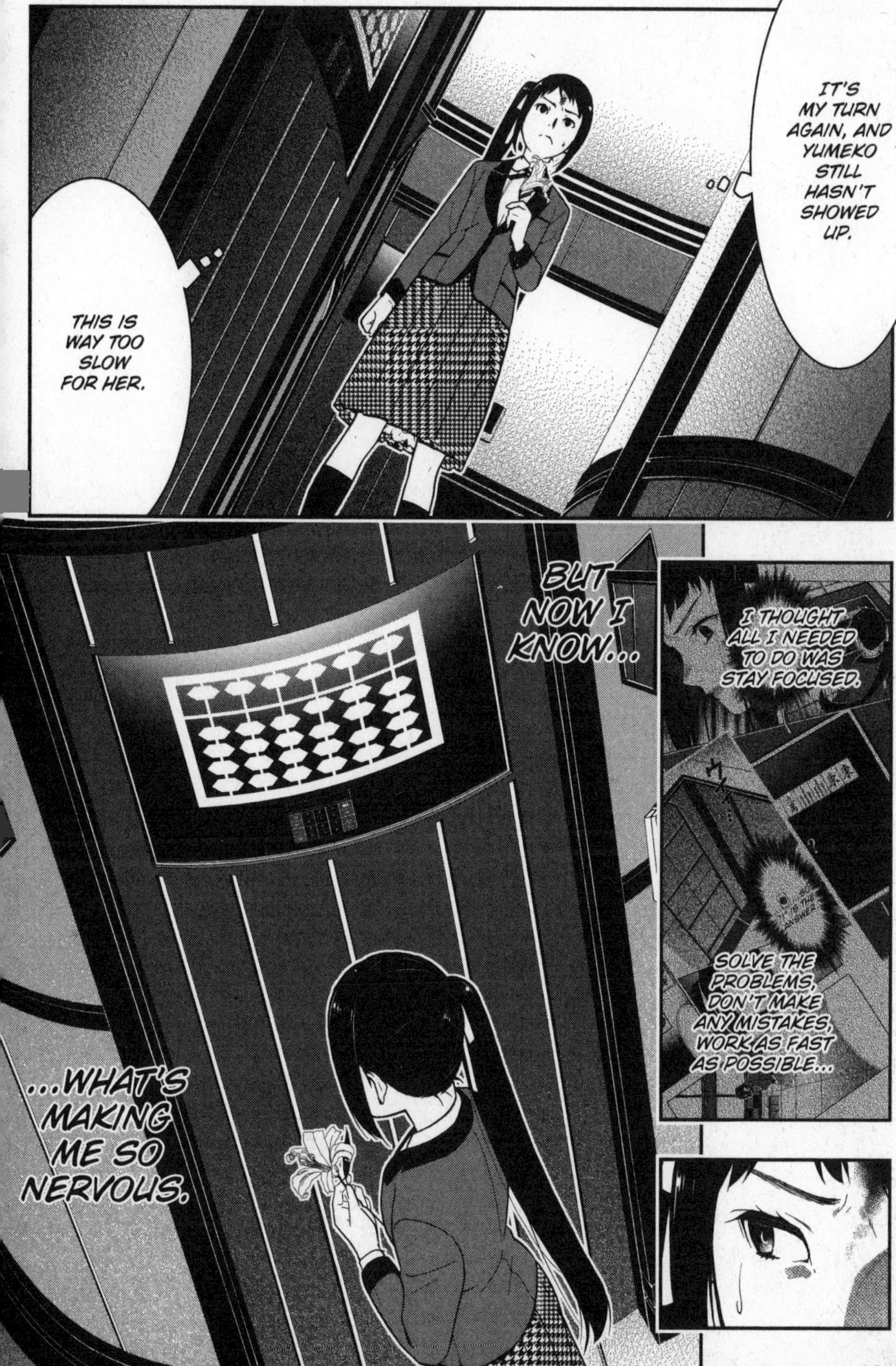
IT'S MY TURN AGAIN, AND YUMEKO STILL HASN'T SHOWED UP.
THIS IS WAY TOO SLOW FOR HER.
I THOUGHT ALL I NEEDED TO DO WAS STAY FOCUSED.
SOLVE THE PROBLEMS, DON'T MAKE ANY MISTAKES, WORK AS FAST AS POSSIBLE...
BUT NOW I KNOW...
...WHAT'S MAKING ME SO NERVOUS.

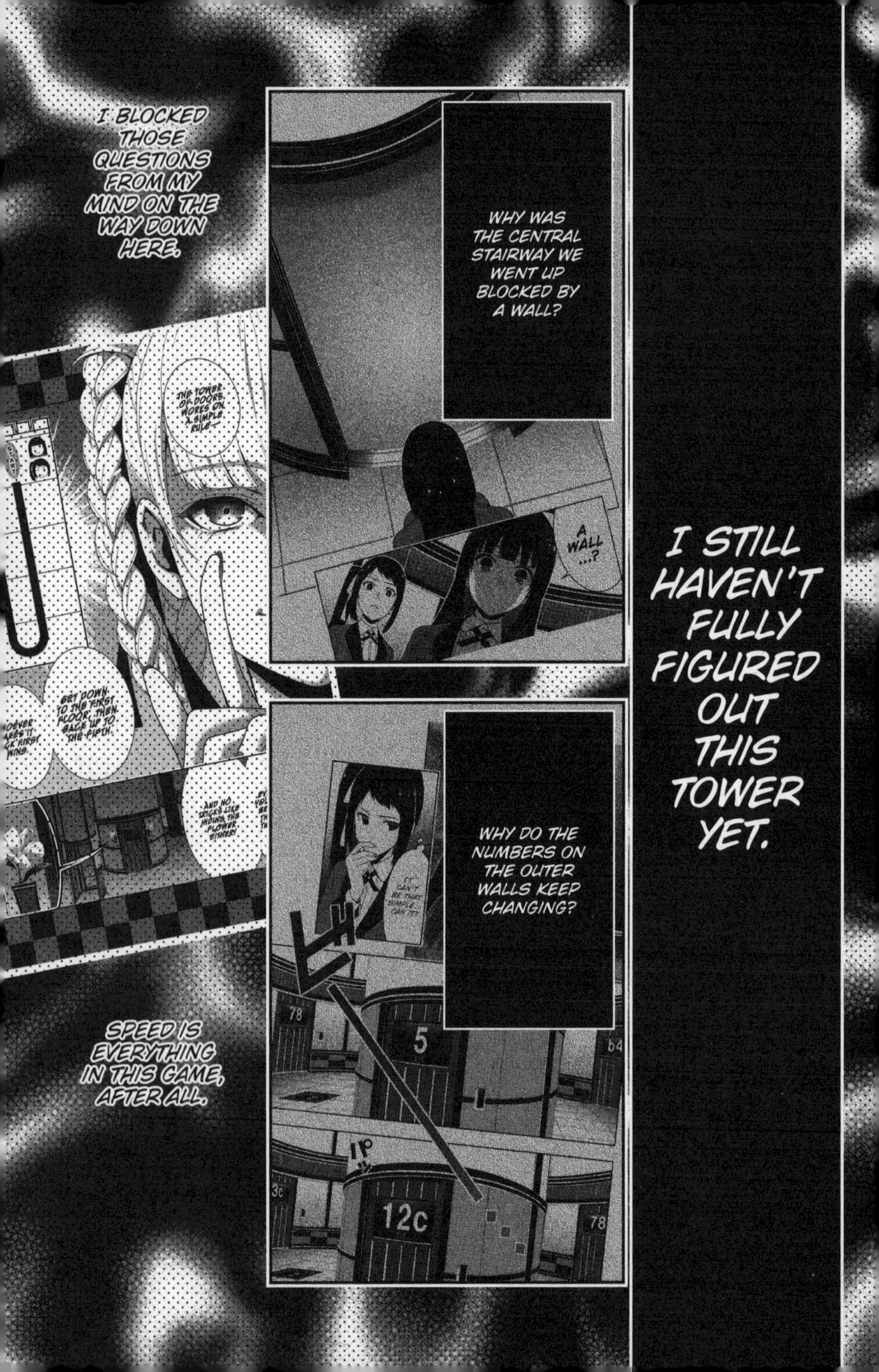
I STILL HAVEN'T FULLY FIGURED OUT THIS TOWER YET.
WHY WAS THE CENTRAL STAIRWAY WE WENT UP BLOCKED BY A WALL?
A WALL ...?
WHY DO THE NUMBERS ON THE OUTER WALLS KEEP CHANGING?
IT CAN'T BE THAT SIMPLE... CAN IT?
5
12c
78
I BLOCKED THOSE QUESTIONS FROM MY MIND ON THE WAY DOWN HERE.
THE TOWER OF DOORS WORKS ON A SIMPLE RULE—
GET DOWN TO THE FIRST FLOOR, THEN BACK UP TO THE FIFTH.
...AND NO TRICKS LIKE HIDING THE FLOWER, EITHER!
SPEED IS EVERYTHING IN THIS GAME, AFTER ALL.

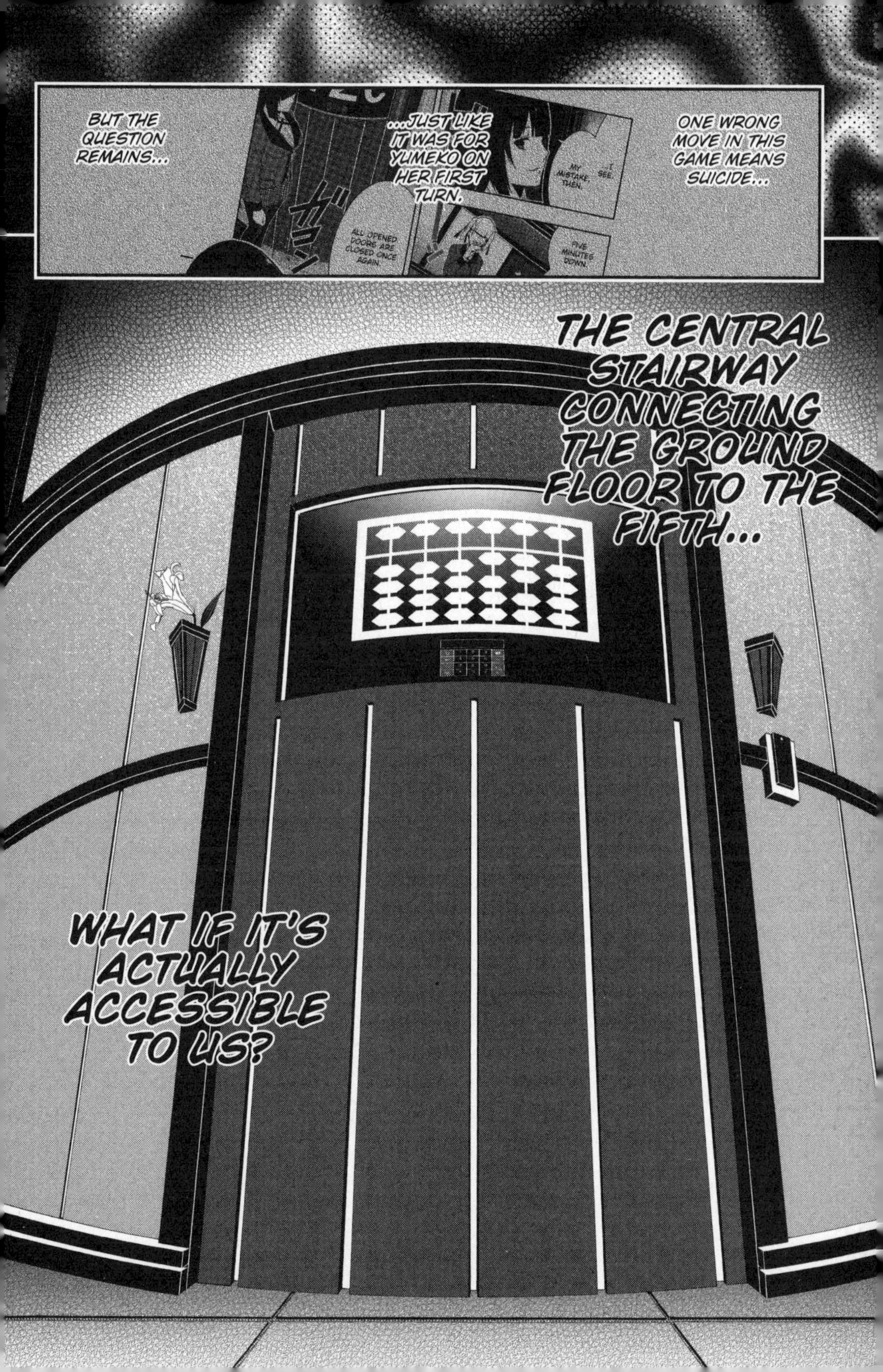
ONE WRONG MOVE IN THIS GAME MEANS SUICIDE...
I SEE.
MY MISTAKE, THEN.
FIVE MINUTES DOWN.
ALL OPENED DOORS ARE CLOSED ONCE AGAIN.
...JUST LIKE IT WAS FOR YUMEKO ON HER FIRST TURN.
BUT THE QUESTION REMAINS...
THE CENTRAL STAIRWAY CONNECTING THE GROUND FLOOR TO THE FIFTH...
WHAT IF IT'S ACTUALLY ACCESSIBLE TO US?

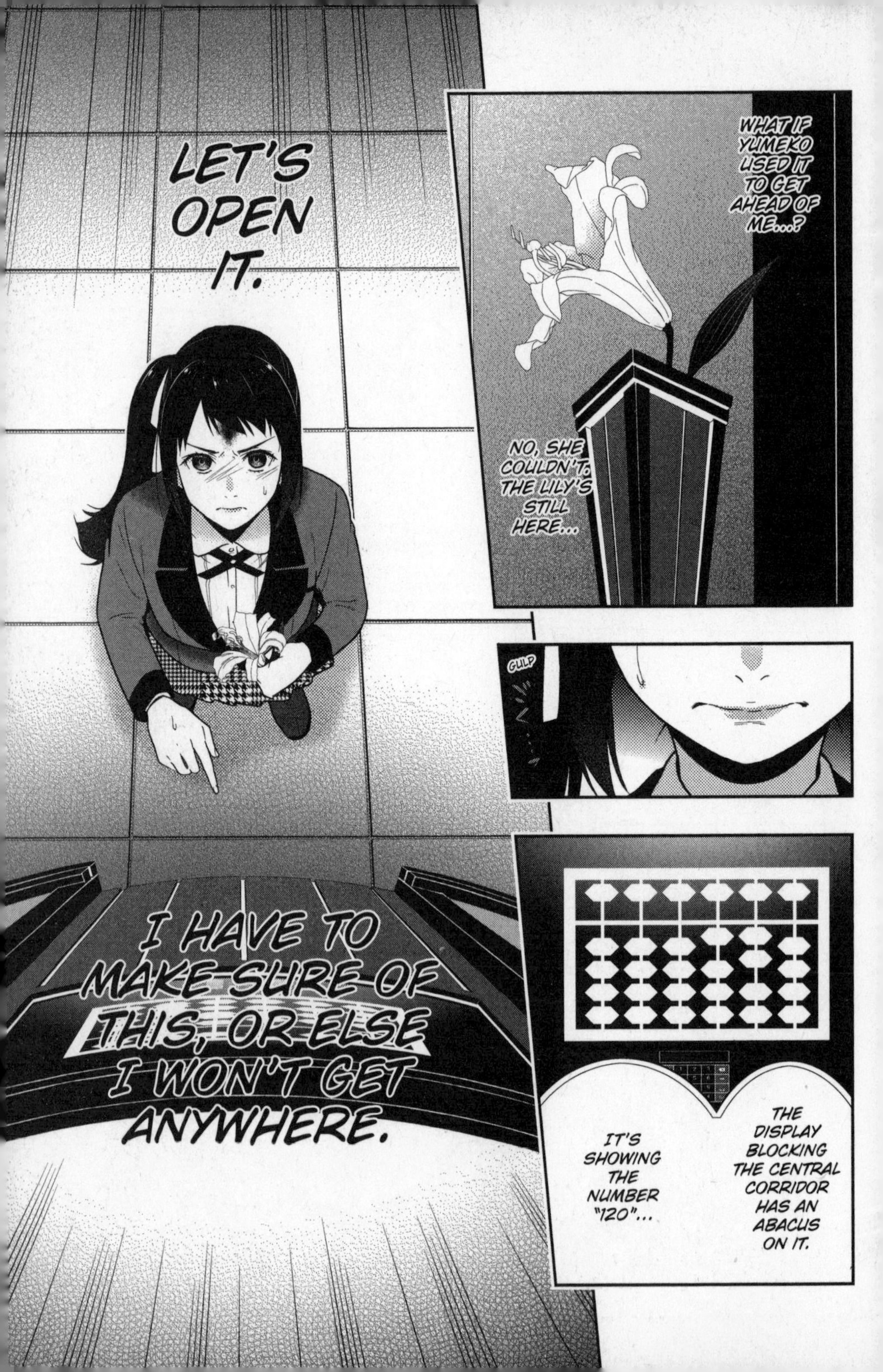
WHAT IF YUMEKO USED IT TO GET AHEAD OF ME...?
NO, SHE COULDN'T. THE LILY'S STILL HERE...
GULP
THE DISPLAY BLOCKING THE CENTRAL CORRIDOR HAS AN ABACUS ON IT.
IT'S SHOWING THE NUMBER "120"...
LET'S OPEN IT.
I HAVE TO MAKE SURE OF THIS, OR ELSE I WON'T GET ANYWHERE.

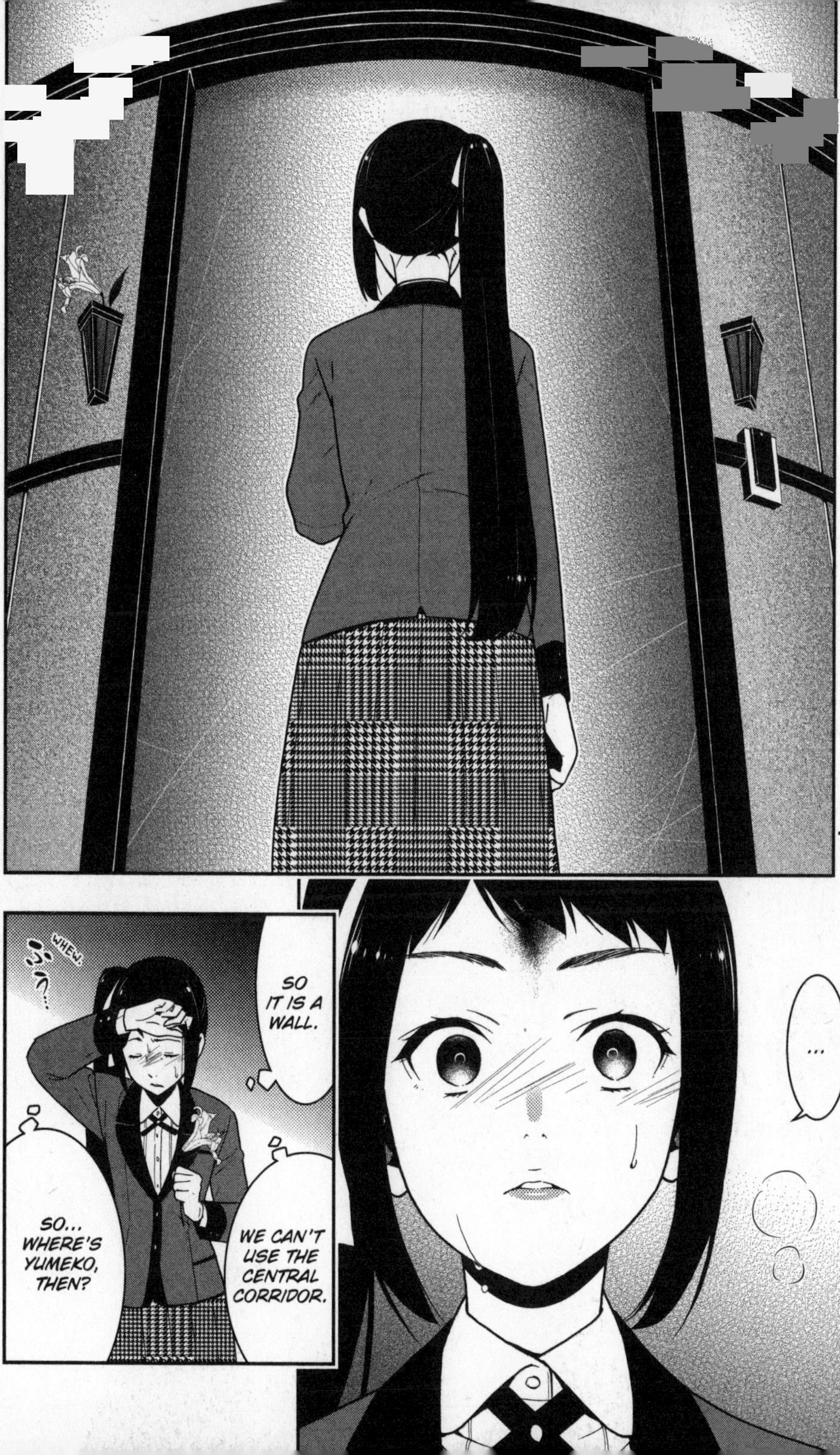
...
SO IT IS A WALL.
WHEW.
ふぅ…
WE CAN'T USE THE CENTRAL CORRIDOR.
SO... WHERE'S YUMEKO, THEN?

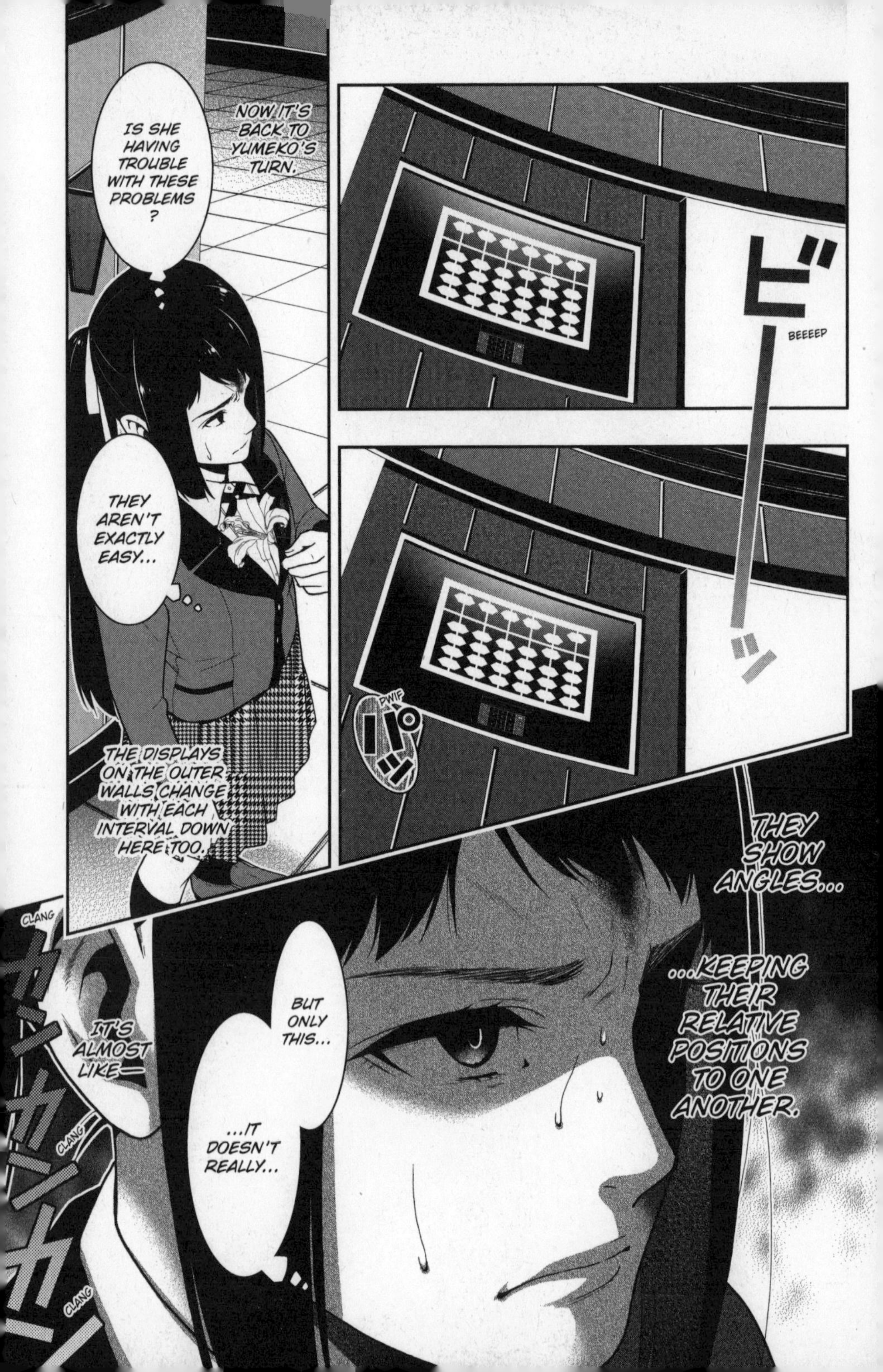
BEEEEP
PWIP
NOW IT'S BACK TO YUMEKO'S TURN.
IS SHE HAVING TROUBLE WITH THESE PROBLEMS?
THEY AREN'T EXACTLY EASY...
THE DISPLAYS ON THE OUTER WALLS CHANGE WITH EACH INTERVAL DOWN HERE TOO.
THEY SHOW ANGLES...
...KEEPING THEIR RELATIVE POSITIONS TO ONE ANOTHER.
BUT ONLY THIS...
...IT DOESN'T REALLY...
IT'S ALMOST LIKE—
CLANG
CLANG
CLANG

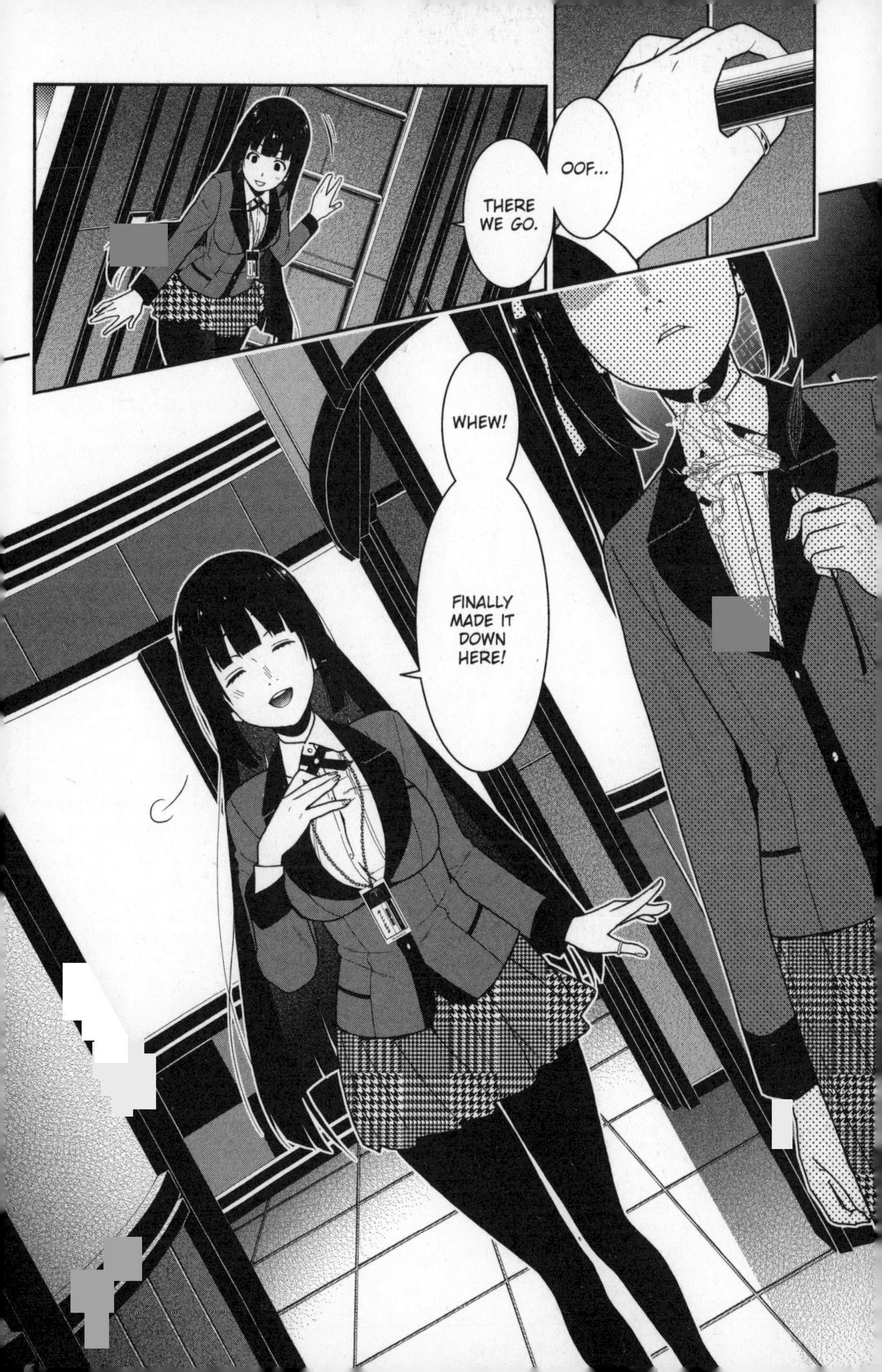
OOF...
THERE WE GO.
WHEW!
FINALLY MADE IT DOWN HERE!

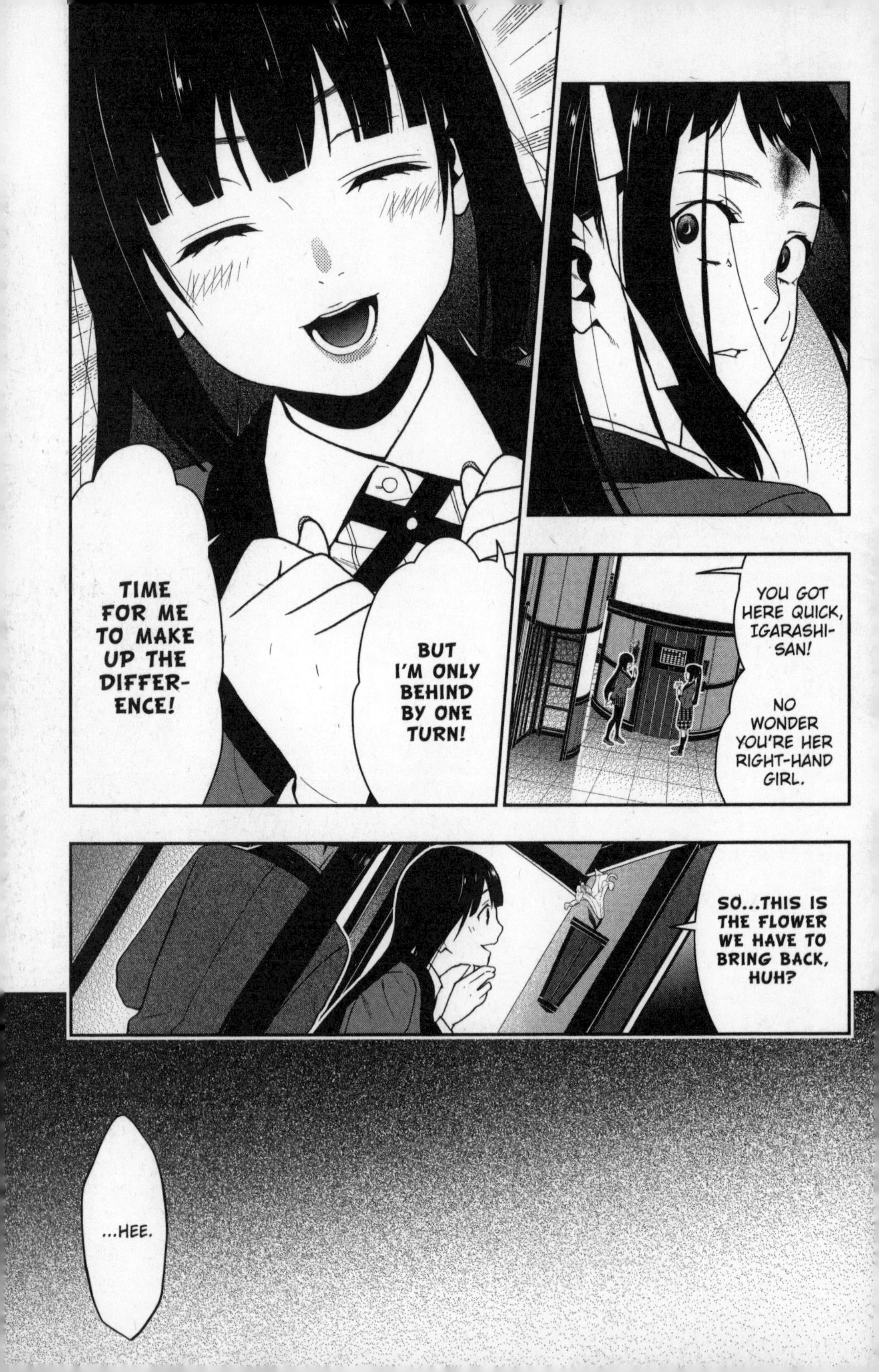
YOU GOT HERE QUICK, IGARASHI-SAN!
NO WONDER YOU'RE HER RIGHT-HAND GIRL.
BUT I'M ONLY BEHIND BY ONE TURN!
TIME FOR ME TO MAKE UP THE DIFFERENCE!
SO...THIS IS THE FLOWER WE HAVE TO BRING BACK, HUH?
...HEE.

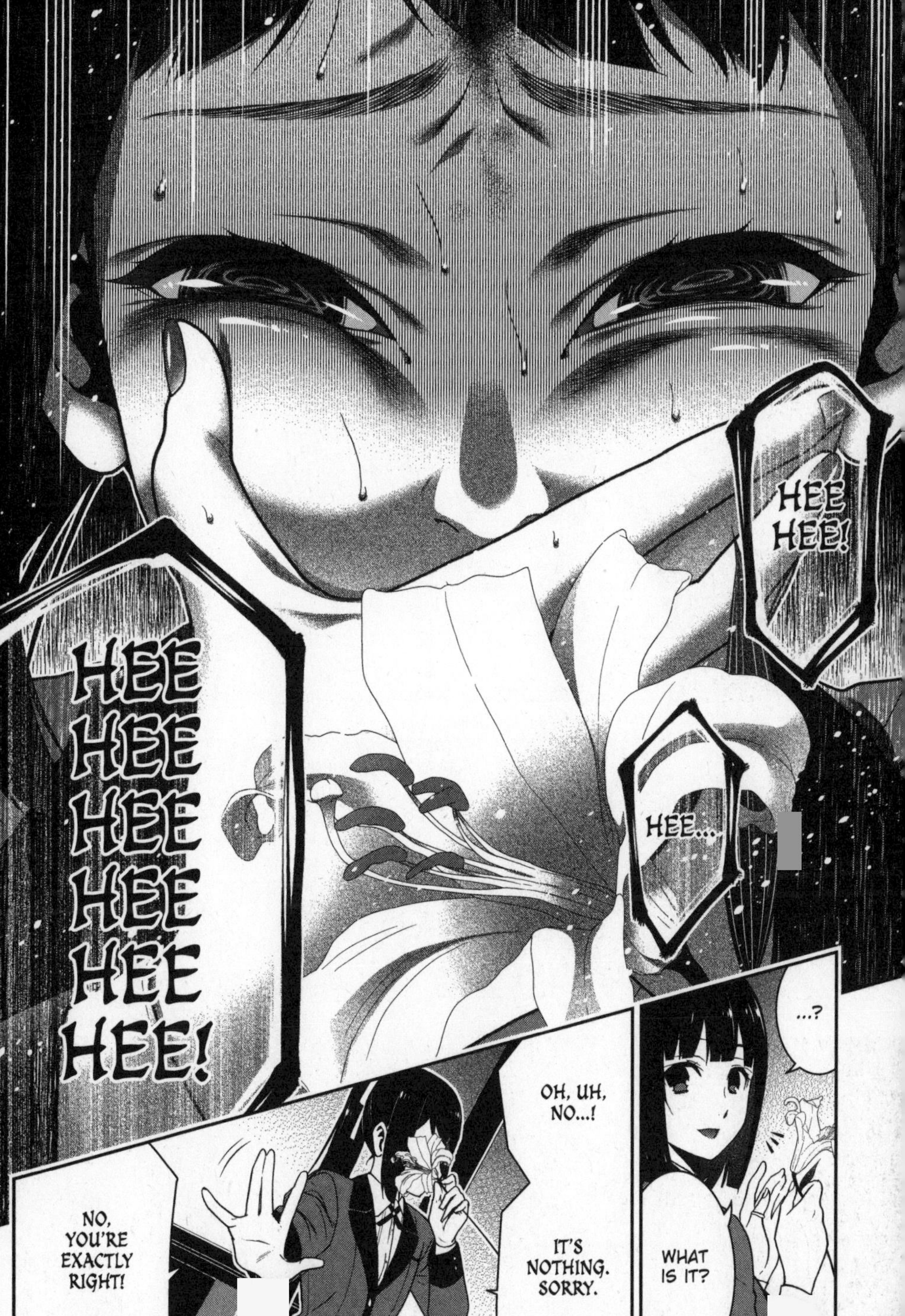
HEE HEE!
HEE...
HEE HEE HEE HEE HEE HEE!
...?
WHAT IS IT?
OH, UH, NO...!
IT'S NOTHING. SORRY.
NO, YOU'RE EXACTLY RIGHT!

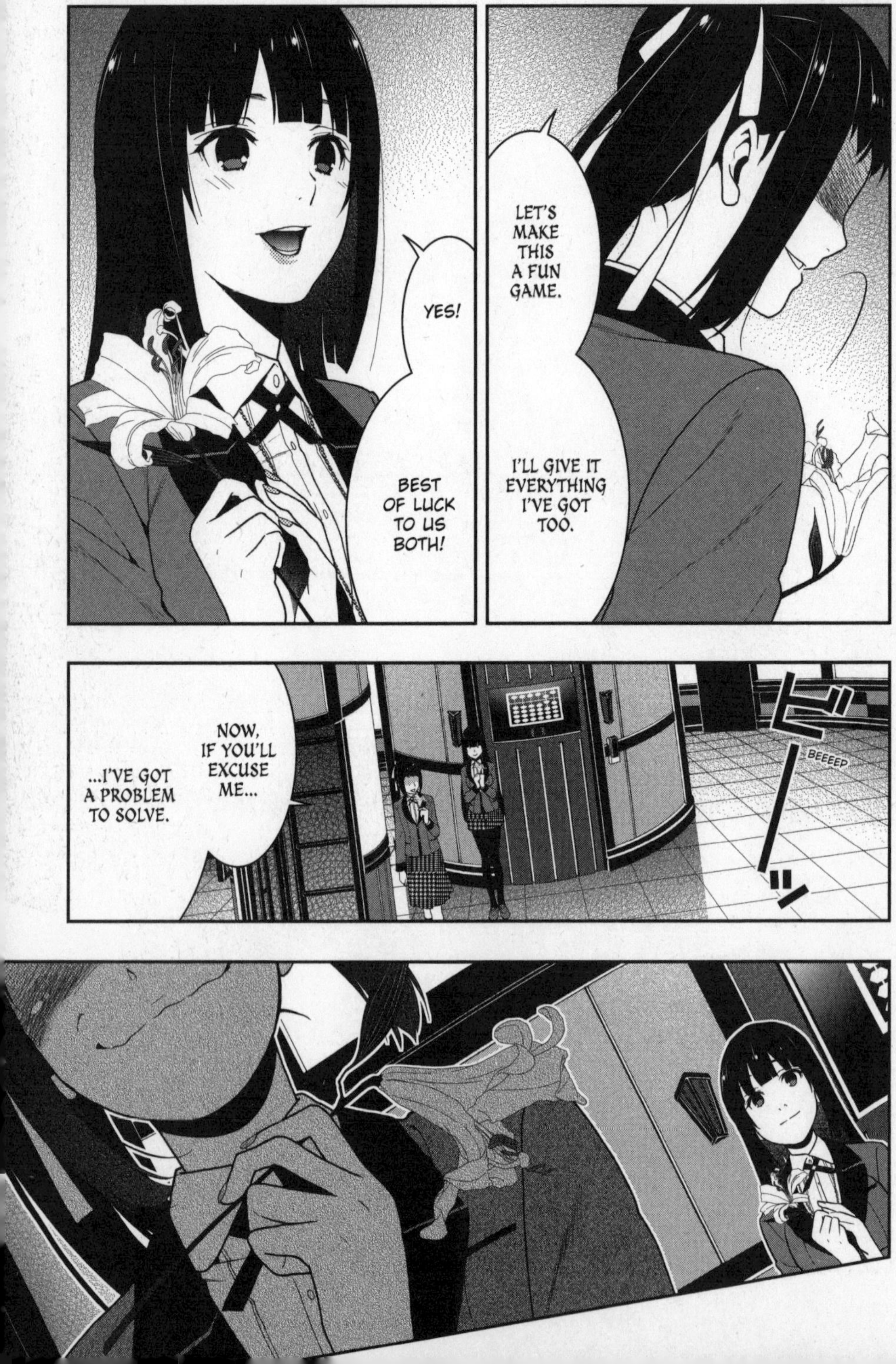
LET'S MAKE THIS A FUN GAME.
I'LL GIVE IT EVERYTHING I'VE GOT TOO.
YES!
BEST OF LUCK TO US BOTH!
BEEEEP
NOW, IF YOU'LL EXCUSE ME...
...I'VE GOT A PROBLEM TO SOLVE.

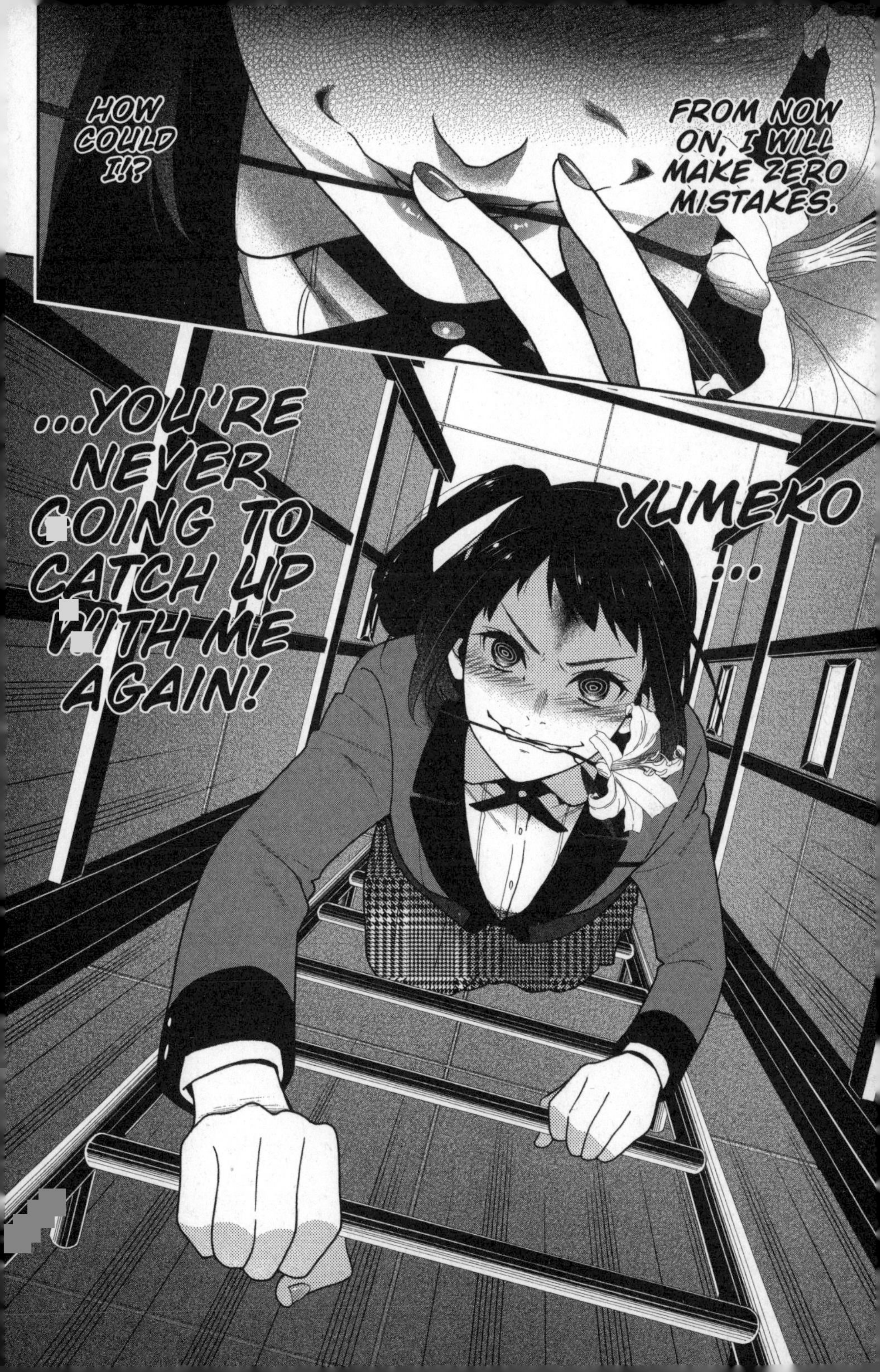
FROM NOW ON, I WILL MAKE ZERO MISTAKES.
HOW COULD I!?
YUMEKO...
...YOU'RE NEVER GOING TO CATCH UP WITH ME AGAIN!

KAKEGURUI

— Compulsive Gambler —

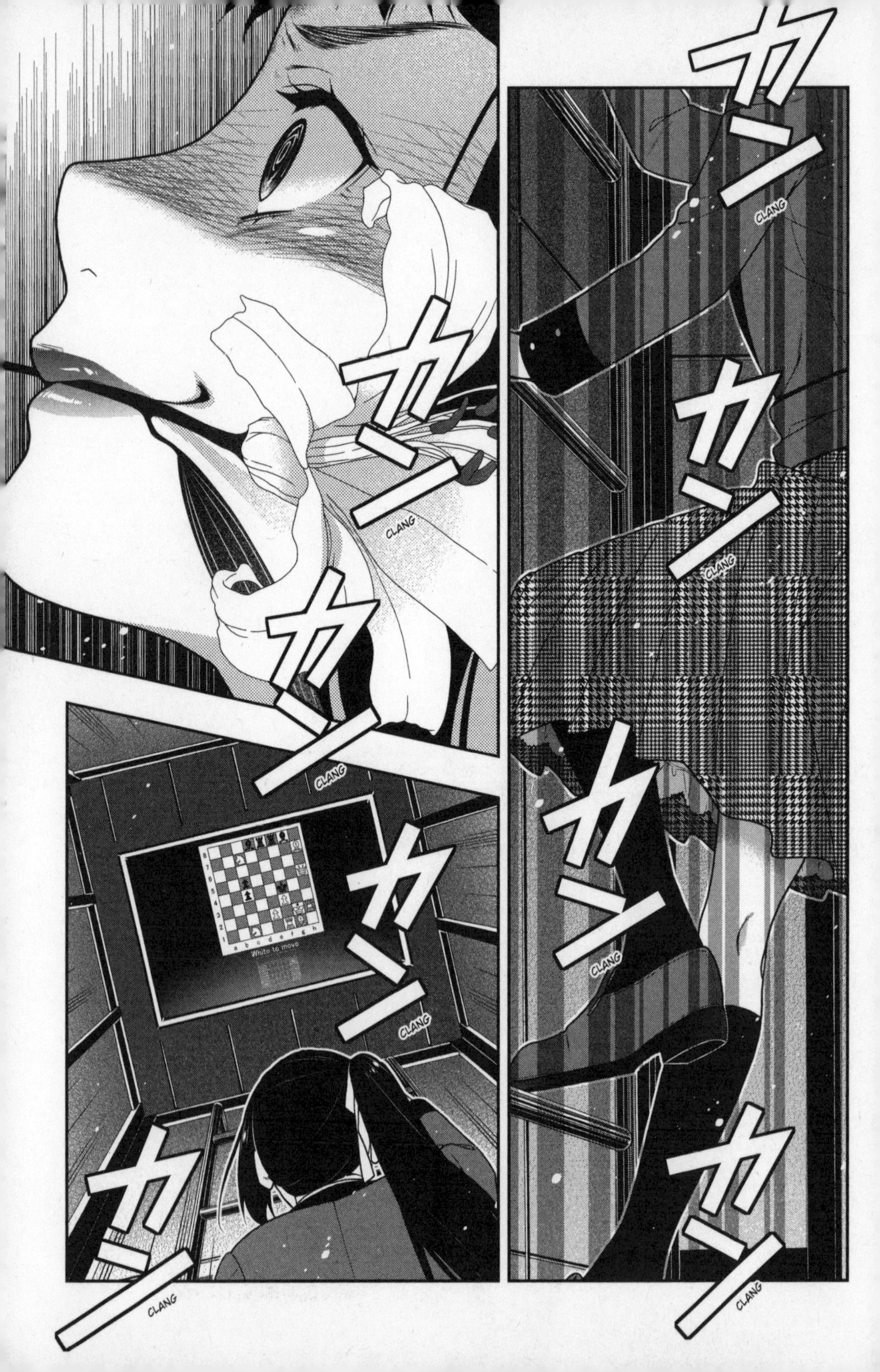

カーン
CLANG
カーン
CLANG
カーン
CLANG
カーン
CLANG
カーン
CLANG
カーン
CLANG
White to move
カーン
CLANG
カーン
CLANG

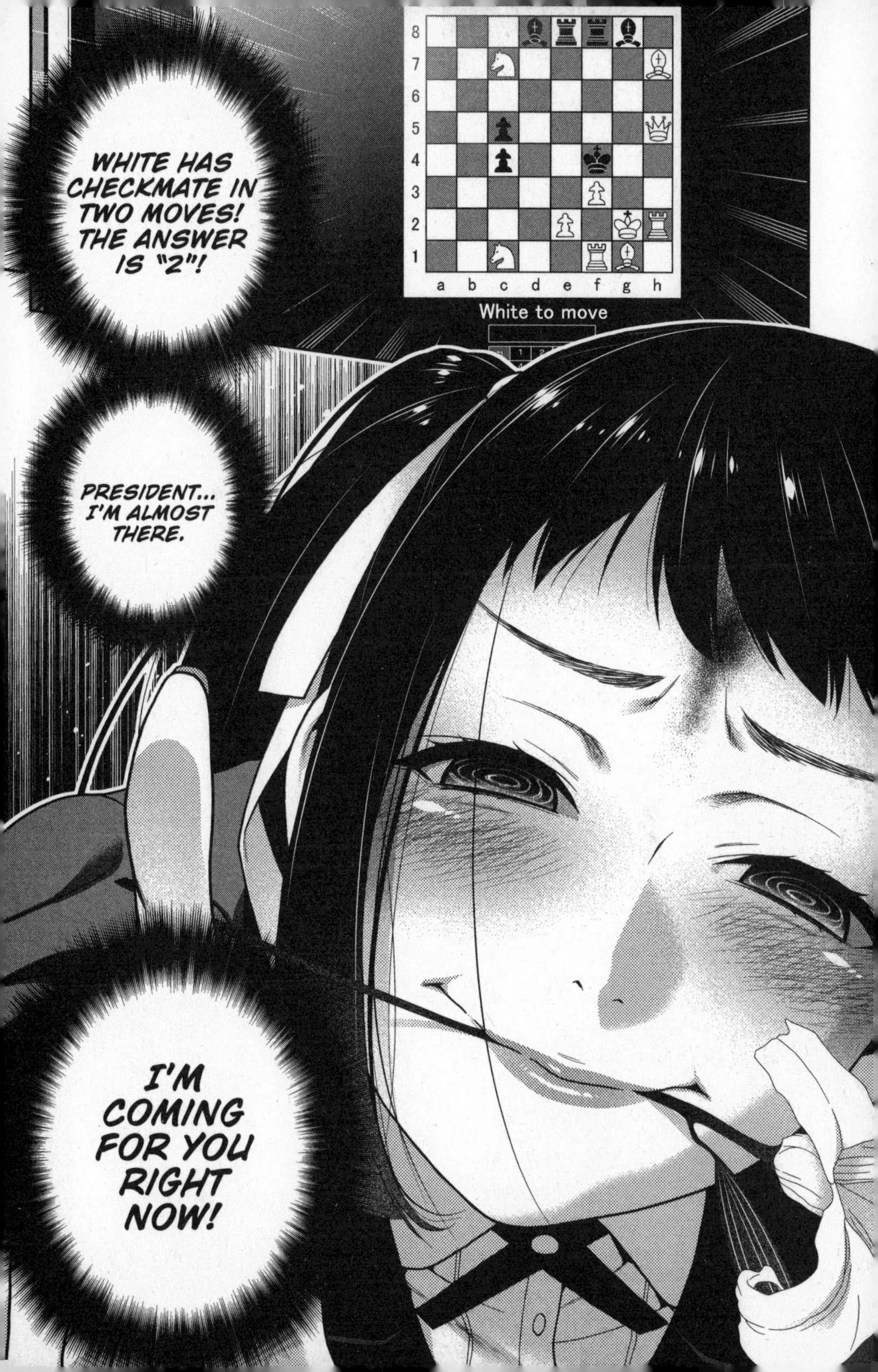
White to move
WHITE HAS CHECKMATE IN TWO MOVES! THE ANSWER IS "2"!
PRESIDENT... I'M ALMOST THERE.
I'M COMING FOR YOU RIGHT NOW!

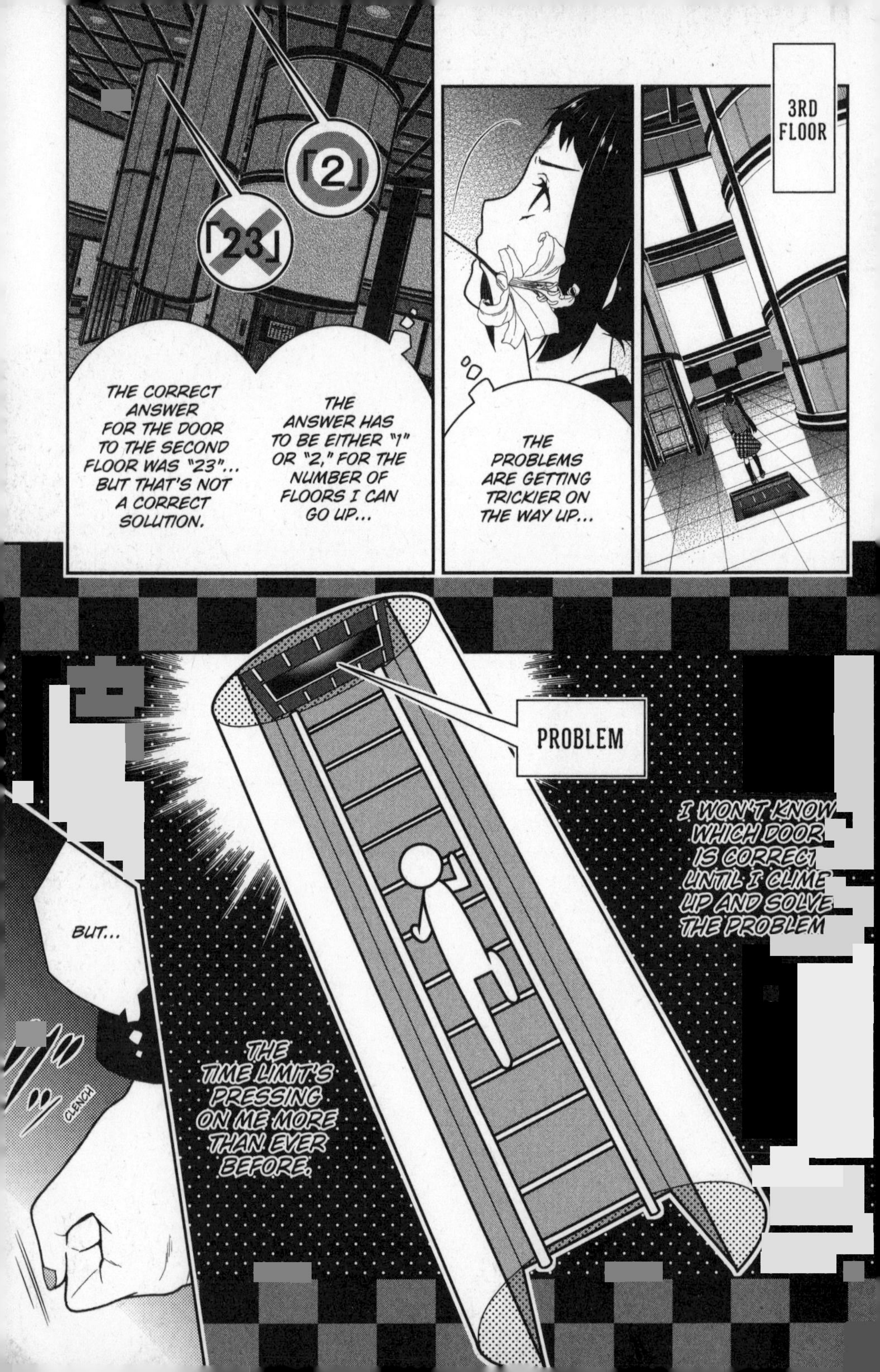
3RD FLOOR
THE PROBLEMS ARE GETTING TRICKIER ON THE WAY UP...
「2」
「23」
THE CORRECT ANSWER FOR THE DOOR TO THE SECOND FLOOR WAS "23"... BUT THAT'S NOT A CORRECT SOLUTION.
THE ANSWER HAS TO BE EITHER "1" OR "2," FOR THE NUMBER OF FLOORS I CAN GO UP...
PROBLEM
I WON'T KNOW WHICH DOOR IS CORRECT UNTIL I CLIMB UP AND SOLVE THE PROBLEM
BUT...
THE TIME LIMIT'S PRESSING ON ME MORE THAN EVER BEFORE.
CLENCH

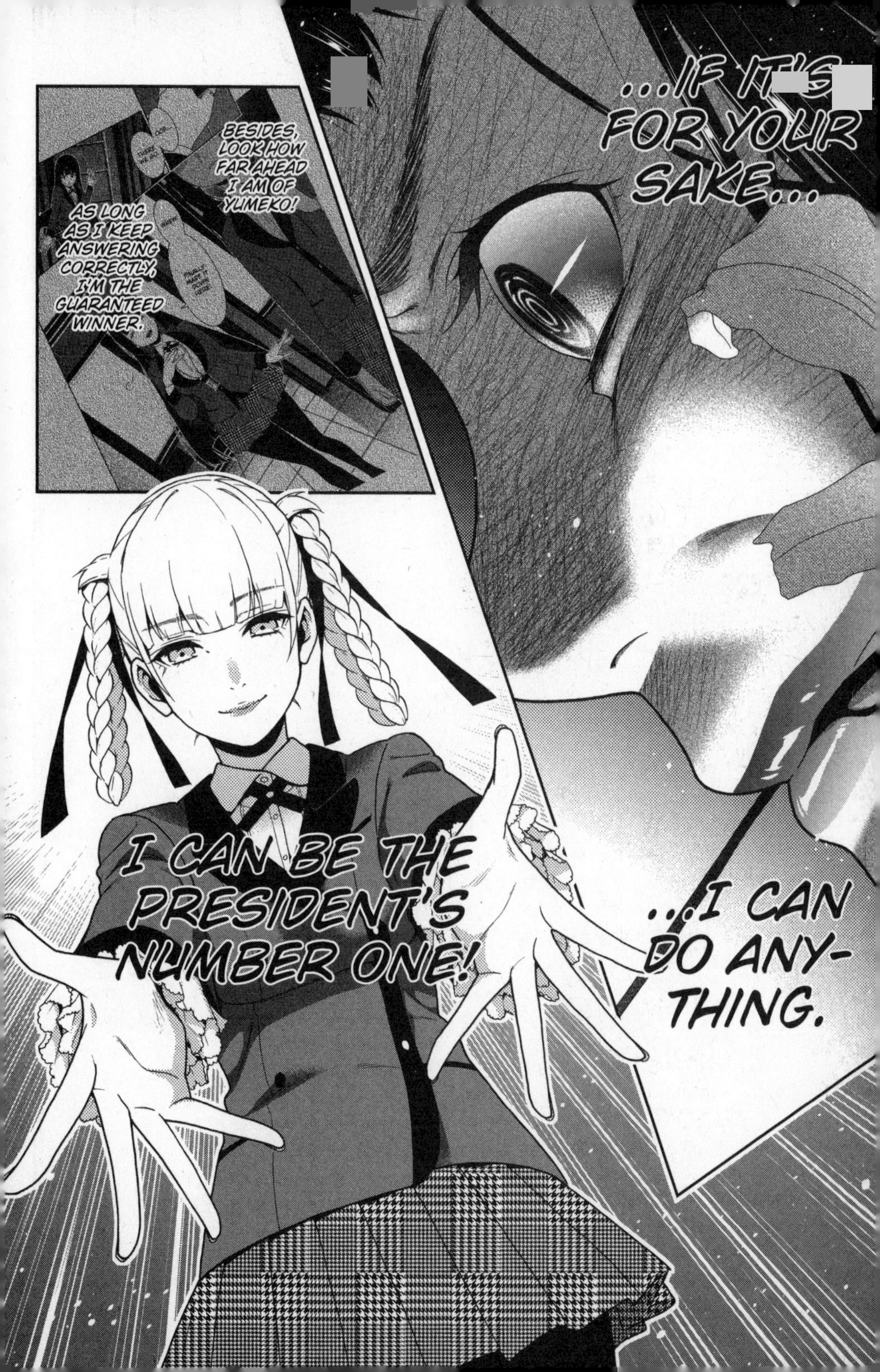
...IF IT'S FOR YOUR SAKE...
...I CAN DO ANY-THING.
BESIDES, LOOK HOW FAR AHEAD I AM OF YUMEKO!
OOF—
THERE WE GO
WHEW!
FINALLY MADE IT DOWN HERE
AS LONG AS I KEEP ANSWERING CORRECTLY, I'M THE GUARANTEED WINNER.
I CAN BE THE PRESIDENT'S NUMBER ONE!

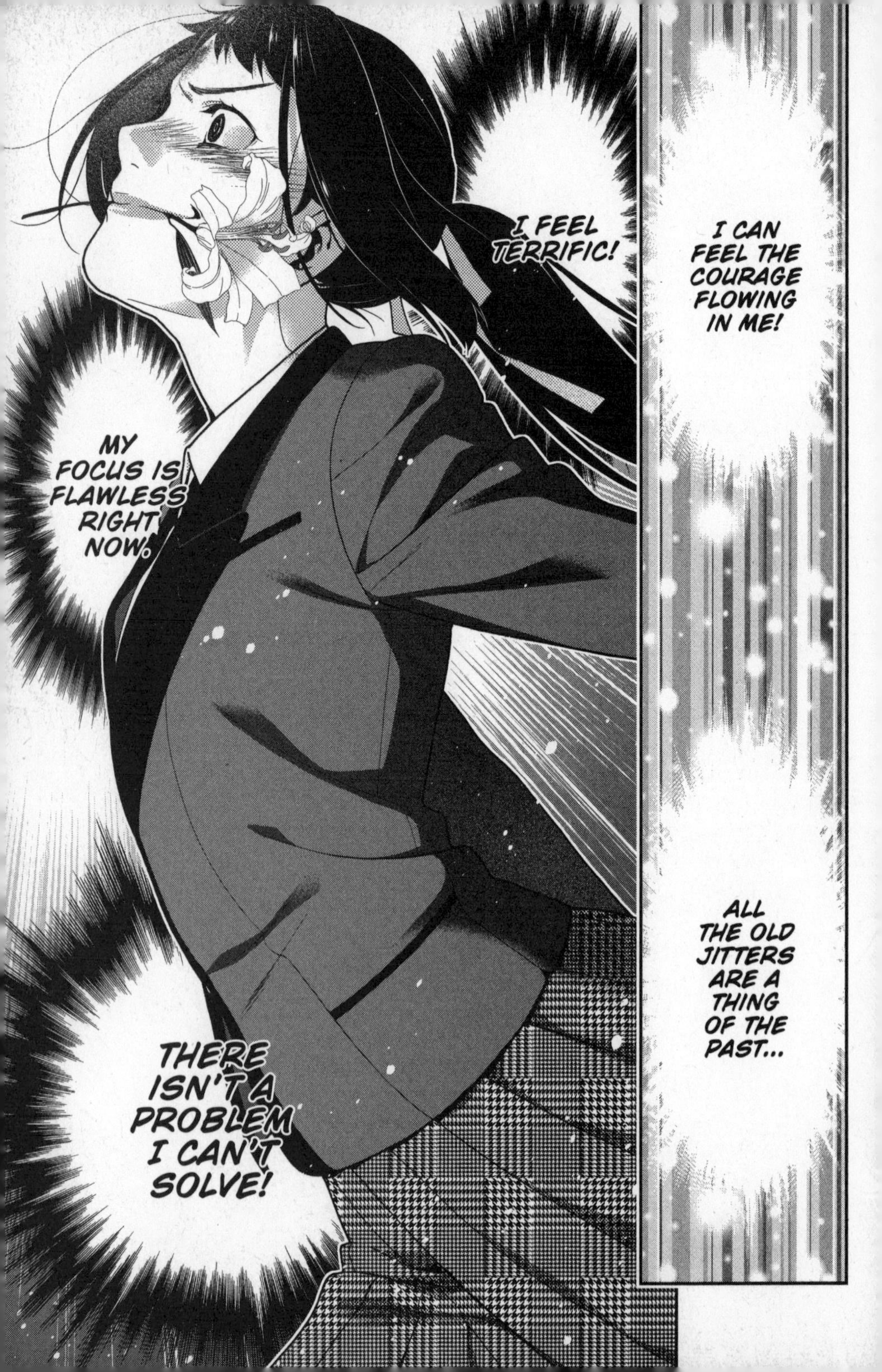
I CAN FEEL THE COURAGE FLOWING IN ME!
ALL THE OLD JITTERS ARE A THING OF THE PAST...
I FEEL TERRIFIC!
MY FOCUS IS FLAWLESS RIGHT NOW.
THERE ISN'T A PROBLEM I CAN'T SOLVE!

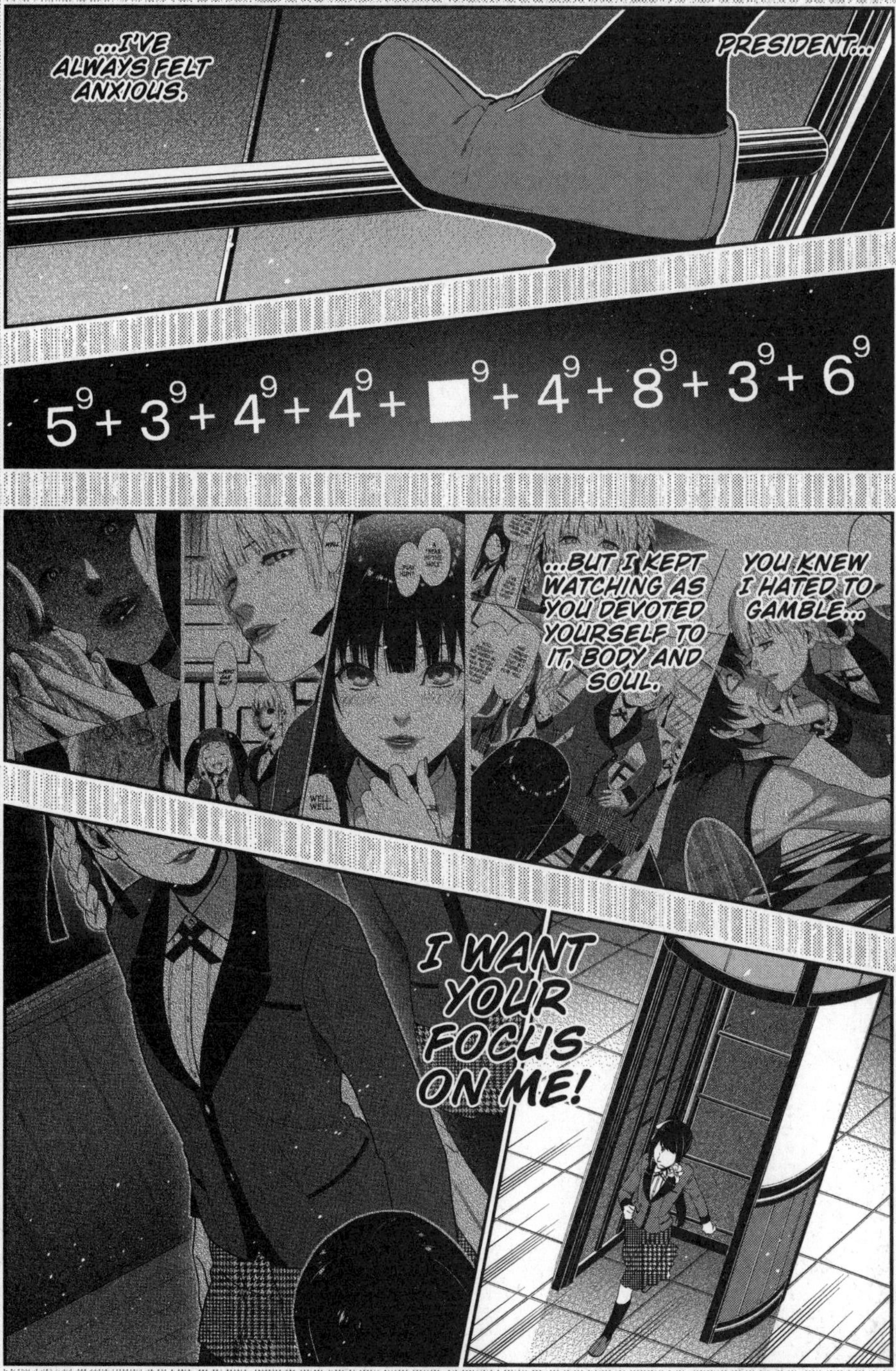
PRESIDENT...
...I'VE ALWAYS FELT ANXIOUS.
$5^9 + 3^9 + 4^9 + 4^9 + \square^9 + 4^9 + 8^9 + 3^9 + 6^9$
YOU KNEW I HATED TO GAMBLE...
...BUT I KEPT WATCHING AS YOU DEVOTED YOURSELF TO IT, BODY AND SOUL.
WELL WELL
I WANT YOUR FOCUS ON ME!

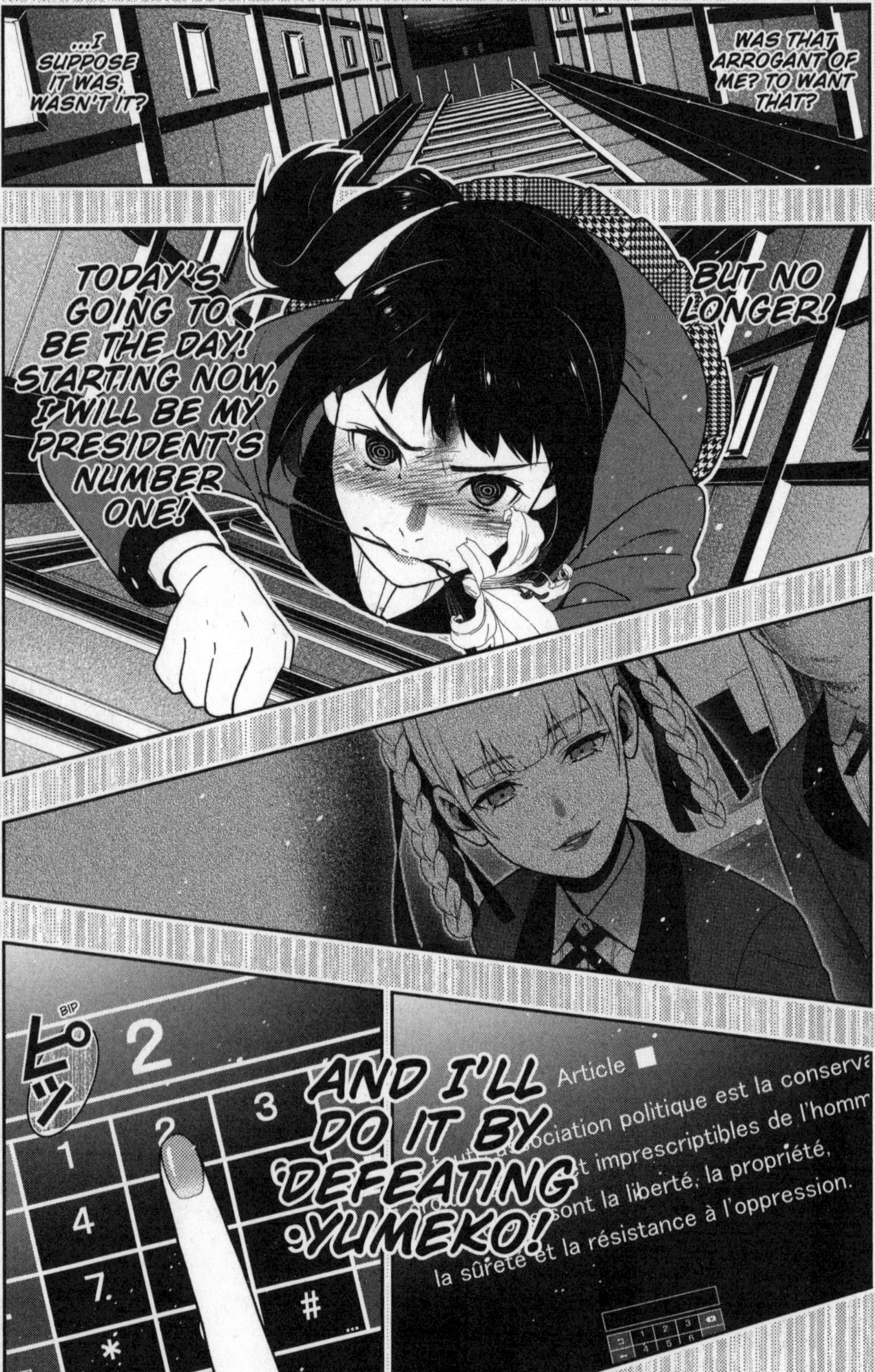
WAS THAT ARROGANT OF ME? TO WANT THAT?
...I SUPPOSE IT WAS, WASN'T IT?
BUT NO LONGER!
TODAY'S GOING TO BE THE DAY! STARTING NOW, I WILL BE MY PRESIDENT'S NUMBER ONE!
Article
ociation politique est la conserva
imprescriptibles de l'homm
sont la liberté, la propriété,
la sûreté et la résistance à l'oppression.
AND I'LL DO IT BY DEFEATING YUMEKO!
ピッ
BIP
2
3
1
2
4
7
#
*

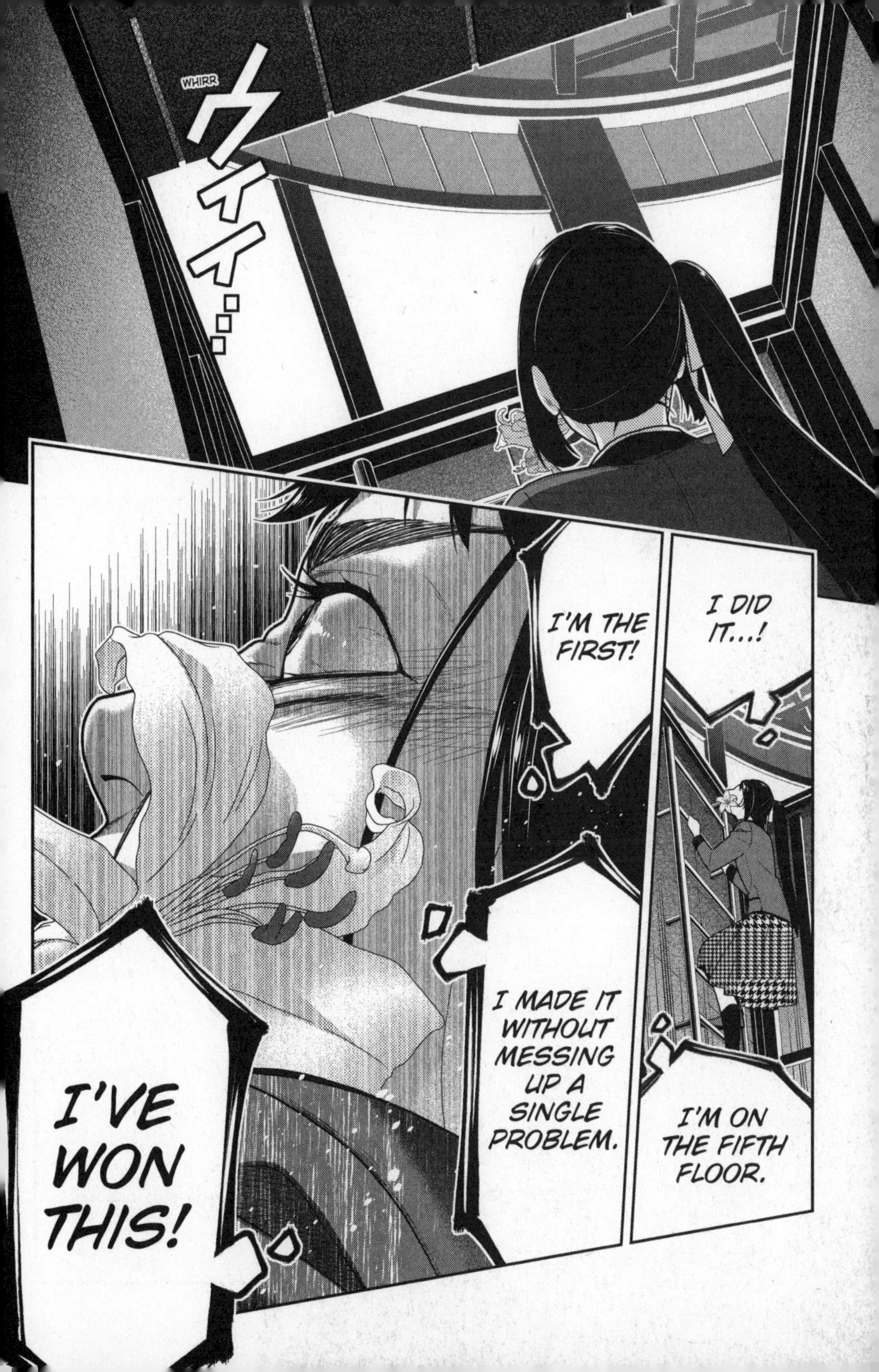
WHIRR
I DID IT...!
I'M ON THE FIFTH FLOOR.
I'M THE FIRST!
I MADE IT WITHOUT MESSING UP A SINGLE PROBLEM.
I'VE WON THIS!

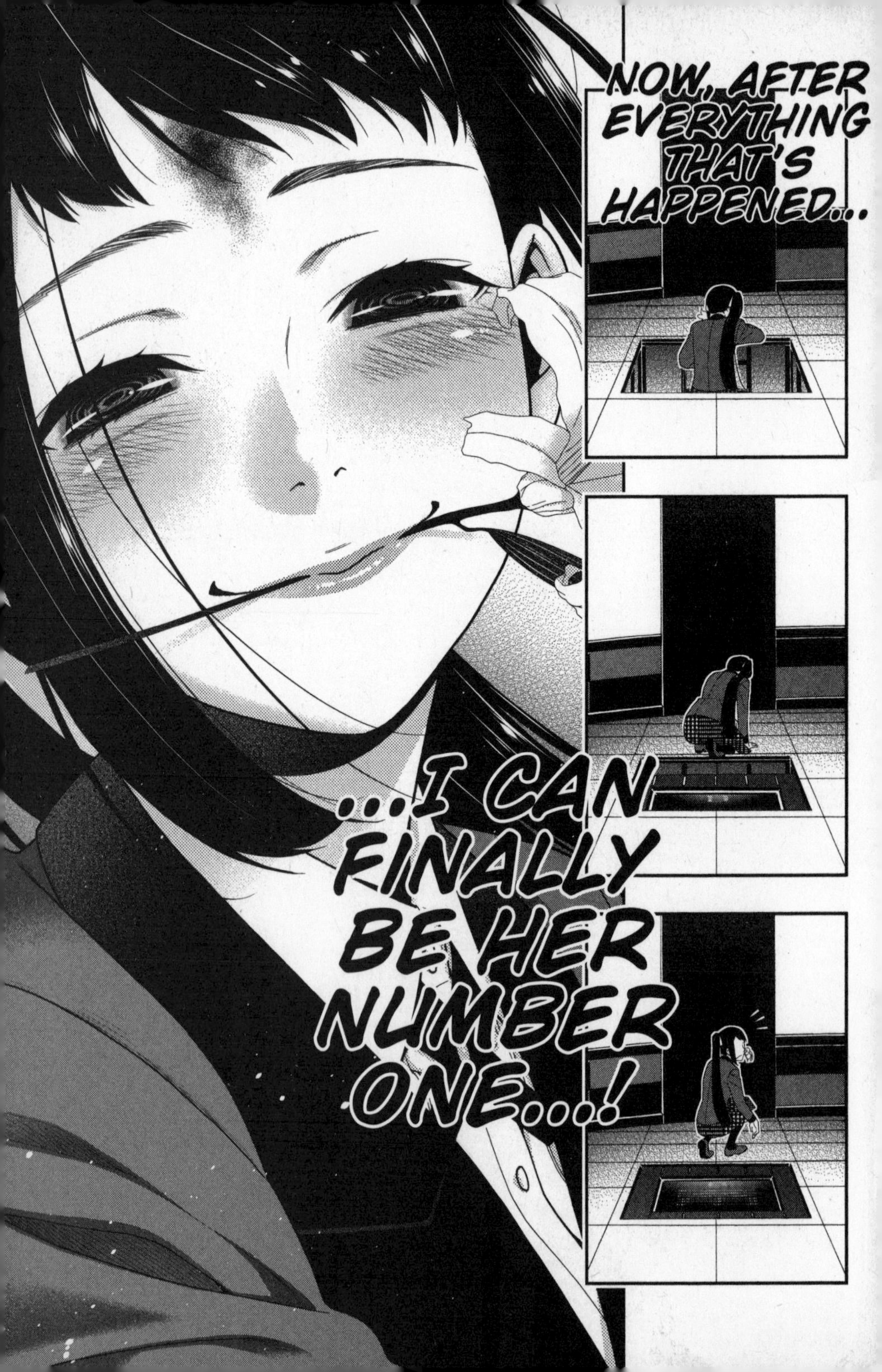
NOW, AFTER EVERYTHING THAT'S HAPPENED...
...I CAN FINALLY BE HER NUMBER ONE...!

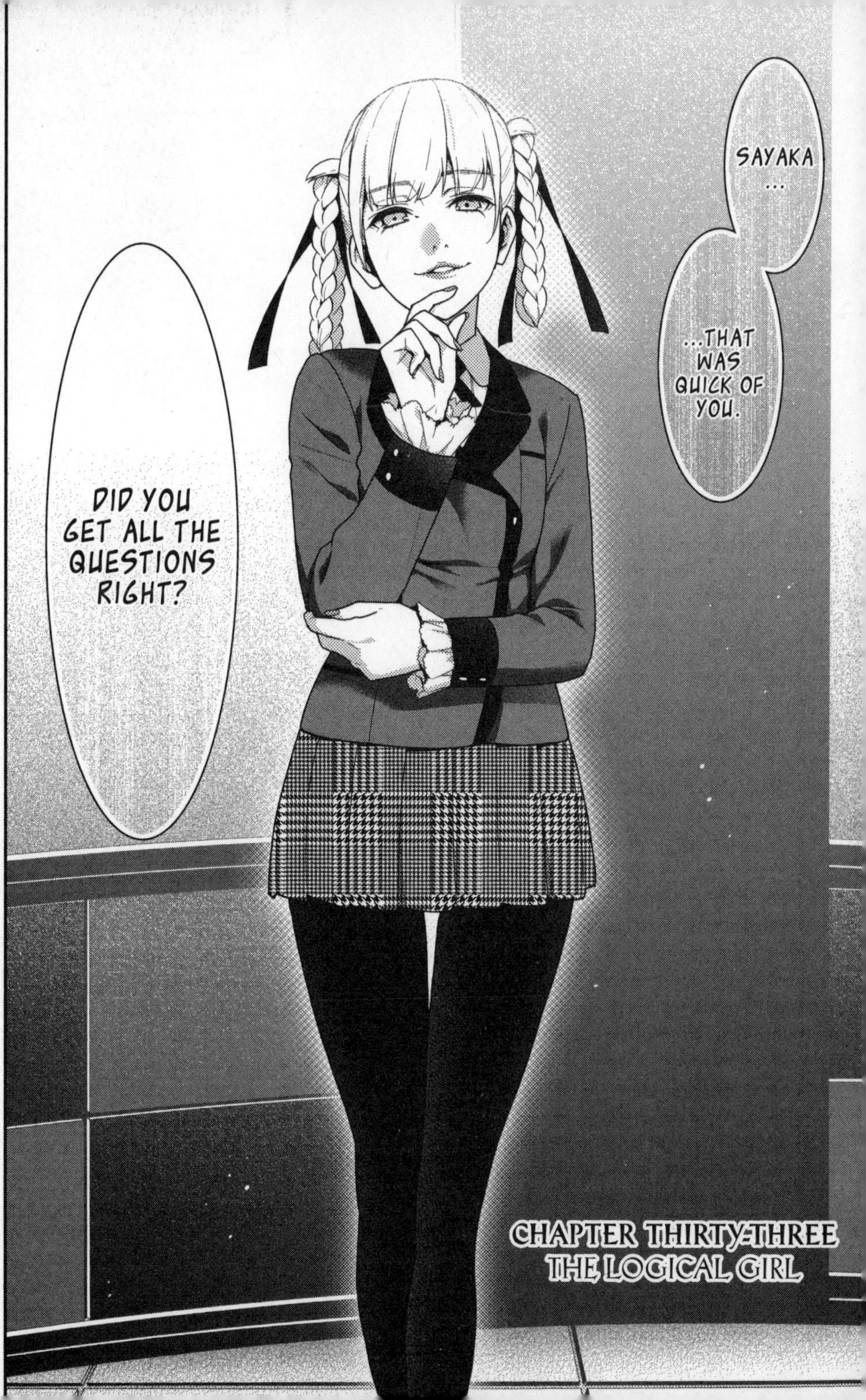
SAYAKA ...
...THAT WAS QUICK OF YOU.
DID YOU GET ALL THE QUESTIONS RIGHT?
CHAPTER THIRTY-THREE
THE LOGICAL GIRL

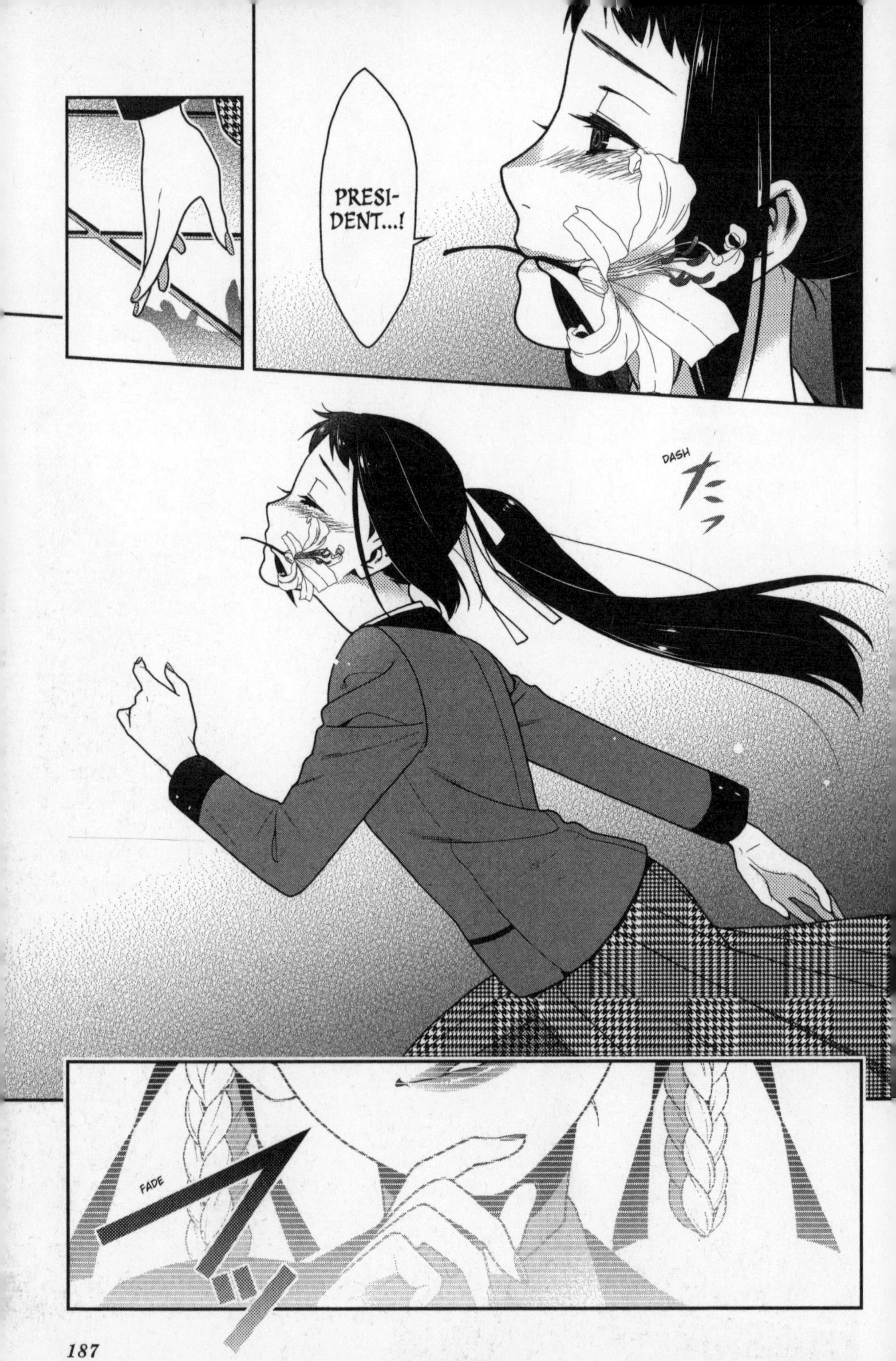
PRESI-
DENT...!
DASH
FADE

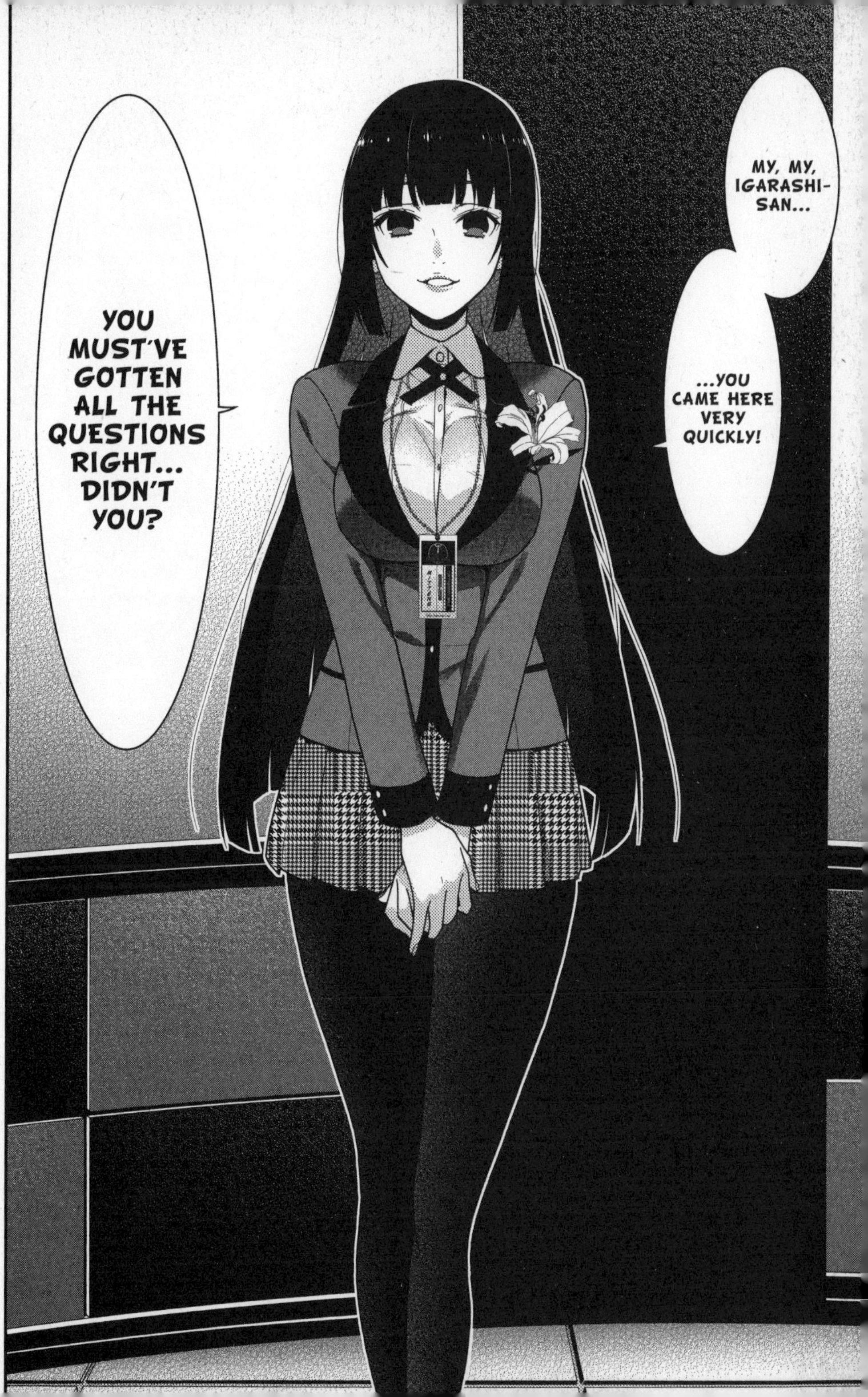
MY, MY, IGARASHI-SAN...
...YOU CAME HERE VERY QUICKLY!
YOU MUST'VE GOTTEN ALL THE QUESTIONS RIGHT... DIDN'T YOU?

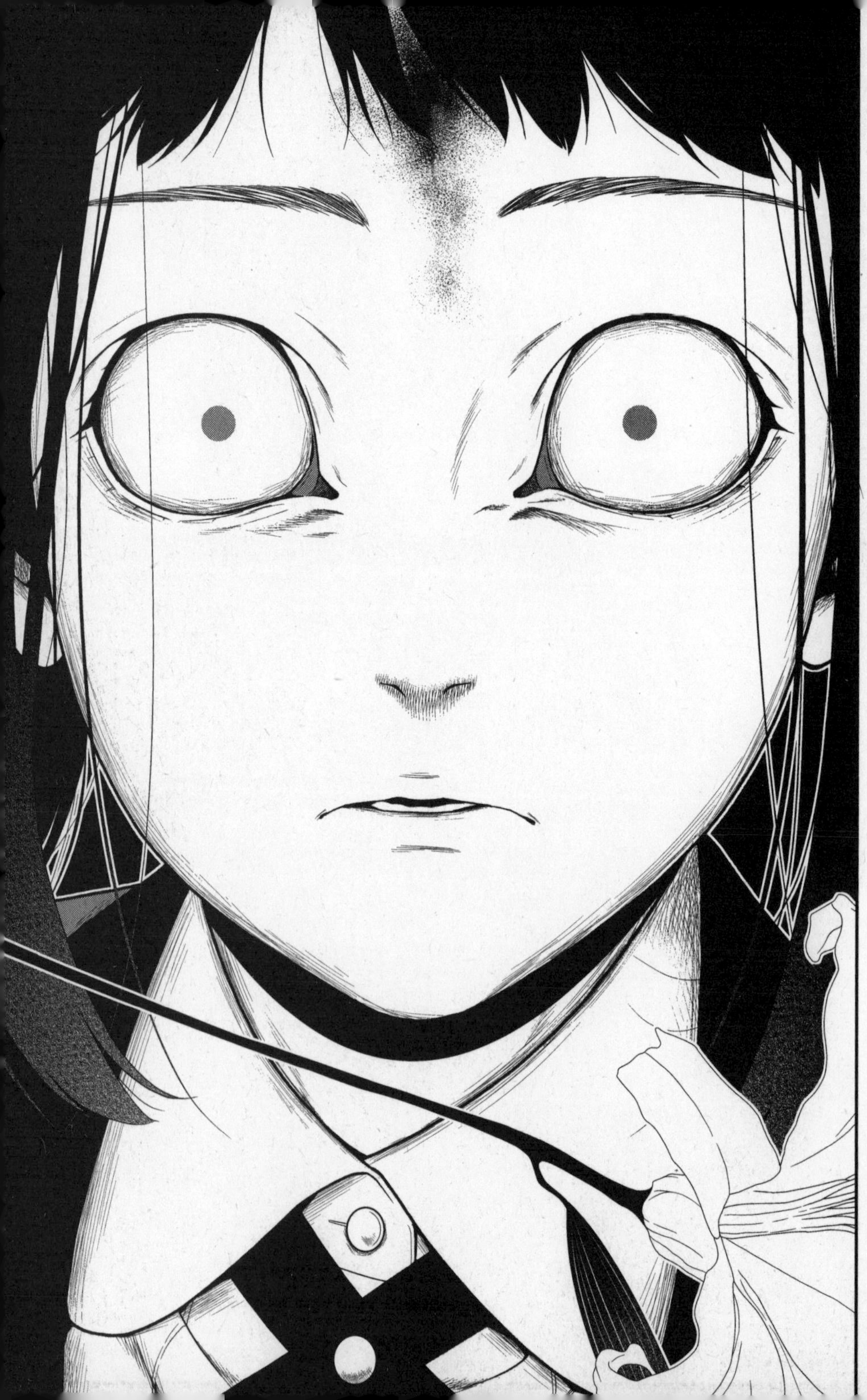

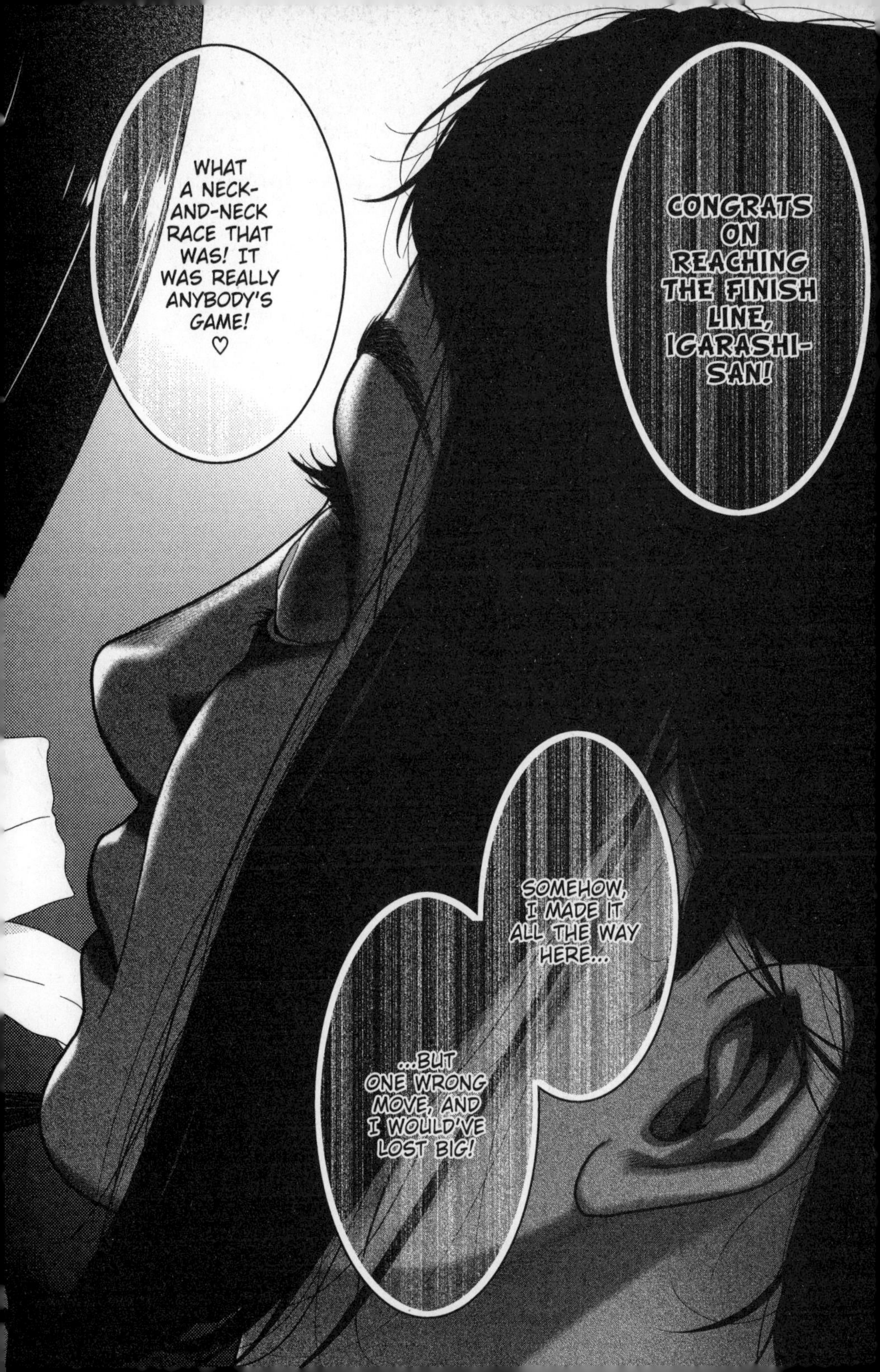
CONGRATS ON REACHING THE FINISH LINE, IGARASHI-SAN!
WHAT A NECK-AND-NECK RACE THAT WAS! IT WAS REALLY ANYBODY'S GAME! ♡
SOMEHOW, I MADE IT ALL THE WAY HERE...
...BUT ONE WRONG MOVE, AND I WOULD'VE LOST BIG!

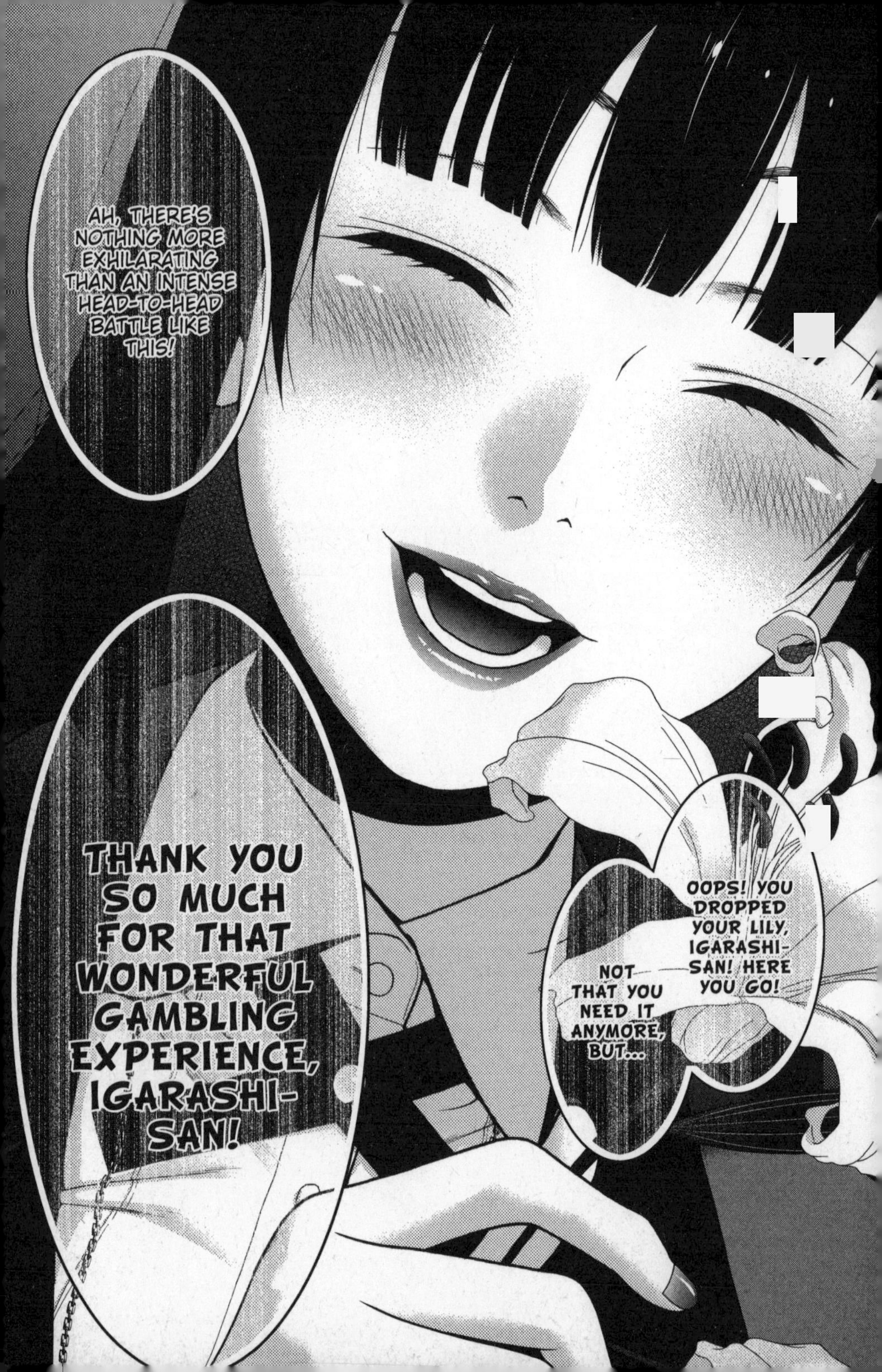
AH, THERE'S NOTHING MORE EXHILARATING THAN AN INTENSE HEAD-TO-HEAD BATTLE LIKE THIS!
OOPS! YOU DROPPED YOUR LILY, IGARASHI-SAN! HERE YOU GO!
NOT THAT YOU NEED IT ANYMORE, BUT...
THANK YOU SO MUCH FOR THAT WONDERFUL GAMBLING EXPERIENCE, IGARASHI-SAN!

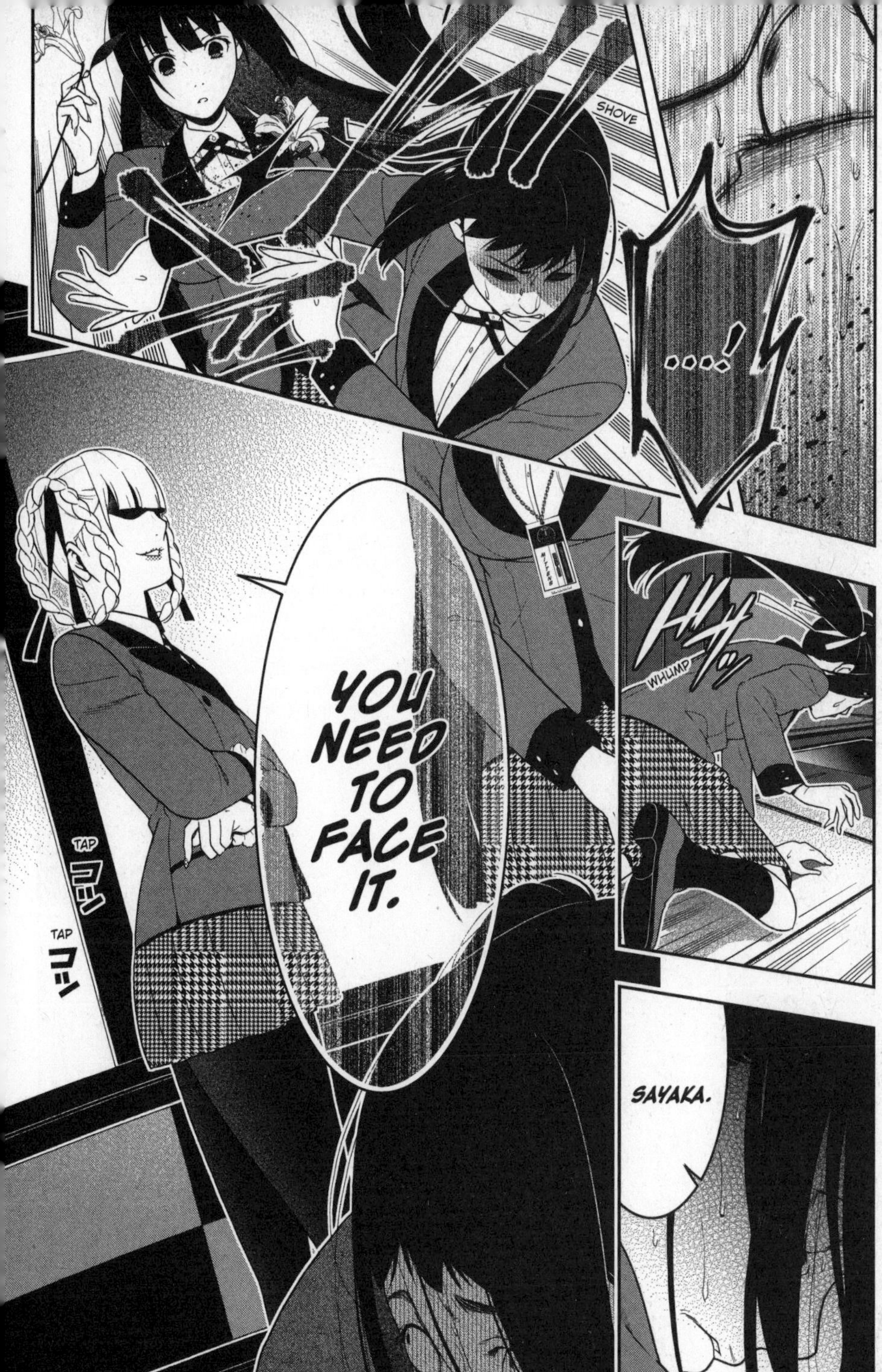
SHOVE
...!
WHUMP
YOU NEED TO FACE IT.
TAP
TAP
SAYAKA.

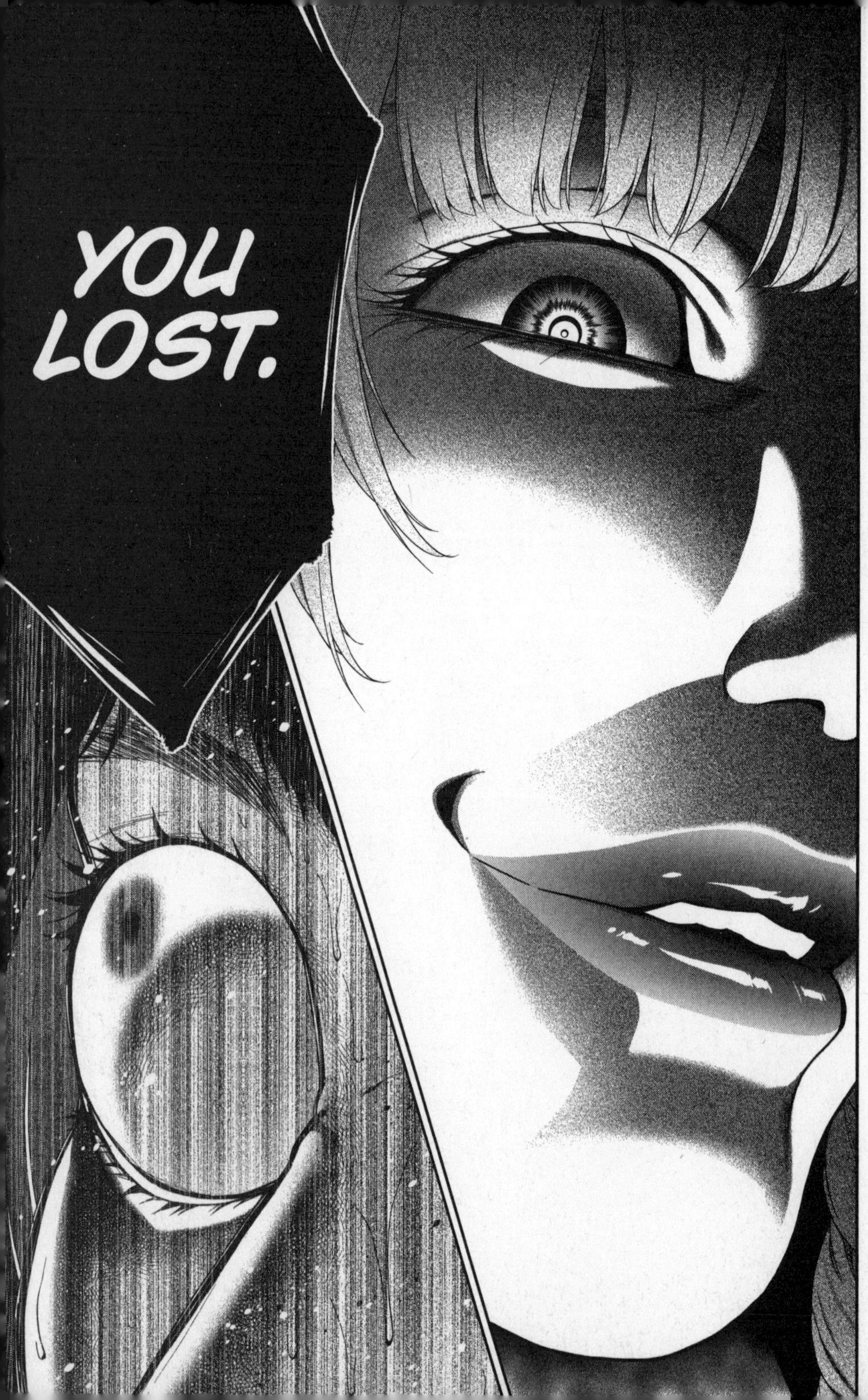
YOU LOST.

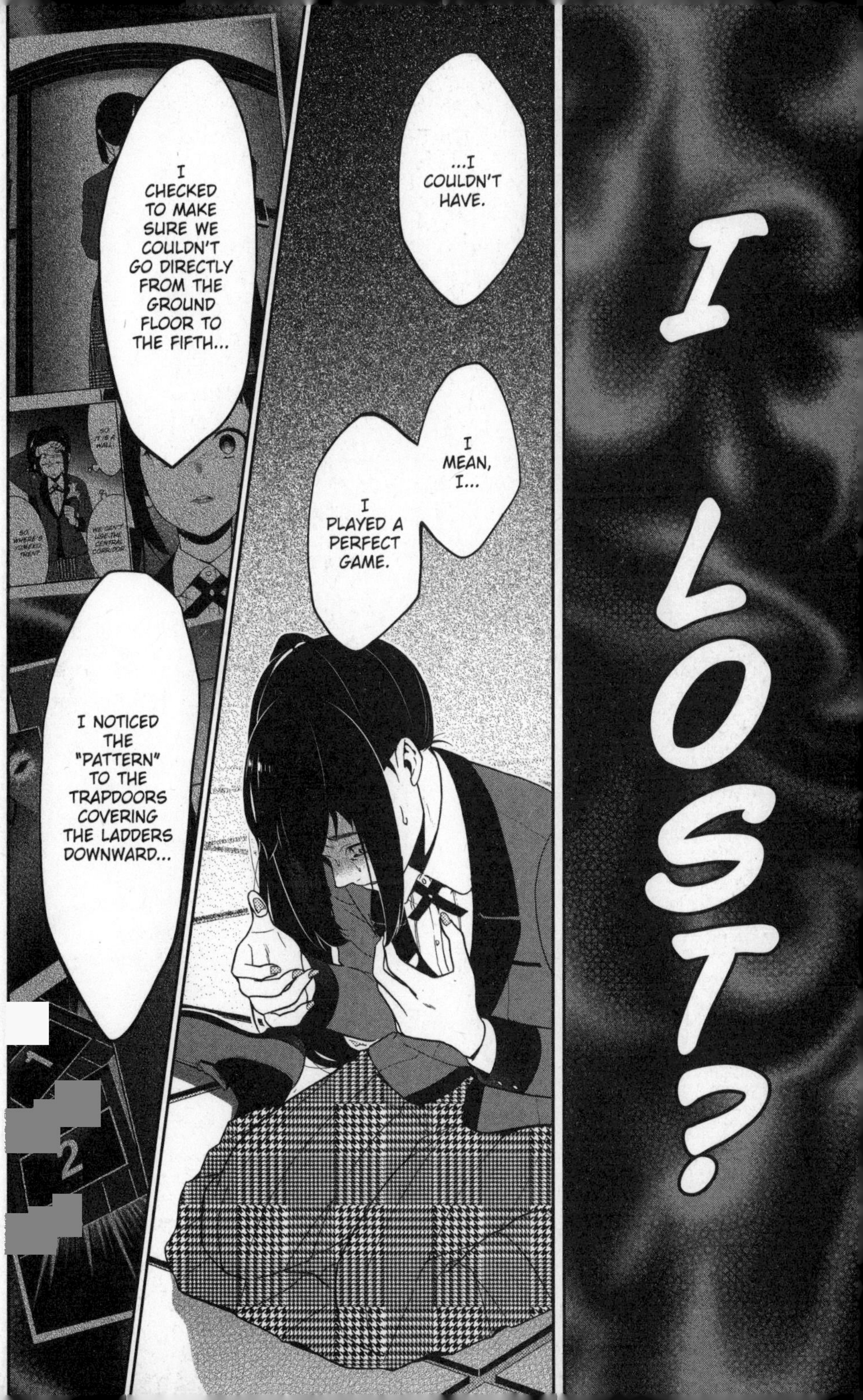
I LOST?
...I COULDN'T HAVE.
I MEAN, I...
I PLAYED A PERFECT GAME.
I CHECKED TO MAKE SURE WE COULDN'T GO DIRECTLY FROM THE GROUND FLOOR TO THE FIFTH...
SO IT IS A WALL
WE CAN'T USE THE CENTRAL CORRIDOR
I NOTICED THE "PATTERN" TO THE TRAPDOORS COVERING THE LADDERS DOWNWARD...

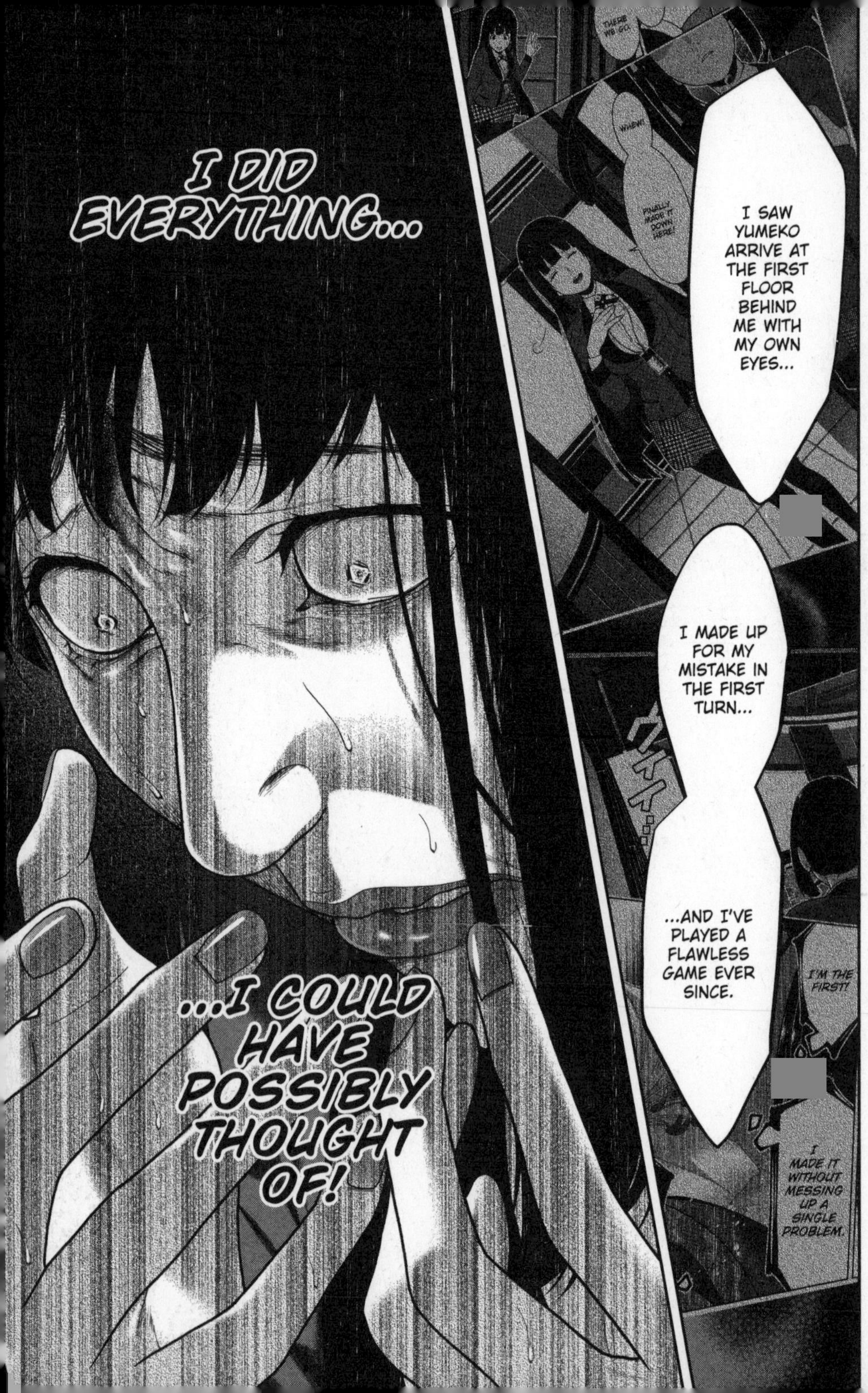
THERE WE GO.
WHEW!
FINALLY MADE IT DOWN HERE!
I SAW YUMEKO ARRIVE AT THE FIRST FLOOR BEHIND ME WITH MY OWN EYES...
I MADE UP FOR MY MISTAKE IN THE FIRST TURN...
...AND I'VE PLAYED A FLAWLESS GAME EVER SINCE.
I'M THE FIRST!
I MADE IT WITHOUT MESSING UP A SINGLE PROBLEM.
I DID EVERYTHING...
...I COULD HAVE POSSIBLY THOUGHT OF!

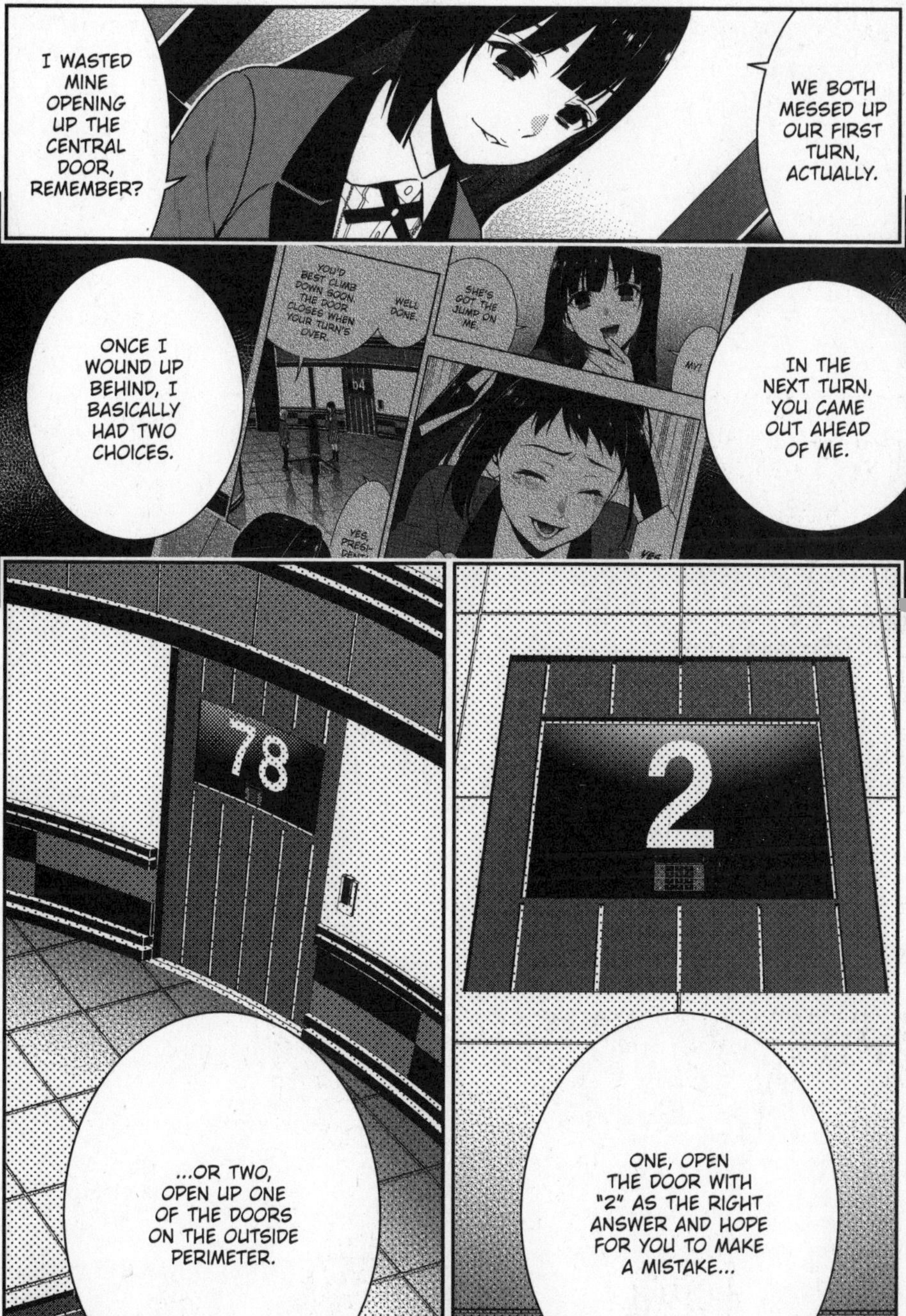
WE BOTH MESSED UP OUR FIRST TURN, ACTUALLY.
I WASTED MINE OPENING UP THE CENTRAL DOOR, REMEMBER?
IN THE NEXT TURN, YOU CAME OUT AHEAD OF ME.
MY!
SHE'S GOT THE JUMP ON ME.
WELL DONE.
YOU'D BEST CLIMB DOWN SOON. THE DOOR CLOSES WHEN YOUR TURN'S OVER.
ONCE I WOUND UP BEHIND, I BASICALLY HAD TWO CHOICES.
2
ONE, OPEN THE DOOR WITH "2" AS THE RIGHT ANSWER AND HOPE FOR YOU TO MAKE A MISTAKE...
78
...OR TWO, OPEN UP ONE OF THE DOORS ON THE OUTSIDE PERIMETER.

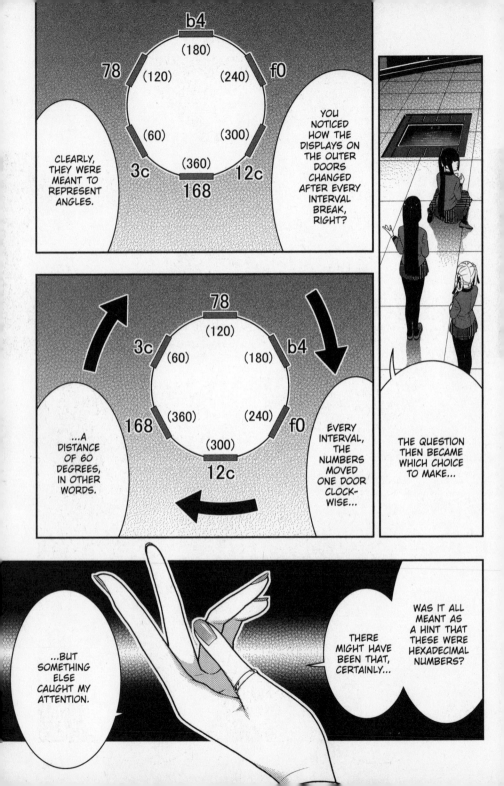

Panel 1 (diagram):

b4

(180)

78 (120) (240) f0

(60) (300)

(360)

3c 168 12c

YOU NOTICED HOW THE DISPLAYS ON THE OUTER DOORS CHANGED AFTER EVERY INTERVAL BREAK, RIGHT?

CLEARLY, THEY WERE MEANT TO REPRESENT ANGLES.

Panel 2 (diagram):

78

(120)

3c (60) (180) b4

(360) (240)

168 (300) f0

12c

EVERY INTERVAL, THE NUMBERS MOVED ONE DOOR CLOCK-WISE...

...A DISTANCE OF 60 DEGREES, IN OTHER WORDS.

THE QUESTION THEN BECAME WHICH CHOICE TO MAKE...

Panel 3:

WAS IT ALL MEANT AS A HINT THAT THESE WERE HEXADECIMAL NUMBERS?

THERE MIGHT HAVE BEEN THAT, CERTAINLY...

...BUT SOMETHING ELSE CAUGHT MY ATTENTION.

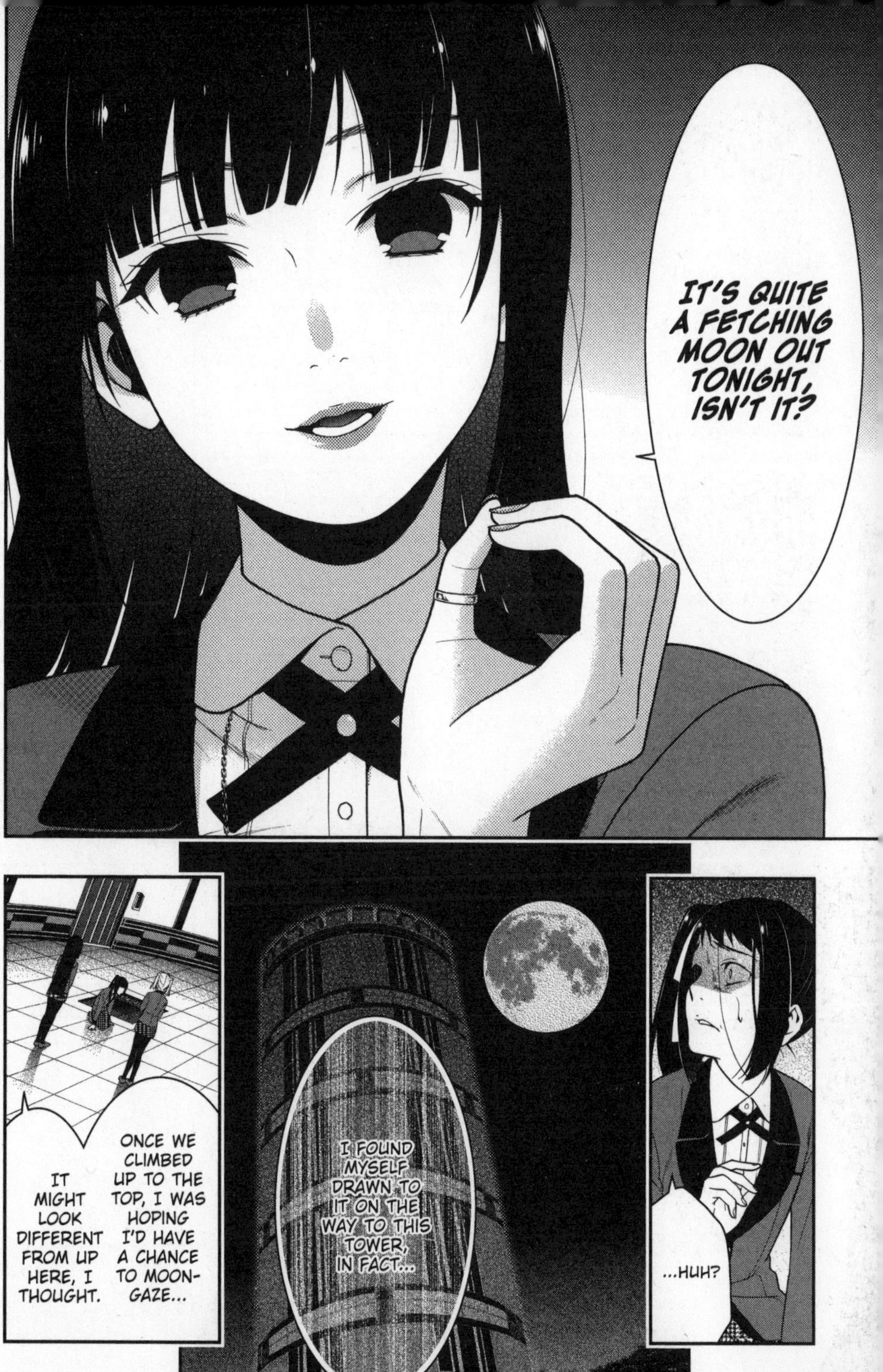
IT'S QUITE A FETCHING MOON OUT TONIGHT, ISN'T IT?
...HUH?
I FOUND MYSELF DRAWN TO IT ON THE WAY TO THIS TOWER, IN FACT...
ONCE WE CLIMBED UP TO THE TOP, I WAS HOPING I'D HAVE A CHANCE TO MOON-GAZE...
IT MIGHT LOOK DIFFERENT FROM UP HERE, I THOUGHT.

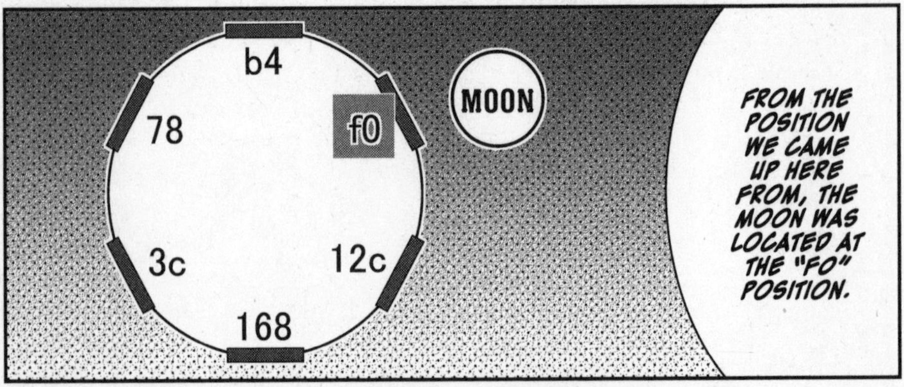
FROM THE POSITION WE CAME UP HERE FROM, THE MOON WAS LOCATED AT THE "F0" POSITION.
MOON
b4
f0
78
12c
3c
168

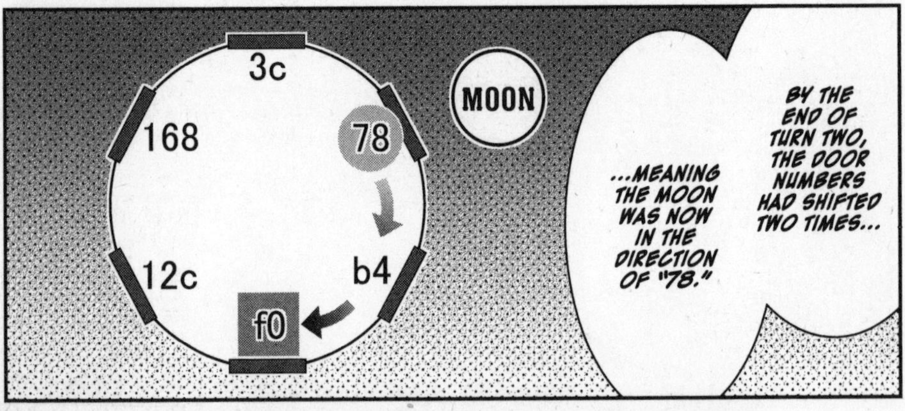
BY THE END OF TURN TWO, THE DOOR NUMBERS HAD SHIFTED TWO TIMES...
...MEANING THE MOON WAS NOW IN THE DIRECTION OF "78."
MOON
3c
78
168
b4
12c
f0

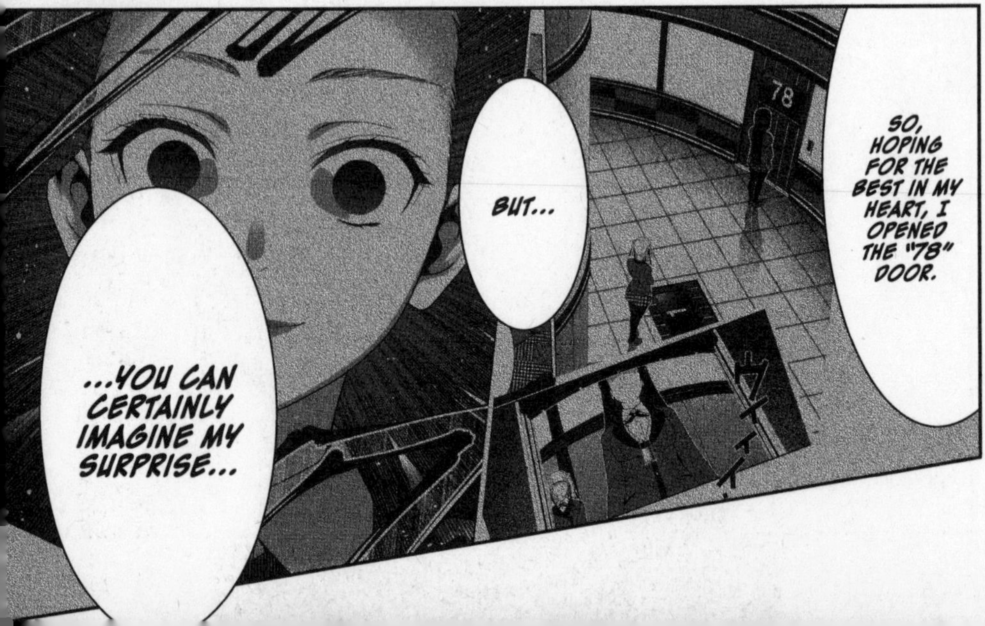
SO, HOPING FOR THE BEST IN MY HEART, I OPENED THE "78" DOOR.
78
BUT...
...YOU CAN CERTAINLY IMAGINE MY SURPRISE...

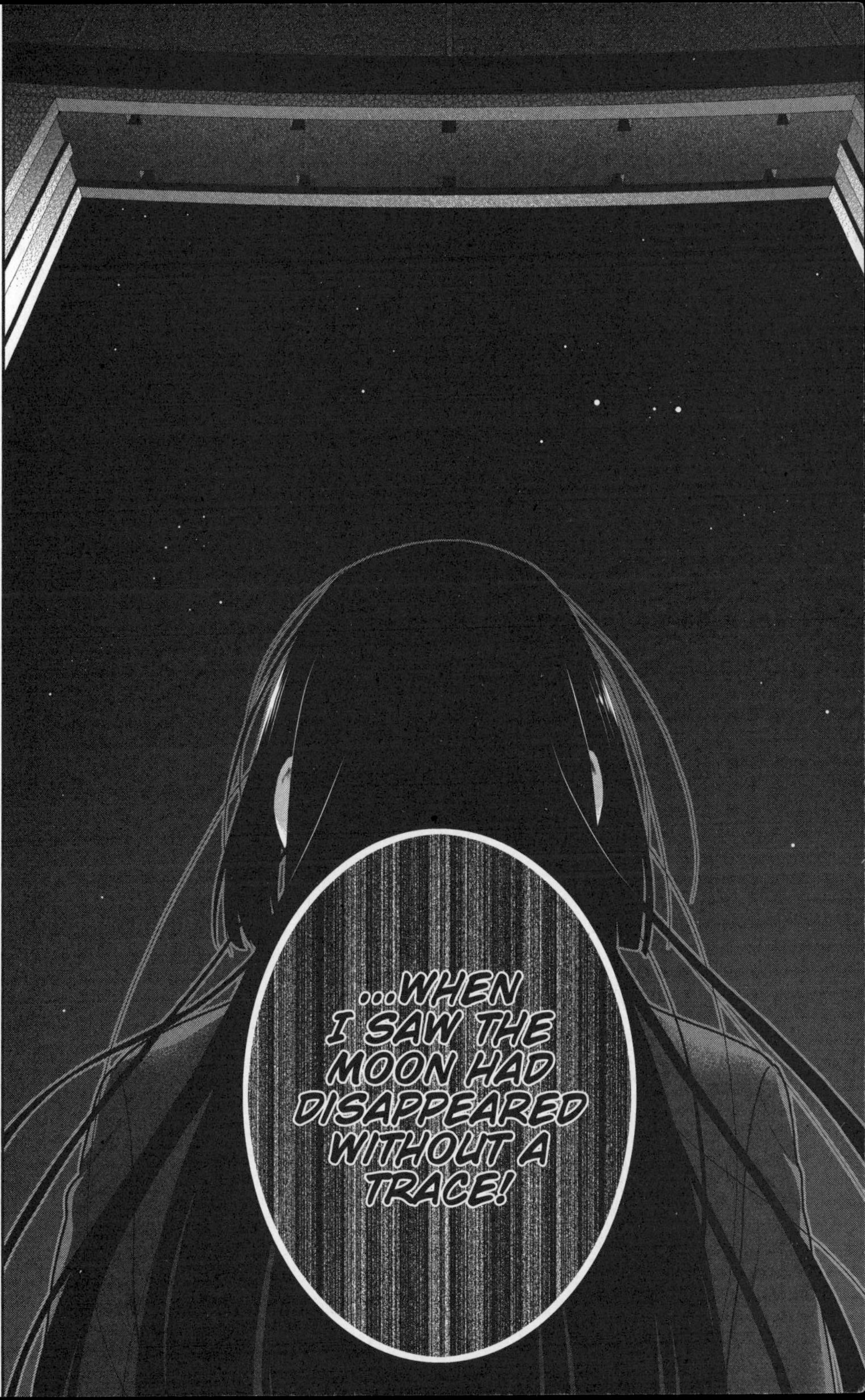
...WHEN I SAW THE MOON HAD DISAPPEARED WITHOUT A TRACE!

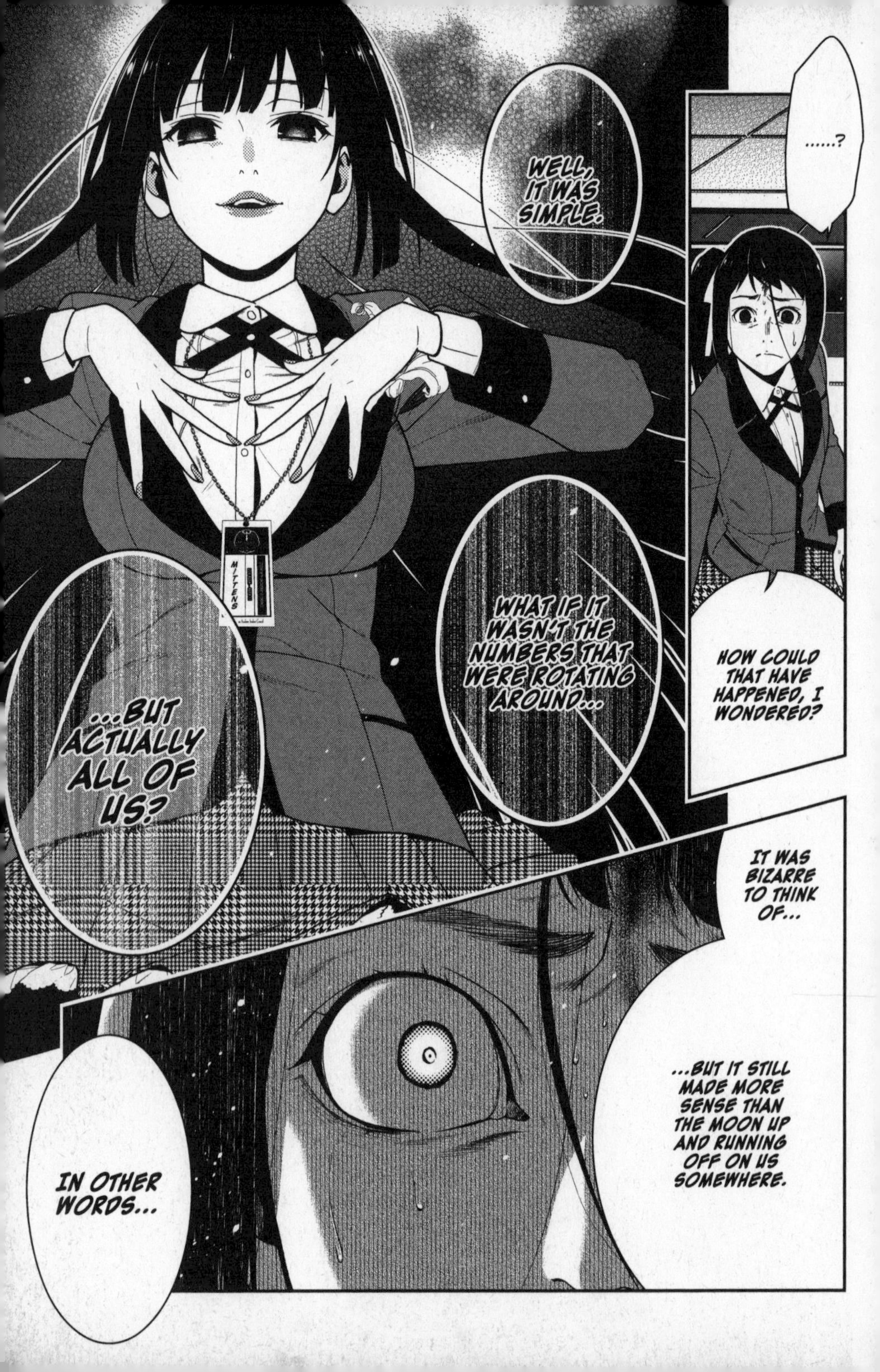
......?
HOW COULD THAT HAVE HAPPENED, I WONDERED?
WELL, IT WAS SIMPLE.
WHAT IF IT WASN'T THE NUMBERS THAT WERE ROTATING AROUND...
...BUT ACTUALLY ALL OF US?
IT WAS BIZARRE TO THINK OF...
...BUT IT STILL MADE MORE SENSE THAN THE MOON UP AND RUNNING OFF ON US SOMEWHERE.
IN OTHER WORDS...

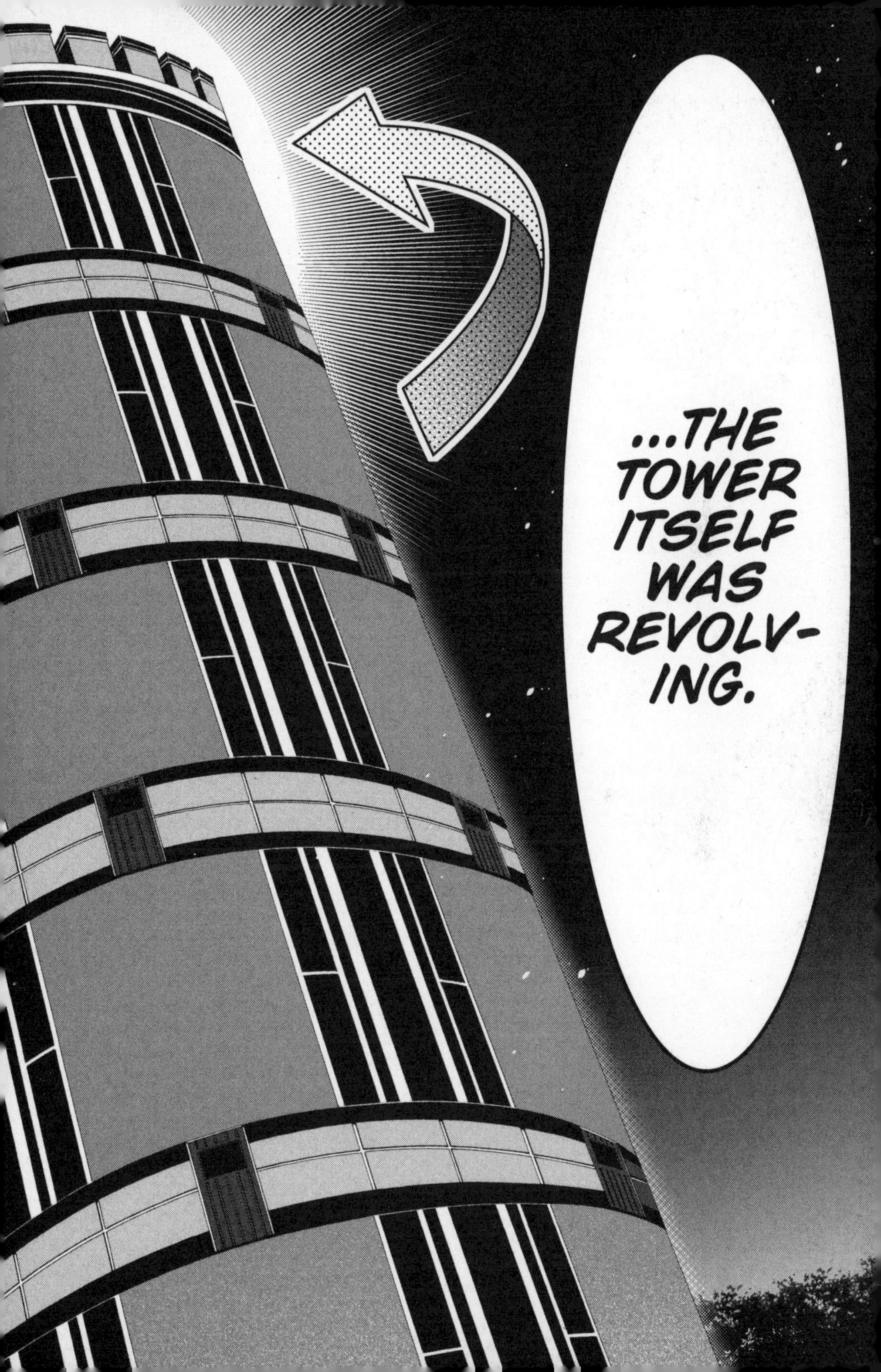
...THE TOWER ITSELF WAS REVOLV-ING.

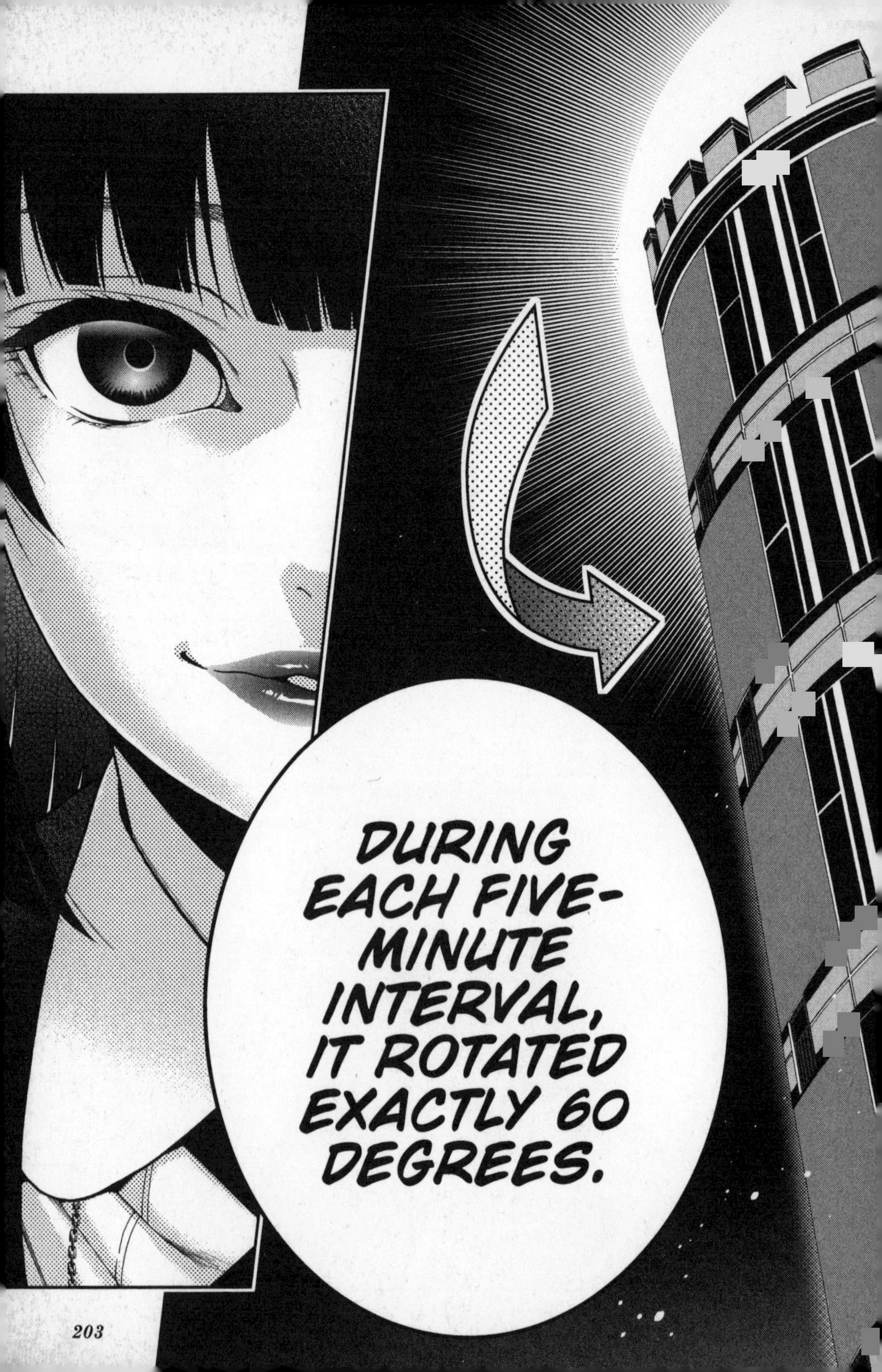
DURING EACH FIVE-MINUTE INTERVAL, IT ROTATED EXACTLY 60 DEGREES.

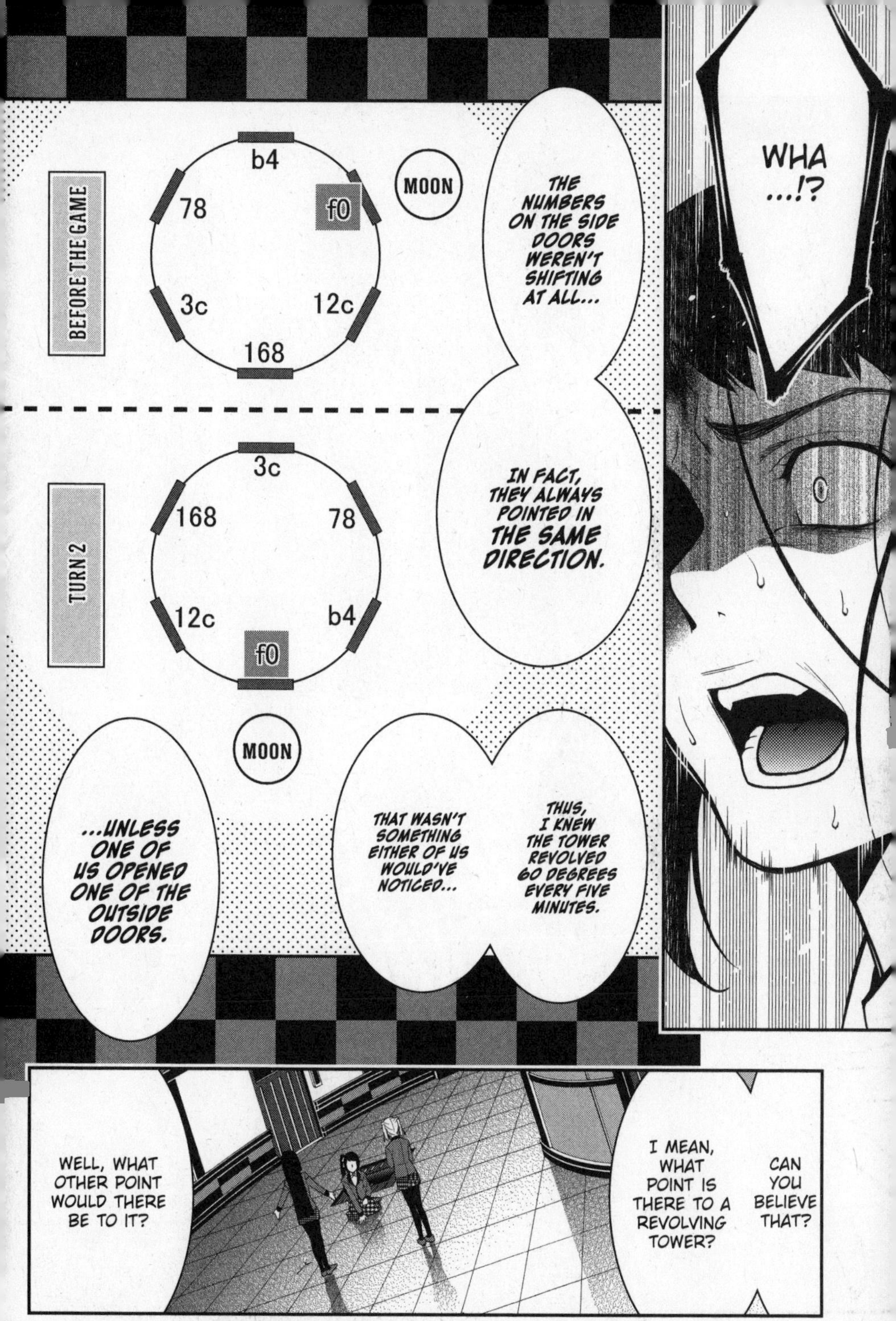

WHA ...!?
THE NUMBERS ON THE SIDE DOORS WEREN'T SHIFTING AT ALL...
IN FACT, THEY ALWAYS POINTED IN THE SAME DIRECTION.
BEFORE THE GAME
b4
78
f0
3c
12c
168
MOON
TURN 2
3c
168
78
12c
b4
f0
MOON
THUS, I KNEW THE TOWER REVOLVED 60 DEGREES EVERY FIVE MINUTES.
THAT WASN'T SOMETHING EITHER OF US WOULD'VE NOTICED...
...UNLESS ONE OF US OPENED ONE OF THE OUTSIDE DOORS.
CAN YOU BELIEVE THAT?
I MEAN, WHAT POINT IS THERE TO A REVOLVING TOWER?
WELL, WHAT OTHER POINT WOULD THERE BE TO IT?

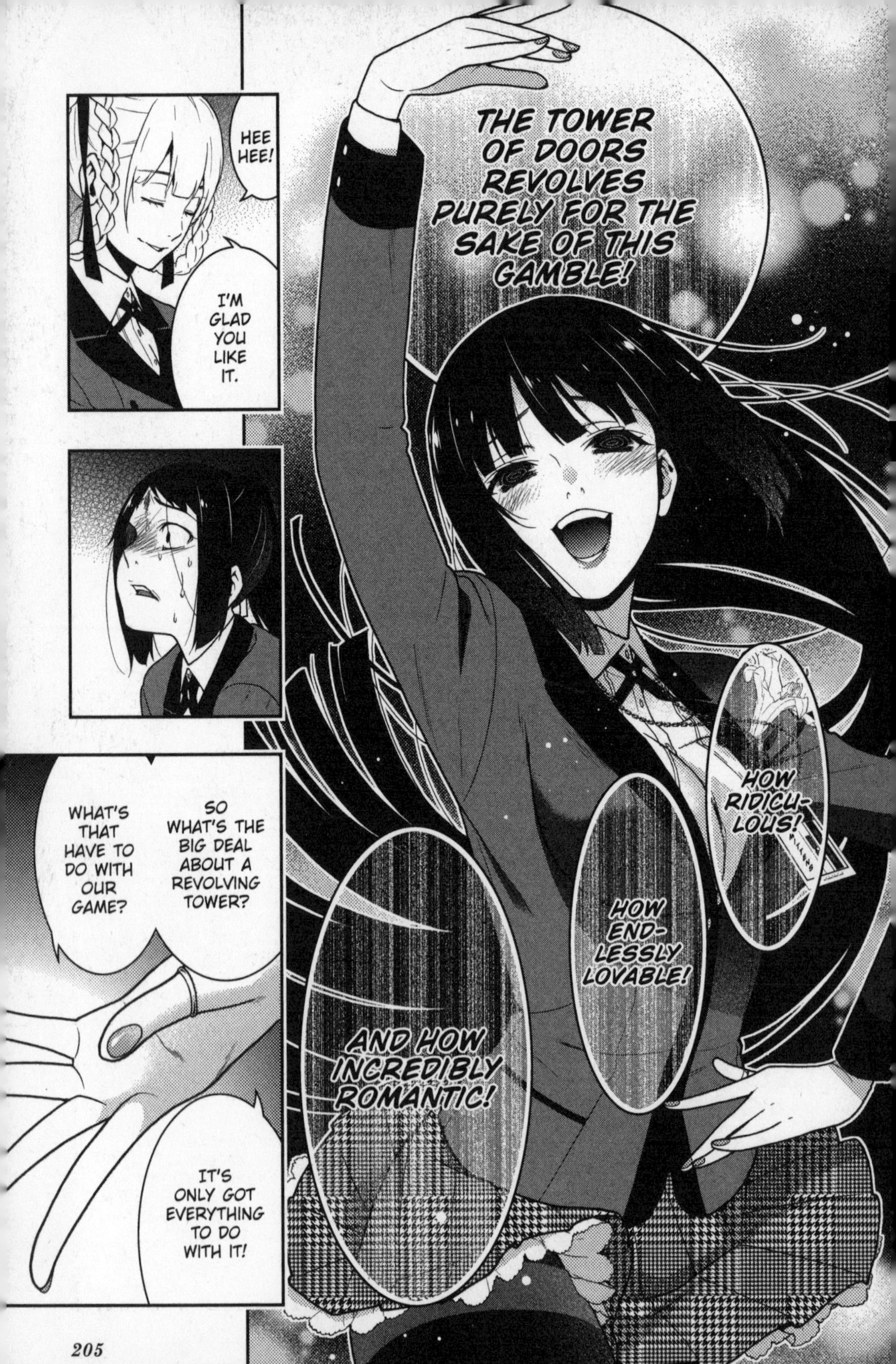
THE TOWER OF DOORS REVOLVES PURELY FOR THE SAKE OF THIS GAMBLE!
HOW RIDICU-LOUS!
HOW END-LESSLY LOVABLE!
AND HOW INCREDIBLY ROMANTIC!
HEE HEE!
I'M GLAD YOU LIKE IT.
SO WHAT'S THE BIG DEAL ABOUT A REVOLVING TOWER?
WHAT'S THAT HAVE TO DO WITH OUR GAME?
IT'S ONLY GOT EVERYTHING TO DO WITH IT!

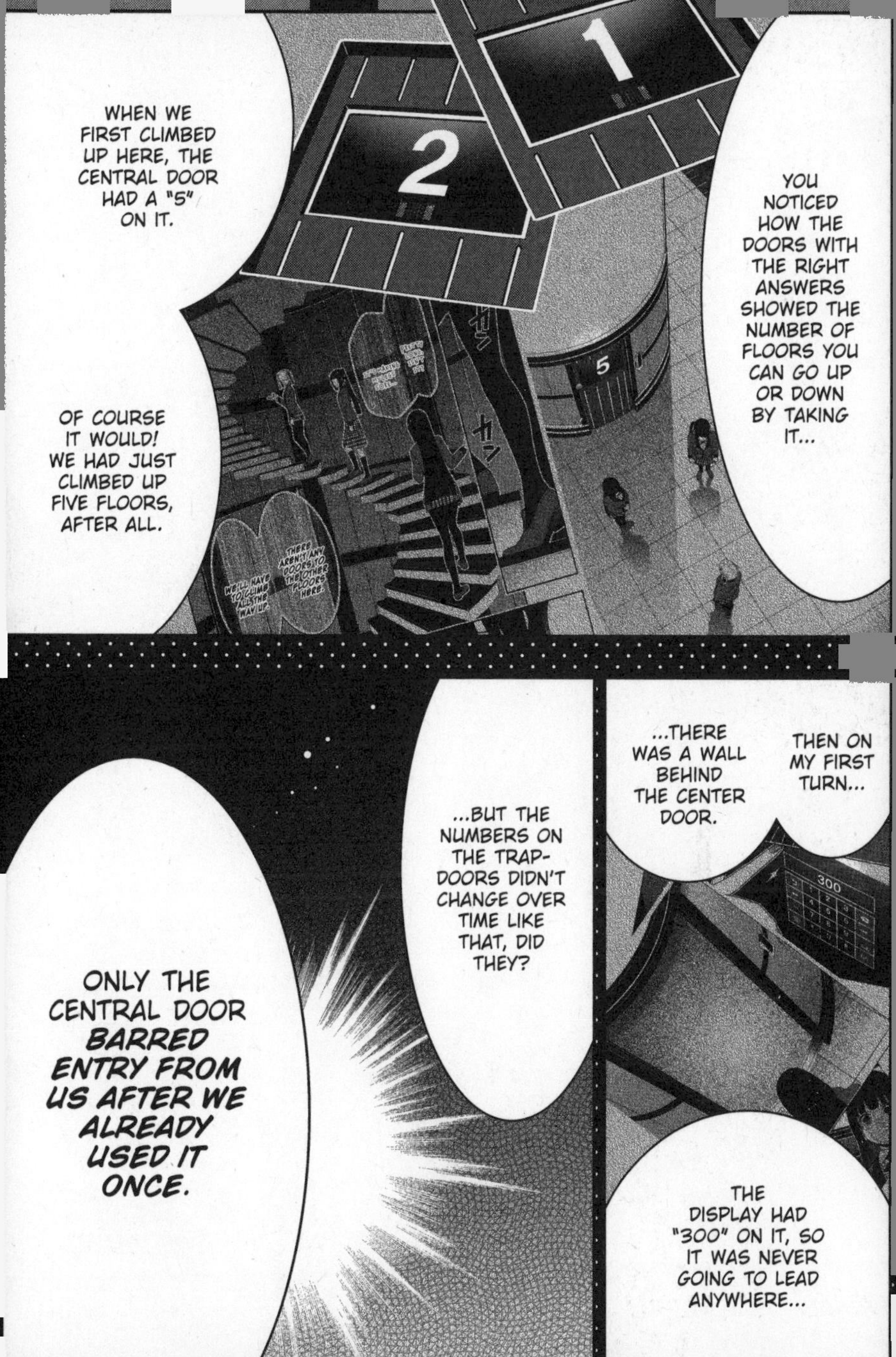
YOU NOTICED HOW THE DOORS WITH THE RIGHT ANSWERS SHOWED THE NUMBER OF FLOORS YOU CAN GO UP OR DOWN BY TAKING IT...
1
2
WHEN WE FIRST CLIMBED UP HERE, THE CENTRAL DOOR HAD A "5" ON IT.
5
PRETTY LONG, ISN'T IT?
IT'S MAKING MY LEGS SORE...
THERE AREN'T ANY DOORS TO THE OTHER FLOORS HERE.
WE'LL HAVE TO CLIMB ALL THE WAY UP.
OF COURSE IT WOULD! WE HAD JUST CLIMBED UP FIVE FLOORS, AFTER ALL.
THEN ON MY FIRST TURN...
...THERE WAS A WALL BEHIND THE CENTER DOOR.
300
THE DISPLAY HAD "300" ON IT, SO IT WAS NEVER GOING TO LEAD ANYWHERE...
...BUT THE NUMBERS ON THE TRAP-DOORS DIDN'T CHANGE OVER TIME LIKE THAT, DID THEY?
ONLY THE CENTRAL DOOR BARRED ENTRY FROM US AFTER WE ALREADY USED IT ONCE.

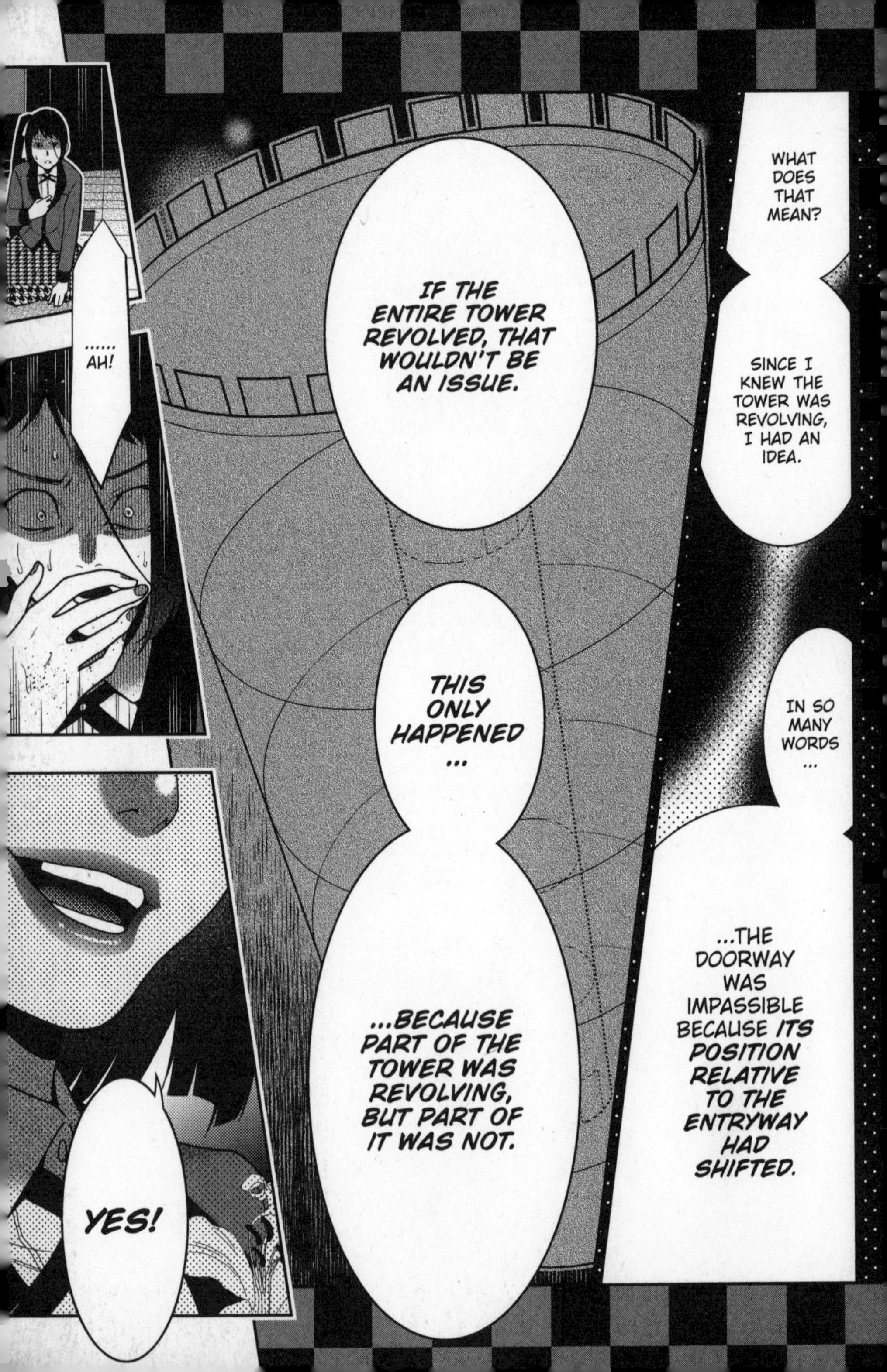
WHAT DOES THAT MEAN?
SINCE I KNEW THE TOWER WAS REVOLVING, I HAD AN IDEA.
IN SO MANY WORDS...
...THE DOORWAY WAS IMPASSIBLE BECAUSE ITS POSITION RELATIVE TO THE ENTRYWAY HAD SHIFTED.
IF THE ENTIRE TOWER REVOLVED, THAT WOULDN'T BE AN ISSUE.
THIS ONLY HAPPENED...
...BECAUSE PART OF THE TOWER WAS REVOLVING, BUT PART OF IT WAS NOT.
......AH!
YES!

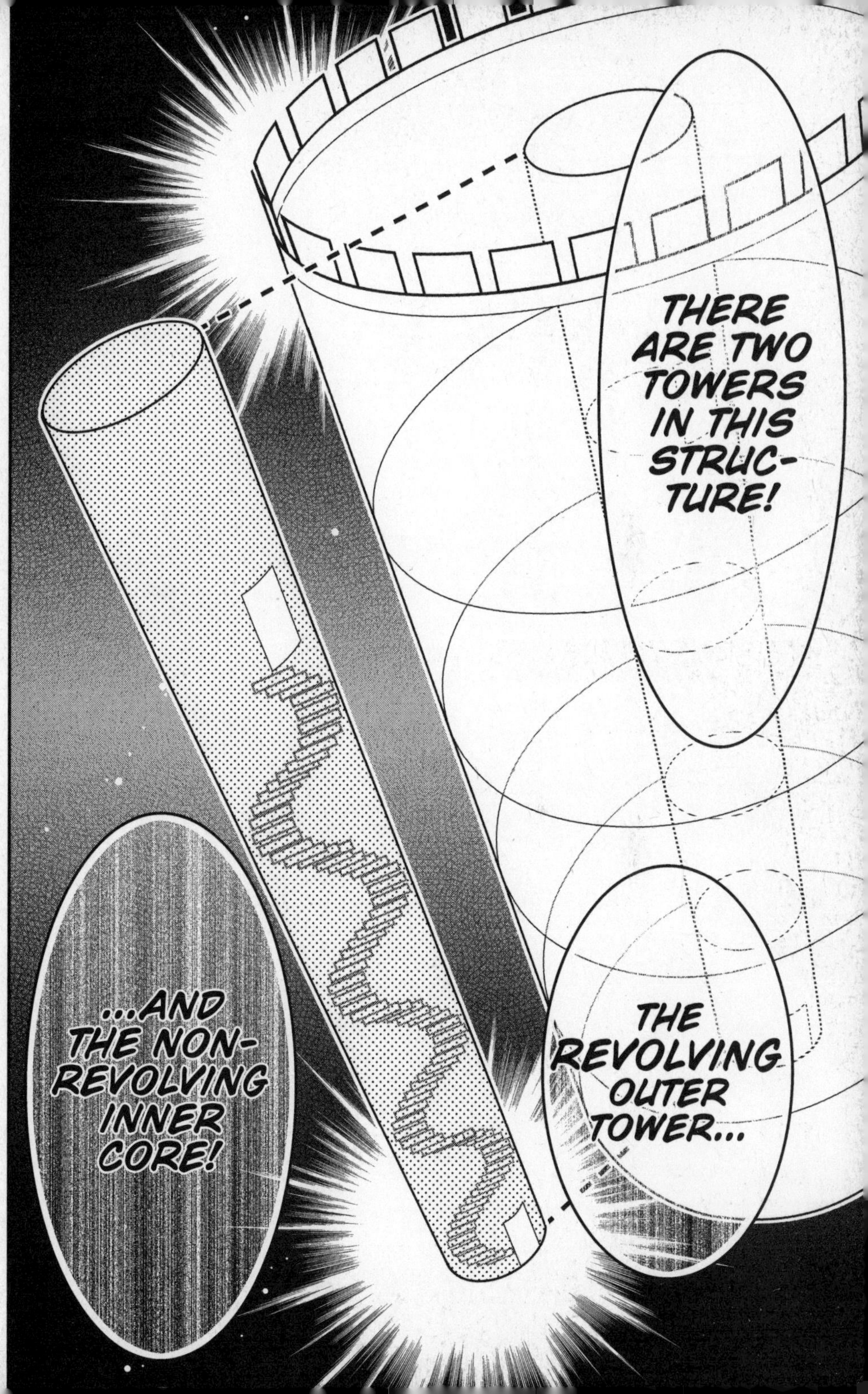
THERE ARE TWO TOWERS IN THIS STRUC-TURE!
THE REVOLVING OUTER TOWER...
...AND THE NON-REVOLVING INNER CORE!

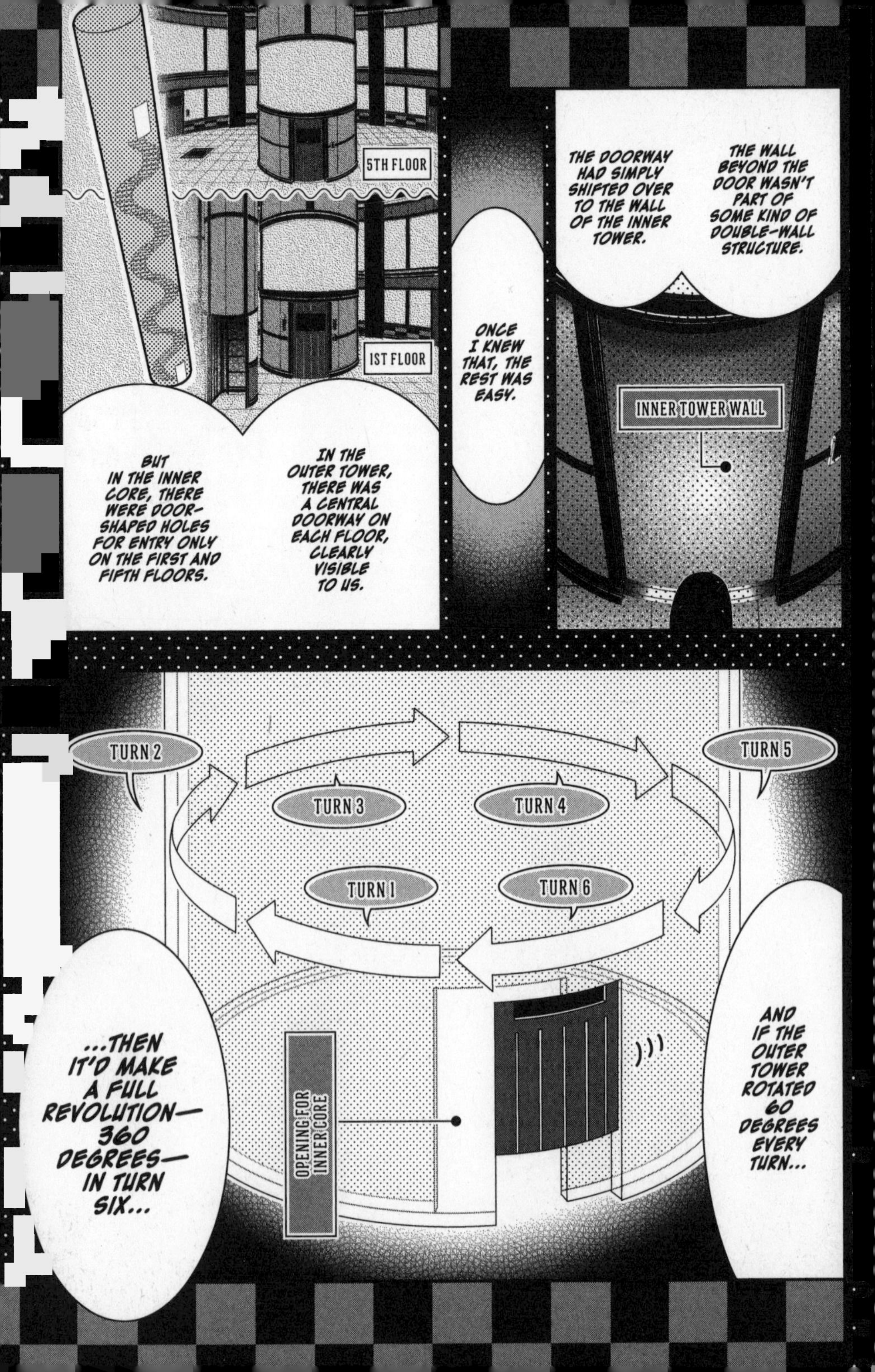
THE WALL BEYOND THE DOOR WASN'T PART OF SOME KIND OF DOUBLE-WALL STRUCTURE.
THE DOORWAY HAD SIMPLY SHIFTED OVER TO THE WALL OF THE INNER TOWER.
INNER TOWER WALL
ONCE I KNEW THAT, THE REST WAS EASY.
5TH FLOOR
1ST FLOOR
IN THE OUTER TOWER, THERE WAS A CENTRAL DOORWAY ON EACH FLOOR, CLEARLY VISIBLE TO US.
BUT IN THE INNER CORE, THERE WERE DOOR-SHAPED HOLES FOR ENTRY ONLY ON THE FIRST AND FIFTH FLOORS.
AND IF THE OUTER TOWER ROTATED 60 DEGREES EVERY TURN...
TURN 5
TURN 4
TURN 3
TURN 2
TURN 6
TURN 1
OPENING FOR INNER CORE
...THEN IT'D MAKE A FULL REVOLUTION—360 DEGREES—IN TURN SIX...

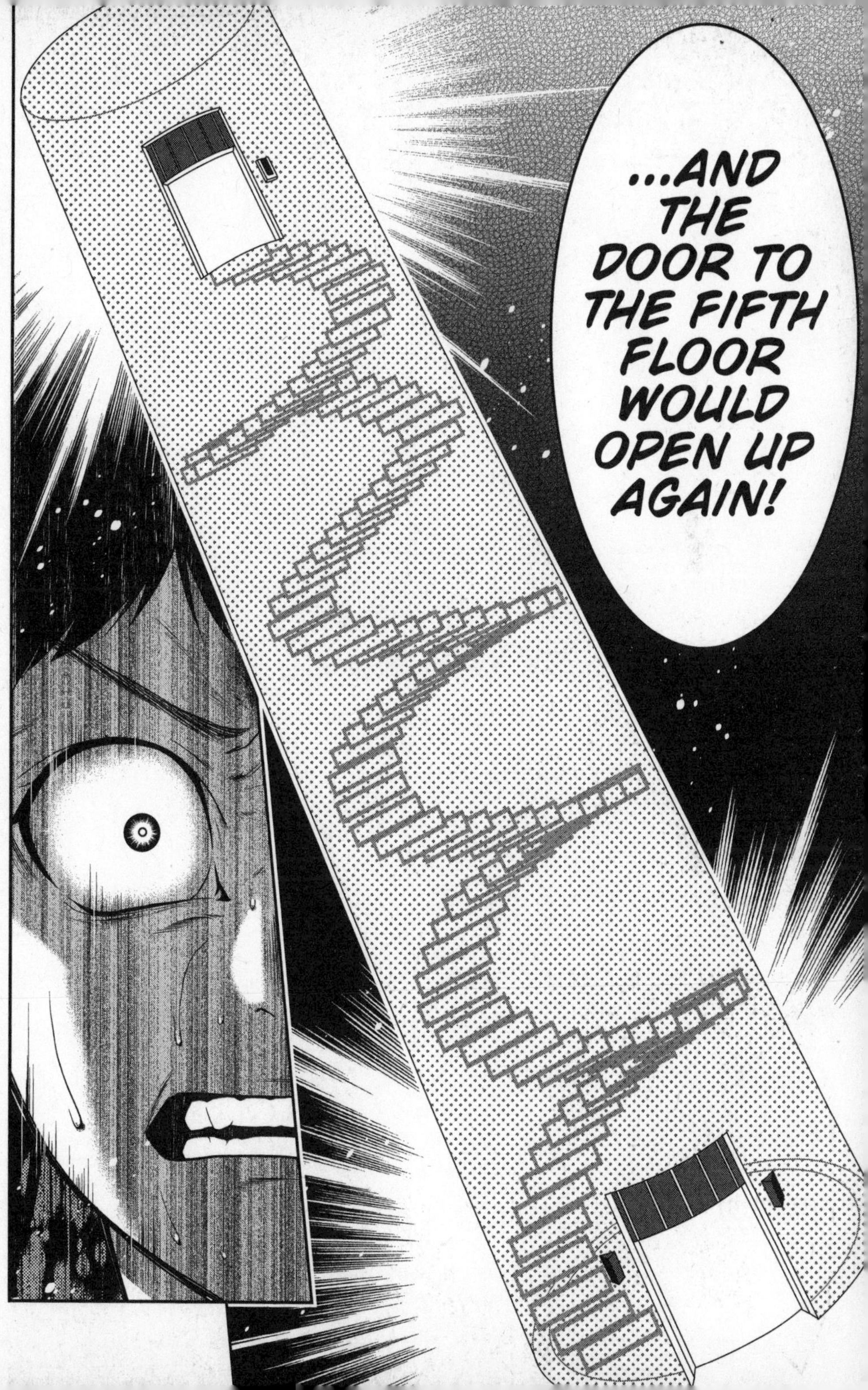
...AND THE DOOR TO THE FIFTH FLOOR WOULD OPEN UP AGAIN!

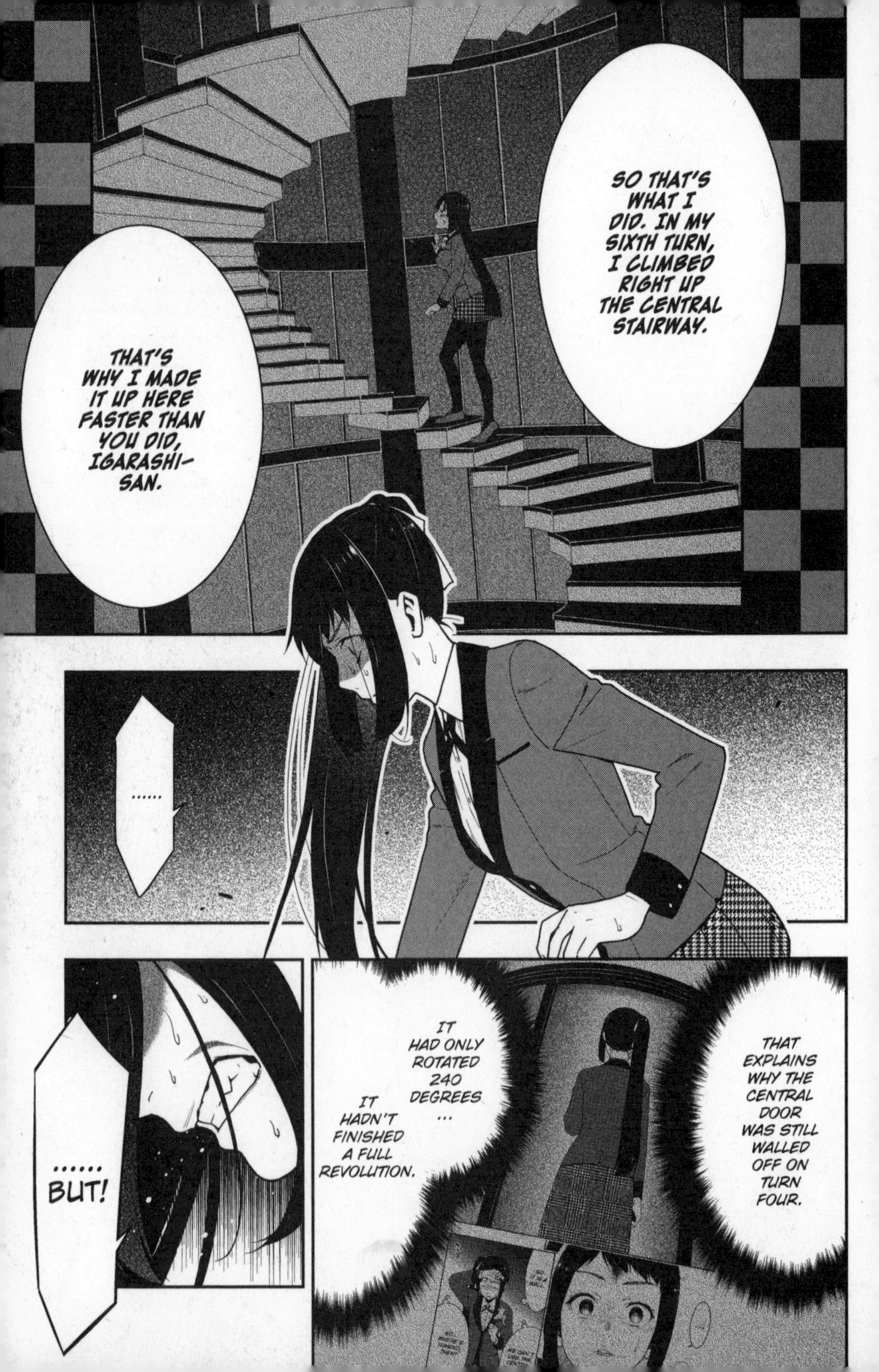
SO THAT'S WHAT I DID. IN MY SIXTH TURN, I CLIMBED RIGHT UP THE CENTRAL STAIRWAY.
THAT'S WHY I MADE IT UP HERE FASTER THAN YOU DID, IGARASHI-SAN.
......
THAT EXPLAINS WHY THE CENTRAL DOOR WAS STILL WALLED OFF ON TURN FOUR.
IT HAD ONLY ROTATED 240 DEGREES...
IT HADN'T FINISHED A FULL REVOLUTION.
...... BUT!

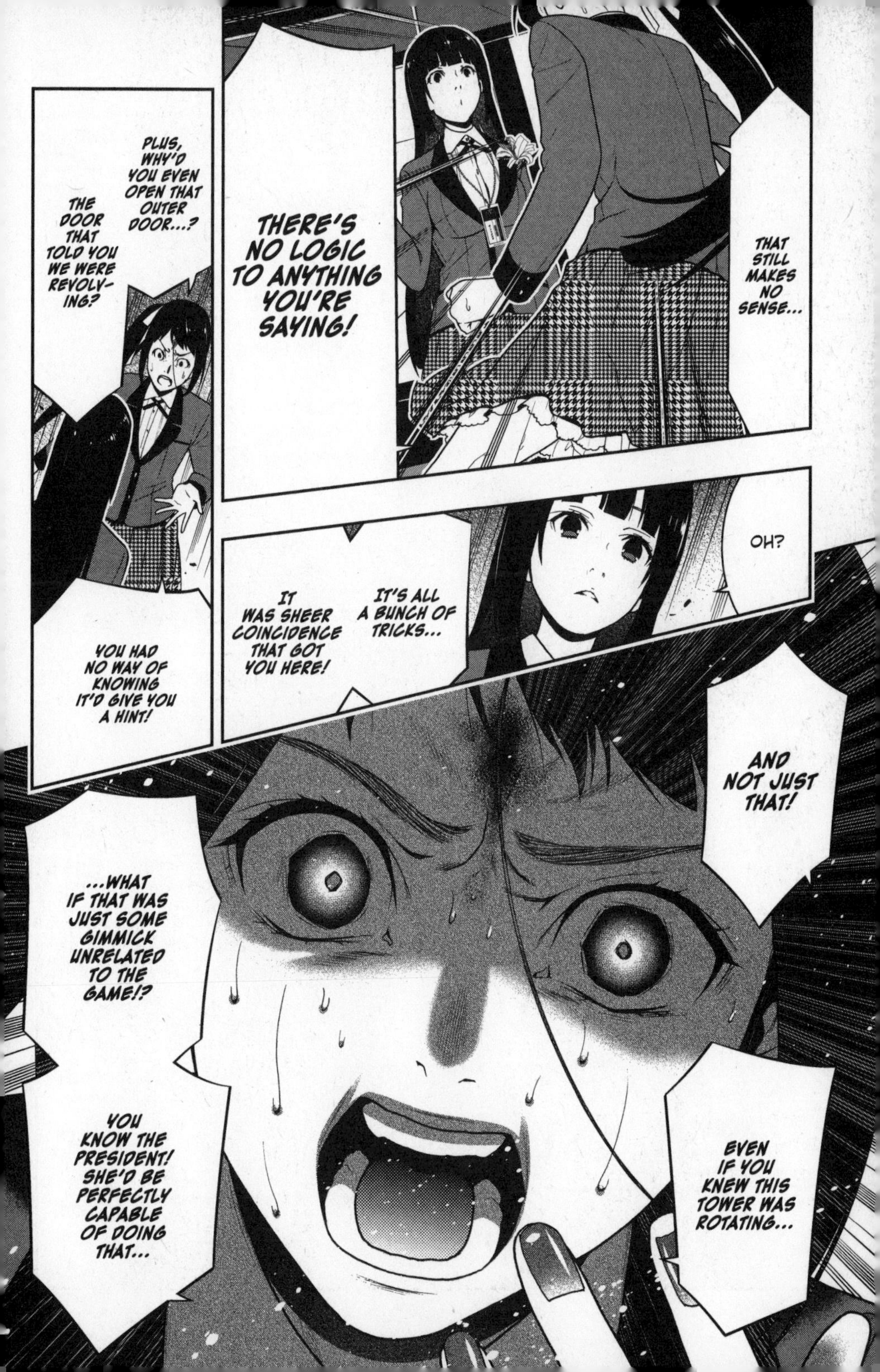

THAT STILL MAKES NO SENSE...
THERE'S NO LOGIC TO ANYTHING YOU'RE SAYING!
OH?
IT'S ALL A BUNCH OF TRICKS...
IT WAS SHEER COINCIDENCE THAT GOT YOU HERE!
PLUS, WHY'D YOU EVEN OPEN THAT OUTER DOOR...?
THE DOOR THAT TOLD YOU WE WERE REVOLVING?
YOU HAD NO WAY OF KNOWING IT'D GIVE YOU A HINT!
AND NOT JUST THAT!
EVEN IF YOU KNEW THIS TOWER WAS ROTATING...
...WHAT IF THAT WAS JUST SOME GIMMICK UNRELATED TO THE GAME!?
YOU KNOW THE PRESIDENT! SHE'D BE PERFECTLY CAPABLE OF DOING THAT...

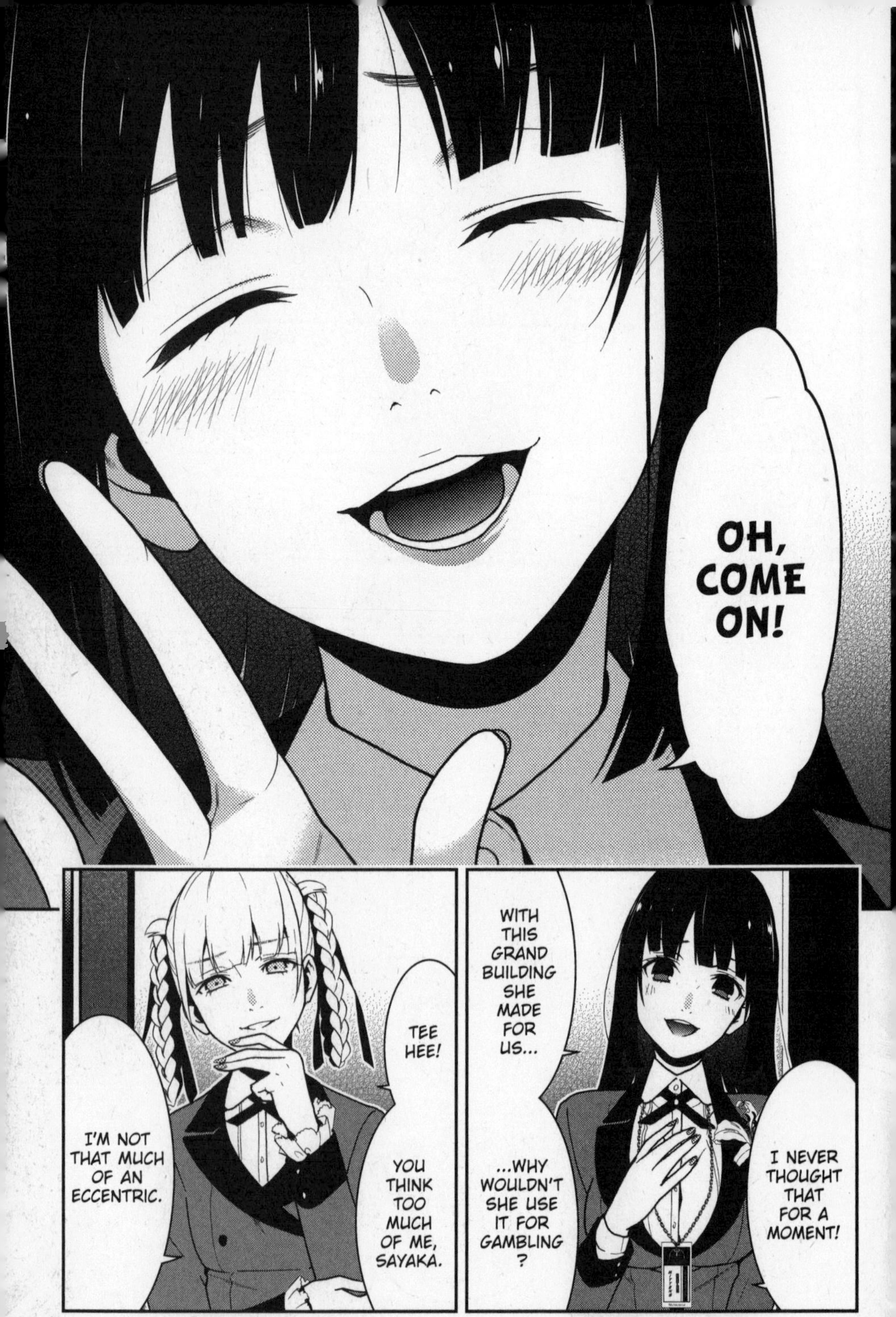
OH, COME ON!
I NEVER THOUGHT THAT FOR A MOMENT!
WITH THIS GRAND BUILDING SHE MADE FOR US...
...WHY WOULDN'T SHE USE IT FOR GAMBLING?
TEE HEE!
YOU THINK TOO MUCH OF ME, SAYAKA.
I'M NOT THAT MUCH OF AN ECCENTRIC.

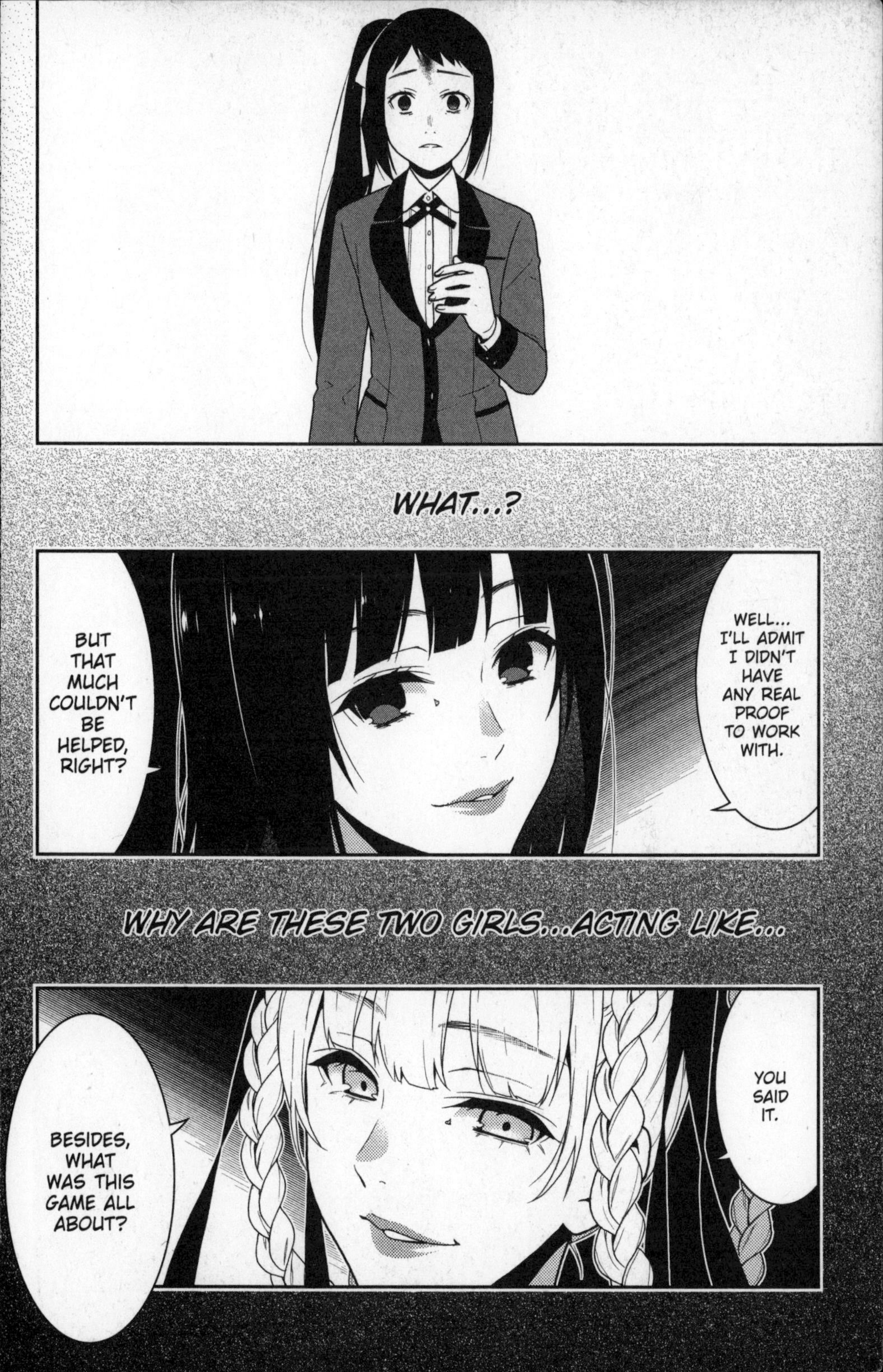
WHAT...?
WELL... I'LL ADMIT I DIDN'T HAVE ANY REAL PROOF TO WORK WITH.
BUT THAT MUCH COULDN'T BE HELPED, RIGHT?
WHY ARE THESE TWO GIRLS...ACTING LIKE...
YOU SAID IT.
BESIDES, WHAT WAS THIS GAME ALL ABOUT?

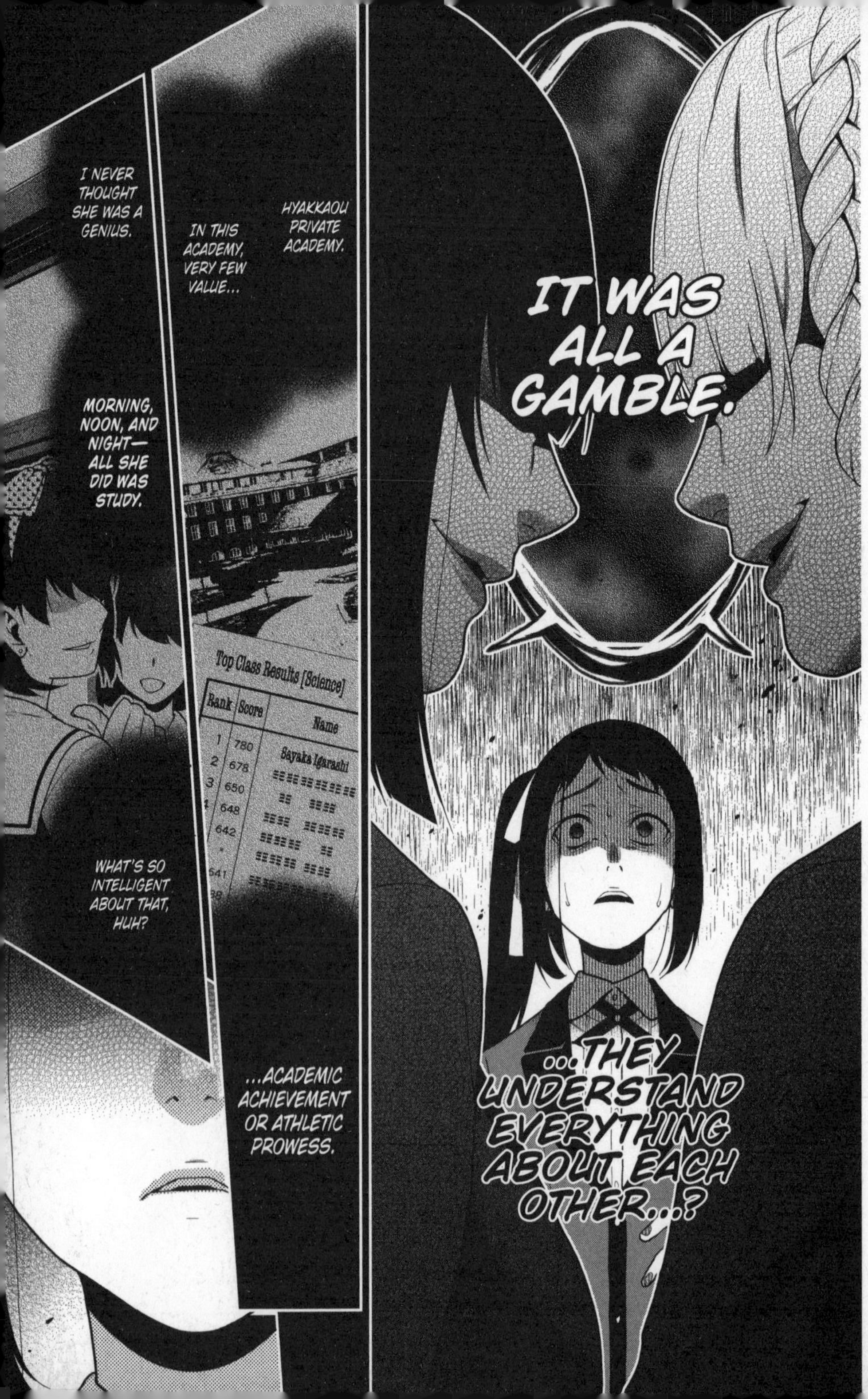
IT WAS ALL A GAMBLE.
...THEY UNDERSTAND EVERYTHING ABOUT EACH OTHER...?
HYAKKAOU PRIVATE ACADEMY.
IN THIS ACADEMY, VERY FEW VALUE...
Top Class Results [Science]
Rank Score Name
1 780 Sayaka Igarashi
2 678
3 650
648
642
641
...ACADEMIC ACHIEVEMENT OR ATHLETIC PROWESS.
I NEVER THOUGHT SHE WAS A GENIUS.
MORNING, NOON, AND NIGHT—ALL SHE DID WAS STUDY.
WHAT'S SO INTELLIGENT ABOUT THAT, HUH?

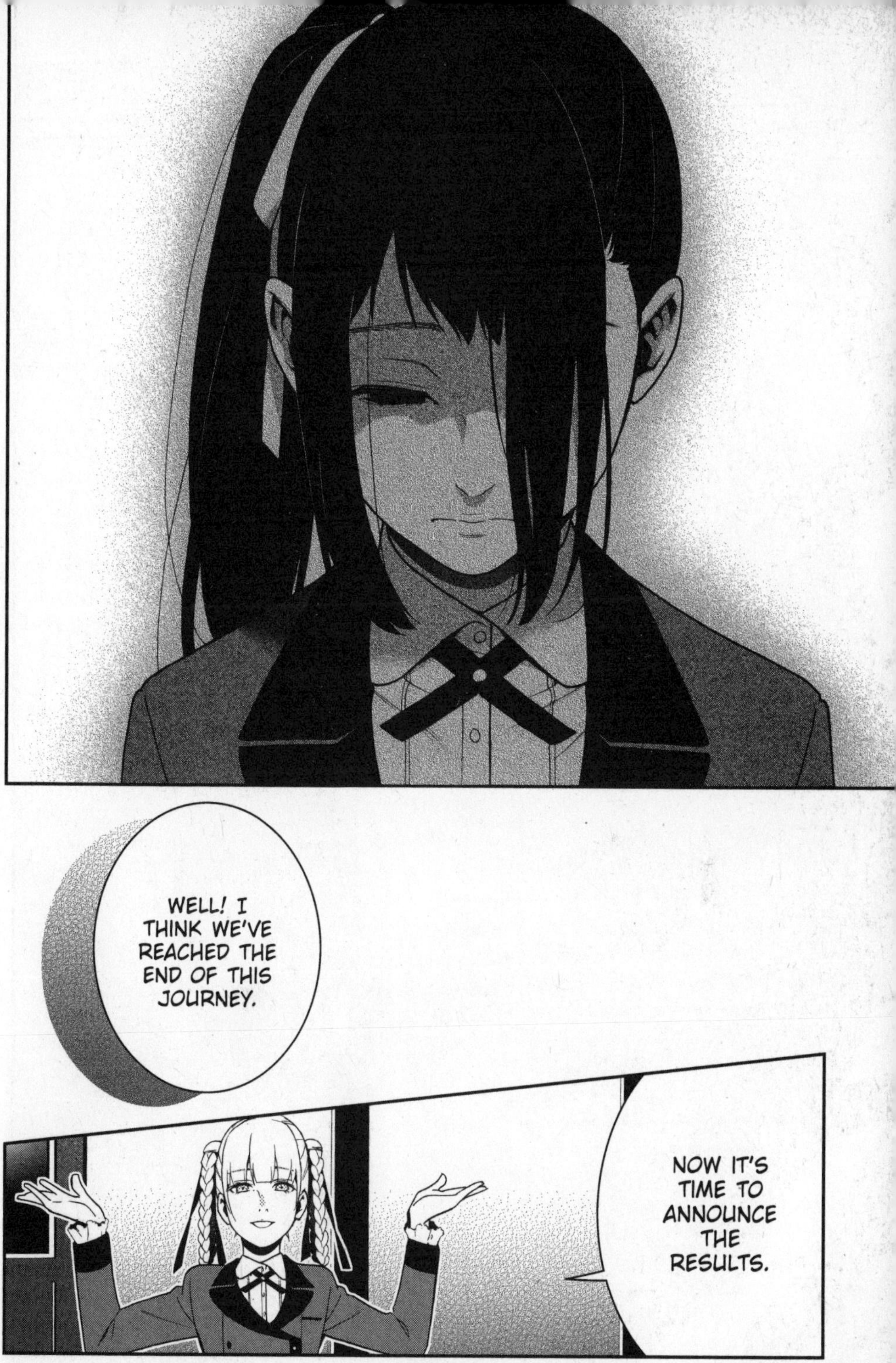
WELL! I THINK WE'VE REACHED THE END OF THIS JOURNEY.
NOW IT'S TIME TO ANNOUNCE THE RESULTS.

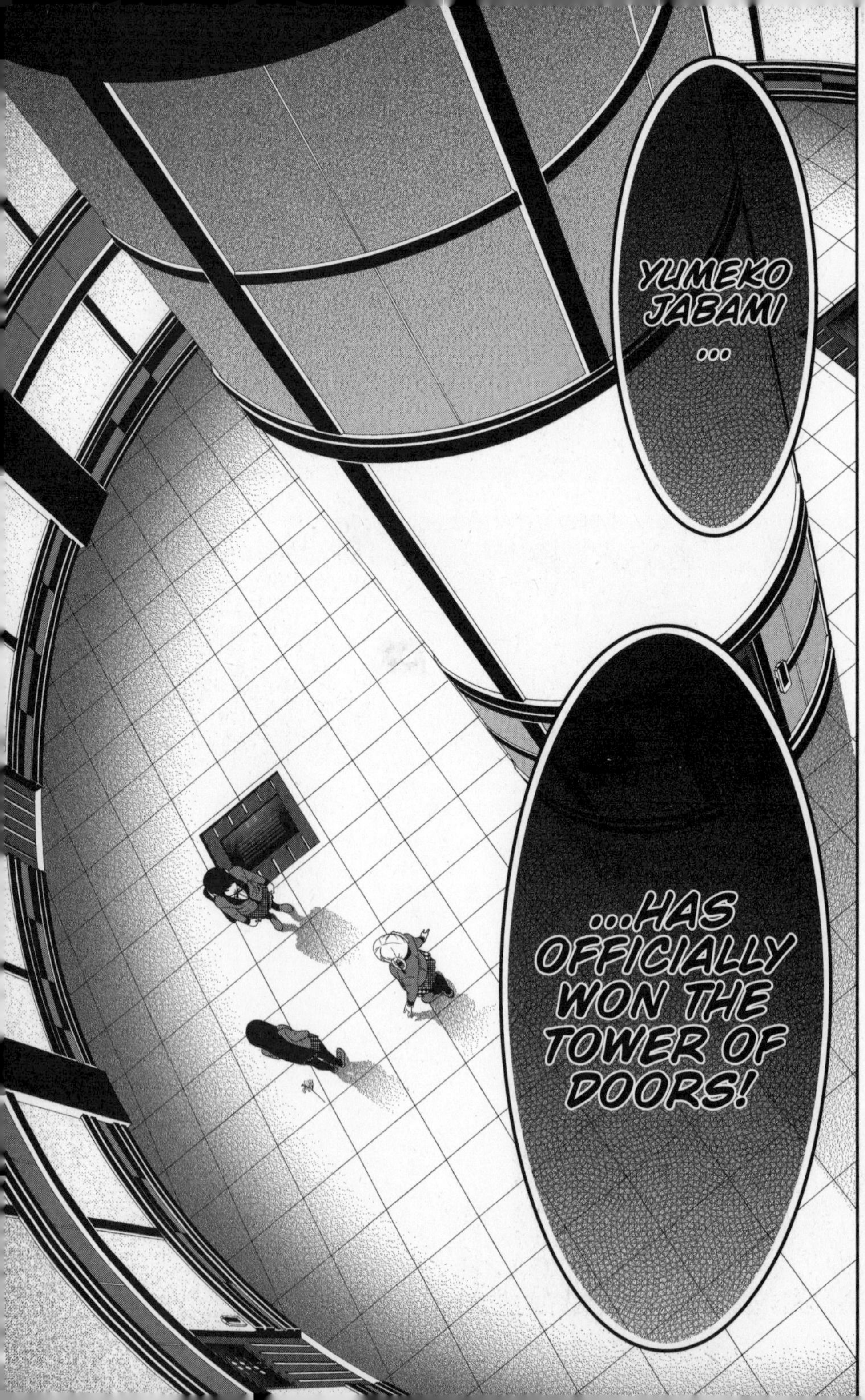
YUMEKO JABAMI ...
...HAS OFFICIALLY WON THE TOWER OF DOORS!

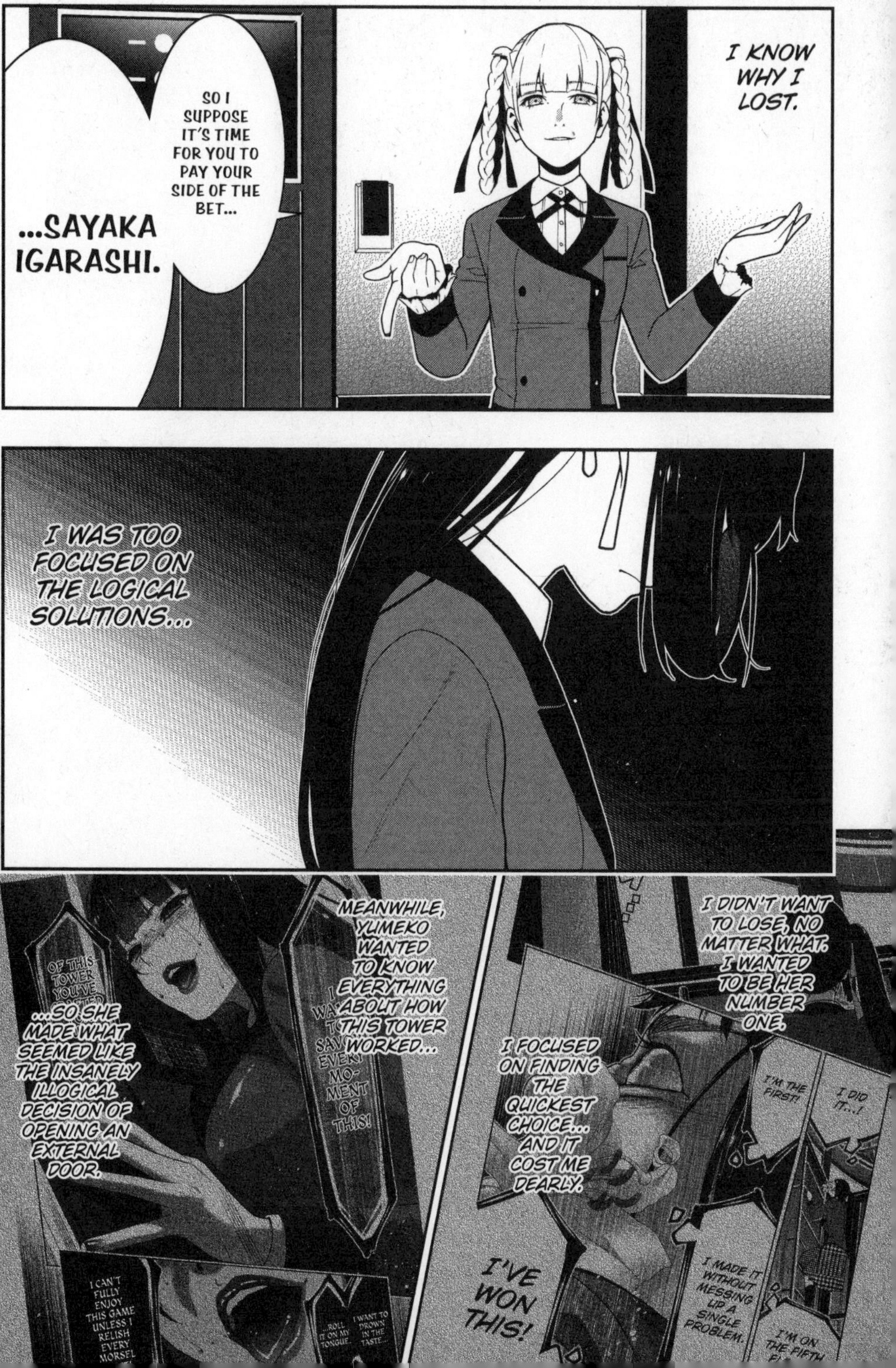
I KNOW WHY I LOST.
SO I SUPPOSE IT'S TIME FOR YOU TO PAY YOUR SIDE OF THE BET...
...SAYAKA IGARASHI.
I WAS TOO FOCUSED ON THE LOGICAL SOLUTIONS...
I DIDN'T WANT TO LOSE, NO MATTER WHAT. I WANTED TO BE HER NUMBER ONE.
I FOCUSED ON FINDING THE QUICKEST CHOICE... AND IT COST ME DEARLY.
I DID IT...!
I'M THE FIRST!
I'VE WON THIS!
I MADE IT WITHOUT MESSING UP A SINGLE PROBLEM.
I'M ON THE FIFTH
MEANWHILE, YUMEKO WANTED TO KNOW EVERYTHING ABOUT HOW THIS TOWER WORKED...
...SO SHE MADE WHAT SEEMED LIKE THE INSANELY ILLOGICAL DECISION OF OPENING AN EXTERNAL DOOR.
I WANT TO DROWN IN THE TASTE...
...ROLL IT ON MY TONGUE.
I CAN'T FULLY ENJOY THIS GAME UNLESS I RELISH EVERY MORSEL

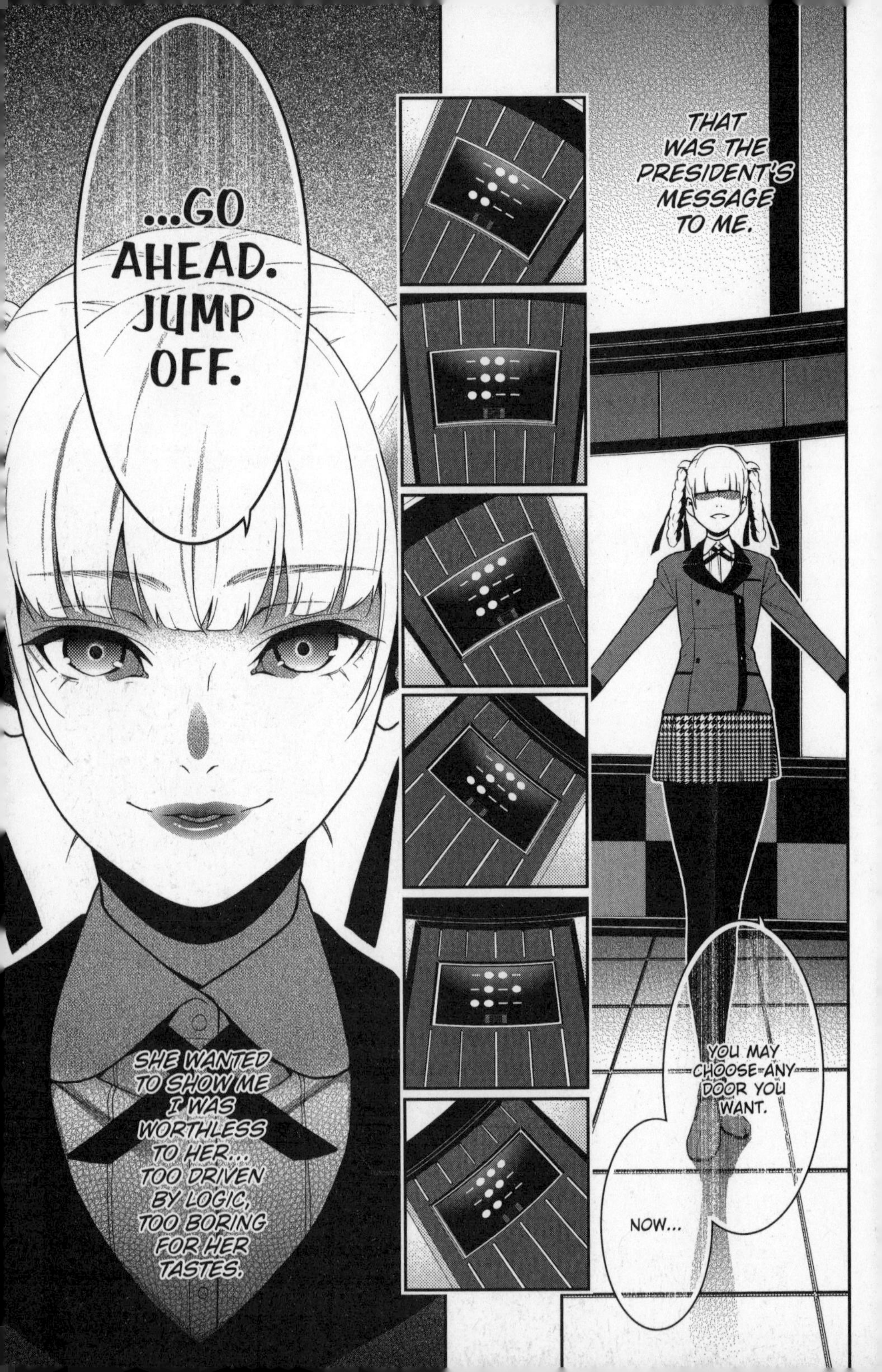
THAT WAS THE PRESIDENT'S MESSAGE TO ME.
YOU MAY CHOOSE ANY DOOR YOU WANT.
NOW...
...GO AHEAD. JUMP OFF.
SHE WANTED TO SHOW ME I WAS WORTHLESS TO HER... TOO DRIVEN BY LOGIC, TOO BORING FOR HER TASTES.

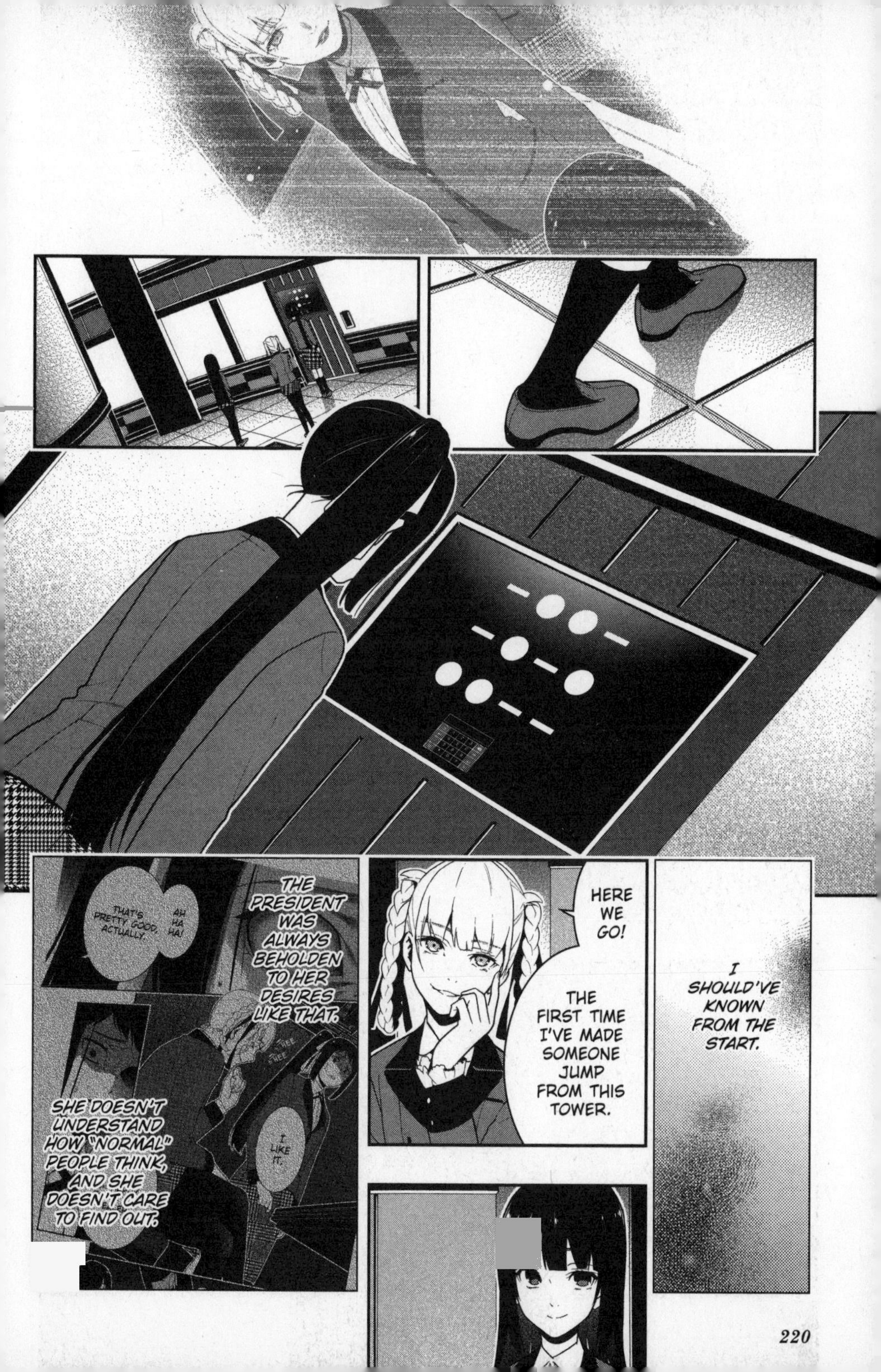
I SHOULD'VE KNOWN FROM THE START.
HERE WE GO!
THE FIRST TIME I'VE MADE SOMEONE JUMP FROM THIS TOWER.
THE PRESIDENT WAS ALWAYS BEHOLDEN TO HER DESIRES LIKE THAT.
AH HA HA!
THAT'S PRETTY GOOD, ACTUALLY.
I LIKE IT.
SHE DOESN'T UNDERSTAND HOW "NORMAL" PEOPLE THINK, AND SHE DOESN'T CARE TO FIND OUT.

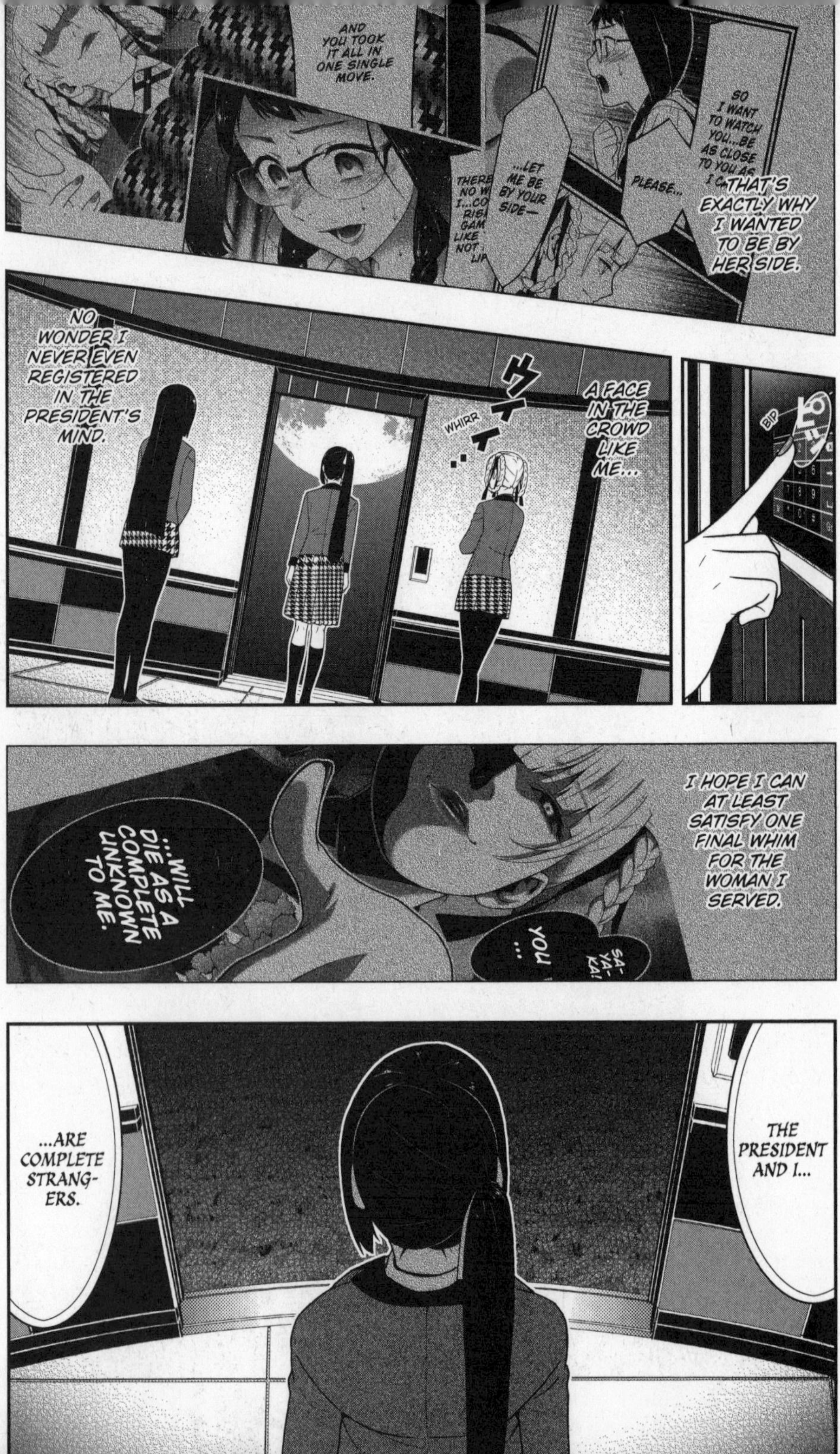
SO I WANT TO WATCH YOU...BE AS CLOSE TO YOU AS I C...
THAT'S EXACTLY WHY I WANTED TO BE BY HER SIDE.
PLEASE...
...LET ME BE BY YOUR SIDE—
AND YOU TOOK IT ALL IN ONE SINGLE MOVE.
BIP
A FACE IN THE CROWD LIKE ME...
WHIRR
NO WONDER I NEVER EVEN REGISTERED IN THE PRESIDENT'S MIND.
I HOPE I CAN AT LEAST SATISFY ONE FINAL WHIM FOR THE WOMAN I SERVED.
SA-YA-KA!
YOU...
...WILL DIE AS A COMPLETE UNKNOWN TO ME.
THE PRESIDENT AND I...
...ARE COMPLETE STRANGERS.

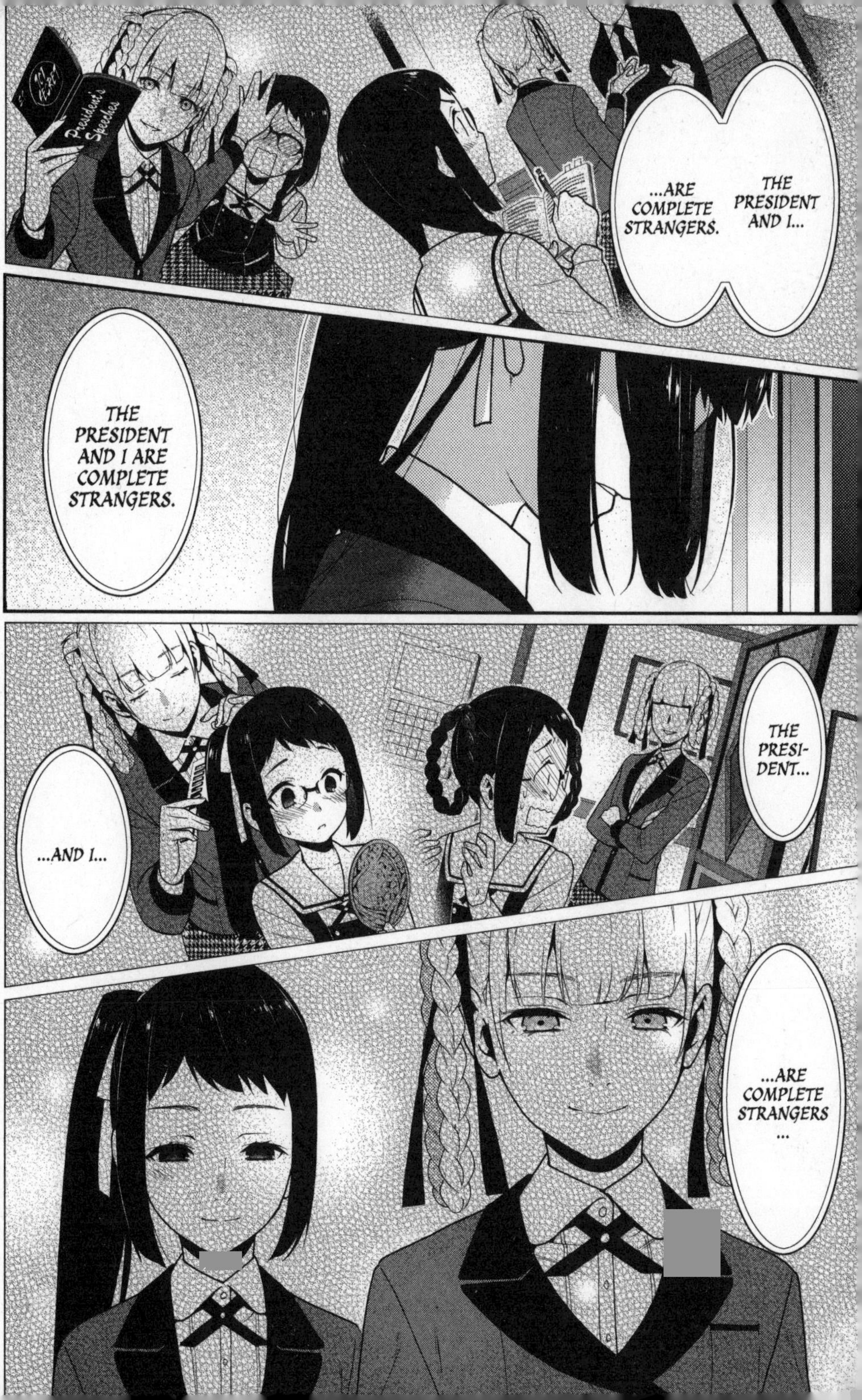
THE PRESIDENT AND I...
...ARE COMPLETE STRANGERS.
President's Speeches
THE PRESIDENT AND I ARE COMPLETE STRANGERS.
THE PRESI-DENT...
...AND I...
...ARE COMPLETE STRANGERS ...

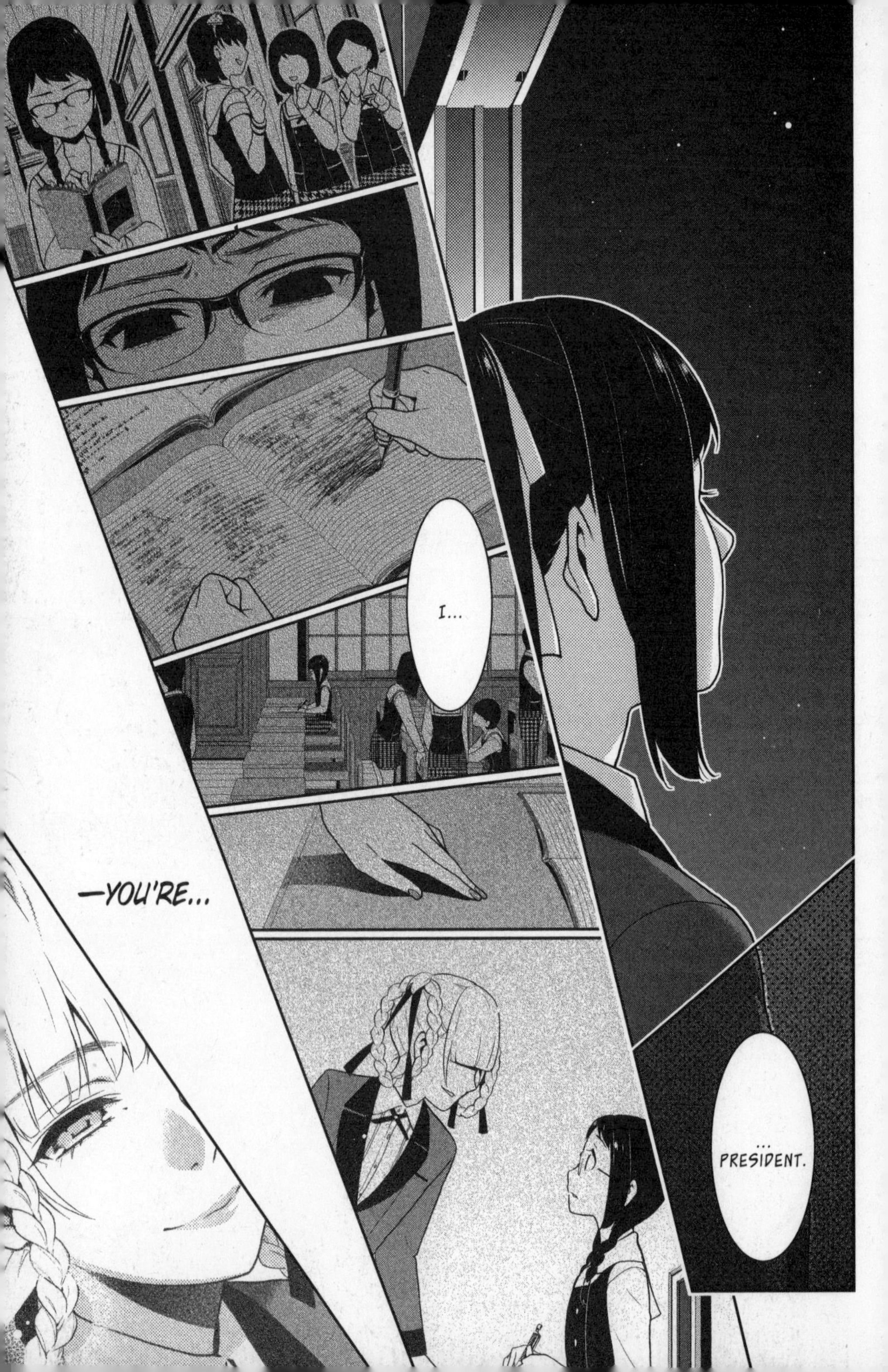
I...
...PRESIDENT.
—YOU'RE...

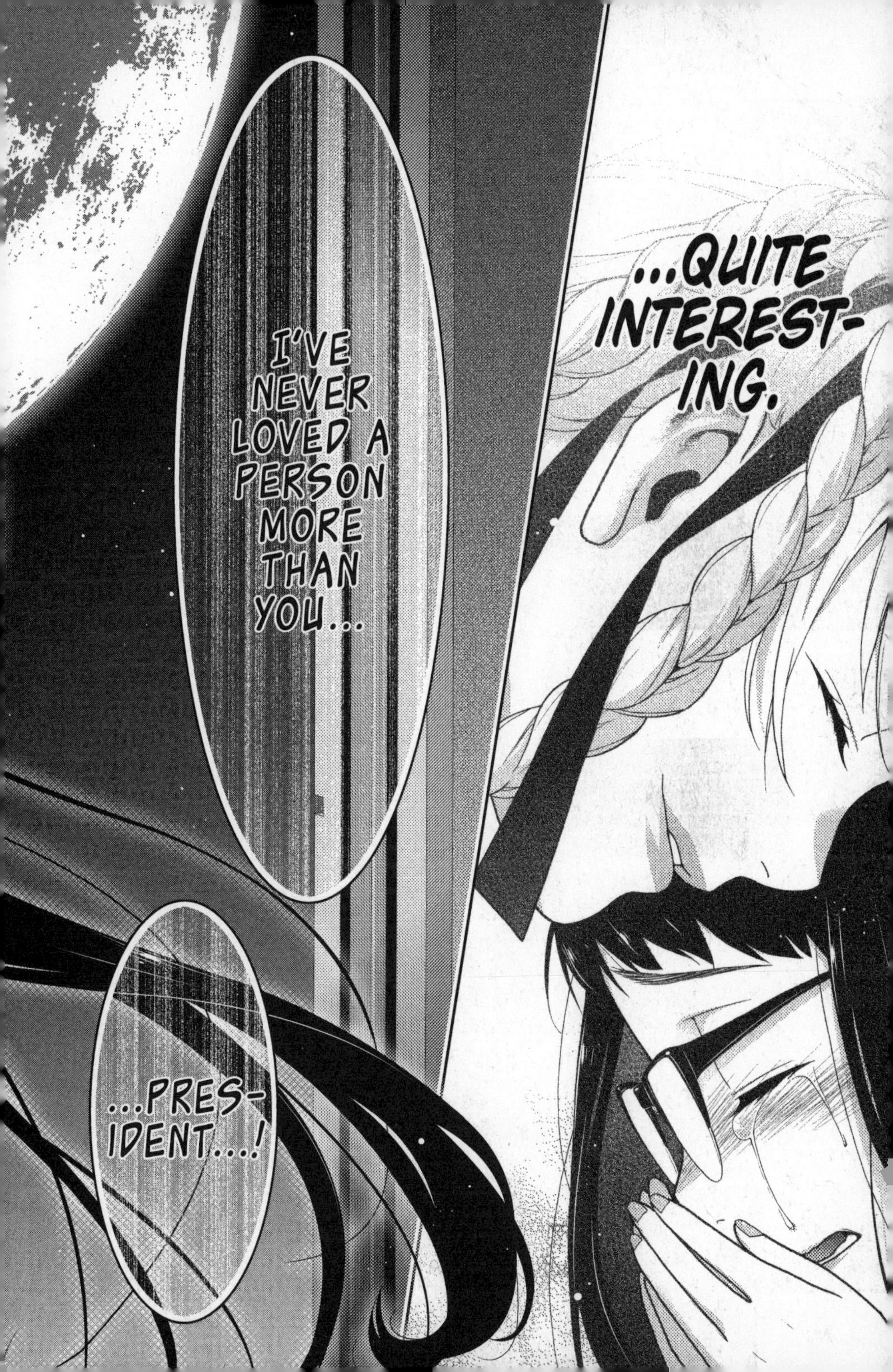
...QUITE INTEREST-ING.
I'VE NEVER LOVED A PERSON MORE THAN YOU...
...PRES-IDENT...!

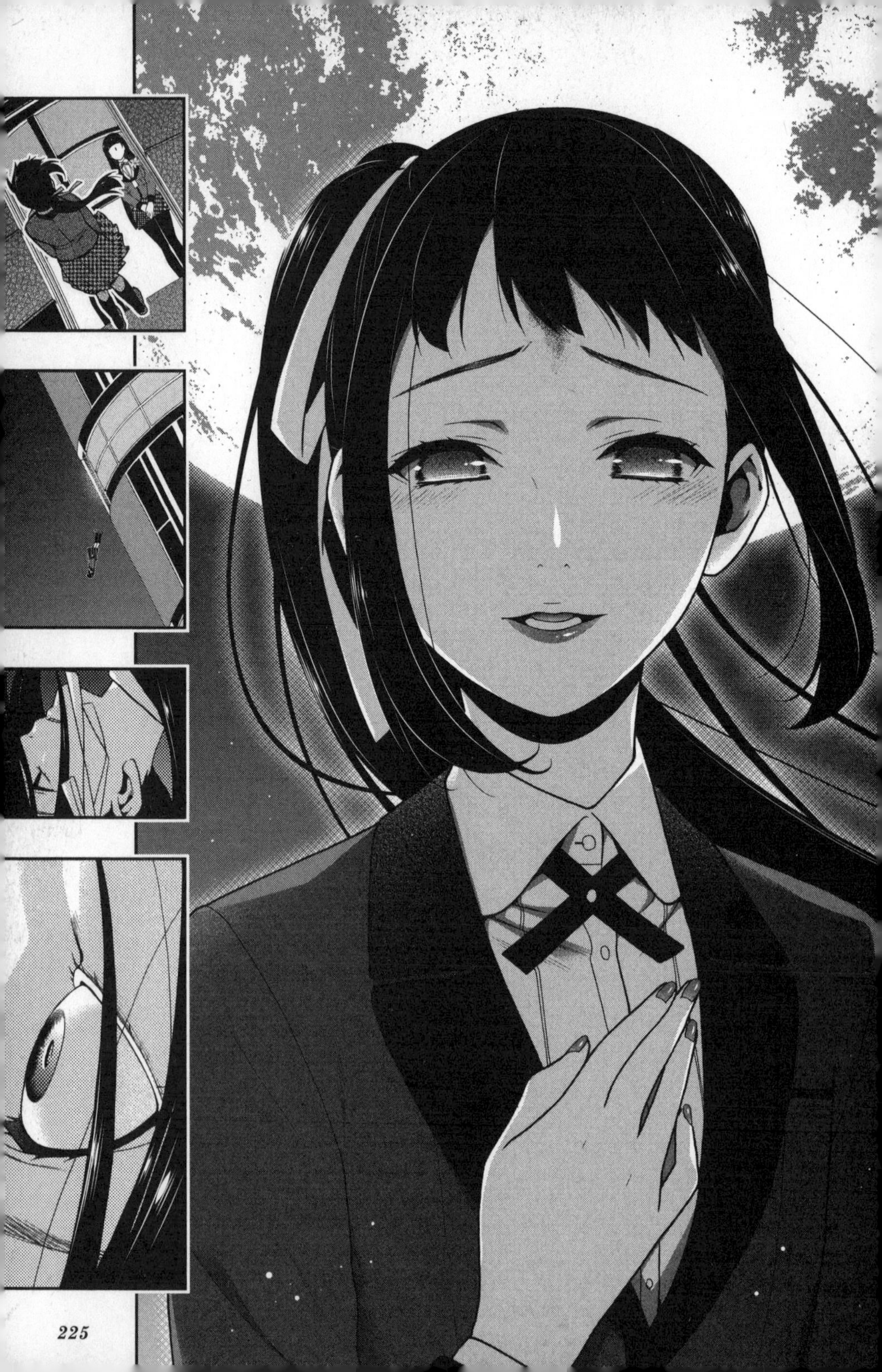

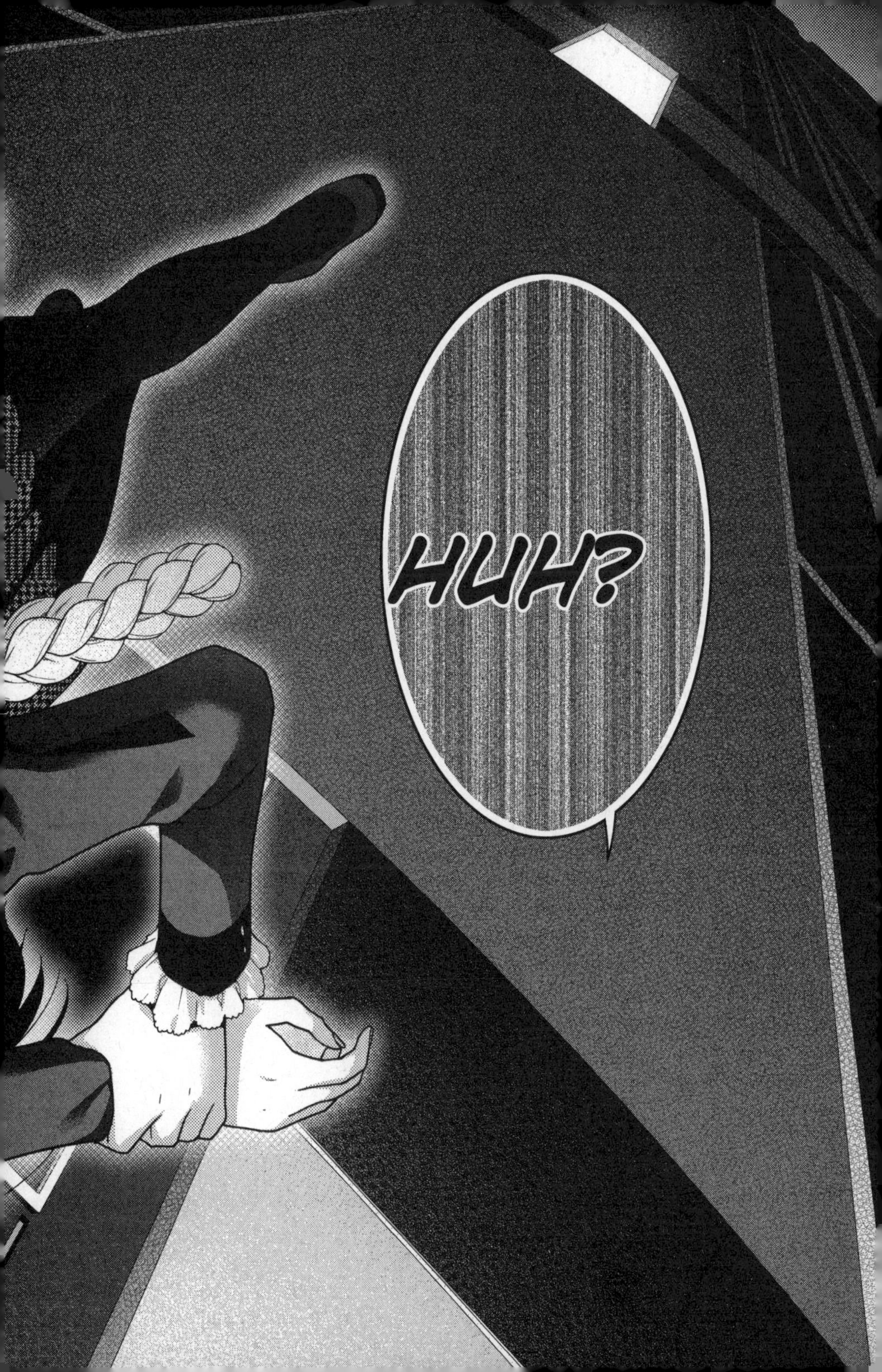
HUH?

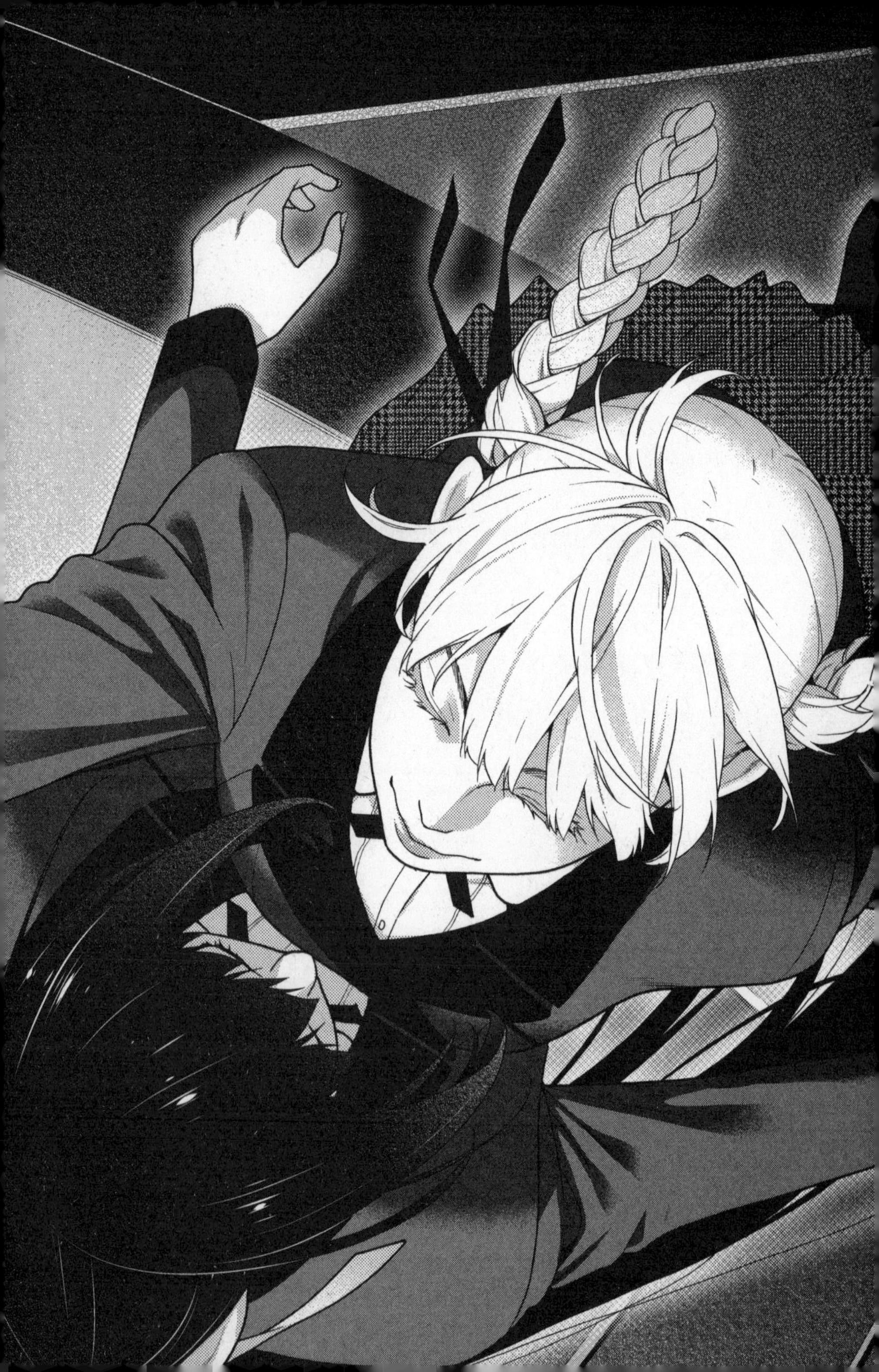

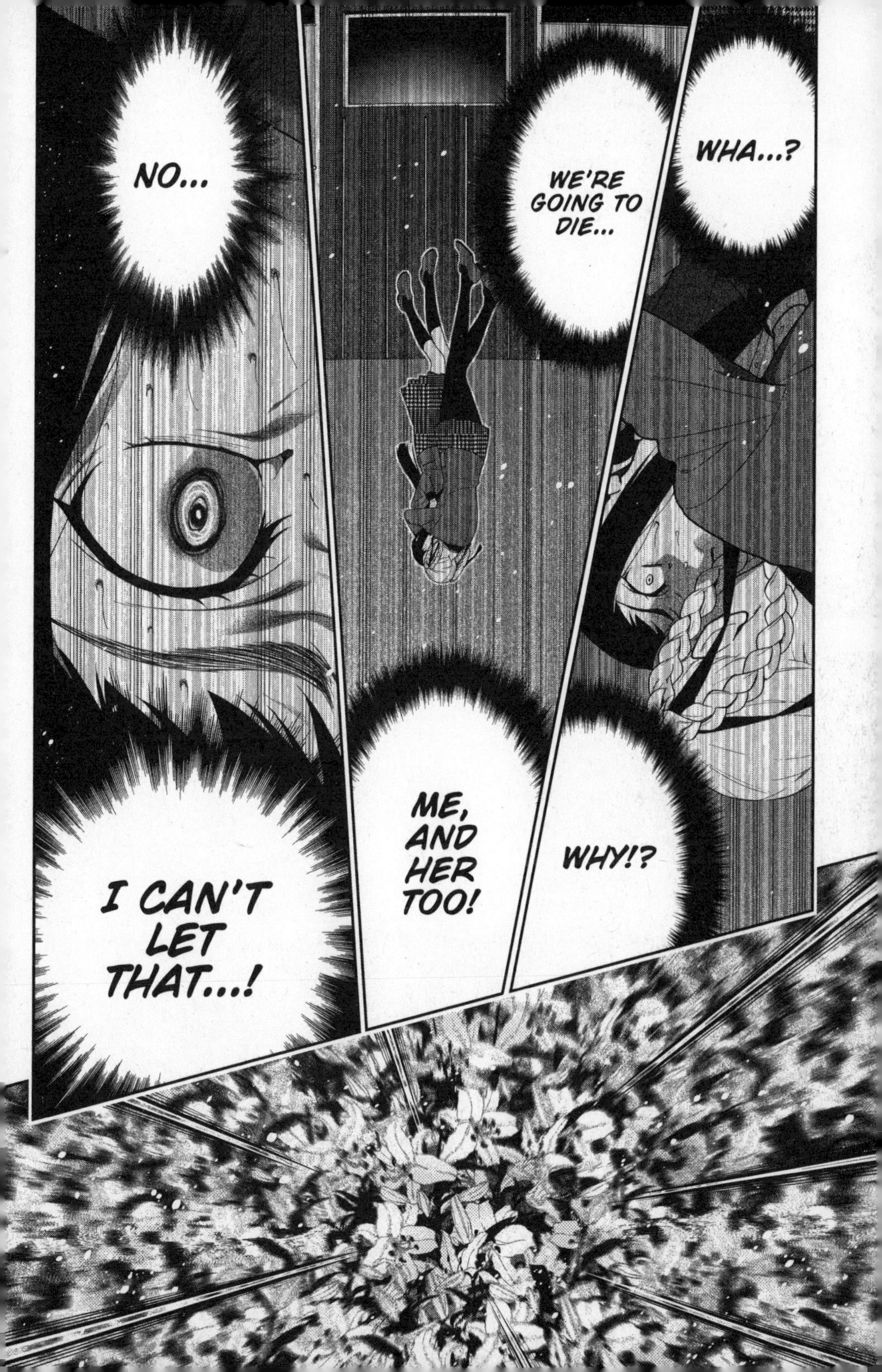
WHA...?
WHY!?
WE'RE GOING TO DIE...
ME, AND HER TOO!
NO...
I CAN'T LET THAT...!

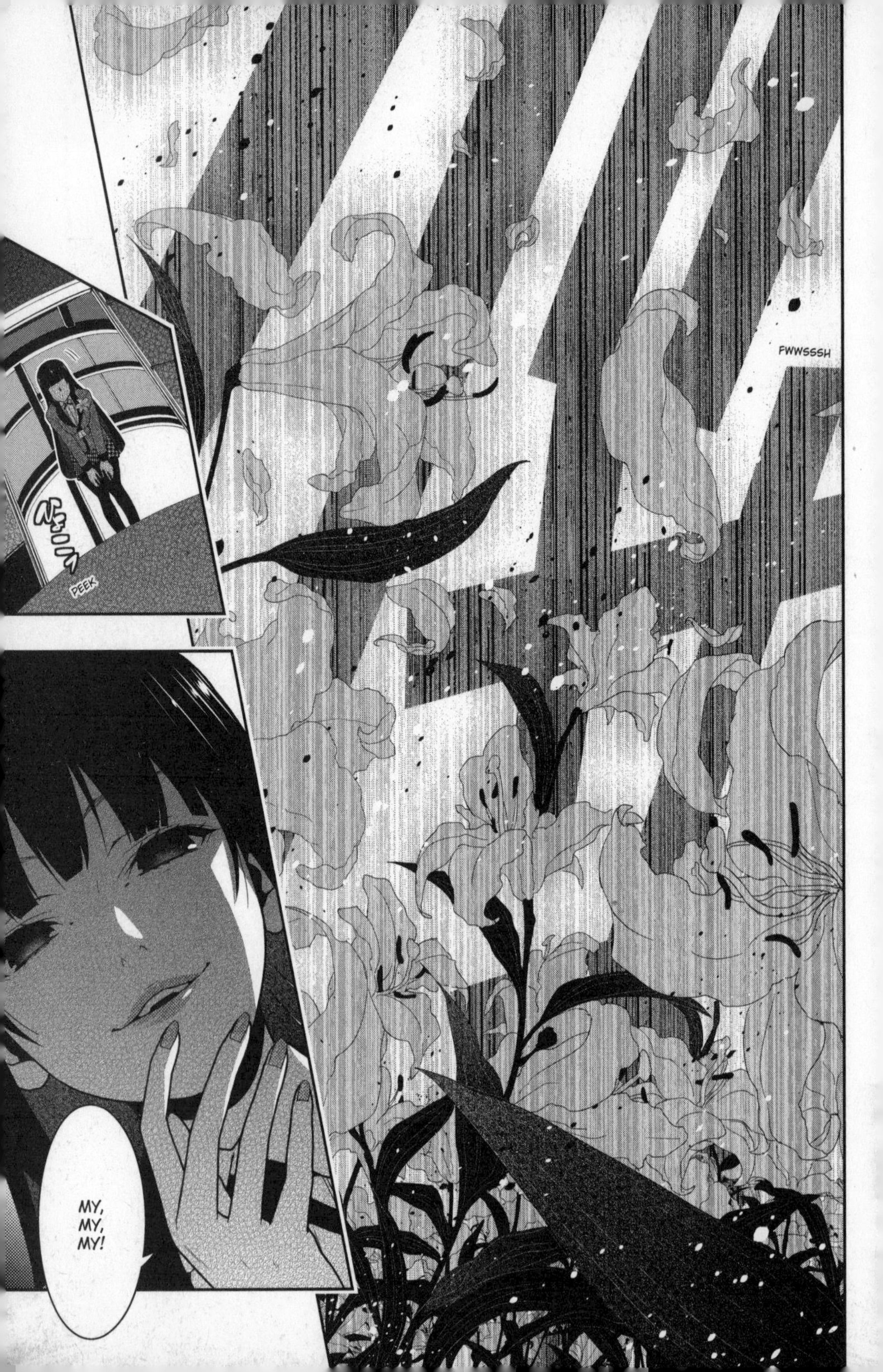
FWWSSSH
PEEK
MY, MY, MY!

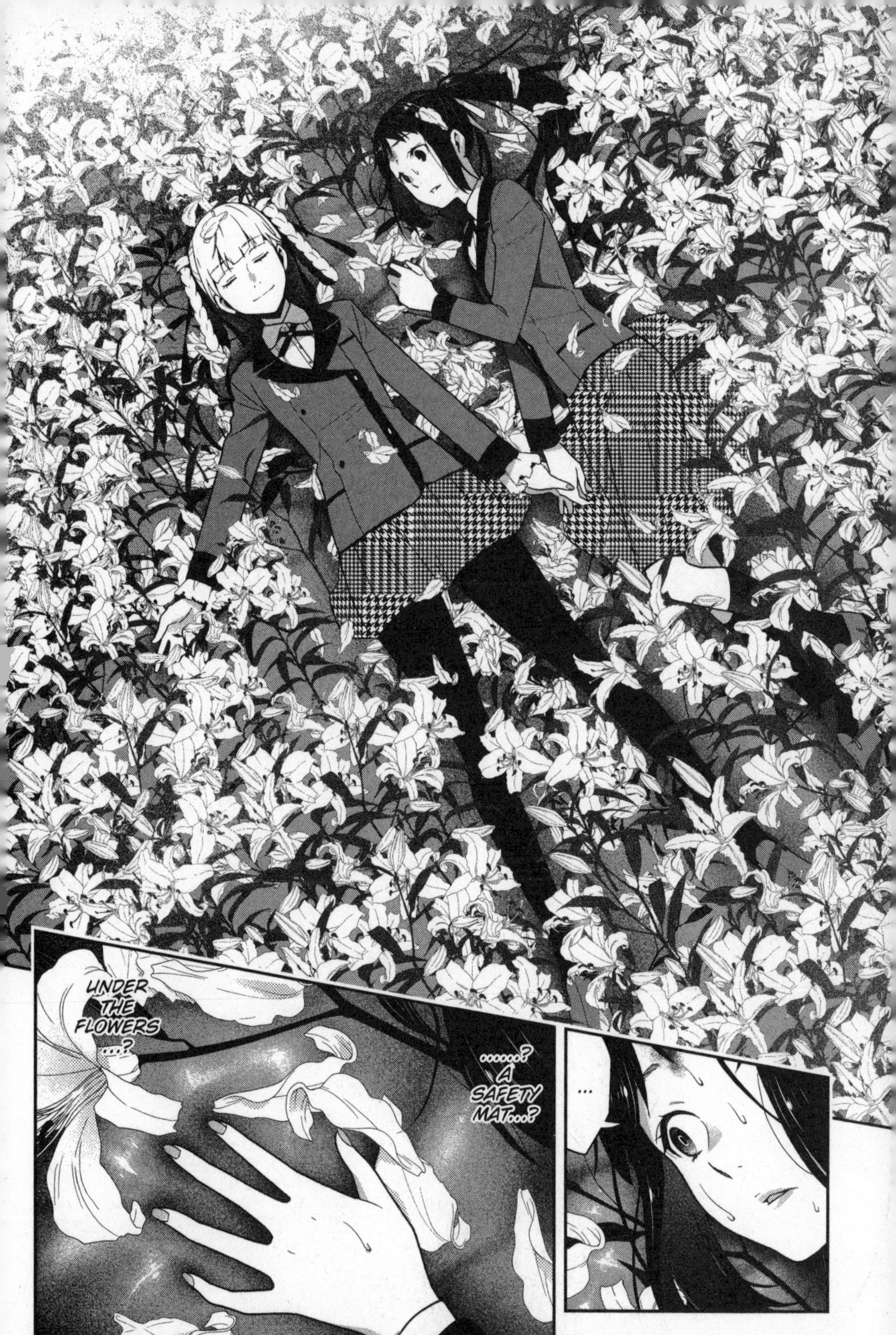
...
UNDER THE FLOWERS...?
......? A SAFETY MAT...?

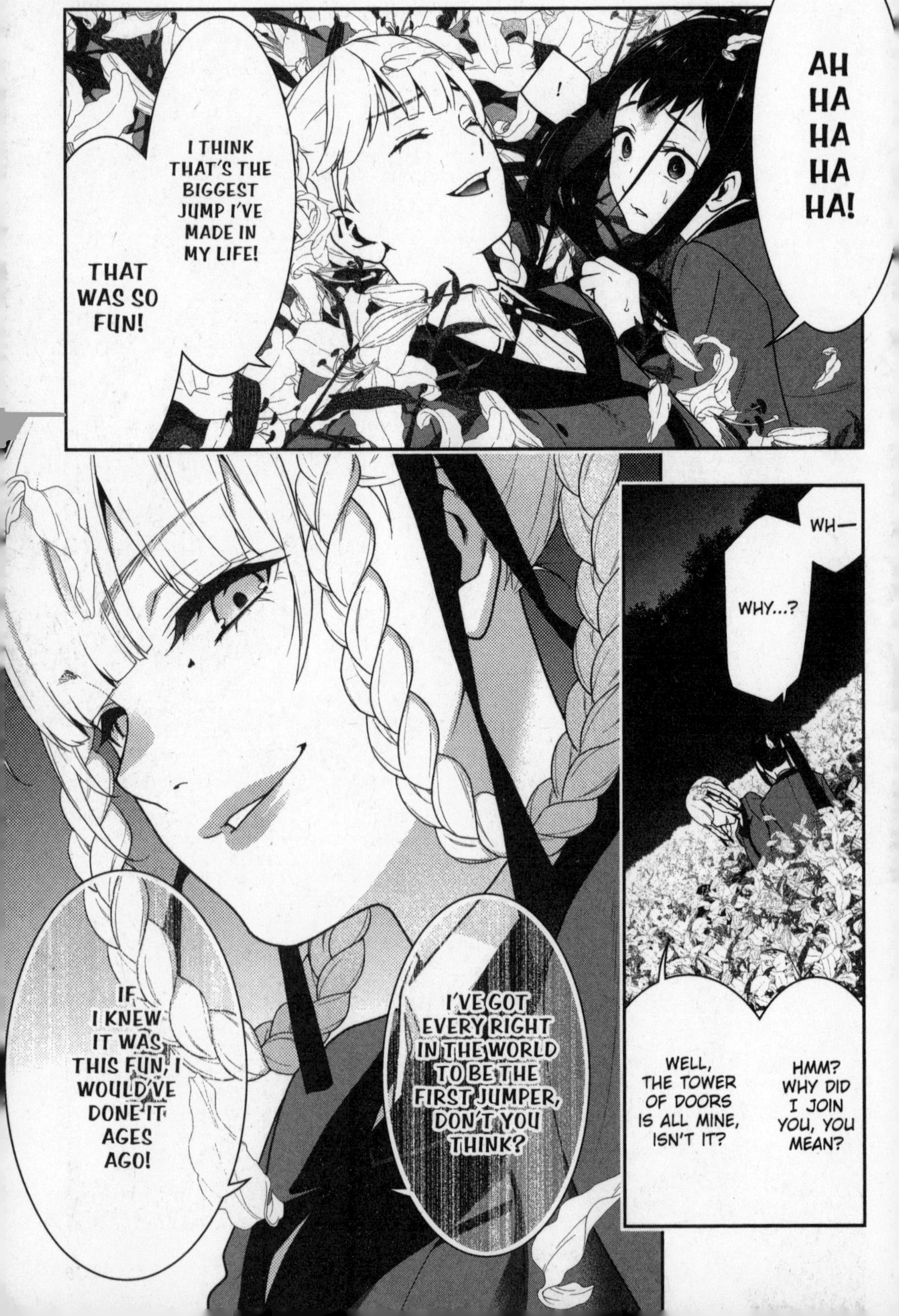
AH HA HA HA HA!
!
I THINK THAT'S THE BIGGEST JUMP I'VE MADE IN MY LIFE!
THAT WAS SO FUN!
WH— WHY...?
HMM? WHY DID I JOIN YOU, YOU MEAN?
WELL, THE TOWER OF DOORS IS ALL MINE, ISN'T IT?
I'VE GOT EVERY RIGHT IN THE WORLD TO BE THE FIRST JUMPER, DON'T YOU THINK?
IF I KNEW IT WAS THIS FUN, I WOULD'VE DONE IT AGES AGO!

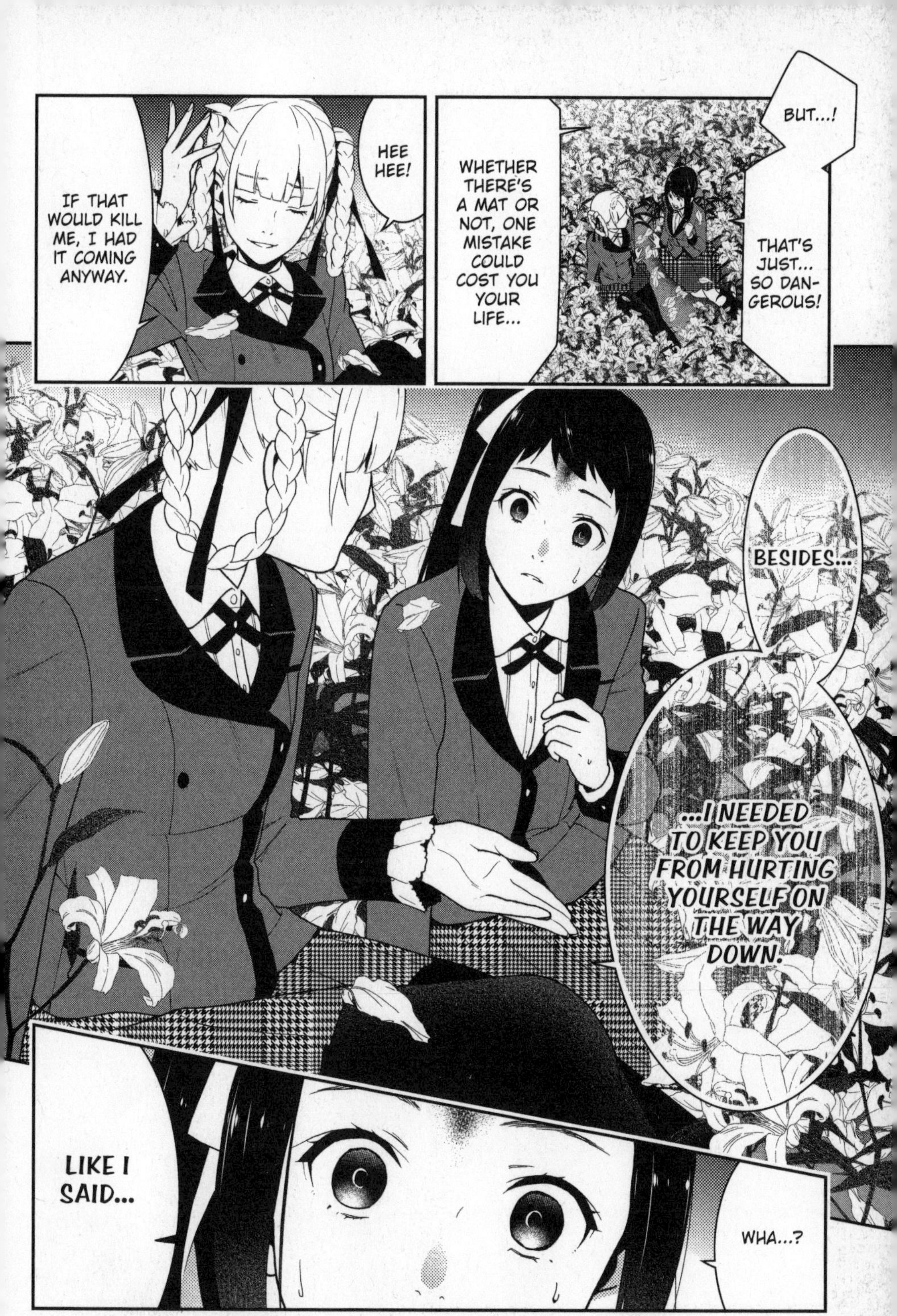
BUT...!
THAT'S JUST... SO DANGEROUS!
WHETHER THERE'S A MAT OR NOT, ONE MISTAKE COULD COST YOU YOUR LIFE...
HEE HEE!
IF THAT WOULD KILL ME, I HAD IT COMING ANYWAY.
BESIDES...
...I NEEDED TO KEEP YOU FROM HURTING YOURSELF ON THE WAY DOWN.
WHA...?
LIKE I SAID...

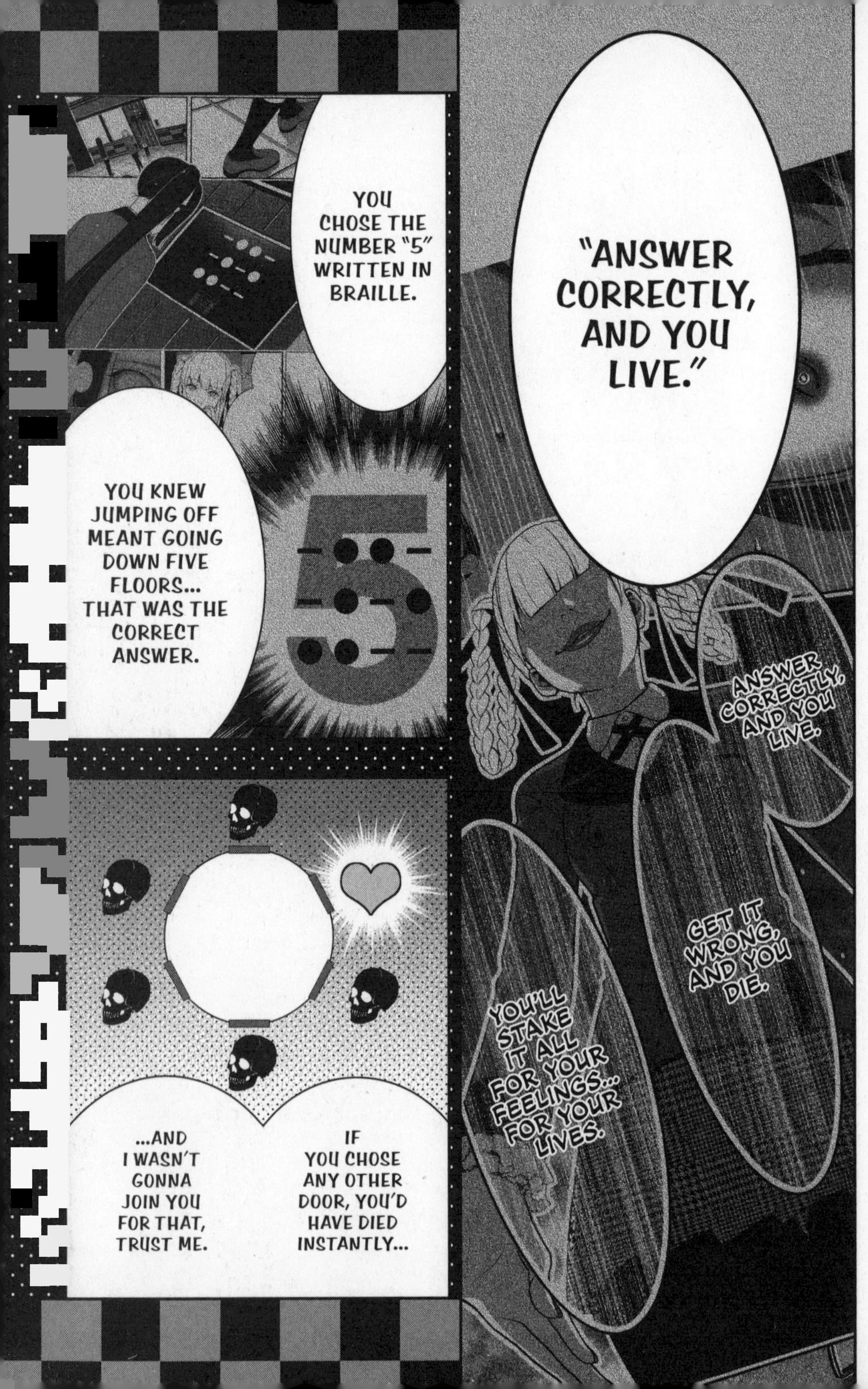
"ANSWER CORRECTLY, AND YOU LIVE."
ANSWER CORRECTLY, AND YOU LIVE.
GET IT WRONG, AND YOU DIE.
YOU'LL STAKE IT ALL FOR YOUR FEELINGS... FOR YOUR LIVES.
YOU CHOSE THE NUMBER "5" WRITTEN IN BRAILLE.
YOU KNEW JUMPING OFF MEANT GOING DOWN FIVE FLOORS... THAT WAS THE CORRECT ANSWER.
IF YOU CHOSE ANY OTHER DOOR, YOU'D HAVE DIED INSTANTLY...
...AND I WASN'T GONNA JOIN YOU FOR THAT, TRUST ME.

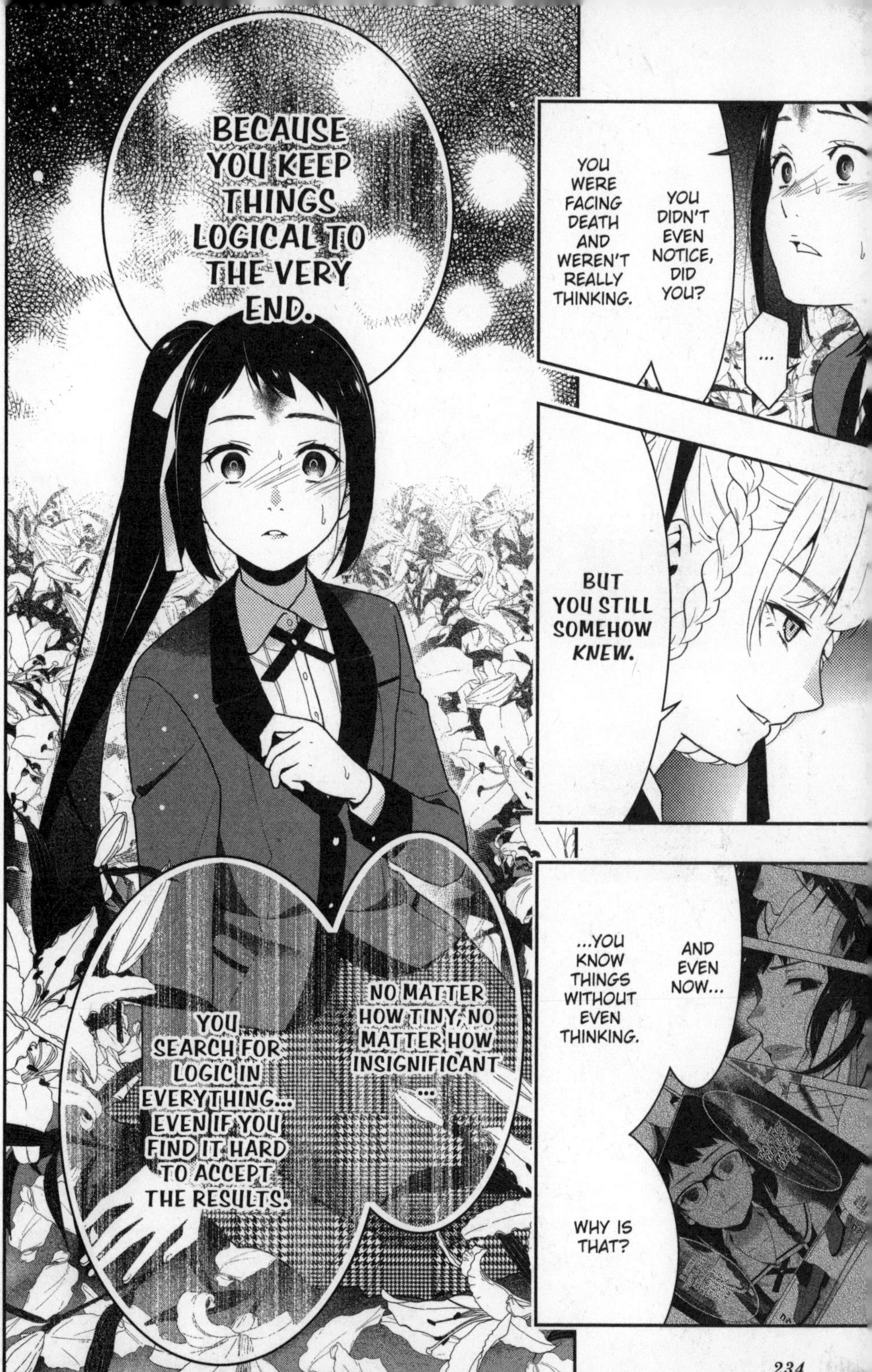
YOU DIDN'T EVEN NOTICE, DID YOU?
YOU WERE FACING DEATH AND WEREN'T REALLY THINKING.
...
BUT YOU STILL SOMEHOW KNEW.
AND EVEN NOW...
...YOU KNOW THINGS WITHOUT EVEN THINKING.
WHY IS THAT?
BECAUSE YOU KEEP THINGS LOGICAL TO THE VERY END.
NO MATTER HOW TINY, NO MATTER HOW INSIGNIFICANT...
YOU SEARCH FOR LOGIC IN EVERYTHING... EVEN IF YOU FIND IT HARD TO ACCEPT THE RESULTS.

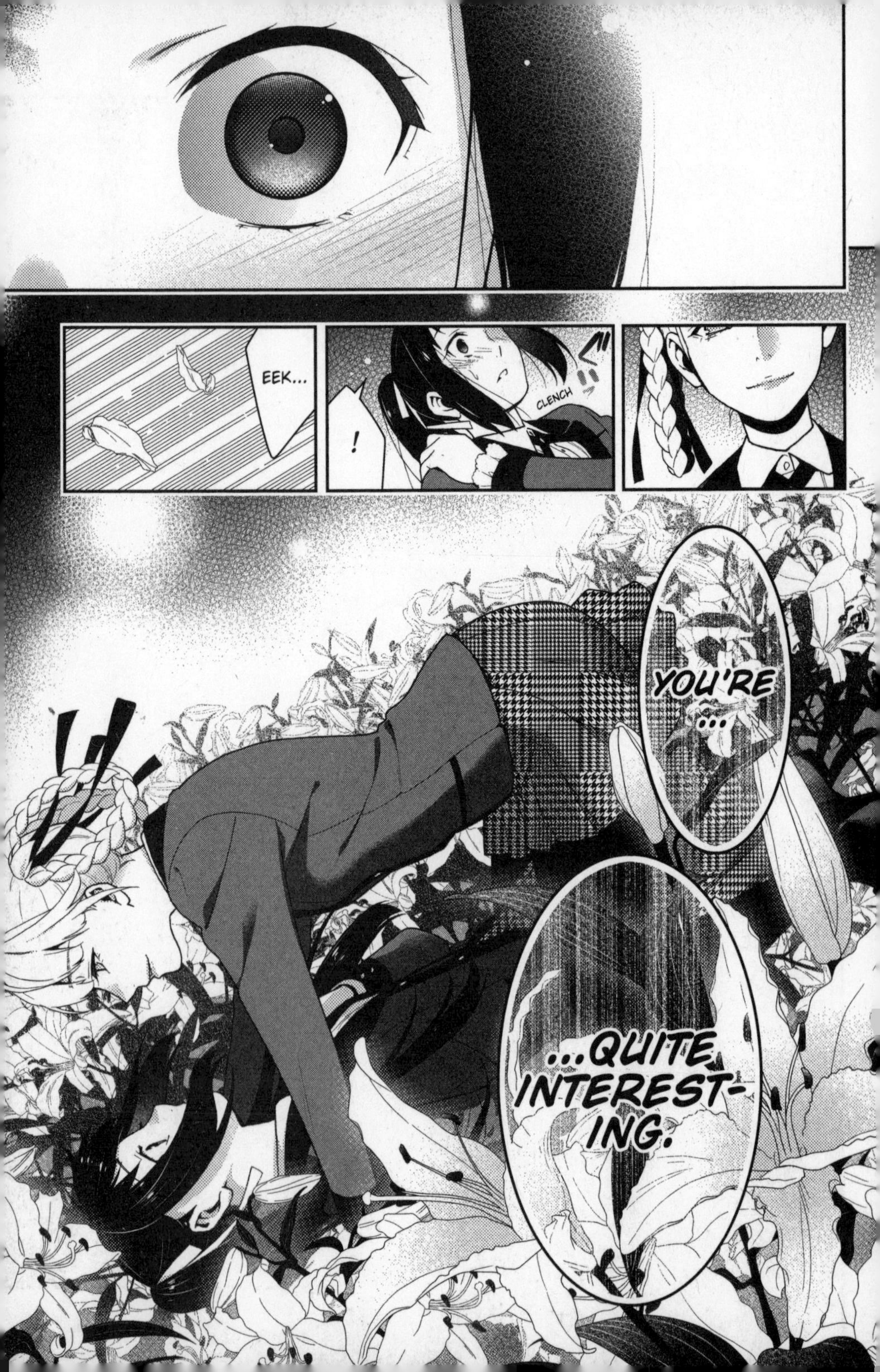
CLENCH
!
EEK...
YOU'RE ...
...QUITE INTEREST-ING.

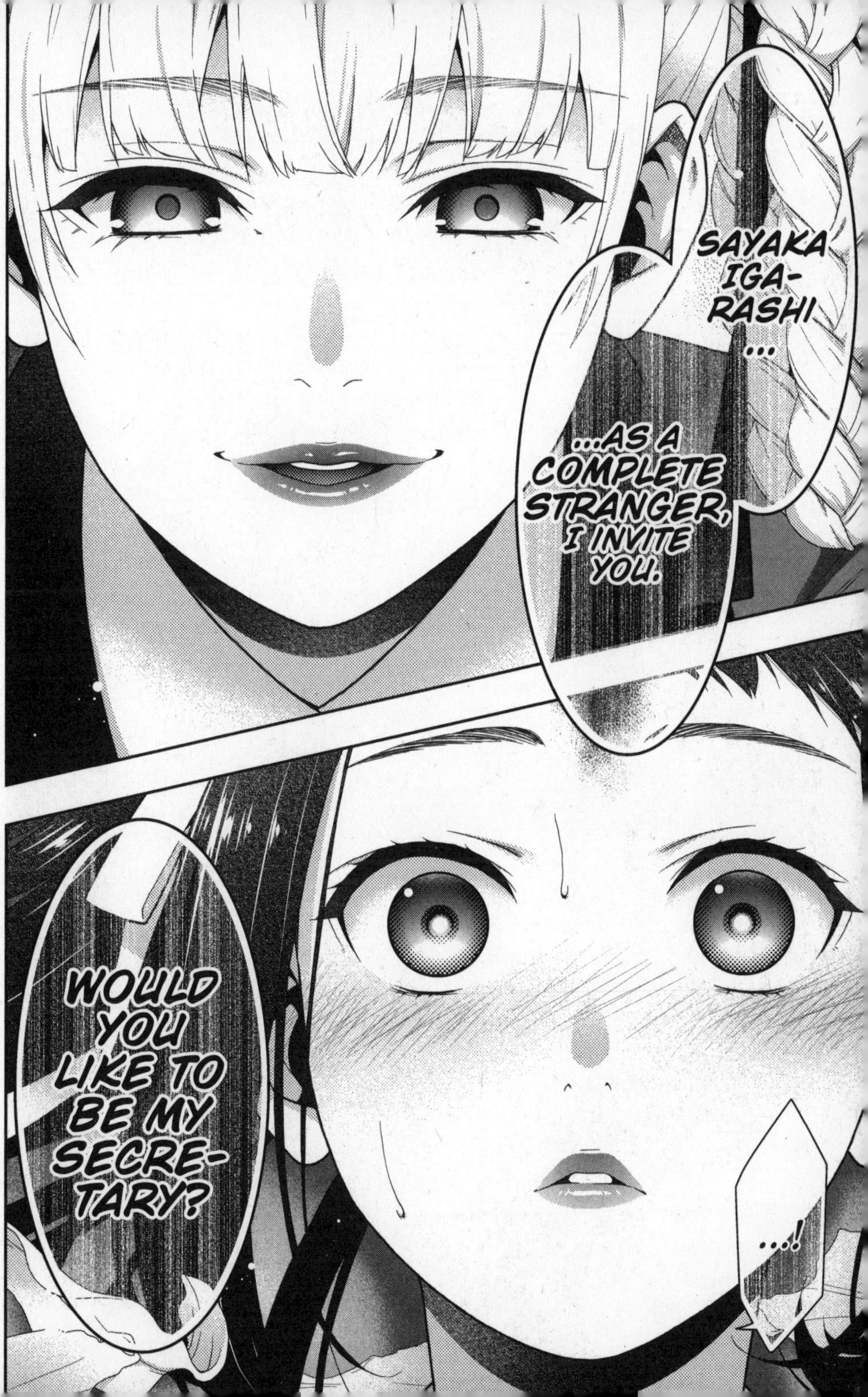
SAYAKA IGA-RASHI...
...AS A COMPLETE STRANGER, I INVITE YOU.
WOULD YOU LIKE TO BE MY SECRE-TARY?
...!

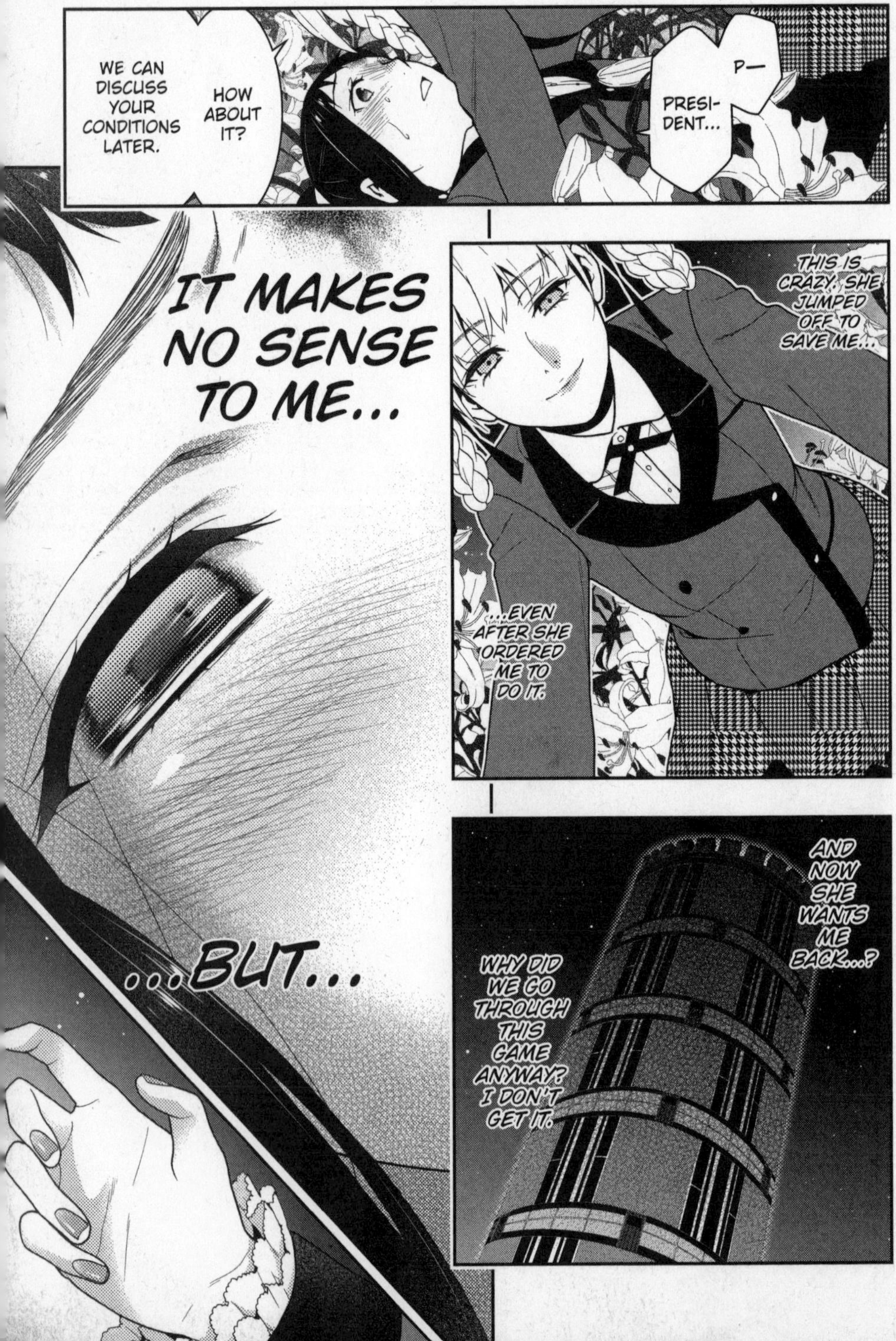
P— PRESIDENT...
HOW ABOUT IT?
WE CAN DISCUSS YOUR CONDITIONS LATER.
THIS IS CRAZY. SHE JUMPED OFF TO SAVE ME...
...EVEN AFTER SHE ORDERED ME TO DO IT.
AND NOW SHE WANTS ME BACK...?
WHY DID WE GO THROUGH THIS GAME ANYWAY? I DON'T GET IT.
IT MAKES NO SENSE TO ME...
...BUT...

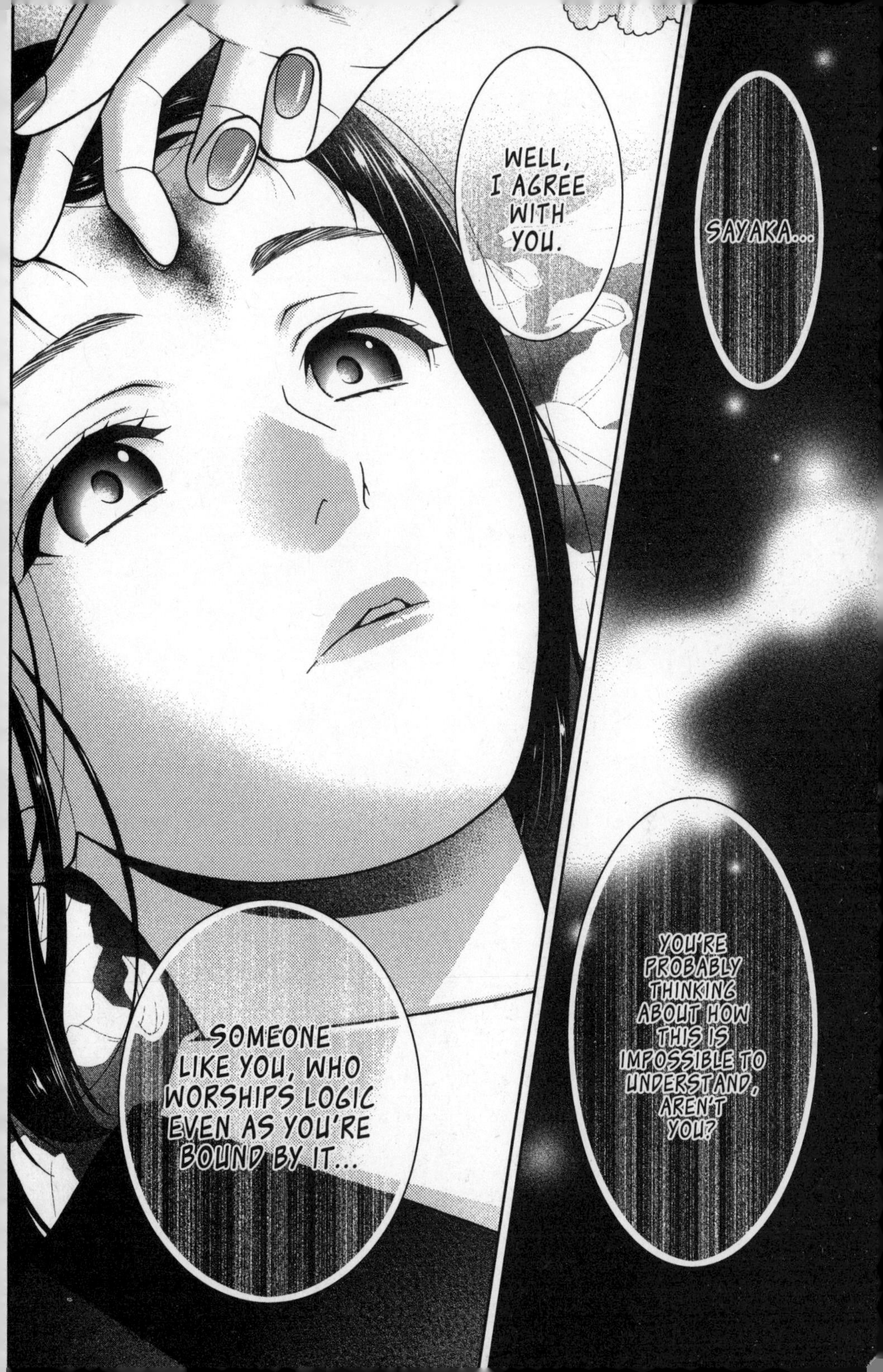
SAYAKA...
YOU'RE PROBABLY THINKING ABOUT HOW THIS IS IMPOSSIBLE TO UNDERSTAND, AREN'T YOU?
WELL, I AGREE WITH YOU.
SOMEONE LIKE YOU, WHO WORSHIPS LOGIC EVEN AS YOU'RE BOUND BY IT...

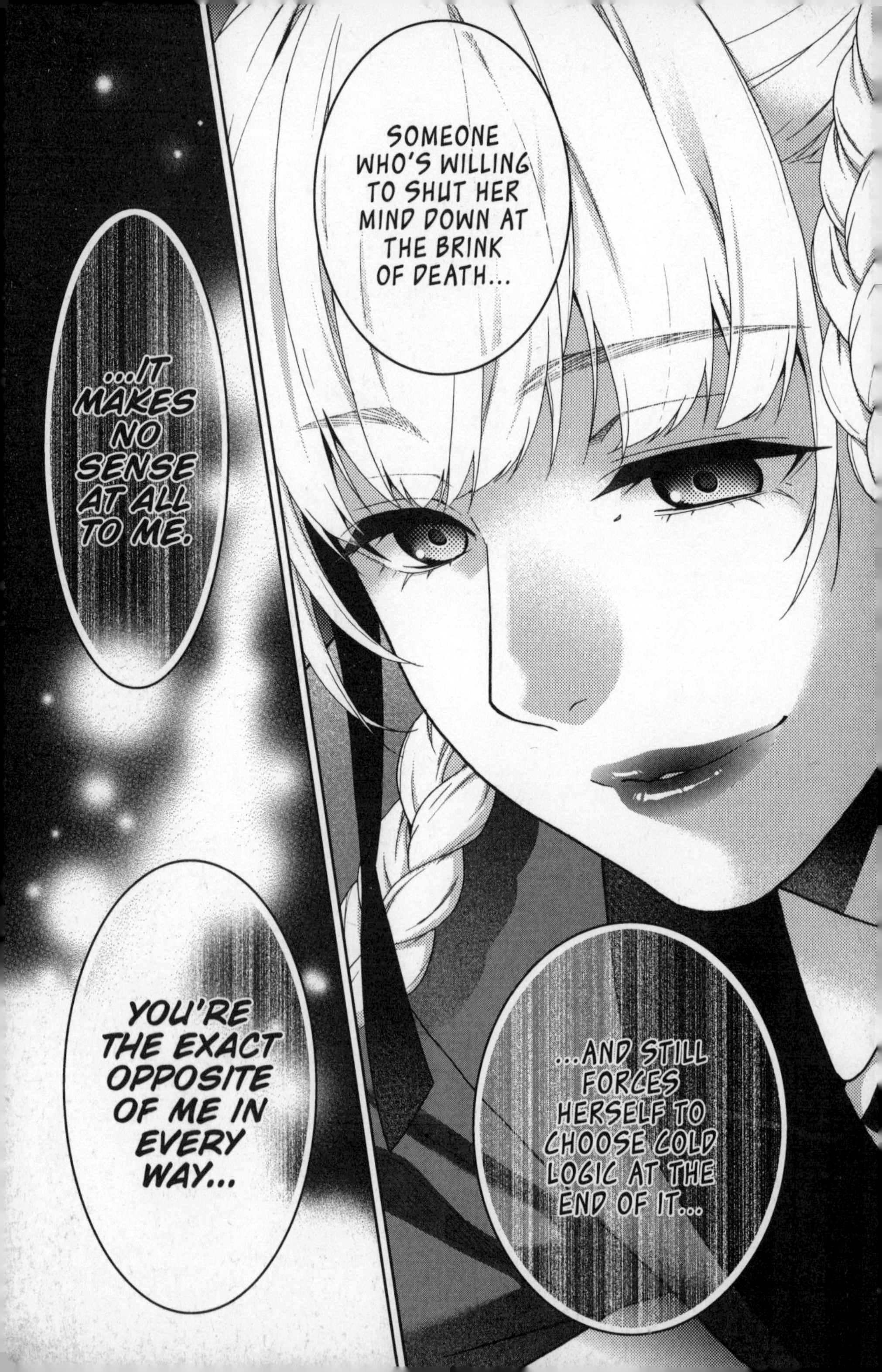
SOMEONE WHO'S WILLING TO SHUT HER MIND DOWN AT THE BRINK OF DEATH...
...AND STILL FORCES HERSELF TO CHOOSE COLD LOGIC AT THE END OF IT...
...IT MAKES NO SENSE AT ALL TO ME.
YOU'RE THE EXACT OPPOSITE OF ME IN EVERY WAY...

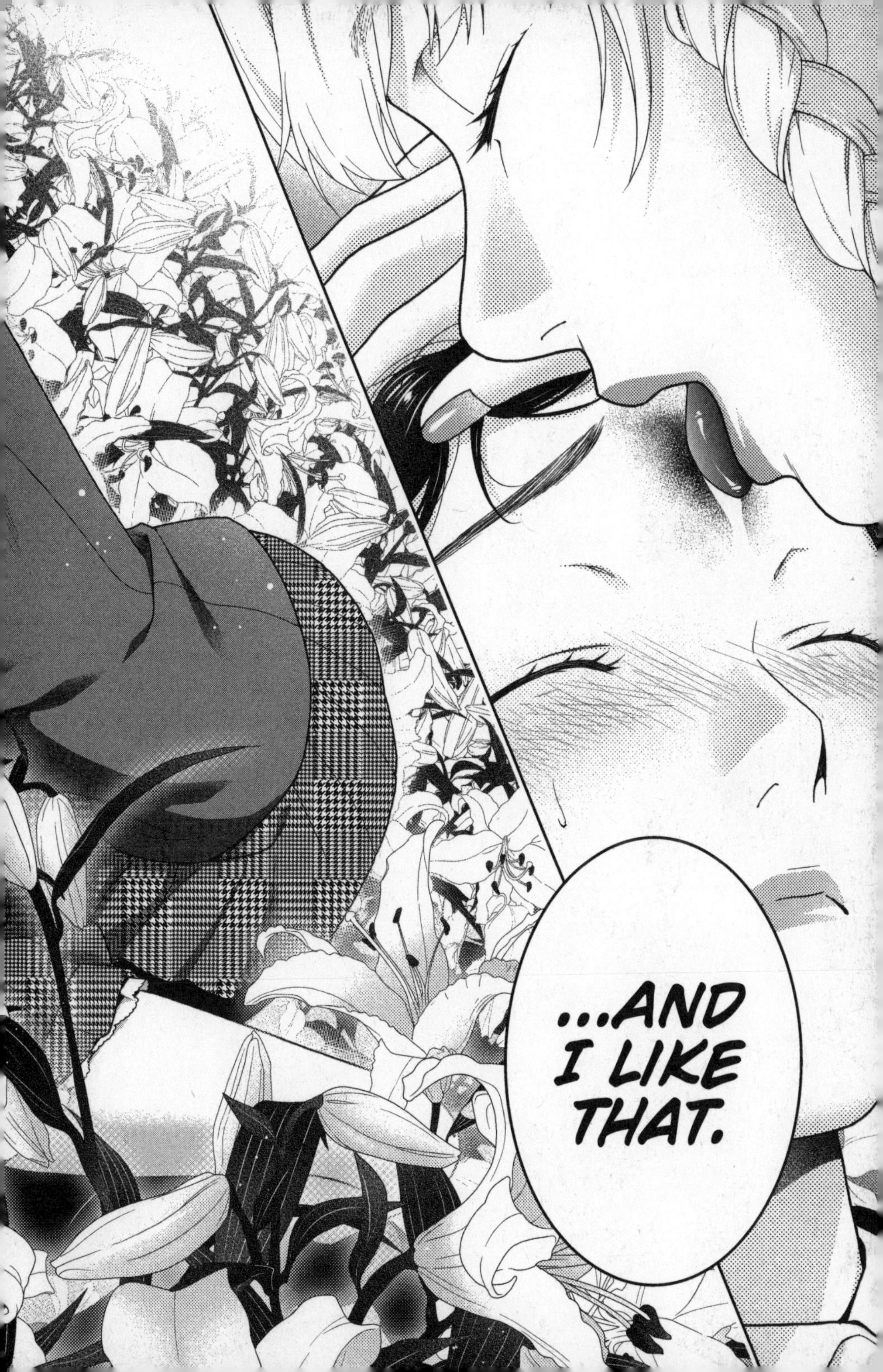
...AND I LIKE THAT.

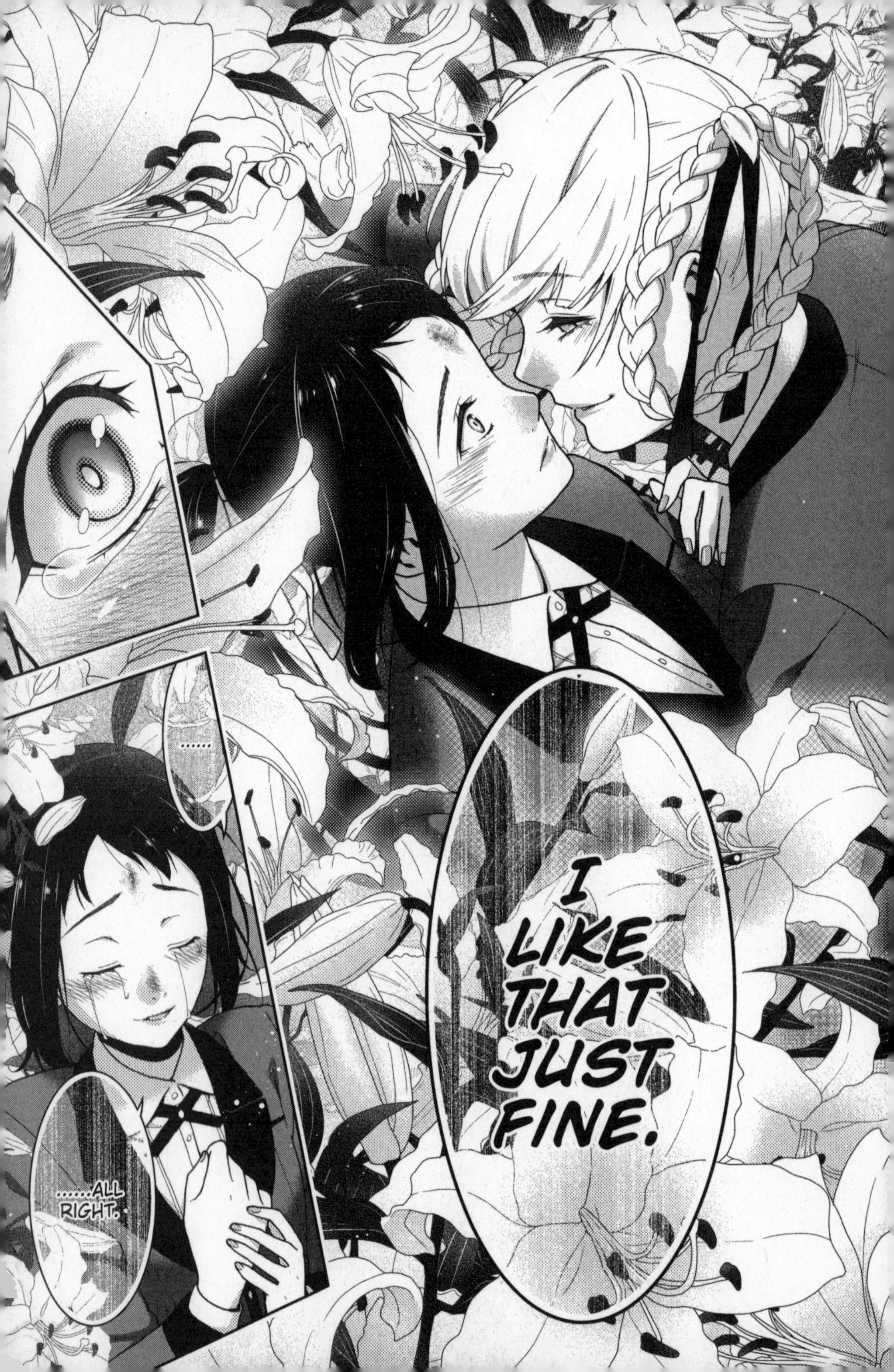
I LIKE THAT JUST FINE.
......
......ALL RIGHT.

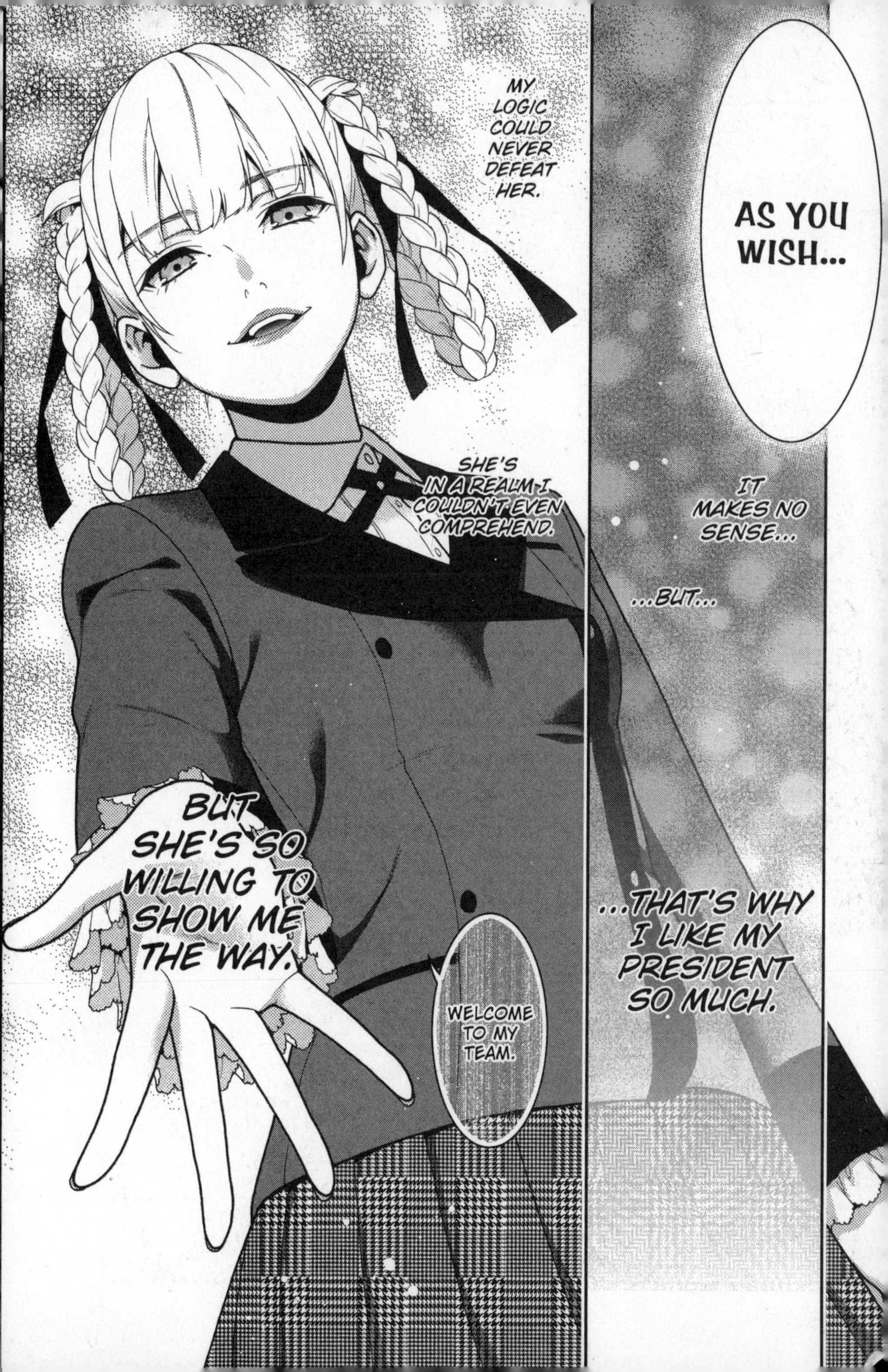
AS YOU WISH...
IT MAKES NO SENSE...
...BUT...
...THAT'S WHY I LIKE MY PRESIDENT SO MUCH.
MY LOGIC COULD NEVER DEFEAT HER.
SHE'S IN A REALM I COULDN'T EVEN COMPREHEND.
BUT SHE'S SO WILLING TO SHOW ME THE WAY.
WELCOME TO MY TEAM.

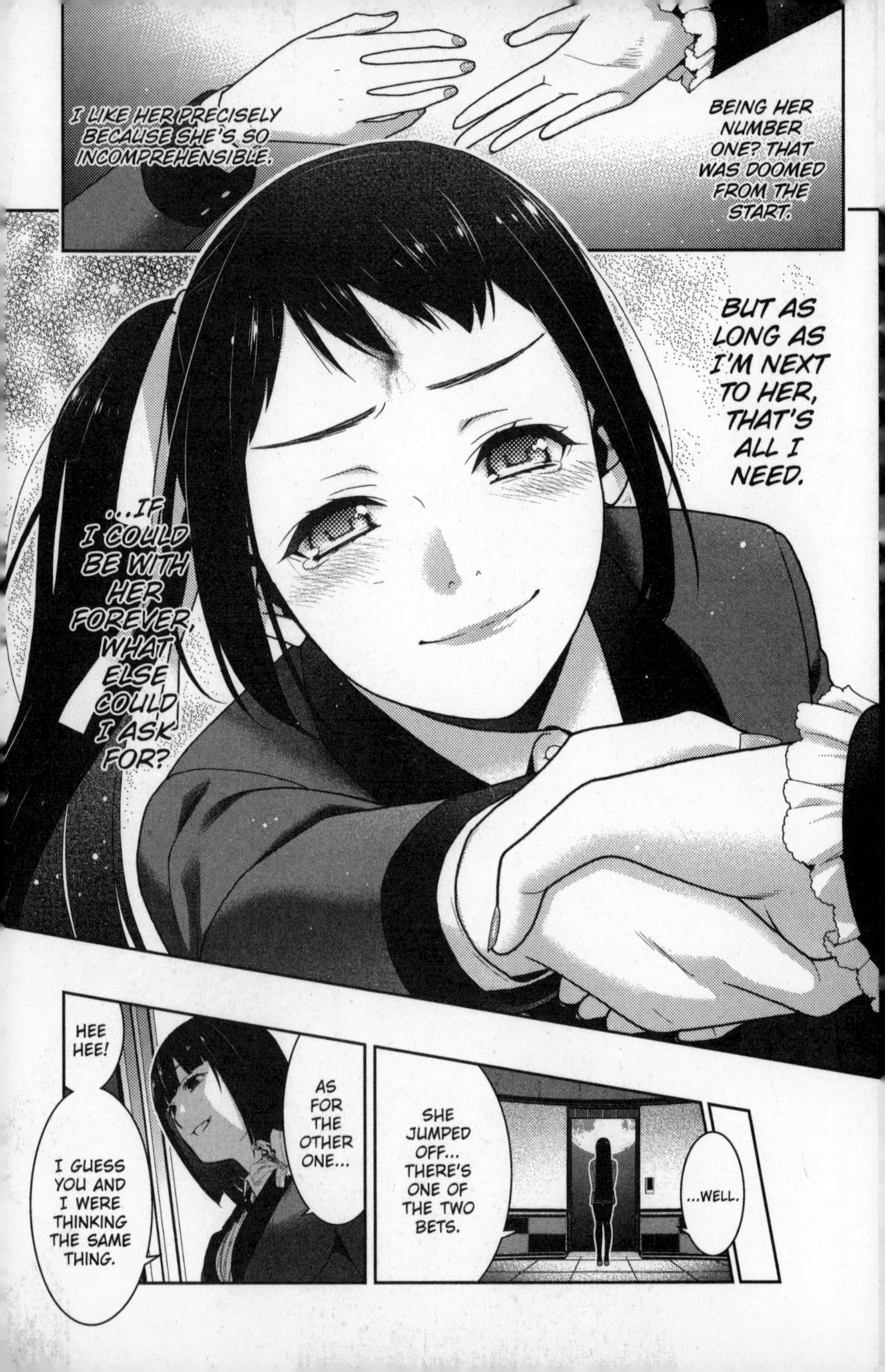
BEING HER NUMBER ONE? THAT WAS DOOMED FROM THE START.
I LIKE HER PRECISELY BECAUSE SHE'S SO INCOMPREHENSIBLE.
BUT AS LONG AS I'M NEXT TO HER, THAT'S ALL I NEED.
...IF I COULD BE WITH HER FOREVER, WHAT ELSE COULD I ASK FOR?
...WELL.
SHE JUMPED OFF... THERE'S ONE OF THE TWO BETS.
AS FOR THE OTHER ONE...
HEE HEE!
I GUESS YOU AND I WERE THINKING THE SAME THING.

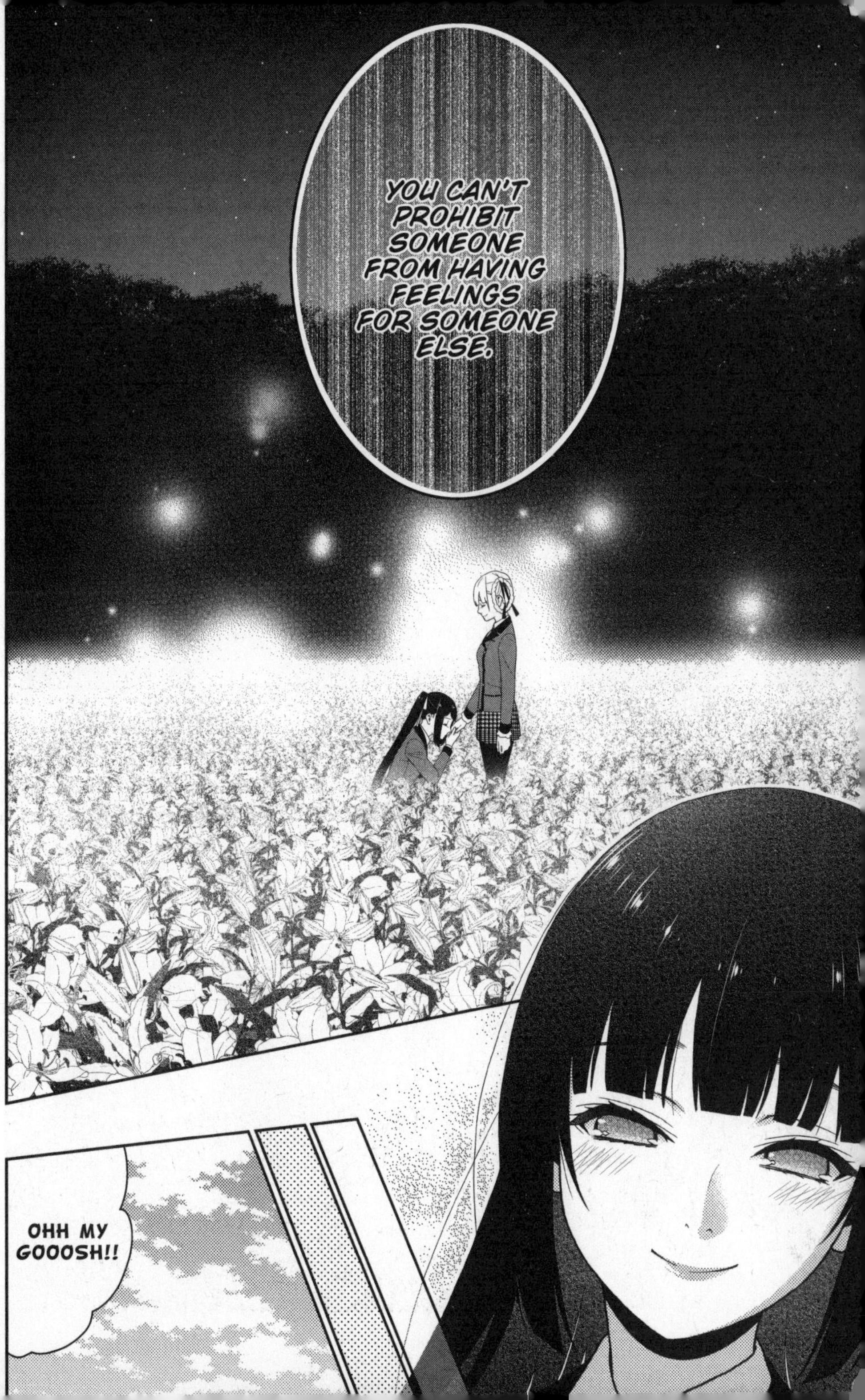
YOU CAN'T PROHIBIT SOMEONE FROM HAVING FEELINGS FOR SOMEONE ELSE.
OHH MY GOOOSH!!

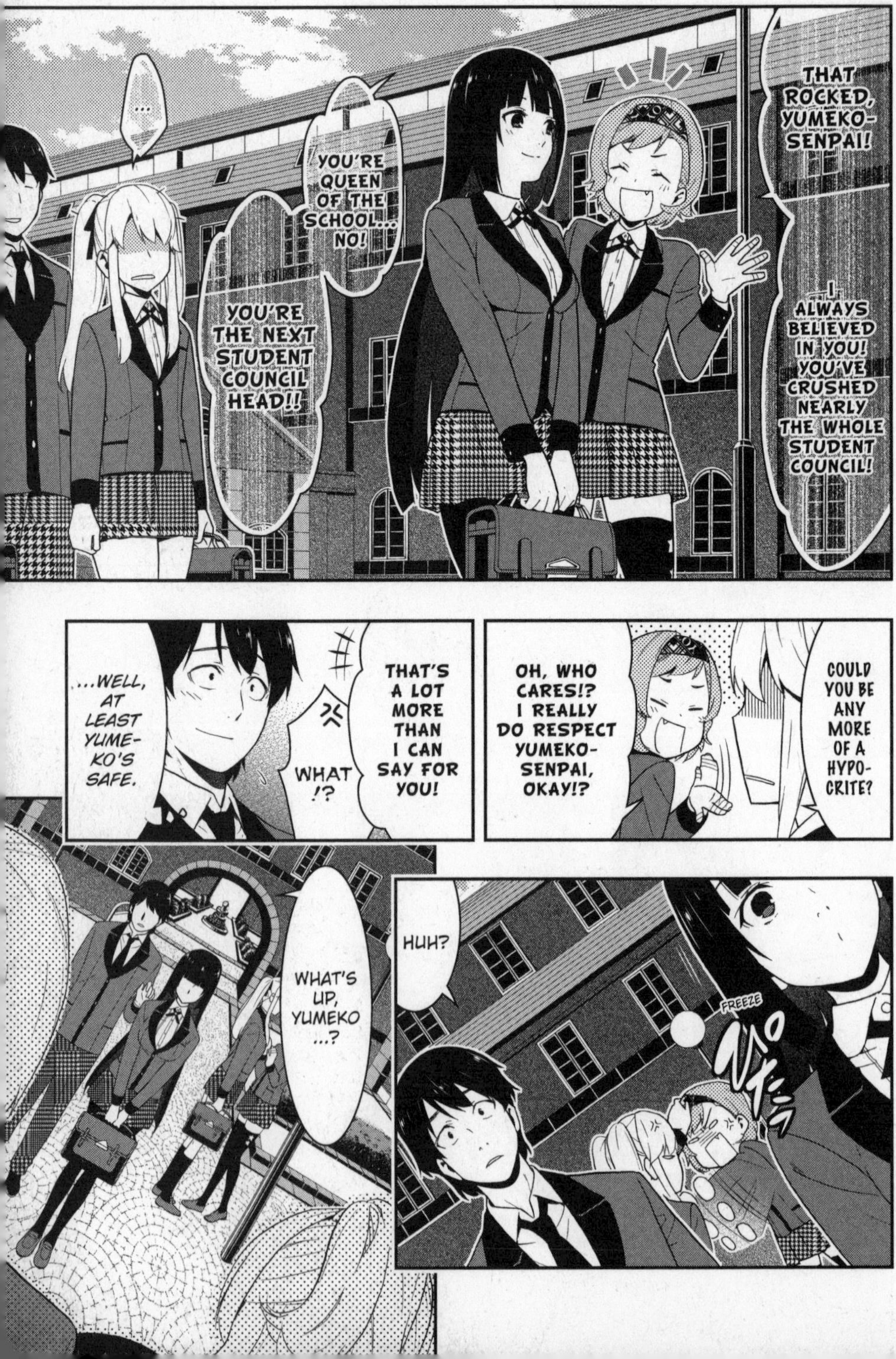
THAT ROCKED, YUMEKO-SENPAI!
I ALWAYS BELIEVED IN YOU! YOU'VE CRUSHED NEARLY THE WHOLE STUDENT COUNCIL!
YOU'RE QUEEN OF THE SCHOOL... NO!
YOU'RE THE NEXT STUDENT COUNCIL HEAD!!
...
COULD YOU BE ANY MORE OF A HYPO-CRITE?
OH, WHO CARES!? I REALLY DO RESPECT YUMEKO-SENPAI, OKAY!?
THAT'S A LOT MORE THAN I CAN SAY FOR YOU!
WHAT!?
...WELL, AT LEAST YUMEKO'S SAFE.
FREEZE
HUH?
WHAT'S UP, YUMEKO...?

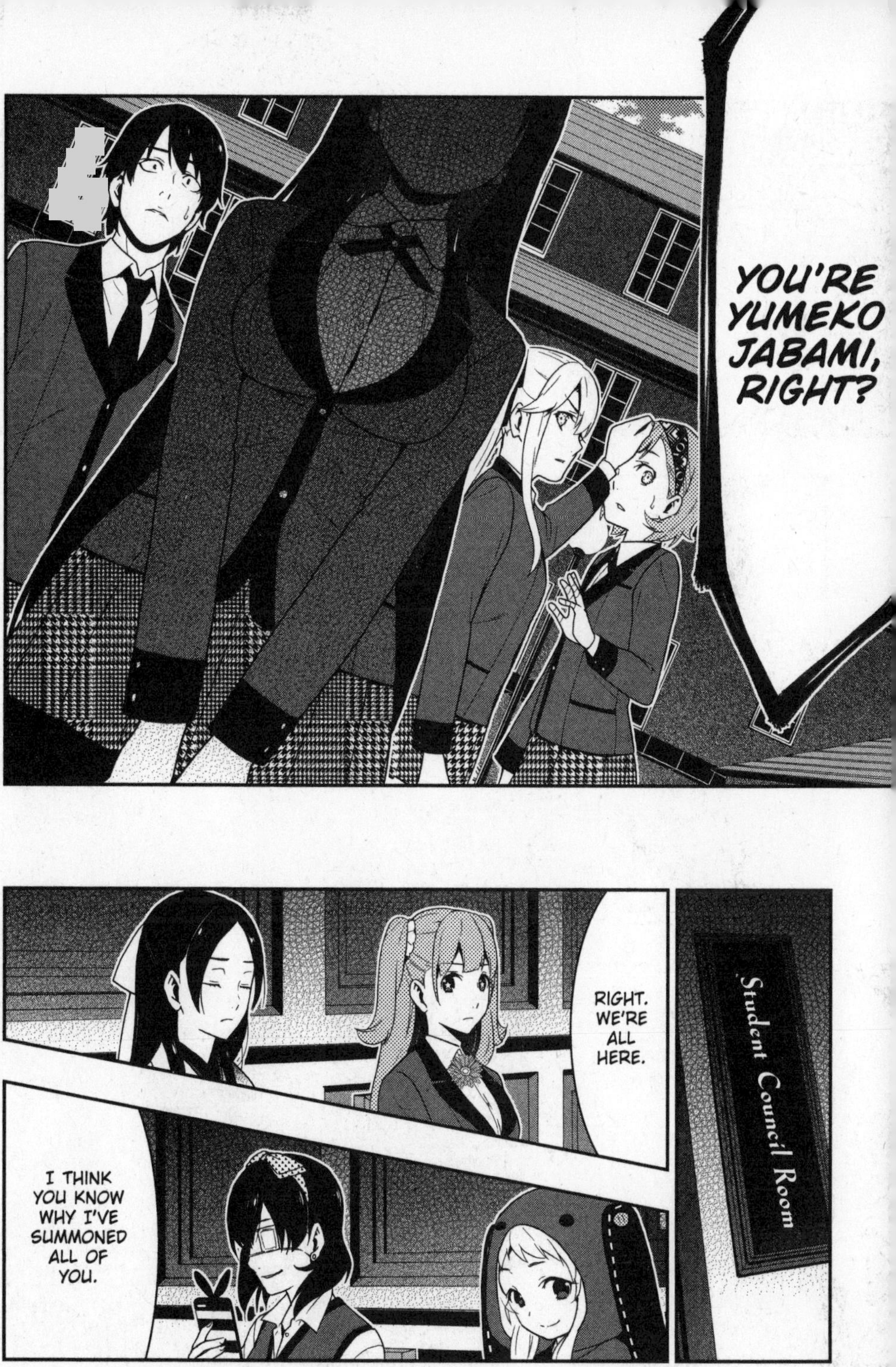
YOU'RE YUMEKO JABAMI, RIGHT?
Student Council Room
RIGHT. WE'RE ALL HERE.
I THINK YOU KNOW WHY I'VE SUMMONED ALL OF YOU.

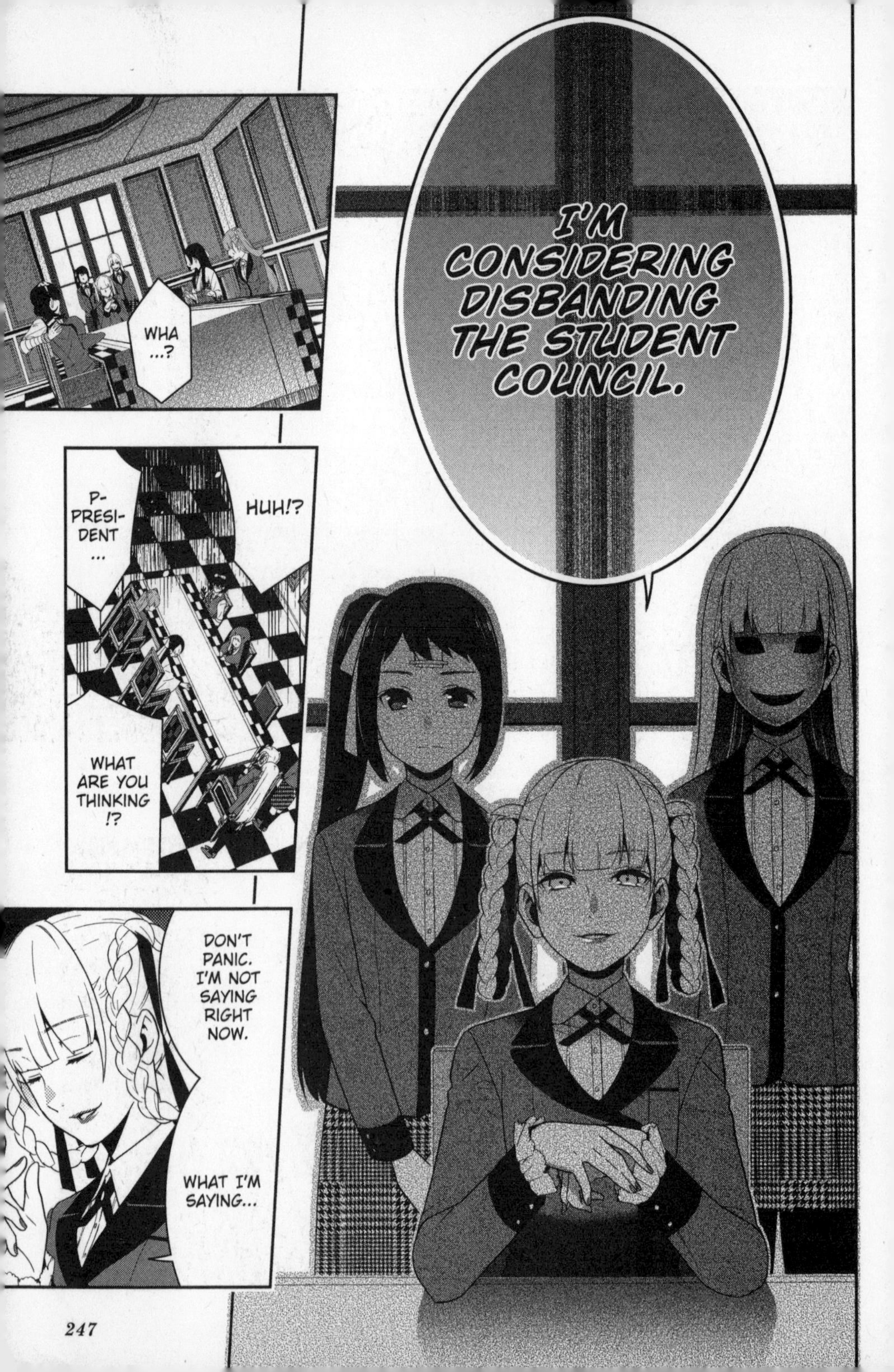

I'M CONSIDERING DISBANDING THE STUDENT COUNCIL.
WHA ...?
HUH!?
P-PRESIDENT ...
WHAT ARE YOU THINKING !?
DON'T PANIC. I'M NOT SAYING RIGHT NOW.
WHAT I'M SAYING...

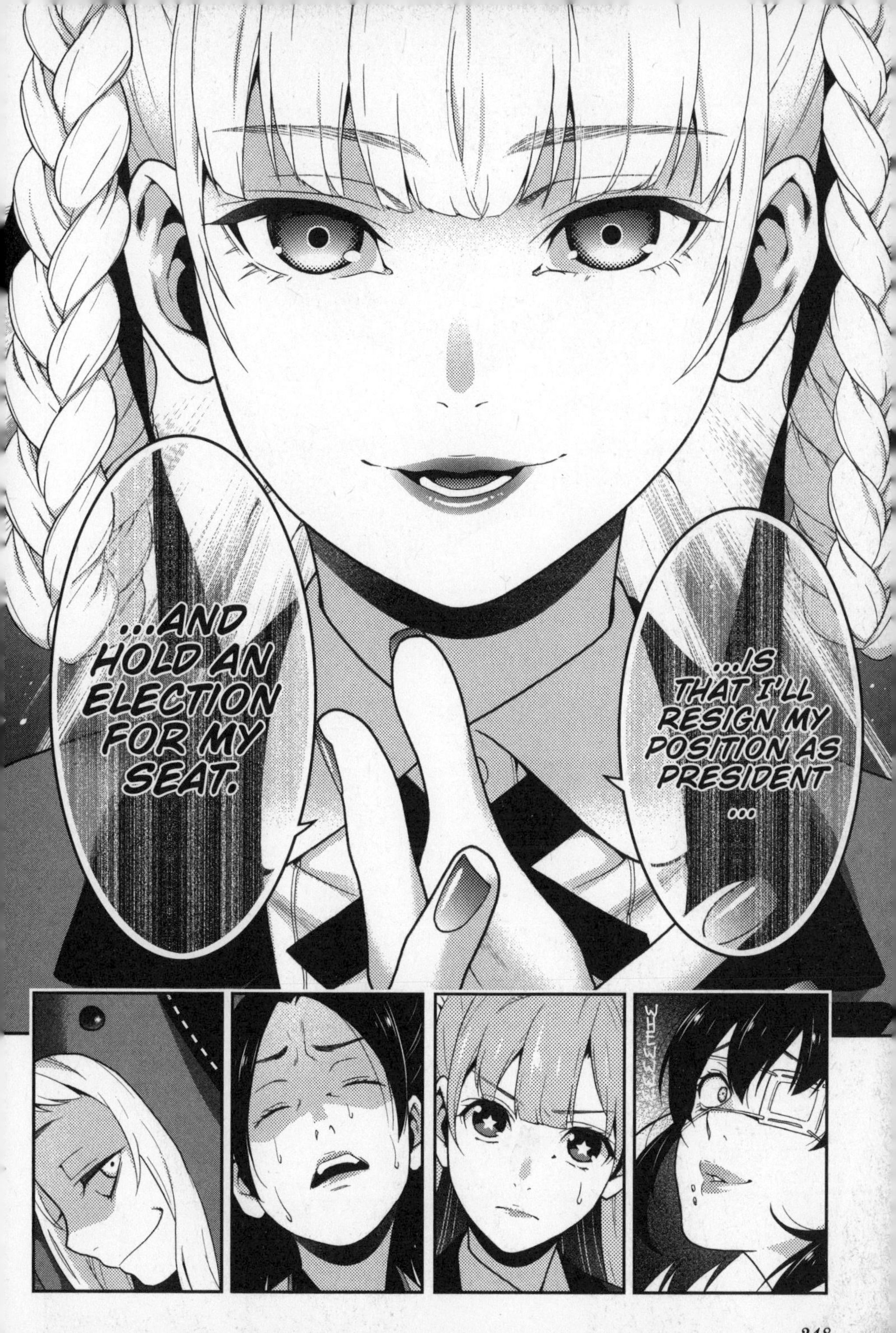
...IS THAT I'LL RESIGN MY POSITION AS PRESIDENT ...
...AND HOLD AN ELECTION FOR MY SEAT.
WHEWW

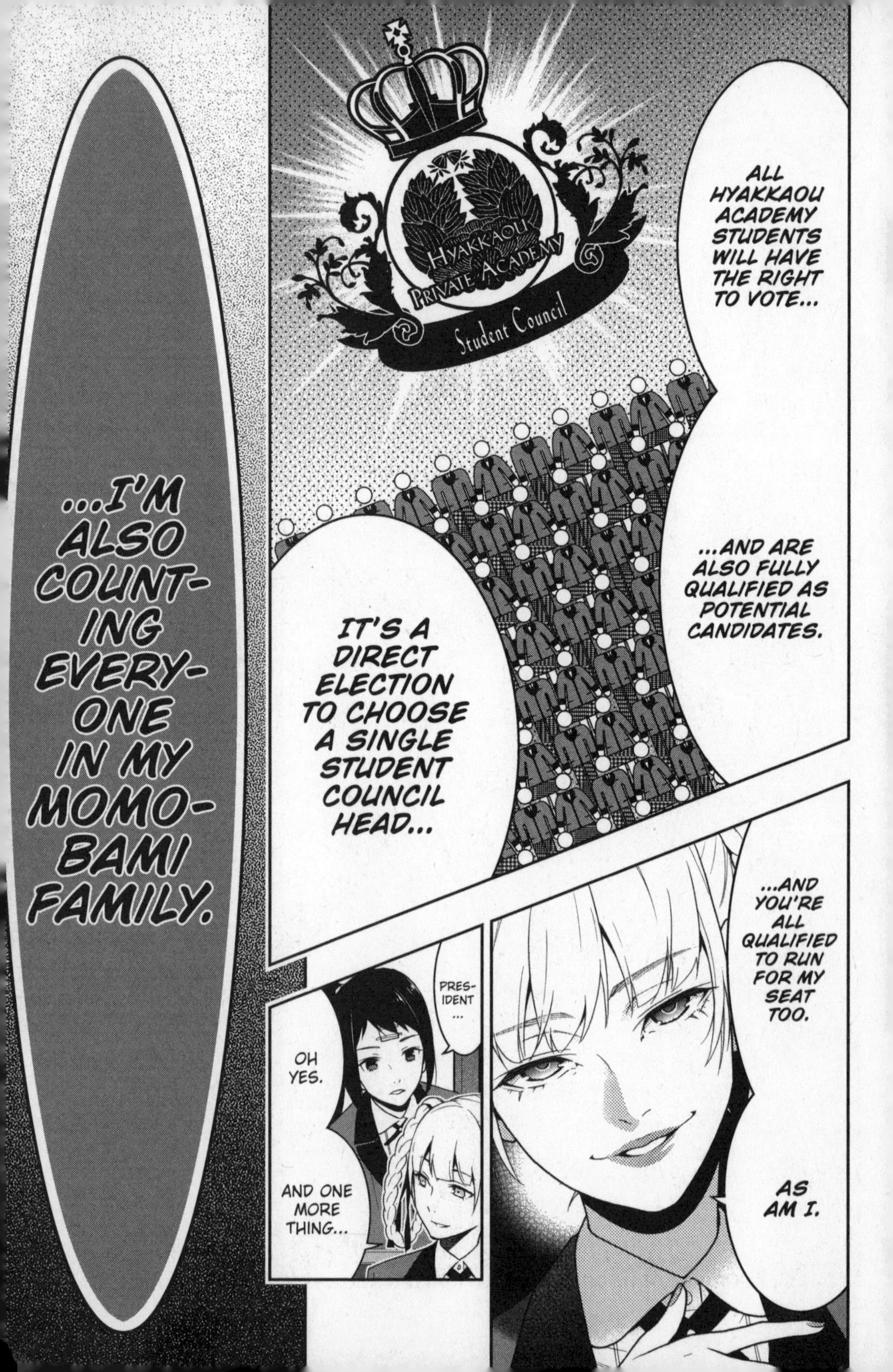
HYAKKAOU PRIVATE ACADEMY
Student Council
ALL HYAKKAOU ACADEMY STUDENTS WILL HAVE THE RIGHT TO VOTE...
...AND ARE ALSO FULLY QUALIFIED AS POTENTIAL CANDIDATES.
IT'S A DIRECT ELECTION TO CHOOSE A SINGLE STUDENT COUNCIL HEAD...
...AND YOU'RE ALL QUALIFIED TO RUN FOR MY SEAT TOO.
AS AM I.
PRESIDENT...
OH YES.
AND ONE MORE THING...
...I'M ALSO COUNTING EVERYONE IN MY MOMOBAMI FAMILY.

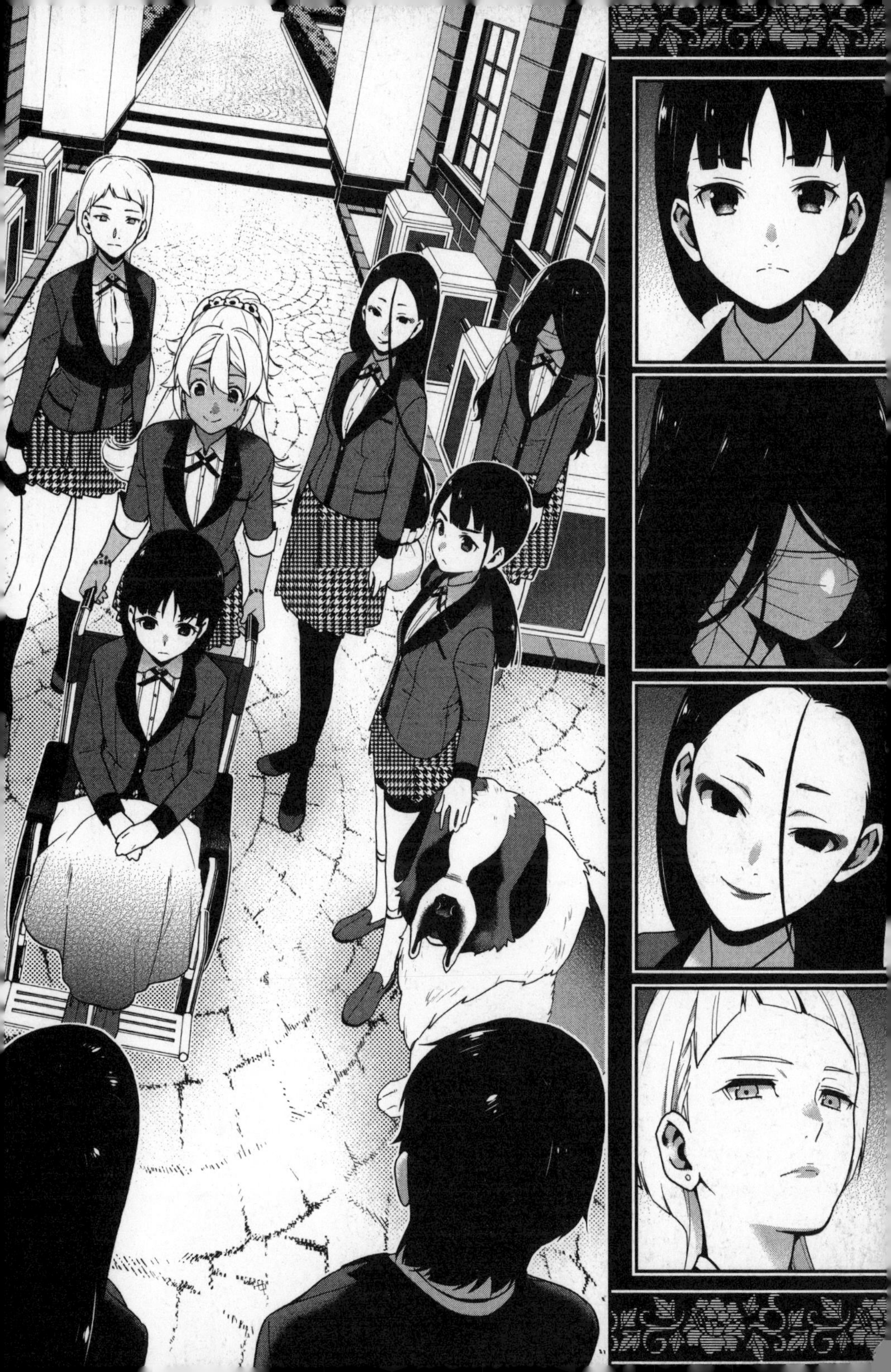

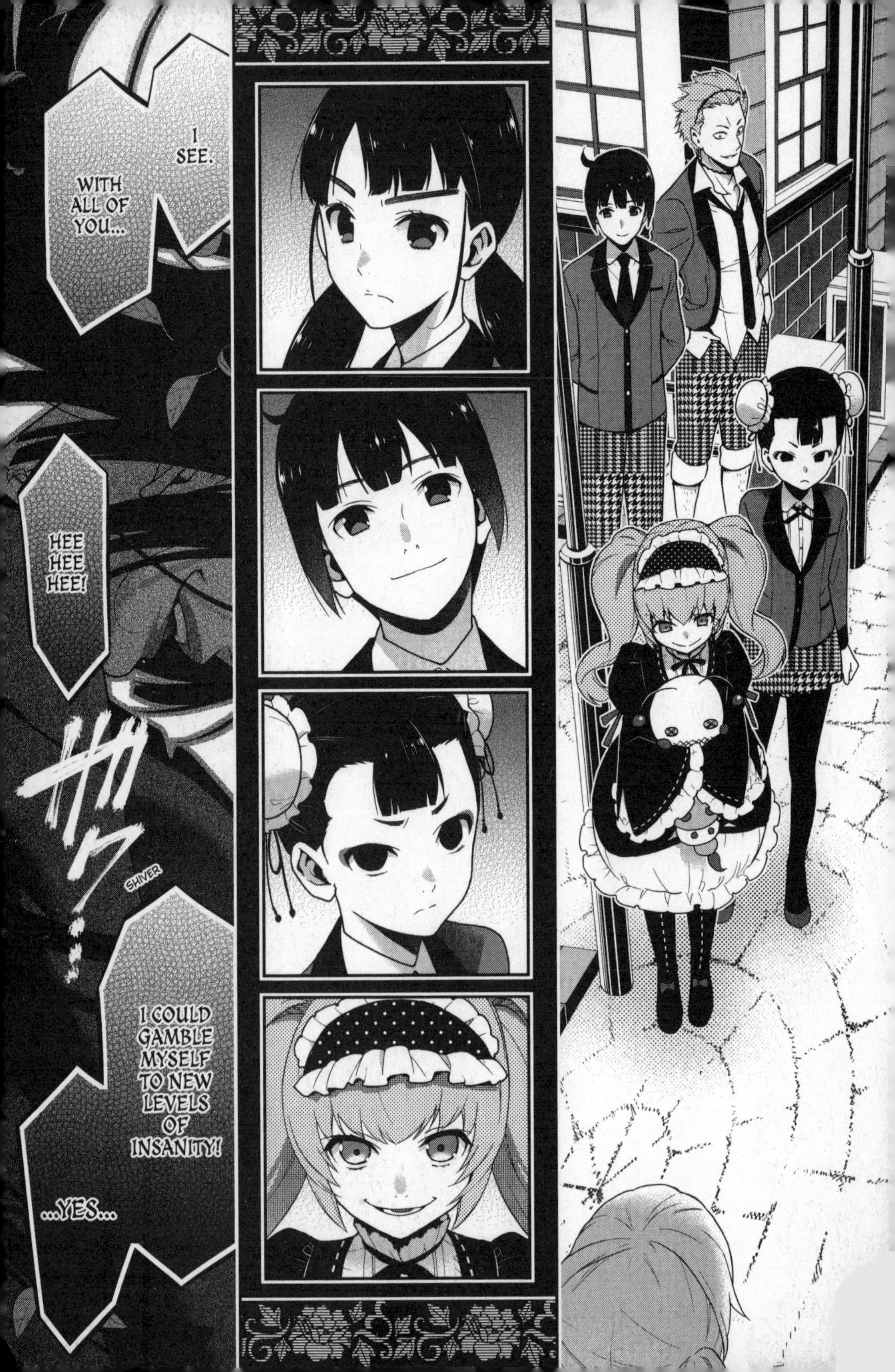
I SEE.
WITH ALL OF YOU...
HEE HEE HEE!
SHIVER
I COULD GAMBLE MYSELF TO NEW LEVELS OF INSANITY!
...YES...

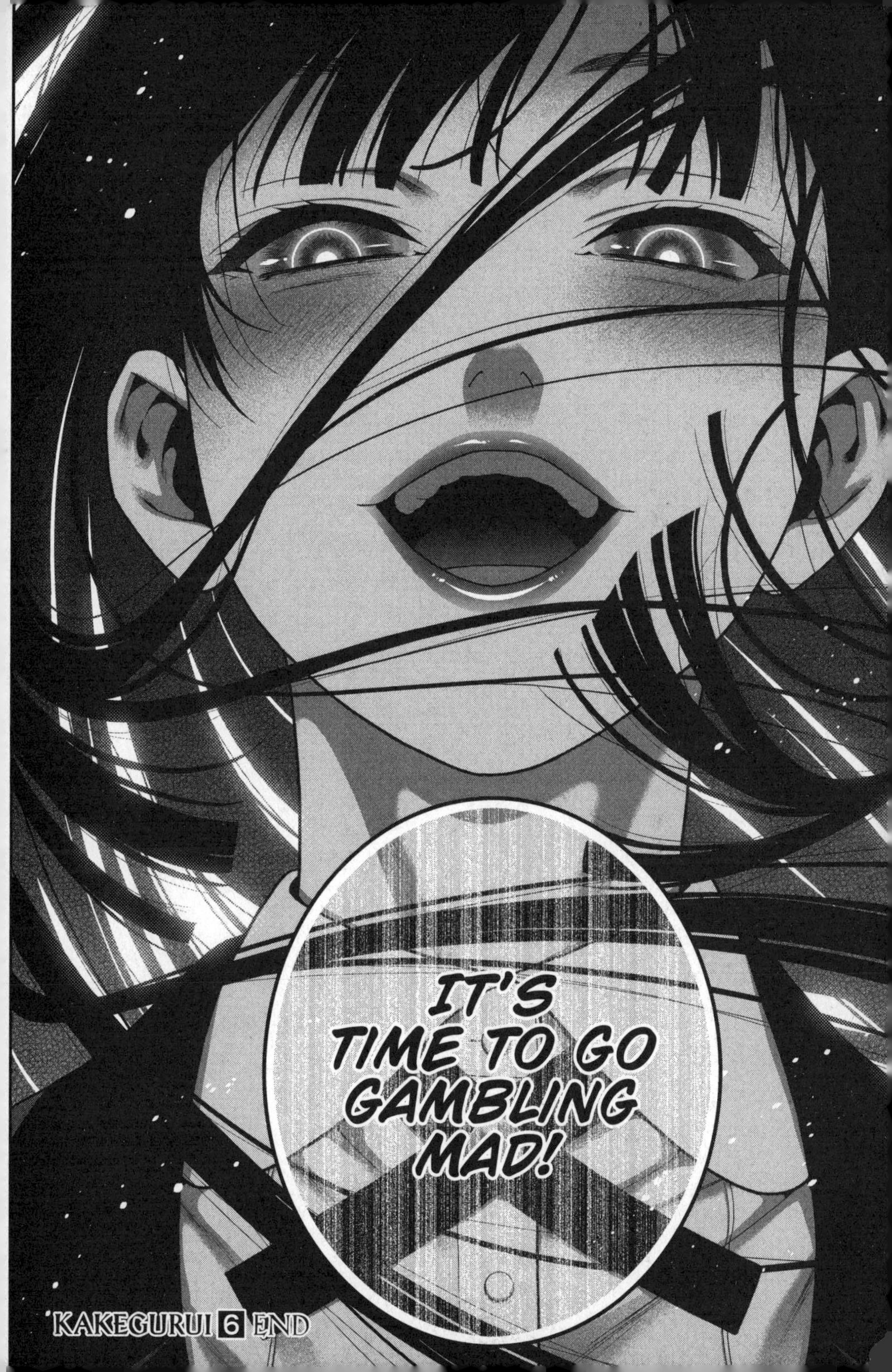
IT'S TIME TO GO GAMBLING MAD!
KAKEGURUI 6 END

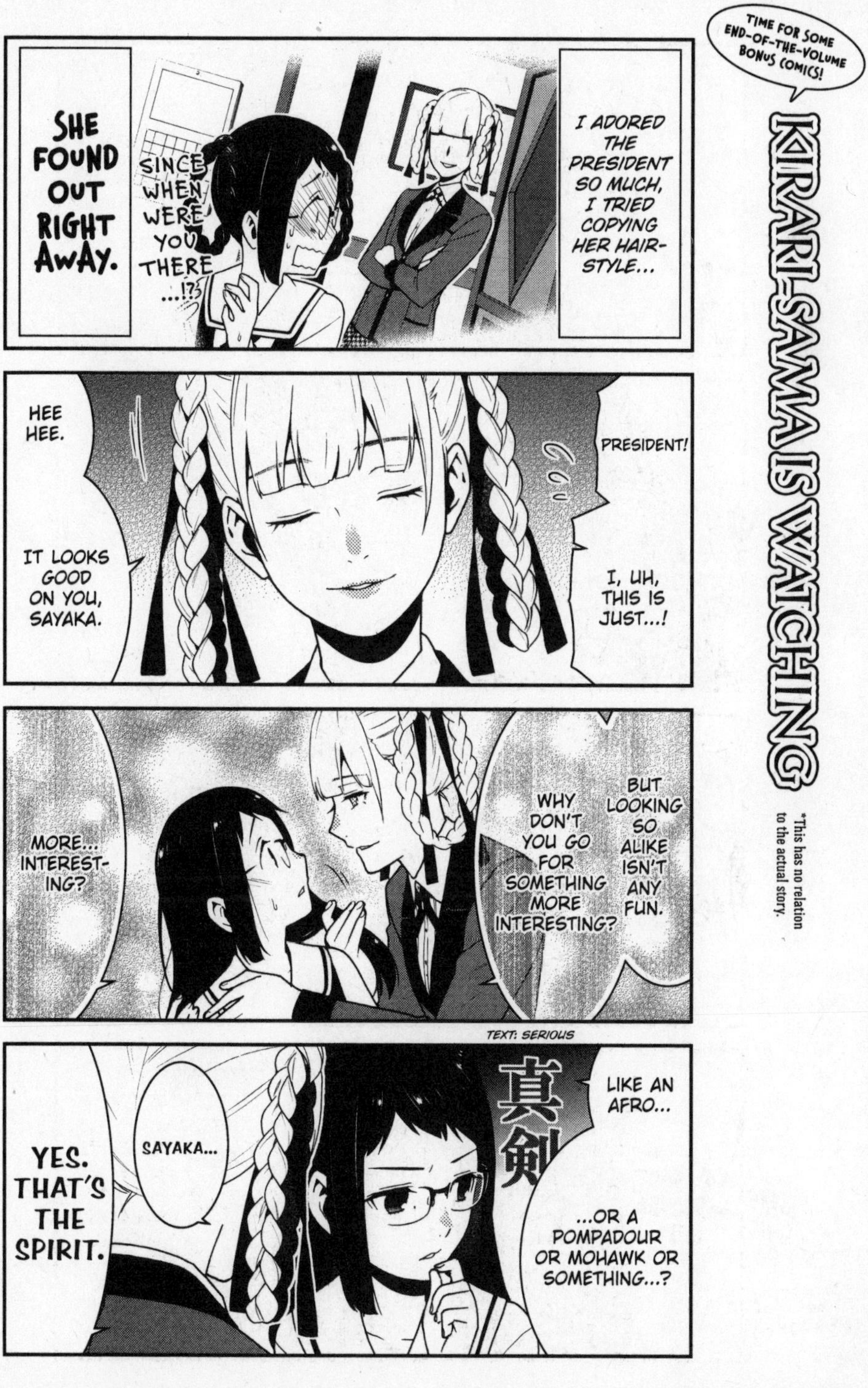
TIME FOR SOME END-OF-THE-VOLUME BONUS COMICS!
KIRARI-SAMA IS WATCHING
*This has no relation to the actual story.
I ADORED THE PRESIDENT SO MUCH, I TRIED COPYING HER HAIR-STYLE...
SINCE WHEN WERE YOU THERE ...!?
SHE FOUND OUT RIGHT AWAY.
PRESIDENT!
I, UH, THIS IS JUST...!
HEE HEE.
IT LOOKS GOOD ON YOU, SAYAKA.
BUT LOOKING SO ALIKE ISN'T ANY FUN.
WHY DON'T YOU GO FOR SOMETHING MORE INTERESTING?
MORE... INTERESTING?
TEXT: SERIOUS
真剣
LIKE AN AFRO...
...OR A POMPADOUR OR MOHAWK OR SOMETHING...?
SAYAKA...
YES. THAT'S THE SPIRIT.
JUST WHAT I HOPED FOR!

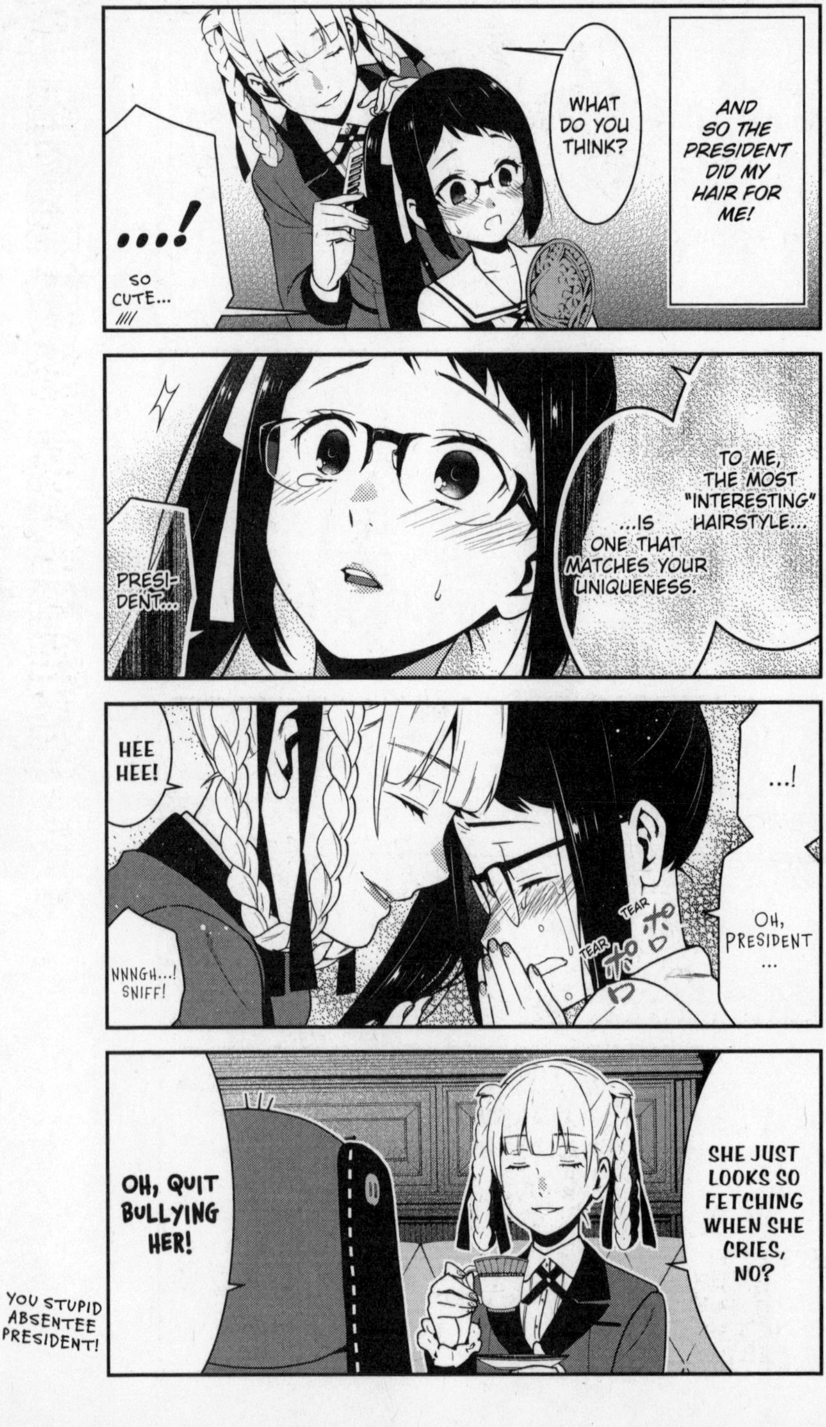
AND SO THE PRESIDENT DID MY HAIR FOR ME!
WHAT DO YOU THINK?
...!
SO CUTE... ////
TO ME, THE MOST "INTERESTING" HAIRSTYLE...
...IS ONE THAT MATCHES YOUR UNIQUENESS.
PRESI-DENT...
...!
OH, PRESIDENT ...
TEAR
TEAR
HEE HEE!
NNNGH...! SNIFF!
SHE JUST LOOKS SO FETCHING WHEN SHE CRIES, NO?
OH, QUIT BULLYING HER!
YOU STUPID ABSENTEE PRESIDENT!

GAMBLING, THAT IS MY RAISON D'ÊTRE.

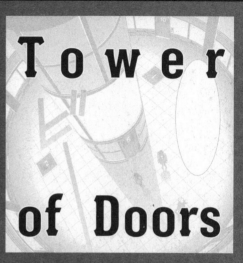

The Tower of Doors is a building constructed by Kirari Momobami exclusively for the purpose of gambling. There is no purpose to any aspect of its structure apart from its use in betting matches. If the way it worked ever got leaked to the public, I doubt it could ever be used again in its current configuration. It would have been a colossal waste of time and effort if it weren't for Yumeko and Igarashi-san taking up the banner for it—something I'm sure made the president pretty happy.

Thank you for picking up Volume 6 of *Kakegurui*. I had wanted to more fully depict Igarashi-san's feelings for the president ever since they began to come to the surface in Volume 2. Seeing them take final form like this fills me with a sense of relief. A lot of people pitched in to make Volume 6 happen. Naomura-sensei and his assistants have made the art in this book even more attractive, and even more overwhelming, than ever before. Sasaki-sama and Yumoto-sama, our editors, continue to refrain from tossing us aside even after all the trouble we cause for them. Everyone at the café continued to give impeccable service to this guy here as he alternated between writing numbers on the sides of tower art and seemingly staring into space. Thanks also go out to Tanaka and, of course, to all my readers. We also couldn't have released this without the support of countless other people, and I'd like to take this space to thank them all.

By the way...*Kakegurui* is officially going to become an anime! I'll let someplace else cover all of the details, but as a soon-to-be viewer, I simply can't wait for it. Be on the lookout for Volume 7 too!

Homura Kawamoto

Afterword

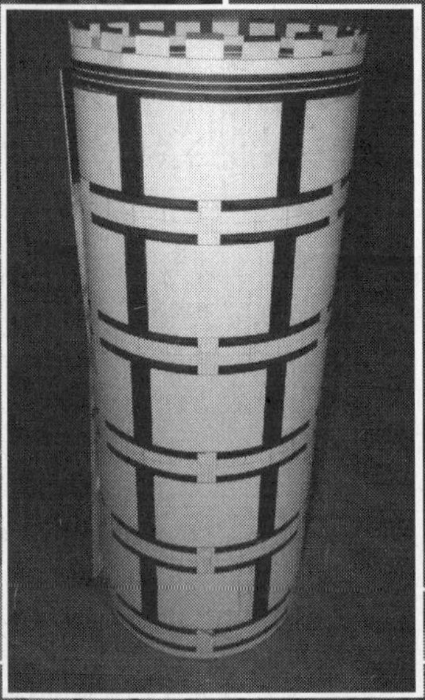

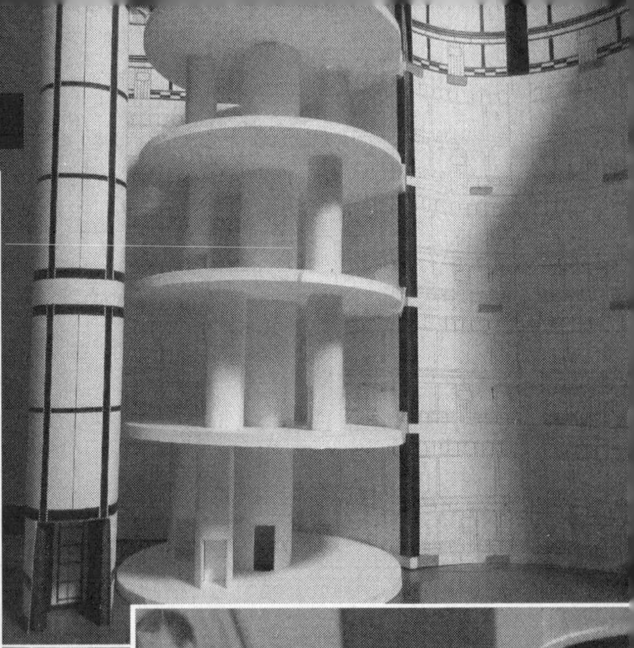

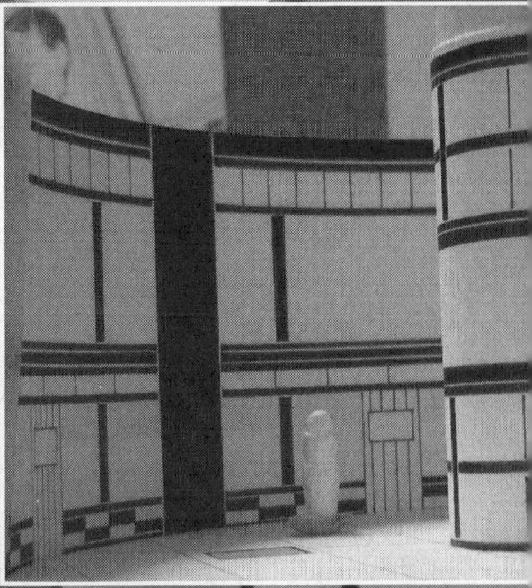

SPECIAL THANKS:

My editors / Kawamoto-sama / Imoutoko / H2-sama / AO-sama / M-sama / Everyone

Toru Naomura (artist), February 2017

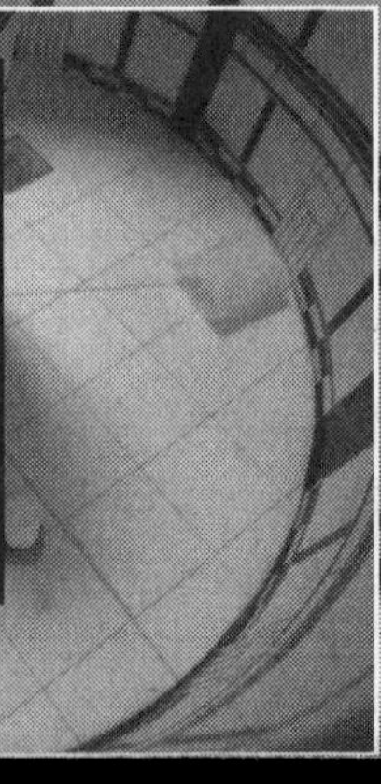

Thanks to all of you for picking up Volume 6 of *Kakegurui*.
The Tower of Doors this volume is set around is purely the work of imagination, but since we needed it to be a place you could realistically gamble against someone in, erstwhile assistant H2-sama built a model for us. This was a huge help as we figured out how the passageways would be positioned, the size and proportions, how the tower should look, and how participants would move between floors. Thank you, H2-sama! Also thanks to AO-sama, who just loves my bell-beans (inside joke), for all the hard work!
To Kawamoto-sensei, my editors Yumoto-sama and Sasaki-sama, and everyone else:
Thank you so much for everything.
I'm starting to feel these days like I'm truly blessed to have everyone I know around me.
I hope to see you soon in the next volume.

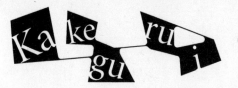

⑥

STORY: **Homura Kawamoto**
ART: **Toru Naomura**

Translation: Kevin Gifford
Lettering: Anthony Quintessenza

KAKEGURUI Vol. 6 ©2017 Homura Kawamoto, Toru Naomura/SQUARE ENIX CO., LTD. First published in Japan in 2017 by SQUARE ENIX CO., LTD. English translation rights arranged with SQUARE ENIX CO., LTD. and Yen Press, LLC through Tuttle-Mori Agency, Inc.

English translation ©2018 by SQUARE ENIX CO., LTD.

Yen Press
1290 Avenue of the Americas
New York, NY 10104

Visit us at yenpress.com
facebook.com/yenpress
twitter.com/yenpress
yenpress.tumblr.com
instagram.com/yenpress

First Yen Press Edition: July 2018
The chapters in this volume were originally published as ebooks by Yen Press.

Yen Press is an imprint of Yen Press, LLC.
The Yen Press name and logo are trademarks of Yen Press, LLC.

The publisher is not responsible for websites (or their content) that are not owned by the publisher.

Library of Congress Control Number: 2017939211

ISBNs: 978-0-316-44759-1 (paperback)
        978-0-316-44760-7 (ebook)

10 9 8 7 6 5 4 3 2 1

WOR

Printed in the United States of America

⑥

K
A
K
E
G
U
R
U
I

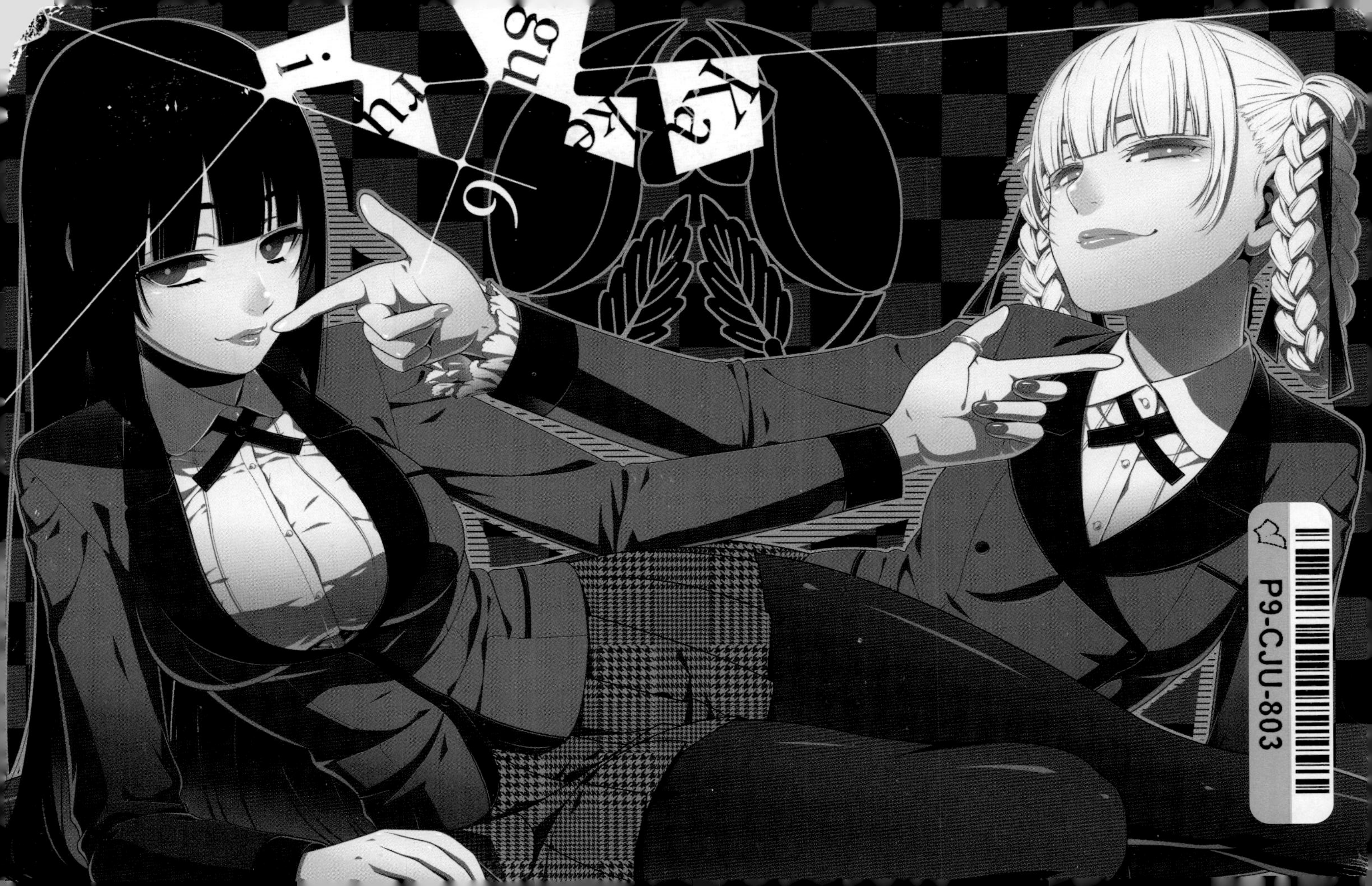
Kakegurui
6